Public Sector Economics

Public Sector Economics

Second Edition

ROBIN W. BOADWAY

Queen's University
Kingston, Ontario

DAVID E. WILDASIN

Indiana University
Bloomington, Indiana

Little, Brown and Company
Boston, Toronto

To Bernie, Kathy, Andrew, John, and Ben

Library of Congress Cataloging in Publication Data

Boadway, Robin W., 1943–
  Public sector economics.

  Includes bibliographical references and index.
  1. Finance, Public. 2. Finance, Public—United
States. I. Wildasin, David E. II. Title.
HJ141.B62 1984   336.73   84–896
ISBN 0-316-10052-8

Library of Congress Catalog Card No. 84–896

ISBN 0-316-10052-8

9 8 7 6 5 4 3 2

MV

Published simultaneously in Canada
by Little, Brown & Company (Canada) Limited

Printed in the United States of America

Preface

The study of public finance is challenging, as it combines both normative and positive economic analysis. On the one hand, it seeks to answer the question: What should the role of the public sector be in influencing resource allocation in a market economy? The determination of a set of normative rules to guide public sector decision-making requires making use of the tools of modern welfare economics. As such, one might classify public finance as applied welfare economics. On the other hand, public finance involves the positive study of how the activities of government (e.g. taxation, expenditures, transfers) influence resource allocation, relative prices, and welfare in the economy. The sheer size and pervasiveness of the public sector ensure that it will play a significant role in determining how the economy's resources will be allocated by the pricing mechanism. In the positive analysis of the effects of public sector decision-making, it must be recognized that government actions will influence prices and outputs on several markets simultaneously. In other words, a satisfactory analysis of the impact of public sector decisions on the economy must take into consideration some of the general equilibrium effects of the actions.

In recent years, considerable scholarly research has been devoted to both the normative and positive analysis of public finance. New journals devoted entirely to these problems have sprung up, and more space has been devoted to them in existing journals. While much of this literature is quite technical, the results obtained are often of fundamental importance in furthering our knowledge of public sector economics and in revising previously held beliefs, and, as such, they should be accessible to the student. *Public Sector Economics* combines the traditional subject matter of public finance with the significant recent developments in the field in a way that is comprehensible to a student with a basic knowledge of conventional microeconomics. In addition, we have tried to meld the principles developed in theory with the practice as represented by the actual fiscal system. The existing system of taxes, government expenditures, and social insurance are described and their effects in the economy are inferred on the basis of the theoretical analysis and empirical research. Also, we are able to indicate some of the structural deficiencies of existing programs on the basis of first principles.

In writing this second edition, we have had three objectives in mind. The first is to present in as non-technical and intuitive a manner as possible what we regard as important and sometimes complex analysis. While we do not ignore such important dimensions of public sector economics as uncertainty, general equilibrium, and dynamic aspects, we have tried to simplify the presentation. The second objective is to incorporate some of the more important policy debates from the political forum into the text. This includes such topics as indexation of the tax system for inflation; the desired structure of social security, unemployment insurance, and medical care; flat-rate taxation; expenditure taxation and the taxation of capital income; and redistributive transfers. The third objective is to update our discussion of principles to include the most recent theoretical and empirical developments in the evolving literature. Thus, a new or amended treatment of taxation and savings, fiscal federalism, the investment and financial decisions of firms, labor supply, social insurance and bureaucratic decision-making has been presented.

The book is divided into four parts. The first part comprises an overview of the subject matter of public economics and introduces the methodological tools of welfare economics subsequently used in the rest of the book. Included in this part is a thorough discussion of the notion of economic efficiency and of the circumstances in which markets fail to provide efficient allocations of resources. These "market failures" provide the necessary conditions for public sector intervention in the economy.

The intervention we are primarily concerned with falls into three general areas—public expenditures, taxes, and transfers. The three remaining parts of the book deal with these three areas. In Part II we cover both the normative and positive aspects of public expenditures, including the theory of public goods and externalities, voting models, pricing and investment in increasing returns industries, preference revelation mechanisms and cost-benefit analysis. Part III deals with taxation. Taxes are analyzed from three points of view—the incidence of taxes, the effect of taxes on incentives of households and firms, and the design of an efficient and equitable tax system. The basic structure of the tax system of the United States is described in the context of these principles. In Part IV we are concerned with transfers both to individuals and to governments. Individual transfers can take the form of income transfers to low income persons, transfers in kind, or social insurance programs such as social security, unemployment insurance, or medical insurance. Each of these is analyzed in detail. Transfers to government (e.g. federal-state transfers) can be conditional or unconditional grants. The economic arguments for each of these, and their effects, are presented. In addition we review the literature on the issue of whether resources will be allocated efficiently in a federal system of government when some budgetary decisions are decentralized to lower levels of government and when labor and capital are mobile. It turns out that the existence of such mobility may provide an argument for intergovernmental grants.

In a book such as this, the selection of topics to cover is governed as much by convention as by logic. We have chosen to stress the microeconomic aspects of public finance as that field is normally defined. The theory of regulation has been omitted on the grounds that it is part of the subject matter of industrial organization. Tariffs are left out since they are part of the subject matter of international economics. The macroeconomics of the public sector (e.g. fiscal policy) has been left out since, increasingly, fiscal policy and debt management are being treated as part of a more general field of stabilization policy encompassing both these and monetary policy.

We have provided numerous citations throughout the text to guide students interested in further study of the topics covered. These citations should give readers a good start in familiarizing themselves with major writers, and should be of use to students developing term papers or seeking details of discussions that we, of necessity, have often only sketched. Needless to say, however, we have not provided a comprehensive survey of all relevant recent developments, nor have we been able to refer to all important contributions to the literature. Anyone working in this rapidly growing area will understand how selective we have had to be, especially in our citations to the now-voluminous literature.

In preparing this revised edition we are grateful for the secretarial assistance of Dorothy MacKenzie and Dorothy Edwards. Chii Chii Ashwe helped in preparing the manuscript and provided constructive comments along the way. Several other persons were kind enough to transmit suggestions on this or the earlier edition, including Neil Bruce, John Burbidge, Arthur Burditt, Mark Frankena, Jonathan Kesselman, Harry Kitchen, Wade Locke, Jack Mintz, Vasillios Rapanos, David Robinson, Anthony Scott, Dan Usher, and Sam Wilson. In addition, very helpful comments were received from the formal reviewers, David Starrett, John D. Wilson, Barry Keating, Maryann Keating, and especially Richard Tresch, whose suggestions significantly affected both the content and organization of this book. Finally, our families, Bernie and Kathy, and Ben, Andrew, and John, deserve our gratitude for their continued support of our collaborative efforts.

Contents

Public Sector Economics

1

Introduction to Public Economics

MARKETS AND GOVERNMENTS: EFFICIENCY AND EQUITY

1–1   Governments play pervasive roles in modern economies. The powerful tools of government policy—taxation, spending, borrowing, regulating—bear upon the economic life of every individual and business, in their various roles as consumers, workers, savers, borrowers, employers, and producers. Not surprisingly, the growth of government involvement in the economy has been accompanied by great debate, both at the popular level and among economists, about the proper scope of government activity. In this book, our goal is to show how the tools of economic analysis can be (and have been) fruitfully applied to the study of some of the most important aspects of public policy.

Before launching into a detailed discussion of government policy in a market economy, we provide in this chapter a brief outline of some of the major themes of our study and of some of the main issues that we shall be examining. Paradoxically enough, we begin our discussion with a careful consideration of the functioning of a pure market economy with no public sector. We do this partly for the sake of a review of the basic principles in the economic theory of the household and the firm. There is a more basic reason for this orientation, however: As all readers with some background in economics must know, economists have devoted the greater part of their efforts to the analysis of how an allocation of society's scarce resources is achieved through decentralized markets, and have shown that, under certain circumstances, an allocation of resources so achieved leads to high levels of economic "welfare." More exactly, it has been shown that competitive markets lead to outcomes that are "efficient" in a precise sense. We define "efficiency" in the next chapter; it is enough to say here that this efficiency property is one that many people find very desirable. The idea that markets are efficient has its roots in Adam Smith, and has played an historically important role in the debate about the need for government intervention in the economy. Indeed, we shall let it continue to play that role for us. Once we see how markets can allocate resources efficiently, which is one of our main objectives in the next chapter, we are naturally led to inquire why markets should not simply be left to solve society's economic problems with no government intervention.

The answer to this question is two-fold:

First, we shall find that the conclusion that markets are efficient is valid only under certain assumptions which are not always satisfied in practice. Thus, after presenting a detailed explanation of how markets can function efficiently in an ideal world, we turn in Chapter 3 to a description of possible "market failures" in which the conditions for market efficiency are not met. This leads to a search for a non-market framework through which efficiency can be achieved, and in this way we discover a possible rationale for many kinds of government intervention in the economy.

Second, even though efficiency in resource allocation is important, it is not the only relevant criterion of economic performance. In particular, efficiency does not insure that the distribution of economic well-being or welfare among the members of society is equitable or just. In a market system, the welfare of an individual or household depends on its ownership of scarce resources like labor, capital, etc., from which it derives income, and on the prices paid for the goods it buys. Underlying inequalities in the value of the scarce resources owned by different households mean that the set of consumption opportunities open to them will vary. Some households may be richly endowed, and may therefore have great opportunities to satisfy their wants, while others may do much worse. Obviously, it might be thought desirable to interfere with the market-determined distribution of welfare in order to achieve a more equitable outcome. This provides a second general rationale for government intervention in the economy. We should note immediately, however, that while economic analysis can be used to describe how the distribution of welfare is determined, and how various policies might affect the relative positions of different individuals, it cannot in itself determine what is equitable and what is not. Such judgments are inherently extra-economic, and must be based on moral or ethical considerations.

With this perspective in mind, then, we can examine various government activities and try to determine whether they might contribute to a more efficient and/or a more equitable economic outcome for society. Unfortunately, as we shall see, there may be conflicting objectives which have to be traded off one against the other, raising difficult problems for policy.

GOVERNMENT EXPENDITURES, EXTERNALITIES, AND PRICING POLICIES

1–2   In Part II of this book we will explore some of the issues raised by the market failures discussed in Chapter 3. Suppose we believe that unfettered markets may not efficiently provide highways, defense, education, electricity, or pollution abatement. What useful steps can be taken?

One possibility is that the government can become directly involved in the provision of public services. This can be especially important when markets simply fail to provide certain goods, such as defense and highways, for example. But if the market does not function efficiently, how is the government to do better? Exactly how much defense, or how many highway projects, should be undertaken? Such activities are worth something to the individual members of society, but they are not worth unlimited amounts of scarce resources. Some balance must clearly be struck between the benefits of public services and their costs. The principles of efficient public expenditure, which show how benefits and costs can be properly compared, are developed in Chapter 4.

But not all market failures necessarily justify direct government provision of goods and services. For example, consider the problem of pollution. This is an example of a broad class of situations referred to as *externalities*, where the actions undertaken by households or firms affect others outside of the framework of market transactions.

A specific case would be the noise generated around airports. Airlines have market relationships with their customers, suppliers, and employees, and are paid by them, or pay them, for goods and services supplied. Airlines do not, however, pay residents around airports for absorbing jet noise. This is an economic relationship: The residents are suffering real losses due to noise, and if they had the right to control the use of the airspace above their homes would charge airlines some amount for each flight, just as employees charge a firm for the use of their labor time. But the noise occurs outside, or is external to, the marketplace.

The economic theory developed in Chapter 5, which deals with several different types of externalities, shows that resources are not allocated efficiently in situations like this. Intuitively, this makes sense: There are resources, like peace and quiet in this example, or clean air or water in other pollution examples, that are being used up without markets to govern their allocation. In effect, social costs are imposed by polluters (or other externality-producers) who do not see these costs as relevant to their own decision-making because they are not forced, through the marketplace, to bear them. It is not surprising, then, that inefficiencies result.

What, then, can be done about externalities? One possibility is to have direct government control over the externality-producing industries or households: The government could take over ownership of the airlines (and the steel industry, and the chemical industry, and all other polluting industries). This would require extensive government intervention in broad areas of economic life, however, and would likely entail many other kinds of costs. Government ownership would also entail the sacrifice of those market institutions which are working relatively well in providing incentives for low-cost operation, in their sensitivity to consumer demands, and so on.

A less radical alternative would be to restructure the economic benefits and costs accruing to polluters and other externality-generators. A government could impose environmental quality standards on polluters, for example, and in fact such standards are widely used to deal with environmental problems in the United States and elsewhere. Economic analysis suggests that regulatory standards may have certain drawbacks, however. Other policy instruments, such as taxes or fees based on pollution emissions, have frequently been advocated by economists and deserve careful consideration. These are among the policy issues that we discuss in Chapter 5.

The principles of public expenditure and externality theory are invaluable in understanding the potential role that governments can play in enhancing the efficiency of resource allocation. However, the information required to achieve efficient levels of public expenditure, or efficient control of externalities, is not easily obtained. While markets provide indications of the (marginal) value of scarce resources through the determination of equilibrium prices, this does not occur for public goods like defense or for external effects like pollution.

How, then, can one determine the value or benefit to society from another highway, dam, waste treatment facility, or school? One seemingly simple and straightforward way to discover the value placed by downstream water-users on a treatment facility, or the value to travellers of time saved by a new road, would be to ask the beneficiaries how much these things would be worth to them. Unfortunately, as we shall see, they would have a strong incentive not to reveal this information truthfully. This is a problem of fundamental importance. It means that there is no immediately obvious way of determining what an efficient public policy would be, a fact that sometimes severely limits the applicability of public expenditure theory.

Indeed, in reality, public policy decisions need not be (and often are not) made with any conscious attempt to attain economic efficiency. Political institutions have evolved which resolve such issues without paying direct attention to principles of efficient resource allocation. Thus, whenever government intervention is proposed as a solution to some market failure, it is important to examine the process through which government policy will actually be made and to try to ascertain whether or not it is conducive to greater efficiency. In other words, we must try to understand government itself as a resource allocation mechanism, one which, like the market, may be subject to "failures." However, this non-market mechanism is less well understood than the market mechanism, in part because it has been the subject of economic study for only a few decades. Economists and other social scientists have begun to develop illuminating models of the political decision-making process, whether it occurs through simple referendum voting, representative legislatures, or government bureaucracies. In Chapter 6 we shall examine these institutions and their implications for government policy determination. A general conclusion emerging from this discussion is that political processes offer only imperfect solutions to the problem of information-gathering and efficient decision-making. We will also consider some new approaches to this problem, which, while yet to be implemented in practice, demonstrate the potential for more satisfactory decision-making procedures.

Governments of course influence the allocation of resources in many ways other than the provision of public goods and services, and control of externalities. In addition, governments often operate, or at least regulate, public enterprises in industries such as utilities, transportation, and others. In these industries, different sorts of problems can arise in the functioning of the market. It is sometimes a characteristic of the technology in such industries, for example, that lowest-cost production is achieved only in very large scale operations, operations so large that a competitive industry structure, with many firms engaging in price competition, is unattainable. In such cases, so called "natural monopoly" will tend to emerge if market forces are left unchecked, but this will generally be incompatible with economic efficiency and may possibly be undesirable on equity grounds as well. The problem, then, is to evaluate alternative public policies to deal with market failure, and to study the functioning of publicly run enterprises if the government does assume control of the industry. We do this in Chapter 7, which deals with such questions as the proper pricing of the product of public enterprises, whether such enterprises should be subsidized, and how much capacity they should have.

Our discussion in Part II concludes with a treatment of cost-benefit analysis. The fact that governments are heavily involved in programs and projects of all kinds, whether justified in terms of market failure or not, means that economic decisions of many kinds are constantly being made in the public sector. It is clearly important to try to determine how these decisions can be made as efficiently as possible. In particular, attempts have been made to systematize public sector decision-making through careful assessment of the social benefits and costs generated by prospective government programs. We therefore examine the principles of cost-benefit analysis, and focus on a number of the more challenging problems that arise in its application. For example, many public projects are long-lived: Dams, highways, port facilities, and water treatment plants are all expected to operate for extended periods of time. How does one evaluate the future flow of benefits and costs associated with such projects? Or, consider the fact that the benefits from, say, an agricultural irrigation project are highly uncertain: The project may not have much value if rainfall turns out to be adequate; if technological change in agricultural methods or changing farm prices induce farmers to switch to different crops with different water requirements; or, indeed, if farmers remove their land from agricultural production altogether. How should such risks be taken into account in project evaluation? These are among the important issues explored in Chapter 8.

TAXATION

1–3   Whether justifiable in terms of market failures or not, the fact is that governments are engaged, to a very substantial degree, in a wide range of resource-using activities. The amount of government expenditure in the advanced western economies has grown dramatically during this century, and such expenditures require reallocations of resources, toward the government and away from those uses to which they would otherwise be put in the private sector. Taxation is the principal mechanism through which this transfer of resources from the private to the public sector occurs, and the analysis of taxation is one of the major tasks of economists who are concerned with public sector economics.

In Part III of this book we devote five chapters to different aspects of taxation. In the first of these, Chapter 9, we introduce the general problems to be discussed and explain how taxes are important both for efficiency and equity. Taxes, unfortunately, can disturb the efficiency of resource allocation in markets that are otherwise functioning well. Income taxes, for example, may dull the incentives for individuals to undertake income-producing activities, such as working or saving. Other taxes, such as those on business, influence investment decisions or corporate financial policy. The incentive (or disincentive) effects of taxes are discussed more extensively in Chapter 11.

Chapter 10 introduces several important concepts of equity in taxation. Taxes have major effects on the distribution of welfare, and all would agree that tax burdens ought to be apportioned on a just and fair basis. The problem is to make operational this fine-sounding but rather vague goal. Consider, for example, whether individuals with higher incomes should pay higher taxes. If we agree that they should, how much higher should their taxes be? Of course, this begs the question of income as a proper object of taxation. Why not tax wealth or consumption expenditures? The latter possibility, in particular, is a live policy issue at the present time, one which definitely raises serious equity issues.

The discussion of equitable taxation is, at base, concerned with the distribution of the real burden of taxation among the members of society. This real burden can take the form of valuable resources sacrificed by individuals, or, ultimately, of losses in well-being or satisfaction of economic wants. It is extremely important to realize that this real burden, or incidence of taxation, need not coincide exactly with the flow of cash payments of taxes from the private to the public sector. To illustrate this idea with some examples, consider a tax on business income. Does this necessarily reduce the net income of a business and its owners? Suppose that the business is able to charge higher prices for its product, or pay lower wages to its workers, after the tax is imposed. Whether or not this would be possible would depend on market conditions, but to the extent that it occurred, it would protect the net income of the business at the expense of consumers or workers. Such shifting of real tax burdens is a possibility with any tax, and the amount of shifting must be determined before anyone can determine the true economic incidence of a tax. The analysis of tax shifting and tax incidence has been the subject of much economic research, and Chapter 12 discusses it fully.

As we have already noted, taxes tend to distort the efficient allocation of resources through the marketplace. One would expect, however, that some systems of taxation result in more disruption of economic efficiency than others, which suggests the following problem: If the government is able to use a mix of taxes—say, taxes on wage income, on interest income, on specific commodities such as tobacco, alcohol, and gasoline, and so on— how much efficiency loss will occur under each possible combination of tax rates, and what system of rates will result in the least efficiency loss? These issues are discussed in Chapter 9, and in Chapter 10 where we take up the related problem of an equity-efficiency tradeoff.

This tradeoff arises as follows. Suppose that we value a more equal distribution of economic welfare, and that a household's welfare is largely determined by its income. It follows that a tax system that imposes relatively greater burdens on high-income households, and leaves untaxed (or even augments) the income to low-income households, will result in a more egalitarian society. The difficulty suggested by common sense is that a more egalitarian society may also be a poorer one: If higher incomes are taxed heavily, there will be little incentive for people to work harder to increase their incomes, and this will tend to make a society poorer as a whole. How, then, is a balance to be struck between the competing goals of efficiency and equity? Not surprisingly, the answer depends on how much these conflicting goals are valued. While we as economists cannot specify how this value judgment should be made, economic analysis at least permits a systematic discussion of the problem.

We conclude our discussion of taxation in Chapter 13, where we examine the current tax structure in the United States. The main components of this system, as in many countries, are taxes on individual and corporate incomes; both have been the subject of considerable controversy and change in recent years. Laws affecting such taxes have been amended, in some cases very substantially, in order to achieve greater equity, efficiency or other goals. We describe the most important characteristics of the tax system, including recent changes, and try to assess their economic consequences. We also consider some of the proposed reforms of the tax system that have been advocated by economists and others, focusing especially on their equity and efficiency justifications.

INTERPERSONAL AND
INTERGOVERNMENTAL TRANSFERS

1–4   As mentioned earlier, a large and traditional function of government is to spend resources on various public goods and services. A less traditional but increasingly important government function is the *transfer* of resources from some individuals or organizations in the economy to others. Transfers to individuals and to other governments are the subjects of the two chapters in Part IV.

Transfers to individuals are made through many different programs and have many different objectives. One goal of some transfer programs is to protect the poor. Transfers to low-income individuals take several forms. In some cases, transfers are made in cash, while in other cases they take the form of transfers of specific goods. The United States food stamp program, which has grown enormously in recent years, provides one example of an in-kind transfer program. Other examples are provision of medical services to the poor, rent subsidies, and public housing.

One important policy issue, obviously, is how cash and in-kind transfers differ in their impacts on the poor, and whether there is some important reason for favoring one kind of transfer over the others. Beyond this, there is a more general question about transfers to the poor, one that directly parallels the equity-efficiency tradeoff in taxation mentioned earlier: How much do income maintenance programs dull the incentive for the poor to earn income by working? The notion that welfare programs encourage recipients of transfers to reduce their efforts to find work has received much popular attention; it has also been the subject of considerable theoretical and empirical analysis by economists. These and other issues involving redistributive transfers are discussed in Chapter 14.

In Chapter 14 we also discuss "social insurance" policies, including old-age security, unemployment insurance, and public health insurance programs. These transfers, while in some cases designed to benefit lower-income households, are often justified on other grounds. In the case of medical insurance, an obvious major purpose is to protect individuals against the economic hardship of ill-health. Social Security insures a lifelong income and insures against other risks as well. Similarly, unemployment insurance protects workers against adverse business fluctuations that can cause their employers to shut down operations and lay off workers temporarily or permanently. In all of these cases, it is important to ask whether and how public programs are able to achieve results unattainable through private insurance and other arrangements.

We must also consider possible unintended adverse consequences of these programs. For example, it has been claimed that social security, now an enormous program with nearly universal coverage in the United States and in other countries, has led to large reductions in private saving and earlier retirement by older workers. These potential effects are the subject of some debate among economists, and warrant thorough analysis. Similarly, it has been argued that unemployment insurance increases the incentive for firms to lay off workers and that it may reduce the incentive for unemployed workers to seek and obtain new employment. In the case of health insurance, an important issue is the degree to which government payment of medical expenses increases the demand for health care and reduces the incentive for doctors and patients to economize on the provision of medical services. All of these possible problems with social insurance programs are being studied by economists from both theoretical and empirical perspectives, and form the central focus of our discussion.

Finally, we take up the issues raised by fiscal federalism. In many countries, including the United States, government expenditure and taxation responsibilities are divided among different levels of government. What economic advantages or disadvantages result from this federal structure? Some would argue that federalism allows a healthy diversity in the public sector, offering greater freedom of choice for individuals and a more sensitive response to their wants. The ability of people and goods to move relatively freely across sub-national political boundaries, however, may mean that interjurisdictional variations in tax and expenditure policy will disturb the geographical pattern of resource allocation, to the detriment of economic efficiency. Moreover, many governmentally-provided goods and services produce benefits which can "spill over" the boundaries of smaller, lower-level jurisdictions. If the decision-makers in particular jurisdictions have no incentive to take into account the benefits of public programs accruing to non-residents, they may not make efficient public expenditure decisions.

Thus, while a federal system may have certain significant benefits, it can create difficulties as well. One method that has evolved to deal with these problems is the transfer of funds from higher-level to lower-level governments. In the United States, for example, the federal government transfers money both to state and local governments on a large scale, and states also transfer resources to localities. It has been suggested that such intergovernmental transfer programs can offset inefficiencies from interjurisdictional spillovers, and can alleviate problems resulting from inefficient migration. These increasingly important issues of fiscal federalism are taken up in Chapter 15.

CONCLUSION

1–5   As this brief introduction to our subject indicates, the scope of public economics today is very broad, and the issues raised in the economic evaluation of public policy are sometimes deep and complex. Quite often we shall have to admit that our understanding of major issues is less satisfactory than it should be. The fact is that public economics is limited by the state of the art in theoretical and empirical economics. But then this is probably a more or less permanent state of affairs, one to be expected in any evolving intellectual discipline. We can look forward to gradual improvement in the application of economic analysis to problems of public policy, and as a result to improvement in the policies themselves. We hope that readers of this book will be motivated to push their studies further and deeper, by examining some of the work of the many scholars upon whose ideas we have freely drawn and to which we have referred throughout the book.

I

The Rationale for Collective Decision-Making

2

Economic Efficiency and the Competitive Price System

INTRODUCTION

2–1   The purpose of an economic system is to allocate the scarce resources of an economy to the production of goods and services for the use of individuals in the society. In a mixed economy, such as that of the United States, two primary mechanisms are relied upon to fulfill that task. One is the market pricing system, by which privately owned and managed firms respond to prices determined by the demand and supply levels in individual markets, and undertake that level of economic activity which is in their own self-interest. The collection of all such firms operating under the institutions of the market mechanism is called the *private sector*. Resource allocation decisions are also taken by the government, or the *public sector,* through its activities of levying taxes, undertaking expenditures for goods and services, making direct money transfers to households and firms, and establishing regulations for the operation of the private sector. The public sector's decision-making actions encompass a significant share of the resources of the economy directly and influence the behavior of the private sector indirectly.[1] It is the purpose of this book to analyze the ways in which public sector decisions are taken and the effects such decisions ultimately have on the well-being of individual households of the economy.

An economy could rely entirely upon the private sector for allocating resources, but none do. The reason has to do not so much with the virtues of public sector decision-making *per se* but with the vices of the unfettered operation of a *laissez-faire* market economy. The first part of this book develops in some detail a rationale for public sector activity based upon the inadequacies of the market pricing system as a mechanism for allocating

Footnotes are found in the Chapter Notes at the end of each chapter.

resources. As a precondition for judging the effectiveness of private markets, it is necessary first to set down the criteria according to which the allocation of resources might be judged. The criteria used are two. The first is the notion of economic efficiency, which is conventionally employed by economists to judge the merits of various resource allocations and to prescribe policy. The other is the notion of equity which, although economists have traditionally had little to say about it for reasons given below, is nonetheless an important criterion used by public sector decision-makers in choosing among alternative policies. The following sections will describe in more detail the interpretation of these terms and will analyze the virtues of the pricing mechanism in achieving them. The justification for public sector economic activity occurs when circumstances exist which prevent the private market mechanism from attaining the desired level of economic efficiency and/or equity in the allocation of resources. The following chapter will discuss these circumstances.

The fourth section will serve to introduce some important methodological concepts and tools which can be used to analyze the efficiency aspects of resource allocation. In particular, we shall stress the use of market prices and the concepts of producers' and consumers' surpluses as measures of the benefits and costs of allocating resources in a particular way. These tools and their relationship to demand and supply curves will be used repeatedly in later chapters in developing the criteria for efficient resource allocation within the public sector and for analyzing the effects of public sector decisions on the efficiency of the allocation of resources in the private sector (e.g. taxes). In the fifth section we extend our discussion to consider efficient resource allocation over time and the role of markets in an intertemporal economy.

THE CONCEPT OF PARETO OPTIMALITY

2–2   Ever since Adam Smith's time the virtues of the competitive market system as a mechanism for the allocation of an economy's resources have been recognized. Self-interested individuals and firms who are able to buy and sell in free markets at given prices are led, as it were, by the "invisible hand" to specialize in those activities in which they have a comparative advantage over others. In such circumstances all participants gain from voluntarily trading in competitive markets, and the value of output produced from society's resources is maximized. Much of the field of welfare economics has been devoted to refining these concepts of gains from trade, comparative advantage, and the maximization of the value of the output of the economy under the general rubric of the notion of economic efficiency. This section and the following one will present a synopsis of the current theory of welfare economics and the role of the competitive price system in achieving an efficient use of the economy's resources.

Central to an understanding of modern welfare economics is the notion of Pareto optimality, named after the Italian economist Vilfredo Pareto (1848–1923), to whom its discovery is attributed. A *Pareto optimum* is defined as a state of affairs such that no one can be made better off without at the same time making at least one other person worse off. In the context of the economy, a Pareto-optimal allocation of resources among uses exists if it is not possible to reallocate resources so as to improve the well-being (or utility) of one person without making at least one other person worse off (i.e., reduce their utility). As will become evident, to achieve a Pareto-optimal allocation of resources is very difficult and demanding. In the real world, there are a number of reasons why it normally will not be attained. We may still be interested in using the concept of Pareto optimality to judge among arbitrary allocations of resources which are not optimal. A change in resource allocation is said to constitute a *Pareto improvement* if at least one person is made better off as a result of the change and no one is worse off. A Pareto optimum is therefore a situation in which no Pareto improvement is possible.

Unfortunately, most changes in the economy cannot be judged according to the Pareto principle, as stated above, since they involve some persons being made better off and others worse off. Indeed, this is perhaps the most important problem in welfare economics. The difficulty is that when some persons gain and others lose from an economic change, any judgment as to whether the change improves society's economic welfare involves making interpersonal comparisons between the gainers and losers. That is, inasmuch as society's welfare consists of the aggregate welfare of the individual members, it would seem that one would have to attach quantifiable weights to the gains and losses of welfare to individuals from a change before judging whether actual social welfare has risen or fallen. Economists *qua* economists have resisted prescribing such weights, since to do so would be to make a value judgment of a sort to which an economist claims no particular expertise.

In seeking to avoid making such interpersonal welfare comparisons, economists have attempted to extend the use of the Pareto principle to such circumstances in a variety of ways. One such way is to judge a move not according to whether an actual Pareto improvement is attained but according to whether a *potential Pareto improvement* occurs. For a potential Pareto improvement to occur, the gainers from the change must be hypothetically able to compensate the losers and still be better off. The change is potentially an improvement, since if the gainers actually did compensate the losers everyone would be better off. The notion of a hypothetical compensation test is not without its ambiguities. The welfare economics literature is filled with research devoted to the problems, and we can only briefly mention some of them here. More detailed surveys may be found in Mishan (1960) and Graaf (1957). The issue that arises is the form that the hypothetical compensation payments take. They may take the form of transfers of particular bundles of goods as in Kaldor (1939), Hicks (1939), and Scitovsky (1941), or transfers of general purchasing power as in Samuelson (1950). In the former, the process of making compensation payments does not affect the production of goods, while in the latter it does. Whether or not the compensation criterion is satisfied may depend upon what form the hypothetical payments are allowed to take. Also, the hypothetical compensation test may be ambiguous in the sense that the compensation criterion might be satisfied both for the change from situation one to situation two and for the reverse move from situation two to one. The possibility of such a reversal is known as the *Scitousky Paradox*. In other words, not all changes can be ordered by the hypothetical compensation test.

The notion of a hypothetical compensation criterion as a method for judging changes in social welfare naturally suggests measuring the changes in well-being of all individuals according to the common measuring stick of money, as strongly advocated by Harberger (1971a), for example. If the change in one individual's utility is valued by him to be worth $1000 and that of another is −$500, one would naturally assume that the former could compensate the latter and still be better off. Economists almost universally follow this procedure of measuring changes in individuals' welfare in monetary terms and aggregating the individual changes to measure society's welfare change. One justification for doing this would be that it indicates whether a hypothetical compensation test might be satisfied.[2]

An alternative way to justify treating a dollar's worth of benefits or losses the same for all individuals is to assume that the responsibility for securing the optimal distribution of income lies with the political decision-makers. According to this view, the economist ought to proceed as if those responsible for income redistribution were fulfilling their task and that the marginal utility of a dollar is actually the same to all. A change might then be judged according to whether the net gains in monetary terms are positive or negative. A Pareto-optimal allocation will then exist when no economic change will result in a net gain. In the analysis that follows, in judging social welfare we shall frequently follow the convention of treating a dollar's worth of utility as having the same weight for all persons.

Our interest in the concept of Pareto optimality results from the fact that it is the normative basis according to which the allocation of resources is to be judged. We shall accept as a basic value judgment that any Pareto-improving change constitutes an improvement in social welfare.[3] The concept of *economic efficiency* is derived directly from the Pareto principle. An efficient allocation of resources is defined as a Pareto-optimal one: It is not possible to make anyone better off without at the same time making someone else worse off. Similarly, a gain in economic efficiency is equivalent to a Pareto improvement. One might also consider a potential Pareto improvement to represent a gain in economic efficiency. We shall for the most part adopt the convention of measuring changes in economic efficiency in monetary terms by aggregating the monetary benefits and losses accruing to all members of society. One ought to bear in mind that to interpret this convention as changes in social welfare requires accepting that a dollar's worth of benefits can be treated as being worth the same to society no matter to whom it accrues, for one of the reasons stated above.

We now turn our attention to the matter of the efficiency of the competitive price system as a mechanism for allocating resources. Under certain circumstances, the allocation of resources resulting from the operation of competitive markets under *laissez-faire* conditions will be Pareto-optimal.[4] The conditions required for the efficiency of competitive markets will not always be satisfied, and that provides the rationale for considering a role for government in the allocation of resources.

THE EFFICIENCY OF COMPETITIVE MARKETS

2–3   The principle of Pareto optimality can be translated into specific conditions called efficiency conditions, those that must be satisfied if resource allocation in actual economies is to be efficient. In static neoclassical economies, with which we shall be concerned in this section, these conditions can be classified as *exchange efficiency, production efficiency,* and *overall efficiency* conditions. These are purely technical conditions devoid of any institutional content and independent of any resource allocation mechanism. The question we ask is how well does the private price mechanism work in achieving the efficiency conditions. It turns out that under certain assumptions about the technology of production and the preferences of individuals, the private price mechanism operating under conditions of perfect competition will allocate resources in such a way as to satisfy the efficiency conditions. The abstract model of the economy used in this section is chosen specifically to illustrate the efficiency of the competitive price system. In section 2-5 the analysis is extended to an intertemporal economy.

In order to present the analysis geometrically, all economic variables will be restricted to two dimensions. The economy will be assumed to consist of two individuals (A and B), two produced goods (X and Y), and two primary factors of production (labor L and capital K), where the latter are taken to be in fixed supply. The economic problem is to characterize the set of conditions under which labor and capital are divided between the production of X and Y, and the outputs of X and Y are allocated to A and B in such a way that no other configuration of factor and output allocations could make either A or B better off without making the other worse off. Fortunately, the results derived geometrically for the two-dimensional case generalize in a straightforward manner to the many-person, many-good, many-factor case. This will be so indicated in the following analysis.

Exchange Efficiency Conditions

Exchange efficiency is defined to exist when, for any given bundle of X and Y goods available, this bundle is divided up between A and B in such a way that it is not possible, by reallocating X and Y, to make either A or B better off without making the other worse off. The exchange efficiency conditions therefore abstract from the production side of the economy by taking the available quantities of X and Y as arbitrarily given. These conditions can apply regardless of what happens on the production side.

They merely ensure that, once produced, a given output of X and Y is allocated efficiently or optimally between A and B, or in the more general case, that whatever output of many goods is produced, they are allocated efficiently among the many consumers.

The derivation of the exchange efficiency conditions and the optimality of competitive markets can both be illustrated using the construct of an Edgeworth box diagram as in Fig. 2–1. This diagram shows all possible allocations of X and Y between A and B (assuming no X or Y is wasted). The distances $O_A \overline{X}$ and $O_A \overline{Y}$ along the horizontal and vertical axes represent the total quantities of X and Y available to the economy. Any point within the box $O_A \overline{Y} O_B \overline{X}$ represents a potential division of X and Y between A and B, where A's allocation is measured northeast from the origin O_A and B's allocation is measured southwest from O_B.

For example, consider the point e. Using the origin O_A, e represents an allocation of X_A and Y_A to individual A. Similarly, from origin O_B, individual B obtains X_B and Y_B where $X_A + X_B = \overline{X}$ and $Y_A + Y_B = \overline{Y}$, the total amounts available. In this way any point in the box represents a particular allocation of X and Y to A and B. Our task is to find which of these points satisfies the exchange efficiency conditions.

Figure 2–1

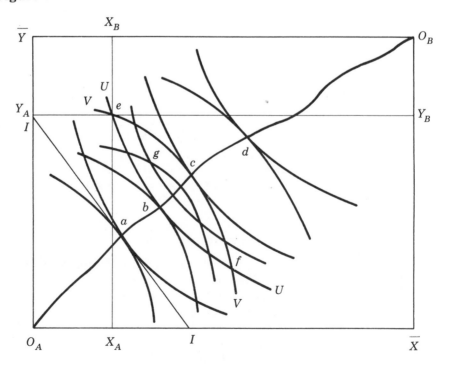

To characterize exchange efficiency requires that we be able to judge when an individual is "better off" or "worse off." We assume that each individual is the best judge of his own welfare, as reflected in his preferences for X and Y. Each is assumed to have a set of well-defined preferences that can be represented by a series of indifference curves or an indifference map. An indifference curve, such as UU for individual A or VV for B, represents the combinations of X and Y among which the individual is indifferent. Thus, A is indifferent between points e and b in the Edgeworth box. For A all points to the northeast of UU are preferred (make A better off) to all points on UU, and all points on UU are preferred to all points to the southwest. A similar property holds for VV measured from B's origin O_B. An indifference curve for each individual could be drawn through *any* point within the box; that is, all possible allocations to A and B can be ranked in order of preference. The slope of an indifference curve at any point on it represents the amount of Y the individual must be given in order to compensate him exactly for a small reduction in X so as to keep him as well off as before the change. It is called the marginal rate of substitution of Y for X and is denoted by MRS^A_{XY} for A or MRS^B_{XY} for B.[5] It is useful to think of MRS^A_{XY} as being the relative value that A places on the last (or marginal) unit of X compared with that placed on the last (or marginal) unit of Y. This interpretation is illustrated in Fig. 2–2, which depicts an indifference curve for a typical individual. The marginal rate of substitution MRS_{XY} at a point q is the slope at q. It is the amount of X that must be given up (ΔX) in order to offset exactly the effect on utility

Figure 2–2

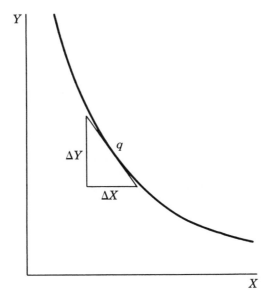

of an increase in Y of ΔY. Suppose we denote by MU_X the marginal utility of X to the individual. It is the change in utility (however "measured") per unit change in X. From a small change in X of ΔX the total change in utility is $MU_X \cdot \Delta X$. Similarly, MU_Y is the marginal utility of Y. The change in utility from a small change of ΔY is $MU_Y \cdot \Delta Y$. Since the change of ΔX and ΔY must leave the individual with the same level of utility as before, these changes in utility must be offsetting so $MU_X \cdot \Delta X = MU_Y \cdot \Delta Y$. Or, since we have defined the ratio $\Delta Y / \Delta X$ as the MRS_{XY},

$$\frac{MU_X}{MU_Y} = MRS_{XY}. \tag{2-1}$$

There are two properties of indifference maps or preference orderings which are important. First, indifference maps do not measure utility levels associated with different allocations of X and Y; they simply order them. We can say that for A, e is preferred to a in Fig. 2–1, since it is on a higher indifference curve, but we cannot say by how much it is preferred. Indifference curves may be arbitrarily numbered in order as one moves from the origin, but the numbers so attached serve only to order the curves and not to attach weights to them. Any arbitrary numbering scheme which orders the indifference curves according to individual preferences would serve just as well. The efficiency conditions do not in any way require that utility levels be measurable. Utility is assumed to be an ordinal, not a cardinal, phenomenon. (For a thorough discussion of the "measurability" of utility, see Alchian [1953].) It is, however, possible and often convenient to choose *some* numbering scheme and use it to embody in mathematical form the information represented by the indifference curves. Thus, we frequently assume that a household's preferences can be represented by a *utility function:*

$$U = U(X, Y)$$

that shows the utility number $U(X, Y)$ attached to any particular consumption point (X, Y). Any numbering scheme that attaches a higher number to higher levels of utility will serve as well.

The second assumed property of indifference curves is that they are convex to the origin. That is, individual preferences have the property that, as one acquires more and more X and less and less Y, the marginal rate of substitution of Y for X diminishes. The more X one has and the less Y, the less is the relative value placed on the marginal unit of X compared to that placed on the marginal unit of Y. This assumption is a hypothesis about individual preferences that is generally reasonable but which might be violated in particular cases.[6] It is a property which is critical for establishing the efficiency of the competitive price system.

It is apparent from Fig. 2–1 that a point such as e does not satisfy the condition of exchange efficiency as defined. From the properties of indifference curves, any point within the lens *ebfc* is preferred by both *A* and *B* to the point *e*. A reallocation of $\overline{X}$ and $\overline{Y}$ from *e* to, say, *g* puts both *A* and *B* on higher indifference curves than *UU* and *VV* and makes them both better off. Nor is *g* a point of exchange efficiency, since a lens could be formed from the indifference curves intersecting there and further reallocation could make both *A* and *B* better off. The only exchange efficiency points in the box are those for which such a lens could not be drawn, and those are points of tangency between indifference curves of *A* and *B*. Points such as *a, b, c,* and *d* are exchange-efficient since one cannot find another allocation of $\overline{X}$ and $\overline{Y}$ which makes one person better off without making the other worse off. The common condition that holds for all these points is that the slopes of the two indifference curves are equal, or

$$MRS_{XY}^A = MRS_{XY}^B. \tag{2--2}$$

In the more general case of many goods and many persons, the exchange efficiency conditions require that the *MRS* between any pair of goods must be the same for all individuals, or

$$MRS_{i,j}^h = MRS_{i,j}^k \tag{2--3}$$

for all individuals *h* and *k* and all pairs of goods *i* and *j*.

In Fig. 2–1, the locus of all points of tangency between *A*'s and *B*'s indifference curves has been drawn in as the line from O_A to O_B. It is called the *contract curve* of the Edgeworth box diagram. Since any point along the contract curve satisfies the exchange efficiency conditions, in principle there are a great many allocations which are exchange efficient. If the goods *X* and *Y* are infinitely divisible, there are an infinite number of exchange-efficient allocations for any given bundle of *X* and *Y* the economy produces. Each point differs from the other by having either *A* or *B* better off and the other worse off. This same information may be represented in a *utility possibility curve* as in Fig. 2–3. Imagine the indifference curves of *A* and *B* to be numbered according to some arbitrary scheme with the property that a higher indifference curve gets a higher number. The utility possibility curve of Fig. 2–3 then represents the combinations of utility levels so numbered attainable by *A* and *B* along the contract curve of Fig. 2–1. It has the property that it slopes downward to the right but its exact shape depends upon the arbitrary numbering scheme for ordering the utility levels U^A and U^B. The points *a, b, c, d, e, f,* and *g* are also shown in the diagram.

As Figs. 2–1 and 2–3 both clearly indicate, a movement from *e* to a point along the contract curve between (and including) *b* and *c* represents a Pareto improvement as does a movement from *e* to *g*. In each case at least one of *A* or *B* is better off and neither is worse off. A move from *e* to *a* is *not* a Pareto improvement, since *B* becomes better off, but *A* worse off. However, such a move represents a *potential* Pareto improvement in

Figure 2–3

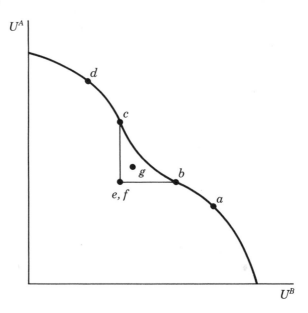

the sense that, from the point *a*, *B* could afford to compensate *A* by giving *A* enough *X* and *Y* to return him to the indifference curve *UU* and still be better off himself. *B* could compensate *A* until both were at point *b*, which is a Pareto improvement over *e*. In a like way, any point on the contract curve may be viewed as being potentially better than any point off it.

Having characterized the exchange efficiency conditions in terms of the shapes of indifference curves, it remains to show how the competitive price system ensures their satisfaction. The indifference maps used here are hypothetical constructs used to represent what preferences might look like if we could observe them. Fortunately, it is never actually necessary to observe the indifference maps of *A* and *B* in order to deduce the efficiency of competitive markets. In this economy *A* and *B* will reveal, through their behavior in competitive markets, their marginal rates of substitution between goods. This property of the voluntary revelation of relative marginal values on competitive markets is critical for the operation of the competitive pricing mechanism, and the lack of it in certain circumstances turns out to be one of the most important rationales for public sector decision-making in the economy.

The allocation of *X* and *Y* by the market price mechanism will satisfy the exchange efficiency conditions if two conditions hold. First, *A* and *B* must behave as price-takers. That is, they must behave as if they had no influence on the prices of *X* and *Y*. Second, *A* and *B* must face the same set of relative prices, p_X and p_Y, for marginal purchases of the two commodities.

Competitive markets will satisfy both these conditions. In a competitive economy, A and B will both face budget lines that are linear (since relative prices are fixed for each) and that have the same slope (since both face the same price ratio). In Fig. 2–1, suppose the line II represents A's budget line. Its slope is the price ratio facing A, and its distance from O_A is determined by the share of income in the economy accruing to A from, say, his share in the ownership of labor and capital. He elects to consume at the point a at which $MRS_{XY}^A = p_X/p_Y$, since that is on the highest attainable indifference curve. At the same time, individual B faces the same price ratio and selects a point on his budget line at which $MRS_{XY}^B = p_X/p_Y$. Since both are setting their MRS to a common ratio, the exchange efficiency conditions are satisfied:

$$MRS_{XY}^A = \frac{p_X}{p_Y} = MRS_{XY}^B. \tag{2–4}$$

In this simple two-person economy, where all income accrues to either A or B and where all X and Y must be consumed by the two persons, II must also represent the budget line from O_B for B. B will choose the allocation a from O_B, which is the same as the point chosen by A. If the budget lines of the two individuals led them to choose different points in the Edgeworth box, the economy could not be at a competitive market equilibrium since the amounts of X and Y which the two are demanding would not sum to the supplies available. Relative prices would therefore have to change until the two chose a common point of tangency within the box. Since all points of tangency lie on the contract curve, the competitive price system achieves exchange efficiency. Which exchange efficiency point along the contract curve (or utility possibility curve of Fig. 2–3) is arrived at depends upon how the income from the production of X and Y is divided between A and B. Changes in the distribution of that income will cause movements along the utility possibility curve.

One important inference may be drawn from this discussion which we shall make use of later on: In a competitive economy satisfying the exchange efficiency conditions, the relative prices reflect the relative marginal evaluations that all consuming individuals place on those goods. We may therefore use the price of a commodity as the monetary measure of its *marginal benefit*, and we shall speak of the price of a commodity as measuring its marginal social value. In terms of our definition of the marginal rate of substitution in Eq. (2–1), the following holds:

$$\frac{p_X}{p_Y} = \frac{MU_X}{MU_Y}, \text{ or, } \frac{MU_X}{p_X} = \frac{MU_Y}{p_Y}. \tag{2–5}$$

Thus, we may write prices (in dollars) as proportional to marginal utilities (however measured), or $p_X = \lambda MU_X$ and $p_Y = \lambda MU_Y$ where the factor of proportionality λ converts dollars to utility and is conventionally called the *marginal utility of income.* Provided we use the same monetary measuring standard for all commodities, the use of prices as marginal benefits for commodities will be consistent with price ratios reflecting marginal rates of substitution.

Production Efficiency Conditions

Production efficiency conditions abstract from the demand side of the economy and concentrate solely on production or supply. *Production efficiency* holds if it is not possible to reallocate factors of production among various uses in such a way as to increase the output of one good without at the same time reducing the output of some other good. The derivation of the production efficiency conditions follows a procedure analogous to that of the exchange efficiency conditions.

   Consider an economy with given supplies of labor and capital, $\bar{L}$ and $\bar{K}$, which may be used to produce outputs of X and Y. We abstract from the production and use of intermediate goods and assume that output is produced from primary factors of production alone. Figure 2–4 measures labor along the horizontal axis and capital along the vertical axis, and has O_X and O_Y as origins for measuring the use of L and K by the two "industries" X and Y. The Edgeworth box has axes of length $\bar{L}$ and $\bar{K}$. Labor and capital

Figure 2–4

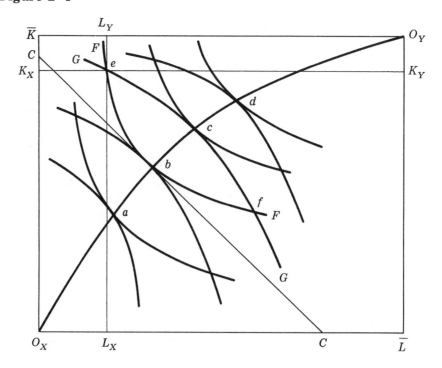

are assumed to be fully employed so any point in the box represents a particular allocation of those factors to X and Y production. For example, the point e represents an allocation of L_X and K_X to industry X, and L_Y and K_Y to industry Y where $L_X + L_Y = \overline{L}$, and $K_X + K_Y = \overline{K}$.

Each industry, when employing a particular amount of labor and capital, will be able to produce some maximum amount of output, this amount being determined by the state of technology relating inputs to outputs. This relationship is often summarized mathematically using a *production function*. For instance, the equation

$$X = f(K_X, L_X) \tag{2-6}$$

shows how much output of good X will be forthcoming when industry X uses K_X and L_X of capital and labor. Much of the information about the technology of production represented by a production function can also be displayed geometrically by the map of isoquants corresponding to each industry. For industry X, FF represents one of a series of isoquants drawn from the origin O_X. Each isoquant shows those combinations of L_X and K_X which are required to produce a given level of output of X. As one moves northeast from one X isoquant to another, the level of output rises. In an analogous way, GG represents one of many isoquants for industry Y measured from O_Y. Moving southwest from O_Y, successive isoquants represent higher levels of output of Y. Of course, output levels associated with each isoquant are measurable, unlike utility levels of indifference curves.

The slope of an isoquant at any point indicates the increase in K required to compensate for a small reduction in L and still maintain the same given level of output. It is called the *marginal rate of technical substitution* of K for L and is denoted $MRTS_{LK}^X$ and $MRTS_{LK}^Y$ for industries X and Y respectively.[7] The interpretation of the $MRTS_{LK}$ is analogous to the interpretation put on the MRS_{XY} earlier. It is the relative value to the industry of the last unit of labor relative to the last unit of capital. The value to an industry of an incremental increase in labor is the increase in output that results or the *marginal product of labor* denoted MP_L. The value of an increment of capital is the *marginal product of capital, MP_K*. By exactly analogous reasoning to that used in Fig. 2–2 for indifference curves, the $MRTS_{LK}$ is given by the following:

$$MRTS_{LK}^X = \frac{MP_{LX}}{MP_{KX}}; \quad MRTS_{LK}^Y = \frac{MP_{LY}}{MP_{KY}}. \tag{2-7}$$

Isoquants are assumed to be convex to the origin. That is, the $MRTS_{LK}$ falls as one substitutes L for K along an isoquant. This follows directly from the hypothesis of diminishing marginal products. As L rises relative to K, MP_L falls and MP_K rises. Therefore, by Eq. (2–7), $MRTS_{LK}$ must fall.

The production efficiency conditions are satisfied when a rearrangement of $\overline{L}$ and $\overline{K}$ between X and Y cannot increase the output of one without reducing the output of the other. Consider the point *e*. It is obviously an inefficient point since within the lens *ebfc* both industries will be on a higher isoquant producing more output. Only at points of tangency between isoquants can the output of one industry not be increased without decreasing the output of the other. Points *a, b, c,* and *d* are all allocations of $\overline{L}$ and $\overline{K}$ which are production-efficient. The contract curve $O_X abcd O_Y$ is the locus of all production-efficient points for the given supplies of $\overline{L}$ and $\overline{K}$ and the given technologies of production. Production efficiency is therefore characterized by a situation in which

$$MRTS_{LK}^X = MRTS_{LK}^Y. \qquad (2-8)$$

In the more general case, production efficiency requires the marginal rate of technical substitution between any two factors of production to be the same in all industries.

An alternative way to depict the locus of production-efficient points is by a *production possibility curve* that shows the combinations of *X* and *Y* which may be produced in the economy. It is constructed by taking the outputs of *X* and *Y* associated with each point on the contract curve and plotting them in a diagram as in Fig. 2–5. The points *a–f* correspond to the points *a–f* in Fig. 2–4. The slope of the production possibility curve is called the *marginal rate of transformation* of *Y* for *X* or MRT_{XY}. It is the increase in $Y(\Delta Y)$ that can be obtained by reducing the output of *X* by ΔX. To give it a more analytical interpretation, imagine that, starting from a given point on the production possibility curve, the output of *X* is reduced

Figure 2–5

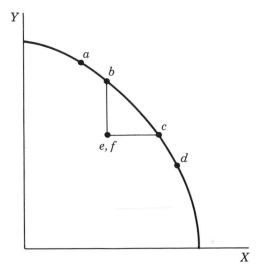

and that of Y increased by shifting a small amount of labor from X to Y. The decrease in X's output will be given by $\Delta X = MP_{LX} \cdot \Delta L$ and the increase in Y's output will be given by $\Delta Y = MP_{LY} \cdot \Delta L$. Since ΔL is the same in both cases, the MRT_{XY} is given by:

$$MRT_{XY} = \frac{\Delta Y}{\Delta X} = \frac{MP_{LY}}{MP_{LX}}. \qquad (2\text{-}9)$$

Using a similar line of reasoning, but supposing K to be transferred from X to Y, it is easy to show that the marginal rate of transformation is also equal to the ratio of the marginal products of capital in the two industries:

$$MRT_{XY} = \frac{MP_{KY}}{MP_{KX}}. \qquad (2\text{-}10)$$

The market price mechanism will ensure satisfaction of the production efficiency conditions provided all firms are price-takers for factors of production and all firms pay the same factor prices. In other words, production efficiency will result from the operation of competitive factor markets. To see this, suppose that the prices paid for labor and capital are w (the wage rate) and r (the rental) respectively. Firms will always be motivated to produce their outputs at a minimum cost. Suppose, for example, that X is going to produce the level of output given by the isoquant FF in Fig. 2–4. At the going factor prices w and r, the minimum cost combination of L and K is that at which an isocost line is tangential to the isoquant FF where an isocost line has a slope of w/r.[8] Any other point on FF will lie on a higher isocost line and so will not be chosen. In Fig. 2–4 the minimum cost isocost line is given by CC. It is tangential to FF at the point b. At that point, the slope of the isocost line, w/r, equals the slope of the isoquant $MRTS_{LK}^{X}$. The Y industry faces the same factor prices w and r and minimizes costs in the same way by selecting a point of tangency between an isoquant and an isocost line. Since the slope of its isocost line is the same as that for industry X, cost minimization yields the following:

$$MRTS_{LK}^{X} = \frac{w}{r} = MRTS_{LK}^{Y}. \qquad (2\text{-}11)$$

In other words, the production efficiency conditions will be satisfied. In the two-industry model of Fig. 2–4, the wage-rental ratio will adjust until both industries choose the same point of tangency in the box diagram. This competitively determined point of tangency will be on the contract curve and will correspond to a point on the production possibility curve.

Just as goods' prices can be interpreted as marginal benefits to consumers, so factor prices can be interpreted as representing the marginal value of factors of production to firms. We know from the elementary theory of the firm that competitive firms hire factors of production until the price of the factor equals the value of the marginal product of that factor,[9] or

$$w = p \cdot MP_L = VMP_L$$

$$r = p \cdot MP_K = VMP_K.$$

(2–12)

Therefore, not only does the ratio of factor prices (w/r) reflect the relative marginal values placed on them $(MRTS_{LK})$, but also factor prices themselves are a measure of the marginal value of the factor of production to the firm.

Overall Efficiency Conditions

The production efficiency conditions determine the infinite number of combinations of X and Y which can be produced efficiently in an economy with given supplies of L and K. The exchange efficiency conditions give the infinite number of ways in which each (X, Y) combination can be allocated to individuals A and B so that both cannot be made better off. There is therefore a double infinity of allocations that satisfy the exchange and production efficiency conditions. The overall efficiency conditions serve to restrict considerably the number of those allocations which are Pareto-optimal.

The satisfaction of the production efficiency conditions implies that labor and capital are being used efficiently and the economy is operating at some point along its production possibility curve. Each point along the curve has associated with it a marginal rate of transformation which determines the rate at which X can be converted into Y at the margin, or $MRT_{XY} = (\Delta Y/\Delta X)_{production}$. The satisfaction of the exchange efficiency conditions implies that the output of X and Y from production is allocated between the consumers A and B in such a way that they have a common marginal rate of substitution, MRS_{XY}. This MRS_{XY} indicates the rate at which consumers are willing to substitute X for Y at the margin and still be as well off; or, $MRS_{XY} = (\Delta Y/\Delta X)_{consumption}$. The overall efficiency condition requires that these two be identical:

$$MRT_{XY} = MRS_{XY}.$$

(2–13)

That is, the rate at which Y can be substituted for X in production must equal the rate at which Y can be substituted for X in consumption. If these two are not equal, it is possible to make both A and B better off by a change in production and allocation. For example, suppose $MRT_{XY} > MRS_{XY}$. This means that the increase in Y which can be attained by foregoing a small amount of output of X on the production side exceeds the amount of Y required to compensate for the reduced X on the consumption side. Therefore, both persons could be made better off by increasing Y at the expense of X, compensating each for his loss of X and having some Y left over to make both better off. The opposite holds if $MRT_{XY} < MRS_{XY}$. Only if Eq. (2–13) holds will it not be possible by reallocating resources to make one better off without making the other worse off. Therefore, Eq. (2–13) is the condition which must hold if resource allocation is to be Pareto-optimal.

A Pareto-optimal allocation of resources for the two-dimensional case is shown in Fig. 2–6. The curve PP is the production possibility curve derived from the contract curve of the Edgeworth box of $\overline{L}$ and $\overline{K}$. At the point a on PP the output combination (X_0, Y_0) is produced with an MRT_{XY} given by the slope of PP at a. The outputs X_0, Y_0 are then used to construct the Edgeworth box for the allocation of X and Y to A and B. A's indifference map is drawn from the origin O, B's is drawn from the origin a, and the contract curve is the line joining O and a. A Pareto optimum (if it exists for a) will be that allocation of X_0 and Y_0 between A and B such that the common MRS_{XY} equals the MRT_{XY}. One such point, of which there may be many, is shown at b. In general, there may be at least one point of Pareto optimality associated with all outputs of X and Y along PP. That is, there may be an infinite number of them, each of which will differ in the relative levels of utility of A and B.

Figure 2–6

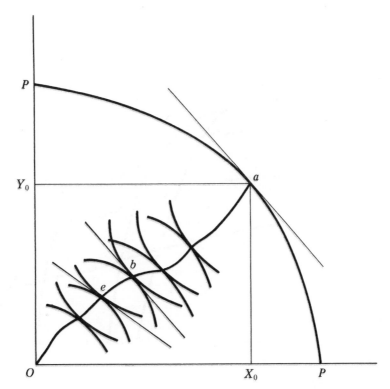

The same point may be illustrated using the device of utility possibility curves introduced above in Fig. 2–3. There we saw that a utility possibility curve could be constructed for the contract curve Oa in Fig. 2–6 by arbitrarily numbering the indifference curves for both A and B in order of their level of utility and plotting the utility levels so numbered on a diagram. In Fig. 2–7, the curve cd represents the utility possibility curve associated with the contract curve Oa in Fig. 2–6 and the points b and e represent the same allocations in the two diagrams. Point e does not satisfy the overall optimum conditions since it has an MRS_{XY} which is less than the MRT_{XY} of the output combination a. There will be another output combination at which more Y and less X is produced which can make both A and B better off than at e. It will have an Edgeworth box and a contract curve associated with it which will yield a utility possibility curve such as gh in Fig. 2–7. There will be a point f on that utility possibility curve which is Pareto-optimal and which is superior to e. In a similar way, utility possibility curves may be drawn for contract curves associated with any output along PP. Several of these are shown in Fig. 2–7. For points such as e which do not satisfy the overall efficiency conditions, there will always be a utility

Figure 2–7

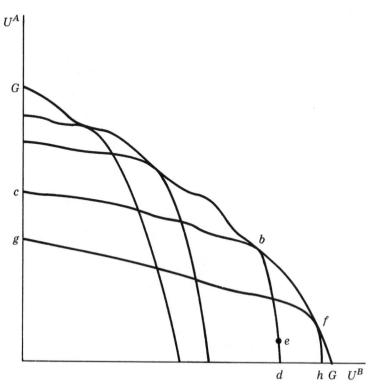

possibility curve which passes to the northeast of it and makes both better off. For points such as *b* and *f* which are Pareto-optimal, no utility combination to the northeast can be attained. The curve *GG* is the envelope of all points of Pareto optimality, such as *b* and *f*, and is called the *grand utility possibility curve*. It shows all the infinite combinations of U^A and U^B which may be attained given the resources, tastes, and technology of the economy.

In the following chapters we shall frequently have recourse to the terms efficiency and equity as criteria either for judging resource allocation or as policy objectives. Their meaning can be indicated using the grand utility possibility curve *GG* of Fig. 2–8. It is conventionally said that any change which moves the economy from a non-Pareto-optimal point such as *d* to a Pareto-optimal point such as *a*, *b*, or *c* improves the efficiency of the economy. It does so in the sense that the gainers could compensate the losers with transfers of income and still be better off. More generally, efficiency is improved whenever the gain to the gainers exceeds the loss to the losers. Policy decisions based on efficiency criteria alone would favor any change which involved a move from *d* to any point on *GG*. However, a move along the grand utility possibility curve from, say, *a* to *b* cannot be judged on

Figure 2–8

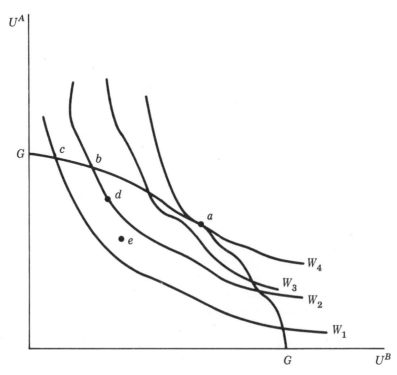

efficiency grounds. Both are Pareto-optimal and therefore efficient. Any such judgment must be made on equity grounds; that is, by weighting the relative changes of utility of A and B. Since this involves interpersonal comparisons of utility, it requires the sort of value judgment that economic analysis alone is incapable of making. As we shall see, public sector resource allocation decisions are, in fact, sometimes taken with the equity criterion in mind as, for example, when the tax system is used to redistribute income. While the economist may refrain from the value judgments required to make such decisions, he may take those value judgments as given from elsewhere in the political decision-making process and apply economic analysis using the equity criterion thus selected. The conceptual tool for introducing equity into the analysis of resource allocation problems, formally defined by Bergson (1938), is the *social welfare function*, which "measures" social welfare as a function of the utility levels achieved by the individuals of society. It is denoted W and written as:

$$W = W(U^1, U^2, \ldots, U^i, \ldots.) \tag{2-14}$$

where U^i refers to the utility level of the ith person. In the two-person case, the social welfare function may be depicted by the contour lines W_1, W_2, W_3, and W_4 in Fig. 2-8, each one representing a successively higher social welfare level. If this were the social welfare function, a would be the maximum level of social welfare attainable, or the *optimum optimorum*, as it is called. The concept of a social welfare function brings out clearly the conflict that may arise between the equity and efficiency criteria. It is obvious in Fig. 2-8 that b is socially preferred to c. Starting at c, a policy of redistributing income from A to B might recommend itself, especially since one would ideally like to arrive eventually at the point a. However, the process of income redistribution may itself introduce distortions into the economy which prevent the economy from moving along the grand utility possibility curve. Thus, as one redistributes income, the economy may move from c to d. Since d is clearly on a higher social welfare contour than c, the gains in equity more than offset the losses in efficiency. Further redistribution may move the economy from d to e. The gain to B, as valued by the social welfare function, is more than offset by the loss to A, so the move should not be taken. This illustration is only conceptual in the sense that the social welfare function is not known, and cannot be known on the basis of economic reasoning alone. Nonetheless, it does show the nature of the conflict between equity and efficiency considerations that is likely to arise whatever value judgment is taken regarding equity. It is a conflict which we shall return to when discussing the use of the tax system for redistributing income in Part III of this book.

    It remains for us to indicate how the market price system in the model of the economy with which we are dealing ensures satisfaction of the overall optimum conditions. What is required, in addition to the conditions required for the satisfaction of the exchange and production efficiency conditions, is that the markets for X and Y be competitive. All producers must be price-takers and must face the same market prices for each commodity as other producers. Also, producers and consumers must face the same set of relative prices for commodities. Under these circumstances, profit-maximizing firms in industries X and Y will both hire labor and capital until the cost of the factors equals the value of their marginal product as in Eq. (2–12). Since the same price, w, is paid for labor in both X and Y, the VMP_L is the same in both X and Y, or

$$p_X \cdot MP_{LX} = p_Y \cdot MP_{LY}. \tag{2-15}$$

Rearranging this equation gives:

$$\frac{p_X}{p_Y} = \frac{MP_{LY}}{MP_{LX}} = MRT_{XY}. \tag{2-16}$$

That is, the MRT_{XY} equals the ratio of goods' prices. Since the ratio of goods' prices also equals MRS_{XY} for both consumers, the overall efficiency conditions (2–13) are satisfied.

There is an alternative way of looking at the correspondence between relative prices and MRT_{XY} which is useful in what follows. Profit-maximizing competitive firms produce that output at which price equals *marginal cost,* denoted MC. The marginal cost is the change in total resource costs (ΔC) associated with a small change in output. Thus, $MC_X = \Delta C_X/\Delta X$ and $MC_Y = \Delta C_Y/\Delta Y$. Suppose that at some point on the production possibility curve, a small amount of resources valued at ΔC is transferred from the X industry to the Y industry. From the fact that the change in resource costs in $X(\Delta C_X)$ and that in $Y(\Delta C_Y)$ both equal ΔC, we may take the ratio of marginal costs and deduce the following:

$$\frac{MC_X}{MC_Y} = \frac{\Delta C_X/\Delta X}{\Delta C_Y/\Delta Y} = \frac{\Delta Y}{\Delta X} = MRT_{XY}. \tag{2-17}$$

The MRT_{XY} is the ratio of the marginal costs of X and Y, and therefore is the ratio of prices of X and Y.

In a Pareto-optimal economy, the prices p_X and p_Y can be interpreted as social or efficiency values in monetary terms. We have already seen how these prices can be taken as a measure of marginal benefits to all consumers when the exchange efficiency conditions are satisfied. In a similar way, when the overall conditions are satisfied these same prices measure the marginal opportunity cost of the resources used to produce the commodity. This interpretation of market prices as marginal benefits and costs is a property of an efficiently operating economy. When, for one reason or another, the economy is not operating efficiently, we shall have to reassess the role of market prices as reflecting social benefits and costs. This will be particularly important in the discussion of cost-benefit analysis in Part II.

CONSUMERS' AND PRODUCERS' SURPLUS AND
THE MEASUREMENT OF WELFARE CHANGE

2–4   The conditions of Pareto optimality characterize an economically efficient allocation of resources in which the gains from engaging in production and exchange opportunities are completely exploited. In many public finance applications we are interested in comparing two (not-necessarily optimal) allocations of resources to see what gains or losses in economic welfare are involved in moving from one to the other. Policy prescriptions are ultimately based on the notion that the policy change will improve social welfare. In some cases, the change in social welfare will be inferred from an actual attempt at measurement (as when a cost-benefit analysis is performed). In other cases, where exact measurement is difficult, the methodology of welfare analysis will be employed qualitatively in the advocacy of one policy or another. In either case, it is important that we determine at the outset the set of analytical tools appropriate for indicating (conceptually or actually) the changes in economic welfare likely to result from various public sector decisions. The basic tools for analysis are none other than simple demand and supply curves. These curves are the devices from which we can determine changes in economic welfare to demanders, or *consumers' surplus,* and changes in economic welfare to suppliers, or *producers' surplus.* It is the purpose of this section to examine the use of consumers' and producers' surpluses to evaluate the welfare changes arising from various policy-induced changes in the allocation of resources.

Fundamental to the use of demand and supply curves for the measurement of welfare change is the fact that prices can be interpreted as monetary measures of the marginal benefits of goods to households and of the marginal cost of production to firms. As we have seen in Section 2–3, this is because households allocate their income among the purchase of various goods in such a way that the marginal value in monetary terms equals the price for each good. Similarly, competitive firms will produce to the point at which price equals marginal cost. This interpretation of price allows us to develop the notions of consumer and producer surplus using demand and supply curves as follows:

Consider first the demand side. Let us measure the gain in welfare to consumers from a fall in the price of a good; all other prices and income will be held constant. Fig. 2–9 depicts the market demand curve for good X, drawn on the assumption that all other prices and incomes are fixed. (Ignore the right-hand side diagram in this Fig., for now). Initially, the price of X is p_X^1 and the quantity consumed is X_1. Suppose that the price falls to p_X^2 and demand rises to X_2. At the price p_X^1, the consumers placed a value of X_1a on the last unit consumed. As the price falls, the consumers consume additional amounts of X which are "worth" less to them; that is, for which they would have been willing to pay less and less. When the price has fallen to p_X^2, the last unit consumed is worth X_2b. If we imagined that the price fall occurred gradually, the marginal value of each additional

Figure 2–9

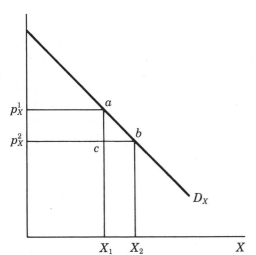
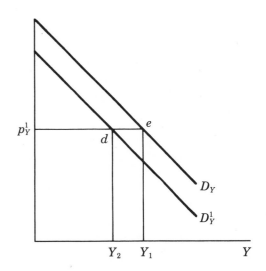

unit consumed would be the vertical distance to the demand curve. Adding up the values of the entire increment in consumption in going from X_1 to X_2, the total value placed on these goods by the market is X_1abX_2. This is approximately the maximum amount of money that the consumers would have been willing to pay for the $X_2 - X_1$ units of output.[10] In fact, the consumers have had to pay only X_1cbX_2 for these extra units of output, so they have acquired a net surplus of abc on the additional consumption. In addition, they are paying $p_X^1acp_X^2$ less for the original X_1 units consumed. Thus, in total, they are paying $p_X^1abp_X^2$ less than what they previously paid for X_1 units plus what they would have paid for $X_2 - X_1$ extra units.

This area, $p_X^1abp_X^2$, is referred to as the *consumers' surplus* of the price fall. It is conventional to view it as a monetary measure of the welfare change from a price reduction to consumers as a whole, but we ought to be cautious about its interpretation. Since the aggregate demand curve of Fig. 2–9 is the sum of the demand curves of all households, the consumers' surplus is the sum of the monetary surplus obtained by each household from the price fall. No distinction is drawn among households. A dollar's worth of surplus to one household is treated as having the same weight as a dollar's worth to another, regardless of their income levels. Thus, distributive or equity implications are disregarded entirely. In using the consumers' surplus as a measure of welfare change this should be borne in mind.

The consumers' surplus measure is the fundamental tool for measuring welfare change to consumers due to price and income changes. There is an alternative, but equivalent, way to represent the same welfare change geometrically which is useful in some applications, such as cost-benefit analysis. We shall refer to it as the *total benefit* method. It will be illustrated using Fig. 2–9 for the special case of an economy consisting of only two goods, X and Y. The price of X will be assumed to fall from p_X^1 to p_X^2 with the price of Y and income unchanged. Good Y could be thought of as a composite of all goods other than X. Initially, the demands are X_1 and Y_1. When p_X falls, the demand curve for Y shifts to, say, D_Y^1 and the new demands are X_2 and Y_2. As we have seen, the increase in consumer welfare is $p_X^1 abp_X^2$, the change in consumers' surplus. We can arrive at an equivalent measure of welfare change as follows: Since the consumers' incomes have not changed, the increase in expenditure on X, or $X_1 cbX_2 - p_X^1 acp_X^2$, equals the reduction in expenditures on Y, or $Y_2 deY_1$. Substitute this into the welfare change measure $p_X^1 abp_X^2$ as follows:

$$p_X^1 abp_X^2 = p_X^1 acp_X^2 + abc$$

$$= X_1 cbX_2 - Y_2 deY_1 + abc \qquad (2\text{–}18)$$

$$= X_1 abX_2 - Y_2 deY_1.$$

The first term, $X_1 abX_2$, is, as we have seen, the maximum amount of money the consumers would have paid for the additional $X_2 - X_1$ units of good X. We refer to it as the *total benefit* of the increased demand. The second term is the reduced expenditures on Y, whose price has not changed. We refer to this as the loss in total benefit on the market for Y. Since p_Y has not changed, the value of each unit of Y lost is p_Y. The same principle applies to cases in which there are many commodities such as Y whose demands change in reaction to a change in the price of X. The change in consumers' welfare from a change in price of X would then become:

$$X_1 abX_2 + \sum_i p_i \Delta Y_i \qquad (2\text{–}19)$$

where the Y_is are all other commodities and p_i is the price of Y_i. The above analysis is applicable when the price of one good changes while income and all other prices are held constant.

Let us briefly discuss the welfare changes associated with changes in income and other prices. A *ceteris paribus* change in income shifts the consumer's budget line out parallel and causes a change in welfare equal to the amount of the income change. In terms of demand curves, consider again the case of an economy with two goods, X and Y. When income changes, the demand curves for X and Y may both shift. For goods that are normal the demand curve shifts right. The welfare change is the increase in expenditures as illustrated in the next example.

Suppose now that both income of consumers and the price of one good, say p_X, change. To estimate the welfare change, one should imagine that the two changes occur sequentially, and sum up the welfare change occurring at each step. For example, consider an income rise accompanied by a fall in the price of good X. The welfare change would be similar to that obtained from an income rise followed by a price reduction. First, welfare would increase by the amount of the increase in income. Then, the price reduction would cause a further increase in welfare which would correspond to the consumer's greater surplus from a price fall starting at the higher income.

This is illustrated in Fig. 2–10 using market demand curves. Initially X_1 and Y_1 are demanded at the prices of p_X and p_Y. When income rises, the demand curves shift right to D'_X and D'_Y (assuming X and Y are normal goods). The welfare change at this stage is the increase in total expenditure $X_1abX_2 + Y_1deY_2$. Next, at the higher level of income, the price of X falls to p'_X. The demand for X rises to X_3 and, assuming an elastic demand for X, the demand curve for Y shifts left to D''_Y. The welfare change of this price fall is the consumers' surplus $p_Xbcp'_X$ or, equivalently, the total benefit $X_2bcX_3 - Y_3feY_2$. By combining these two welfare changes, we obtain the welfare change of the combined income and price change:

$$X_1abcX_3 + Y_1dfY_3. \tag{2-20}$$

Next consider the welfare change from a simultaneous change in the price of two goods. To analyze this case it is useful to imagine the consumer spending his income on three goods, X, Y, and Z, as depicted in Fig. 2–11.

Figure 2–10

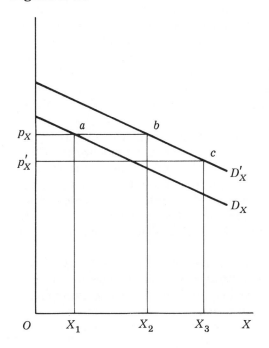
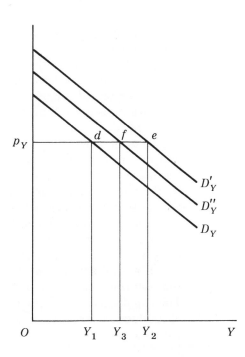

Figure 2–11

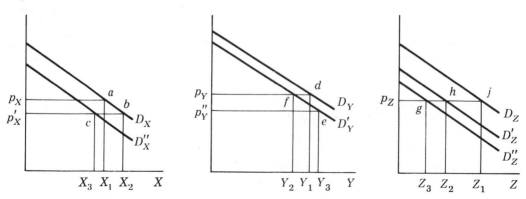

Initially, prices p_X, p_Y, and p_Z are in effect and X_1, Y_1, and Z_1 units are consumed. Imagine now a fall in the prices of goods X and Y, with p_Z unchanged. Taking the two price changes sequentially, p_X falls to p_X', causing the demand for X to rise to X_2, and the demand curves for Y and Z to shift to D_Y' and D_Z'. The welfare change from this step is the consumers' surplus area $p_X abp_X'$, or $X_1 abX_2 - Y_2 fdY_1 - Z_2 hjZ_1$. Next, the price of Y falls to p_Y'', causing the demand for Y to rise to Y_3 along the new demand curve D_Y' and shifting the demand curves for X and Z to D_X'' and D_Z''. The welfare change from this step is $p_Y fep_Y''$, or $Y_2 feY_3 - X_3 cbX_2 - Z_3 ghZ_2$. The aggregate welfare change from the combined price change is the sum of these two welfare changes. It can be expressed in two forms, in terms of consumers' surpluses or in terms of total benefits. In the former case, the welfare change is the sum of the consumers' surpluses $p_X abp_X' + p_Y fep_Y''$. That is, it is the sum of the consumers' surplus from the initial fall in p_X plus the consumers' surplus from the subsequent fall in p_Y, *conditional* on the already lowered price p_X'.[11] The equivalent welfare change measure in terms of total benefits is $X_1 abX_2 - X_3 cbX_2 + Y_2 feY_3 - Y_2 fdY_1 - Z_3 gjZ_1$.

To summarize, the utility of consumers will change whenever the prices and/or income facing them change. If we treat a dollar's worth of real income as worth the same for all, the change in welfare can be approximated by the sum of consumers' surplus changes plus the income change, where the consumers' surpluses are evaluated as if the price and income changes occurred in an arbitrary order. Equivalently, it is the sum of total benefits and total expenditures arising from the price and income changes as illustrated in the above example.

In a similar way, we can define the concept of *producers' surplus* as representing the welfare change resulting from price changes to suppliers. The suppliers can be firms producing goods or households supplying factors of production (such as labor). This concept is illustrated using Fig. 2–12, which depicts the aggregate supply curve for labor L at various wage rates

Figure 2–12

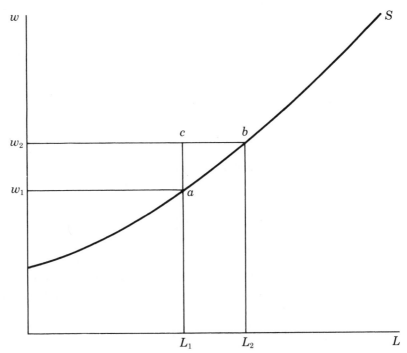

w. If the wage rate rises from w_1 to w_2, the labor supply rises from L_1 to L_2. The producers' surplus of the wage increase is the area w_2baw_1. This is the sum of the additional wage payment to the original workers (w_2caw_1) plus the excess of the wage payment for the new workers (L_1cbL_2) over the minimum amount they would have been willing to work for (L_1abL_2).[12] We refer to L_1abL_2 as the *total cost* of the additional work supplied.

The supply curve in Fig. 2–12 could also have been interpreted as the aggregate supply curve for a commodity by a competitive industry. In this case the area L_1abL_2 would be interpreted as the total cost to the economy of an increase in supply from L_1 to L_2. The industry supply curve may rise either because of increasing factor prices facing the industry as the industry output rises, or because of diminishing returns to scale as the industry expands. The distinction is discussed in the classic paper by Viner (1931). In either case, the supply curve is the true opportunity cost of supplying the additional output ($L_2 - L_1$), and w_2baw_1 is the producers' surplus. If the supply curve rises due to rising factor prices, the factor owners receive the surplus. If there are diminishing returns to scale, as the output expands the owners of the firms in the industry will receive the surplus as an increase in rent.

To complete this section, let us apply these concepts of consumers' and producers' surplus, and total benefits and costs, to an example of the measurement of welfare change associated with economy-wide changes in resource allocation. The example will illustrate the equivalence between two approaches to the measurement of welfare changes:

1. Add up the changes in consumers' and producers' surpluses to all parties involved;
2. Measure the total benefit and total cost of the change and subtract the latter from the former.

In many cases it will turn out that the latter method is simpler to apply, as we shall see in the discussion of cost-benefit analysis in Chapter 8. It ignores the transfer of money that actually takes place in each situation and concentrates solely on changes in areas beneath the demand and supply curves.

The simplest example to consider is the welfare change from introducing an excise tax into the economy: Suppose that producer prices in the economy are fixed so as to avoid introducing producers' surplus (the latter will be considered again in Chapter 9). In addition, assume that excise tax revenues are removed from the economy, so that the tax collections represent a net resource loss to society. (Alternative dispositions of the tax revenues will be subsequently considered.)

Fig. 2–13 illustrates this case where X is the taxed good and Y is a composite representing all other goods in the economy. The initial prices

Figure 2–13

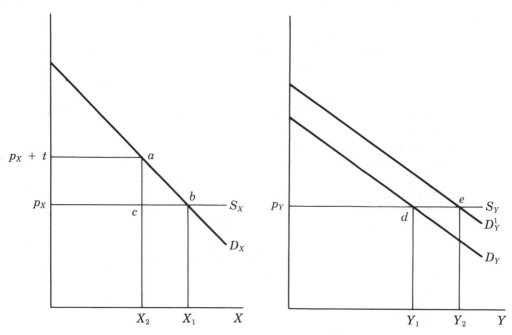

are p_X and p_Y, and these equal the fixed marginal costs of producing X and Y. A tax of t is imposed on X causing the price of X to rise to $(p_X + t)$. On the assumption that X and Y are substitutes, the demand curve for Y shifts right to D_Y^1. Since the tax revenue is assumed to be removed from the economy, the only change facing consumers is the rise in price of X. All other prices (including factor prices) and consumer incomes remain fixed by the assumptions we have made. Using aggregate consumers' surplus as the welfare change measure, society is worse off by the loss of consumers surplus $(p_X + t)abp_X$. There is no change in producers' surplus, so the welfare change from the tax is $-(p_X + t)abp_X$.

Using total benefits and costs as the criteria yields the same welfare change measure. The change in total benefit to consumers is $-X_2abX_1 + Y_1deY_2$. However, additional resource costs of Y_1deY_2 are incurred in the production of Y, while resources worth X_2cbX_1 are saved in the X industry. In addition, there is a social cost of $(p_X + t)acp_X$, the tax revenues collected, since we assume they are lost to society. By combining these amounts, we obtain $(Y_1deY_2 - X_2abX_1) + (X_2cbX_1 - Y_1deY_2) - (p_X + t)acp_X = (p_X + t)abp_X$.

Matters are slightly more complicated when the tax revenues are assumed to be returned to the consumers as lump-sum income transfers. In this case, the consumers face the loss in consumers' surplus from the price rise as before, but benefit from the increase in transfer income of $(p_X + t)acp_X$. Thus, the net change in surplus is $-(p_X + t)abp_X + (p_X + t)acp_X = -abc$. This welfare change is referred to as the dead-weight loss of the tax and will be discussed further in later chapters.

Using the total benefits and costs, the same results can be obtained by noting that the total benefit from the tax-*cum*-transfer change is $-X_2abX_1 + Y_1deY_2$. Total cost changes are $-X_2cbX_1$ on the market for X and Y_1deY_2 in the market for all other goods. Subtracting total costs from total benefits yields $-abc$ as before.

EFFICIENCY IN AN
INTERTEMPORAL ECONOMY

2–5   (a) The Efficiency Conditions
in a Two-Period Intertemporal Model

So far the discussion has not dealt in any explicit way with the fact that economic activity takes place over time; the analysis has been static (referring to a single moment of time), or atemporal (not referring to time at all), as opposed to dynamic or intertemporal. However, as we show in this section, many of the ideas of Section 2–3 can be extended directly to a dynamic economy. We begin by presenting the simplest such extension, one in which the economy exists for only two periods of time, called "present" and "future," and in which there are only two corresponding commodities: present consumption (C_p) and future consumption (C_f). As in the previous discussion, the arguments can be generalized to the many-commodity, many-time period case, and we briefly discuss later the nature of some of these generalizations.

Just as in the atemporal analysis of the preceding sections, we assume that consumers, as of the present moment, have preferences over the two consumption goods C_p and C_f representable by a utility function

$$U = U(C_p, C_f). \tag{2-21}$$

This should be thought of as the consumer's present evaluation of the consumption patterns (C_p, C_f) extending from the present until the end of the consumer's lifetime; it may be called the consumer's *lifetime utility*. The consumer's preferences may also be represented by indifference curves with the same properties as in the atemporal case as shown in Fig. 2–14. At any point on an indifference curve, the slope is the marginal rate of substitution of present for future consumption, MRS_{fp}. As before, MRS_{fp} may be also considered to be the ratio of the marginal utilities of consumption, MU_f/MU_p. As one obtains more C_f and less C_p the MRS_{fp} falls due to the assumed property of diminishing marginal utility of consumption. Along the 45° line in Fig. 2–14, C_p and C_f are equal. In this case, the term $(1/MRS_{fp} - 1)$, is often called the *rate of pure time preference* since it is the proportionate increase in consumption in the future that is required to compensate for a given reduction in consumption now.[13] It indicates the

Figure 2–14

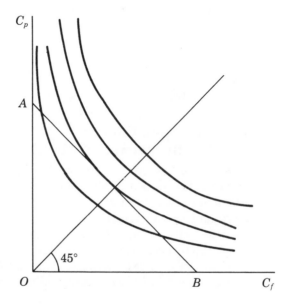

premium that the individual places on present consumption over future consumption because of the time factor alone.

On the production side, one could draw a production possibility curve between C_f and C_p indicating the rate at which future consumption goods could be produced by abstaining from present consumption. Resources which could otherwise have been used to produce consumption goods are instead invested to produce consumption goods at some future date. The production possibility curve might have the same shape as *PP* in Fig. 2–6. At any point, its slope would be the marginal rate of transformation, MRT_{fp}, or the rate at which C_f could be transformed into C_p at the margin $(\Delta C_p / \Delta C_f)$.

The conditions for Pareto optimality are exactly equivalent to those derived for the case of two goods X and Y. The overall efficiency condition is:

$$MRS_{fp} = MRT_{fp} \tag{2–22}$$

where MRS_{fp} is the marginal rate of substitution for all individuals in society (by exchange efficiency). Also, the production efficiency conditions must hold at an optimum, so that factors of production are properly allocated within those industries producing present consumption goods and those producing investment or future consumption goods.

Perfectly functioning markets can insure that a Pareto-optimal allocation of resources can be achieved in an intertemporal economy. This requires, in particular, perfect capital markets which allow consumers and firms to lend or borrow as much as they desire, in the present period, at the market rate of interest, r. With such markets, a consumer with an income in the present period of Y_p, and a future (non-interest) income of Y_f, can choose any pattern of present and future consumption that satisfies the following budget constraint:

$$C_f = Y_f + (Y_p - C_p)(1 + r); \tag{2–23}$$

that is, future consumption equals future income, plus savings $Y_p - C_p$ carried forward from the present, plus interest on the savings. Note that if the consumer borrows in the present period (i.e. present savings $Y_p - C_p$ is negative), the interpretation of (2–23) is that future consumption is lower than future income by the amount of principal plus interest on the consumer's debt.

If we divide (2–23) through by $(1 + r)$ and rearrange, we get a slightly different version of the budget constraint:

$$C_p + \frac{C_f}{1 + r} = Y_p + \frac{Y_f}{1 + r}. \tag{2–24}$$

This equation shows that the *present value* of two-period consumption must equal the present value of two-period income discounted at the interest rate r.[14] The budget line AB in Fig. 2–14 is a curve representing Eq. (2–23) or (2–24). The slope of AB is $(1 + r)^{-1}$. The consumer maximizes utility over the two periods by choosing the point on the budget at which his indifference curve is tangential to the budget line, or

$$MRS_{fp} = \frac{1}{1 + r}. \tag{2–25}$$

At the same time, on the production side the competitive market mechanism will ensure that the rate of return on investment is the interest rate r. In other words $MRT_{fp} = (1 + r)^{-1}$ Combined with Eq. (2–25), this ensures that the optimality condition of equation (2–22) is satisfied.

The market interest rate r reflects marginal values and costs just like any other price. In particular, $(1 + r)^{-1}$ reflects the marginal value that consumers place on future consumption relative to present consumption. At the same time, $(1 + r)^{-1}$ is the marginal cost of producing future consumption relative to present consumption. That is, $(1 + r)^{-1}$ units of present consumption can be sacrificed to produce one more unit of future consumption.

(b) Extensions:
Many Periods and Many Generations

The above model of a two-period economy can be generalized in a number of ways. We now discuss two extensions: First, we consider a consumer with a multi-period lifetime; second, we examine an economy with several generations of consumers rather than just one.

The Multiperiod Lifetime. Explicit consideration of a T-period economy, as opposed to the two-period model just discussed, does not raise any new, fundamental issues. This extension is worthwhile, however, because it helps one to develop a better intuitive appreciation of the model and, in particular, of its implications for consumer behavior.

Consider the choice problem of a consumer who lives for T periods, and whose preferences are defined over the entire lifetime stream of consumption $C_1, \ldots, C_t, \ldots, C_T$, as represented by a utility function

$$U = U(C_1, \ldots, C_t, \ldots, C_T). \tag{2–26}$$

The consumer has a non-interest (e.g., wage) income in period t of Y_t, and is able to lend and borrow as much as desired in period t at a fixed interest rate, with interest r_{t+1} to be received or paid in period $t + 1$. Let S_t be the amount of savings carried forward from period t to $t + 1$; if the consumer is in debt in period t, S_t is negative, corresponding to a loan balance that is due in the next period. The consumer is constrained to pay off all debts in period T; this is what prevents the consumer from indefinitely borrowing large amounts throughout life to finance high levels of consumption. By the same token, assuming for now that the consumer has no interest in events occurring after his lifetime (such as the consumption of a surviving spouse or children), any positive savings carried into period T will certainly be spent and consumed then. Thus,

$$C_T = Y_T + (1 + r_T)S_{T-1}, \tag{2-27}$$

or,

$$\frac{C_T}{1 + r_T} = \frac{Y_T}{1 + r_T} + S_{T-1}. \tag{2-28}$$

To see how S_{T-1} is determined, recall that in period $T - 1$, the consumer has a wage income of Y_{T-1}, savings of S_{T-2} carried forward from $T-2$, and interest income of $r_{T-1}S_{T-2}$. S_{T-1} is the part of this income and wealth that is not spent; i.e.

$$S_{T-1} = Y_{T-1} + (1 + r_{T-1}) S_{T-2} - C_{T-1}. \tag{2-29}$$

This can be substituted into (2–28); upon division by $1 + r_{T-1}$ and rearranging we have

$$\frac{C_{T-1}}{1 + r_{T-1}} + \frac{C_T}{(1 + r_{T-1})(1 + r_T)}$$

$$= \frac{Y_{T-1}}{1 + r_{T-1}} + \frac{Y_T}{(1 + r_{T-1})(1 + r_T)} + S_{T-2}. \tag{2-30}$$

One can similarly solve for S_{T-2} by using a relation like (2–29), and substitute into (2–30). Dividing this time by $1 + r_{T-2}$, and continuing the process back to period 1, we get the budget constraint

$$C_1 + \frac{C_2}{1 + r_2} + \ldots + \frac{C_T}{\prod\limits_{t=2}^{T}(1+r_t)} = Y_1 + \frac{Y_2}{1 + r_2} + \ldots + \frac{Y_T}{\prod\limits_{t=2}^{T}(1+r_t)}. \tag{2-31}$$

Comparing (2–31) with (2–24), we see that the lifetime budget constraint in both cases has the same interpretation: The present value of lifetime consumption on the left-hand side must equal the present value of lifetime wage income, or what we may call *lifetime wealth,* on the right-hand side. Notice that the discount factors applied to consumption in each period in effect determine the price of future consumption relative to period 1 consumption. To provide for $1 of consumption in period 3, for instance, requires that one sacrifice $[(1 + r_2)(1 + r_3)]^{-1}$ dollars worth of period 1 consumption, since this sum, saved in period 1, would grow to $1 by period 3. Thus, the price of C_3 relative to C_1 is $[(1 + r_2)(1 + r_3)]^{-1} < 1$.

The budget constraint (2–31), though easily interpreted, has important and perhaps surprising implications. It means, for instance, that the timing of lifetime income *per se* has no effect on the set of attainable consumption streams $C_1, \ldots, C_T$, provided that lifetime wealth remains unchanged. This means, for example, that a consumer is made no better or worse off if $1000 of income in year 1 is postponed until year 3, and simultaneously augmented by the amount $1000 \times [(1 + r_2)(1 + r_3) - 1]$ (as would be the case if one seized the consumer's $1000 and required that it be saved for two years before releasing it, with interest), since this leaves lifetime wealth unchanged. The reason the consumer is indifferent to such a retiming of income is that it can be perfectly offset by appropriate capital market transactions. To continue the example, if the consumer wishes to use the $1000 in year 1, he need only borrow $1000 for two years, paying back the loan balance with the extra year 3 income; at that time he will end up no better or worse off for having been forced to save $1000 for two years.

The conclusion that consumption decisions depend on lifetime wealth rather than the pattern over time of income itself is, in fact, a major feature of *life-cycle savings* models (for example, Ando and Modigliani [1963], Friedman [1957] and Hall [1978]. Such models essentially assume that consumers make intertemporal choices in the manner just described, and that the lifetime income stream $Y_1, \ldots, Y_T$ assumes a characteristic form. Generally the assumption is that wage income is low or even negative early in (economic) life, as an individual enters the labor force with few skills and little experience, or, indeed, stays out of the labor force while investing in the acquisition of skills through costly education and training. Wage income then is assumed to rise over time until at roughly ages 45–60 earnings reach a peak beyond which they remain approximately constant until retirement. At this point, of course, wages drop to a low level, possibly zero. An income stream of this form is pictured by the solid line of Fig. 2–15.

How would a consumer with such a lifetime income path act? It would certainly be possible to spend each dollar of income as it accrues, so that C_t could equal Y_t for each t. However, many consumers would probably prefer a smoother stream of consumption, having the same present values such as that represented by the dashed line in Fig. 2–15. The rationale here is that a consumption stream that tracked the income stream exactly would entail very low consumption in, say, period 6, at which point the marginal utility of extra consumption might be very high compared to that in period 4. The consumer would then find it advantageous to reduce consumption in period 4 and use the resulting savings to augment consumption later.

Figure 2–15

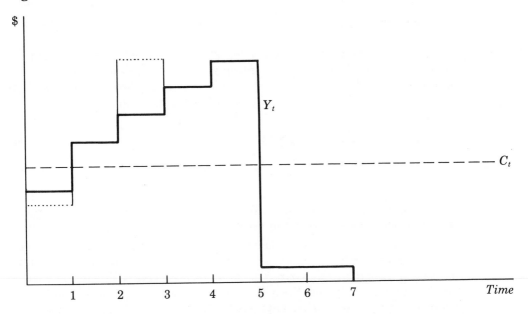

Notice that the Y_t and C_t paths of Fig. 2–15 combine to show the amount of saving out of wage income that a household undertakes. The early years of the life cycle are characterized by little saving, or possibly borrowing, while the middle years are spent building a reserve to finance retirement consumption and to pay off any debts incurred earlier. This is the conventionally-assumed form of life-cycle savings. Notice also that this savings pattern is sensitive to the time path of income. According to our earlier discussion, if the income stream were changed by reducing Y_1 and increasing Y_3 in such a way as to leave lifetime wealth unchanged, as shown by the dotted lines in Fig. 2–15, the consumption path C_t would remain unchanged. This would entail greater borrowing in period 1, to be offset by greater saving in period 3. This example clearly reveals that a chief function of saving and borrowing in a life-cycle model is to "unhook" the time path of consumption from that of income by rearranging the time pattern of resources at the consumer's disposal.

To complete our discussion of the multiperiod model, we briefly note that a market equilibrium has the same efficiency properties as in the two-period case. Between periods 1 and t, consumers are just willing to substitute C_1 for C_t at the marginal rate

$$MRS_{1t} = \frac{-\Delta C_1}{\Delta C_t} = \frac{MU_t}{MU_1} \qquad (2\text{–}32)$$

where MU_t is the marginal utility of consumption in period t. According to the budget constraint, an extra unit of C_1 costs $\prod\limits_{s=2}^{t} (1 + r_s)^{-1}$ units of C_t, and in equilibrium the consumer will equate MRS_{1t} to this relative price. On the production side, profit-maximizing firms will choose levels of output of C_1 and C_2 so that the marginal rate of transformation MRT_{1t} is equated to the relative price ratio. Thus, in equilibrium,

$$MRS_{1t} = \frac{1}{\prod\limits_{s=2}^{t} (1 + r_s)} = MRT_{1t} \quad t = 2, \ldots, T, \tag{2-33}$$

which are the necessary and sufficient conditions for efficiency. Compare this with equations (2–22) and (2–25).

An Economy with Several Generations. So far we have considered an intertemporal economy with one consumer, and we have seen how resource allocation over the time horizon of this consumer can be efficiently carried out through the market. Presumably the consumer's planning horizon is the time until death. What happens to the economy after that time?

The answer, if we wish to be strict about our interpretation of the model, is that the economy simply ceases to exist when its single consumer dies. While this may be a logically acceptable interpretation of the model, it is not an economically meaningful one. In reality, the economy continues to exist, with economic activity carried on by succeeding generations for perhaps an indefinite period of time. What can we say about the intertemporal efficiency of markets in such a world?

One way to proceed is as follows: Suppose, as before, that consumers have lifetimes over which they plan their lifetime consumption. In contrast to the simple life-cycle model, however, suppose consumers have children who will survive them, and that these consumers are altruistic toward their children. Specifically, assume that each generation of consumers gets utility both from their own lifetime *consumption* and from the lifetime *utility* of the succeeding generation. If we label the current generation as generation 1, their children as generation 2, and so on, this assumption implies that increases in consumption at any point in the life cycle of generation 2 (*ceteris paribus*), by increasing generation 2's lifetime utility, will also increase generation 1's utility. Moreover, the fact that generation 1 cares about 2's lifetime *utility* rather than the consumption *per se* means that 1 "respects" 2's preferences; 1 will regard any change in 2's lifetime consumption as desirable or not according to whether generation 2 itself sees the change as desirable. This implies that if generation 2 finds and exploits an opportunity to rearrange its consumption within its lifetime budget constraint in a way that improves its lifetime utility, this rearrangement would be seen as desirable by the parents as well; it is also true that in choosing a consumption path that maximizes own-lifetime utility subject to a lifetime budget constraint, generation 2 is making exactly the intertemporal choices that generation 1 would make for them, if it could.[15]

It is now clear that generation 2, and consequently the altruistic generation 1, would be made better off (*ceteris paribus*) if generation 2's lifetime wealth were to be increased somehow, since lifetime wealth limits the lifetime consumption path and thus lifetime utility. Therefore, generation 1 must be willing to pay something to bring about an increase in 2's wealth. For instance, if generation 2 were very poor, generation 1 might be willing to pay relatively much to attain an increase in 2's lifetime wealth. But, with well-functioning capital markets, this willingness to pay can in fact be tangibly expressed in the marketplace: Generation 1 can give or bequeath wealth to generation 2. In fact, this is a new margin of utility-maximizing choice for generation 1. It will increase its gifts and bequests to generation 2 so long as the benefits, in the form of higher lifetime utility for generation 2, exceed the costs, in the form of lower own-lifetime consumption. In general, of course, the optimal bequest (let us ignore *inter vivos* gifts for simplicity) will depend on various exogenous factors. For instance, one would expect that an increase in generation 1's lifetime wealth would normally increase the optimal bequest, and that an increase in generation 2's would decrease it.[16]

This model of intertemporal consumption and bequest planning has some striking properties. Because generation 2 will act to maximize its lifetime utility by making precisely the consumption choices that generation 1 would prefer, it in effect acts as an agent for generation 1. We can therefore model 2's choice of lifetime consumption as if that choice is being made by generation 1. The only obstacle that would stand in the way of a fully satisfactory choice of consumption paths for both generations, as seen from the perspective of generation 1, is that the lifetime wealth of generation 2 may not be "right." If generation 2's wealth were too low, for instance, generation 1 might not be satisfied with the overall allocation of consumption across generations. Generation 1 might wish to sacrifice some own-consumption for the sake of 2's consumption, even though 2 would be choosing its lifetime consumption as 1 would prefer *conditional* on 2's low wealth. However, because it is possible for generation 1 to transfer wealth to generation 2 through bequests, this potential obstacle is obviated. We can, in effect, regard the choice of consumption paths for these two generations as being made by generation 1, subject to an overall limit imposed by the combined wealth of both generations. In short, in an economy with altruistic parents who respect the preferences of their children, and with capital markets that permit intergenerational transfers, the choices made by generations 1 and 2 can be modelled as if they reflected the behavior of a single consumer, a consumer who maximizes utility by choosing a consumption stream spanning two generations, subject to a wealth constraint that limits the present value of consumption by both generations to the present value of the stream of income received by both generations.[17]

This in itself is a somewhat remarkable conclusion. However, if generation 2 cares about *its* offspring's lifetime utility, the conclusion is incomplete. The consumers in generation 2 will face the same problem as generation 1: How should the amount of the bequests left to generation 3 be determined? Generation 2 will solve this problem just as generation 1 does, by reducing own-consumption and increasing bequests until the gain from a marginal increase in generation 3's utility is just offset by the loss from a further reduction in own-consumption. Now note that since generation 1 respects generation 2's preferences, *including* generation 2's altruistic attitude toward its children, the bequests chosen by generation 2 are in fact desirable from the viewpoint of generation 1. Thus, generation 1's utility depends, indirectly, on the consumption of generation 3. An improvement in 3's lifetime consumption path makes 2 better off, and this in turn makes 1 better off. Because each generation respects its survivor's preferences, however, generation 3 will make its consumption decisions, conditional on its wealth, in just the way generation 1 would prefer. And, because generation 1 respects 2's altruism toward 3, generation 3's wealth will be adjusted by bequests from 2 to exactly the level that 1 would prefer. In effect, then, all three generations will be making lifetime consumption and bequest decisions in a way that achieves for them, subject to their combined wealth constraint, exactly what generation 1 would prefer. We could thus model decision-making over three generations as if all decisions were taken by generation 1. And, of course, the logic of the argument can be pushed as many generations into the future as one desires.

The consequence of this argument is that intertemporal decision-making for a whole sequence of generations can be treated as if it were carried out by a single life-cycle consumer whose preferences are defined over the consumption paths of each of the generations in the sequence. Because these generations act as if there were such a single agent who makes decisions for all generations, this model could be referred to as one of *dynastic* utility maximization. This can be seen, effectively, as an extension of the life-cycle model to an intergenerational context, and the behavioral and efficiency implications of the single-generation life-cycle model carry over directly.

For example, consider the effect of a forced transfer from generation 1 to generation 2, where the money taken from 1 grows at the market rate of interest until it is paid out to 2. If 1 left the bequest to 2 unchanged, 2's lifetime wealth would be increased and 1's lifetime wealth would fall. This would throw 1 out of equilibrium, however. Previously, generation 1 had planned a bequest for generation 2 so that the marginal dollar of bequests would increase 2's lifetime utility just enough to compensate 1 for the associated reduction in own-lifetime consumption; however, with an increased lifetime consumption for 2 and a decreased consumption for

1 resulting from the transfer, this marginal balance is disturbed. To restore it, generation 1 will reduce its bequest to 2. In fact, because the transfer does not alter the combined lifetime wealth of generations 1 and 2, generation 1 will reduce its bequest by precisely enough to preserve the originally-planned, two-period consumption stream. Thus, the previously-established life-cycle result—that a within-lifetime forced transfer is entirely offset by a reduction in savings, leaving the lifetime consumption path unchanged—has a direct extension to the intergenerational economy. Reductions in bequests now play the key equilibrating role that leaves the intergenerational consumption path unchanged.

The efficiency of intertemporal resource allocation can be established in this model as well. Of course, the marginal rates of substitution in consumption that are equated to the relative prices of consumption in future periods must be those of the "as if" dynastic utility-maximizer. Given this interpretation, however, it can easily be established that an intertemporal market equilibrium will be efficient, satisfying the usual set of marginal conditions relating substitution in consumption over time to transformation in production over time (see (2–33)). Thus, all of the important properties of a single-consumer life-cycle model can be established in the dynastic utility maximization model of an intergenerational economy.

CHAPTER NOTES

1. For example, the share of total government expenditures in Gross National Product is now over 33 percent. Of this, nearly two-thirds is spent by the federal government, with state and local governments accounting for about 20 and 15 percent, respectively. See Table 3–4 in the next chapter.

2. One must be careful in using this justification for aggregating monetary net benefits over individuals. In general, there may not be a one-to-one correspondence between the satisfaction of the compensation criterion, and the sign of aggregate net benefits as measured in the conventional way as discussed in Section 2.4 below. This point is developed in Boadway (1974); see also the comments by Smith and Stephen (1975) and Foster (1976).

3. We also assume that each individual knows best how to pursue his own self-interest.

4. The converse will also be true—each Pareto-optimal allocation of resources will correspond to a competitive equilibrium. See Arrow (1951a) for a rigorous proof.

5. The slope of an indifference curve is actually negative. Therefore, we define these marginal rates of substitution to be the negative of the slopes to make them positive in sign.

6. There are some circumstances when preferences will definitely not be convex. For instance, consider the indifference curves describing preferences for consumption of housing in two different cities. One can expect that the consumer will prefer to consume any given amount either in one city or the other, rather than having half of a dwelling unit (or living half the time) in each. If so,

indifference curves will be concave. In principle, such preferences can generate demand behavior that is incompatible with the existence of a competitive equilibrium price system, so that there may not be any market equilibrium corresponding to a particular efficient allocation of resources. (Advanced theory has shown, however, that this problem may become insignificant when there is a large number of consumers.) However, for our purposes in this book, there are no special problems concerning non-convex preferences that we need to emphasize, so we make the standard assumption of convex preferences throughout.

7. As with the marginal rate of substitution, the marginal rate of technical substitution is defined to be the negative of the slope of an isoquant.

8. An isocost line is defined by the equation:

$$\overline{C} = wL + rK$$

where $\overline{C}$ is any arbitrary cost, and L and K are the combinations of labor and capital that may be purchased at the wage rate w and the rental r.

9. That is, the price of the factor is the marginal cost of hiring an additional unit of the factor. The value of the marginal product is the marginal benefit to the firm of hiring one more unit. At the optimum, the firm equates the marginal cost and the marginal benefit.

10. This is only approximate, since if we actually extracted that money from the consumers, it would be as if their income had changed, and the demand curve would shift. From a theoretical point of view it is more appropriate to use what is known as a compensated demand curve for this exercise (see Hicks [1943]). A well-known article by Willig (1976) shows that the error committed in using ordinary rather than compensated demand curves to measure consumers' surplus depends on the size of the income elasticity of demand. For many purposes, this error will be insignificant. Oftentimes in public finance, however, especially in the analysis of taxation, one is crucially concerned not with a total change in consumers' surplus but with the size of a *part* of the change (e.g. the deadweight loss triangle, as discussed in Chapter 9). In such cases a greater degree of precision is required, and the error involved in using the ordinary demand curve may be quite important. For further discussion of this point, see Hausman (1981a).

11. If the price changes were assumed to have occurred in the opposite sequence with P_X changing first and then P_Y, the sum of consumers' surpluses would be slightly different if the demand curves D_Y, D_X etc. are ordinary demand curves. This is known as the problem of *path dependency*. If these demand curves are compensated ones, however, the order in which the price changes occur will not affect the measure of consumer's surplus change at all, i.e. the measure will be *path independent*. Under many circumstances, however, the discrepancies introduced by the path dependence of measures derived from ordinary demand curves will be quite small and can be ignored. For further discussion of path independence, see, e.g. Silberberg (1972).

12. Once again, if we actually extracted the surplus from the workers, the appropriate supply curve to measure the amount that could be extracted would be the compensated supply curve. The producers' surplus associated with S underestimates the above if the income effect is negative, and overestimates it if positive; the size of the error depends on the income elasticity of labor supply. This elasticity may in fact be large and negative; indeed, economists have

sometimes concluded that the ordinary labor supply curve is backward-bending, because the income effect of higher wages induces workers to enjoy more leisure, and this more than offsets the substitution effect which induces workers to take less leisure. Whether this is the true situation or not, it is clear that income effects may not be negligible in the analysis of labor supply, and we should therefore be particularly careful about the interpretation of labor supply schedules when using them for welfare analysis.

13. If a unit of C_p foregone grows at the rate of $(1/MRS_{fp}-1)$, it will yield $\Delta C_f = 1 + (1/MRS_{fp}-1) = 1/MRS_{fp}$ units of future consumption. Such a rate of growth exactly compensates the consumer for a delay of consumption from the present to the future, since $\Delta U = MU_f\Delta C_f + MU_p(-1) = MU_f/MRS_{fp} - MU_p = 0$. For further discussion of this model of intertemporal choice, see Hirshleifer (1976).

14. The notion of present value is discussed in detail in Chapter 8.

15. This is in contrast to other possibilities that arise if generation 1 does not respect its survivor's preferences. For example, parents may prefer to see their children be more frugal, saving earlier in life to support consumption when older. In such a case, a rearrangement of generation 2's consumption path, involving a reduction in early consumption followed by an increase in later consumption, might well be regarded as undesirable by generation 2 itself and as desirable by generation 1. As one can imagine, such conflicting preferences can alter the efficiency and other properties of the intertemporal economy. For instance, government policies that discourage early consumption by generation 2 might well make generation 1 better off; this could provide a rationale for government interference with freely-functioning intertemporal markets. Such a rationale cannot be justified if generation 1 does respect 2's preferences.

16. We generally observe older generations making transfers to younger ones, i.e. bequests. It is theoretically possible, however, that older generations would prefer to *receive* transfers from younger generations. This might conceivably be achieved by having the old die with negative net worth, thus passing along debts (negative bequests) to their heirs. Such behavior is generally not possible, however, both because the older generation would be declared bankrupt, prior to death, as soon as its net worth became negative, and also because the heirs would not be legally responsible for repayment of any outstanding debts in excess of the value of the deceased's assets. Another way that the flow of intergenerational transfers might be reversed is by "persuasion," overt or in the form of social norms, on the part of the older generation. They may, for instance, be supported in old age by their children. (Of course, this might more appropriately be analyzed as a form of altruism on the part of children, as opposed to a choice on the part of the older generation to achieve negative bequests.) In any case, it would appear, as an empirical matter, that desired bequests are in fact positive, so that a reverse flow of intergenerational transfers seems not to arise in practice. Therefore, in the remaining discussion, we ignore this possibility.

It is interesting to note that other models can be constructed in which reverse flows of wealth would be much more important. Consider, for instance, an economy consisting of an infinite sequence of generations of consumers, each of whom lives for two periods. When young, a consumer is endowed with $\bar{y}$ units of resources which, however, cannot be stored or saved until old age. If the economy has a constantly growing population, then it would increase the welfare of every generation if the young would reduce their current consumption at any time and give some to the old. This would ensure, for every household, some consumption in both periods of life. Of course, this requires a constant net wealth transfer from the young to the old. If the young are selfish, they have no incentive to undertake such a transfer. In a world such as this, an economy can be locked into a pattern of consumption that is regarded by every generation as inferior to a feasible alternative. A government program of forced transfers from young to old, such as social security, could improve intertemporal resource allocation in this economy. For the original discussion of this problem see Samuelson (1958).

17. This overall constraint can be presented somewhat more formally as follows: Let $PV_1(Y^1)$, $PV_1(C^1)$, and $PV_1(B)$ be the present value as of the beginning of generation 1's lifetime, of its lifetime income stream, lifetime consumption stream, and bequests to generation 2, respectively. These present values are computed using market interest rates as shown in more detail in 2–31. Then the budget constraint for generation 1 is:

$$PV_1(Y^1) = PV_1(C^1) + PV_1(B).$$

Similarly, let $PV_2(\cdot)$ represent a present value computed as of the beginning of generation 2's lifetime. Then, ignoring (for simplicity) any bequests made by generation 2 itself, its lifetime budget constraint is

$$PV_2(Y^2) + B = PV_2(C^2)$$

where Y^2 and C^2 are the lifetime income and consumption paths, respectively. Now note that the present value as of the beginning of *generation 1's* lifetime of the *second generation's* income Y_2 is just $PV_1(Y^2) = PV_1[PV_2(Y^2)]$. Similarly, $PV_1(C^2) = PV_1[PV_2(C^2)]$. Using these relations, if one expresses $B = PV_2(C^2) - PV_2(Y^2)$ and substitutes into generation 1's budget constraint, one has, after rearranging,

$$PV_1(Y^1) + PV_1(Y^2) = PV_1(C^1) + PV_1(C^2).$$

This is just the "lifetime" budget constraint that would confront a decision-maker planning the two-generation consumption stream (C^1, C^2) given the income stream (Y^1, Y^2).

3

Market Failure and the Rationale for Government Intervention

INTRODUCTION

3–1 In the previous chapter we outlined the circumstances under which the competitive price mechanism would lead to an efficient or Pareto-optimal allocation of resources. The conditions required, including the specification of technology and preferences, are much more stringent than those likely to exist in the real world. Even if we ignore the complications that arise due to the fact that markets are rarely, if ever, perfectly competitive, there are still a number of compelling reasons why a *laissez-faire* economy may be inefficient. In this chapter we will catalog in detail the reasons for the inefficiency of the market mechanism, or *market failure*. Except for the case of a natural monopoly we shall specifically ignore the complications that arise out of the nonexistence of competition *per se*; that is, the problems of monopolistic or oligopolistic behavior and monopsonistic behavior. Such problems, though they may give rise to government intervention via legislation or regulations to enforce competition, are traditionally considered to be the subject matter of the field of industrial organization.

The failure of the price system to allocate resources efficiently is of prime interest to us for two reasons. First, it implies that market prices do not necessarily reflect marginal social benefits or costs and market profitability does not necessarily reflect net social benefits. We shall later have recourse to devising pseudo- or shadow prices to measure social values in such cases. Second, and more fundamentally, the failure of private markets to allocate resources efficiently provides an *a priori* reason for considering other supplementary mechanisms for allocating resources directly (e.g., public provision of goods and services) or for considering corrective devices for interfering with the price mechanism so as to induce markets to function more efficiently (e.g. taxes and subsidies). The basic theme of the first part of this book is that government intervention in the market economy is ultimately rationalized by a failure of the market mechanism to allocate resources efficiently and, as we discuss below, equitably.

In keeping with the mainstream of modern economic reasoning, this rationalization of public sector activity based on market failure rests on a basic acceptance of an individualistic view of society's goals. That is, the efficiency of the allocation of resources is to be judged ultimately by the Pareto principle with reference to the preferences of all the individuals in society rather than using the preferences of some independent organic entity called "the State." The relevant goal of economic society is to satisfy the aggregate desires of the individuals that make up the society. The state is viewed as the sum total of the individuals in society rather than as being an entity unto itself with its own goals and desires. As a consequence, the criterion by which we judge government decision-making is the same as that by which we judge market decision-making; that is, by how well it accords with the preferences of individuals in society.

A word of caution is required regarding the interpretation of the arguments of this chapter. The mere existence of market failure does not by itself justify public sector intervention. Market failure is a necessary but not a sufficient condition for government action. It is necessary because without it the market would be operating satisfactorily and there would be no need for intervention. It is not sufficient, though, because it may be the case that government intervention is inefficient as well, introducing its own distortions. As we shall see, it may be the case that the same sorts of problems which beset the market mechanism and prevent it from allocating resources efficiently will also beset the government. What is really required is an assessment of the relative merits of resource allocation by freely operating markets versus government intervention in each particular case of market failure. In many cases government intervention may improve the allocation of resources. In others it may not. Often the uncertainties of the situation may be such that there is wide disagreement over whether government intervention is beneficial or otherwise. Many elections have been fought over just such questions. The best we can hope to do is to elucidate the types of inefficiencies that can arise in markets and the types of measures governments might take to correct them. Whether any particular real-world case of market failure should be subjected to collective intervention is a matter for empirical judgment. Our intention here is to provide a strong theoretical basis for making an informed judgment. We therefore proceed to discuss individually the main classes of market failure that arise in actual economies.

PUBLIC GOODS

3–2   Our analysis of the efficiency of the market mechanism assumed that each individual's utility was dependent upon only those quantities of commodities purchased by that individual, and that each producer's production of output was determined solely by those factors of production purchased by that producer. In practice that may not be the case. Some commodities exhibit the property that they simultaneously provide benefits to more than one individual at the same time; that is, they are *jointly consumed*. Typical examples of goods which are consumed simultaneously by a particular populace are the services of defense, law enforcement, radio and television, and flood control. Such goods are called *public goods* and they possess certain properties which render the market mechanism an inefficient device for allocating resources to them. So-called *pure public goods* have the property of joint consumption or *nonrivalness* in consumption by several individuals, a term attributable to Musgrave (1969a). That is, one individual's consumption of the good does not detract from the benefits simultaneously accruing to other individuals from the same good. In addition, the use of public goods may be *nonexcludable*. It may be impossible, or at least very costly, to exclude particular individuals from the consumption or use of the existing output of the public good.

These properties both imply difficulties for the market pricing mechanism. The latter operates by excluding those individuals from the consumption of a good who are not willing to pay the going price. In that way markets ensure that the existing quantity is rationed to those who value it the most. With nonexcludability, sellers cannot exact a price from users since the latter can consume it free of charge in any case. Since a voluntary price cannot be enforced on rational individuals, any price charged for the use of nonexcludable public goods will have to be coercive, as with taxes. This failure of the voluntary pricing system due to nonexcludability is referred to as the *free-rider problem*.

Even if public goods use were excludable the market mechanism would have difficulties. Although all individuals simultaneously consume the same quantity of the output, they will generally derive different total and marginal benefits from the same output. Therefore, the price that could be exacted from each individual at the margin would differ from person to person. Furthermore, even if individuals could be excluded from enjoying the public good it is clear on efficiency grounds that they ought not be. The reason is that, due to the joint consumption property, the marginal cost of allowing one more individual to consume the public good is zero. Any pricing scheme which excludes individuals is inefficient.

The existence of pure public goods, or goods simultaneously consumed by all individuals in a given population (local, regional, national, world) provides perhaps the strongest case for public sector intervention. Unfortunately, precisely those problems which render the market inefficient also pose problems for the government decision-maker. We saw that because of the properties of joint consumption and nonexcludability rational individuals will not voluntarily pay a price to use a public good but will behave as free-riders. For exactly the same reason they will not be willing to reveal their marginal preferences for public goods voluntarily if they will be coercively taxed according to the preferences they reveal. Conversely, if the government seeks to elicit their preferences for the purposes of determining the quantity to produce without at the same time relating those preferences to any tax to be charged, there may be an incentive to overstate the benefits received. With an unwillingness to reveal their true preferences, individuals present the government planner with an informational problem, since in order to know how much of a public good to produce, the planner must know what magnitude of benefits are generated by varying quantities of it. Thus, while we can prescribe so-called normative rules for determining the efficient amount of each public good to produce as we do in Chapter 4, informational problems may preclude the planner from exactly following these rules. Since he cannot rely on preferences being revealed directly by the users, some indirect means must be used such as voting behavior or surveys of users. In Chapter 6 we discuss the mechanisms that are used for determining the output of public goods as well as some that have been suggested.

The same problem of jointness of use arises in a number of other contexts, each of which have the same implications for the efficiency of the market mechanism as that of the pure public good case. The analog of a pure public good on the production side is a *public intermediate good* or factor of production used simultaneously by a group of firms. The fruits of new discoveries, public information, weather reports, and manpower training programs might be examples. Once again the jointness in use of public intermediate goods prevents the market from extracting a price from firms unless they can be excluded. If they can be excluded, they ought not to be on efficiency grounds. The public sector therefore often assumes the responsibility for the provision of public intermediate goods. As with public goods, informational problems regarding the benefits generated by public intermediate goods are prevalent although it has been argued that the problems are not as insurmountable as in the public goods' case. The reason is that, as Musgrave (1969b) pointed out, the benefits of public intermediate goods may accrue to firms as pure profits or rents and these may, in principle, be observable. There are also innumerable instances of goods which might be termed *impure public goods* because they are neither private nor purely public but somewhere in between. Public goods have the property of nonrivalness in use while private goods are completely rivalrous. That is, any additional consumption of a private commodity by one person comes entirely at the expense of foregone consumption by someone else. Impure public goods may be partially rivalrous. Given the quantity of the public good, allowing an additional individual to use that commodity does not prevent the previous users from using it, but it does reduce the benefits attained by previous users. Thus, there is some opportunity cost involved in admitting more users. This phenomenon of partial rivalness is typically called *congestion* in the economics literature. The opportunity cost of allowing more use of the public good, or the reduction in benefits to those already consuming it, is called the *congestion cost.*

It is useful to distinguish between two ways in which the consumption of the good may be increased. Greater use of a congested facility may arise because another individual user is added to share in the consumption of the fixed amount of the public good, or because existing individuals can use the facility more intensively (e.g. the number of trips on a highway). By a congested public good we shall mean the former. Public goods exhibiting congestion as more users are added may be of various sorts. One example is the local public good such as fire or police protection. As more persons are covered by a given size of fire or police station, the benefits per person may fall because of, say, a higher probability that the services will be in use elsewhere when required. One may even regard the archetypal public good, defense, as being subjected to congestion for the same reason. As the population rises, an individual may feel that the security he receives from a given level of defense expenditures falls. Another category of congested public goods is what Buchanan (1965a) has called *club goods* such as swimming pools, golf courses, tennis courts, etc. These are typically public goods subject to congestion for which exclusion is possible. The analysis of congested public goods involves determining not only how large the facility ought to be, but also how many users ought to be admitted to using it.

The other sort of congested public facility, that for which the quantity of services used by individuals can be varied, are called *variable-use public facilities.* Examples of these include roads, bridges, and recreation facilities for which the amount of use by individuals may be varied.[1] Because of the variability of use, these goods are fundamentally different from public goods whose quantity is "consumed" in fixed amounts by all. Since their use can be varied, individuals can increase their intensity of use until their marginal benefit equals the marginal cost of additional use. Provided excludability is possible, which may or may not be the case, variable-use public facilities could be provided by the private sector, and as such are not unlike movie theatres, restaurants, etc. Where exclusion is not possible or costly, as with roads, market provision is not feasible and, therefore, public provision is often used. Public provision may also be used where the private sector would not provide the facility competitively due to, say, economies of scale. Indeed, variable-use facilities provided with increasing returns to scale are identical to increasing returns to scale industries discussed later in Section 3–4 and again in Chapter 7.

It is also useful to distinguish those public goods for which location or nearness is important. For example, one must be near a television station or fire station to benefit from it. Public goods of this sort are typically classified in geographic terms such as local public goods, regional public goods, or national public goods depending upon the geographical area served (see Breton [1965]). Such public goods provide an economic rationale for

multilevel or federal systems of government and will be discussed fully in
Part IV. In addition, the existence of local public goods provides a potential
mechanism for the revelation of preferences for public goods in the form
of labor mobility between regions (or "voting with the feet"). As originally
suggested by Tiebout (1956), persons may reveal their preferences for local
public goods by migrating to localities providing the most favorable mix
of public goods and taxes according to their preferences. Such information
may assist local public decision-makers to decide on the levels of public
goods to provide. The Tiebout model is discussed in more detail in Chapter 15.

EXTERNALITIES

3–3   Another phenomenon closely related to public goods and arising out of the
jointness of use property is that of externalities. An *external economy* is
said to be emitted when an activity undertaken by an individual or firm
yields benefits to other individuals or firms in addition to the benefits
accruing to the emitting party. The benefits so generated are typically
nonexcludable and thus are unpriced; that is, they are external to the
pricing system. Because the emitting party is not being reimbursed for the
external benefit generated, there is no inducement to take that benefit into
consideration when deciding upon the level of activity to undertake. The
individual or firm chooses that level of activity at which the private marginal
benefits from the activity just equal the marginal costs of undertaking it,
thus ignoring the marginal benefits which simultaneously spillover to other
parties. As we shall consider in Chapter 5 in more detail, the result is a
misallocation of resources or a failure of the market economy to generate
a Pareto optimum. Examples of such external economy-producing activities
include the allocation of resources by firms to the discovery of knowledge
or inventions, the training by firms of labor, and the prevention of communicable disease by individuals. Each of these activities yields potential
benefits to others which are not captured in the decision-making processes
of firms or individuals.

Analytically, the study of external economies is identical to that of
public goods, and the distinction between them is one of degree rather than
of kind. In both cases, the same commodity or activity enters the utility
functions of several persons or the production functions of several firms
simultaneously. Institutionally, there are likely to be differences. Externalities
arise as an *unintended* byproduct of individual or firm behavior, as emphasized
by Mishan (1971b). The private benefit to the individual is presumably
relatively large compared to the external benefits generated, large enough
to provide enough incentive for individuals or firms to undertake the activity
in the first place. With public goods, on the other hand, the benefits to any
single individual would be relatively small compared with the cost of providing
the services of the good, so that individuals might not voluntarily provide
any of it for themselves (e.g. defense). This difference accounts for the fact

that, while typically the remedy for market failure due to public goods is for the public sector actually to undertake to provide the good, the remedy for externalities is often to provide incentives to the private sector to produce the correct amount. This may be done by subsidizing the activity to "internalize" the external benefits.

Because of the similarity of their properties to public goods the correction of external economies involves the same informational problems as does the provision of public goods. There is no incentive for the beneficiaries of the external economy to reveal their true preferences. If the revelation of their preferences is directly reflected in a tax price to be charged, they will grossly underestimate the benefits (since they can receive the benefits at zero price in any case). Alternatively, if the revelation of their preferences is to be used solely to determine, say, the extent of the subsidy to be provided to the emitter without implying any charge to the recipients, it will be in the interest of the recipients to overstate the benefits they receive. The same mechanisms for the relevation of preferences for public goods will apply to externalities as well.

Externalities may be detrimental as well as beneficial. The activities of an individual or firm may damage or produce disbenefits to other parties without the emitting party having to consider the opportunity cost of inflicting the damage. Such damages are called *external diseconomies*. The most common examples of external diseconomies are pollution by factories, automobiles, airports, noise, etc., highway congestion,[2] and the overuse of an unpriced common property resource, such as a fishing ground of limited capacity. In each of these cases the emitting party (the polluter, road user, fisherman) pursues his activity in such a way as to equate the marginal benefit from the activity to the marginal cost, but neglecting the cost imposed on others. The result is once again a misallocation of resources.

The ultimate cause of external diseconomies can conceptually be traced to a lack of definition of property rights, often due to the costs of enforcing them. The so-called common property resource problem arising from, say, the depletion of a fishing ground occurs because, although the fishing ground is a scarce resource with a limited capacity for supplying fish, the use of that resource is not rationed by a price. As Knight (1924) pointed out in a seminal contribution to the subject, and as we shall see in Chapter 5, if the property were privately owned and a competitive price charged, there would be no external diseconomy problem and the fishing ground would be used efficiently. The rent charged for the use of the fishing ground would exactly reflect its scarcity value. Similarly, the pollution problem arises because of a difficulty in enforcing property rights in the use of, say, the atmosphere. In the case of air there is obviously a problem of excludability and implementation of property rights.

Because of the inability of those damaged by an external diseconomy such as pollution to exclude the damagers from the use of the atmosphere, or because of the lack of enforcement of property rights in general, the government may decide to intervene in the market mechanism to attempt to provide the damaging parties with the correct incentive to take into consideration the entire social opportunity costs of their activities. This may be done in various ways: By taxing the activities at the appropriate rate, by subsidizing the damaging parties to restrict their activities, or by imposing regulations in the form of quantity controls. These various methods for internalizing external diseconomies are discussed in Chapter 5. Once again, the government has an informational problem in determining the magnitude of the damages being emitted, not unlike the revelation-of-preference problem of public goods and external economies. The problem is administratively complex because normally there will be a large number of both emitting parties and affected parties.

INCREASING RETURNS TO SCALE

3–4   The analysis of the efficiency of competitive markets requires that firms' technologies exhibit constant or decreasing returns to scale. If increasing returns to scale exists in an industry up to relatively high levels of output, the competitive analysis of market behavior breaks down for two reasons. First, the market structure of such an industry would not be such as to induce competitive behavior. Because of the increasing returns or economies of scale, large firms would force small firms out of business by producing at a lower cost, and ultimately the industry would end up as a monopoly if the scale economies continued to large enough outputs. Since monopoly pricing does not set prices equal to marginal costs, the overall Pareto-optimal conditions are violated and efficiency of resource allocation is not attained.

A second problem arises when increasing returns to scale prevail. Even if a competitive market structure did exist, or if firms could be coerced into behaving as firms in a competitive industry do, the private sector could not profitably sustain marginal cost pricing. With increasing returns to scale, the average cost curves of a firm will everywhere slope downward, yielding marginal costs that are less than average costs. Pricing at marginal cost would be equivalent to pricing below average cost and therefore firms would be unable to cover costs. Because of this the private sector could not behave according to the Pareto-optimizing rules.

There are several potential policy measures the government might take in these circumstances. They might decide to do nothing, thereby allowing society to sustain the loss in economic welfare associated with the monopoly. On the other hand, society would gain whatever innovative advantages the monopoly might have due to its size. Or the government might decide to regulate the monopoly by prescribing its price or rate of return. If so, the price can at best be set at average cost to prevent the firms from incurring a loss. Some loss in welfare due to inefficiency is incurred in this situation as well but, in principle, less than would be incurred under the do-nothing remedy. The loss may not be too big if the rate at which the firm's costs decline is not great, or if the firm actually runs into increasing costs at large outputs. Finally, the public sector might decide to operate the monopoly as a public enterprise and set its prices on welfare or efficiency grounds rather than on grounds of financial profitability.

There are problems with this latter approach as well. If the public enterprise is to price at marginal cost, its production losses must be financed somehow out of government revenues raised elsewhere (e.g. taxes) and the raising of the latter imposes inefficiencies of its own. Also, it is sometimes argued that public enterprises are run less efficiently than regulated private industries since the former have no incentive to minimize costs of production. If so, this must be taken into consideration in choosing a policy for dealing with increasing returns industries. Different industries may justifiably be treated differently if the perceived net benefits of different policy options differ. For example, airlines may be regulated while urban commuter services and passenger trains may be public enterprises. Some countries such as the United Kingdom have used the public enterprise remedy much more frequently than the United States, which has tended to use the regulation remedy. A full analysis of the problems that arise in increasing returns industries is provided in Chapter 7. Analytically, of course, there is no difference between increasing-returns-to-scale industries and what we have characterized as variable-use public facilities.

RISK AND UNCERTAINTY

3–5   The conclusions of Chapter 2 on the efficiency of the competitive price system were based on a model in which perfect certainty existed. Both consumers and producers were assumed to know with certainty the prices of all goods and factors that would prevail now and in the future. In the real world, future events are of course uncertain and, as a consequence, so are future prices, subject as they are to the vagaries of changing weather, tastes, population, technology, and to accidents of various sorts. The analysis of the optimality of competitive markets in economies characterized by uncertainties is unfortunately beyond the scope of this work. We can only point out some of the main results that have been achieved in that field.

It has been demonstrated by Arrow (1970) that in a world of uncertainty there is a set of circumstances in which the competitive pricing mechanism will yield an efficient allocation of resources. The conditions required are very stringent. Assume the future can be classified according to various "states of the world" each of which yields its own particular climate, technology, tastes, etc. Also, assume that each individual is able to attach subjective probabilities to each of the states of the world happening, and that the probabilities all sum to unity. An individual endowed with a given amount of resources will know the allocation of resources that endowment would provide him with in each possible state in the future. Suppose now that there exist markets for "claims" to each type of commodity or factor in each possible future state of the world. These markets are often called *contingency markets.* A purchase of a contingency claim to a good in state *s* is equivalent to purchasing a claim to a quantity of that good should the state *s* actually occur. If the state *s* does not occur, nothing is received. An insurance policy on, say, a car is an example of a contingency claim. One pays a premium for the claim to receive the proceeds of the policy should a certain state, i.e. an accident, occur. Given their initial endowments of commodities or income, individuals can purchase various contingency claims on the future states at the going price established for these claims on contingency (or future) markets.

Assume that individuals behave so as to maximize their expected utility, denoted *EU*. It has been shown by Friedman and Savage (1948) that under certain reasonable assumptions individuals will behave in this way. The expected utility is defined as:

$$EU = \sum_{s=1}^{S} \pi_s U_s(x_{1s}, \ldots, x_{ns}) \tag{3-1}$$

where U_s is the utility function in state *s*, π_s is the probability of state *s* occurring, and x_{is} is the consumption of good *i* in state *s*. Suppose the contingency markets result in prices for contingency claims denoted by p_{is} for each commodity *i* in each future state of the world *s*. If the individual has a given income of *Y*, that income can be used to purchase and sell contingency claims to the future according to a budget constraint of the form:

$$Y = \sum_{i=1}^{n} \sum_{s=1}^{S} p_{is} x_{is}. \tag{3-2}$$

The individual will choose the combination of x_{is} that maximizes expected utility, Eq. (3–1), subject to the budget constraint, Eq. (3–2). The individual will set his expected marginal rate of substitution, or the rate at which, say, x_{is} can be substituted for x_{jr} so as to keep *EU* the same, at the price ratio p_{jr}/p_{is}. All individuals will behave in exactly the same way. Similar to the efficiency of competitive markets described in Chapter 2, the existence of competitive contingency markets will result in a Pareto-optimal allocation of resources in the following sense: It will not be able to increase the expected utility of one person without at the same time reducing the expected utility of someone else.[3] The market will have resulted in allocating *risk* efficiently. Those most willing to bear the risk of an uncertain outcome will be able to bear more risk by appropriate "speculation" on contingency markets. Those desiring to avoid risk can do so by appropriate "hedging" against uncertainty.

Market failure results because in the real world a complete set of such contingency markets does not exist. It is true that some commodities have future markets, and insurance policies allow one to purchase claims against certain contingencies (e.g. accidents, death) in the future. But, in general, relatively few commodities have anything near complete markets for future claims contingent on the state of the world. The stock market, which is the prime vehicle for trading in the risk of individual enterprises, is not a perfect futures market. One can indeed buy claims to the future profits of a corporation by the purchase of shares. But, the portfolio of shares of an individual provides a fixed proportion of claims to future profits of firms regardless of the state of the world that occurs. That is, the proportions in which one holds the shares of various firms are the same, regardless of which state is to result.

There are at least two important reasons why perfect contingency markets have not developed. One is that the transaction costs of establishing such markets might be high relative to the number of traders. The other reason is the phenomenon of *asymmetric information,* also known as the *principal-agent problem.* This refers to the fact that individuals who wish to take out, say, insurance against future possible states of the world possess information that insurers do not. The insured persons (the *agents*) can exploit this informational advantage in dealing with the insurers (the *principals*) in various ways. Two ways in which the principal-agent problem manifests itself in market breakdown are known as the *moral hazard* problem and the *adverse selection* problem.

Moral hazard occurs when the insured can, through actions unobservable to the insurer, influence either the probability of a loss occurring, or the magnitude of the loss. For example, a person can influence the probability of an accident by the degree of preventive action taken. If the quantity of preventive action is not observable to the insurer, market failure can result as shown by Pauly (1974) and Marshall (1976). Alternatively, the standard example of how the insured influences the size of the loss is medical insurance. In the event that illness occurs, the insured can overuse medical services. This sort of moral hazard has been investigated by Arrow (1963), Pauly (1968), Zeckhauser (1970), and Feldstein and Friedman (1977). Perfect contingency markets cannot develop in the presence of moral hazard.

Adverse selection occurs when there are several different types of insured persons, distinguished from one another by the probabilities of a bad state of nature occurring. Thus, some persons might be high risk and others low risk, and the insurers cannot tell one from the other. Automobile insurers cannot tell careful from careless drivers except imperfectly through such indicators as age, sex, and family status. As Rothschild and Stiglitz (1976) have shown, an equilibrium may not exist in the presence of adverse selection and, even if it does, it may not be efficient.

A problem related to adverse selection is the simple lack of information by market participants. The derivation of the Pareto-optimality of competitive markets assumed that individuals and firms had complete knowledge regarding the availability and attributes of all goods and factors. Such will not always be the case. Consumers may not know the implications of various products for their health or safety, nor will they have full information on the relative merits of various competing consumer items. Firms do not always know the quality of the labor force they are hiring. The provision of information has the attributes of a public good, especially the joint consumption property. Thus, information on product safety and health hazards is often publicly provided (e.g. the Food and Drug Administration). Similarly, the education system provides, in addition to its training role, an informational function known as *screening*.[4] That is, by attaching levels of achievement to persons coming out of the education system (e.g. degrees, diplomas, grades), information is being provided to prospective employers regarding the potential productivity of the person. Presumably, the practice of licensing various professions or trades plays a similar screening role, however imperfect it is. The dissemination of information can, for our purposes, be considered as a particular type of public good.

Due to the nonexistence of perfect contingency markets, Pareto optimality does not exist in the real world, and this may influence government behavior. We shall discuss in Chapter 8 the manner in which the existence of uncertainty or risk should be taken into consideration in public sector resource allocation decisions. As well, the influence of taxes on the incentive to assume risk is considered in Chapter 11.

TAX DISTORTIONS AND MARKET INEFFICIENCY

3–6   The government itself prevents the attainment of Pareto optimality through the market mechanism when it imposes distortionary taxes to finance its activities. As we shall see later, this contribution of taxation to allocative inefficiency must be taken into consideration when deciding upon the size and nature of public sector resource allocation decisions. Typically, taxes are levied on economic transactions of one sort or another and, as such, they drive a wedge between the prices paid by demanders and received by suppliers.

The levying of distortionary taxes may be unavoidable but the government will have some control over the amount of inefficiency that it induces in the economy, since it has control over what type and mix of taxes to levy. There is a long tradition of scholarly interest in the question of what sorts of taxes impose the least efficiency losses on the economy. We shall pursue that question in detail in Chapter 9. In the meantime, we must recognize that the existence of taxes prevents a Pareto optimum from being achieved, and this implies that market prices need not accurately reflect marginal social values.

INCOME DISTRIBUTION

3–7   Besides the question of what combination of private and public sector activity is required to produce a Pareto optimum, there is the question of which Pareto optimum to aim for. In principle there are an infinite number of Pareto optima possible, each one associated with a different distribution of utility among the members of society corresponding to the various points on society's grand utility possibility curve. Some judgment, explicitly or implicitly, must be made regarding the relative merits of the various Pareto-optimal allocations.

If the economy were of the sort discussed in Chapter 2, in which a purely private sector market economy is efficient, a policy of *laissez-faire* could be used to select the point on the grand utility possibility curve by default. That is, given the distribution of ownership of resources, skills, and tastes that has evolved, the competitive market mechanism would achieve some Pareto optimum without any public sector guidance.

However, once market failure due to, say, public goods exists, the choice of a Pareto optimum by default is no longer possible. Because there is no institution equivalent to the price mechanism for financing public goods, the government must choose the set of taxes with which to finance them. Unlike market prices, which perform an allocative or rationing function by regulating how much each individual consumes, the taxes used to finance public goods play no such role. Once the quantity of a public good is selected, that quantity is consumed by all individuals regardless of how it is financed. The choice of a method of financing is thus based more on distributive or equity grounds than on allocative grounds. The government cannot avoid deciding upon how the tax system is to impinge upon the relative utility levels of different members of society. In practice, as well as using progressive income taxes to finance public expenditures, governments also decide to influence the welfare distribution arising out of market forces directly by reallocating incomes through the taxation of some and the transfer of the proceeds to others. That is, governments engage in purely redistributive activities.

The question of income distribution or the choice of the "best" point on the grand utility possibility curve is perhaps the most intractable normative problem with which the study of public finance has to deal. There can be fairly widespread agreement that Pareto optimality or efficiency is a good thing, since it is based upon a set of individualistic moral premises that seem to be widely accepted, viz. that each person knows best his own set of preferences, and making one person better off according to his preferences without making any other worse off according to his improves society's well-being. However, to choose among Pareto optima requires making a comparison between the welfare levels attained by different individuals in society, trading the gains of some against the losses of others. There is no agreed method for making such a value judgment about interpersonal welfare comparisons. For that reason, much of economic policy prescription has involved an analysis of the efficiency of various actions leaving the question of equity to be judged elsewhere. In this regard, one role of the economist might be to analyze the effects on relative utility levels and on efficiency of various courses of action and leave the choice among them to the policy-maker. This latter role is important in selecting, say, the appropriate income tax schedule. The more progressive the schedule is, the more income redistribution is attained; but, at the same time, the greater are the distorting effects of the tax on efficiency in terms of distorting the supply of labor and capital. Some judgment must be made regarding the relative weights to be given to efficiency losses and equity gains from increasing the progression of the income tax.

There have been some recent attempts to avoid partially such a conundrum by positing the notion of *Pareto-optimal income redistribution.*[5] The basic idea is that of interdependent utility functions among individuals which is a form of externality. Suppose an individual's utility depends not only upon his own consumption but also upon the consumption of income received by others. For example, out of a feeling of benevolence, a rich person may feel better off if the utility attained by a poor person is increased. In these circumstances, there may be some potential for making everyone better off by transferring income from one person to another. If a rich person obtains more benefit from a marginal increase in income to the poor than from a marginal increase in his own income, both can be made better off by a transfer of income from rich to poor. That is to say, the grand utility possibility curve may look like that of Fig. 3–1 for the two-person economy. There is a limit to how much B can be made better off at the expense of A and vice versa. Between O_A and P^B, both B and A can be made better off by transfers of income from B to A. Similarly, between O_B and P^A, both can be made better off by transfers from A to B. A much more detailed analysis of this phenomenon will be presented in Chapter 5.

The government may or may not have a role in affecting Pareto-optimal redistribution. If a particular individual A benefits from a transfer of his income to a particular individual B, that transfer will be made voluntarily, as with private contributions to charity. However, the improvements in the well-being of B (the "poor") may be of a public good nature in the sense that it simultaneously benefits many persons of type A (the "rich"). A one-dollar donation by a rich person to the poor will benefit all the rich as well as just the donor. Since the individual donors have no incentive to take this external benefit into account, there will be no incentive to make the efficient quantity of transfers. There is a gain to be had by the collective provision of such transfers or the subsidization of individual transfers. The problem is not unlike the free-rider problem that arises with any public good.

The existence of utility interdependence effectively narrows the locus of Pareto-optimal allocations to $P^B P^A$ on the grand utility possibility curve of Fig. 3–1, but does not eliminate the requirement to choose a point on the locus. Ultimately some choice must be made among the various efficient allocations on some other, noneconomic grounds. There have been several attempts to construct formal normative theories (or social welfare functions) of how such decisions ought to be taken. Some of these theories, such as utilitarian, and Rawlsian, are discussed later in Chapter 10. The positive theory of how equity decisions are, in fact, taken by governments operating

Figure 3–1

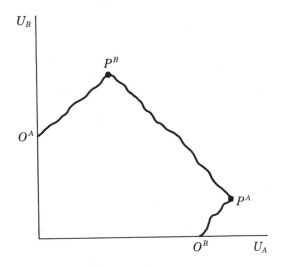

under democratic constitutions is not yet well developed. Some discussion of this issue will be presented in Chapter 6.

INTERTEMPORAL EFFICIENCY AND EQUITY

3–8   While Section 2–5 described how competitive markets could bring about an intertemporally efficient allocation of resources, it is quite an open question whether real economies reasonably approximate the conditions assumed there. Moreover, an efficient outcome might be deemed undesirable on other grounds.

Let us take the last point first. Suppose that the households currently alive are dynastic utility maximizers, and that capital markets allow the borrowing, lending, and intergenerational transfers that result in efficiency. One might still object that the desires of future generations are represented only by the current generation's feelings of altruism toward them, and that the current generation is too selfish to provide adequately for subsequent generations. Therefore, government intervention on behalf of future generations is called for. Note that this argument is essentially based on an ethical judgment about the distribution of welfare over time: One would like the current generations to do more, even if it makes them worse off, in order that future generations might benefit. The argument can take other forms, however, such as a desire for faster economic progress and growth than the market would otherwise provide. Such views are often expressed in the context of less developed countries. When these considerations are important, what role might the government play?

One possibility is to attempt to increase the saving carried out in the private sector in order to augment the wealth in the hands of future generations. Note, however, that the likely effectiveness of such policies will depend crucially on whether they are based on a correct understanding of household intertemporal decision-making. As discussed in Section 2–5, if one forces dynastic utility-maximizing parents to save more for the sake of their children, they may simply respond by reducing the bequests they would otherwise have made, leaving the future generations in an unchanged position. Clearly, a more sophisticated policy, such as subsidization of saving or bequests, would be called for in this type of economy.

The problem of intergenerational equity can be even more severe in economies where parents are not so foresighted as the dynastic model assumes. If consumers are life-cycle savers, then they will leave no bequests intentionally, and thus make no intentional provision for subsequent generations. Of course, a life-cycle saver whose lifetime is uncertain may, during the working years, accumulate enough wealth to finance consumption over quite a long retirement period. If this person only survives for a short period of time after retirement, or does not live long enough even to reach retirement, then he will die leaving some wealth behind as an *unintentional* bequest. But, aside from such accidents, non-dynastic life-cycle savers will not provide for a stock of wealth or capital for the next generation.

Also, capital market institutions may arise which make it possible to minimize such accidents. For example, much saving takes the form of contributions by workers to retirement annuity programs. These programs guarantee a worker a certain income stream, in the form of annuity payments, beginning at retirement and ending upon the death of the worker (or possibly the worker's spouse). The company providing the annuity program sets a benefit level based on the probabilities of survival to various ages, thus offering a statistically (or *actuarially*) fair return on contributions to the participants (except for administrative costs). The worker can then choose a contribution level during the working years that guarantees any desired level of income in retirement. He will receive these payments only for a short time if he dies early, and receive them for a long time if he is more fortunate. The net effect of this system is to relieve the worker of the risk of surviving for a long time after retirement, exhausting his savings, and not being able to finance much consumption; or, of dying early and leaving a large unintentional bequest. Thus, when workers only save for own-lifetime consumption, and especially when market institutions exist that make it possible to avoid unintentional bequests resulting from early death, the current generation may make very little provision indeed for future generations. Government intervention on equity grounds may therefore be desired, the need for such intervention presumably being greater than if the current generation consisted of dynastic utility-maximizers who would carry out at least some capital accumulation on behalf of future generations.

Interestingly, the scope for government policy to redistribute income across generations may be greater when consumers are non-dynastic life-cycle savers, because their behavioral response to government policies is likely to differ from the dynastic utility-maximization case. For example, consider a forced transfer of income from the current generation to a subsequent generation. Given that no bequests (or at least no intentional bequests) are being made voluntarily by the current generation, they cannot then reduce their bequests in order to offset the intergenerational transfer set up by the government policy. This is in complete contrast to what happens with intergenerational consumption planning by dynastic utility maximizers.

Of course, one would not necessarily prefer to redistribute in favor of future generations, as we have so far assumed. In fact, a common rationale for social insurance programs is that older people are deserving of transfers from the current younger generations. Obviously, we cannot hope to determine here which view on intergenerational equity is more appropriate. We may note, however, that public policies designed to redistribute in favor of the elderly will generate behavioral responses in the private sector, for reasons already spelled out above, that may partially or completely negate the effect of the policies. Thus, whatever the underlying ethical judgments, we may conclude that attempts to alter the intertemporal distribution of welfare must take carefully into account private sector intertemporal behavior. This will emerge as a major consideration in our discussion of public old-age security programs in Chapter 14.

So far we have emphasized intergenerational equity. There are also important intertemporal efficiency issues that may prompt public intervention. Perhaps the most crucial problems arise from an absence of complete markets. Central to our argument about the efficiency of intertemporal resource allocation through the marketplace is the existence of capital markets in which households and firms may lend or borrow as much as desired at fixed interest rates. There may be important institutional obstacles to such capital market transactions, however. A well-known and important example of such an institutional constraint is the inability of consumers to incur as much indebtedness as desired in order to finance current consumption or other outlays. This problem, which is familiar to students, arises in the following way: A consumer at an early stage in the life-cycle wishes to invest in the acquisition of knowledge and skills through education and training. This investment requires the sacrifice of wage income that could be earned currently, and may build debt to meet expenses such as tuition; this investment is, however, expected to yield a return in the future in the form of higher earnings. In the absence of any borrowing, undertaking the investment might entail a sufficiently low current consumption stream that the consumer would decide against it, whereas the investment would be attractive if it could be financed by borrowing at the going interest rate. A lender, however, may be unwilling to lend at this rate because the loan, unlike a mortgage on a house or a corporate bond, is not secured by any tangible asset that reverts to the creditor if the borrower defaults. The borrower cannot make a binding contract to pledge his future earnings to repayment of the debt, since such an arrangement amounts to indentured servitude and is not legally enforceable. Yet, could such a pledge be made, it might result in transactions which are beneficial both to creditor and debtor. That they are precluded by legal constraints means that full intertemporal efficiency cannot be achieved. This breakdown in efficiency is often used as an argument to support public intervention in education. If markets result in underinvestment in education, then policies which increase the amount of education, such as subsidization of educational expenses, may improve resource allocation.

Finally, we must note that even if adequate capital markets exist, some would question whether households are sufficiently forward-looking and rational in their economic behavior to ensure that market outcomes will be either efficient or, again, equitable. It could be that the life-cycle savings model, and *a fortiori* the intergenerational planning model of dynastic utility maximization, simply assumes far too much sophistication on the part of consumers. Instead, people may thoughtlessly spend for today and make no plans for the future; or, if they do think about the future, they may not engage in the careful comparison of benefits and costs of consumption in different periods assumed in the life-cycle model. They may, instead, follow some simple rule of thumb: They may always save $X\%$ of each dollar of disposable income, as the simple textbook Keynesian consumption function posits. Perhaps they may let their saving be determined passively by institutional forces, such as the proportion of net income paid out as dividends by the corporations they own, or the size of the required employer and employee contributions to their company pension plan. For such consumers, the idea of intertemporal efficiency may not even make sense, since this concept requires the existence of indifference curves (i.e. well-defined preferences) over present and future consumption for which a marginal rate of substitution may be defined. However this may be, the point is that it might be hard to accept as being other than arbitrary the intra- and intergenerational time paths of consumption and saving produced by such behavior. The potential scope for government policy seems correspondingly larger in this type of economy. For instance, forcing shortsighted consumers to save for their own retirement might keep them from arriving at old age penniless and starving, and this might be regarded as ethically desirable. In fact, we could make an intertemporal equity argument for *intra*generational transfers of the same type that was made earlier for *inter*generational transfers.

The foregoing discussion has considered the possible roles for government policy in quite different economic environments, ranging from economies populated by the most sophisticated and rational of consumers to those populated by extremely shortsighted ones. Which sort of economy exists in reality? This is fundamentally a problem to be resolved by positive empirical economic analysis. Economists of varying persuasions have considered each of the above possibilities and, as one might expect, have come to varying conclusions about policy. At present it is fair to say that decisive empirical tests of competing hypotheses about consumer behavior have not yet been carried out, so that the positive issues of how intertemporal decisions are made, and how the private sector will respond to various policies, remain open. Our later discussions of the effects of taxes, social security, and public expenditures on, for example, investment and saving, economic growth, capital accumulation, and factor pricing, will all reflect the importance of these basic issues.

GOVERNMENT EXPENDITURES IN THE UNITED STATES

3–9   Having discussed why government intervention in a market economy might be desirable, let us now turn to a description of the size and purposes of government activities actually carried out at the federal, state, and local levels in the United States.

To begin with, it is useful to survey the pattern of aggregate public expenditures as it has evolved over the past half-century. We shall consider how total public expenditures of all levels of government have changed both absolutely and in relation to population and private sector expenditures, and how the shares of expenditures of the three levels of government have changed.

Table 3–1 depicts public expenditures by all levels of government in absolute terms, as a percentage of gross national product, and per capita, for selected years from 1922 to 1982. The data are to a certain extent self-explanatory. Total expenditures have risen dramatically over this period, both absolutely and in relation to the size of the economy. There was a substantial drop in public expenditures following World War II, as defense expenditures fell sharply. This is revealed clearly in the data in Table 3–2, which also shows that defense expenditures relative to all government expenditures continued to fall until the mid-1970s. Since then, defense has held a roughly constant share of about 14% of government expenditures. (Observe, however, the recent increase in the defense share.) As the defense share of the total public budget has declined, the share of other programs has increased. In particular, transfer payments to persons, especially at the federal government level, have increased greatly in the postwar period. The transfer programs involved include welfare, food stamps, and, particularly, social security. Table 3–3 documents this growth. Thus, the recent history of government expenditure reflects overall growth relative to the economy, and a change in the composition of government expenditure away from defense and toward transfer payments. Clearly, the redistributive role of the government has expanded greatly since World War II, and especially during the 1970s. Against this backdrop, the recent (1982) reduction in transfer payments as a share of the budget may be of some importance.

The rise in the percentage of gross national product used for government expenditures could reflect many things. One simple interpretation is that the income elasticity of demand for public goods and services is greater than unity. As incomes rise, individuals are willing to spend a larger proportion on such things as education, roads, health, and transfer payments of various sorts. This explanation of the rise in the relative importance of

Table 3–1   Total Government Expenditures in Selected Years, 1929–1982

Year	Total Expenditures* ($ Millions)	Expenditures as % of GNP**	Expenditures per Capita†
1922	9,297	12.5	85
1927	11,220	11.8	95
1932	12,437	18.3	100
1936	16,758	19.4	131
1942	45,576	40.4	341
1944	109,947	48.9	821
1946	79,707	21.7	581
1952	99,847	27.0	646
1957	125,463	26.0	742
1962	176,240	28.4	955
1967	257,800	30.3	1,311
1972	399,098	31.3	1,924
1977	680,329	32.5	3,156
1979	832,385	31.1	3,797
1980	958,657	33.1	4,243
1981	1,109,815	33.5	4,860
1982	1,196,897‡	35.5‡	5,192‡

*Fiscal Year Basis. Sources: Tax Foundation (1973), Table 5, p. 17; Tax Foundation (1981), Table 6, p. 18; Tax Foundation, private communication, 1983.

**Calendar Year Basis. Sources: Tax Foundation (1973), Table 20, p. 33; Tax Foundation (1981), Table 23, p. 36; Tax Foundation, private communication, 1983.

†Fiscal Year Basis. Sources: Tax Foundation (1973), Table 6, p. 18; Tax Foundation (1981), Table 7, p. 19; Tax Foundation, private communication, 1983.

‡Tax Foundation estimates.

public expenditures is incomplete for at least three reasons, however. First, many government services are of the nature of capital expenditures which serve to a great extent as factors of production, or intermediate inputs for industry. For example, publicly provided transportation facilities (e.g. roads, waterways, airports) are of this sort, as is education. The derived demand for these services is analogous to an investment demand rather than a consumption demand. The growth in the demand for public investment-type expenditures has not been studied in any systematic way, so we lack a complete theory which satisfactorily explains their continued rise.

A second factor which might contribute to explaining the rise in public expenditures is the change in the relative costs of public versus private goods and services. An income elasticity of demand is defined as the proportional change in demand resulting from a proportional change in income with all prices held constant. Suppose, however, the price of private goods has fallen over time relative to the cost of public services. This could lead

Table 3–2 Defense Expenditures, in Total and as a Percentage of Total Government Expenditures, Selected Fiscal Years, 1942–1982

Year	Total Defense Expenditures ($ Millions)*	Defense Expenditures as % of Total Government Expenditures**
1942	23,937	52
1944	76,696	70
1946	43,176	54
1952	43,796	44
1957	43,368	35
1962	51,097	29
1967	69,101	27
1972	76,550	19
1977	97,501	14
1979	117,681	14
1980	135,856	14
1981	159,765	14
1982	187,418	15

*Source: Tax Foundation (1981), Table 75, p. 93; Tax Foundation, private communication, 1983.

**Calculated from Table 3–1.

to a rise in the proportion of income devoted to public expenditures even if the income elasticity of demand for public goods and services did not exceed unity. Baumol (1967) has argued that technical progress has produced much greater improvement in productivity in the private sector than in the public sector, causing the relative costs of private goods to fall compared with public goods. Public services, especially those which are labor-intensive,

Table 3–3 Transfer Payments to Persons, in Total and as a Percentage of Total Government Expenditures, Selected Calendar Years, 1939–1982

Year	Total Transfer Payments ($ Millions)*	Transfer Payments as a % of Total Government Expenditures**
1939	2,526	14.3
1949	11,722	19.7
1959	25,209	19.2
1969	62,762	21.9
1979	239,949	31.8
1982	323,939	27.1

*Source: Tax Foundation (1981), Table 20, p. 33; Tax Foundation, private communication, 1983.

**Source: Calculated from Tax Foundation (1981), Table 20, p. 33 and Table 23, p. 36; Tax Foundation, private communication, 1983.

may be unlikely to experience significant productivity improvements over time. If the price elasticity of demand for public goods were low, this would also contribute to the rising share of public expenditures in the GNP.

A final factor which may also have contributed to the relative rise in public expenditures is the rise in population. We discuss in Chapter 4 the phenomenon of economies of scale in the use of public goods. As the number of users of a public good rises, the effective price per person of public goods may fall, and the demand would then be expected to rise. Unfortunately, we have no available data which would show the importance of this or any of the other factors in the growth of public expenditures.

It is also interesting to consider the change in relative importance of the three levels of government. Table 3–4 shows the proportion of total public expenditures made by the federal, state, and local governments over the period 1922–1982. These data show considerable variation, especially before and after the Great Depression and World War II. Prior to that time, local governments accounted for as much as half, or even more than half, of total government expenditures. The relative importance of local governments declined sharply during the Depression years, and even more during World War II, over which period federal expenditures became much more important. The federal government's share dropped off after World

Table 3–4 Shares of Federal, State, and Local Government in Total Government Expenditures, Selected Fiscal Years, 1922–1982*

Year	Federal Share (%)	State's Share (%)	Local Share (%)
1922	40.5	13.6	46.0
1927	31.5	16.8	51.7
1932	34.3	20.6	45.1
1936	54.7	18.8	26.5
1942	78.0	9.8	12.2
1944	91.4	3.7	4.9
1946	83.5	7.7	8.8
1952	71.7	13.4	15.0
1957	65.2	16.3	18.5
1962	64.4	16.6	19.1
1967	64.7	17.5	17.8
1972	60.7	20.3	19.0
1977	63.2	20.3	16.5
1979	64.4	20.3	15.4
1980	64.2	20.0	15.8
1981	64.6	19.9	15.5
1982	65.7**	19.2**	15.1**

*Source: Tax Foundation (1981), Table 7, p. 19; Tax Foundation, private communication, 1983.

**Tax Foundation estimates.

War II, of course, but only fell to about 70 percent of the total in 1952, with a further decline to about 60 percent in 1972. Since that post-war low, the federal share has risen again, so that it now accounts for about two-thirds of total public expenditure. This federal government growth has been accompanied by a decline in local government expenditures, which, after World War II, never regained their previous importance. Meanwhile, the share of the states has fluctuated between 15 and 20 percent, aside from the war years, showing some gradual increase in the postwar period.

Let us now consider the structure of government expenditures in more detail. Table 3–5 provides a breakdown of expenditures by function for 1981–82, showing the relative importance of different activities by each

Table 3–5   Government Expenditure by Function and Level of Government, 1981–1982*

| | | Expenditures ($ Millions) | | |
Function	Total	Federal	State	Local
National Defense and International Relations	204,275	204,275	—	—
Postal Service	21,761**	21,761**	—	—
Space Research	6,181	6,181	—	—
Insurance Trust Expenditures	267,576	228,110	34,664	4,802
Education and Libraries	166,057	11,484	42,301	112,272
Public Welfare	78,821	22,564	41,513	14,744
Hospitals & Health	52,766	12,507	19,398	20,860
Social Insurance Administration	5,409	3,123	2,278	8
Veterans Services	15,023	14,959	64	—
Transportation	44,451	5,276	20,962	18,212
Public Safety (Fire, Police, Correction)	37,094	2,422	9,825	24,846
Natural Resources	45,486	38,974	5,165	1,348
Sewerage & Sanitation	14,934	—	359	14,575
Parks & Recreation	8,783	1,375	1,362	6,046
Housing & Urban Renewal	16,008	7,910	488	7,610
Administration	28,264	6,040	8,308	13,917
Interest on Debt	121,786	101,816	9,015	10,955
Other	46,614	21,507	9,564	15,543

*Source: US Department of Commerce (1983), Table 9, p. 31 and Table 11, p. 33.

**Gross of Postal Service Revenue of $21,696,000. Source: US Dept. of Commerce (1983), Table 4, p. 19.

level of government and for the public sector as a whole. It also shows the relative importance of each level of government for any given function. We shall discuss briefly the nature of the various types of expenditures undertaken by each level of government.

(a) Federal Government Expenditures

As shown in Table 3–5, federal government expenditures are dominated by three categories: national defense and international relations, insurance benefits, and interest on debt. About 29 percent of the budget in 1981–82 was devoted to national defense and international relations, while insurance benefits comprised over 32 percent. Interest on debt, which is self-explanatory, was almost 13 percent of the budget. Lesser amounts were spent on public welfare, natural resources, education, and health, and still less on a number of other functions as shown. We shall briefly outline the purposes to which the expenditures in each functional category are put.

(i) *National Defense and International Relations; Veterans Services.* These expenditures include outlays for military personnel, operations and maintenance, and capital outlays. Lesser amounts go to research and development, atomic energy defense activities, construction, and military assistance to other countries. In the international relations area, by far the largest item of spending is foreign economic assistance, much of which is bilateral. Remaining dollars in this area contribute multi-lateral assistance through various international organizations. Veterans services include health care for veterans and other veterans benefits as well.

(ii) *Postal Service; Space Research.* Like defense and international relations, these are purely federal government functions. The postal service is subsidized from general government revenues, but the amount of subsidy is gradually diminishing over time. Whether or not such government enterprises should be subsidized is open to debate; the issues involved are discussed in Chapter 7. The same issue of subsidization is beginning to arise concerning some aspects of the space program, notably the Space Transportation System, or "space shuttle," as they become increasingly routinized and commercialized. The dividing line between government space research and the private telecommunications industry is becoming blurred, with uncertain implications for the type and level of government involvement in the future.

(iii) *Insurance Trust Expenditures; Social Insurance Administration.* These expenditures, financed mainly by the federal payroll tax, represent payments to social security and unemployment insurance beneficiaries. The social security system pays benefits to retired persons, surviving family members of deceased workers, and disabled workers, while the unemployment insurance program provides benefits for a period of time to workers who have lost their jobs. These programs, particularly social security, have grown spectacularly in recent years, and have become the focus of much controversy. The difficult and important issues that they raise are discussed in Chapter 14.

(iv) *Education and Libraries.* The federal government plays only a small role in education, principally devoting its efforts to promoting equal educational opportunities. Assistance is offered to university students under some programs; other programs aid disadvantaged children at the preschool, primary, and secondary levels.

(v) *Public Welfare.* The federal government provides assistance to low-income households through a variety of programs, although primary responsibility for general welfare payments rests with the states. Among specific federal activities are Medicare, which provides medical benefits for the aged, and the Food Stamp program, which provides transfers in the form of coupons redeemable for food. The Food Stamp program has increased in size rapidly in recent years. These programs are discussed further in Chapter 14.

(vi) *Health.* Federal government involvement in health (other than the Medicare program mentioned above) includes an increasing outlay of funds to support research into health problems, to assist students training to be health professionals, and to support programs that prevent illness and control health problems in areas such as occupational health, communicable disease, and consumer safety. The federal government also contributes to the construction and modernization of certain health facilities. However, over 75 percent of health expenditures are undertaken by state and local governments.

(vii) *Transportation.* The main components of direct transportation expenditures by the federal government are for air and water transportation. Expenses for air transportation include the costs of federal airports and airway programs; air traffic control and navigation systems; and the activities of the Federal Aviation Agency and the Civil Aeronautics Board. Water transportation outlays include assistance to the ship-building and shipping industries through subsidies; the Coast Guard; the St. Lawrence Seaway Development Corporation; and various port facilities. The federal government also provides funds to the national rail passenger service, Amtrak.

(viii) *Public Safety.* Federal government expenditures on police activities include the costs of operating the Federal Bureau of Investigation; the Immigration and Naturalization Service; Bureau of Narcotics; Secret Service; and some correctional institutions. Public safety is primarily a function of lower-level government, however. Local governments alone spent almost ten times as much as the federal government in this area in 1981–82.

(ix) *Natural Resources; Parks and Recreation.* A significant portion of the disbursements in this area are devoted to agriculture, including in particular commodity purchases designed to stabilize the prices of various agricultural products. Some of these purchases are eventually resold or transferred to aid programs. Agricultural support payments tend to vary from year to year, and in the most recent years they have been reduced considerably. The federal government also funds a variety of types of agricultural research, and farm crop and mortgage insurance. Other major components of this category of expenditures are programs to provide hydroelectric power, water supplies, flood control, and irrigation; the management of national forests and parks; soil conservation and reclamation programs; and recreation programs.

(x) *Housing and Urban Renewal.* Some direct services are provided under this category, including planning and management assistance to communities, research directed at community development programs, various area and regional development programs, and disaster relief and insurance. The federal government also incurs some expenses from providing mortgage insurance, through the Federal Housing Administration, to those individuals inadequately served by private mortgage markets. The Housing and Community Development program provides housing assistance to those in need. Finally, rural housing programs exist to provide low-interest housing loans to rural families with low income.

(b) State Government Expenditures

Direct outlays at the state level vary considerably from state to state. The division of responsibilities between state and local governments is decided upon separately by each state, since local governments all derive their powers from the state. In general, state governments' spending activities are heaviest in the areas of education, public welfare, insurance benefits, transportation, and health. Our remarks will be directed towards aggregate state expenditures rather than at particular states.

Spending on education makes up nearly 20 percent of state direct expenditures. The major part of this cost is devoted to higher education, primarily the operation of state universities, colleges, junior colleges, and other post-secondary school institutions. State funds are also used for local school supervision, and for state schools for the handicapped and other special programs.

Public welfare accounts for over 19 percent, and social insurance benefits account for over 16 percent, of state spending. Some states assume responsibility for general relief welfare programs, while others delegate it to local governments. Moreover, some states provide supplementary payments to individuals receiving federal public assistance. Public welfare payments also include vendor payments for medical care programs. Insurance benefits include a variety of transfer methods. All states have unemployment insurance programs and public employee retirement pensions. Most operate workers compensation programs, and some have their own social insurance plans.

State transportation spending takes almost 10 percent of the budget, of which the bulk goes to state highways for construction and maintenance, land purchase, and equipment. The remainder is devoted mainly to toll roads and bridges. The data on expenditures are gross of the revenue received by user charges, such as road tolls.

Health disbursements are about 9 percent of total state outlays. Most of this money is devoted to public hospital construction and operation. Lesser amounts are used for public health facilities, and as payments to private hospitals for the care of patients on public support.

State governments are also involved in a number of functions of lesser magnitude as indicated by Table 3–5. Natural resources spending includes the operation of state parks and recreational facilities. Public safety expenses are for the operation of state prisons and similar institutions, and for the provision of state police.

(c) Local Government Expenditures

As with state spending, local government expenditures vary from state to state, and they also vary from locality to locality. In the aggregate, the main functional outlays by local governments are for education; local services such as police, fire, sewerage, and sanitation; transportation; health; and public welfare. Most of these expenditures are self-explanatory, so we shall mention the main components of each very briefly.

Education is by far the most important local government function, taking about 36 percent of all local government spending. This represents mainly the provision of primary and secondary schooling including such health, recreation, and library services as are administered by local school systems. Local police protection, fire protection, sewerage, and sanitation take up another 13 percent of the budget of local governments, while transportation, public welfare, and health each take around 5–7 percent. Local transportation outlays maintain roads, urban transit, and parking facilities. Public welfare expenditures are primarily for general relief by those local governments that have been given responsibility by the states for welfare. Some local governments also supplement welfare payments made by the federal government. Health spending is for the operation and and provision of hospital and public health facilities. Lesser amounts are spent on natural resources, housing and urban renewal, interest on debt, insurance benefits, and libraries.

Much of the specialization of functions by level of government that we have just described is a longstanding feature of the United States fiscal system. In Chapter 15 we discuss some of the economic reasons for such a pattern of activities. We also discuss there the very important fiscal interconnections among the different levels of governments, especially intergovernmental transfers, that we have ignored here for the sake of simplicity. As we now proceed to discuss the economic principles underlying government expenditures, the reader will find it helpful to keep in mind the areas of government activity sketched out here, and to see how much of this activity might be explained by such principles.

CHAPTER NOTES

1. Some of the above club goods also have variable use by members. Buchanan's original analysis emphasized the optimal number of members rather than the intensity of use of the facility.

2. Analytically, the phenomenon of highway congestion is the same as a congested variable-use public good.

3. This is not an unambiguous notion of efficiency. *Ex ante* it will not be possible to increase one person's expected utility without reducing that of another. However, *ex post,* once the state of the world has been determined, it would generally be possible to reallocate commodities so as to raise every person's utility.

4. For discussions of the screening functions of education systems, see Arrow (1973) and Stiglitz (1975). For a broad discussion of the phenomenon of screening or signalling, especially on labor markets, see Spence (1974).

5. This notion has appeared several times in the literature. See, for example, Hochman and Rogers (1969), Marglin (1963a), and Thurow (1971).

II

Public Expenditure Theory, Externalities, and Public Enterprise Pricing

4

The Theory of Public Goods

INTRODUCTION

4–1   Public expenditure theory may be conceptually divided into two categories: Normative analysis and positive analysis. Normative analysis is concerned mainly with deriving rules for the efficient allocation of resources in economies with commodities exhibiting the joint consumption property. The normative approach will be the substance of this chapter. The positive aspect of public expenditure theory is involved with the implementation of those rules by the public sector. It includes, primarily, a study of the mechanisms that could or do exist for allocating resources to public expenditures in the face of the free-rider problem. This positive analysis, or the theory of public choice, is presented in Chapter 6.

Normative public goods analysis proceeds by applying the Pareto criterion to an economy containing one or more public goods. That is, one wants to find the marginal conditions which must be satisfied if resources are to be allocated in such a way that it is not possible to make one person better off without at the same time making another worse off. We begin by presenting a geometric derivation of these efficiency conditions in a two-person two-good economy analogous to that of Chapter 2 except that one of the goods is a pure public good. This analysis was originally attributable to Samuelson (1954, 1955), and the conditions we shall derive are often called the *Samuelson conditions*. The analysis will also allow us to indicate clearly the source of the failure of competitive markets.

THE OPTIMAL PROVISION OF
PURE PUBLIC GOODS

4–2   A Pareto optimum exists if it is not possible to make one person better off without at the same time making at least one other person worse off. An equivalent way to characterize Pareto optimality is as follows: For any given level of utility for all persons in the economy but one, a Pareto-optimal allocation of resources will put the remaining person at the highest utility level possible. For example, in the two-person exchange economy of Fig. 4–1, suppose individual A is at the utility level of indifference curve II. The allocation of resources which allows B to attain the highest level of utility consistent with A being on II is given by the point of tangency between B's indifference curve JJ and II. This will be a point on the contract curve $O_A O_B$. Any other Pareto-optimal allocation could be attained by selecting a different initial level of utility for A, and the same tangency condition would hold. The derivation of the Pareto optimality conditions for public goods involves performing that type of conceptual experiment for an economy which has public goods.

A simple economy consisting of two individuals, A and B, and two goods, a private good X and a public good G, will suffice. The private good is allocated between A and B in such a way that supply equals demand:

$$X_A + X_B = X \tag{4–1}$$

Figure 4–1

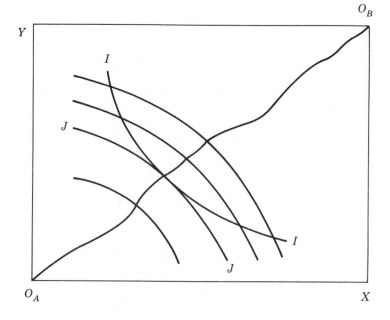

However, recall from Section 3–2 that the public good has the property that it is consumed *simultaneously* by both individuals in its entirety. We may therefore write:

$$G_A = G_B = G \qquad\qquad (4\text{--}2)$$

Since we need not distinguish between the amount of public good produced, G, and the amount consumed by each individual, there will be no need to carry the subscripts A and B on G. Equation (4–2) characterizes what we have called the joint consumption property. Both persons "consume" the services of the same physical commodity G. That is not to say that they derive the same utility from doing so. The fact that they do not is one of the main sources of the government's informational problem.

Both the public and the private good are produced according to production functions by employing factors of production. On the production side, there is no difference between an economy producing X and G and the one producing two private goods in Chapter 2. An Edgeworth production box similar to Fig. 2–4 could be used to derive exactly the same production efficiency conditions as in a purely private goods economy. That is, the marginal rate of technical substitution between any two factors must be the same in the production of both X and G. Since the production efficiency conditions remain intact, they can be satisfied by a competitive private sector producing both private and public goods, selling the private goods to consumers, but selling the public goods to the public sector. Therefore, the existence of public goods does not imply the public *production* of those goods. Only the public *provision* of them may be required.

If we assume the production efficiency conditions to be satisfied in the provision of X and G, we may represent the combinations of X and G which can be produced by the economy given its supplies of factors of production and technology in a production possibility curve such as PP in the top diagram of Fig. 4–2. Both A and B benefit from the consumption of the private and public good and we may draw indifference maps for each of them. The top diagram in Fig. 4–2 depicts A's indifference curves drawn from the origin O_A while the bottom diagram shows B's indifference curves drawn from O_B.[1]

To derive the Pareto optimality conditions, we shall take an arbitrary level of utility for A and find the allocation of resources which maximizes the utility level of B. Suppose A has the utility level given by the indifference curve II. Any combination of G and X_A leaving A on II is permissible. Our first task is to find the combinations of G and X_B available to B that are consistent with the combinations of G and X that may be produced, and with the combinations of G and X_A which must be available to A (to keep A on II). Consider any point on PP such as C. The output of G produced here ($O_A E$) can be consumed by both A and B since it is a public good. The output of X is EC and must be divided between A and B. To maintain a utility level of II, A requires ED of it, leaving CD for B, the vertical distance

Figure 4–2

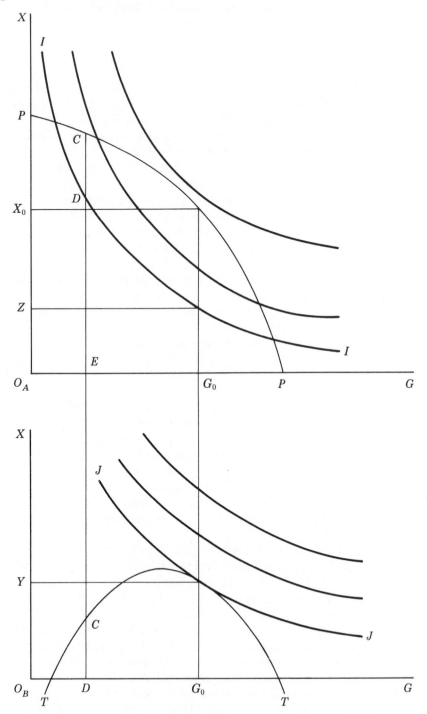

between the production possibility curve *PP* and the indifference curve *II*. In a similar way, for any point on *PP* we may obtain the combination of *X* and *G* available to *B* by vertical subtraction of *II* from *PP*. The resulting consumption opportunities for *B* are given by *TT* in the lower diagram of Fig. 4–2. The maximum level of utility that *B* can attain is that of indifference curve *JJ*, which is tangential to *TT*. This entails an output of the public good given by $O_A G_0$ ($= O_B G_0$), and an output of the private good of $O_A X_0$, of which $O_A Z$ is consumed by *A* and $Z X_0$ ($= O_B Y$) is consumed by *B*.

Our purpose is to deduce the conditions which characterize this Pareto-optimal allocation of resources. At the point of tangency between *JJ* and *TT*, the slope of *B*'s indifference curve equals the slope of *TT*. The slope of *B*'s indifference curve is his marginal rate of substitution of the private good for the public good (MRS_{GX}^B). Since *TT* was derived from subtracting vertically *II* (with a slope of MRS_{GX}^A) from *PP* (with a slope of MRT_{GX}), the slope of *TT* is by elementary geometry the difference between the slopes of *PP* and *II* ($MRT_{GX} - MRS_{GX}^A$). Therefore, at the optimal allocation the following equality holds:

$$MRS_{GX}^B = MRT_{GX} - MRS_{GX}^A$$

or,

$$\sum_{i=A,B} MRS_{GX}^i = MRT_{GX}. \tag{4–3}$$

Equation (4–3) represents the efficiency condition for the optimal supply of public good *G*, and is conventionally referred to as the Samuelson condition. Intuitively it makes a great deal of sense, for it says that at the optimum, the marginal cost of supplying the last unit of *G* in terms of *X* foregone (MRT_{GX}) just equals the sum of the marginal benefits that all users of the increment of *G* simultaneously obtain in terms of $X(\Sigma\, MRS_{GX}^i)$. The same condition can easily be shown to hold algebraically in the more general case, in which there are many consumers (see Samuelson [1954]). More generally, in an economy with many persons, many public goods, and many private goods, a condition such as Eq. (4–3) must hold for each of the public goods in terms of any arbitrary private good. The usual Pareto-optimal conditions hold among all private goods.[2]

In an economy in which money is used as the unit of account we may interpret the efficiency conditions in terms of monetary marginal benefits and marginal costs. The marginal rate of transformation is the ratio of the marginal cost of producing *G* to the marginal cost of producing *X*, or

$$MRT_{GX} = \frac{MC_G}{MC_X}. \tag{4–4}$$

Similarly, the marginal rate of substitution for an individual is the ratio of marginal utilities of the two goods which in turn is the ratio of the marginal benefits in monetary terms of G and X,[3] or:

$$MRS_{GX}^A = \frac{MU_G^A}{MU_X^A} = \frac{MB_G^A}{p_X}. \tag{4–5}$$

In an economy in which competitive producers follow marginal cost pricing and therefore satisfy the production efficiency conditions, $p_X = MC_X$ and Eqs. (4–3), (4–4), and (4–5) imply:

$$\sum_{i=A,B} MB_G^i = MC_G. \tag{4–6}$$

That is, the sum of the marginal benefits to all individuals from G must equal the marginal cost of producing it.

This latter version of the efficiency conditions in terms of marginal benefits and marginal costs lends itself readily to a diagrammatic interpretation using the constructs of demand and supply curves. In Fig. 4–3 the supply curve shows the marginal cost of producing G for various points along the production possibility curve PP. The curves D^A and D^B represent the "demand" curves for G by the two individuals, in the sense that they show the marginal benefit placed on G by the individuals (MB_G^i), or the

Figure 4–3

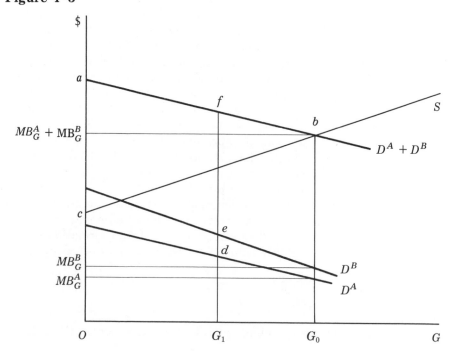

price that they would pay for each output of G if they had to pay a price. There are alternative ways in which the demand curves could be drawn. For example, they might be compensated demand curves obtained by taking the slopes of the indifference curves II and JJ in Fig. 4–2 at various points. Or, they might be what Hicks (1956) has called marginal evaluation curves obtained by taking the slopes of indifference curves along a hypothetical budget line tangential to II and JJ. (See Buchanan [1968] for this interpretation.) Finally, they might be ordinary demand curves generated by a price-consumption line passing through II and JJ at the optimal point. As we shall show in the Appendix to Chapter 9, if income effects for G are zero, the three will be equivalent. Otherwise, they will all intersect the optimal point G_0 at different slopes. To show how the optimal point G_0 is determined, we add the individual demand curves vertically (rather than horizontally, as with private goods), to derive the "aggregate" demand curve $D^A + D^B$. For instance, at the level G_1 of the public good, we add the distances $dG_1 = MB_G^A$ and $eG_1 = MB_G^B$ to find the point f, which is thus equal to the sum of MB_G^A and MB_G^B. The optimal output of G occurs at the point at which the aggregate demand curve $(D^A + D^B)$ intersects the supply curve. At this point, Eq. (4–6) and also Eq. (4–3) are satisfied.

The net social benefit from producing the optimal amount of the public good can also be illustrated with the aid of Fig. 4–3. The total benefits to A and B respectively are the areas beneath the demand curves D_A and D_B between O and G_0. Adding these areas together, the total benefit generated by the public good is the area beneath $D^A + D^B$ or $OabG_0$. The total cost is the area beneath the supply curve or $OcbG_0$. Therefore the net benefit generated by producing the public good is the area abc. How this benefit is distributed among various individuals in society depends upon the nature of the pricing or taxing scheme used to finance G. We return to this question in Chapter 6, where we also consider whether or not the full gain abc will be exploited in practice.

The analysis of Fig. 4–3 suggests a pseudo-market interpretation of the supply of public goods known as *benefit pricing* or the *Lindahl solution*.[4] If individuals in the economy are all endowed with given incomes, ordinary demand curves for G could be drawn which would show the quantity that each would hypothetically purchase at various prices. Inversely, such demand curves would show each individual's willingness to pay for a marginal unit of the public good at various levels of provision. Under a system of benefit pricing, consumers are charged a per-unit price for the public good equal to their marginal benefit or willingness to pay at the level actually provided.

Since individual tastes and incomes may differ, each may well have a different benefit price from the others at any given G. At the optimal point G_o, the sum of the individual benefit prices $(MB_G^A + MB_G^B)$ would just equal the marginal cost. Thus in Fig. 4–3, A would pay MB_G^A per unit of G and B would pay MB_G^B per unit of G. Unlike the private goods pricing mechanism, each individual would be paying a price for the same good, and each person's price would be different.

While the above benefit pricing scheme may naturally suggest itself as an analog to the market mechanism for allocating public goods, the analogy is not particularly helpful, nor is it operational. In the first place, the government must know the individual marginal benefit schedules in order to assign the benefit prices. These schedules are not, however, directly observable. The problem is that each individual realizes that the benefit price eventually assigned to him can be minimized by falsely understating his demand or marginal benefit schedule. Each individual has an incentive to do so since the understatement of any one individual's demand will have only a small effect on the aggregate demand and thus on the level of G selected, while significantly reducing the individual's benefit charges. Unfortunately, when every individual reasons this way, the combined effect of many understated marginal benefit schedules is to lower the aggregate demand substantially, and to reduce the amount of G provided significantly below the optimum. Each individual acts as a free rider, failing to reveal his true preferences for the public good. The upshot is an inefficient level of provision of the good. (Of course, even if exclusion by price is feasible, it would be inefficient to exclude anyone from the consumption of a non-rivalrous good. As noted earlier, this follows because the cost of adding one more consumer to the consuming group is zero, while the benefit would be positive. Properly-determined Lindahl prices would not, however, actually exclude anyone.) In the second place, prices do not play the same allocative role with public goods as they do with private goods. Prices are a rationing device in the case of private goods, since they determine who consumes how much. With public goods this is not the case. Since everyone by definition consumes the same quantity of G once it has been provided, a pricing scheme plays no allocative role. The only function of a pricing scheme would be to determine how the costs of financing the public good are to be shared among the users.

While on efficiency grounds there is no reason to prefer benefit pricing to any other financing scheme, on equity grounds there may be, depending upon the value judgment that is made about distribution. It has been argued that when people buy a private good, they pay an amount equal to the value of the marginal unit times the number of units consumed, and that this is fair and equitable. Similarly, under a scheme of benefit pricing, each individual's total charge is equal to the marginal benefit of the public good times the quantity consumed, and again it could be argued that this is a fair way of sharing the costs of the good. However, just as there is an infinite number of Pareto-optimal allocations of resources in a private goods economy, so it is in a public goods economy as well, each such allocation differing from the other by having a different distribution of welfare or utility. Some persons will be better off and some worse off in comparing any two efficient allocations. The financing scheme in conjunction with the initial ownership of resources will determine which of the Pareto-optimal allocations is achieved (assuming one is achieved). Recall that in deriving Eq. (4–3) we began by arbitrarily selecting II as A's level of utility. Any other level could have been chosen and the same conditions (4–3) would have resulted. If a lower level of utility had been chosen for A, a higher level of utility would have resulted for B, and vice versa. We could summarize the alternate levels of utility achievable in a grand utility possibility curve identical to that of Fig. 2–7. The choice among these various optima must be made on equity grounds, and that may or may not require a scheme of benefit pricing.

Note that even though Eq. (4–3) holds for all Pareto-optimal allocations, that does not imply that the optimal allocation G_0 will be the same for all. In general, it will not. In that sense, equity and efficiency considerations are inextricably intertwined. There is no single efficient level of G. It depends upon the distribution of utilities which in turn depends upon the financing scheme for public goods. In Fig. 4–3, for example, if individual A's demand for G is highly income-elastic while B's demand is less so, then the aggregate demand curve $D^A + D^B$ would shift up in a situation where A's endowment has been increased at the expense of B's. While D^B would shift downward, D^A would shift upward by a more-than-offsetting amount. Under these assumptions, the efficient level of G is increased as income is redistributed in favor of A and away from B. Other outcomes are clearly possible under different assumptions about tastes.

There is a comparative static property of the above model which is of considerable importance in the application of the notion of public goods to some problems discussed later, such as the theory of clubs and fiscal federalism. Suppose that a third person C is added to the above economy of two persons. The previous resources of the economy were owned by A and B, who obtained a certain income from them and had a certain demand for public goods. Individual C, upon joining the economy, is assumed to have his own income generated from his own factors of production (e.g. labor) which is brought with him. Let us consider what happens to the output of public goods in the economy and the level of well-being of its members when the population rises by one. Initially, let us ignore all changes that may occur in the incomes of A and B and concentrate on the demand side as illustrated in Fig. 4–4. Before C is added, the demand curves of A and B result in an optimal level of output of public goods at the amount G_0 as above. The addition of C admits a third person to the use of G at no extra resource cost. But since C presumably obtains some benefit from the public goods, the sum of the marginal benefits ($\Sigma\ MB_G^i$) will now exceed the marginal cost and the efficiency condition will be violated at the level of output G_0. As shown in Fig. 4–4, the new aggregate demand curve $D^A + D^B + D^C$ intersects the supply curve at the higher output G_1.

It is easy to see that everyone can be better off in these new circumstances. For example, under a benefit pricing scheme both A and B would now face a lower price for G and thus, with given incomes, must reach a higher level of indifference. The net benefits generated by the addition of the third individual equal *abdc* in Fig. 4–4. The reason why A and B can be made

Figure 4–4

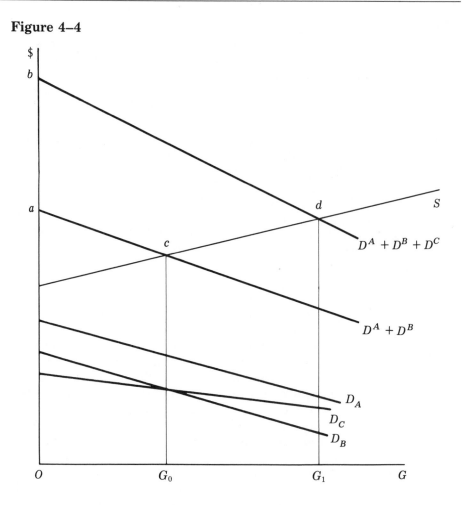

better off is not hard to find. The addition of another individual adds another source of tax revenue without reducing the benefits achieved by the previous users. With more persons to share in the cost of G, the cost per person can be reduced for all users. This phenomenon, which we shall call *economies of scale in consumption* of public goods, turns out to be of paramount importance in the theory of clubs discussed below and in the theory of fiscal federalism discussed in Part IV. The implication is that per-person utility can be increased continuously as population rises.

This analysis of economies of scale in consumption of G assumed that when individual C joined the economy he brought with him his own income or factors of production and that the incomes of A and B were not affected. However, in the real world, there may well be some offsetting influences to economies of scale in consumption on the production side. To consider the simplest case, suppose that the economy's factors of production include a fixed factor, land, and a variable factor, labor, and that when C joins the economy he brings with him only labor. As more and more persons join the economy, the ratio of labor to land rises. If the production side of the economy exhibits diminishing marginal products of the usual sort, the average output of the economy per person will initially rise, reach a maximum where the average product of labor equals the marginal product of labor, and then fall. If the labor force population is beneath the point of maximum average product, the addition of one more worker will not only allow economies of scale in consumption of G, it will also increase the average incomes in the economy. However, if the labor-land ratio is already so high as to be beyond that which maximizes the average product, additional units of labor, while they do involve economies of scale in consumption, tend to set up an offsetting influence on welfare by reducing per capita output and incomes in the economy. This offsetting tendency naturally raises the question of an optimal population size which we shall return to in Part IV. Yet another tendency offsetting economies of scale in consumption is discussed in the following section.

IMPURE PUBLIC GOODS

4–3   In practice, it might be argued that very few public goods are pure in the sense assumed above. First, the joint consumption property might be partly violated. Although all individuals may consume the services of the same quantity of the public good, the benefit obtained from the public good falls as more persons share in its consumption. As pointed out in Chapter 3, this phenomenon is known as congestion. We shall speak of congested public goods as those for which the use exhibits only partial rivalness. Second, the intensity of use of the services of a public good may be variable to individual consumers, as with a bridge or road. One could argue that it is debatable whether or not such facilities whose use is variable by consumers should be termed a public good or not (e.g. a road). That is purely a semantic issue. They do share with pure public goods the property that several consumers simultaneously use the same facility. The variable-use public good may, of course, be subject to congestion as well. We shall discuss each of these in turn.

Congested Public Goods: No Variability of Use

The derivation of the optimality conditions for the output of congested public goods is a straightforward extension of that for pure public goods. First consider an economy (or community) consisting of a given number of individuals N. Each person will have a set of preferences for the public good relative to other goods which is contingent upon the total number of users N. As N rises, the preference map of each will change. Given the number of users, the analysis of the optimality conditions for the provision of the public good follows exactly that for pure public goods in Section 4–2 above. The optimal amount will be given when the sum of the marginal benefits from the last unit supplied just equals the marginal cost of supplying it. These Samuelson conditions therefore apply more generally than to the pure public good case.

What does differ in the congested public good case is the analysis of the comparative static effects of adding additional persons to the economy, or group of users, since the benefit each individual obtains from the use of public goods depends upon the number of users. The congestion property implies that as more users are added, the benefit that previous users obtain from a given level of output of the public good is decreased. In terms of the demand curves of Fig. 4–4, as person C is added, the demand curves of persons A and B shift downward. This reduction in per-person benefits tends to offset the advantages generated from economies of scale in consumption of the public good due to the sharing of costs. It also suggests that there may be an optimal number of users of the public good.

These offsetting elements form the basis of what Buchanan (1965a) has called *the theory of clubs.* A club good is a congested public good for which exclusion is possible and which may be replicated within an economy for different groups of persons or different clubs. The analysis of the theory of clubs is concerned both with the optimal output of a club good or congested public good and with the optimal number of users or members. We have already suggested that given the number of users the optimal output of a congested public good is given by the Samuelson condition, Eq. (4–3). What remains to be found are the conditions for the optimal number of users. To obtain these in the simplest form, assume that all individuals who are potential members of this club have identical preferences and that they all contribute equally to the financing of the public goods.[5]

Consider now the situation of a representative individual user as the total number of users N increases on a given size of facility $\overline{G}$. Figure 4–5 depicts this case. The curve TB represents the total benefits received by a typical user as the number of users increases. The curve may rise initially and then begins to fall, reflecting the reduced benefits to any one user from having more users share the same public good. The slope of the TB curve reflects the marginal benefit from having additional users, or $MB = \Delta TB/\Delta N$. The marginal benefit is negative and defines the *marginal congestion cost* imposed on a typical individual. Since there are N individuals, the marginal congestion cost imposed by one more user is the reduction in benefits to all of them, or $N \cdot MB$.

Let us assume that the total cost of the given amount of public good, C, is divided equally among all consumers, so that the cost incurred by each person is C/N, shown in Fig. 4–5. Since C is a constant for any fixed level of G, C/N is a rectangular hyperbola. The slope of the C/N curve is the change in cost to each individual as an additional user is added, or the marginal cost, MC. It, too, is negative, since additional users contribute their share of the cost of the public good and therefore reduce the cost to

Figure 4–5

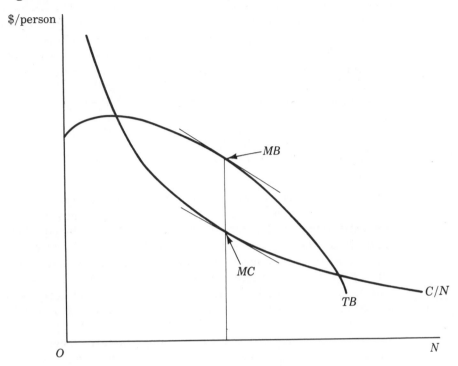

others. Since each additional user pays the going share price C/N, the payments required from all of the prior N users is reduced by that amount in total, or by C/N^2 each. The MC, or the slope of C/N, is therefore $-C/N^2$.[6]

Per capita net benefits will be maximized when $TB - C/N$ is at a maximum, or when $MB = MC$.[7] This gives:

$$MB = -\frac{C}{N^2}$$

or,

$$-N \cdot MB = \frac{C}{N}. \tag{4–7}$$

Equation (4–7) says that the optimal number of users is reached when the per-person tax price (C/N) just equals the marginal congestion costs ($-N \cdot MB$). This is what one might expect intuitively, since C/N is the benefit from adding one more user in terms of tax savings for existing users, while $-N \cdot MB$ is the opportunity cost of adding one more user, or the marginal congestion costs imposed on all users.

The above condition (4–7) for the optimal number of users of the club good was derived for an arbitrary level of output $\overline{G}$. The optimal provision requires both the correct level of output and the correct number of users. That is, it requires the simultaneous satisfaction of both the Samuelson condition $N \cdot MRS_{GX} = MRT_{GX}$ and the above condition, Eq. (4–7). Consider the simple case in which the public good can be produced with constant marginal costs. In that case, the total cost C will equal $G \cdot MRT_{GX}$ where G is the level of output. Combining this equality with the two optimality conditions we obtain:

$$\frac{C}{N} = G \cdot MRS_{GX} = -N \cdot MB. \qquad (4–8)$$

When the club good is both optimally provided and optimally utilized, the per-person tax price (C/N) will equal the output times the marginal rate of substitution of each person $(G \cdot MRS_{GX})$. This will also equal the marginal congestion cost imposed by each user $(-N \cdot MB)$, and each user's net benefits will be maximized. In other words, a scheme that practices benefit pricing, and that prices according to marginal congestion costs simultaneously, will be optimal in both size of facility and number of users, and will have just enough revenues to cover total costs when the facility can be produced at constant cost.

From the above analysis we may immediately recognize the potential optimality of the competitive provision of club goods or congested public goods by the market. If exclusion is possible without cost and if the costs of providing the good are constant, the competitive market mechanism can be relied upon to provide an economy of many individuals with the correct size of facility and the correct number of members, and, therefore, the correct number of such facilities for the entire population.[8] The competitive provision of such facilities would result in zero profits on their operation. Market failure in the provision of such goods will result if exclusion (and therefore market pricing) is not possible, if the size of the optimal facility is so large relative to the population that competition does not prevail, or if the facility can be produced at decreasing costs. In each of these cases there is a *prima facie* case for collective provision, but in so doing the government may face severe informational problems as in the pure public goods case.

Variability in the Use of Public Facilities

A number of authors (e.g. Oakland [1972b], Sandmo [1973]) have distinguished between the sorts of public goods discussed above and those whose intensity of usage can be varied by the users. Many publicly-provided facilities appear to be of the latter sort, such as parks and recreation facilities, bridges, and roads. In these cases the public sector provides a facility whose services can be used simultaneously and in varying amounts by individuals. The individuals may themselves incur a marginal cost in the use of such facilities, such as fuel for transportation or time taken to use the facility, but the inclusion of such costs is not germane to the analysis.

We may distinguish, as in the public goods case, between those facilities whose services are available at no opportunity cost and those that are subject to congestion in the sense that additional users reduce the benefits obtained by previous users. Consider the former case first. Figure 4–6 depicts the demand curve D for the use of the services X of a facility of a particular size. The only costs incurred are for the provision of the facility itself, since we assume that there are no costs of providing services. There are two issues involved in the optimal provision of variable-use public facilities. One is the optimal use of services from a given size of facility and the other is the optimal size of the facility itself. Since there is no congestion, the opportunity cost of using additional services is zero. The use of services ought to be extended to the point at which marginal benefits from the use equal zero, or X_0 in Fig. 4–6. This optimal use of the facility is obtained by charging no price and the issue of excludability or otherwise is unimportant.

Consider now the question of the optimal size of the facility. First of all we can estimate whether the facility of the size shown in Fig. 4–6 should be constructed at all. At its optimal use level X_0, the total benefit

Figure 4–6

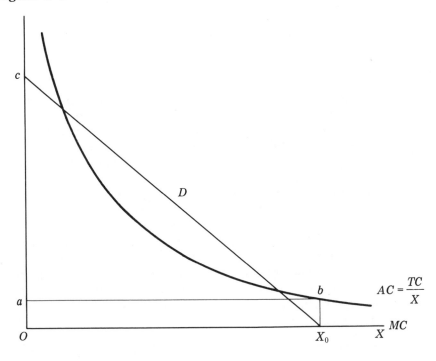

of the facility is approximately the area beneath the demand curve OcX_0. The total cost of the facility is not shown directly in the diagram. However, the average cost curve is the rectangular hyperbola labeled AC. By the relationship between the average and total costs ($AC = TC/X$), the total cost is the area $OabX_0$. The public facility provides a positive net benefit to society if the area OcX_0 is larger than the area $OabX_0$. Since the former is not directly observable, it must be inferred from other sources or empirically estimated.

Even if the net benefit to society is positive, that does not imply that this size of facility ought to be provided. Other sizes may provide greater net benefits. In order to know the optimal size of the facility something must be known of the effect on benefits of changes in the size of the facility. In the simplest case, the demanders may benefit from the services of the facility but not from the size *per se*. The only function of size may be to relieve congestion. For example, using a large uncongested bridge may not give greater benefits than using a small uncongested bridge. If that is the case, a reduction in the size of an uncongested facility is always beneficial since it reduces costs without reducing benefits. In fact, the size of the facility should be reduced until the savings in costs is just offset by the reduction in benefits due to congestion, in which case the analysis of the following section applies. One can only justify building an uncongested facility if there are indivisibilities which impose a minimum size on the facility, or if there are direct benefits to be had from the size of the facility *per se*. In a broader context, an uncongested facility might be built now if it is expected to become congested in the future due to an increase in its use through, say, population growth. Or, a facility might be built which is uncongested over certain periods and congested over other, "peak," periods. Typically, uncongested facilities are subject to some sort of indivisibility which prevents their being built smaller, as is the case with roads and bridges. In such cases, the minimum size is called for.

The optimal provision and use of congested facilities involves slightly more complicated considerations than the above, not unlike the club good case discussed earlier. (Indeed the term "club good" has been taken by some, e.g. Oakland [1972b], to apply to these congested variable-use public facilities as well as to congested public goods discussed above.)

Let us consider, for example, the problem of highway construction and utilization. First we suppose that a highway of size K has been built, and we study its optimal utilization. Then we turn to the choice of K, that is, the level of investment in highway facilities.

Beyond the construction costs of the road, which, taking K as given, we may treat as fixed costs, there are two other (variable) costs of highway use. On the one hand, there are various monetary costs in the form of fuel, vehicle wear and tear, etc. Let us suppose that these monetary costs *per trip* are a constant C, independent of the level of road use. On the other hand, and in many cases more importantly, there is a cost in time incurred by travelers on the road. Let us for simplicity suppose that each road user places the same value on a marginal unit of time saved; that is, each traveler would be willing to pay a certain amount, the same for all travelers, to shorten the trip by one minute. Then let $T(X,K)$ be the travel time cost incurred by each user when X travelers use the road and when the road is of size K. $T(X,K)$ is expected to be increasing in X because, as more and more travelers use the road, traffic speeds fall and travel times increase. This indeed is the basic congestion phenomenon that we wish to analyze. Also we expect $T(X,K)$ to be decreasing in K: the bigger the highway, the less time is incurred per trip at any given number of trips. Given a road of size K, then, the total variable cost incurred when X trips are taken is $X \cdot [C + T(X,K)]$, and the average cost per trip is just $C + T(X,K)$. This average cost curve is illustrated in Fig. 4–7, where we assume that congestion of the highway begins once the number of trips taken rises above X_0.

Now consider the social marginal cost of a trip. If one more traveler is added to the highway, that traveler will incur money and time costs of $C + T(X,K)$. In addition, however, the traveler will slow down the flow of traffic slightly, increasing the travel time for each of the other X travelers by $\Delta T(X,K)/\Delta X$, the change in T caused by a one-unit increase in X. The cost of the extra trip to all parties is therefore $C + T(X,K) + X \Delta T(X,K)/\Delta X = SMC(X)$. As shown in the figure, this obviously exceeds the average cost, the difference, $X \Delta T(X,K)/\Delta X$, being the *marginal congestion cost* imposed by an extra traveler at each level of utilization.

Let D be the demand curve for trips, showing desired highway usage at any given price per trip. Then X^* is the optimal level of utilization of

Figure 4–7

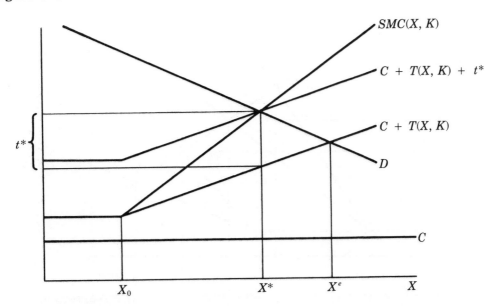

the highway. In the absence of tolls or other corrective mechanisms, however, X^e trips will be taken, since each individual user ignores the cost to other travelers of his presence on the highway and considers only the average cost $C + T(X,K)$ in deciding whether a trip is worth taking. Thus the equilibrium level of utilization is too high. Suppose, however, that one computes the marginal congestion cost imposed at the efficient level X^*, $X^* \Delta T(X^*,K)/\Delta X$, and imposes a toll t^* of this amount per trip. Then the cost to each traveler of taking a trip rises to $C + T(X,K) + t^*$, and, as shown in the figure, this would reduce the number of trips taken to the efficient level, X^*.

How does one evaluate the benefits of highway investment? Essentially, the gain from expanding a highway is the resulting savings of travel time that occurs because higher travel speeds can be achieved. The exact magnitude of this benefit depends, however, on how the highway is utilized before and after the investment. Figure 4–8 shows that when the highway size increases from K to K', the average and marginal cost-per-trip schedules shift rightward. If no congestion tolls are imposed either before or after the investment, the effective price of trips to users will fall from p^e to $p^{e'}$, and the level of use will increase from X^e to $X^{e'}$. The benefit from the investment can be computed as a change in total travel benefits minus total costs or, equivalently, as a change in consumer surplus resulting from a fall in price; in either case, the benefit is the area $p^e b d p^{e'}$. If, on the other

Figure 4–8

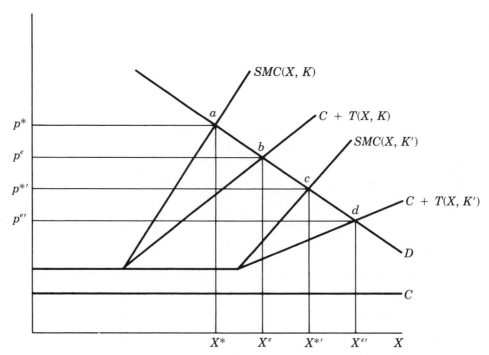

hand, an optimal toll is charged both before and after the investment, the benefit would be the area p^* a $cp^{*'}$. It is interesting to observe that the benefit from additional investment is higher when the road is not properly priced (see Wheaton [1978]). Whether or not tolls are imposed, however, the optimal amount of investment occurs when the appropriately-measured benefit from an incremental expansion of the road is equated to its cost.

Unfortunately it is difficult to estimate the magnitude of the benefits from highway use, and we might like to know whether there are other more operational signals of the correct size of the facility. For example, can we expect, as in the club good case discussed earlier, that when the facility is of optimal size and when the pricing of services is set correctly to the marginal congestion costs, total revenues will just cover total costs? Oakland (1972b) has demonstrated that there is one set of circumstances such that the optimal size of facility will be that for which the correct pricing scheme will generate just enough total revenue to cover the total costs of the facility. Two basic conditions are required:

1. The size of the facility can be expanded at constant costs.
2. The congestion that individuals are subject to, which depends upon the total use of the facility and its size, has the property that a proportionate increase in total use and size of facility will have no effect on the congestion costs borne by an individual user.[9]

Unfortunately, the proof of this proposition requires the use of calculus. We might just note some of its implications here. If exclusion is possible and without cost, the competitive provision of such facilities by the private sector may be possible. Indeed, one might interpret such privately-operated facilities as movie theatres, restaurants, and the like as being analytically identical to congested public facilities. Where exclusion is not possible except at great cost, or where the size of the facility is large relative to the total demand for it so that the market provision of several competing facilities is not feasible, market failure results. Of course, with exclusion not possible or costly, the public sector will not be able to enforce the optimal use of the facility either, as, for example, with congested roads.

CHAPTER NOTES

1. The exchange efficiency conditions derived from an Edgeworth box diagram as in Chapter 2 have no analogous interpretation in this economy. There is no exchange of X for G by a consumer individually in this economy since each consumer takes the same level of G as given. Only X can be reallocated between the two.

2. One can easily see that an analysis quite similar to that just given applies as well to public inputs or factors of production. Suppose that G is a publicly-provided good which simultaneously enters the production function of two or more firms. Examples might include port facilities, agricultural research, etc. A marginal unit of G enhances production for the affected firms, and one can

define the marginal physical product and marginal value product of the public input just as one does for ordinary inputs. Using money as a unit of account, the social benefit from the marginal unit of G is thus the sum across firms of its marginal value product, which should be equated at an optimum to the marginal cost of the input. This result directly parallels (4–3) above and (4–6) below. As one would expect, an informational problem also arises for public inputs, just as for public goods, namely the problem of assessing the marginal benefits to the firms. That problem may in some cases be somewhat less severe for a public input, however, since it may be possible to observe or estimate the change in profits of the affected firms resulting from a marginal increase in the input. Provided that equilibrium input and output prices are unchanged as a result of a change in G, this change in the profits measures precisely the marginal value product of G. For further discussions of public inputs, see Meade (1952), Kaizuka (1965), and Sandmo (1972).

3. The marginal utility of a dollar to the individual is used to convert the ratio of the marginal utilities of the two goods into the ratio of marginal dollar values. In the process, the marginal utility of a dollar appears in both the numerator and denominator in Eq. (4–5) and cancels out.

4. See Lindahl (1958). A good discussion of the Lindahl solution may be found in Musgrave (1959).

5. We also abstract from the production side by assuming that all members have given incomes. That is, joining or changing clubs does not involve changing location and income.

6. This slope may be obtained directly by the use of elementary calculus:

$$MC = d(C/N)/dN = -C/N^2.$$

7. Alternatively, one might want to maximize not per capita benefits, $TB - C/N$, but total benefits, $N(TB - C/N)$. In general, a different answer will be attained. The latter will call for larger N and lower per capita benefits $(TB - C/N)$. This is so because, at the optimum,

$$\frac{d[N \cdot (TB - C/N)]}{dN} = 0, \text{ or } (TB - C/N) + N(MB - MC) = 0.$$

The facility should be expanded beyond the point at which $MB = MC$. The last user not only influences per capita net benefits but also adds to total benefits by the amount of his own net benefit $(TB - C/N)$. It will be more appropriate to maximize per capita net benefits when the population is large enough such that a large number of club goods of the optimal size can be replicated. For a discussion of this, see Ng (1973). If club goods can be replicated, the above analysis can be extended to the case in which the population consists of persons of different preferences. In that case, like persons will tend to join the same club and the size of each club will be determined by the tastes of its members.

8. We might also expect that if persons have different tastes the market would provide a mix of club good types. Likes would tend to congregate together in the same club.

9. This is equivalent to the algebraic statement that the congestion function is homogeneous of degree zero in total use and the size of the facility.

5

Externalities

INTRODUCTION

5–1   An externality is said to exist if an activity of one party (a household or firm) affects the utility or production possibilities of another party without being priced.[1] The fact that it is not priced implies that the "emitting" party has no incentive to take into consideration the effect, beneficial or detrimental, on the "affected" party. That being the case, the emitting party may devote an inefficient amount of resources to pursuing the activity. The purpose of this chapter is to outline the various types of externalities that can occur and to consider various mechanisms (public or private) for "internalizing" or pricing them.

Throughout the analysis, there are a number of ways of classifying externalities to which we shall refer. First, externalities may benefit or harm the affected party. In the former case they are called external economies and, in the latter, external diseconomies. Second, externalities may be unilateral or reciprocal. A unilateral externality is from one party (or parties) to another party (or parties) in one direction only. Reciprocal externalities exist when each party both emits and receives an externality from the other party. The most celebrated sort of the latter is the so-called internal-to-the-industry external diseconomy arising in the unpriced use of common property resources to be discussed in Section 5–4. Finally, externalities must be distinguished, especially for policy purposes, according to whether there are many parties involved on one side or the other, or few parties. The more parties to the externality there are, the greater will be the free-rider problem and, therefore, the stronger will be the *a priori* case for public sector intervention.

The general cause of the existence of externalities is usually taken to be a lack of enforcement of property rights, either because exclusion is not possible, or because property rights have not been assigned or cannot be assigned without great difficulty (Coase [1960]). For example, party A and party B both have access to the use of the atmosphere. However, party A pollutes the air that party B uses without any account being taken of the damage done. If one or the other party could be assigned ownership rights to their share of the atmosphere and could exclude the other from its use, the externality would be internalized. If B owned the rights to use the air, he could charge A for its use and there would be no externality problem. A would be forced to take the price of the air into account in deciding how much use to make of it. Provided there were enough parties of types A and B, a competitive situation would arise and resources would be optimally allocated. Similarly, if A owned the air, he would have the right to do with it as he wished. If B wanted clean air, he would have to purchase it from A (who would have to forego polluting it) and once again the externality would be internalized. The above scenario is, of course, an absurd one because of the difficulty of defining and enforcing property rights on the use of the atmosphere. However, it does serve to illustrate that the source of the external diseconomy problem can be characterized as a lack of enforcement of property rights.

In a similar way, external economies exist because the emitters are unable to enforce property rights on the entire fruit of their activities. As with public goods, this may result from an inability to exclude the affected parties. This inability to exact a price for the external benefits of an activity means that the emitting party does not have an incentive to undertake the optimal level of the activity.

The analysis of the optimal level of externality-producing production or consumption activities bears a close similarity to the analysis of public goods presented above. The essence of the public good case is that several persons simultaneously consume the same good and, therefore, in determining the benefit from marginal increases in the provision of that good, one must aggregate the marginal benefits that all users simultaneously obtain. In the external economy case, an activity of the emitting party has a similar joint-consumption property (Buchanan [1965b]). It simultaneously benefits the emitter and the affected party or parties. To determine the optimal undertaking of the activity, one must weigh the marginal cost of the activity against the marginal benefits of the activity to all those who enjoy it (the emitter and all affected parties). At the optimum the two will be equal. That is, the following Samuelson-type conditions must hold:

$$MC = MB_A + \sum_{j=1}^{h} MB_j \qquad (5\text{--}1)$$

where MC is the marginal resource cost of expanding the activity, MB_A is the marginal benefit to the emitting party A, and MB_j is the *marginal external benefit* to each of the h affected parties.[2] If the externality goes uncorrected, party A will weigh only the marginal benefits and costs incurred privately and will select the level of activity such that:

$$MC = MB_A. \tag{5-2}$$

By convention, the right-hand side of Eq. (5–2) is called the *marginal private benefit* of the activity, while the right-hand side of Eq. (5–1) is called the *marginal social benefit*. The two differ by the amount of the marginal external benefit. The failure to take into account the external benefits provided jointly to other parties will result in an incorrect choice of the level of activity.

The external diseconomy case is identical to the above except that the affected parties are damaged rather than helped. The same optimality condition of Eq. (5–1) holds except now the terms MB_j will be negative, reflecting the detrimental effect of the externality on the affected parties. Often this condition will be written in the following form:

$$MC + \sum_{j=1}^{h} MD_j = MB_A \tag{5-3}$$

where MD_j is the *marginal external damage* imposed on individual j and is merely the negative of MB_j. The left-hand side of Eq. (5–3) is often called the *marginal social cost* of A's activity. As before, the emitting party A will behave according to Eq. (5–2) and an inefficient allocation of resources will result.

No new problems are encountered if the externality is reciprocal. In that case, an equation such as (5–1) must hold for each party in its role as emitter of an externality. Once again an inefficient allocation of resources results, since the emitting parties all behave according to Eq. (5–2) rather than Eq. (5–1). The fact that party A is benefiting from externalities emitted by party B does not influence the fact that A will behave according to incorrect rules.

THE TYPES OF EXTERNALITIES

5–2   We defined externalities as being unpriced effects of activities of one party on those of another without specifying the type of party involved. They may be either households or firms, and it is useful to classify externalities according to whether the emitting and affected parties are one or the other. The following is a taxonomy of externalities categorized according to the type of activity producing the externality and the type of party being affected.

Producer-Producer Externalities

A producer-producer externality exists when the production activities of one firm influence the production possibilities of another firm or firms either beneficially or detrimentally. There are several well-known examples of this. An upstream firm pollutes the water with waste and this adversely affects a downstream firm which uses water in its production process. An oil exploration company discovers oil in some geographical location; the information becomes available and valuable to others exploring nearby. A firm trains its labor force, part of which then moves to take employment with another firm, to the benefit of the latter. A firm employs a fleet of trucks on a congested road; this increases the travel time for other firms. A fisherman takes his catch from a fishing ground, making it more difficult for other fishermen to catch fish. This latter is the classic case of the internal-to-the-industry external diseconomy arising from an unpriced common property resource.

In each of the above cases, the firm undertaking the activity emits an external economy or diseconomy on another firm or firms without capturing the benefits or incurring the costs through the pricing mechanism. Consequently, a misallocation of resources is likely to result. In the case of external economies, the emitting firm does not take into consideration the entire benefits of its actions; as a result it may undertake too little of the activity. With external diseconomies, too much of the activity may be undertaken.

The amount of the externality emitted may depend upon either the total level of output being produced or the amounts of particular factors of production used by the emitting firm. For example, suppose the emitting firm produces output X and the affected firm output Y. Let X be produced using inputs of labor, L_X, and capital, K_X, according to the production function:

$$X = f(L_X, K_X). \tag{5-4}$$

If the X-firm is a profit maximizer in a competitive industry, it will pay factors according to the values of their marginal product; i.e., letting w and r be the prices of labor and capital, and p_X the price of good X,

$$w = p_X \cdot MP_{L_X}^X \tag{5-5}$$

$$r = p_X \cdot MP_{K_X}^X. \tag{5-6}$$

Suppose the firm producing Y receives an externality, the level of which depends upon the X-firm's use of capital. The production function for Y is:

$$Y = g(L_Y, K_Y, K_X). \tag{5-7}$$

Assume for the moment that the Y-firm is the only one affected by K_X. It takes the level of K_X as given (since that is determined by the X-firm) and maximizes profits by paying labor and capital the value of their marginal products. Nonoptimality arises because K_X is contributing to the output of Y, but the X-firm is not taking it into consideration. At the optimum, the marginal cost of using K_X, which is its price r, should equal the sum of its marginal contributions to production of both X and Y, or:

$$r = p_X \cdot MP_{K_X}^X + p_Y \cdot MP_{K_X}^Y = p_Y \cdot MP_{K_Y}^Y. \tag{5–8}$$

The term $p_Y MP_{K_X}^Y$, the marginal external effect, is the value of the marginal product of K_X in the production of Y and may be positive or negative. The X-firm, in considering only the marginal private benefits of K_X, rather than the marginal social benefits inclusive of the marginal external effect, is behaving in a nonoptimal or inefficient manner.

More generally, there may be many firms affected by the externality. Suppose we label them $Y_1, \ldots, Y_n$. In this case, the marginal social benefits of the use of K_X include not only the benefits accruing privately to the X-firm itself, but also the marginal external benefits received by all n firms, $Y_1, \ldots, Y_n$. The optimality condition for the use of K_X must be amended to include all externalities generated:

$$r = p_X \cdot MP_{K_X}^X + \sum_{i=1}^{n} p_i \cdot MP_{K_X}^i \tag{5–9}$$

where p_i is the price of Y_i and $MP_{K_X}^i$ is the marginal product of K_X in the production of Y_i.

Some complicating factors, pointed out originally by Meade (1952), may arise in the above circumstances. Suppose the K_X enters Y's production process as an external economy. There are two potential complications to the above analysis. First, the return to K_X in the production of Y may be reflected as a profit to the producers of Y. In that case there may be entry of firms into the industry to compete for the profit, and the benefit of the external effect will show up as producers' and consumers' surpluses. In Meade's analysis of the problem, he assumed that the production function g in Eq. (5–7) had constant returns to scale in L_Y and K_Y alone, so that the payments to these factors just exhausted the revenue generated on the sale of Y and no pure profits were obtained. In this case, no incentive exists for entry. The influence of K_X on the production of Y, what Meade termed the *creation of atmosphere*,[3] operated by shifting the isoquants of Y toward the origin. The optimality conditions Eq. (5–8) or Eq. (5–9) continue to hold for this case.

The second complicating factor arises if the external benefit emitted by the X-firm on firms of type Y is not purely public or nonrivalrous. This corresponds to what Meade called the *unpaid factor*. In this case, a given amount of a "factor" of production is provided externally by the X-firm to the producers of Y where the latter are now many firms within a competitive industry. If the use of the services of the externality is unpriced, the firms in the Y-industry will use them as if they were freely available (i.e. not scarce). However, because of the rivalry in the use of the external effect, there is an opportunity cost involved in each firm's use, the reduction in benefits to other users.[4] Not only will the emitting industry producing X be behaving nonoptimally (by ignoring the benefits of K_X to the Y-industry), but so will the members of the using industry (by ignoring the opportunity cost imposed on others by their use of the externality). The analysis of the externalities arising out of the competitive use of the unpaid factor is the same as that for a common property resource, which we discuss further in Section 5–4 below.

In the case in which the external effect is a diseconomy, a different sort of problem arises, originally discussed in the classic article of Coase (1960), and more recently by Baumol (1972), and Baumol and Bradford (1972). This is the *nonconvexity problem* of externalities. Suppose that the affected firm producing Y is a part of a wider industry of similar firms, but the Y-firm suffers from its being located near the X-firm. In the absence of the X-firm, the Y-firm would be able to compete profitably in the industry. However, the existence of the X-firm nearby causes the Y-firm's profits to fall due to the external diseconomy associated with K_X. It may be that the unfettered operation of the X-firm will cause a level of externality great enough to make the Y-firm's profit negative and, therefore, force it out of business despite whatever other locational advantages it may possess. At the same time, if the X-firm's activity level were restricted by forcing it to take into account the marginal external costs of the damage done to the Y-firm, the latter might be allowed to stay in business. Should the X-firm's output be so restricted? The answer is that one cannot say *a priori*. If the incremental value of the output of Y produced (over the alternative zero level) exceeds the loss in the value of X produced due to the reduction of its level of output, then correcting the X-firm's behavior and allowing firm Y to stay in business would be optimal. But if not, or if the costs of changing locations are low for the Y-firm, then the X-firm ought to be allowed to act uncorrected. As Coase pointed out, total gains and losses in the two situations must be compared. The satisfaction of the marginal optimality conditions is not sufficient.

In the above analysis it was assumed that the magnitude of the external effect depended upon the use of K_X in the production of X. It could as well depend upon the total output of X. In the fishing ground case, the external diseconomy posed on other fishermen is presumably a function of the total catch of each. The preceding discussion is still valid with some minor amendments. The production function for Y now reads:

$$Y = g(L_Y, K_Y, X). \tag{5–10}$$

While the marginal cost to the X-firm of producing its output includes the payments to labor and capital it hires, the marginal social benefits include both the price received from the sale of its output (marginal private benefits) and the unpriced marginal external benefits (positive or negative) to the Y-firm or firms.

There are two ways of viewing the nonoptimal behavior of the X-firm. One is to recognize that, in maximizing profits, the X-firm chooses the level of output which satisfies the condition:

$$p_X = MC_X. \tag{5-11}$$

The optimizing production of X is that which recognizes all the marginal social benefits generated by the production of X, or:

$$p_X + p_Y \cdot MP_X^Y = MC_X \tag{5-12}$$

where $p_Y \cdot MP_X^Y$ is the value of the marginal product of the output of X to Y's production process (once again, positive or negative).

An equivalent way of viewing the optimality condition (5–12) is in terms of the marginal productivity criteria for hiring L_X and K_X. The social values of marginal output increases of X accrue both as p_X and as the marginal external value to the Y-firm. Therefore, the social values of the marginal products of L_X and K_X should be equated to the factor prices:

$$w = (p_X + p_Y \cdot MP_X^Y) \cdot MP_{L_X}^X \tag{5-13}$$

$$r = (p_X + p_Y \cdot MP_X^Y) \cdot MP_{K_X}^X. \tag{5-14}$$

These two ways of viewing the externality process are identical. In the external economy case, the X-firm is hiring too few factors and producing too little output. In correcting the X-firm's behavior, one can operate by giving the correct incentives to produce output (e.g. by subsidizing the production of X as discussed in Section 5–3), or by giving appropriate incentives to hire labor and capital (e.g. by subsidizing the use of L_X and K_X at the same rate). Either remedy will serve to internalize the externality correctly.

If, as in the fishing ground case, the externality is reciprocal so that the X-firm's activities affect the Y-firm's production possibilities, and vice versa, no new problems arise. Both the X-firm and the Y-firm will be emitting marginal external benefits which are not being accounted for. The behavior of both must be corrected.

Producer-Consumer Externalities

The activities of firms may give rise to effects on the utility of individuals which are not captured in the price system (in addition to those outputs of the firm which are priced). The most obvious example of this is factory pollution of, say, the air which imposes damages on individuals living nearby. The analysis of this case is a straightforward extension of the discussion above. As a result of their profit-maximizing behavior firms will choose that level of output and the input configuration such that price equals marginal cost. If, however, a firm producing X emits an externality on n consumers which varies with the level of output, the ith consumer's utility function will look as follows:

$$U^i = U^i (X^i, Y^i, Z^i, \ldots, X) \tag{5-15}$$

where X^i, Y^i, Z^i, ... are the quantities of X, Y, Z, etc. consumed by the ith individual, and X is the aggregate output of X. The optimal allocation of resources dictates that the external benefits accruing to consumers from the output of X ought to be included along with the value of the output sold by a firm producing X (the private benefits) in choosing a level of output. For the X-firms this condition should be:

$$p_X + \sum_{i=1}^{n} MB_X^i = MC_X \tag{5-16}$$

where MB_X^i is the marginal benefit to consumer i from the firm's output of X. That is, the marginal social benefit of producing X must be equated to the marginal cost. In the event that the externality is a diseconomy, one may wish to rewrite Eq. (5–16) as:

$$p_X = MC_X + \sum_{i=1}^{n} MD_X^i \tag{5-17}$$

where MD_X^i is the marginal damage done to individual i and is the negative of the marginal benefit (which is itself negative). Thus, the price of X ought to be set to the marginal social cost of production.

Equivalently, the social value of the marginal product of labor and capital used in X should be:

$$w = (p_X + \sum_{i=1}^{n} MB_X^i) \cdot MP_{L_X}^X \tag{5-18}$$

$$r = (p_X + \sum_{i=1}^{n} MB_X^i) \cdot MP_{K_X}^X. \tag{5-19}$$

Firms will neglect the marginal external benefits emitted. If they are positive, X will tend to be underproduced, while if they are negative, X will tend to be overproduced.

The level of externality emitted by a firm on individuals may depend not upon its total output but on the quantity of a particular input used. In this case, the input appears as an argument in the utility function. If the externality depends upon K_X we obtain:

$$U^i = U^i(X^i, Y^i, Z^i, \ldots, K_X). \tag{5-20}$$

Optimality in the use of K_X requires that the firm equate the cost of using it, r, with the marginal social benefits of its use:

$$r = p_X \cdot MP^X_{K_X} + \sum_{i=1}^{n} MB^i_{K_X}. \tag{5-21}$$

In a competitive economy, the firm will neglect the latter term, the marginal external benefits. The internalization of the externality requires that an appropriate incentive be given to the X-firm in its hiring of K_X.

The converse of production-consumption externalities might be called consumption-production externalities. While they are perhaps much rarer in practice than the other types, they could nevertheless occur, and their analysis is a straightforward extension of the above reasoning. If a consumer's activity affects a firm, optimality calls for an equating of the marginal costs of pursuing the activity (the market price of the good consumed, say) with all the marginal social benefits produced; that is, the marginal private benefit to the individual plus the values of the marginal product of the individual's activity to the affected firms.

Once again, any of the above may be reciprocal, in which case both parties are behaving incorrectly. Efficient resource allocation calls for corrective action to be taken *vis-a-vis* all emitting parties.

Consumer-Consumer Externalities

One consumer's consumption of goods (or supply of factors) may directly influence the level of utility of other consumers without going through the pricing mechanism. Conceptually, these externalities might be divided into those which are "physical" and those which are "psychic," though the distinction may often be blurred. Pollution of various sorts might be regarded as physically affecting the well-being of consumers as, for example, the discomfort arising out of air pollution generated from the use of automobiles by other consumers. Psychic external effects may arise from feelings of altruism on the one hand, or avarice and envy on the other. Consumer A may "feel" better off if consumer B consumes adequate food and shelter; or, he may feel worse off if B drives a flashy car. Fortunately for the economist, no distinction need be drawn between these two cases, since analytically they are identical. In both cases, the consuming activities of one person enter into the utility function of the other, contributing either positively (external economy) or negatively (external diseconomy).

It is convenient to distinguish two ways in which one person's consumption can effect another person's utility: Via the level of consumption of particular items or via the level of utility attained by the former person. In the first case, one individual's consumption of a good, such as automobiles, directly influences the level of utility attained by others, say, by air pollution. If individual A's consumption of X affects the utility of B, B's utility function may be written:

$$U^B = U^B(X^B, Y^B, Z^B, \ldots, X^A).\qquad(5\text{--}22)$$

Individual A's consuming activity benefits not only himself but, as with public goods, also benefits individual B. The appropriate optimality condition to be satisfied if A's consumption of X^A is to be efficient is:

$$p_X = MB^A_{X^A} + MB^B_{X^A}.\qquad(5\text{--}23)$$

There may well be several persons affected by the external effect in which case the marginal external benefit will be a summation of terms such as $MB^B_{X^A}$ over them all. Since A will neglect the last term in Eq. (5–23), which may be positive or negative, nonoptimal behavior will result. If the external effects are economies, there would be a tendency for A to undertake too little of the X activity, and the opposite for diseconomies. Whether or not the external effect is psychic or physical is of no consequence for this result, or for the corrective policy prescription to be applied.

The other sort of consumer-consumer externality is the so-called utility interdependency case discussed briefly in Section 3–7. This case, which fits more squarely into the category of psychic externality, occurs when individual A benefits (or suffers) from the level of utility attained by individual B. Thus, if A is altruistic, he may feel better off the better off is B. We may write A's utility function as follows:

$$U^A = U^A [X^A, Y^A, Z^A, \ldots, g(X^B, Y^B, Z^B, \ldots)]\qquad(5\text{--}24)$$

where g is a function which reflects B's preference orderings or indifference map.[5] The important characteristic of g is that it has all the properties of B's utility function; that is, A's altruism respects B's preferences. The importance of this property will become obvious shortly.

Whether or not resources will be optimally allocated when utility interdependence is of the type shown in Eq. (5–24) is not obvious. There may be an opportunity for improving efficiency by making interpersonal income transfers, or Pareto-optimal income redistributions. The general problem of utility interdependence can be illustrated geometrically for the two-person two-good case. It will be sufficient for us to consider only the exchange efficiency conditions so that the analysis is conducted for a given bundle of goods, $\overline{X}$ and $\overline{Y}$. The Edgeworth box diagram of Fig. 5–1, based on the discussion in Schall (1972) (see also Archibald and Donaldson [1976]) shows the various allocations of $\overline{X}$ and $\overline{Y}$ possible to the two individuals A and B. In the general case we are considering, assume each individual obtains utility both from their own consumption mix and also from that of the other. Then we can write the utility function as:

$$U^A = U^A(X_A, Y_A, X_B, Y_B) \tag{5–25}$$

$$U^B = U^B(X_B, Y_B, X_A, Y_A). \tag{5–26}$$

We assume that X_B and Y_B enter with positive marginal benefits into U^A; that is, there is a marginal external economy arising from B's consumption of the commodities. The same holds for X_A and Y_A in U^B. The points within the Edgeworth box diagram satisfy the market clearing conditions $X_A + X_B = \overline{X}$, and $Y_A + Y_B = \overline{Y}$.

Consider now the construction of A's indifference map drawn from the origin O_A. An indifference curve shows the combinations of X_A, Y_A, X_B, and Y_B which leave him equally well off. As one moves northeast from O_A, A receives more and more of X and Y and B receives less and less.

Figure 5–1

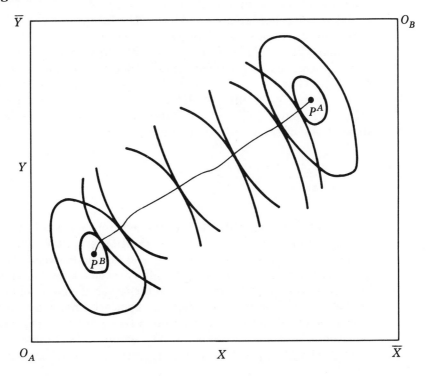

Initially A is better off in moving northeast since he values his additional consumption of X and Y more than he values the X and Y foregone by B. Eventually, however, there comes a point at which A has so much X and Y relative to B that the value to A of obtaining additional X and Y at the expense of B is outweighed by the loss in utility to A from B's loss of X and Y. Further increases in A's consumption make him worse off. The point P^A represents the maximum utility level attainable by A. To the northeast of P^A, A is absolutely worse off despite having more of X and Y to consume privately. Similar preferences hold for B, whose indifference map is drawn from the origin O_B. The maximum utility level attainable by B is at the point P^B.

The contract curve joining all points of tangency between P^A and P^B represents the locus of points satisfying the exchange efficiency conditions in this economy. At all points along $P^A P^B$ the slopes of indifference curves are equal. The slope of an indifference curve here, however, is not the usual marginal rate of substitution between X_A and Y_A for A because in this diagram each point along an indifference curve also represents a different allocation of X_B and Y_B which affects A's utility. The slope of an indifference curve is instead given by:[6]

$$-\frac{\Delta Y_A}{\Delta X_{A/\overline{U}^A}} = \frac{MU^A_{X_A} - MU^A_{X_B}}{MU^A_{Y_A} - MU^A_{Y_B}} \qquad (5\text{--}27)$$

where $MU^A_{X_A}$ is the marginal utility of X_A to A, etc., and $\overline{U}^A$ implies that utility is being held constant. Without the utility externality, as explained in Section 2–1, the slope of an indifference curve is simply the ratio of the marginal utilities, MU_{X_A}/MU_{Y_A}. The difference here is due to the fact that a small increase in X_A implies a small reduction in X_B and the latter reduces A's utility. The same holds for Y. Therefore, a change in Y_A of ΔY_A entails a change in A's utility of $MU^A_{Y_A} \cdot \Delta Y_A + MU^A_{Y_B} \cdot \Delta Y_B = (MU^A_{Y_A} - MU^A_{Y_B}) \Delta Y_A$ since $\Delta Y_A = -\Delta Y_B$. In an analogous way, we may derive the slope of one of B's indifference curves to be:

$$-\frac{\Delta Y_B}{\Delta X_{B/\overline{U}^B}} = \frac{MU^B_{X_B} - MU^B_{X_A}}{MU^B_{Y_B} - MU^B_{Y_A}} \qquad (5\text{--}28)$$

The utility possibility curve obtained from all points between O_A and O_B was presented in Fig. 3–1. As mentioned there, Pareto-optimal transfers are possible at all points between O_A and P^B and between O_B and P^A. That is, both persons can be made better off by income transfers in these ranges. Whether these will be made voluntarily, or if some collective transfer mechanism will be required, depends upon whether many persons benefit from a given transfer. If so, there is a free-rider problem and an *a priori* case could be made for public sector action. Unfortunately, as with any other public good problem, there are severe informational problems here.

There is no way that the public sector can know if such utility interdependencies exist and, if so, whether they are strong enough to justify
redistribution on purely efficiency grounds. Preferences for redistribution
will only be revealed through the political process.

Along the contract curve $P^A P^B$ no Pareto-efficient income redistribution
is possible; yet there are still utility interdependencies or consumer-consumer
externalities. It is of some interest to know if and when the competitive
market mechanism will be efficient in these circumstances. The exchange
efficiency condition that must be satisfied is equality between the slopes
of indifference curves, or, from Eq. (5–27) and (5–28):

$$\frac{MU_{X_A}^A - MU_{X_B}^A}{MU_{Y_A}^A - MU_{Y_B}^A} = \frac{MU_{X_B}^B - MU_{X_A}^B}{MU_{Y_B}^B - MU_{Y_A}^B}. \tag{5–29}$$

In a competitive market economy in which there are many persons of types
A and B, and in which the externality goes uncorrected, individuals set
their own private marginal rates of substitution equal to the given price
ratio:

$$\frac{MU_{X_A}^A}{MU_{Y_A}^A} = \frac{p_X}{p_Y} = \frac{MU_{X_B}^B}{MU_{Y_B}^B}. \tag{5–30}$$

In general, satisfaction of Eq. (5–30) by the market will not imply
satisfaction of the exchange efficiency condition Eq. (5–29). However, there
is one set of circumstances in which it will. Suppose that X_B and Y_B enter
into A's utility function in such a way that A's marginal rate of substitution
between X_B and Y_B is identical to that of B, the consumer of X_B and Y_B.
This is equivalent to saying that A respects B's preferences and benefits
from the level of utility achieved by B as determined by B's own preferences
for X_B and Y_B. That is, Eq. (5–25) may be written in the form of Eq. (5–
24). Similarly, suppose B's benefits from X_A and Y_A reflect A's preferences
so that B benefits from the level of utility achieved by A. Algebraically,
this property of respecting the preferences of others, called *nonpaternalism*
by Archibald and Donaldson (1976), implies the following equalities:

$$\frac{MU_{X_B}^A}{MU_{Y_B}^A} = \frac{MU_{X_B}^B}{MU_{Y_B}^B} \; ; \quad \frac{MU_{X_A}^A}{MU_{Y_A}^A} = \frac{MU_{X_A}^B}{MU_{Y_A}^B}. \tag{5–31}$$

These conditions along with Eq. (5–30) imply that Eq. (5–29) will be satisfied.
In other words, if utility interdependencies are nonpaternalistic, no market
inference is called for except that which is required to make Pareto-optimal
income transfers.[7] On the other hand, if the consumer-consumer externalities
are not of the nonpaternalistic sort, the exchange efficiency conditions will be
violated. Therefore, some corrective action may be called for by the government such as subsidizing or taxing those commodities which emit the

externality. We turn to the possible corrective measures in the following section.

CORRECTIVE DEVICES FOR EXTERNALITIES

5–3   The various types of externalities discussed in Section 5–2 all have a common analytical framework. Parties emitting an externality incur a marginal cost in undertaking an activity and obtain a private marginal benefit. They behave so as to equate the marginal cost and the marginal private benefit, neglecting the marginal external benefits received by the affected parties. The efficient allocation of resources requires that the marginal cost of an activity be equated with all the marginal benefits generated by it, or the marginal social benefits. In theory, one way to obtain a Pareto optimum is to introduce some mechanism or corrective device for ensuring that the emitting party has an incentive to take the external effects fully into consideration in deciding upon the level of activity to undertake. The purpose of this section is to consider the various mechanisms which have been suggested in the literature for pricing or internalizing externalities. A simple geometric model, similar to that of Turvey (1963), will be used for describing the operation of the various mechanisms and their limitations. An alternative geometric treatment may be found in Tulkens and Schoumaker (1975).

Consider the case of party A emitting an external diseconomy on party B as a result of undertaking an activity X_A. A or B may be either firms or individuals for the purposes of this analysis. Figure 5–2 depicts the various marginal cost and benefit curves to the two parties. MC_X is the marginal cost of activity X to A and is assumed to be constant. MB_A is the marginal benefit to A from undertaking activity level X_A. If A is an individual, MB_A will be the demand curve of A for X_A. For simplicity, we assume that income effects are negligible so that MB_A is invariant to changes in the level of income or utility. Later, we shall relax this assumption. If A is a firm, the problem of income effects does not arise. The curve MD_B represents the marginal damage done to party B. It is simply the negative of the marginal benefit of activity X_A to party B defined that way so as to put it into the positive quadrant. Once again, if B is an individual, income effects are assumed to be negligible so that MD_B will not shift with changes in income or utility. Marginal damages are assumed to increase with the level of X_A in the diagram although this is not necessary for the analysis. Both A and B are assumed to behave as competitive price-takers, although there are only two of them. They can be thought of as representative individuals taken from two groups. Also, in this analysis A alone determines the level of X_A. B is a passive party treating the external effect as being given from the outside.

When party A is allowed to maximize its own net benefits with the external diseconomy unpriced, the level of activity of X_A chosen will be

Figure 5–2

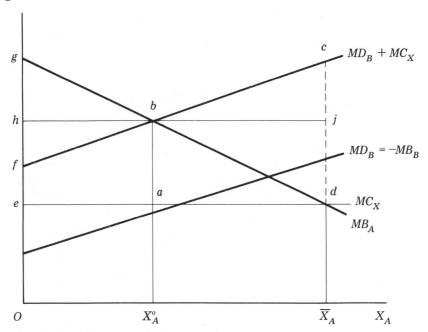

that at which $MB_A = MC_X$, or $\overline{X}_A$. This will be an inefficient choice of X_A since no consideration is being given to the marginal external diseconomy that is being simultaneously conferred upon B. The efficient allocation of resources is that for which $MC_X = MB_A + MB_B$ or, since $MB_B = -MD_B$,

$$MB_A = MC_X + MD_B \tag{5–32}$$

That is, marginal benefits to A from the activity X_A should equal marginal social costs. In the diagram, this efficient outcome can be determined by adding vertically the curves MD_B and MC_X to give a marginal social cost curve, $MD_B + MC_X$. Where it intersects the MB_A curve, at point b, is the optimal point. This gives an optimal activity level X_A^o which is less than $\overline{X}_A$. We can calculate the total gain to society in monetary terms from correcting the externality by comparing the benefits to A and B at $\overline{X}_A$ and X_A^o. In moving to X_A^o, A loses total benefits equal to $\overline{X}_A db X_A^o$ and B gains (by a reduction in damages) $dcba$. At the same time resources valued at $\overline{X}_A da X_A^o$ are released for use elsewhere. The total net gain to society is the sum of these changes, or

$$-\overline{X}_A db X_A^o + dcba + \overline{X}_A da X_A^o = bcd. \tag{5–33}$$

In order to induce A to behave efficiently, it is necessary to make it take into consideration the marginal damage done to B. There are four ways that this might conceivably be accomplished in this simple model. For the moment we ignore any informational problems involved with knowing the magnitude of the marginal damages done. The four remedies will be considered in turn.

1. Taxation of X_A

Suppose that the government levies a tax on A's use of X_A at a rate which is equal to the marginal damage done to B at the optimum, or ab. From A's point of view, the marginal cost of activity X_A has been increased to $MC_X + ab$ so that the curve labeled hj now represents the marginal cost. A will equate this marginal cost to its marginal benefits and will select the optimal output X_A^o.[8] Tallying up the net gains and losses for each of the parties involved, using the notion of consumer's surplus, we obtain the following:

Gain to B = $abcd$ (reduction in damages)

Gain to A = $-ehbd$ (loss of consumer's surplus)

Gain to government = $ehba$ (tax revenues)

Net social gain = bcd

As is easily checked, we could obtain the same net social gain measure by using the notion of total benefit and total cost rather than consumer's surplus.

2. Subsidization of A to Reduce X_A

An alternative measure that might be taken is to offer A a subsidy at the rate MD_B (evaluated at X_A^o) per unit of X_A on the reduction of its output below $\overline{X}_A$. The decision to produce a unit of output implies the foregoing of the subsidy on that output. The opportunity cost to A of each level of activity is therefore the marginal cost MC_X plus the foregone subsidy MB_X or dj, the same opportunity cost as in the taxation scheme. That is, starting at $\overline{X}_A$, the marginal benefit to A from reducing output is the saving in cost MC_X and the receipt of the subsidy dj. The line hj is like a marginal benefit line for reductions in X_A starting from $\overline{X}_A$. Similarly, MB_A is the "cost" to A of restricting activity of X_A. A will select the point b at which the marginal gains from reducing X_A just offset the marginal costs (reduction in benefits). Once again we may tally up the net gains to each party from the move from $\overline{X}_A$ to X_A^o:

Gain to B = $abcd$ (reduction in damages)

Gain to A = bjd (gain in subsidy—loss in consumer's surplus)

Gain to government = $-abjd$ (subsidy payments)

Net social gain = bcd

The subsidization scheme yields exactly the same net gain to society as the taxation scheme, so both are equally efficient. The only differences lie in the allocation of gains and losses. A is better off under a subsidy and the rest of society is worse off; with the tax, the opposite holds. The affected party B is indifferent between the two except as it may affect the tax he must pay to the government. Some additional difficulties may accompany the subsidy solution, however. One is that the subsidy payment is defined with respect to a reference level $\overline{X}_A$. The government must know the activity level $\overline{X}_A$ in order to know how much subsidy to pay. No such requirement exists with the taxation remedy.

A second difficulty accompanies subsidies when the number of externality-producing agents is variable, namely that subsidies might encourage participation in the damaging activity (Baumol and Oates [1975]; Burrows [1979]). To see this, consider a competitive industry whose output is accompanied by pollution that damages nearby households. Suppose that each firm has identical costs of production, and that firms can enter and exit the industry freely, so the industry long-run supply curve S in Figure 5–3 is flat at a height equal to minimum average cost. Then a long-run competitive equilibrium occurs at price p_0, industry output of Q_0, and firm output of q_0. Let MD be the marginal damage per unit of output imposed on households; assume that MD is constant regardless of the amount of pollution and that it is the same for all firms. Then $S + MD$ in panel (b) of the figure shows the marginal social cost of production, and Q^* is the efficient level of output. This could be achieved with a tax of MD per unit

Figure 5–3

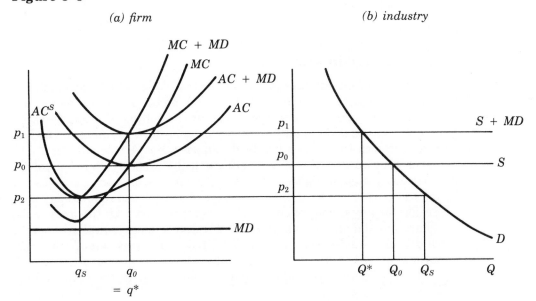

of output imposed on every firm; this would raise the marginal cost and average cost of production by MD per unit, to $MC + MD$ and $AC + MD$, respectively. A new long-run equilibrium is achieved when the price rises to p_1. In this equilibrium, industry output is Q^*, and individual firm output is $q^* = q_0$. Notice that the reduction of pollution and output arises entirely from the exit of firms from the industry.

Now, suppose instead that firms are subsidized in the amount MD for every unit reduction in output below q_0, and that this subsidy is available both to the firms in the industry in the initial equilibrium and to any firms that may subsequently enter, i.e. the program treats all firms in the industry uniformly. Each unit expansion of output now costs the firm an extra MD in foregone subsidy, so the effective marginal cost is $MC + MD$, as in the tax case. But average cost, *net of the subsidy,* is now (by definition)

$$\frac{TC(q) - MD(q_0 - q)}{q} = AC(q) - MD\left(\frac{q_0}{q} - 1\right) \tag{5-34}$$

(where $TC(q)$ is the total cost of producing q), which is shown by the curve AC^S in panel (a). Now the new long-run equilibrium will be achieved when price falls to minimum average cost, such that each firm produces q_S and entry has occurred to compete away all profits. With more firms in the industry, industry output has *expanded* to Q_S, which means that the total amount of pollution has risen as a result of the program. Clearly, the possibility of entry renders the subsidy solution to the externality problem a counterproductive one. Note, however, that this analysis does not invalidate the discussion above, illustrated in Fig. 5–2, since there the possibility of entry is implicitly denied. For some externality problems such as consumer-consumer externalities, this is the relevant assumption and that analysis remains applicable.

3. Liability for Damages to A

The correction of externalities in this simple model may also be accomplished by assigning property rights or liability for damages to one party, and allowing the payment for damages done, or the selling of property rights to be accomplished, via legally imposed compensation payments or by bargaining between the parties involved. Suppose that A is legally liable for damages done so that B is effectively given the property rights involved. Furthermore, suppose that compensation payments for such damages can be imposed costlessly by the legal system. A is then required to pay compensation for any damages done to B at the rate given by the area under B's marginal damage curve MD_B. A effectively faces marginal costs of expanding X_A equal to the curve $MD_B + MC_X$ and selects point b, the point of optimal activity level X_A^o. At this output level, A must pay to B a sum equal to *efba* to undertake the activity. Compared with the activity level

$\overline{X}_A$, the optimal level attained by imposing legal liability on A will cause the following net gains and losses to be registered:

Gain to B = *efcd*   (reduction in damages + payment from A)

$$\frac{\text{Gain to } A = -efbd \quad \text{(loss in surplus + payment to } B)}{\text{Net social gain} = bcd} \qquad (5\text{--}35)$$

Once again, the net gain to society is the area *bcd*, but the distribution of the net gain differs. B is much better off under this scheme than under the others, and A is much worse off as a result of the assignment of property rights. In effect, B receives an amount equal to the total damage done by the externality.

4. Property Rights to A

Giving the property rights to A (or not recognizing B's property rights) implies that B has no legal recourse to A's undertaking the level of activity which is privately optimal (i.e. $\overline{X}_A$). Nonetheless, since $\overline{X}_A$ is nonoptimal there are still net gains to be obtained for A and B combined by restricting the output level. These net gains are maximized at the level X_A^o. If costless bargaining is possible, it would clearly be in B's interest to compensate A voluntarily to reduce its output. In Fig. 5–2, B would be willing to pay an amount up to the area beneath the marginal damage curve MD_B to reduce the level of X_A. At the same time A would be willing to reduce its output if it received at least the area between the marginal benefit curve MB_A and the marginal cost curve MC_X. Bargaining to reduce X_A would be possible as long as the maximum amount that B would be willing to pay to secure a reduction in $X_A(MD_B)$ exceeds the minimum amount that A would be willing to receive to reduce X_A, $(MB_A - MC_X)$. Bargaining would continue until these two amounts are equal. The efficient outcome, X_A^o, would result. The fact that efficiency in the allocation of resources will result no matter who is given the property rights (and assuming costless bargaining) is known as the *Coase theorem*. The setting of property rights will, of course, affect the distribution of utility or gains, but not the efficiency of resource allocation.[9]

The determination of the gains and losses to A and B when the optimum is achieved by bargaining is ambiguous. B would be willing to pay an amount up to *abcd* to have A reduce his activity level to X_A^o. A must receive a minimum of *abd* in order to do so. The difference between the maximum that B would pay and the minimum that A would accept is the area *bcd* (the net gain). The actual compensation paid by B to A will be between *abd* and *abcd*. The exact amount will depend upon the bargaining strengths of the two and cannot be predicted from our analysis.

While all these remedies for external diseconomies appear to lead to efficiency in our simple idealized model, in the real world some of them will be ruled out. The most important complication is that in the real world the externality may involve many parties of types A and B simultaneously. A polluting factory may affect several individuals at the same time. The externality will have all the characteristics of a "public bad." In particular, the free-rider problem will preclude a bargaining solution of the type described above. Those individuals being damaged will not willingly reveal the extent of their true damages if the amount they must pay to secure a reduction in pollution will depend upon it. Bargaining-type solutions are therefore out of the question and a collective or coercive method of correcting the externality such as taxation or subsidization will be required.[10] As already mentioned, subsidy schemes may be more difficult to implement than tax schemes because of the requirement to set a benchmark level X_A on which to base the subsidy payments. One is therefore left with taxation as the simplest scheme in the many-party case.

The free-rider problem will, as usual, render the government's informational problem difficult. The correct tax rate is that which equals the marginal damage done at the optimal output. The magnitude of that is not available from any data generated by market behavior. A problem similar to that involved in determining the optimal output of public goods is evident. Ultimately the political process determines the level of public goods chosen. In the externality case, the determination of the final level of an externality-producing activity such as X_A may be the result of a trial-and-error process. That is, the tax may be set, the resultant level of X_A observed, and the tax reset until an acceptable level of X_A is finally attained.

In some cases, an alternative institutional method for correcting externalities might be used; it is ultimately equivalent to the tax solution, but has the advantage that the desirable amount of the activity can be attained directly rather than by trial-and-error. Suppose that the government at the outset determines that a particular activity level of X_A is the most socially acceptable according to some political criterion. For expositional purposes suppose that X_A is a pollution-producing activity and that the activity can be costlessly monitored by the government.[11] Then, as suggested by Dales (1968), the government may be able to create an artificial market for "pollution rights" by making firms purchase the right to undertake the polluting activity X_A. If the quantity of such rights has been fixed at the acceptable level and if there are many firms, the price of those rights will be established by competitive bidding of firms wishing to undertake the activity. The market for pollution rights will ensure that only the quantity of X_A that the government selects will be undertaken, and also that the distribution of pollution rights among the firms will be optimal in the sense that only those firms which can afford to pollute will do so. The firms who obtain the greatest benefits from their polluting activities will be the ones allowed to pollute most. At the margin, since all firms will be paying the same price for the pollution rights, the marginal benefit of all firms from the polluting activity will be identical. From an efficiency point of view this is clearly desirable. The price paid for pollution rights will play exactly the same role as the tax of ab levied on polluting activities in Fig. 5–2.

In practice, governments often pursue corrective policies which do not operate via the price system or via financial incentives for the emitting party. For example, the government may impose common quantity restrictions on each of a group of firms, limiting the amount of pollutants it may emit. The disadvantage of such schemes is that they lead to an inefficient use of resources. Efficiency, in general, does not call for each firm to emit the same level of pollution. Different firms can afford, from a social point of view, to emit different levels.

Figure 5–4 illustrates this for the case of two firms A and C engaging in a polluting activity (X_A and X_C). For simplicity, the firms are assumed to face fixed marginal costs for activity X and emit damages of a fixed amount on party B. They may be two firms out of many operating on a given stream and emitting effluent waste. The marginal benefit curves for activities X_A and X_C are MB_A and MB_C. For some reason, C gets more benefit from emitting the effluent than does A. They may produce different products and emit differing amounts of effluent per unit of output. The efficient activity levels X_A^o and X_C^o are as shown. The government may decide to attain the same total level of effluent-producing activity by regulating equal quantities on the two firms, X_A^R and X_C^R. As a consequence A will be emitting too much and C too little. There will be a net loss of abc from producing too much effluent in A and a net loss of efg from producing too little in C. One could only justify the regulation policy in

Figure 5–4

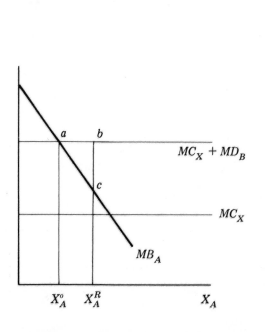
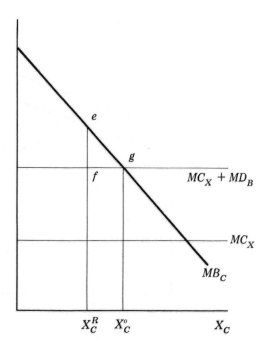

this case either because the costs of regulating are less than the costs of operating another scheme, or because the uncertainties involved in operating, say, a taxing scheme were such that one did not know what tax rates to impose to approach the efficient solution. For example, the government may have little knowledge of the positions of the marginal benefit curves of Fig. 5–4. The use of a tax system would involve a trial-and-error process which might take too long to implement.

If the externalities involve individuals, the above analysis must be amended to the extent that income effects are important, as emphasized by Mishan (1967, 1971b). Suppose, for example, that the activity X_A is a normal good to A so it has positive income effects. At the same time, suppose the diseconomy is a normal "bad" to B. That is, increases in income shift the marginal damage curve up. Figure 5–5 illustrates the influence of income effects upon the optimal allocation of resources attained under different corrective devices. Superscript 1 refers to a corrective scheme which favors A and disfavors B (such as giving property rights to A). The optimal allocation of X_A will be X_A^1 where $MB_A^1 = MC_X + MD_B^1$. Now suppose we consider an alternative scheme denoted by superscript 2 which

Figure 5–5

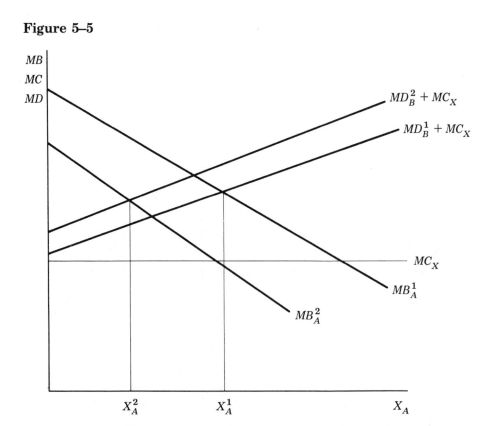

favors *B* relatively more and *A* less (such as giving property rights to *B*). *A* will achieve lower real income since he must pay damages to *B*. Therefore, *A*'s marginal benefit curve will be lower at MB_A^2. Also, since *B* is receiving compensation from *A* rather than paying it, he has a higher real income and, therefore, his marginal damage curve is higher. The optimal level of output attained under schemes which favor emitters (*A*) relative to those affected (*B*) is higher than under schemes which favor *B* relative to *A*.[12]

The preceding analyses of corrective devices may be extended in an analogous way for external economies. It can be shown that an external economy can be internalized either by bargaining between the emitting and affected parties, or by subsidizing the activity of the emitting party at a rate equal to the marginal external benefit generated. The latter solution is more feasible when large numbers are involved and voluntary bargaining fails due to the free-rider problem.

Governments often do use the subsidy remedy for external economies as, for example, in the case of education or health. Another interesting case is that of industrial research and development, where subsidy schemes may coexist with the patent system to encourage firms to undertake research activities. The patent system does so by ensuring that the firm captures at least some of the fruits of the research in the form of profits or rents. It is easy to see that, in principle, the patent system is inferior to the subsidy system on efficiency grounds. Patents operate by excluding users from the use of innovations or knowledge obtained from research and development. This is inefficient since, once the new discovery has been made, there is no social marginal cost involved in allowing others to use it and dissipate its rent. Therefore, it ought to be made freely available rather than used exclusively. However, making it freely available would drastically reduce the incentive to undertake the research in the first place. Hence, a subsidy scheme would be required. The case for the use of the less efficient patent system rather than a subsidy system must lie in the relative costs of implementing the two schemes, or in the fact that the subsidy system is much more informationally demanding than the patent system. The government must know which firms to subsidize, and in practice there will be a great deal of uncertainty as to which subsidies will "pay off" in the form of successful innovation. With the patent system, the risk of failure lies entirely with the innovating firm rather than the government.

COMMON PROPERTY RESOURCES

5–4 The common property resource problem has enjoyed a prominent position in the history of the analysis of externalities since it was the center of an early famous debate between Pigou (1918) and Knight (1924).[13] In its simplest form the common property resource problem arises due to the existence of a factor of production, the services of which are scarce, but which is used free of charge by a group of competitive firms that are part of a larger industry. One might call the group of firms a competitive sub-industry which is a small enough part of the industry as a whole to be considered a price-taker. This special treatment of the common property resource problem falls into the category of an internal-to-the-industry external diseconomy; in fact, in this simple case, it is internal to the subindustry. In terms of our previous classification, it is analogous to a congested public intermediate good, or Meade's unpaid factor, although the common property resource may be a primary factor of production (as in the fishing ground case) rather than a produced one (as in the congested highway case). We can obtain considerable insight into the general common property resource problem by analyzing this simplest case of a subindustry using a common property resource of a given size. One can think of a fishing ground of limited capacity being exploited by a group of competitive fishermen who face fixed prices for their output and variable inputs. The problem arises because they treat as free the services of the fishing ground which are in reality scarce.[14]

Suppose that the subindustry produces an output X according to a production function of the form:

$$X = f(L, T) \tag{5-36}$$

where L is a variable input and T is a fixed factor. For simplicity we shall assume that the subindustry production function (5-36) exhibits constant returns to scale in L and T. In this analysis, T will be a common property resource available in fixed supply $\overline{T}$ and used by all members of the sub-industry. For the given amount of T we may draw the subindustry production function (5-36) as the total product curve (TP) of Fig. 5-6. From the TP curve we may deduce the average and marginal products of labor (AP_L, MP_L) as varying amounts of labor are added to the fixed T. For example, when L_1 of labor is used, the AP_L is the slope of the ray from the origin Oa, and the MP_L is the slope of the tangent to the TP curve bc.

If labor is available to the subindustry at a fixed wage rate w, the subindustry's average and marginal cost curves may also be obtained from TP since labor costs are the only costs of production incurred by the sub-industry. The average costs (AC) are given by:

$$AC = \frac{w \cdot L}{X} = \frac{w}{AP_L}. \tag{5-37}$$

Similarly, the marginal costs (MC) are:

$$MC = \frac{w \cdot \Delta L}{\Delta X} = \frac{w}{MP_L}. \tag{5-38}$$

These curves are drawn in Fig. 5-7.[15] The subindustry is assumed to face

Figure 5–6

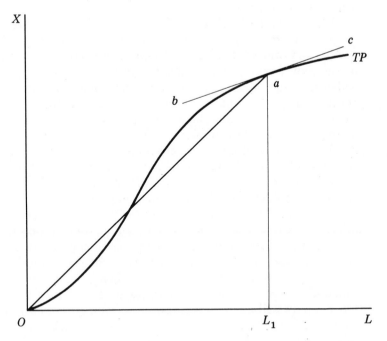

Figure 5–7

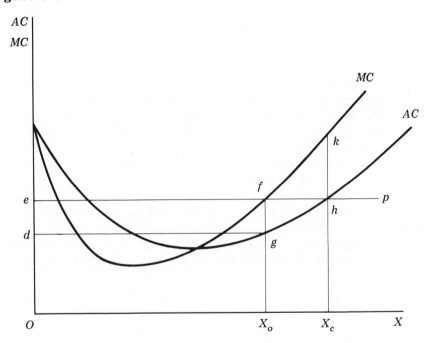

a fixed price for its output p. That price is also shown in the diagram as a horizontal demand curve.

We immediately observe that if the subindustry were operated as a single profit-maximizing venture, it would produce the output X_o where $p = MC$, and this would be the optimal output. The profit earned, *defg*, would be the rent accruing to the fixed factor T based upon its marginal product. This profit-maximizing optimal solution will be obtained, as Knight (1924) pointed out, if the common property resource T is solely owned and, either the owner of T operates the subindustry as a single firm or T is rented so as to maximize rental profits.

The common property resource problem arises when the fixed factor T is not solely owned, and when it is treated by users as if it were not a scarce resource, but a free one. This will arise when the subindustry is composed of many small firms, each one hiring its own labor, but able to gain access to the services of T free of charge. Suppose that there are so many firms that each firm employs but a small proportion of the entire labor used in the subindustry, and does not perceive the effect that its additional use of labor has on the MP_L for the subindustry as a whole. That is, each firm behaves as if its own production function exhibited constant returns to scale in labor alone. It believes that a doubling of its labor inputs will double its output. The competitive entry of firms into the subindustry will result in a situation in which each firm receives no profits but simply recovers its labor costs in the revenues earned on the sale of output.

For the entire subindustry, payments to labor in this competitive situation will just equal the value of output. That is, $wL = pX$, or:

$$w = \frac{pX}{L} = p \cdot AP_L. \tag{5-39}$$

Labor in the competitive subindustry will be receiving the value of its average product. This is also what individual firms perceive the value of their marginal product to be, since they believe they face constant returns in L, so that $AP_L^i = MP_L^i$ for firm i. However, for the subindustry as a whole, the marginal product of labor does not equal the average product. Beyond some point, as more labor is used, the marginal product of labor for the subindustry falls as in Fig. 5–6.

In Fig. 5–7, the free exploitation of T will produce a competitive equilibrium at the output X_c. Profits will be zero, so the rent on the scarce common property resource T will have been competed away or dissipated. Using Fig. 5–6 we may construct a "total revenue" curve from the equality between total revenues and total labor costs, $pX = wL$, or:

$$X = \frac{w}{p}L. \tag{5-40}$$

For given prices w and p this total revenue expression (5–40) appears as a ray from the origin Oa with a slope of w/p. At the industry competitive equilibrium, point a, $w/p = X/L = AP_L$. However, the marginal product of labor, the slope of bc, is less than that. Therefore,

$$\frac{w}{p} > MP_L. \tag{5–41}$$

Labor has been hired beyond the point at which its wage rate equals the value of its marginal product. The common property resource T is being overused. One could likewise show that, at point a, the marginal product of T is positive but is receiving no return since it is not priced. The efficiency loss occurring from this overuse of T is the area fkh in Fig. 5–7, the amount by which the resource cost of producing X_oX_c exceeds the benefit or price paid.

We have already pointed out that one remedy for the overexploitation of the common property resource T is to bring it under sole ownership and allow the owner to maximize its rent. The above analysis suggests an alternative remedy which was suggested by Pigou (1918). The industry could be induced to use T efficiently if a tax were imposed on the output of X by each firm at the rate fg, which is the difference between MC and AC at the optimal output X_o. Then the net price received by each firm would be Od, and firms would set this price to average labor costs, thereby establishing an equilibrium at g, where output is optimal. The informational requirements for determining the rate fg are equivalent to that for the sole owner. The appropriate tax rate is that which maximizes the tax revenues $defg$.

Matters are complicated considerably when the subindustry is large enough to influence either the product price of its output, p, or the price of its inputs, w. In the former case, the subindustry would face a downward-sloping demand curve such as D in Fig. 5–8. The competitive output is that at which the revenues just cover variable labor inputs. That will occur at the output X_c where D intersects AC. As before, the competitive output will exceed the optimal output X_o at which $p = MC$. The welfare cost due to the overexploitation of the common property resource is the area acd.

The profit-maximizing output achieved under sole ownership (or the tax revenue-maximizing output) differs from both of these. To obtain it we construct the marginal revenue curve MR. The profit-maximizing output will be X_m where $MC = MR$. This is less than the optimal output and causes a welfare loss of eaf due to underuse of the common property resource. The sole ownership or Knightian remedy will be more or less efficient than the competitive solution according to whether acd is more or less than eaf.

The optimal output X_o can be achieved by setting a tax of the rate ab on the price received for the output of each firm. The tax rate is the difference between the marginal and average costs of production. In order

Figure 5–8

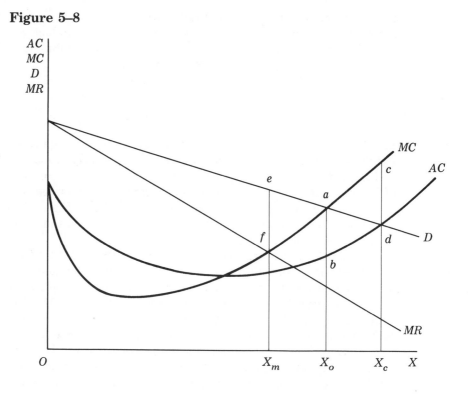

to know the correct tax to set, the government must know the industry cost curves, and that information will generally not be costlessly available to it.

Similar problems arise when the industry has an influence over the price of its variable inputs, here the wage rate w. If w rises as the subindustry's output expands, the subindustry's average cost curve will now slope upward for two reasons. AC will rise as output rises, due to the diminishing marginal product of adding labor to fixed T as before, and also due to the increasing wage rate. The former cause of the rise in AC is called *technological externalities* (that is, externalities to individual firms in the subindustry). The latter are called *pecuniary externalities*.[16] The individual firm in the competitively organized subindustry will perceive neither the pecuniary nor the technological externalities which cause AC to rise. Being small relative to the entire subindustry, the firm will behave as if it could expand output at constant costs by hiring more labor. Entry will occur until profits are eliminated, or until $p = AC$.

If the subindustry were operated on a monopolistic profit-maximizing basis, the sole owner would take into consideration marginal increases in costs arising from both pecuniary and technological externalities. By exploiting the fact that by hiring more labor its wage rate is increased, the firm would be exercising its monopsony power over the purchase of labor.

The price-taking behavior required for the efficient operation of markets would be violated.

The optimal output is determined where the price equals the true marginal costs of production; that is, the marginal cost of expanding output when input prices are treated as fixed but costs rise due to technological externalities. Those cost increases which are due to rising factor prices are not true opportunity costs, but merely transfer payments from the firm to the owners of factors of production. That is, they are increments of producers' surplus.

The situation is depicted in Fig. 5–9. The curve AC is the average cost curve of the subindustry, rising as X increases due to both technological and pecuniary externalities. We ignore problems of monopoly on the output side so that the output price is fixed at p. The competitive industry which dissipates the rent on the common property resource will produce an output X_c at which $p = AC$. The curve labeled MC_1 is the curve marginal to AC, rising above it due to the fact that marginal product falls. As above it is defined by Eq. (5–38) where now, however, w will differ at various points along it. Thus, the divergence between MC_1 and AC is solely due to differences between MP_L and AP_L and no account is taken of the rise in w as an influence on MC. The curve MC_1 is thus the true marginal cost curve, and the optimal output is that at which $p = MC_1$, or X_o.

The sole owner will, however, recognize that an expansion in X will increase costs due both to the diminishing marginal product of labor and

Figure 5–9

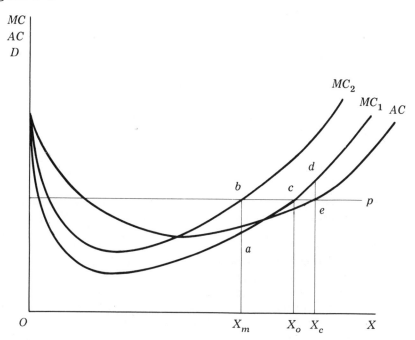

to increases in labor costs w. The marginal costs of expanding output to the sole owner, MC_2, can therefore be defined as[17]

$$MC_2 = w\frac{\Delta L}{\Delta X} + L\frac{\Delta w}{\Delta X}$$

$$= MC_1 + L\frac{\Delta w}{\Delta X} \tag{5-42}$$

where the first term on the right-hand side reflects the influence of technological externalities and the second represents pecuniary externalities ($\Delta w/\Delta X$ is the rise in w due to an incremental expansion in X). The curve MC_2 is shown in Fig. 5-9, intersecting AC at its minimum point.[18] The sole owner will produce the level of output X_m where $p = MC_2$. As can be seen, this output is suboptimal and may be better or worse than the competitive solution depending upon the relative sizes of the welfare losses incurred, *abc* and *cde*.

Once again the government could, in principle, induce optimality of behavior by the competitive industry by setting a tax on the output of X at the rate of $MC_1 - AC$ at the output X_o. Unfortunately, the informational requirements for finding the optimal tax are likely to be severe. The cost curves and the optimal output must be known in advance. The task of the government is all the more difficult if both p and w are variable to the subindustry. Or, in the more general case, more than one industry may use the common property resource and the government must know the characteristics of all users.

CHAPTER NOTES

1. For a thorough discussion of the definition of the concept of externalities, see Buchanan and Stubblebine (1962).
2. Alternatively, these conditions might be written in terms of a numeraire good, or

$$MRT = MRS_A + \sum_{j=1}^{h} MRS_j$$

where MRT is the marginal rate of transformation between the externality-emitting activity and a numeraire good, and MRS_j is the marginal rate of substitution to individual j of the activity for the numeraire good. Conditions (5-16), (5-23), and other similar expressions given below can likewise be stated in terms of a numeraire good.

3. The example used by Meade was that of an afforestation scheme which increased the rainfall on neighboring wheat fields. The rainfall provided an external benefit to the farmers of the sort described here. The fruits of research and development activity is another example of this sort of externality.

4. The example of an unpaid factor used by Meade is that of the bees owned by bee-keepers feeding upon the apple blossoms of a neighboring apple farmer. The contrived nature of this example may well indicate that this type of externality is not too frequently found in practice.

5. We need not use U^B directly as an argument in U^A. The function g may be any function which produces exactly the same indifference map as U^B; that is, the marginal rate of substitution between any pair of commodities is the same for g as for U^B. Algebraically, g is any arbitrary monotonic transformation of U^B.

6. Algebraically, this can be shown as follows. Totally differentiate Eq. (5–25) and set $dU^A = 0$ (since we are considering movements along a given indifference curve):

$$dU^A = 0 = MU^A_{X_A} dX_A + MU^A_{Y_A} dY_A + MU^A_{X_B} dX_B + MU^A_{Y_B} dY_B.$$

Since $dX_A = -dX_B$ and $dY_A = -dY_B$, rearrangement gives:

$$\frac{-dY_A}{dX_A} = \frac{MU^A_{X_A} - MU^A_{X_B}}{MU^A_{Y_A} - MU^A_{Y_B}}.$$

7. It is interesting to recall Section 2–5's discussion of altruistic parents in an intertemporal economy. There we assumed that parents care about the lifetime utility achieved by their children, which means that they respect their children's preferences. Rather amusingly, this means in the present terminology that such parents exhibit nonpaternalism. The conclusion that exchange efficiency conditions are not violated with nonpaternalism is the foundation of the intertemporal efficiency property of competitive markets mentioned in Section 2–5. In addition, the fact that consumers optimize the level of their bequests (and the fact that parents care only about their *own* children, so that public good considerations are absent) ensures that no opportunities for Pareto-preferred intergenerational wealth redistribution are missed.

8. This assumes that it is not more beneficial for A to cease operations and move or undertake an alternative activity yielding higher net benefits. If so, we have the so-called nonconvexity problem mentioned above in Section 5–2. Turvey (1963) discusses the possible nonoptimality of the taxation remedy when party A changes activities as a result of the tax. The point is that it may be cheaper to have B relocate rather than to force A to change behavior by the tax. In this case, the marginal analysis that we are pursuing is not sufficient.

9. The problem of nonconvexities can arise in schemes which enforce property rights with legally sanctioned forced compensation payments (assuming the absence of costless bargaining). For example, forcing A to pay B for the damages done by an activity might cause A to relocate or undertake an alternative activity. It may have been cheaper to allow A to undertake the activity and have B relocate. This is discussed in detail by Coase (1960). Coase provides several examples of these cases in which the marginal analysis fails and one must look at the total costs and benefits of alternate courses of action. The point is also made geometrically in Turvey (1963).

10. If costless bargaining were possible, the externality problem would not arise in the first place so the question of corrective measures is irrelevant. Indeed, if corrective measures (e.g. taxation or subsidization) were undertaken when

bargaining is possible, bargaining itself would take the economy away from the corrected Pareto-optimal allocation of resources. This point, which is unimportant in practice, was made in Buchanan and Stubblebine (1962).

11. The requirement that the activity be monitored by the government is also required in the taxation case since the tax paid will depend upon the amount of activity undertaken.

12. The taxation and subsidization remedies directly affect only the income of the emitting party A. If the activity is a normal good, the taxation remedy will result in a lower optimal output than the subsidy remedy will since under the tax A's marginal benefit curve will be further to the left.

13. A useful summary of the debate may be found in Mishan (1971b).

14. The fishing ground problem has a history of its own despite its similarity to the Pigou-Knight controversy. For example, see Gordon (1954), Scott (1955), and Cheung (1970). A dynamic analysis of the overexploitation of a fishing ground of limited capacity was done by Smith (1968).

15. In some applications, the average cost curve may eventually bend backwards. In this case, the marginal cost would go to infinity when the average cost curve becomes vertical. An example of this is road congestion. Suppose the variable X, the output, is the flow of traffic on a highway measured as vehicles per minute passing through a given point on the road. And suppose the cost per trip is the time it takes to take a trip of specific distance on the highway. Then, initially, as the flow of traffic increases, the road becomes more congested and the speed decreases, or the time per trip increases. There eventually comes a point at which the flow of vehicles on the road is at a maximum. This is the capacity of the road. Any attempt to put more vehicles on the road will not increase the flow, but decrease it, and increase the time it takes to travel a given distance. In other words, beyond the capacity, the average cost curve will bend backwards. A detailed discussion of this phenomenon is found in Walters (1961). Some of the implications of the analysis for road tolls are discussed in Johnson (1964). A recent application of this sort of model to estimate the deadweight loss that occurs from the absence of optimal pricing and investment policies on highways is found in Kraus, Mohring, and Pinfold (1976).

16. The distinction between technological and pecuniary externalities was made by Viner (1931). The distinction was further elaborated by Scitovsky (1954).

17. Algebraically, the total cost is $TC = wL$. The marginal cost to the sole owner is:

$$MC_2 = \frac{dTC}{dX} = w\frac{dL}{dX} + L\frac{dw}{dX}.$$

The social marginal cost ignores pecuniary externalities. It is:

$$MC_1 = \frac{dTC}{dX\big|_{\overline{w}}} = w\frac{dL}{dX}.$$

Therefore, $MC_2 = MC_1 + L(dw/dX)$.

18. This is proven as follows. The average cost is defined as $AC = wL/X$. At the minimum point of the AC curve,

$$\frac{d(wL/X)}{dX} = 0 = \frac{L}{X}\frac{dw}{dX} - \frac{wL}{X^2} + \frac{w}{X}\frac{dL}{dX}.$$

Rearranging this yields:

$$L\frac{dw}{dX} + w\frac{dL}{dX} = \frac{wL}{X}$$

or,

$$MC_2 = AC.$$

6

Resource Allocation Mechanisms for Public Goods

INTRODUCTION

6–1   The discussion of the public goods phenomenon in the previous chapters has been devoted primarily to the determination of the optimality conditions for the provision of such goods. While considerable insight has been gained into the normative rules that would guide an all-knowing and Pareto-optimizing government, in the real world decision-makers face near-insurmountable problems. As we have already stressed, the combined properties of joint consumption and nonexcludability prevent the market price mechanism from being used to determine the preferences of individuals for marginal changes in public goods output (even assuming that the individuals themselves have enough information to make such an assessment). With nonexcludability, individuals will not voluntarily reveal their preferences for public goods if a pricing scheme is going to be based on their stated preferences, since they cannot be excluded from consuming it for free. Rational individuals will be free-riders. Even if they could be excluded, they ought not to be, since the joint consumption property implies that there is no marginal opportunity cost to allowing individuals to consume it.

Two problems naturally arise, both of which we shall discuss in this chapter. First, given that ordinary markets cannot be used to allocate public goods,[1] by what mechanism do governments actually choose quantities of public goods? The study of how such decisions are made, or the positive analysis of public goods' determination, is often called the *theory of public choice*. It treats the political mechanism, especially voting behavior, as the means by which the preferences of individuals for public goods are rationally transmitted to policy-makers and, as such, is an extension of economic analysis into political decision-making. While the analysis of the determination of public goods' output through the political process is still in its early stages, even the abstract models developed thus far are suggestive of the fruitfulness of the approach. We shall present in Section 6–2 a summary of the properties of public goods determination that can be deduced from particular voting models. Of special interest is the question of the optimality properties of various voting models. That is, under what conditions will the public goods' output decisions that are motivated by voting behavior be optimal?

A second question arises out of the failure of the price mechanism to allocate public goods. Can one devise alternative mechanisms which will induce individuals to report their preferences accurately? It turns out that, in principle, one can construct a planning mechanism that will provide an incentive for individuals to report their true preferences to the government. An example of such a mechanism will be developed in Section 6–3 below.

VOTING MODELS

6–2   In the real world, optimal resource allocation to public goods cannot be secured voluntarily through the operation of the price mechanism or by bargaining, because of the free-rider problem. Some coercive form of collective decision-making, which binds all individuals to a method of resource transfer, is required. Ideally, one would like the decision-making mechanism to be one that respected the preferences of individuals in the society and that at the same time operated efficiently (without excess cost). Political processes are typically relied upon to fulfill this function. Democratically-elected governments are coercive in the sense that, having decided upon the level and allocation of public expenditures, they can determine the price or taxes to be paid by each citizen. At the same time, to the extent that they must rely upon the votes of the citizens to be elected to office, there is an incentive for governments to try to choose those public expenditures which the citizens prefer and to provide them at least cost.

Our concern here is with how well political processes perform that task. As yet, there is little consensus on the answer to that question. At least part of the reason lies in the fact that no satisfactory model exists to demonstrate how the political process transmits the preferences of citizens to the government through the voting process. There have been several abstract ·and elementary "voting" models developed over the last thirty years which have yielded some fruitful insights into the way collective decisions are taken. Many of them have been models of "direct democracy." That is, they have assumed that citizens vote directly upon the decisions being taken (e.g. the level of output of a public good) rather than voting for representatives who themselves vote on such decisions ("representative" democracy). The following discussion presents a summary of the main results obtained from these elementary voting models.

(a) The Optimal Constitution

The analysis of any voting process to determine the level of public expenditures and individual taxes presupposes a voting rule to determine when a proposed measure passes. The question of what *ex ante* voting rule would, before any measures are taken, be written into the constitution of a direct democracy by utility-maximizing citizens was first considered by Buchanan and Tullock (1962). They considered the voting process as a mechanism for exploiting the gains from trade in public goods (and externalities). The greater the proportion of voters required to support the measure, the closer would the voting process come to exploiting all the gains from trade (i.e. ending up on the contract curve) but the costlier would be the decision-making process in terms of the time and costs involved in getting the requisite number to agree. There is therefore a trade-off between exploiting the gains from trade and the costs of decision-making in choosing an "optimal constitution" or voting rule.

More specifically, Buchanan and Tullock define an *external cost function* and a *decision-making cost function* for the representative citizen as follows: The external cost associated with a voting rule is defined as being the expected loss in utility in future voting decisions compared with the situation in which all gains from trade are collectively exploited (a Pareto optimum). By this definition, an external cost to an individual will include any expected reduction in utility both due to departures from Pareto optimality (external economies and diseconomies, public goods, etc.) and due to adverse redistributions of income. The curve C in Fig. 6–1 shows how external costs for a representative citizen are expected to fall as the proportion of voters required for a decision rises, falling to zero with unanimity. The reason C rises as n falls is that the less people are required to agree, the more likely is it that actions will be taken that impose costs on this individual, including taxes and income redistribution decisions as well as inefficient resource allocations. The decision-making costs of a voting rule include the time and effort required to secure agreement. As the proportion n of votes required increases, the decision-making costs rise. Strategic behavior becomes much more important as unanimity is approached. The curve D depicts the decision-making costs function. Citizens are presumed to choose a voting rule or constitution to rule over all future decisions. The representative individual of Fig. 6–1 will prefer that voting rule which minimizes the expected total costs $(C + D)$ of the collective decision-making process. That will be the voting rule given by n_o, what Buchanan and Tullock have called the optimum constitution.

Some conceptual problems arise with this process for choosing a constitution. In order to define the external cost function C the representative voter must know his utility in the Pareto-optimal situation when all gains

Figure 6–1

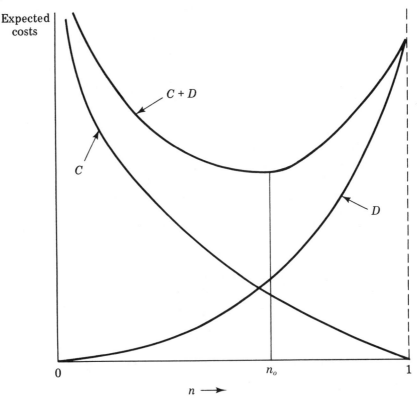

Expected costs

$C + D$

C

D

0

n_o

1

$n \longrightarrow$

n = proportion of votes needed
to pass a proposal

from collective agreements are realized. Unfortunately, there is an infinite number of potential Pareto-optimal solutions, each of which will differ in utility for the individual. How then shall the individual select the benchmark against which to measure the cost of less-than-unanimity rules, particularly since one of those costs is that likely to result from pure redistribution? No satisfactory answer may be given to this question. It would perhaps be more useful to treat as a benchmark the utility level before the gains from trade are exploited. Another problem is that of the rule to be used in selecting the optimal constitution. There is nothing to guarantee that n_0 will be the same for all individuals. Nonetheless, the notion of individuals having a preferred voting rule *ex ante* is useful as a device for indicating that there is nothing superior *a priori* about any particular voting rule such as majority rule or unanimity. It will depend upon the costs of decision-making, the perceived gains from internalizing externalities and public goods, and the expectations of the voting mechanism being used to redistribute income from an individual.

Voting models must assume some decision rule and almost always that is majority rule (passage requires over 50 percent of the votes). The main exception is in the models of representative democracy, where plurality rules determine the choice of representative (the candidate with the most votes wins). Even in these models, majority rule is typically required of the spending decisions taken by representatives. Although there is no reason *a priori* why the optimal constitution should require majority rules, one can contrive circumstances under which it would in fact be chosen. For example, suppose the costs of decision-making are negligible except when n is very high. Furthermore, suppose the expected changes in utility, as measured from existing levels rather than perceived optimal levels, arise solely from pure redistributions and not from collective gains from trade; and that any redistributive vote will either cause a rise or an equal decline in utility, depending upon whether the individual is in the majority or minority. Without knowing which decisions will be collectively taken, an individual X may expect one of the four outcomes to occur with equal probability:

A. X supports a motion which is defeated.
B. X opposes a motion which is carried.
C. X supports a motion which is carried.
D. X opposes a motion which is defeated.

If the expected gain from motions which X supports equals the expected loss from motions which he opposes, then X will prefer the voting rule which maximizes the probability of either C or D occurring (or equivalently minimizes the probability of A or B). It can be shown (Rae [1969]) that the voting rule which does that is majority rule. Unfortunately, many real-world decisions are not likely to have such properties. The expected losses of being in the minority may well exceed the expected gains of being in the majority, or vice versa. If issues involve net gains from a more efficient resource allocation as well as purely redistributive gains, the expected gain from being in the majority may well exceed the expected loss from being in the minority, and a greater-than-majority rule might be desired.

A constitution may well stipulate more than just the voting rule. It may also impose limitations upon the sorts of decisions or policy instruments governments may act upon. For example, there has been some lobbying in the United States to impose a constitutional requirement on governments to balance their budgets, or to restrain them from increasing particular tax rates above a certain maximum (e.g. property tax rates). The economic rationale for such constitutional limitations have not been fully worked out despite the large amount of public debate that has taken place. However, the literature does contain at least one example of the kind of analysis that might lead one to constrain the taxing powers of government. Brennan and Buchanan (1980) have studied the consequences for the desired taxing powers that would arise if the government were assumed to be a tax revenue-maximizing institution. While one may view this as an unrealistic way to characterize government behavior, the analysis is interesting for its methodological approach to the question of the optimal constitution.

The Brennan-Buchanan prescriptions can be summarized readily, although space precludes us from explaining how the logic of these consequences was arrived at. It is assumed that, at the stage of setting the constitutional rules, the population perceives that the government will act in the post-constitutional period so as to maximize its own tax revenues. Given this assumption, Brennan and Buchanan argue that the representative citizen would be best served if the governments of the future were constrained in the following ways: The constitution should as far as possible limit the government to levying narrow-based taxes rather than broad-based ones; deficit financing should be prevented; taxing powers should be decentralized to lower levels of government wherever possible, and taxes thus levied should be on tax bases mobile across jurisdictions rather than on immobile tax bases; taxes should not be levied on wealth; and tax bases which are complementary with the provision of public services should be encouraged. Whether or not a constitution which contained these sorts of strictures could ever be written or enforced remains an open question.

One final important example of the economics of constitution-making is the appropriate design of a constitution for a federal state. At issue here is the assignment of government functions (e.g. defense, police, social welfare, etc.) to the various levels of government. This topic will be considered in much more detail in our discussion of fiscal federalism in Chapter 15.

(b) The Bowen-Black Majority Voting Model

One of the earliest models of public goods' output determination through the voting process was presented by Bowen (1943). He showed that in a model in which tax shares were given, the output of public goods which would be preferred by a majority would be uniquely determined and, under certain assumptions, would even be optimal.[2] Assume that a public good can be produced at constant marginal cost MC and that the cost of the public good is to be equally divided among all N members of the society. To each individual, then, the *marginal tax-price* of the public good, i.e. the cost to each person of one more unit of the good, is MC/N. If MRS^i is the marginal benefit to individual i from the public good, the optimal output of public goods is given when $\Sigma_i MRS^i = MC$, or $\Sigma MRS^i/N = MC/N$; that is, when the *mean* marginal benefit of the N individuals equals the per person cost of the public good.

Figure 6–2 shows the MRS^i curves for a number of individuals as well as the mean or average MRS^i, denoted $\Sigma MRS^i/N$. Each individual's most-preferred output of public goods is that at which his MRS^i curve intersects his tax price curve MC/N, since at such an output level the *individual* marginal benefits and costs of the public good are equal. Suppose that

Figure 6–2

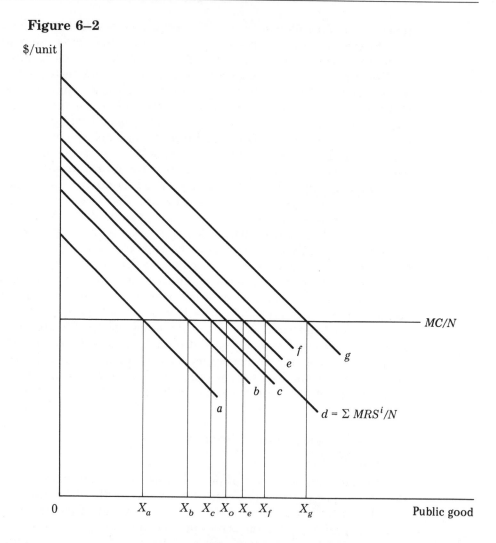

preferences for the public good are normally distributed about the mean $\Sigma\ MRS^i/N$. If each individual is allowed to vote for his most-preferred output, the output which will secure the most votes is X_o, that of the mean voter labeled d. Furthermore, since at this output $\Sigma\ MRS^i\ =\ MC$, the output of public goods will be optimal.

Most mechanisms do not operate by asking voters to indicate their most-preferred output. Instead they require the voters to vote "yes" or "no" to a particular level as opposed to, say, the prevailing level, or to vote upon an incremental change. In the model of Fig. 6–2, it is easy to see that the most preferred output of the *median* voter would be preferred by a majority over any other output, and a process of incremental changes in G would eventually end up at X_o. All individuals would vote to increase G from 0 to X_a since that would represent a move closer to all persons' preferred output. Similarly, all but a would vote to move from X_a to X_b (6 to 1), all but a and b would vote to move from X_b to X_c (5 to 2), and all but a, b, and c would vote to move from X_c to X_o (4 to 3). Once at X_o, no majority would agree to change. A move to X_e would be opposed by four persons (a, b, c, d). The preferences of d, the median voter, would rule. Since with a normal distribution of preferences for the public good, the median voter has the mean preferences, the allocation eventually attained under majority rule would be optimal.

If the preferences for public goods were not distributed normally, but were skewed, the mean preferences and the preferences of the median voter would differ. Since the preferences of the latter would prevail under majority voting, a nonoptimal outcome would result. For example, if preferences were distributed in a way similar to income, the mean would exceed the median, and majority voting would result in too small an output of the public good.

The analysis of Black (1948) generalized the circumstances under which majority rule would result in the preferences of the median voter ruling. He showed that, under majority rule, the preferences of the median voter will be preferred by a majority over all other options or potential outcomes when preferences of all voters are "single-peaked." The meaning of single-peaked preferences is illustrated in Fig. 6–3. In this diagram, possible outcomes are ordered along the horizontal axis. The relative preferences of five individuals for the various outcomes are ordered in the vertical direction. The absolute height of the preference orderings is irrelevant to the analysis. All that is important is the shape of each curve reflecting an ordering of preference of each outcome relative to each other. Preferences are assumed to be single-peaked if one can order the outcomes in such a way that the preference orderings over such outcomes yields a single-peaked curve for all voters as in Fig. 6–3.[3]

Figure 6–3

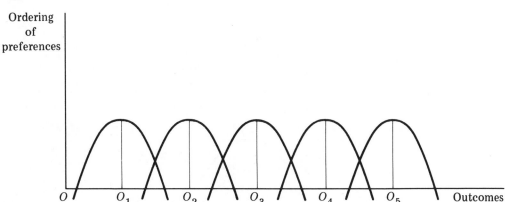

For example, each of the voters in the Bowen analysis has single-peaked preferences when the output of the public good is measured along the horizontal axis. To see this, plot the "consumer's surplus" attained by the consumer at each level of output of the public good. In Fig. 6–4, the consumer's surplus is the area beneath *MRS* less the area beneath *MC/N* at each output level. It reaches a maximum at the point of intersection and is single-peaked.

Black's proposition is that whenever all preferences are single-peaked, majority voting will select the output most preferred by the median voter over all other outcomes. (Of course, if there are an even number of voters, there will be a tie between the two median voters which must be arbitrarily broken.) The proof of this statement follows directly from recognizing that each individual will always prefer outcomes closer to his peak over those further away. Movements from O to O_1 will be preferred by all voters, from O_1 to O_2 by voters 2–5, and from O_2 to O_3 by 3, 4, and 5. However, any move beyond O_3 will be opposed by at least 3 voters (1, 2, and 3). Thus, a majority will always prefer the median voter's most-preferred outcome O_3 over any other.

The absence of single-peaked preferences may give rise to a problem called *cyclical majorities* or intransitivity of social preferences under majority rule. The problem is best illustrated by an example. Suppose A, B, and C must choose among three outcomes X, Y, and Z by majority rule. The preference ordering of A, B, and C is given in Table 6–1 and illustrated in Fig. 6–5. It is obvious that the preference orderings are not single-peaked for all individuals, and there is no way of ordering X, Y, and Z along the horizontal axis so that they will be. Consider now the effects of majority voting among the various pairs of outcomes. In a vote between X and Y, X would win by two votes (A, C) to one (B). Between Y and Z, Y would win by two votes (A, B) to one (C). And between X and Z, Z would

Figure 6–4

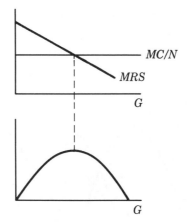

Table 6–1 Preference Orderings

	Person		
Ordering	A	B	C
1	X	Y	Z
2	Y	Z	X
3	Z	X	Y

win by two votes (*B*, *C*) to one (*A*). Therefore, no one outcome can command majority support over all others and the outcome is uncertain. Repeated votes can result in cyclically alternating outcomes. Social preferences established through majority rule are said to be intransitive. The definition of transitivity of preferences is that if *X* is preferred to *Y* and *Y* to *Z*, then *X* will be preferred to *Z*. This property, which is a condition of rationality for individual voters, is not satisfied for this collective decision process.

Single peakedness is thus an important property for individual preferences to have; as we have seen, it arises quite naturally when a single-dimensional issue is to be decided, such as the level of provision of a single public good as portrayed in Figure 6–2. However, this useful condition is virtually certain to fail when decisions must be taken over multi-dimensional issues (Plott [1967], Kramer [1973]).

Figure 6–5

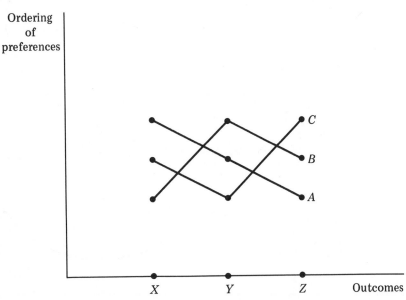

To demonstrate this, consider the problem facing three voters, *A*, *B*, and *C*, who must determine, say, the level of provision of two public goods, G_1 and G_2. Any point in the plane of Fig. 6–6 shows a possible outcome that might be chosen. Each individual is presumed to be able to rank all of these possible outcomes, and we represent voter *A*'s preferences, for example, by the closed curves u_0^a, u_1^a, etc., around the point G^a. The interpretation of this construction is that G^a is *A*'s most preferred combination of G_1 and G_2, that all points on the locus u_0^a are inferior to G^a but indifferent to one another, that all points on u_1^a are less-preferred than the points on u_0^a but indifferent to one another, and so on. In other words, one can think of the curves u_0^a, u_1^a as contour lines on a hill, the peak of which is G^a; points on contour lines closer to G^a are higher up the hill and are more preferred; points on lower contour lines are less preferred. With these preference curves for voter *A*, we can predict how *A* will vote on any pair of issues; for example, point *III* is clearly inferior to point *I* and *A* would always vote for *I* in a contest against *III*.

The preferences of the other two voters, *B* and *C*, are similarly represented in Fig. 6–6. With these preference maps, we can describe how a voting procedure will determine the outcome of any sequence of votes. We shall

Figure 6–6

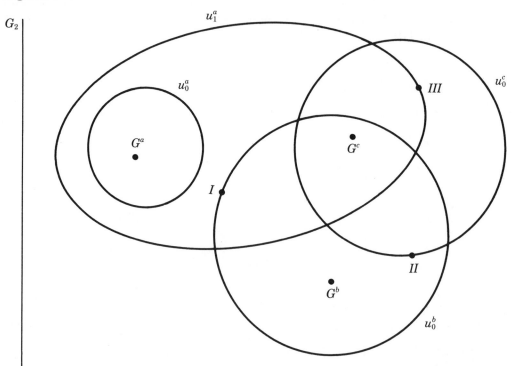

assume that each proposal to be voted upon is a *simultaneous* specification of the levels of both G_1 and G_2, as represented by a point in Fig. 6–6. We wish to analyze the process of simple majority voting over an *agenda,* that is, a given sequence of proposals.

Suppose that at an initial starting point such as *I* with given levels of G_1 and G_2, an alternative *II* is put forward. Since *II* is preferred by individuals *B* and *C*, it defeats *I*. Now suppose *III* is put forward for consideration. Clearly *III* is preferred to *II* by both *A* and *C*, and thus it wins. Notice that so far, in a sequence of only two votes, the group has moved from a fairly "centrist" alternative at *I* to an apparently rather "extreme" outcome at *III*.

The process need not stop at *III*, however. Just to illustrate two possibilities, it is clear that the original alternative *I* can defeat *III*, demonstrating the possibility of cycling; also G^c can defeat *III*. It should be evident, in fact, that no alternative is an equilibrium, in the sense that it can defeat every other alternative in a majority vote. This means that the process need never terminate. Obviously, in practice, voting procedures do terminate. One lesson that is clear from this example is that the rule that determines when the process stops, whether after one vote, three votes, etc., can be quite important. Equally clear is the fact that the choice of the sequence of alternatives put before the electorate can be crucial. In the above example, starting from *I*, the sequence of votes *I* vs. *II*, *II* vs. *III*, *III* vs. G^c, ending after three votes, is excellent from the viewpoint of *C*. If these voters are members of a committee chaired by *C*, this individual, as an astute chairman, might in fact attempt to engineer precisely this agenda. In any case, it is obvious that a majority rule process can be used to "arrive" at many (G_1, G_2) combinations if the agenda provides for the appropriate sequence of proposals. Indeed, it has been shown (McKelvey [1976, 1979]) that essentially *any* outcome is achievable if the agenda is properly designed.

We must conclude that for multi-dimensional issues, majority voting is open to cycling and, indeed, can produce virtually any conceivable outcome; the eventual outcome depends in an essential way upon the *process* by which votes are taken, i.e. the agenda, as opposed to the underlying structure of preferences. This in itself may be considered an undesirable feature of majority voting. Finally, we should note that many issues decided by referenda or by representatives are in fact multi-dimensional; this would be true of any defense appropriations bill, for example. Thus the problems of majority voting are of potential practical importance.

Despite its limitations when multi-dimensional issues are to be decided, considerable use has been made of the Bowen-Black median voter model in both the theoretical and empirical literature. One common application (see, e.g. Barr and Davis [1966], Borcherding and Deacon [1972], and Bergstrom and Goodman [1973]) has been the estimation of demand functions for local public goods on the assumption that the preference of the median voter rules. The analysis typically proceeds in two stages. In the first stage, individuals are assumed to determine their most desired level of public expenditures given their predetermined tax shares or tax rates. Any departures from the most desired level of expenditures will make an individual less well off, the more so the further are the actual expenditures from the desired. In other words, individual demands for public goods are single-peaked. The second stage selects the median voter from the population and attempts to estimate the demand by the median voter for public services of various types by using cross-section data from several local governments. Usually the median voter is assumed to be the one with the median income or tax base. Extra variables are added to capture differences between jurisdictions. A typical estimating equation is that used by Bergstrom and Goodman:

$$\log E = c + \alpha \log n + \delta \log \tau + \varepsilon \log \hat{Y} + \Sigma \beta_i X_i \qquad (6\text{--}1)$$

where E is local expenditures on a particular category, n is local population, τ is the tax share of the median person, $\hat{Y}$ is median income (often approximated by mean income), and X_i are other relevant variables such as percentage of dwellings owner-occupied, employment-to-residency ratio, population density, and population change. Estimates using cross-sections of municipalities have typically found positive income elasticities of demand (0.2 to 1.0) and slightly negative price or tax share elasticities. For a review and critique of these empirical studies, see the survery articles by Romer and Rosenthal (1979a) and Inman (1979).

Most issues of expenditure and taxation decided by legislative voting are of the nature of choices between two alternatives with a majority being required to win. Even so there are various processes by which apparently independent choices among alternatives can be made to depend upon one another, such as vote-trading or logrolling. The role of these was discussed by Buchanan and Tullock and we turn to them now.

(c) The Buchanan-Tullock Model

The work of Buchanan and Tullock (1962) builds upon and extends the results of the simple majority-rule direct-democracy models of Bowen and Black. They explore the implications of two important attributes of the political decision-making process. First, under majority rule, each individual's vote is given equal weight in deciding an issue, regardless of the intensity of the preferences of the voter (or, in economic terms, regardless of how much the voter would pay to have the decision passed or defeated). Second, issues are not decided independently of one another. Instead, there is a continuous stream of issues being voted on, one after the other, and this naturally gives rise to the process of logrolling or vote-trading over time. One of the main contributions of their work is to consider the positive effects and the optimality properties of the process of logrolling which is assumed to exist in political processes. Let us consider these two problems in turn, using for illustration some of the examples constructed by Buchanan and Tullock.

In a model of majority voting, when all individuals' preferences (both for and against) are assumed to be of equal intensity (in monetary terms), a majority in favor of a measure always indicates that the gainers benefit by more in aggregate than the losers lose. That is, majority voting and only majority voting is Pareto-optimal.[4]

To use the example of Buchanan and Tullock, a locality consisting of three individuals is to receive a grant of one dollar from a higher level of government to be used for road improvements to the three persons. Each person is assumed to obtain a dollar's worth of benefits from each dollar's worth of expenditures on the road. A majority vote is to be used to divide the dollar among expenditures on the three roads. It is apparent that the likely outcome will be that those two of the three persons who form the majority will vote in favor of spending one-half dollar on each of their roads and none on that of the dissenter. The total benefits produced will be one dollar and that will be Pareto-optimal.

Suppose, however, that preferences differ, so that one dollar of expenditure on roads yields benefits of ten dollars, five dollars, and one dollar to each of the individuals respectively. A majority vote will again result in the one dollar expenditure being divided evenly among the two in the majority, but the benefits generated will depend upon which of the two form the majority. There are three possible combinations of pay-offs in benefits from dividing the expenditures between alternate pairs:

$$(5, 2\frac{1}{2}, 0) \qquad (5, 0, \frac{1}{2}) \qquad (0, 2\frac{1}{2}, \frac{1}{2}). \tag{6-2}$$

Any one of these is liable to happen under majority rule, depending upon which two persons form the majority. Unfortunately, none of the three is Pareto-optimal. Under the first option, the total benefits generated from the one dollar is seven and one-half dollars; and it is even less under the others. The maximum benefits from the one dollar would be achieved by devoting it entirely to the road of the first person, which yields ten dollars in benefits. This outcome cannot occur under simple majority rule since only the first person would agree to it. Therefore, with differing intensities of preferences, simple majority rule will not generally yield a Pareto optimum.

Suppose, however, that full side-payments or vote purchasing is allowed. This, of course, assumes that such side-payments for votes could be enforced, so secret balloting is precluded. It also assumes that there is no free-rider problem on the part of those wishing to "purchase" votes. If the benefits are of a public goods' nature, the free-rider problem will preclude the efficient operation of vote-trading. However, if full vote-trading could take place, it is evident that a Pareto-optimal allocation can occur. Each person can register his intensity of preferences by the amount he is willing to pay for others' votes. In the example above, individual *A* could afford to pay either of the other two voters to induce them to vote with him. The likely outcome is one of the following:

$$(5, 5, 0) \qquad (5, 0, 5) \qquad (0, 5, 5). \tag{6–3}$$

The first individual may end up bribing the second, the third, or both the second and third voters. In each case the total benefits are ten dollars, the maximum that can be achieved. The outcome will be Pareto-optimal, but the distribution of benefits will be indeterminate. It all depends on who forms the majority, and on relative bargaining strengths.[5]

Full vote-trading is clearly not possible in practice. Even if it were not illegal, it would presumably be very difficult to institutionalize voluntarily due to free-rider problems. Nonetheless, as Buchanan and Tullock argue, there are ways in which partial vote-trading is accomplished implicitly through the political process, and which also allow for differences in intensities of preferences to be at least partially registered. One way this is done is through the phenomenon of *logrolling*. Logrolling refers to the explicit or implicit trading of votes that occurs in a decision-making body, and which takes a sequence of votes over time. One person agrees to vote for another person's desired measure if the latter votes for a measure the former strongly prefers. An implicit form of logrolling occurs in the formation of platforms of political parties, where a party attempts to take a stand on a group of issues that caters to the strong preferences of minorities.

Buchanan and Tullock argue that logrolling is beneficial to the extent that it enables the political process to take into account the differences in intensities of preferences of voters. However, they construct an example to show that it may also lead to a general level of expenditure which is too high from an efficiency point of view. Suppose there are one hundred farmers in a locality, each of which is served by a separate access road which requires maintenance. Maintenance of a specific road must be passed by a majority of voters and, if passed, is financed out of general tax revenues levied equally on all farmers. If each road's maintenance is voted on separately and no logrolling takes place, no road improvements would pass under general tax financing. Each road improvement benefits only one person but the cost is borne by several.

Suppose vote-trading agreements can take place. In order to have his road repaired, each farmer must agree to support the road repairs of fifty other farmers in order to get the fifty-one votes required for his own. The benefit to this farmer is the benefit of having his own road repaired. The cost to him of the agreement is his share of the repairs to be done on the fifty other roads he agrees to support. In the general case, each of the farmers will attempt to secure an agreement with fifty other farmers and the agreements will probably be overlapping since all one hundred farmers want to get their own roads repaired. In the end each farmer will have secured agreement to have his road repaired. In determining the level of road repairs on each road, the benefit to the farmer whose road is being repaired is weighed against the costs to fifty-one farmers of repairing it. The costs incurred by the other forty-nine farmers not included in that particular agreement are neglected. Overall, the cost to all farmers will exceed the benefits from the chosen level of repairs on each road. The logrolling process will have resulted in overexpenditure.

Whether that overexpenditure is a characteristic of political processes in general is still to be established. The tendency to overexpenditure is reduced to the extent that the logrolling process is not as efficient an operation as the above. Also, if the benefits from outlays are of a public goods nature rather than being specific to each farmer, the above analysis is not appropriate. In that case, those in the majority will not only neglect the contribution of the minority to costs, but will also neglect the benefits generated for the minority. Finally, Downs (1957) has argued that there is an opposite tendency in collective decision-making to underspend, because the benefits of public expenditure are more indirect than the costs or taxes and thus relatively undervalued.

The possibility of vote-trading to exploit the potential gains from trade through the political process enhances the importance of redistribution of income through transfers in an individual's preferred choice of a constitutional rule. In the extreme case of perfect vote-trading, a Pareto-optimum is always attained under any voting rules; the only questions remaining in deciding on a constitution are how are the gains from trade to be distributed among citizens and whether or not the constitution allows governments to undertake purely redistributive transfers.

The former question cannot be satisfactorily answered owing to the basic indeterminacy of perfect vote-trading equilibrium. However, a move to a Pareto optimum through collective choice can be expected to make everyone better off.

As to the second question, Buchanan and Tullock provide an ingenious argument to show why rational individuals might want to allow purely redistributive transfers to be made collectively, even though at any given time in the future they may be transferrers of income (losers) rather than recipients (gainers). At the time of setting the constitutional rules, individuals do not know their future stream of lifetime earnings with certainty. There may be periods in which their income is abnormally low or abnormally high. If individuals have diminishing marginal utilities of income, the utility they may lose in a bad year is not compensated by the utility they will gain in a good year. Therefore, they would like to take out some form of lifetime income insurance. Unfortunately, private insurers will not be efficient at providing such insurance. This partly owes to the imperfections in the capital market. Typically, individuals are unable to borrow against their "human" capital (i.e. their future stream of earnings). More important, income insurance is plagued by the problem of moral hazard. That is, individuals, by their own behavior, can influence their stream of income and thus their ability to collect insurance. There will be a built-in incentive to "cheat" the insurance company by not working and collecting compensation. Thus, private insurance companies would not provide such insurance except at a high cost, and individuals may rationally choose to give the public sector the responsibility for income insurance.[6]

One problem remains. How is an individual to be sure that, after giving governments the right to take redistributive measures out of a motive of "income insurance," the voting rule will not be used for arbitrary income transfers from a minority to the majority, who happen to form a coalition at any given point in time solely for the purpose of income redistribution? One answer to that problem is that individuals recognize that as the political process continues over time, they may be in the minority the next time. Over the long run, no individual can expect to be a net gainer from arbitrary redistributive transfers. Therefore, the government may be prevented in effecting redistributive measures that take income discriminately from particular persons and transfer it to others. Such redistribution as does occur tends to take place through general laws (e.g. income tax laws) applying the same schedule to all persons.

(d) The Downs Model

The Buchanan and Tullock model treats the political process as an analog to the bargaining process for internalizing the gains from trade in public goods and for effecting transfers from one group to another through political agreement or coalition. Like-minded voters agree to make spending and taxing decisions which they perceive to be in their interest. The model of political decision-making developed by Downs (1957), while retaining the assumption of self-interest on the part of voters, emphasizes the role of political parties as the institution through which the bargaining or coalitions of like-minded voters are effected. It is an explicit model of representative democracy in which political parties are independent entities whose objective is to gain office by maximizing votes. Downs does not pose the prior constitutional choice problem as do Buchanan and Tullock. Rather he takes as given a constitution that calls for a representative form of democracy in which political parties periodically compete for office, and while in office, pursue their own goals. Individual voters do not vote on each expenditure and tax issue. Instead they vote for a political party that presents them with a complete program of taxes and expenditures. While such a model precludes the sort of logrolling on a series of issues found in Buchanan and Tullock, the process of choosing a political platform that simultaneously encompasses all sorts of expenditure decisions is an explicit form of vote-trading. The political party, in an attempt to maximize votes, must endeavor to take into consideration the differences in intensities with which different individuals view various expenditures. While we cannot do full justice to the Downs model of political decision-making, we can summarize some of the more important aspects of it.

In the simplest version there are two types of decision-makers: Voters and political parties. Voters are assumed to behave so as to maximize their expected utility. In the two-party system they will vote for the party whose platform and performance are expected to yield the highest level of utility in the ensuing period. Things are slightly more complicated in multiparty systems. Voters who favor a third party may decide not to vote for it if they have a subpreference between the two main parties and if they think the third party has no chance of winning. Political parties, on the other hand, have as their objective the gaining of power and they pursue this objective by maximizing votes. The simplest case to consider is the two-party case. In a world of relative certainty, one might expect that one party could take the majority position and stay in office forever. There are several reasons why this may not happen, according to Downs, and these will be reflected in the strategy of the opposition party.

(i) *Matching of Policies* If the preferences of all voters are single-peaked over the spectrum of political platforms (e.g. left, center, right, etc.) and if the distribution of voters according to their most preferred point on the spectrum (i.e. the peak) is unimodal, a phenomenon known as the *Hotelling principle* or the *principle of minimum differentiation* will result, and the political system will be stable. Fig. 6–7 illustrates the case where preferences are single-peaked and unimodally distributed over a spectrum which can be ordered from left to right. The vote-maximizing party will

Figure 6–7

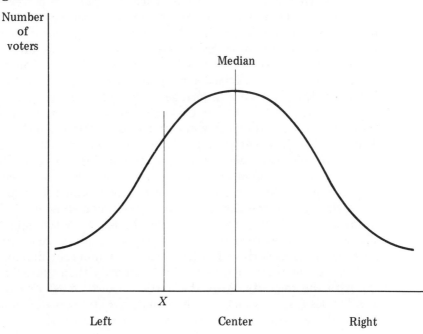

choose the position given by the median voter. The optimal strategy for the party in opposition at a given point of time would be to take a position closely matching that of the party in power. To take a position some distance away from the median would unnecessarily forfeit many of the votes between the two parties. For example, a position X will capture all the votes to the left of X but would lose all those to the right of the median and some between X and the median. The opposition party can capture all of one "tail" of the distribution curve, by taking a position arbitrarily close to the party in power. The party in power may then change hands, due to such things as uncertainty on the part of either the party (not knowing the preferences of voters) or the voters (uncertain as to the impact of policies on utility), or due to perceived inadequacies in the performance of administrative duties by the party in power. Under these circumstances, the two-party system would appear to be stable, with the two parties being rather similar in platform and near the median. The difference between the two parties may be more perceptible if voters at the tail tend to abstain from voting. This is particularly evident the more distant the two parties are from the tail and the less difference there is between them. If the distribution of votes is not unimodal, there may be an incentive for many parties to form and the system may be less stable.

(ii) *Cyclical Majorities* If the preferences of voters are not single-peaked, the cyclical majority problem may result quite apart from whether or not voters are unimodally distributed. If the party in power is required by circumstances to reveal its policies first, the opposition party may always be able to choose a stand that will defeat the party in power owing to the intransitivity of preferences. For example, if platforms can roughly be divided among left (L), right (R), and center (C), and if there are three types of representative voters whose preferences are not all single-peaked, the preferences over platforms may be intransitive if the population is more or less evenly divided among the three types of voters. This will happen if the preference orderings of the three groups are ($L > C > R$), ($C > R > L$), and ($R > L > C$). If the party in power selects policies on the right, the opposition can win with a center platform; if the party chooses center, left will defeat it; and, if left, right will defeat it. To the extent that more than two parties can exist, this problem may be eliminated.

(iii) *Coalition of Minorities* Downs argues that when issues are multidimensional, there are some circumstances in which the opposition party can always defeat the party in power by taking a stand on different issues in favor of minority groups of voters who feel very strongly about them. The circumstances required are the following: More than half the voters must be in the minority on at least one issue, and they must hold stronger preferences for those views when in a minority than those for which they are with the majority. Also, the party in power must reveal its position on all issues first, at least on all those that have strong-preferenced minorities. Under these circumstances, in a world of certainty the opposition party will always be able to defeat the incumbent party by selecting an appropriate mix of minority policies, and power will change hands regularly.

The following example will illustrate how the opposition can form a "coalition of minorities" to defeat the party in power. Suppose that each issue has only two alternative outcomes: a majority position and a minority position. In the simplest case, suppose there are three voters (*A*, *B*, *C*) and two issues. On the first issue *A* and *B* are in favor, but *C* is strongly opposed; on the second, *B* and *C* are in favor, and *A* is strongly opposed. If the·incumbent party takes the majority position on each issue, the opposition will win by taking the minority position on each issue, since both *C* and *A* will favor it. On the other hand, if the incumbent party takes the minority position on each issue, the opposition can defeat it by matching the incumbent's position on one issue but taking the majority position on the other. For example, if the opposition takes the minority position on the first issue, but the majority on the second, it will win the votes of *B* and *C*. More complicated examples with more voters and more issues could be constructed to give the same results, provided the above assumptions hold.

The likelihood of a coalition-of-minorities strategy being successfully pursued in the real world is tempered by a number of considerations. First, there must be enough diversity of both views and intensities of preferences over various issues among the electorate. If a broad consensus exists, the phenomenon cannot occur. It is also required that the incumbent reveal its platform first. If not, the ability of the opposition to adopt a strategy will be limited. In any case, for various reasons, such as credibility, parties may be reluctant to change their platforms drastically from election to election as would be required. Furthermore, in the real world there is a great deal of uncertainty about the future, both on the part of voters and political parties. Part of this uncertainty is capitalized on by pressure groups who seek to influence the opinions of the electorate in specific ways. Thus, even if the requisite lack of consensus exists in the electorate, it is by no means certain that it will be manifested in frequent changes of the party in power.

Finally, we might briefly inquire into the optimality properties of the Downs model. Can we expect it to yield a Pareto-optimal allocation of resources? In a world of perfect certainty, the answer is apparently "yes." If a party adopted a non-Pareto-optimal strategy, it could always be defeated. By the definition of Pareto optimality, there must exist another strategy which would make everyone better off without, at the same time, making anyone worse off, and the vote-maximizing party would choose it.

However, perfect certainty does not characterize the real world. As we have already noted, voters do not know the exact effects of policies upon their utility, and political parties do not know the preferences of voters for their policies. This has led Downs to argue that the political process is likely to cause an underprovision of public goods, and to result in a public sector which is too small relative to the optimum. He argues that the benefits of public goods are less directly perceived than the benefits of private goods, and therefore people are not as aware of them, although they are aware of the taxes they pay to support them. This relative lack of awareness is heightened by the fact that people are made more aware of the benefits of private goods through advertising, whereas no equivalent supply of information is provided on behalf of public goods. As we saw earlier, Buchanan and Tullock argued the opposite, viewing the logrolling process as contributing to an overextension of the public sector. The question of whether the public sector is too big or too small remains a matter of great debate. Unfortunately, since we have not yet succeeded in obtaining a reliable way to measure the preferences of individual consumers for public goods, the issue remains unresolved.

(e) Bureaucrats vs. Voters: The Romer-Rosenthal Model

The Downs analysis enriches the simplest referendum voting models by introducing political parties. Voting models can be extended in other ways as well. For example, it has often been argued that bureaucracies have important interests in the outcome of the political process, and that they will act, if possible, to further these interests. One common hypothesis is that bureaucrats prefer that their agencies should have budgets that are as large as possible. Of course, this sets up a conflict with voter-taxpayers who, while presumably valuing the goods and services produced by the agencies to some extent, nevertheless find that the marginal costs of additional expenditures eventually exceed the marginal benefits. They will therefore attempt to restrain the budget size once it rises beyond some level.

In analyzing public expenditure determination in economies with budget-maximizing bureaucrats, it is therefore natural to specify the process through which the conflict between voters and bureaucrats is resolved, and then to study the properties that such a process may possess. As an example of such an analysis, let us review the study by Romer and Rosenthal (1979b) which builds on the earlier work by Niskanen (1971). They consider voter-bureaucrat interactions in the following simple setting: Bureaucrats prepare a proposed level of agency funding which is put before the electorate in a referendum, where it is either accepted or rejected by a simple majority. If it is rejected, the level of expenditure will be set at a *reversion* level that is specified in some way exogenous to the model. For instance, the reversion level might be last year's budget, or it might be zero (in which case a rejection of the bureaucracy's proposal means that the agency would shut down), or it might be determined in some more complex way. Romer and Rosenthal examine the bureaucrat's problem, namely to develop a proposal to put before the voters, and explain how the level of expenditure is finally determined. They then contrast the implications of this model with the simple Bowen-Black majority voting model discussed above. We now summarize the main features of the analysis:

First, the bureaucrats must ascertain how the voters will respond to any particular proposal. Consider any individual voter whose preferences over a private good Y and agency expenditure X are represented by the indifference curves of Fig. 6–8. Each voter must pay some known part of the cost of the bureaucracy's expenditure, and thus, with limited income, faces a tradeoff between X and Y as represented by the budget line AB. Its slope is the negative of the voter's marginal tax-price for X, as determined by the financing plan in effect. Given the preferences and budget line shown, the voter would most prefer the level X^* for the agency budget. Suppose, however, that the reversion level for X is X_R, which would result in the utility level $U^0 < U^1$. Then, clearly, the voter would vote for any level of X between X_R and X_B in preference to X_R, and, in particular, would vote for a level of expenditure up to X_B if the sole alternative is X_R. The intuition here is obvious: If the level of public service provided at the reversion point is sufficiently low, one would be willing to accept a level of expenditure considerably above one's optimum in order to avoid it.

Figure 6–8

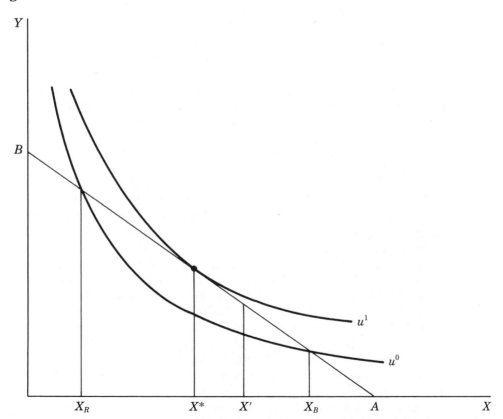

Now suppose that Fig. 6–8 represents the preferences of the voter with the median most-preferred level of expenditure X^*. In a Bowen-Black world of simple majority voting equilibrium, X^* would be the level of expenditure actually selected. However, it is clear that this median voter would in fact vote for levels of X greater than X^* such as X', if the alternative were the reversion level X_R. Moreover, all of the voters whose most-preferred levels of X exceed the median voter's X^* would also vote for levels of X at least somewhat above X^* as well: They would prefer increases in X in any case, and they would especially prefer levels of X greater than X^* as compared with the reversion level X_R. But this means that there is some level of X greater than X^* that would be favored, in a contest against X_R, by the median voter plus all of the above-median voters—i.e. a majority of voters. If the bureaucracy correctly chooses such an X, it will prevail against X^*, and the resulting level of expenditure will exceed the Bowen-Black equilibrium level.

All of this is on the assumption that $X_R < X^*$. Now suppose $X_R > X^*$. Then the bureaucrats need only choose a proposal larger than X_R to ensure that the reversion level, greater than the median voter's preferred level, will win. Only if the reversion level is actually equal to the median voter's most-preferred choice will the Bowen-Black equilibrium be achieved; this level of expenditure thus serves as a lower bound on the possible outcomes.

It is interesting to see how the level of X finally chosen depends on the reversion level X_R. As already noted, the maximum level of X that the voter in Fig. 6–8 would vote for in a contest against X_R is higher, the lower is X_R. This is true in particular for the median voter, and it is also true for all of the above-median voters. Thus, the lower is X_R, the greater is the level of X that the bureaucracy can propose that will secure majority approval. The best situation for the bureaucrats occurs when $X_R = 0$. To give a common-sense example, one may well be tempted to vote for a level of school funding that one regards as excessive if the alternative is to have no schools at all.

The fact that the reversion level helps to determine the level of funding for the bureaucracy is a major conclusion emerging from this analysis. It demonstrates that the details of the procedure by which political decisions are made need to be specified before definite conclusions about the outcome of the procedure can be established. Unfortunately it is not possible to make any definite statements about the normative properties of decisions made by this "voters vs. bureaucrats" procedure. We can say that the process will lead to inefficiently high levels of expenditure if we know that the median voter's preferred X^* is efficient; but, as noted in the discussion of the Bowen-Black model, the median voter outcome is optimal only under restrictive assumptions. In general, we may conclude that if the median voter's preferred level of X is greater than the optimal level, then the voters vs. bureaucrats equilibrium will be even more inefficiently high. But if the median voter's preferred level is inefficiently low, the interaction of voters with budget-maximizing bureaucrats may lead to either more or less efficient decisions.

INCENTIVE MECHANISMS FOR
PREFERENCE REVELATION

6–3   The inability of the competitive price system to allocate resources to public goods efficiently arises from the lack of incentive that individuals have to reveal their true preferences. Rational individuals will understate their true preferences if the price they are required to pay for public goods equals the marginal value they report. On the other hand, they will have an incentive to overstate their preferences if the tax revenue they will be assessed is unrelated to the level of output of the public good. This preference revelation problem is somewhat reduced if individuals are assumed to bear a predetermined proportion of the total costs of the public good. They will then most prefer the level of output of the public good at which their marginal benefit equals their personal marginal cost (i.e. the overall marginal cost times the individual's tax share). This preferred level of output of the public good would be willingly revealed through an appropriate voting mechanism, and under some conditions an optimal output of the public good would result, as we have seen in Section 6–2.

The conditions required for voting processes to achieve optimality are quite stringent even if we neglect such things as uncertainty and lack of information by voters, the lack of incentives for voters to take the effort to inform themselves, and the costs of taking decisions by voting. For example, in the simple model of Bowen (1943), we require that the distribution of preferences of voters in the economy be normal. The inability of either the competitive market or voting to assure an efficient output of public goods has led some authors to devise alternate mechanisms designed to induce individuals or firms to reveal their true preferences for public goods. While such mechanisms are far from being operational, they are of theoretical interest since they do offer a way out of the free-rider dilemma posed by Samuelson and others. We shall present an example of such a mechanism for revealing the preferences for a public good, the essence of which is common to similar mechanisms proposed by several authors, including Clarke (1971), Groves and Loeb (1975), Tideman and Tullock (1976), and Groves and Ledyard (1977).[7] In each of these, the taxing of an individual (or firm) is such that the amount of tax paid on the marginal unit of output of the public good is the difference between the marginal cost of the public good (MC) and the sum of the marginal benefits to all users of the public good other than the one being taxed. The individual will have an incentive to have the public good expanded until the marginal benefit he receives (MB_i) just equals his marginal tax payment ($MC - \sum_{j \neq i} MB_j$). This is just the Samuelson optimality condition.

For this mechanism to operate, the individual consumers of a public good, say G, must communicate their *reported demand curves* to a planner. The planner does not, of course, know whether the reported demand curves are true ones, but is assumed to choose a level of G at which the sum of the reported marginal benefits equals marginal cost. The individuals know the planner will act this way. Thus, in Fig. 6–9, AD represents the reported

Figure 6–9

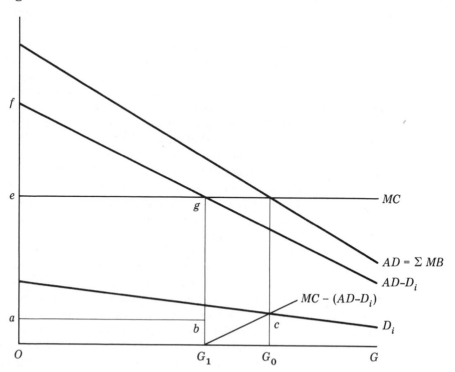

aggregate demand for the public good (or the sum of the reported marginal benefits of all users), while MC is the marginal cost of the public good, assumed constant for the sake of simplicity. The planner will choose to provide G_0 of G. The curve D_i is individual i's reported demand curve, while $AD\text{-}D_i$ is the vertical sum of reported demand curves for all individuals other than i.[8]

If individual reported demand curves are true ones, then G_0 is clearly the optimal level of G. The problem, then, is to devise a taxing mechanism that ensures that each individual will choose to reveal his true demand curve to the planner, whether or not other consumers are truthful. Such taxes can be computed as follows: First, consider the outcome of the planner's behavior if individual i reported a zero marginal benefit for G at all levels of G—or, equivalently, if i simply were "absent" from the process. In this case, G_1 would be chosen because at G_1, $MC = AD - D_i$. Now, with G_1 so defined, individual i's tax can be described. It has two components:

1. An amount which is unrelated to the individual's preferences. For example, the individual might be assessed a tax price based on G_1 as determined by everyone else's preferences such as the area $OabG_1$. This tax payment, denoted by A_i, does not affect this individual's reporting of preferences

and is levied solely to generate lump-sum revenue to finance the public good. The relative size of A_i for different individuals could be determined by equity considerations.

2. A tax equal to the amount of money that would be required to be paid to all other individuals to induce them to expand the output of G beyond G_1. This tax equals the difference between the costs of expanding beyond G_1 and the revealed benefits of all other persons, or the area beneath the curve $MC - (AD - D_i)$ in Fig. 6–9. We denote this tax by B_i.

The lump-sum part of the tax payments A_i is the same for individual i no matter what preferences are revealed. However, the tax payment B_i depends upon the demand curve D_i revealed by individual i. Given the preferences of all others, individual i's preferences will determine how far G_0 is above G_1 (since G_0 is determined by $AD = MC$). The marginal cost to i of expansions beyond G_1 is the area beneath $MC - (AD - D_1)$. The marginal benefit is the area beneath his true demand curve. Individual i will desire the output of G to rise to the point at which the marginal cost of further expansions to him equals his marginal benefit. That will be achieved if the demand curve D_i revealed to the planner is his true demand curve. This is so since the planner will expand output to the point at which $MC = AD$, which is equivalent to the point at which $D_i = MC - (AD - D_i)$ (private marginal benefits equal private marginal costs).

This same principle holds regardless of the preferences revealed by other persons $(AD - D_i)$. Individual i will always have an incentive to reveal his true preferences. Since all individuals face the same sort of taxing mechanism they also have an incentive to reveal their true preferences. Thus, AD will reflect the true aggregate demand for G and G_0 will be the optimal output.

There are a number of problems with implementing such a mechanism, many of which are common to other sorts of collective decision-making rules. The most obvious problem is that the above analysis assumes that individuals will be willing to take the time and effort to ascertain the benefits that various public goods provide to them and to report those benefits fully to the planner. Since each voter is one of millions, his impact upon the output of the public good will be small, and the benefit he obtains from the correct revelation of preferences is also likely to be small. It may, therefore, not be worth his while to devote energy to determining these preferences. A similar problem exists with ordinary voting or referendum rules. Another problem common to most social choice rules is that non-optimality will result if individuals form coalitions and exercise their joint strength to their collective benefit. The mechanism does not specify any rules for determining the lump-sum part of the tax payment, A_i. Finally, the process discussed above need not result in a balanced budget. There is no guarantee that the total taxes collected from all individuals ($\Sigma A_i + \Sigma B_i$) just equals the cost of provision of public goods. If a surplus is generated it must somehow be disposed of, and any deficit must be met by taxation. Therefore these mechanisms cannot be relied on completely for the operation of the public sector. The magnitude of the net surplus or deficit generated can be manipulated through trial and error by changing the magnitudes of the lump-sum portion of tax payments, A_i.

The specific form of the incentive mechanism presented in Fig. 6–9 is not the only possible one. Other mechanisms have been proposed in the literature which differ in the way they compute A_i or in the benchmark used for computing B_i. We shall briefly outline two such mechanisms, one suggested by Groves and Loeb and the other discussed by Tideman and Tullock.

(a) Groves and Loeb

The problem considered by Groves and Loeb (1975) is that of a public input demanded by several firms. We may analyze this case using Fig. 6–9 if we interpret G as the public input, D_i as the value of the marginal product or rent of G to the ith firm, and AD as the sum of the D_i for all firms.[9] An important assumption here is that the number of user firms is fixed even though a positive profit is generated by G for each of them.

The taxing mechanism suggested by Groves and Loeb is slightly different from that described above. The total tax price charged to firm i, T_i, is given by the following formula (equivalent to Eq. [13] of Groves and Loeb):

$$T_i = A_i + TC - (TB - TB_i) \tag{6-4}$$

where TC is the total cost of the public input ($= G \cdot MC$ in the constant cost case), TB_i is the total benefit to user i and TB is the total benefit of all users ($= \Sigma \, TB_i$). Thus, $TB - TB_i$ is the total benefit to all users except i, or the area beneath $AD - D_i$. Once again A_i is some lump-sum tax on i which is unrelated to i's revealed demand. In terms of areas in Fig. 6–9, the tax on firm i consists of A_i plus the difference between the area beneath MC and $AD - D_i$, or

$$T_i = A_i + G_1 c G_0 - efg. \tag{6-5}$$

The marginal price facing i for expansions in G is $MC - (AD - D_i)$ exactly as before and, by the same argument, there will be an incentive for true preference revelation.

(b) Tideman and Tullock

The mechanism described geometrically by Tideman and Tullock, which is the same as that devised by Clarke (1971), is depicted in Fig. 6–10.[10] It differs from that discussed above by altering the benchmark output G_1 and by computing the fixed part of the tax A_i as a share of the cost of the output of G_1.

Figure 6–10

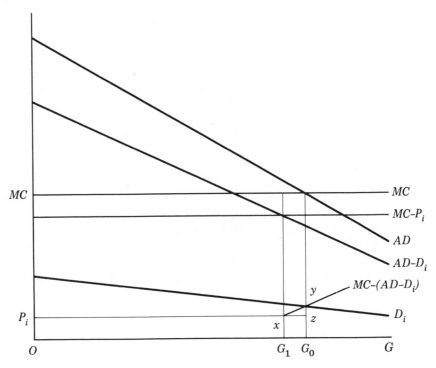

In Fig. 6–10, P_i is the share of individual i in the cost of public good G defined for all individuals so that $\Sigma\, P_i = MC$. The benchmark output of the public good, G_1, is that found by setting $AD - D_i = MC - P_i$. It is the output that would be chosen by all individuals except i if they had to pay a price for G equal to their shares. Note that G_1 in Fig. 6–10 is greater than G_1 in Fig. 6–9. The tax paid by an individual i consists of two parts. The first is the area OP_ixG_1, which is determined by the demands of all other persons except i. Like A_i above, it does not influence the preferences revealed by the individual. The other part of the tax is the amount required to compensate all other voters to go from G_1 to G_0, or the area beneath $MC - (AD - D_i)$, G_1xyG_0. The marginal tax cost to the individual of expansions in the output level of G above G_1 is $MC - (AD - D_i)$, exactly as in the mechanism discussed above. Once again, the individual has an incentive to reveal his true preferences for the same reasons.

For the person depicted in Fig. 6–10, the marginal benefit received from the public good (yG_0) exceeds the tax share P_i. There will be other individuals for whom the opposite holds. For them the output G_0 will be less than G_1. In this case the individual's tax bill is reduced by the area beneath $MC - (AD - D_i)$ as output is reduced. It is easy to show (Tideman and Tullock, pp. 1154–55) that the individual is again induced to reveal his true preferences.

The more complicated form of the Clarke incentive mechanism allows it to have two interesting properties. The first is that the tax revenues gathered over and above the cost of producing the public good will be very small. In Fig. 6–10 individual i's tax payments are $OP_izG_0 + xyz$. Since the sum of the rectangular areas OP_izG_0 over all individuals is just the cost of producing the public good, the extra revenue generated is the triangular area such as xyz for each individual.[11] The second property is that by an appropriate choice of P_i, a Lindahl solution can be generated at which the triangles xyz disappear and the budget is balanced. Such a solution would require a trial-and-error method to generate it, such as that discussed by Tideman and Tullock.

These examples show that, in theory, it is possible to devise mechanisms to induce people to reveal their true preferences for public goods. Unfortunately, these mechanisms are not easily made operational. The administrative costs of applying them to the large number of functions regularly undertaken by governments, and the problems of inducing individuals and firms to take the time to acquire information regarding the benefits they receive from public expenditures make them impractical. Nonetheless they are theoretically interesting for understanding the structure of the free-rider problem.

CHAPTER NOTES

1. Although we shall refer mainly to the provision of public goods in this chapter, the principles involved include all commodities which have the property of joint consumption including externalities and public intermediate goods.

2. Bowen was also one of the first authors to formulate the optimality conditions for the efficient allocation of public goods, $\Sigma\, MRS = MRT$.

3. A formal analysis of the optimality properties of the majority voting rule which explicitly introduces properties of the utility function and the distribution of income is presented in Stiglitz (1974). It is also useful to note that the distribution of preferred public good levels depends on the tax system as well as incomes and tastes. For example, if a system of Lindahl prices for the public good were somehow established, this distribution would collapse to a point, with all individuals preferring a common—and efficient—level of provision. In some crude sense, the degree to which most-preferred levels of public good provision differ among households is an indicator of the extent to which individual marginal tax-prices depart from perfect benefit prices.

4. We have already seen in (b) above that majority voting also gives Pareto-optimal allocation of resources for the case in which tax shares are predetermined and preferences are normally distributed.

5. Buchanan and Tullock (1962, pp. 186–188) also show that with full vote-trading, *any* decision rule will be Pareto-optimal.

6. Of course, the problem of moral hazard does not go away with the collective provision of "income insurance" to low-income earners. There will still be some incentive to earn a low income and collect the public sector transfer payments.

7. The technique was originally developed in the context of counter-speculation policy in private goods by Vickrey (1961). For an extensive recent treatment of incentive mechanisms, see Green and Laffont (1979).

8. Shifts in these demand curves due to income effects are neglected here. The existence of income effects poses certain technical problems. These problems are briefly discussed in Tideman and Tullock (1976, p. 1154).

9. When the users are firms rather than individuals, the problem of income effects does not occur.

10. Our discussion here maintains the assumption that the level of public good provision is continuously variable. However, it is possible to modify the analysis to deal with discrete choices. Many public good problems have this characteristic, as, for instance, when one must decide whether or not to build a school of a given size, whether or not to zone a particular lot for industrial use, etc. The relevant version of the "Clark tax" system for discrete choice is discussed by Tideman and Tullock.

11. For those individuals for whom $P_i > D_i$ at the output G_1 the triangular area is to the left of G_1 and beneath P_i.

7

Public Enterprise Pricing and Investment Rules

INTRODUCTION

7–1   Governments are sometimes directly involved in the provision of private or marketable goods. For example, the public sector may operate enterprises in the public utility field (electricity, water, telephones, communications) or in transportation (railways, airlines, buses). There are various other services for which the government may set user charges such as toll roads, day-care centers, and education and health services of various sorts. Governments become involved in the provision of excludable commodities because, for some reason, the private sector does not provide the optimal amount. Two reasons may be singled out as the most prevalent.

(i) *Natural Monopoly*   Some industries are natural monopolies in the sense that they exhibit increasing returns to scale up to relatively large outputs (i.e. outputs that are large relative to market demand). In a *laissez-faire* economy, such an industry would become a monopoly and would set a price above marginal cost, thereby violating the Pareto-optimum conditions and producing too little output. In fact, as we shall see below, in a natural monopoly situation the firm could not set a price equal to marginal cost and still cover the total cost. For a firm to break even, it must receive a price equal to average cost; but, with increasing returns, marginal cost is less than average cost, so the firm must incur a loss with marginal cost pricing. Natural monopolies, if left to maximize profits, would in fact be likely to charge a price above average cost, thereby restricting output even below the breakeven level.

In these circumstances, there are several alternative policies the government might pursue in an attempt to induce an output closer to the efficient level. The pricing policies of the natural monopoly firm might be regulated, as is often done in the United States. At best, regulation can restrict the pricing policies of the firm to that which covers average cost. Unless some price discrimination is possible, as discussed below in Section 7–2, this implies that the firm is still producing below the efficient point (where price equals marginal cost). Nonetheless, many of the principles discussed in this chapter apply equally well to the problems of regulation of natural monopolies.

Alternatively, the government itself may decide to set up its own public enterprise to produce and sell the output of natural monopoly industries. These industries are often referred to as *nationalized industries*. They are relatively more prevalent in the United Kingdom and other European countries and, to a lesser extent, in Canada than in the United States. In this case, the government could, if it so desired, charge a price equal to marginal cost and cover the deficit from general tax revenues. As we shall see below, there may well be some reasons why it would actually choose to charge a price in excess of marginal cost. These reasons have to do with the fact that the raising of tax revenues itself imposes efficiency or welfare costs on the economy.

On efficiency grounds, the case for establishing a public enterprise rather than relying on regulation of privately operated natural monopolies is not clear cut and depends upon the specific circumstances. All things considered, a public enterprise will, in principle, provide greater net benefits compared with the regulated monopoly if it is socially desirable to set price below average cost. On the other hand, many writers have argued that because of the absence of the profit-maximizing, and therefore the cost-minimizing, motive in public enterprises, the latter would be run less efficiently than private regulated industries (see Leibenstein [1966]). This inefficiency, called *X-inefficiency*, would have to be weighed against the gain in efficiency from setting a price below average cost and selling more output. These various gains and losses, which will be illustrated geometrically below, are often very difficult to evaluate in practice, and some judgment must be made on the basis of limited information.

There is one circumstance in which the decision may be somewhat more straightforward. It may be the case that even average cost pricing is not possible; that is, there may be no price that can be charged that will cover the average cost of producing the level of output demanded at that price. If price discrimination is not possible, the enterprise could not be operated in the private sector without a subsidy. In this case, the government may well decide to operate the industry as a public enterprise. Then the investment problem to be solved is whether or not it is socially beneficial to operate the industry at all.

(ii) *External Benefits* The second reason for which public enterprises are established to sell "private" goods is when the good being sold is accompanied by significant external benefits. On efficiency grounds, this constitutes the reason for public provision of, say, university education and certain health services. There may well be other grounds for public provision of these services, such as equity. Indeed, Musgrave (1959) has also defined a category of publicly-provided goods as *merit goods,* those goods provided by the state on the paternalistic grounds that individuals ought to consume them, but would not act in their own self-interest and purchase them without substantial subsidization. This may, of course, be one of the reasons for public provision of these goods; however, on normative grounds it is hard to justify the provision of merit goods and still maintain the two basic premises of neoclassical welfare economics: That individuals are rational and that individuals know their own interests best.

Once again, there are several possible policies that may be pursued in the presence of externality-emitting goods. Public provision is one such policy and carries with it the possibility of X-inefficiency as above. Or, the goods may be provided by the private sector with the aid of a subsidy from the government. Alternatively, the consumer may be provided with an earmarked grant to be spent on the purchase of such goods from the private sector. This is the basis of the so-called *voucher scheme* for financing education advocated by Friedman (1964). The essence of the voucher scheme is that each individual of school age is entitled to one voucher worth, say, $2000 per year that may be "spent" on the school of his choice. Schooling may, in fact, cost more than $2000 per year, and the difference must be made up by the consumer. The private sector "education" industry then competes for the consumers' demand for educational services.

The voucher scheme differs from a direct subsidy scheme to individual schools, since the former treats each individual identically whereas the latter does not. If the subsidy were *ad valorem,* it would reduce the price of education to all individuals, thereby providing relatively more benefits to those who purchase the most education. If the purchase of education has a positive income elasticity of demand, it would benefit high-income groups relative to low-income groups. The voucher scheme, on the other hand, is a grant fixed in size for all income groups. Thus, relative to the subsidy scheme it would help low-income groups relative to high-income groups. Of course, compared to universal free education, it would be of less benefit to low-income groups if the value of the voucher were less than the per-pupil cost of education. Furthermore, depending upon the nature of the external benefit from education, the voucher scheme may not be an efficient scheme in the Pareto-optimal sense. A subsidy of some sort could always be found to match the external benefits of education. However, the voucher scheme that pays the same lump-sum, ear-marked grant to every pupil is a particular form of per-pupil subsidy which would be efficient only if the monetary magnitude of the external benefit from education were the same for all pupils.

The analysis applicable to this latter rationale for public provision of private or excludable goods has already been discussed in Chapter 5. Public provision at a price below the marginal cost of goods which exhibit external economies is analytically identical to subsidization of private sector production, and the principles of subsidizing external benefits are applicable here. This chapter therefore concentrates on the analysis of problems arising out of natural monopolies, or increasing-returns-to-scale public enterprises. We begin by reviewing the essence of the marginal cost pricing controversy of the 1950s. A number of special problems in the pricing and investment criteria for public enterprises are considered, many of which have applicability elsewhere in public finance.

THE MARGINAL COST PRICING PROBLEM

7–2   The marginal cost pricing problem in increasing-returns-to-scale industries is readily illustrated using the cost curves of Fig. 7–1. Consider a firm monopolizing the output X of an increasing-returns-to-scale industry. Assume that the prices of all inputs into the production process are fixed so that the average cost (AC) and marginal cost (MC) curves slope downward solely due to increasing returns to scale.[1] If, in addition, the firm has an influence on its input prices as it produces more and more output, the AC and MC curves defined for fixed input prices will shift upwards as X increases. From a social welfare point of view, one should not count an increase in input prices as part of the marginal cost of producing X, since it includes an element of producers' surplus or rent which does not constitute a real opportunity cost. This phenomenon of rising cost curves due to rising factor prices (or pecuniary diseconomies) was discussed earlier in Section 5–4. In other words, the MC curve of the firm is drawn as if the firm were a price taker in the input market at each level of output X. The industry demand (D) and marginal revenue (MR) curves facing the firm are also drawn in Fig. 7–1.

As was discussed in Chapter 2, the overall efficiency conditions for Pareto optimality would be satisfied in a decentralized economy if all firms charged a price equal to marginal cost. In Fig. 7–1 this would occur at the output X_o and price p_o. We know from elementary economic theory that whenever a firm has a decreasing average cost curve, average costs will exceed marginal costs.[2] Therefore, average costs will exceed price and total costs (OC_ohX_o) will exceed total revenues (Op_ocX_o). In order to achieve Pareto optimality, increasing-returns firms would have to operate at a loss.

If the firm were to operate as a profit-maximizing natural monopolist it would set $MR = MC$ and produce at an output of X_m and price p_m. The approximate cost to society of having the wrong output and price can be depicted geometrically in Fig. 7–1. We apply here the notions of total benefits and total costs as developed in Chapter 2. The loss in total benefits to consumers from consuming X_m rather than X_o is the area beneath the demand curve X_macX_o. On the other hand, the saving in resource costs from the reduction in output from X_o to X_m is the area beneath the MC

Figure 7–1

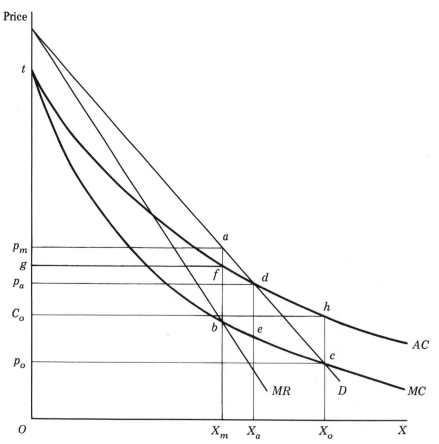

curve $X_m bc X_o$. Therefore, the net cost to society is the difference between these two areas abc.

The same net cost to society can be determined by using the notions of consumers' and producers' surplus. Suppose we calculate the net loss in surplus in going from the optimal output X_o to the monopoly output X_m. We may identify two parties involved in the gains or losses: the consumers and the monopolist, the latter being the recipient of all the producers' surplus. The loss in consumers' surplus in the price rise from p_o to p_m is $p_m acp_o$. The monopoly profit at p_m is $p_m afg$, or equivalently $p_m aX_m O - tbX_m O$ (since the total cost is also the area beneath the marginal cost curve). The loss at p_o is given by $tcX_o O - p_o cX_o O$. Thus, the gain to the monopolist in going from X_o to X_m is $p_m aX_m O - tbX_m O - p_o cX_o O + tcX_o O$, or $p_m abcp_o$. The net loss to society is the consumers' loss less the producer's gain, $p_m acp_o - p_m abcp_o$ or abc as before. The identification of this area as the welfare loss of monopoly is due to Harberger (1954) and has been the subject of a great deal of empirical analysis since then.

A regulated firm, which was instructed to set price equal to average cost and thereby earn just the normal return on capital, would produce X_a at the price p_a. By the same reasoning as above, the net loss to society from average cost pricing would be the triangular area *dec*. This can be thought of as the cost of operating an increasing-returns-to-scale industry as a regulated private firm. It is not necessarily the total net benefit to be obtained from nationalizing the industry for at least two reasons: First, publicly-operated firms may not in fact operate at $p = MC$ because of the opportunity cost of raising revenues through taxes to finance the loss. This problem of raising revenue to cover costs will be taken up shortly. Second, the AC curve may differ for public and private enterprises, since neither may operate using the lowest cost techniques of production. For public firms, as discussed above, inefficient production ("X-inefficiency") may occur as a result of lack of incentives for public firms to minimize costs. For private firms, the mechanics of the regulatory process may induce firms to operate inefficiently.

This latter source of inefficiency, the so-called Averch-Johnson effect, operates as follows: Prices are not regulated to be set equal to average costs of production; instead, they are set so as to allow firms to achieve a target rate-of-return on capital. This is often referred to as *rate-of-return regulation*. Rate-of-return regulation induces profit-maximizing firms to use too much capital relative to labor. The reason for this is as follows: The regulatory price is set so that the firm's rate of return on capital, $(R - C)/K$, is equal to some level s where R is revenues, C is non-capital costs, and K is capital. This regulatory constraint restricts the return that the firm may make *per dollar* of capital; but it does not directly constrain the total profit of the firm. The firm will have an incentive to exploit the regulatory constraint by expanding its capital stock to increase the total return arising from a given rate-of-return. The end result, as shown by Baumol and Klevorick (1970), is that the firm is induced to hire more capital, and also to use a technique of production that is more capital-intensive than that which minimizes costs. That is, it chooses a capital-labor ratio at which the marginal rate of technical substitution between capital and labor differs from the wage-rental ratio facing it. The output produced is most likely increased by the regulatory constraint as intended, but the output is produced at too high a cost. Thus, one sort of inefficiency is introduced in the process of attempting to eliminate another.

There is another potential difficulty which may be encountered in a natural monopoly. As Fig. 7–1 is drawn, it is obvious that the total benefits exceed the total costs of operating the firm, and the firm should indeed stay in operation. It is conceivable, however, that the demand curve D may everywhere fall below the average cost curve, in which case no private firm could possibly cover costs. Figure 7–2 illustrates this. There is no possible price that could be charged such that $p = AC$. Nonetheless, it is quite possible that the firm might still produce a positive output. At a price of $p_o(= MC)$ and an output of X_o the total benefit to consumer is the area

Figure 7–2

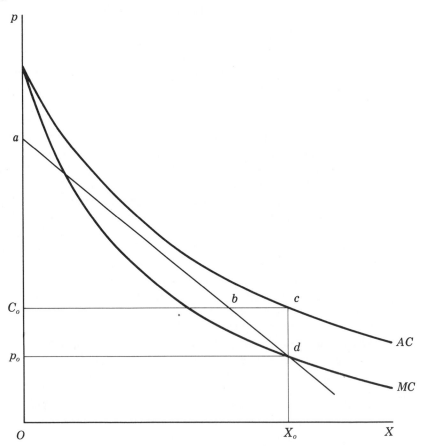

$OadX_o$. The total cost is the area beneath the marginal cost curve or, equivalently, the average cost times the output OC_ocX_o. The firm should produce X_o if $OadX_o > OC_ocX_o$, or $C_oab > bcd$.

Suppose now that the public sector has decided to operate the industry, and that it has been established that the total benefits from so doing exceed the total costs. If the firm is to follow marginal cost pricing, the operating losses must be made up somewhere. There are two ways, in theory, of meeting total costs without imposing distortions elsewhere. First, if perfect price discrimination were possible, the firm could charge each user the maximum amount they would be willing to pay and collect an amount of revenue equal to the total benefits of consumers $OadX_o$ in Fig. 7–2. There are obvious practical problems with imposing price discrimination, especially perfect price discrimination, but it serves as a useful benchmark against which to compare alternative schemes. The second method of covering costs is to levy lump-sum taxes. As discussed later in Chapter 9, lump-sum taxes are simply taxes which are levied on some item which is invariant in quantity. For example, if labor is fixed in supply, a wage tax is a lump-sum tax. Or, a head (or poll) tax is a tax of a given amount levied on each person. Lump-sum taxes have the characteristic of being nondistortionary and, therefore, are ideal taxes from an efficiency point of view (see Chapter 9).

In the real world, governments do not rely on lump-sum taxes. For one thing, the types of lump-sum taxes which are feasible may not be very satisfactory from an equity point of view. In particular, if one of the roles of taxation is to redistribute income, lump-sum taxes may not be desirable since, typically, they are not progressive. In the real world, distortionary taxes are levied. In addition to transferring purchasing power to the public sector, actual taxes impose net welfare or efficiency losses on society. The nature of these efficiency losses will be discussed in considerably more detail in Chapter 9. For now, we only need to recognize that such losses do exist, and we must take them into account whenever tax revenue must be raised.

There are alternative distortionary ways of raising revenues to cover costs which have been advocated at various times in the past. Several types of imperfect price discrimination are possible and are used in practice. For example, marginal cost pricing combined with a fixed license fee is sometimes used for telephone services. While such a scheme does not impose distortions on the marginal use of the service, it will impose an infra-marginal distortion to the extent that, for some individuals, the license fee exceeds the total benefit they would receive from the service. They are therefore precluded from using the service, even though the marginal cost of allowing them to use it may be very small. Other sorts of price discrimination impose a similar sort of infra-marginal distortion. Utility pricing schemes often employ price discrimination schedules, based either on quantity consumed, on type of consumer, or both. Thus, the price charged for the first X units may exceed the price charged for the next Y units and so on. Also, residential consumers may pay a different amount from industrial users since their elasticity of demand is presumed to be different. Such schemes, though falling short of pricing the last units at marginal cost, are more efficient than uniform pricing and allow greater use of the good in question.

Price discrimination has the advantage of increasing use by charging a low price at the margin. However, it is not always a feasible method of allocating resources, since it requires that different units of sale can be appropriately classified for discrimination, and that resale cannot be engaged in easily. Therefore, uniform pricing may be required, in which case the revenue to cover costs must be made up in some other way. There are two alternative ways this may be done: First, the public enterprise may follow a scheme of average cost pricing and incur the welfare or efficiency loss of *dec* in Fig. 7–1. Of course, if the demand curve is entirely below the *AC* curve as in Fig. 7–2, this is not possible. Let us assume, however, that it is possible. If the government tries to pursue average cost pricing on all its enterprises, this is equivalent to putting a particular set of distortions between price and marginal cost within the public sector. From an analytical or theoretical point of view, setting price above marginal cost in the public sector is equivalent to imposing a commodity tax on competitive industries in the private sector. Both cause a distortion between price and marginal cost that causes a net welfare loss. Therefore, one can look at the problem of raising revenue for public enterprises as part of the more general problem of raising revenue for all public sector activities, including the provision of public goods, by choosing the appropriate set of distorting taxes. In this case, the marginal cost pricing problem in decreasing cost industries is really part of the overall "optimal tax" problem to be considered in detail in Chapter 9. (See also Baumol and Bradford [1970]).

Economic efficiency may not be the only criterion that may be used for public utility pricing. Feldstein (1972b) has argued that equity or income distribution ought to be taken into consideration as well. This analysis suggests that if the marginal social utility of income diminishes as income rises, goods with the highest income elasticities should be priced higher for equity reasons. Whether public utility pricing policy ought to be used as a tool for income redistribution is something upon which not all economists would agree. There are other sorts of taxes (e.g. progressive income tax) which might be better suited for the task than commodity taxes.

In the real world, public-enterprise pricing and output decisions must often be taken on a piecemeal or decentralized basis, with policies elsewhere being taken as given. One interesting question which has been widely discussed in welfare economics is that of determining pricing rules in one industry (say, a public enterprise) when distortions exist elsewhere in the economy over which the decision-maker has no control. This general sort of problem is called the *theory of second best*, to which we now turn.

THE THEORY OF SECOND BEST

7–3   The Pareto optimality or efficiency conditions discussed in Chapter 2 were derived under the assumption that there were no restrictions on meeting these conditions in any sector of the economy. A "first-best" or Pareto optimum exists when all the efficiency conditions hold in every industry. As we saw in Chapter 2, these conditions will be satisfied in decentralized competitive economies under some circumstances. Suppose, however, that these conditions are violated in some sector of the economy. For example, price may not equal marginal cost due to monopoly, externalities, or taxes. Furthermore, suppose that the public-sector decision-maker whose behavior we are analyzing has no control over these distorted sectors and must take their nonoptimal behavior as given. The theory of second-best seeks to establish pricing rules for the controllable sectors of the economy, given that distortions exist elsewhere. Obviously, a first-best optimum cannot be achieved. What, then, does the second-best optimum look like? In particular, should the authorities nonetheless continue to set prices equal to marginal cost in the controllable sector, even though prices may not equal marginal costs elsewhere? The answer to this question, first explicitly discussed in a celebrated article by Lipsey and Lancaster (1956–7), is generally in the negative. To see this, consider the following simple example.

The economy in this example is composed of three "commodities:" a public enterprise output, X_1, a good, X_2, that has a distortion between price p_2 and marginal cost MC_2, and a composite or numeraire commodity X_3, which includes all other commodities in the economy, none of which are distorted. One might think of X_2 as an urban expressway and X_1 as mass transit. Suppose the price of X_2 is less than the marginal social cost of using X_2, due to the externalities of road use including congestion and pollution. Therefore, we would expect roads to be overused compared with the optimum. Figure 7–3 illustrates the problem by using supply and demand curves where it is assumed that all commodities may be produced at constant cost. We are therefore abstracting from the problem of decreasing costs to concentrate on the second-best aspects of public sector pricing. In practice, both problems may be present. The general analysis of this problem derives from Harberger (1971a).

The demand curves $\overline{D}_1$ and $\overline{D}_2$ represent the demand curves that would exist if marginal cost pricing were pursued in the public sector X_1 ($\overline{p}_1 = MC_1$). The outputs of X_1 and X_2 would then be $\overline{X}_1$ and $\overline{X}_2$, taking into consideration the fact that $\overline{p}_2 < MC_2$ in the second industry. Suppose the distortion between $\overline{p}_2$ and MC_2 is fixed. Recall that ordinary demand curves are drawn under the *ceteris paribus* assumption; that is, all other prices and income are assumed constant. If other prices or incomes do change, the demand curves will, in general, shift. The intuition of the second-best argument is as follows: Since too many resources are being devoted to industry two when marginal cost pricing is followed in industry one, a gain in welfare might be obtained by changing the pricing policy in the latter

Figure 7–3

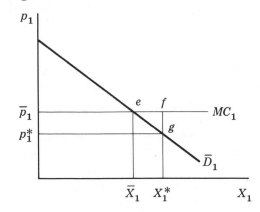
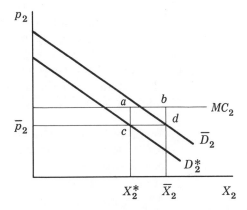

so as to induce a shift of resources out of industry two. Suppose that X_1 and X_2 are substitutes, as is presumably the case with urban transit and road use. A reduction in price of X_1 to, say, $p_1^* < MC_1$ would cause the demand curve of $\overline{D}_2$ to shift to the left to D_2^*. Since we have assumed that both the marginal cost and the divergence between p_2 and MC_2 are fixed, p_2 does not change but the output of X_2 is reduced to X_2^*.

Let us now tally up the total change in social welfare that occurs as a result of reducing the price to p_1^*. We shall use the total benefit method of Chapter 2, although the same result could be obtained by aggregating consumers' and producers' surplus changes. In industry one, the increase in total resource cost from the price reduction is $\overline{X}_1 efX_1^*$, while the increase in total benefit is $\overline{X}_1 egX_1^*$, leaving a net reduction in welfare of the triangular area *efg*. In industry two, the savings in resources are valued at $X_2^* ab\overline{X}_2$ and total benefits fall by $X_2^* cd\overline{X}_2$, the value to consumers of each unit of X_2 lost. Therefore, the net gain in welfare is *abdc*. Provided *abdc* exceeds *efg,* the reduction in price would improve social welfare. More generally, if there are several distorted markets, the area *abdc* will be augmented by similar areas for each distorted market, or $\Sigma_i (p_i - MC_i)\Delta X_i$, where the goods X_i include all those sold on distorted markets elsewhere. The analytical underpinnings for this approach may be found in Harberger (1971a).

If the government is free to set p_1 at any price desired, it will set it so as to maximize social welfare. This is known as the *second-best policy.* In Fig. 7–3, an initial small reduction in the price of X_1 below MC_1 will increase welfare by an area like *abdc* but decrease it by the triangular area *efg*. For a very small change, the triangle will be negligible, so welfare will increase. As p_1 is reduced *efg* becomes larger and larger so that at some point the increase in the triangle will just offset the increase in the rectangle. At that point, the price of X_1 will be at its optimal second-best level.

The theory of second-best outlined above thus suggests that if $p < MC$ for the distorted good, and if the distorted and controllable goods are substitutes, then p_1 should be less than MC_1 at the second-best optimum. One must be careful not to misinterpret this result for policy purposes. Not all prices below marginal cost in industry one would be beneficial. If p_1 is lowered far enough, *efg* may exceed *abdc* and the economy would have been better off had marginal cost pricing been pursued. It is therefore important to have some idea regarding the relative magnitudes involved.

By extension of the above analysis we may derive the following sets of rules for second-best policy in the context of the above simple economy:

1. When $p < MC$ in the distorted sector, in the second-best optimum $p \gtrless MC$ in the control sector according to whether the two are complements or substitutes.

2. When $p > MC$ in the distorted sector, in the second-best optimum $p \gtrless MC$ in the control sector according to whether the two are substitutes or complements.

3. $p = MC$ in the control sector if the two sectors are unrelated in demand.

The real world is more complicated than the above model, and second-best effects may be much more pervasive. Two immediate extensions arise. First, marginal cost curves may not be horizontal. This complicates matters considerably, since it implies that both p_1 and p_2 will change, causing a shift in both demand curves and the supply curves as well. Our geometric techniques can only give approximate results in this case. For example, consider Fig. 7–4, which reproduces the case of Fig. 7–3 except that marginal cost curves are assumed to slope upwards. When the price in industry one is reduced below MC_1, the demand curve $\overline{D}_2$ shifts left to D_2^* and MC_2 shifts to MC_2^*. The gain in welfare in industry two is the area $abdc$ and the loss in industry one is efg. These areas, however, represent only a first approximation, since when p_2 and X_2 change, the demand and marginal cost curves in X_1 will shift and this will induce a further shift in X_2, etc. The areas $abdc$ and efg ignore all these secondary, induced shifts.

The other extension of the analysis is to the case of more than one distorted sector. Suppose X_1 is the control sector and X_2 and X_3 are distorted sectors (and X_4 is all others). X_1 may be urban public transit, X_2 is urban roadways, and X_3 is privately-operated train service. Suppose $p_2 < MC_2$ and $p_3 > MC_3$ and that all three goods are substitute means of transport. The second-best policy problem here concerns the proper pricing in X_1. There are now three influences at work: The welfare loss in departing from marginal cost pricing in X_1, and the induced changes in welfare on the markets for X_2 and X_3 calculated as above.[3] One can see that in the second-best optimum $p_1 \lessgtr MC_1$ depending on whether X_1 is a closer substitute for X_2 or X_3 and depending on the relative magnitudes of the distortion in X_2 and X_3.

Figure 7–4

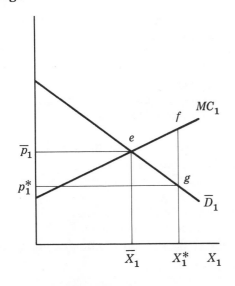
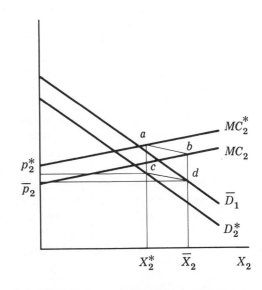

As was mentioned earlier, the second-best problem has much broader applicability than just the problem of public sector pricing. It also plays an important part in cost-benefit analysis, as we shall see in Chapter 8, and in analyzing the welfare effects of taxation, as will be discussed in Chapter 12.

CAPACITY CONSTRAINTS AND THE PEAK-LOAD PROBLEM

7–4   A different set of problems arises for the public enterprise decision-maker (or regulator of natural monopolies) when the commodity being provided is constrained by a capacity limit. At the capacity limit the amount of the commodity that can be provided is fixed; its purchase is rationed by charging the price that will just sell all the available output. The natural question that arises is what should be the capacity of the public enterprise. There are three sorts of circumstances which, in practice, render the investment in capacity decision difficult. First, the capacity may not be continuously variable; instead it may be indivisible and expandable only in discrete steps. Second, the capacity may be increased subject to either falling or rising marginal costs. Finally, the use of the capacity may fluctuate so that at times it is fully used (peak periods) and at other times it is not (off-peak periods). In order to analyze these problems we utilize a simple model of the firm adopted from Williamson (1966) on the peak-load pricing and investment problem. For our purpose, the essential feature of this model is the distinction between variable and fixed inputs.

Consider first the case in which none of the above three problems arises. A firm produces an output X using current or *variable inputs,* and capital or *fixed inputs*. For any given size of capacity, different amounts of output X may be produced by varying the use of variable inputs. In particular, an additional unit of X may be produced by using an amount of variable inputs valued at b dollars where b is a constant. Then, b is the short-run marginal cost ($SRMC$) of producing X up to the capacity which is $\overline{X}$. Figure 7–5 illustrates short-run marginal cost curves for three alternative capacities $\overline{X}$, $\overline{X}_0$, and $\overline{X} + \varepsilon$. The capacity of this firm $\overline{X}$ may be continuously varied at a constant cost of β per unit of capacity. The *long-run marginal cost* curve labeled $LRMC$ is the sum of $b + \beta$. It indicates the marginal cost of producing each level of output when both variable and fixed factors can be varied continuously at the margin.

It is easy to see that the optimal capacity of the firm is $\overline{X}_0$ in the diagram. Suppose the capacity was $\overline{X}$ and, therefore, the price charged to ration the available output was $\overline{X}f$. The total benefit to consumers is $Oef\overline{X}$ and the total cost to the firm is $O(b + \beta)g\overline{X}$, giving a net social benefit of $(b + \beta)efg$. It is obvious that the total benefit can be increased by expanding capacity to $\overline{X}_0$. At $\overline{X}$, the benefit from a marginal expansion in capacity is the price $\overline{X}f$, while the cost is only $\overline{X}g$. At the optimum, the marginal benefit equals the marginal cost $(\overline{X}_0h)$ and net benefits $(b + \beta)eh$ are maximized. The opposite argument holds starting at capacity $\overline{X} + \varepsilon$. A reduction in capacity to X_0 will increase net benefits by hjk.

Note the following property of the optimum capacity $\overline{X}_0$. At this capacity the price is $b + \beta$, and total revenues and total costs are identically $O(b + \beta)h\overline{X}_0$. That is, the firm just breaks even. If either b or β were declining so the firm produced with decreasing costs as output rose, the firm would take a loss at the optimal output. If costs were increasing, the firm would make a profit at the optimum.

Suppose, however, that capacity additions are indivisible and can only be increased by a discrete amount ε at a time. Two possible capacities might be $\overline{X}$ and $\overline{X} + \varepsilon$ in Fig. 7–5 so that the optimum $\overline{X}_0$ is not attainable. A decision must now be made between $\overline{X}$ and $\overline{X} + \varepsilon$ according to which one provides the greatest net benefits. We have already seen above that capacity $\overline{X}$ provides net benefits of $(b + \beta)efg$. Capacity of size $(\overline{X} + \varepsilon)$ gives total consumer benefits of $Oek(\overline{X} + \varepsilon)$ at a total resource cost of $O(b + \beta)j(\overline{X} + \varepsilon)$. Therefore, the net benefit resulting from the capacity $\overline{X} + \varepsilon$ is $(b + \beta)eh - hjk$. Capacity $\overline{X} + \varepsilon$ will be preferred to capacity $\overline{X}$ if $(b + \beta)eh - hjk$ exceeds $(b + \beta)efg$; that is, if $fgh > hjk$. $\overline{X}$ will be preferred to $\overline{X} + \varepsilon$ if $fgh < hjk$. These areas must be estimated before a decision is taken. Notice now that the firm cannot possibly break even despite the fact that constant costs exist. If $\overline{X}$ is chosen, total revenues will exceed total cost and a profit will be generated. If $\overline{X} + \varepsilon$ is chosen, total revenue will be less than total cost and the firm must operate at a loss.

Figure 7–5

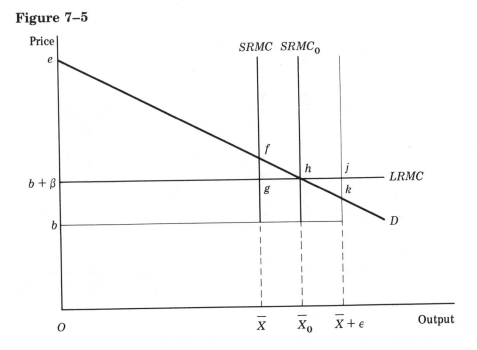

Let us revert to the continuous-capacity case and suppose that the firm faces a fluctuating demand over time for output on the same capacity. To simplify matters, we assume that these are two distinct periods within each cycle of time. Period One, called the *peak period,* lasts for a proportion w_1 of the cycle and period Two, the *off-peak period,* lasts for w_2, where $w_1 + w_2 = 1$. Furthermore, to facilitate the use of demand curves it is assumed that demand in each period is independent of the price in the other. This is an admittedly unrealistic assumption, but as has been shown by Mohring (1970) the results go through even with interdependent demands.

The problem is illustrated in Fig. 7–6. In this diagram, D_1 and D_2 represent the demand curves for the peak and off-peak periods, each drawn as if the period were to last for the entire cycle. Thus, a point on D_1 shows what the demand per cycle would be at the given price if the peak period lasted for the whole cycle. The reason for so defining the demand curves

Figure 7–6

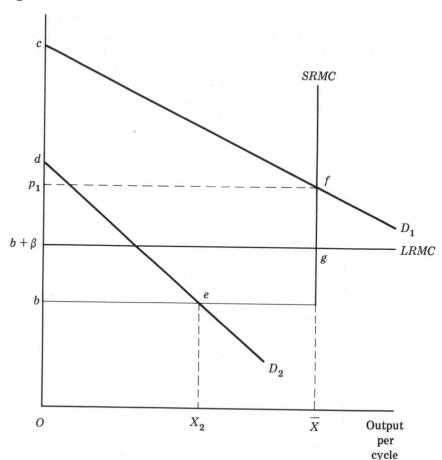

is that the horizontal axis measures outputs per cycle rather than per period. As the figure is drawn, the existing plant could sustain a demand of $\overline{X}$ over the whole cycle. This would imply a price of p_1 under peak-period demand conditions, as shown in the diagram. This price is also applicable for any period within the cycle that uses the plant at the peak rate. Thus, the peak-period price of p_1 will just serve to ration the output of $w_1\overline{X}$ that would occur over the fraction w_1 of the cycle. On the other hand, the off-peak period does not use the entire capacity under a marginal cost pricing scheme.[4] At a price of b (the $SRMC$), the off-peak period would use X_2 per cycle, or w_2X_2 over a proportion w_2 of the cycle.

In order to determine the optimal capacity $\overline{X}$ under fluctuating demand we must equate marginal benefits to marginal costs. The total benefit consumers obtain from the capacity $\overline{X}$ is the sum of the benefits in the two periods: $Ocf\overline{X} \cdot w_1 + OdeX_2 \cdot w_2$. The marginal benefit from expanding $\overline{X}$ is that accruing to the marginal peak users only. Since off-peak users do not use the plant to capacity as it is, they do not benefit from an expansion in capacity. Therefore, the marginal benefit is:[5] $MB = w_1 \cdot \overline{X}f = w_1p_1$. The total cost of providing the outputs $w_1\overline{X}$ and w_2X_2 consist of the capacity costs, $\beta\overline{X}$, and the variable costs in each period, $w_1b\overline{X} + w_2bX_2$. Once again, additional variable costs from expanding capacity occurs only in the peak period. Therefore, the marginal cost from expanding the capacity slightly is the incremental capital cost plus the additional peak-period variable costs:

$$MC = w_1b + \beta. \tag{7-1}$$

At the optimum, $MB = MC$, or:

$$p_1 = b + \frac{\beta}{w_1}. \tag{7-2}$$

The optimum capacity has some properties which are of interest to us:

1. The off-peak price is the $SRMC$, or $p_2 = b$.
2. The peak price exceeds the $LRMC$, or $p_1 = b + \beta/w_1 > b + \beta$.
3. Total revenues equal total costs at the optimum so that the peak users bear the entire cost of capacity.

This latter proposition is easily proven. From the definition of total costs as the sum of variable costs in each period and fixed costs over the cycle, total costs are:

$$TC = \beta\overline{X} + w_1b\overline{X} + w_2bX_2. \tag{7-3}$$

Total revenues are the sum of the revenues from each period. Using Eq.

(7–2), they are:

$$TR = p_1 w_1 \overline{X} + p_2 w_2 X_2$$

$$= (b + \beta/w_1)w_1\overline{X} + bw_2X_2. \tag{7-4}$$

Therefore, from Eqs. (7–3) and (7–4), total revenues equal total costs. To summarize, when capacity is continuously divisible, and when both variable and capacity costs are constant, the optimal capacity is that which equates total revenues and total costs.

The zero-profit condition vanishes once indivisibilities or nonconstant costs are introduced. In this case, the indivisibilities argument is very similar to that presented above for the constant-demand case and is not repeated here. The nonconstant costs can apply either to capacity costs or variable costs. In either case the result is the same. With decreasing costs the enterprise should earn a loss at the optimal capacity, whereas with increasing costs a profit would be earned.

For example, suppose there are economies of scale in expanding capacity so that it may be expanded at decreasing costs. In Fig. 7–7, the curve of long-run marginal costs will decline due to the fall in the marginal capacity cost β. Following the same procedure to find the optimal capacity, the pricing equation in the peak period at the optimum would be given by Eq. (7–2) as before, where β is the marginal capacity cost. Therefore, the total revenue expression (7–4) is the same as before. However, total costs are no longer given by Eq. (7–3). Variable costs are still $w_1 b\overline{X} + w_2 bX_2$; however, fixed costs are no longer $\beta\overline{X}$ since β is only the cost of the last unit of capacity. Infra-marginal units of capacity are evaluated at the marginal cost appropriate to them, which is higher than β. In Fig. 7–7, fixed costs are the area beneath the capacity cost curve, $Ors\overline{X}$. In this case, $TC > \beta\overline{X} + w_1 b\overline{X} + w_2 bX_2 = TR$. Therefore, the optimal capacity must be run at a loss.

Exactly the same sort of problems face the planner here as in the increasing-returns case of Section 7–2. If the firm is operated as a public enterprise, the resources to cover its costs must be obtained somewhere out of government revenues, and the costs of obtaining them must be considered. If the firm is to be operated as a regulated private-sector firm, it cannot possibly be operated at the optimal level since that would imply operating at a loss. The best that can be done is to restrict output and raise peak-period prices until total revenues cover total costs.

The various problems that we have analyzed in this chapter may all occur at the same time. That is, increasing returns might be accompanied by second-best problems, indivisibilities, fluctuating demands, or any combination of these. This makes the public decision-maker's job formidable, and he may well not have the information to take all these considerations fully into account. Our task in this chapter and, indeed, elsewhere in the book, has been to point out those things which, in principle, ought to guide

Figure 7–7

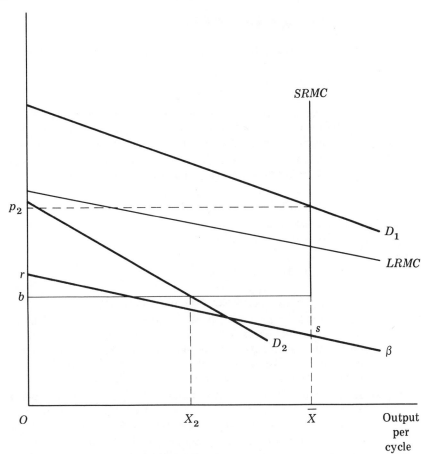

the well-informed policy-maker. The problems of implementing the economist's advice are unfortunately beyond the expertise of economic analysis as it has developed thus far.

CHAPTER NOTES

1. Increasing returns to scale industries have the property that a proportional increase in the inputs causes a greater than proportional increase in the output. For example, consider the neoclassical homogeneous production function $X = f(L, K)$. Suppose both inputs are increased by the multiple λ. Then, $\lambda^k X = f(\lambda L, \lambda K)$ where k is the degree of homogeneity of the function and is greater than unity for the increasing-returns-to-scale case. A well-known property of homogeneous functions is Euler's theorem, which states the following:

$$kX = (\partial f/\partial L)L + (\partial f/\partial K)K$$

Multiplying through by the price we obtain:

$$pkX = p(\partial f/\partial L)L + p(\partial f/\partial K)K.$$

If factors are paid the values of their marginal products, then:

$$pkX = wL + rK.$$

Therefore, since $k > 1$ for increasing-returns industries, $wL + rK > pX$. That is, the value of the output does not cover payments to factors of production. A firm which acts optimally would not make enough to cover costs.

2. The algebraic proof of this is as follows. Let X be the level of output, and TC, AC, and MC be total, average, and marginal costs. Then,

$$AC = TC/Q$$

$$MC = \partial TC/\partial Q = \partial(Q \cdot AC)/\partial Q$$

$$= AC + Q\partial AC/\partial Q$$

If AC is declining, $\partial AC/\partial Q < O$ and $MC < AC$.

3. For example, if $p_1 > MC_1$ in the control sector, there will be an induced shift in the demand curves for X_2 and X_3 to the right. There will be a welfare loss on the market for X_1 (a triangular area), a welfare loss on X_2 (a rectangular area), and a welfare gain on the previously underused good, X_3 (also a rectangular area). At the optimum, the net gain must be maximized.

4. It makes no difference to the main results if the off-peak period does use the capacity output as well. This case, perhaps the more unlikely, is discussed in Williamson (1966). He also generalizes these results to the many-period case.

5. This expression for the marginal benefit is derived from $\Delta(Ocf\overline{X}) \cdot w_1$ where the change Δ is an insignificantly small change.

8

Cost-Benefit Analysis

COST-BENEFIT ANALYSIS AS APPLIED WELFARE ECONOMICS

8-1 The term cost-benefit analysis, in its most general sense, refers to the measurement of the net economic benefits from any change in resource allocation. In the context of public finance, it most often refers to the calculation of net social benefits arising from a specific public expenditure such as a road, a bridge, an irrigation project, or a disease prevention program. Cost-benefit analysis may also be applied to broader programs of expenditures such as post-secondary education, or research and development. Or, it may be applied to changes in laws or regulations such as compulsory seat-belt legislation, or rate-of-return regulation of natural monopolies. Finally, cost-benefit analysis may usefully be applied to private sector projects if it is considered that the market profitability of a project is unlikely to reflect its social profitability; for example, in economies in which market prices do not closely reflect marginal social values. It is often used to evaluate industrial projects in less developed countries for this reason.

We argued in Chapter 2 that the competitive market mechanism was an efficient allocator of resources under certain ideal circumstances. In these circumstances, prices of goods would reflect marginal social benefits in monetary terms, and prices of inputs would reflect marginal social opportunity costs. Profit maximization would naturally lead to an efficient allocation of resources. The need for cost-benefit analysis arises when, for some reason, we cannot rely on profitability to reflect as accurately as we would like the net social benefits of a project. There are a number of general reasons why market profitability may not reflect social profitability, and it is worth cataloging them in detail at the outset.

The most obvious case in which market profitability is deficient is when some benefits or costs incurred as a result of the project do not have market prices. This may occur because some of the benefits are of a *public good or externality nature* which, because of non-excludability and/or nonrivalness, cannot be priced. Thus, for example, it is often argued that the expenditures on immunization or on education provide external benefits to those not actually being immunized or educated, and that, therefore, the profits from providing these services on competitive markets might understate the net social benefits of their provision. A related category of unpriced benefits and costs are so-called *intangibles*. These are benefits and costs that accrue directly to the users of the project and which do not have market prices, possibly because they are unquantifiable. Examples of this category include the benefits of time saved on, say, transportation projects, the benefits of lives saved or disease reduced from health care expenditures, the benefits from the use of recreation facilities, and the cost of noise pollution from airports.

Even when market prices exist for outputs and inputs, these prices may not accurately reflect marginal *social* benefits and costs. If markets have tax distortions, quotas, or regulations, market prices may not indicate social values. Similarly, if inputs are purchased from a monopoly supplier, prices will diverge from marginal costs. In such circumstances, the cost-benefit analyst should calculate a set of prices which do reflect true marginal benefits or costs. These prices, called *shadow prices*, can then be used to calculate the social profitability of the project. A related problem exists when the project induces changes in resource allocations on distorted markets elsewhere in the economy. The net benefit of these induced changes should, whenever possible, be taken into consideration in calculating the benefits of the project. Cases of this sort will be considered below.

A separate class of problems arises when a project has increasing returns-to-scale. In the first place, increasing-returns-to-scale projects which price outputs at marginal cost will always show negative profits. This is because marginal cost will always be less than average cost if cost curves decline with output. Yet it is quite possible that their total benefits (approximately the area beneath their demand curves) will exceed their total costs (the area beneath their marginal cost curves). In such a case the market profitability criterion breaks down. A second problem which frequently arises in practice is that the cost-benefit analyst may have to choose between two indivisible projects which are mutually exclusive, in the sense that only one can be undertaken (either because physically they would require the same fixed factor or location, or because both cannot be operated "profitably"). The choice of building an urban expressway or a subway may be a case in point. The relative profitabilities of the two projects may not reflect their relative net social benefits, since the consumer surplus generated by them may differ.

Finally, there is a set of problems that arises when intertemporal considerations are taken into account. The market interest rate used in calculating the present value of profits may not reflect the true intertemporal discount rate for the society. This will be so if there are distortions in the capital market, such as taxes of various sorts on capital income. In addition, it is often argued that intertemporal externalities of the following sort arise on capital markets. To the extent that members of the current generation benefit from the well-being of future-generation members, saving for future generations has the characteristic of a public good. Each individual's net lifetime savings for future generations confers a benefit upon all other contemporary savers, but, since this external benefit is not reflected in the individual's marginal private benefits and costs, undersaving will result. In other words, the social discount rate is less than the private discount rate. One other problem arising in an intertemporal context is that future outcomes are uncertain. All intertemporal resource allocations involve some risk or uncertainty. To the extent that the costs of private risk-taking differ from the costs to society of public sector risk-taking, the discounting for risk done by competitive capital markets may differ from the discounting for risk that ought to be done on public projects. All these problems will be discussed in detail in this chapter.

We are assuming in this chapter that an appropriate criterion according to which cost-benefit analysis can proceed is that of economic efficiency. That is, it is assumed to be legitimate to ignore questions of interpersonal utility comparison or equity, and to treat a dollar's worth of benefit as being worth the same to society no matter to whom it accrues. The justification for proceeding in this manner and the implications of doing so were discussed in Chapter 2. One either appeals to a separation of the efficiency (or allocative) functions of government from the equity (or distributive) functions and assumes that cost-benefit analysis falls squarely in the first; or, one assumes that a suitable criterion for welfare improvement is that the gainers could be able to compensate the losers and still be better off, and therefore aggregate monetary net benefits are a reliable indicator of a potential Pareto improvement in that sense. Otherwise, one would have to make a value judgment regarding the weights to be attached to each person's gains or losses and weigh them accordingly in applying the techniques of cost-benefit analysis. One example of how this calculation may be made in practice can be found in Weisbrod (1968).

AN APPROPRIATE DECISION RULE

8–2   Before discussing the problems of measurement of costs and benefits that arise in cost-benefit analysis, it is worthwhile formulating a general decision rule according to which the various benefits and costs might be aggregated so as to arrive at a measure of net benefits and, therefore, at a decision as to whether or not to proceed. Typically, projects yield a stream of benefits and costs that stretch over a period of time. In order to obtain a single measure of the net social benefit of a project, it is necessary somehow to aggregate monetary benefits and costs over time. At each point in time all benefits and costs can simply be added together by our assumption that a dollar is judged to have the same value no matter to whom it accrues. However, a dollar received now is not necessarily worth the same as a dollar received next year.

Consider an individual in an economy with competitive capital markets yielding an interest rate r per period of time, say, a year. Assume that it is now year zero. The individual will not value a dollar to be received in year one as much as a dollar to be received now since the dollar now could be saved at the going rate of interest to yield $(1 + r)$ dollars in year one. The individual can always transform present into future dollars at the ratio $1:(1 + r)$. As outlined in Chapter 2, the individual will arrange his intertemporal consumption pattern so that the marginal rate of substitution between year-zero and year-one dollars is $(1 + r)$. That being the case, if we assume all individuals face the same market interest rate and there are no externalities arising from private saving, then for society the following holds at the margin:

$1 in year zero is worth $(1 + r)$ in year one

where r is society's marginal rate of substitution or discount rate between years zero and one. A more convenient way of stating the above equivalence is in the converse way:

$1 in year one is worth $1/(1 + r)$ in year zero.

Therefore, in order to aggregate net dollar benefits in year one with net dollar benefits in year zero, we can reduce or discount all the former by the discount factor $1/(1 + r)$ and add the discounted value of year one net benefits to year zero net benefits.

In a similar way, if the interest rate r also holds between years one and two, one dollar in year two is worth $1/(1 + r)$ dollars in year one. Or, using the above equivalence between years one and zero, one dollar in year two is worth $1/(1 + r)^2$ dollars in year zero. Carrying forward the same procedure to year n, we find:

$1 in year n is worth $1/(1 + r)^n$ in year zero.

If the discount rate changes from period to period so r_t is the one-period discount rate in period t, the value of one dollar in year n must be amended to read:

$1 in year n is worth $\$1/ \prod_{t=1}^{n} (1 + r_t)$ in year zero

where the symbol $\prod$ refers to the product of all terms $(1 + r_t)$. For simplicity we shall assume in what follows that the discount rate is constant over time, since it makes no difference to the principles involved.[1]

The value in year zero of a dollar received in a later year is called the *present value* of the dollar. Using this notion of present value we may aggregate the streams of money benefits (B_t) and costs (C_t) occurring in various years according to the common measuring rod of current dollars. The present value of a project which is to last for T years is:[2]

$$V = \sum_{t=0}^{T} \frac{B_t - C_t}{(1 + r)^t}. \tag{8-1}$$

We have so far taken r to be the market interest rate. As we shall see in Section 8–4, the social discount rate to be used on public projects may differ from the market interest rate. That does not affect the discussion of this section.

The present value of a project is an appropriate yardstick with which to judge its desirability assuming that all benefits and costs are captured in B_t and C_t. It measures the aggregate value in terms of current consumption of all the changes in resource allocation induced by a project, both now and in the future. If $V < 0$ the project ought to be rejected since it would reduce economic welfare. On the other hand, if $V > 0$ the project would increase society's welfare and so might profitably be undertaken. One has to be somewhat careful in the use of the present value criterion, for there often are alternatives to the project under consideration which could yield a higher present value. For one thing, there may be a choice regarding the scale of the project, in which case that scale which maximizes the present value ought to be chosen. Or, there may be some choice as to when the project should be introduced. This may be important when the number of users is expected to grow over time. The project should begin at the time which maximizes the present value. Finally, alternative and mutually exclusive projects may be available, and the one with the largest present value should be chosen.

While, in principle, the present value of a project is the correct measure of the project's net contribution to social welfare, other criteria are often used for assessing the viability of a project. Two common ones are the *internal rate of return* and the *benefit-cost ratio*. These frequently-used measures will, in most circumstances, indicate accurately whether or not a project would make a net positive contribution to social welfare. Unfortunately, they often give incorrect rankings of various projects, each of which yields positive net benefits to society. Since they are often used, it is worth explaining in more detail the merits and disadvantages of each.

The internal rate of return (*IRR*) of a project is defined as the discount rate which makes the present value of a project zero. Denoting the *IRR* by λ, it will be defined by:

$$0 = \sum_{t=0}^{T} \frac{(B_t - C_t)}{(1 + \lambda)^t}. \tag{8-2}$$

Equation (8–2) can be solved for λ but immediately a problem arises. Since Eq. (8–2) is a polynomial of the Tth degree, λ may have as many as T solutions.[3] In fact, the number of solutions it has will depend upon the number of times $B_t - C_t$ changes sign over time.[4] In practice, this is probably not a great problem since, in most cases, projects incur net costs in early years ($B_t - C_t < 0$) and net benefits in later years ($B_t - C_t > 0$). In this case, the sign changes only once and the *IRR* is uniquely determined. If the *IRR*, or λ, exceeds the social discount rate r, this implies that the project has a positive present value ($V > 0$) at the discount rate r, and vice versa. The *IRR* criterion thus consists in comparing λ with the social discount rate r and, provided λ is unique, this will indicate whether or not a project increases social welfare. Of course, if r varies from period to period, the *IRR* criterion may no longer be useful. For example if r_t sometimes exceeds λ and λ sometimes exceeds r_t, then one cannot say from a comparison of λ and r_t whether or not $V > 0$ for the project.

The benefit-cost ratio (B/C) always indicates clearly whether or not social welfare is improved by undertaking the project. It is defined as the present value of the stream of benefits divided by the present value of the stream of costs, or:

$$\frac{B}{C} = \frac{\sum_{t=0}^{T} B_t/(1 + r)^t}{\sum_{t=0}^{T} C_t/(1 + r)^t}. \tag{8–3}$$

It is obvious that B/C will be greater than (or less than) unity as V is greater than (or less than) zero. V is the difference between the present values of benefits and costs while B/C is their ratio.

While both *IRR* and B/C can normally be relied upon to indicate whether or not a project will increase or decrease social welfare (i.e. have benefits in excess of costs), they may rank alternative (mutually exclusive) projects incorrectly in terms of their contributions to economic welfare. They cannot therefore be relied upon as criteria for choosing the project which *maximizes* the contribution to social welfare. In the case of B/C this is due to the fact that the scale of the project is not explicitly considered. To take a simple example, suppose the present values of benefits and costs of project A are \$200 and \$100, while those of project B are \$170 and \$80. The B/C criterion would rank B ahead of $A(\frac{17}{8} > 2)$ whereas the contribution of A exceeds that of B as reflected in the present values (\$200 − 100 > \$170 − 80).

The inconsistencies inherent in the *IRR* criterion are best illustrated with the help of a specific example. To avoid problems of scale, we take two projects with the same initial costs incurred in period zero. Table 8–1 depicts two projects, A and B, each costing \$1000 and yielding a different stream of benefits. The *IRR* is calculated for each, as are the present values (PV) at different discount rates. Figure 8–1 shows the present values of each project at various discount rates. The *IRR* is the value of r at which

Table 8–1

Project	Net Benefits in Year ($)			IRR	Present Value at ($)		
	0	*1*	*2*		*2%*	*5.2%*	*7%*
A	−1000	0	1210	0.10	163	93	57
B	−1000	1150	0	0.15	127	93	75

the present value curve intersects the horizontal axis. The *IRR* criterion ranks project *B* above project *A* (0.15 > 0.10). However, the relative present values of *A* and *B* depend critically upon what discount rate is used. At the low discount rate of 2%, *A* has a higher present value than does *B* but as *r* rises *B* eventually comes to be preferred to *A*. This occurs because of the time profile of the benefits in the two projects. The benefits of project *A* come later than those of project *B*. As the discount rate rises, later benefits are weighted much less than earlier benefits, and, consequently, project *A* fares less well compared with *B*.[5]

The source of the problem with the IRR rule can be detected by means of the following calculation: Consider the case in Table 8–1, in which the discount rate is 2%. This is the rate at which present consumption can be

Figure 8–1

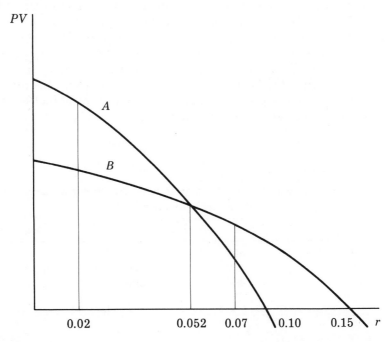

transformed into future consumption and vice versa on capital markets. It is easy to show that if we combine a capital market transaction with the stream of net benefits on project A, we can obtain a stream of benefits which dominates that obtained in project B. For example, if we borrow $1150 in year one for consumption, a total of $1150 (1.02) or $1173 will have to be repaid in period two, leaving $37 for consumption. Therefore, a net consumption stream of $(-1000, 1150, 37)$ can be generated by combining this borrowing transaction with the net benefit stream of project A. As can be seen, this stream dominates that of project B. In general, it will always follow that one can use capital market transactions to convert the net benefits of one project into some other net benefit stream which dominates the net benefit stream of another project with a lower PV. In other words, the present value criterion implicitly takes into account the costs of financing, whereas the IRR rule does not.

Since neither IRR nor B/C rules can adequately choose between two exclusive projects, they cannot be used to determine either the scale of a project or the optimal timing. The ability to vary either the scale or the timing of a project, or both, can be treated as special cases of comparing mutually exclusive projects.

There is one set of circumstances in which one must exercise some caution in the use of the present value criterion. That is when the project evaluator is faced with a fixed capital budget that cannot be exceeded, and when there are several alternative combinations of projects from which to choose. Once again a numerical example serves to illustrate the problem. Suppose the capital budget equals $1000 and there is a choice among the four projects A, B, C, and D shown in Table 8–2. The rankings of the projects in terms of present value at a five percent discount rate are A, C, B, and D. However, should A be undertaken, funds would not be available for either B or C because of the limited size of the capital budget. Funds would permit B and C to be undertaken. Since the combined present value of B and C exceeds that of A and D, the former ought to be undertaken rather than the latter. As this example illustrates, the relevant comparison is between the present values of alternative combinations of projects when capital budget constraints exist.

Table 8–2

Project	Net Benefits in Year ($)		Present Value at r = 5% ($)
	0	1	
A	−800	950	105
B	−500	600	71
C	−400	500	76
D	−200	240	28

EVALUATING INPUTS AND OUTPUTS

8–3   The major problems in cost-benefit analysis involve measuring in monetary terms the benefits (B_t) and costs (C_t) in each period, and in choosing the correct discount rate, r, at which to aggregate the time stream of benefits and costs. This section will discuss the problems involved in evaluating inputs and outputs as they occur, and Section 8–4 will consider the choice of an appropriate social discount rate. There are three broad categories of cases to consider here: the shadow pricing of inputs and outputs whose prices do not accurately reflect marginal social values, the evaluation of intangibles, and the measurement of indirect effects. These are considered in turn below.

Even when prices do reflect marginal social values, they will be insufficient for evaluating benefits and costs if the project itself is large enough to influence input and output prices. In this case infra-marginal values must be estimated, since market prices will only measure the value of the last unit. In the case of project outputs, the appropriate area beneath the demand curve must be estimated. In Fig. 8–2, if the project output is X_1X_2, or ΔX, so that as the price of X is reduced by Δp from p_1 to p_2, the appropriate total benefit of the output is the area X_1abX_2. If the demand

Figure 8–2

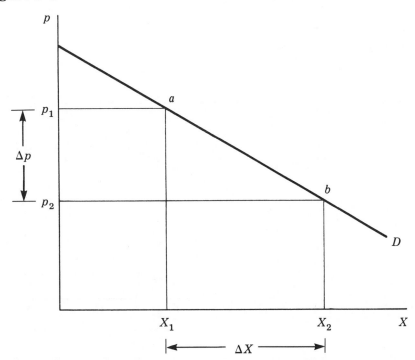

curve is assumed to be linear, the area X_1abX_2 is equal to $\frac{1}{2}(\Delta X) \cdot (p_1 + p_2) = (\Delta X) \cdot \bar{p}$ where $\bar{p}$ is the average of the before and after project prices. Alternatively, if the elasticity of demand is assumed to be constant, the area X_1abX_2 can be approximated by $\eta \bar{X} \Delta p$, where η is the elasticity of demand evaluated at $\bar{X}$, the midpoint between X_1 and X_2. This follows directly from the definition of the elasticity of demand, $\eta = (\Delta X \bar{p})/(\Delta p \bar{X})$.

In a similar way, if the project forces the price of an input Y up, the opportunity cost of the project's input use must be calculated as the area beneath the marginal cost curve of Y. In Fig. 8–3, a project using $Y_1Y_2 = \Delta Y$ units of input Y will cause its price to rise by Δw from w_1 to w_2. The opportunity cost will be the area Y_1cdY_2, or approximately $\bar{w}\Delta Y$ where $\bar{w}$ is the average input price $[=(w_1 + w_2)/2]$. If the marginal cost curve is assumed to have a constant elasticity ε, the area could be approximated by $\varepsilon \bar{Y} \Delta w$, since ε is defined to be $(\bar{w}\Delta Y)/(\bar{y}\Delta w)$.

Two other general problems might be cleared up before moving on to evaluation problems. The first is that, in a period of inflation, there will be a difference between current and real prices on the one hand, and the nominal and real discount rate on the other. If the annual rate of inflation is π, assumed to be constant for simplicity, then the relation between nominal and real prices is given by

$$p_t = (1 + \pi)^t p_0 \qquad\qquad (8\text{–}4)$$

Figure 8–3

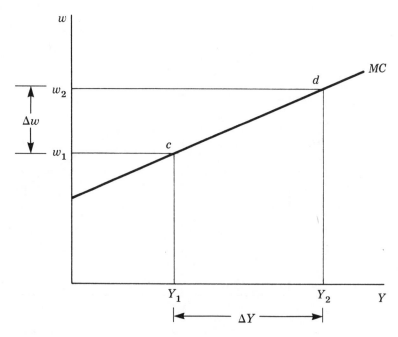

where p_t is the current price in year t and p_0 is the real price using year zero as a base year. At the same time, as shown by Fisher (1930), the relation between the real and nominal discount rates is given by:

$$(1 + i) = (1 + r)(1 + \pi) \tag{8-5}$$

where i is the nominal discount rate, and r is the real discount rate. In performing the cost-benefit analysis one may either use current values and discount by the nominal discount rate, or use real values and discount by the real discount rate. The equivalence between the two is apparent from the following present value formulations:

$$V = \sum_{t=0}^{T} \frac{p_t X_t - w_t Y_t}{[(1 + r)(1 + \pi)]^t} = \sum_{t=0}^{T} \frac{p_0 X_t - w_0 Y_t}{(1 + r)^t} \tag{8-6}$$

where p_t is the current price of benefits or outputs X_t, w_t is the current price of costs or inputs Y_t, and p_0 and w_0 are the real values related to the money values by Eq. (8–4).

The other item of general interest has to do with the treatment of scrap values, and depreciation and interest charges. Frequently, the time span of a project evaluation may be less than the life of the project itself if, for example, one cannot see far enough into the future. If the useful life of the capital installed (or replaced) in the project exceeds the time span of the project evaluation, it is appropriate to include the value of the capital existing at the end of the period as a benefit in year T. This terminal value of capital, called the *scrap value*, theoretically ought to be the present value of the flow of net benefits from the capital after the year T. Scrap value will typically be very difficult to measure since the project life T is usually the furthest in the future that one can foresee with accuracy.

As far as accounting for depreciation and interest charges are concerned, one must beware of double counting. Whether or not depreciation and interest are treated as costs depends upon the method of accounting for capital costs that is used. Two methods are possible in principle. The first, based on the concept of *user costs*, treats as a cost of capital only the current imputed costs associated with using the services of the capital in each period. According to this method, the initial purchase of capital would not be deducted as a cost; instead, the subsequent flow of depreciation and imputed interest ought to be included. The appropriate depreciation to include is the amount by which the value of the capital has declined over the period due to wear and tear, obsolescence and capital loss. The imputed interest charge should be the opportunity cost as expressed in terms of foregone interest on the value of the capital held which otherwise could have earned interest elsewhere in the economy. In practice, however, the appropriate depreciation and interest charges are difficult to measure. Fortunately, an alternative is available, and that is to treat as costs only the initial expenditure on capital. This is referred to as *cash flow*. In principle, the two methods are equivalent, since the initial expenditures on capital should equal the present value of the future stream of depreciation and foregone interest. But since cash flow is readily measurable, it is easier to use in practice. One must, however, be careful to ensure that if capital expenditures are costed on a cash flow basis, *no* deductions may be made for depreciation or interest on the same capital.

We now turn to the specific problems of evaluating inputs and outputs as they occur.

(a) Shadow Pricing

The need for shadow pricing arises when market prices do not reflect social values. A simple example of this occurs when a project uses an input purchased on a distorted market where the distortion takes the form of a divergence between the demand price and the marginal cost. We analyze that case in detail as an example of the principles involved. The analysis is based on Harberger (1969).

Figure 8–4 illustrates the competitive market for an input, X, where the distortion between the demand price and the marginal cost or supply price takes the form of an *ad valorem* tax at the rate t, that is, a tax levied as a proportion of the price of the commodity. The demand curve labeled $D[p(1 + t)]$ depicts the quantity that would be demanded by nonproject users at each demand or gross price $p(1 + t)$. The supply curve $S(p)$ shows how much X would be supplied at various supply or net prices p. It is transformed into the supply curve $S[p(1 + t)]$ by adding the tax payments vertically at each price. This curve then shows the quantities of X that would be supplied at various gross prices $p(1 + t)$, of which the suppliers only receive p. The market equilibrium before the project is undertaken is given by the quantity X_1, the supply price is p_1, and the demand price is $p_1(1 + t)$. The reason for carefully distinguishing between the demand and supply prices is that they both measure marginal values. The demand price $p_1(1 + t)$ measures the value of the last unit of X purchased by demanders, while the supply price, p_1, is the marginal cost of the last unit of X supplied assuming a competitive industry.

Suppose now a project is undertaken which demands an amount ΔG of X, causing the demand curve to shift to $D + \Delta G$ as shown. At the new market-clearing equilibrium, X_s will be supplied at the new (higher) supply price, p_2, and X_D will be demanded at the demand price $p_2(1 + t)$. The required amount ΔG for the project comes from two sources: Supply is increased by an amount X_1X_S or ΔX_S, and demand is reduced by X_DX_1 or ΔX_D. The opportunity cost of the ΔG purchased for the project consists of the costs of supplying the additional ΔX_S, which is the area X_1cdX_S in Fig. 8–4, and the reduction in benefits to demanders from their reduction in use ΔX_D, which is X_DabX_1. If the project is small enough so that the price

Figure 8–4

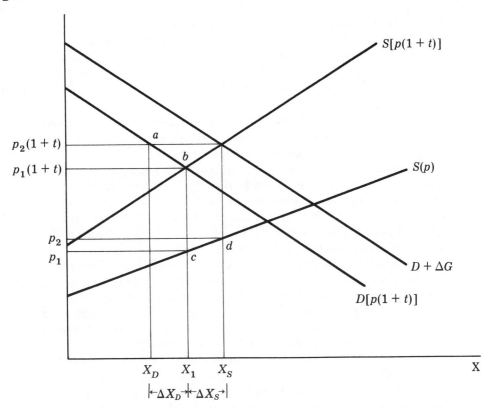

changes are relatively small, the opportunity cost to society of the additional ΔG can be approximated by:

$$\text{Opportunity cost of } \Delta G = p_1 \Delta X_S - p_1(1 + t)\Delta X_D \tag{8–7}$$

where the two terms on the right-hand side of Eq. (8–7) are approximately the areas $X_1 c d X_S$ and $X_D a b X_1$. The shadow price of X to the project, p_G, is defined as the opportunity cost per unit of G. Dividing (8–7) through by ΔG we obtain:

$$p_G = p_1 \frac{\Delta X_S}{\Delta G} - p_1(1 + t) \frac{\Delta X_D}{\Delta G}. \tag{8–8}$$

Since $\Delta X_S + \Delta X_D = \Delta G$, the shadow price p_G is a weighted average of the supply and demand prices, the weights being the proportions of the ΔG which come at the expense of increased supply and reduced demand respectively.[6] We observe that if the supply is completely inelastic or demand is infinitely elastic, $\Delta X_D/\Delta G = 1$ and $p_G = p_1(1 + t)$. Conversely, if supply is perfectly elastic or demand is inelastic, $\Delta X_S/\Delta G = 1$ and $p_G = p_1$. These shadow prices are used to evaluate the inputs used in the project. The costs of the inputs ΔG are entered in the cost-benefit analysis as $p_G \Delta G$.

The principles in the foregoing analysis can be applied to any situation in which demand and supply prices are distorted, whether due to monopoly, quotas, or any other cause. We shall consider three important applications of shadow pricing often encountered: those to labor, foreign exchange, and public funds.

(i) *Shadow Price of Labor*   Labor markets are sometimes characterized by distortions between demand and supply prices, or wage rates. For example, the existence of involuntary unemployment will drive a wedge between the demand price (the wage rate paid) and the supply price (the least wage that unemployed workers would willingly work for). Or, especially in less-developed countries, the wage rate paid for urban work may exceed the wage rate received by rural workers who migrate to the cities in search of employment. The presence of these distortions implies the need to determine an appropriate shadow wage rate for project evaluation.

Additional labor demanded by a project might come from three sources: workers previously employed elsewhere at the market wage, workers involuntarily unemployed, and workers voluntarily unemployed. The shadow wage rate ought to be a weighted average of the wage rates attributable to these three sources, the weights being the proportions of labor drawn from each source. In the case of workers employed elsewhere, the wage rate reflecting the opportunity cost of their foregone use is the wage rate gross-of-tax paid there. For workers voluntarily unemployed, it is the wage rate net-of-tax, since this reflects the amount of money they must be paid in order to induce them (i.e. the marginal workers) to enter the labor force. The appropriate supply price to attach to labor involuntarily unemployed is problematic, since there is no market price which reveals the minimum amount they would be willing to accept in order to work, or, in other words, to forego leisure. It is less than the net-of-tax wage since, by virtue of their being involuntarily unemployed, they would certainly be willing to work for that amount. On the other hand, it is likely to be above zero, since the workers presumably attach some positive value to their leisure time.[7] In the absence of further information it is not possible to know the supply price of involuntarily unemployed labor. In practice, some arbitrary number may have to be chosen above zero (or the level of transfer payments received) but below the net-of-tax wage rate; several alternative numbers could also be tried to test the sensitivity of the results to that chosen. In any case, the overall shadow price of labor will generally not be the price that the project actually pays for it, and, therefore, the measure of costs in the cost-benefit analysis will differ from financial costs actually incurred.

The issue of the appropriate shadow wage rate has been prominent in the literature on project evaluation in developing countries because of the significance of unemployment and the special structural features of labor markets in these countries (see, for example, Little and Mirrlees [1968], Dasgupta, Marglin and Sen [1972], Sen [1972], and Harberger [1971b]). Labor markets are said to be *dualistic* or *segmented*, consisting of a rural agricultural sector with low wages, and an urban industrial sector with much higher wages as well as significant unemployment. Projects undertaken in the urban sector are assumed to draw their workers from the rural area, where their productive output is viewed as being quite low, possibly even zero. One tradition in the literature obtains a shadow wage rate by assuming that a new job created would be filled by a migrant worker whose opportunity cost is the rural wage (e.g., Little and Mirrlees [1968]). The result is a shadow wage rate significantly lower than the urban market wage that has to be paid, and thus a significant incentive to create jobs.

The other tradition, associated with Harberger (1971b) and Harris and Todaro (1970), argues that the migration mechanism implicit in the previous view is unrealistic. In particular, the assumption that the creation of one job in the urban sector would induce one migrant to move from the urban sector cannot be rationalized by viewing labor migration as a proper equilibrating device in an economy with wage differentials and unemployment in the urban sector. Instead, these writers develop a model which would generate *as an equilibrium outcome* the sort of wage differentials and urban unemployment observed in many developing countries. The basic idea behind their model is as follows: Workers are assumed to locate where they can earn the highest expected income. In the rural area where there is full employment, the expected income is simply m, the wage rate there. In the urban area, the expected income is πw where π is the probability of obtaining a job, and w is the urban wage. It is assumed that all jobs are allocated randomly so that π equals the ratio of jobs to urban labor force. At equilibrium, expected incomes are the same in the two regions, or $m = \pi w$. Now, suppose a job is created in the urban sector, to be filled randomly as before. If w and m are given, migration equilibrium requires that the probability of obtaining a job be restored to its original value π when this job is created. In order to do this, $1/\pi$ workers (>1) will migrate from the rural to the urban sector. The opportunity cost of filling the urban job is then the foregone rural output of the migrant workers, or m/π. Since this exactly equals w by the migration equilibrium condition, the shadow wage is equal to the market wage and no adjustment is called for.

The contrast in results in these two cases illustrates the importance of the specification used to explain the existence of wage differentials for computing the shadow wage.

(ii) *The Shadow Price of Foreign Exchange* Many projects use tradable goods as inputs, or produce tradable goods for sale, that is, goods which are either importable or exportable on world markets. In either case, the impact of the project's net use of traded goods is on the market for foreign exchange. Since the foreign exchange market may be distorted due to the existence of tariffs, quotas, or other sorts of controls, the price of foreign exchange or the exchange rate may be distorted. Therefore, project evaluators often construct a shadow price of foreign exchange to measure the opportunity cost of the net foreign exchange requirements of a project.[8]

The simplest case to consider is that in which the world price of exports and imports is fixed on world markets from the point of view of the country under consideration, and there is a common rate of tariff distortion on all import purchases. Then all imports can be treated as a composite commodity subject to a single tariff rate, and the same for exports which have no distortion. Both can be denominated in units of foreign exchange. If the foreign currency under consideration is pounds, then we can think of one pound of foreign exchange as representing one pound of the composite commodity "imports" at world prices. The domestic price of this quantity of imports will be $e(1+t)$ dollars where e is the domestic price of foreign exchange and t is the tariff rate. In terms of Fig. 8–4, the import demand curve for foreign exchange required to purchase the imports is a function of the tariff-inclusive price for foreign exchange $e(1+t)$. This curve is downward sloping, because as the exchange rate e or the tariff rate t rise, imports will be more expensive to domestic residents so less will be purchased. Therefore, the demand for foreign exchange (e.g. pounds) will be less. The supply of foreign exchange would be generated by sales of exports. The export supply curve will give the supply of exports as a function of the existing exchange rate e. Given the world price of exports, the higher the price of foreign exchange e, the higher the price in domestic currency received from the sale of exports, and the more goods produced for export. Therefore, the supply curve of foreign exchange arising from the sale of exports will be upward-sloping just like the supply curve of Fig. 8–4.[9]

Using the same reasoning as above, the shadow price of foreign exchange, p_f, may be written:

$$p_f = e\,\frac{\Delta E}{\Delta G} - e(1+t)\,\frac{\Delta M}{\Delta G} \tag{8–9}$$

where ΔG is the net demand for foreign exchange by the project, ΔE is the change in exports, and ΔM is the change in imports. The amount ΔG will include the foreign exchange used by the project as a whole, that is, the sum of the value of tradables produced less the value of tradables used. This shadow price is a weighted average of the demand and supply prices of foreign exchange, the weights being the proportions of the project's foreign exchange requirements that come at the expense of increased exports and those coming from reduced imports. This, of course, assumes that the exchange rate e is variable according to the demand and supply equilibration for foreign exchange. If the exchange rate is not variable, the freeing of foreign exchange for the project must come from the imposition of additional controls on foreign trade, and the opportunity cost of these controls (e.g. tariffs or quotas) must be treated as part of the cost of obtaining foreign exchange.

The above analysis may be easily extended to the case in which there are many exports and imports, each with a different distortion. For example, if there are n imports denoted $M_i (i = 1, \ldots, n)$, and each has a tariff rate t_i, then the shadow price of foreign exchange becomes:

$$p_f = e \frac{\Delta E}{\Delta G} - \sum_{i=1}^{n} e(1 + t_i) \frac{\Delta M_i}{\Delta G}. \tag{8-10}$$

The principle involved in the computation of the shadow price of foreign exchange is the conversion of foreign exchange into its equivalent domestic monetary value. If countries have tariff distortions, their exchange rates will be overvalued (i.e. e will be lower than it would be in the absence of the tariff). The shadow price of foreign exchange p_f will then typically be greater than e, the actual price of foreign exchange. The value of traded goods will be increased relative to nontraded goods, providing projects with an incentive to produce traded goods and to economize on the use of traded inputs. An alternative way to proceed, one which has similar effects on the relative valuations of traded and nontraded goods, has been advocated by Little and Mirrlees (1968). Instead of converting foreign exchange into domestic values, they suggest evaluating a project entirely in terms of its net foreign exchange contribution. Traded goods are valued at their foreign exchange or world prices exclusive of any tariff revenues. Nontraded goods (and factors) are converted into their *foreign exchange equivalent* by calculating the amount of foreign exchange that is provided or used up indirectly via the general equilibrium interaction of the system. For example, a project may utilize electricity, which is a nontraded good. However, the production of electricity indirectly uses some traded inputs in its production as well as some nontraded ones. In turn, these nontraded inputs will use other traded and nontraded inputs. The ultimate use of foreign exchange is determined by tracing back through the earlier stages of production all the foreign exchange that is indirectly used up in producing the nontraded good, in this case electricity. Special problems arise in the computation of the foreign exchange equivalent of primary or unproduced factors, such as labor. One must compute the foreign exchange foregone in using labor on a project which would otherwise be used elsewhere to produce, directly or indirectly, tradable goods.

(iii) *The Social Opportunity Cost of Public Funds*   Public projects are frequently not self-financing, either because the benefits are not all captured in revenues, or because the project exhibits economies of scale. In this case, funds are raised to cover the costs of the project either through taxation or through issuing of bonds. A cost-benefit analysis must consider not only the shadow pricing of all inputs and outputs, but must also include any additional opportunity costs, or deadweight losses, incurred as a result of the need to meet financial losses through the provision of public funds. An important source of distortion influencing the opportunity cost of public funds is that arising in capital markets. The financing of a public project may use funds that otherwise would have been used for private investment. The opportunity cost of the foregone private investment is the present value of the stream of consumption that the investment would have yielded in the private sector. The excess of this present value over and above the value of funds transferred represents a deadweight loss which should be treated as a cost of the project.

Consider the following model, attributable originally to Marglin (1963b). A project is to be undertaken which requires a sum of capital initially, and incurs benefits at later dates. The financing of the capital expenditures will divert resources from the private sector. Let θ be the proportion of the resources that would have been invested and $(1 - \theta)$ that which would have been consumed. In general, θ will depend upon the method of financing (e.g. taxes, bond issues, etc.). If the project is financed with bonds, some of the bond financing comes from increased savings and some from reduced investment elsewhere, presumably in the private sector. One might expect the proportion θ to differ if the project had been tax-financed. The opportunity cost of the proportion that comes from increased savings is exactly the current consumption foregone. A dollar's worth of foregone consumption is currently valued at one dollar. The opportunity cost of the funds diverted from investment elsewhere is less straightforward. Suppose the gross rate of return to private investment is ρ at the margin. One might expect ρ, the *IRR* of the marginal private investment, to exceed r, the social discount rate, because of the existence of corporate income taxes and personal taxes on capital income (dividends, capital gains, and interest). A dollar's worth of investment yields a perpetual stream of output of ρ each year. If that stream is consumed as it is earned, the present value of the stream of consumption generated is ρ/r.[10] Therefore, the opportunity cost of each dollar of capital expenditures on the project, denoted a, is:[11]

$$a = (1 - \theta) + \frac{\theta\rho}{r}. \tag{8-11}$$

In this case, $a > 1$, so capital financing has a shadow price in excess of its actual dollar amount.

In practice, many other complications may arise which require Eq. (8–11) to be amended. For example, the annual returns to private sector investment ρ might be reinvested, in which case the second term should include the larger stream of consumption generated by the part of ρ reinvested. On the other hand, the returns to the public projects themselves may be partly reinvested. This additional stream of benefits would tend to reduce the opportunity cost of capital financing. These complications are taken up in Marglin (1963b) and Bradford (1975).

In conducting the cost-benefit analysis, one must attribute as a cost of the project the additional opportunity costs of the funds required over and above those required to purchase inputs. That is, if a project uses K dollars worth of capital inputs and finances it entirely out of public funds, the project should be charged with a cost of aK dollars where a comes from Eq. (8–11). Of course, if the physical capital inputs themselves come from distorted markets, that distortion must itself also be taken into consideration by a shadow price calculated from the analog to Eq. (8–8) above. A general rule for evaluating projects when some of the revenue comes from public funds was developed by Feldstein (1972a). Suppose B_t and C_t are the benefits and costs of a project evaluated using the appropriate shadow prices, and D_t is the project's deficit in year t. Then, if r is the social discount rate as above, the present value of the project is:

$$V = \sum_{t=0}^{T} \frac{B_t - C_t - (a - 1)D_t}{(1 + r)^t}.$$
(8–12)

Here a is the opportunity cost of public funds used in the project, D_t, and $(a - 1)D_t$, is the additional opportunity cost incurred in the financing of the losses of the project over and above that incurred by a nondistortionary transfer of funds. The latter real resource transfer, D_t, is already included in the cost terms C_t. The value of D_t may vary from period to period. When revenues exceed costs it would be negative, and the contribution of the project to public funds would reduce the welfare loss by $-(a - 1)D_t$. In addition, there is no reason why a should not vary from period to period.

An alternative way to incorporate capital market distortions in cost-benefit analysis has been advocated by Harberger (1969). He argues that the funds used to finance the project must give a rate of return on the project of at least what they would have earned in the private sector. This rate of return is a weighted average of the rates of return to private investment and private savings weighted by the proportions in which the funds are drawn from foregone investment and foregone consumption in the private sector. If the funds used on a project do not yield at least this rate of return, the project should not be undertaken. In other words, the present value of the project can be written:

$$V = \sum \frac{B_t - C_t}{(1 + r_w)^t}$$

where

$$r_w = \theta\rho + (1 - \theta)r.$$

Feldstein (1972a) has argued that, in general, the use of a weighted average discount rate in the present value formula for a project is inappropriate. This is most obvious for the case of self-financing projects which require no public funds. The appropriate rate at which to discount the future stream of net benefits is the social time preference rate.

(b) The Evaluation of Intangibles

Very often projects of the public sector incur costs or provide benefits of an intangible or nonmonetary nature, such as the saving of time or life, or the emitting of pollution. The task of the project evaluator is to attempt to attach a monetary value to such costs or benefits. The underlying principles to be followed in establishing monetary values for intangibles are identical to those for items bought and sold in open markets: The total benefit of an intangible is the maximum amount of money that users would pay in order to have its services, and the total cost of an intangible is the minimum amount that would be accepted by the bearers of the cost in order to agree willingly to bear it. With marketed inputs and outputs, prices (or the appropriate areas beneath demand and supply curves) serve as indicators of money values. With intangibles, money values must be inferred from some source other than market data, often indirectly from market behavior elsewhere. As an example of how monetary values can, in principle, be attached to intangibles, we consider two examples that are often encountered in actual cost-benefit analyses of transportation and health expenditures: the value of time saved and the value of lives saved or disease prevented.

(i) *The Value of Time Saved*   Transportation projects will typically have as one of the largest benefits the saving of travel time. The principle to be followed is to evaluate the saving of travel time as the amount of money that the beneficiaries of the saving would be willing to pay in order to obtain the saving. Time-saving is valuable since it frees time for engaging in other activities. In evaluating time saved traveling, it is important to specify the alternative use to which the time might be put. Broadly speaking, time saved traveling may be devoted either to work activities or leisure activities. The values of these alternative uses of time will be discussed in turn. A more complete discussion may be found in Harrison and Quarmby (1972).

In a competitive economy in which firms are able to make productive use of the time freed from traveling, the value of time saved is the value of the increase in output that the time saving makes available, or in the wage rate. The appropriate wage to use is the gross-of-tax wage rate since, in a competitive economy, that is the value of the marginal product of labor. A number of imperfections may occur that prevent the firm from fully exploiting the time saved by its workers. The indivisibilities attached to a person's work may prevent a few minutes saved from being put to productive use. The time saved then goes to leisure, and must be evaluated as such. Also, employees may not be indifferent between time put in traveling for an employer and time put in doing other work. In this case, one should in theory impute a money value to the change in utility (although this may be ultimately reflected in a change in the wage rate). In practice, because of the obvious difficulties of measurement, this is often ignored, and the wage rate is taken to be the value of working time saved.

Some of the time saved traveling may be devoted to increased leisure time. For example, time saved commuting may be entirely used up at home, rather than in increased working time. To an individual, the value of substituting leisure time for commuting time is problematic, since that value is not directly reflected in market prices. The wage rate does not accurately reflect the value of leisure time for the following reason: Consider an individual allocating his time between leisure and work so that, at the margin, he is indifferent between taking more leisure or taking more work. The benefit of taking more leisure just equals the opportunity cost, which consists of two items: the foregone wage payments (which yield consumption benefits) and the foregone benefits of working (which is presumably negative). Algebraically:

$$MB_L = w + MB_w \tag{8--13}$$

where MB_L is the marginal benefit of leisure time, w is the wage rate, and MB_w is the marginal benefit of work. Since MB_w is negative, we would expect the marginal benefit of leisure time to be less than the wage rate w.

Equation (8--13) does not exactly capture the opportunity cost of savings in commuting time, since there is presumably some utility or disutility attached to commuting time. If the individual were free to vary his commuting time, he would presumably reduce it to zero. Unfortunately, this is not possible, and the individual must take a fixed amount of commuting time. The benefit of the reduction in that fixed amount of commuting time equals the benefit of the increased leisure time less the benefit of the commuting time foregone (which is likely negative). Therefore, using Eq. (8--13) we obtain:

$$V_C = MB_L - MB_C$$

$$= w + MB_w - MB_C \tag{8--14}$$

where V_C is the value of a reduction in commuting time and MB_C is the marginal benefit from time spent commuting. Since both MB_w and MB_C are negative, if the marginal disutility from work exceeds the marginal disutility from commuting (so $MB_w < MB_C$), then V_C will be less than w as before. However, to repeat, there is no market price that we may use to infer directly the value of commuting time saved, V_C.

Several attempts have been made to estimate V_C using indirect means. (See the detailed discussion in Layard [1972].) For example, suppose that there are two alternative methods of traveling to work which differ in the travel time involved, and in the money or resource costs to the commuter. If the money costs of the two alternative ways of commuting are competitively determined, one can, in principle, obtain the opportunity cost of travel time to the marginal commuter by observing the differences in money costs that are required to offset the time costs between the two modes of transport.

The problem is to find two modes of travel which are close enough alternatives so as to be able to give reliable estimates of the value of time. There will generally be other differences in travel modes than time spent travelling (e.g. comfort), and statistical analysis will have to be used to sort out their contribution to the choice of mode as well. The usual method is to run a regression relating the proportion of trips taken by one of the modes to differences in time cost, differences in money cost, and any other differences deemed appropriate. The coefficient on time cost differences is taken to be the value of time. Estimates of this sort have tended to yield values of V_C which are about one-quarter of the gross wage rate.

The value of time is typically a significant and even determining factor in transportation projects. This was illustrated in one of the most celebrated cost-benefit analyses ever done for a transport project, that of the Victoria Underground Line in London, England, by Foster and Beesley (1963). In attributing the value of time saved to a project, such as a subway, it is usual to distinguish three sorts of beneficiaries: traffic diverted to the project, generated traffic, and undiverted traffic. Diverted traffic represents users who switch from other means of transport to the subway without changing the number of trips taken. Generated traffic represents the increase in trips taken on the subway. Time will also be saved by nondiverted traffic due to reduced congestion. Let us consider the evaluation of each of these in turn.

The general method of measuring the direct benefits to diverted and generated traffic can be illustrated with the aid of Fig. 8–5. The curve D_1 represents the demand curve for a particular type of trip on the existing means of transport before the subway was built. The fare per trip is p_1 and the number of trips taken by the previous means of transport is X_1. When the subway is constructed, the demand curve for trips will shift upward to D_2. People will be willing to pay a greater amount per trip due to the time-saving. The vertical shift in the demand curve represents the amount of money they are willing to pay for time-saving. Suppose now that the fare is reduced to p_2. The number of trips will increase to X_2. In fact, even if fares did not decrease, the number of trips would rise. Let us suppose that all persons who previously took the trip now switch to the new line. We may call the trips OX_1 diverted traffic, and the trips X_1X_2 generated traffic.

The total benefit to diverted traffic is the area *efbd*. It is estimated by the following:

Benefit to diverted traffic = $OX_1 \cdot$ (value of time saved per trip).

To estimate this we need to know the actual time saved per trip as well as the dollar value of each unit of time saved.

The benefit to generated traffic is the area X_1bcX_2. Equivalently, this may be written as $\frac{1}{2}(p_1 + db + p_2)(X_1X_2)$. The distance db is the time saved per trip as before. Provided an estimate can be made of the increase in the number of trips, the total benefit can be estimated.

Figure 8–5

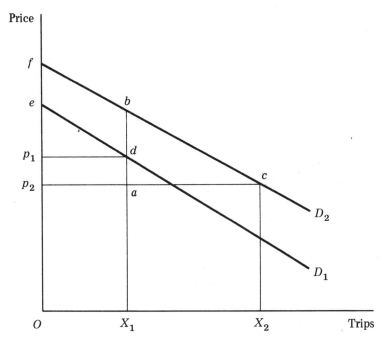

In addition to the above benefits, there will be a resource saving accruing to diverted traffic because of a reduction in trips taken by other means, for example, those who previously drove automobiles save the operating costs of driving. These must be treated as benefits to the project.

For traffic not diverted to the subway, the same sorts of benefits will accrue. Time-savings will occur because of the reduced congestion on alternative means of transport. Also, some savings may accrue in operating costs of traffic not diverted, especially road traffic users' costs.

In order to estimate all the above benefits, the project evaluators must estimate the change in traffic patterns among existing users, the amount of newly generated traffic, the time-savings that would accrue to all existing and potential users, and the savings in resource costs from the diversion of traffic. In addition, in order to attach a monetary value to it, the reckoning of the time saved must distinguish between working time saved and non-working time saved.

(ii) *The Value of Lives Saved or Disease Prevented*   Many projects will directly cause a loss or a saving of lives, or changes in the health of individuals. The most obvious cases are health expenditure programs (such as immunizations, or research and development). However, transportation projects also have an influence on lives or health through accidents. The principles involved in evaluating the savings of life or the reduction of disease are basically the same, so we may confine our analysis to the former.

The measurement of the benefit to society from saving lives is conceptually no different from the measurement of any other benefit. It is the maximum amount that would be paid by the members of society to secure the reduction in lives lost. Conversely, the cost to society of a project that increases the number of lives lost is the minimum amount that would be accepted by those affected.[12] There are a number of different ways in which society benefits from a reduction in lives lost (or incurs costs from an increase in lives lost). Consider a project which has as one of its benefits a reduction in fatalities. Following Jones-Lee (1976), we can distinguish four types of benefits to society:

(a) The resource savings brought about by a reduction in physical damage. This would include such things as damage to vehicles, roads, etc., as well as medical and funeral expenses incurred. To attach a value to this saving, one must predict the reduction in future resource costs expected to be achieved by the project.

(b) One of the costs to society of a fatality is the projected net contribution of the deceased to the rest of society. This includes the present value of the individual's future output less future consumption. This amount (which could be negative) would otherwise have been available to others in society, but no longer will be. If a project reduces fatalities, one benefit to society would be the increased net output available due to the reduced deaths. In order to estimate that benefit, one must predict which types of persons are to comprise the reduced fatalities, since different persons make different net contributions to the rest of society due to differences in age, ability, training, etc.

(c) The reduced risk of death to all members of society may well be the most significant benefit from reducing fatalities. The appropriate method of measuring it will be discussed in detail below.

(d) The reduction in the psychic costs to friends, relatives, etc. that accompanies the death of an individual also benefits society. The estimation of this benefit is obviously problematic, and no satisfactory method has been proposed for obtaining it. Consequently it is usually ignored.

In estimating benefit (c), the benefit to members of society from a reduction in the risk of death, we follow the principle outlined above. It is the maximum amount of money that all individuals would be willing to pay to reduce the risk. Or, the cost of an increase in the risk of death is the minimum amount a person would accept to take the risk. At first sight, it might seem that this amount of money would be very large indeed. If a person is asked how much he would be willing to accept in order to offset the cost of losing his life now, the answer is likely to be extremely large, possibly infinite. If we evaluated the lives lost on a project by posing that question to those whose lives would be lost, the project would never be built. However, for most projects, we cannot designate in advance those persons whose lives will be lost. The best we can do is to estimate for various persons the probabilities of their losing their lives. That being the case, the opportunity cost of the expected loss of life from a project is the amount that all persons affected would be willing to receive in order to accept the possibility of death due to the project. That sum, as we shall argue below, is likely to be finite and of a manageable size when probabilities are low. Therefore, projects causing a certain loss of life, randomly dispersed over the many users, may well be justifiably undertaken, while those with exactly the same loss of life occurring, but to predesignated persons, most certainly will not be. This principle of evaluating loss of life *ex ante* has been challenged by Broome (1978), who has argued that the government should view the loss of life *ex post* and not be concerned with who dies. This alternative view would lead to a much greater value of life than that discussed here.

While it is required in principle to charge the opportunity cost of lives, or to credit the benefits of lives saved, to a project in a cost-benefit analysis, one must be careful to avoid double-counting; these costs or benefits may already be included in the measurement of other costs or benefits. For example, as Mishan (1971c) has pointed out, users of a project voluntarily incur the risk of losing their lives when they drive their automobiles on a highway or take an airplane trip. Suppose we measure the benefits the users obtain from the services of the project by the appropriate demand price or area beneath a demand curve. This demand curve will represent the price that users would be willing to pay for the use of the project's services, knowing that there is a risk of death involved. Therefore, the price they would be willing to pay will already have discounted the costs of the risk of dying, and as such these costs need not be explicitly included in the project evaluation. This will be the case whenever the risks have been voluntarily assumed by users. In the case of a highway, these risks include not only the risk of killing oneself, but also the risk of being killed by another driver.

Projects may affect the risk of death to persons who are affected involuntarily, as with a communicable disease, or an airplane accident in a populated area. In this case, the project evaluation will generally be required to take the opportunity cost of the increased risk of death, or the benefits of the reduced risk, into account.

As with the value of time saved, there is no direct price that project evaluators can rely upon to measure the benefits of a reduced risk of death. One must rely on indirect measures. In estimating the implicit value that individuals place upon the risk of death, one can look for situations in the economy where persons actually do trade off the risk of death for money. One obvious example of this is the differential wage rates offered for jobs which have different risks of death. If two jobs were identical in all nonpecuniary effects save for the differences in the risk of death, then under competitive labor market conditions, the wage differential between the two jobs would represent the amount that must be paid to induce the marginal man to take the higher risk of dying. Thus, in principle, if one had enough wage differential comparisons which satisfied this criterion, the value attached to varying amounts of risk of death could be estimated. In practice, wage differential data may not be completely reliable, since wage differentials may reflect nonpecuniary differences other than the risk of dying. Nonetheless, a statistical regression analysis could be performed relating the wage differentials observed to all measurable differences in occupations in order to isolate the effect of risk of death. This procedure is used by Thaler and Rosen (1975). However, to the extent that different individuals have different attitudes towards risk, the wage differential may not reflect the costs of assuming the risk to the average person, since more risk-averse persons would tend to take the low-risk jobs and less risk-averse persons the high-risk jobs.

These measures of the opportunity cost of an increased risk of death can be used to estimate a "value of life" for project evaluation in the following way: Suppose that a project will have n users and m are expected to die (at random) on the project. Then, the probability of death for each of the n users is m/n. Suppose that from empirical estimates it is found that the amount of money required to compensate each individual for an increased risk of dying of m/n is x dollars. Then the total opportunity cost of the increased probability of dying is xn dollars for all users. If we define the value of life as the opportunity cost per expected death, then it will be xn/m dollars, or x dollars divided by the probability of death. Thus, if the increase in the probability of death is 0.0001 on a project, and each individual must be compensated ten dollars for accepting this risk, the "value of life" to be used as a cost-per-death on the project is $10/0.0001 = \$100,000$. According to Thaler and Rosen, this value is about $200,000 in 1967 dollars using wage differential data.

Similar principles may be applied to measuring the benefits of preventing disease, or to the costs of increased health hazards. However, there is an additional problem to be taken into consideration. Suppose a project changes the risk of, say, disease, but not of death; then the cost picture takes on two aspects. First, there is an opportunity cost arising from the increased risk of exposure to the disease, a cost sustained by all those who might be affected (the *ex ante* cost). Second, there is the psychic cost, or *ex post* cost, borne by those who, in fact, do catch the disease. Both these costs ought, in principle, to be included in a cost-benefit analysis.

(c) Indirect Benefits and Costs

Projects may change social welfare by indirectly affecting total benefits or total costs elsewhere in the economy. In particular, the project may induce changes in resource allocation on distorted markets elsewhere, and this will cause a change in social welfare in the economy by the arguments of the theory of second best, as presented in Chapter 7.

Suppose, for example, that on some related market, price is less than marginal social cost (*MSC*) due to externalities. In Fig. 8–6, *MSC* is assumed

Figure 8–6

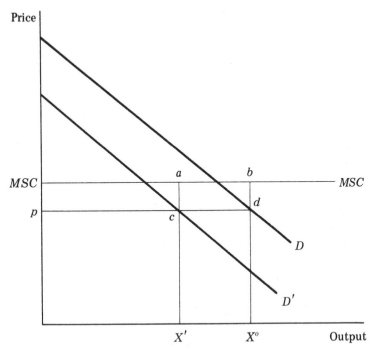

to be constant. The output on this market may be the services of a congested road which is being overused because of an inability to price the congestion. Initially, the output is at X^o, where the price or user cost is p, which is less than MSC. Consider now the introduction of a project which provides substitute services to X and causes the demand curve for X to shift from D to D'. The use of services is reduced to X'.

The cost-benefit analysis of the project should include any net social benefits induced from this change in the resource allocation of X. In this example, since the reduction in social costs from the reduction in X is the area $X'abX^o$, while the reduction in total benefits is only $X'cdX^o$, there is a net social gain of $cabd$ attributable to the project. Such a calculation of indirect benefits or costs should be done for all changes in output on distorted markets induced by the project. Note that for non-distorted markets, output changes can be ignored.

THE SOCIAL DISCOUNT RATE

8–4   Having discussed the measurement of costs and benefits as they occur, it remains to consider the appropriate discount rate at which to aggregate them to a present value. The social discount rate is the rate at which society discounts a marginal addition to consumption in the future relative to the present. We have already discussed how individuals discount future consumption. If the market interest rate net of tax is r, and if we assume capital markets are perfect, individuals will arrange their time stream of consumption such that the marginal rate of substitution between the consumption of any two periods is $1/(1 + r)$. The market interest rate r is the private discount rate. If capital markets are not perfect in the sense that individuals may not borrow freely against future income, such quantity constraints on borrowing may make private discount rates higher than r and unobservable to the project evaluator. This section abstracts from that problem and considers the relationship between the private discount rate r, which determines individual saving behavior, and the social discount rate to be used in cost-benefit analysis.

Since the money net benefits of each individual are being treated identically, and since each individual is assumed to face the same discount rate, r,[13] one might expect that r should also be the social discount rate. However, some economists (e.g. Marglin [1963a] and Sen [1967]) have argued that individual savings for bequests yield external benefits to others which the private saver does not take into consideration in deciding upon their saving pattern. Therefore, the amount of saving done voluntarily will be inefficiently low. To the extent that this is true, the social discount rate may differ from the private rate r.

The problem is an example of an externality arising out of interdependent utility functions, as discussed in Chapter 5. Suppose the utility of each household of the current generation depends not only on its own consumption, but also on the consumption level of all members of the next generation, both its own heirs and the heirs of its contemporaries. In deciding how much to leave for future generations, each household equates the marginal cost of foregoing its own consumption with the marginal benefit to itself of saving for the next generation. However, it neglects the benefit its savings confers upon its contemporaries, who also obtain utility from any saving done for future generations. In other words, the marginal social benefit from a household's saving for future generations exceeds the marginal private benefit to the household. Each household will therefore undersave. It is exactly the same sort of externality as that which arises under voluntary contributions to charity.

The existence of these external economies of savings implies that, on the one hand, private savings will be below the socially efficient amount, and, on the other, the rate at which future consumption should be discounted is r_s, which is below the market interest rate r because of the externality on the capital market. One might add various complications to the above model, but the same basic result remains. Only if such intergenerational externalities were negligible would the appropriate social discount rate be the market rate of interest.

Notice that the above argument uses only the preferences of the current generation to determine the social discount rate. It does not take into consideration the preferences of future generations. In other words, the argument is made purely on efficiency grounds, not equity grounds. The implied social welfare function is one which gives zero weight to future generations' utility except as it influences that of current generations. If the present generation collectively decided to consume all the world's resources during its lifetime, the cost-benefit criterion based upon efficiency would not reject it. To do otherwise would require making an interpersonal utility comparison between generations. Still, whatever the utility comparison turned out to yield, the above efficiency argument would remain valid. There could still be a divergence between r_s and r, and r_s is the appropriate one to use in aggregating social costs and benefits over time.

THE PROBLEM OF RISK AND UNCERTAINTY

8–5   The benefits and costs of a project in the future are rarely known with complete certainty. Instead, one may be faced with several different streams of costs and benefits, and must make an evaluation based upon uncertainty as to which of these will occur. Typically, we can distinguish between a *risky* situation, in which the probabilities of the various outcomes are known, and an *uncertain* situation, in which even these probabilities are not known. Our discussion will concentrate on the former case, not because it is necessarily the most realistic, but because it has been assumed in most analyses conducted so far. If one cannot attach probabilities to various outcomes, one cannot obtain clearcut decision rules for project evaluation, and one will generally end up assuming some probabilities *a priori*. For example, one might assume the worst and use a decision rule which maximizes the return on the worst outcome, called a *maximin* strategy. Or, one might assume that all possible outcomes have an equal chance of occurring and utilize those probabilities. For a survey of these and other decision rules under uncertainty, the reader is referred to an article by Dorfman (1962). For now, we shall assume that somehow probabilities can be attached to the various possible outcomes.

The existence of risk imposes an opportunity cost on the individuals required to bear that risk. We begin with a brief discussion of the costs of risk-bearing before considering how risk might be accounted for in project evaluation. In principle, the cost of risk-bearing is like any other cost—it is the minimum amount of money that must be paid to an individual in order to compensate him for taking a risk. A simple example will illustrate. Figure 8–7 shows the utility curve for an individual where utility, U, depends upon the level of income, Y. The diagram is drawn on the assumption of diminishing marginal utility of income.

Suppose the individual is faced with some risk as regards his level of income. In particular, there is a probability π_1 that income will be Y_1, and a probability π_2 that it will be Y_2, where $\pi_1 + \pi_2 = 1$.[14] The *expected*

Figure 8–7

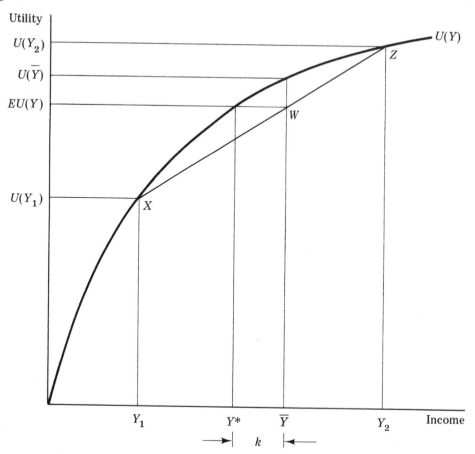

value of this risky situation, in this case the individual's expected income, is defined by:

$$EV = \sum_i \pi_i Y_i = \pi_1 Y_1 + \pi_2 Y_2. \tag{8–15}$$

Since Y_1 and Y_2 have utilities $U(Y_1)$ and $U(Y_2)$ associated with them, we define *expected utility* to be:

$$EU(Y) = \sum_i \pi_i U(Y_i) = \pi_1 U(Y_1) + \pi_2 U(Y_2). \tag{8–16}$$

That is, the expected utility is a weighted average of the utilities of possible outcomes, the weights being the probabilities of each outcome's occurrence.

It has been shown by Friedman and Savage (1948) that, under reasonable assumptions, rational individuals will behave so as to maximize their expected utility. We shall assume that to be the case. For various combinations of

π_1 and π_2, the expected utility of the outcomes Y_1 and Y_2 can be depicted geometrically as the straight line joining X and Z in Fig. 8–7. This follows directly from the formula for $EU(Y)$, Eq. (8–16). The ratio of the line segments WZ/XW will equal the ratio of the probabilities, π_1/π_2, corresponding to that point. Therefore, a risky situation with an expected outcome of $\overline{Y}$ will have an expected utility of $EU(Y)$ in Fig. 8–7. Notice that this is less than the utility that would be achieved from the certain level of income $\overline{Y}$.

The *cost of risk-bearing* is defined as the reduction in expected value that the individual would accept in order to have a certain income rather than the risky expected income. In Fig. 8–7, the utility derived from the risky expected income $\overline{Y}$ is equivalent to the utility received from the certain income Y^*, or $EU(Y) = U(Y^*)$. The cost of risk-bearing, denoted k, is the amount $Y^*\overline{Y}$. Unfortunately, k is not a sum which is directly observable on the market.

There are two ways in which the cost of risk-bearing is important in cost-benefit analysis. The first is in the calculation of the opportunity cost of public funds discussed in Section 8–3. Recall that, for projects which require public funds for their support, the public funds will come either from foregone consumption or foregone investment. The opportunity cost of that part which displaces private investment had to be calculated by taking the present value at the social discount rate of the stream of consumption generated out of the gross returns to capital in the private sector ρ. In the case in which all returns are consumed, this present value is ρ/r, where r is the social discount rate. Suppose, however, that the gross return in the private sector includes a premium to cover the costs of risk-bearing.[15] When the private sector is displaced, in addition to foregoing the annual stream of consumption benefits ρ, the private sector no longer has to incur the cost of risk-bearing on that expected future stream. The net loss in the private sector is thus $\rho - k$ where k is the risk premium, and the opportunity cost of public funds is now amended to read:

$$a = (1 - \theta) + \frac{\theta(\rho - k)}{r}. \tag{8–17}$$

The second problem for which risk is relevant is in the project decision rule itself. Since the benefits and costs of a public project are risky, one might expect that individuals in society have to bear the costs of public risk-bearing, and this ought somehow to be estimated and subtracted from the expected net value of the project in order to determine if social welfare is increased or not (i.e. in order to obtain the "certainty equivalent" value of the project analogous to Y^* in Fig. 8–7). The measurement of this cost of risk-bearing would seem to be extremely difficult, but fortunately there are two reasons why the social cost of risk-bearing on public projects may be negligible. These reasons are the phenomena of *risk-spreading* and *risk-pooling*.[16]

Risk-spreading occurs when the benefits and costs of a project are shared among a large number of individuals. In the case of public projects financed out of general tax revenues, risk-spreading takes place among individual taxpayers. As Arrow and Lind (1970) have argued, as the number of individuals sharing in the benefits and costs of a project increases, the cost of risk-bearing per individual decreases, and so does the total cost of risk-bearing of all individuals. When the number of individuals sharing approaches infinity, provided the project is small relative to GNP and uncorrelated with GNP, the total risk approaches zero. The proof of this proposition requires some mathematics, and we shall content ourselves with an intuitive explanation here using Fig. 8–8, which shows the utility function for a typical individual. In an economy consisting of n taxpayers, all sharing equally in the net benefits of a public project through their tax payments, the typical individual will have possible net-of-tax incomes of Y_1 and Y_2 and an expected income $\overline{Y}$ where the randomness is assumed to be due entirely to the public project. The cost of risk-bearing to this individual is $\overline{Y}Y^*$, and society's total risk is $n\overline{Y}Y^*$.

Figure 8–8

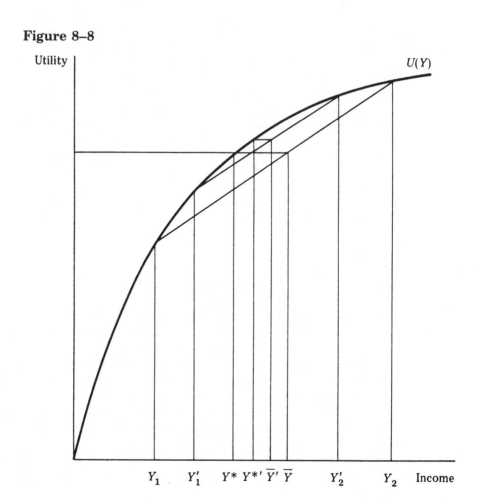

Now suppose the number of individuals doubles to $2n$, with the size of the project unchanged. The potential return to the public project, and the expected value from the project to the individual, are halved, leaving him with possible outcomes Y'_1 and Y'_2, and an expected income of $\overline{Y}'$. The individual cost of risk-bearing is now $\overline{Y}'Y^{*'}$, which is less than half of $\overline{Y}Y^*$, due to the curvature of the utility function. The total risk to society is $2n\overline{Y}'Y^{*'}$, which is less than $n\overline{Y}Y^*$. The Arrow and Lind proof consists in showing that as $n \to \infty$, $n\overline{Y}Y^* \to 0$. That is, the risk-bearing cost of each individual, $\overline{Y}Y^*$, approaches zero at a rate faster than that at which n approaches infinity (as illustrated by the effect of doubling n shown above). In practice, n is, of course, less than infinity, but provided it is large enough, the total cost of risk-bearing may be negligible. If so, the cost-benefit analysis can be conducted purely in expected value terms.

Risk-pooling occurs if the government has many small projects with (relatively) independent probability distributions. In this case, the society has a portfolio of many independent projects and, by the principles of portfolio selection, the risks of each project tend to offset one other. That is, the probability distribution of the public sector portfolio of projects is much less dispersed than the sum of the distribution of individual projects and the cost of risk-bearing will be low. In terms of Fig. 8–8, the dispersion of possible outcomes Y_1 and Y_2 will be small, and so will the cost of risk-bearing. Once again, the government is justified in using the expected present value of a project as an approximate measure of its contribution to social welfare, without taking risk into account.

For large projects or projects which benefit relatively few persons, it may be necessary to include a risk premium in the costs of the project. Measuring the cost of risk-bearing is very difficult and, often, *ad hoc* methods of taking risk into account may be used. For example, low estimates of benefits and high estimates of costs may be used, giving a conservative estimate of net benefits. This is equivalent to the maximin method mentioned earlier in this section. Or, a risk premium may be added to the discount rate. This will tend to reduce the net benefits by more the further in the future they are to occur. This may be justified if the uncertainties of outcomes increase the further into the future they are expected. Finally, some project evaluators may decide to apply a cut-off date to benefits. That is, they might require that a project "pay for itself" in a given period of time, even though benefits are expected to accrue further into the future.

CHAPTER NOTES

1. The same principles are involved if one is working with continuous time rather than with discrete time periods. In this case, the discount factor applicable to one dollar at time t is e^{-rt}. That is to say, one dollar at time t is worth e^{-rt} dollars at time zero. Here, r is the instantaneous interest rate. That is, interest must be calculated at each instant of time rather than periodically. The continuous-time version is often used for analytical convenience.

2. The present value formula measures the value of a stream of returns in terms of current dollars. Of course, one could measure the value in terms of any year's dollars. For example, the value of a stream of returns of year s dollars, V_s, is:

$$V_s = \sum_{t=0}^{T} \frac{B_t - C_t}{(1 + r)^{t-s}} = V\left[\frac{1}{(1 + r)^{-s}}\right].$$

We follow the usual convention of measuring the net benefit of a project by its present value V.

3. For example, consider the case in which $T = 2$. Then, Eq. (8–2) may be written:

$$0 = (B_0 - C_0) + \frac{(B_1 - C_1)}{1 + \lambda} + \frac{(B_2 - C_2)}{(1 + \lambda)^2}$$

or $(1 + \lambda)^2(B_0 - C_0) + (1 + \lambda)(B_1 - C_1) + (B_2 - C_2) = 0$. This may be simplified to read:

$$\lambda^2 + a\lambda + b = 0.$$

This second-degree polynomial may have as many as two solutions.

4. In the example given in footnote 3, suppose that $B_0 - C_0 = -7270$, $B_1 - C_1 = 17,100$, and $B_2 - C_2 = -10,000$. Then λ may take on the values .10 and .25 (or rates of return may be 10% or 25%). The net benefits $(B_t - C_t)$ changes signs twice in going from one year to the next so there are 2 solutions.

5. This inadequacy of the *IRR* can be avoided by calculating the rate of return on the difference between two projects rather than comparing the *IRR* of the two separate projects. If the rate of return calculated on the difference between the streams of returns on A and B is positive, A will have the higher V. This was pointed out by Feldstein and Flemming (1964).

6. The shadow price p_G may be written in terms of elasticities of demand (η) and supply (ε) as follows:

$$p_G = p\,\frac{\varepsilon - p(1 + t)(X_D/X_S)\eta}{\varepsilon - \eta(X_D/X_S)}.$$

This may be proven as follows using differential calculus. The shadow price expression equation (8–8) may be written:

$$p_G = pX_S'\frac{dp}{dG} - p(1 + t)^2X_D'\frac{dp}{dG}$$

where X_S' and X_D' are the derivatives of supply and demand with respect to p and $p(1 + t)$ respectively. Market clearing requires that

$$dG = dX_S - dX_D$$
$$= X_S'\,dp - X_D'(1 + t)dp.$$

Solving this for dp/dG yields:

$$\frac{dp}{dG} = \frac{1}{X_S' - X_D'(1 + t)}.$$

Substituting this into the above expression for p_G gives:

$$p_G = \frac{pX'_S - p(1 + t)^2 X'_D}{X'_S - X'_D(1 + t)}.$$

This may be immediately converted into the elasticity version of the shadow pricing rule by using the definitions:

$$\varepsilon = X'_S p/X_S; \eta = X'_D p(1 + t)/X_D.$$

7. The value attached to leisure time will presumably be affected by transfer payments received by the involuntarily unemployed such as unemployment insurance or welfare. If leisure has a positive income elasticity of demand, the opportunity cost of leisure time will be increased as a result of the receipt of such transfers. Nonetheless, the amount of the transfers received does not reflect the opportunity cost of the leisure time. The latter is unobservable. For a detailed discussion of this point see Mishan (1971a).

8. For a full discussion of the principles involved in constructing a shadow price of foreign exchange, see Dasgupta, Marglin, and Sen (1972). The weighted average shadow pricing rule for foreign exchange is also presented in Harberger (1969).

9. In principle, the supply curve for foreign exchange could bend backwards. This is a common phenomenon in the trade literature (see Kindleberger [1973]).

10. The present value of a perpetual stream of output ρ is $\sum_{t=1}^{\infty} \frac{\rho}{(1 + r)^t}$. With both ρ and r constant, the value of this sum is simply ρ/r.

11. If current expenditures are financed out of bonds or taxes, this opportunity cost must be applied to their financing as well. The financing of both capital and current expenditures is incorporated in the analysis of Feldstein (1972a) discussed below.

12. This approach follows that of Mishan (1971c). In this article, Mishan also discusses other, less sound, methods used to evaluate the value of life such as taking the value of consumption or output foregone due to death, or the value of life insurance purchased. Other discussions may be found in Usher (1973), Thaler and Rosen (1975), and Jones-Lee (1976).

13. In practice, this is not exactly true even with perfect capital markets since different persons pay different marginal tax rates on interest income due to income tax progressivity. Therefore, their marginal time preference rates will be different.

14. The assumption that there are only two possible outcomes is made to facilitate geometrical analysis. The same results may be derived algebraically for the more general case in which several outcomes are possible.

15. We assume that individuals cannot avoid risk entirely via diversification on stock markets or via the ownership of large conglomerated corporations.

16. For discussions of the concepts of risk-spreading and risk-pooling see James (1975), and Layard and Walters (1978).

III

Taxation

9

The Normative Analysis of Taxation: Efficiency Aspects

INTRODUCTION

9–1   In order to undertake public expenditures the government must acquire purchasing power to obtain resources from the economy. In a mixed economy such as that of the United States, there are three main ways in which this is done: The levying of various sorts of taxes, the issuing of public debt, and the creation of money. In this part of the book we consider in some detail the use of taxation to divert resources from the private to the public sector. The issues that arise over the issue of debt and the creation of money are typically of a macroeconomic nature and, as such, fall more within the subject matter of monetary theory and policy than public finance. Our main concern is with the microeconomic or resource allocation effects of public sector activity, rather than with more aggregative issues. The implications of the use of debt for the reallocation of resources across generations raises issues similar to those encountered in the economic analysis of social security, which is discussed in Chapter 14. The economics of debt financing will be considered there. This chapter and the next will discuss the principles of taxation, by which we mean the criteria according to which the government could decide upon an appropriate mix of the various types of taxes, and the extent to which various taxes satisfy these principles.

In the theory of public finance, there are generally considered to be two principal criteria by which taxes are judged: The *efficiency* criterion and the *equity* criterion. The efficiency criterion might be described as follows: In diverting resources to the public sector, taxes of different sorts impose varying degrees of distortions on the workings of the market economy. These distortions impose *welfare losses* or *deadweight losses* on the economy by causing a departure from Pareto optimality similar to the welfare losses discussed earlier in Chapter 2. These welfare losses are also referred to as the *excess burden* or the *welfare cost* of taxation. One aim of the tax system might be to minimize the deadweight loss imposed on society from diverting a given amount of resources to the public sector. The efficiency criterion judges taxes by the deadweight loss per revenue dollar collected. Those which impose less deadweight loss are said to be more efficient in the economic sense. The notion of efficiency is discussed more fully below in this chapter. We shall also discuss the efficiency of various types of taxes and the choice of a most-efficient tax system (the so-called *optimal tax problem*).

The equity criterion is concerned with how the burden of output reduction in the private sector is distributed among the various members of society under various taxing schemes. This burden will, in general, include the deadweight loss imposed by the tax system as well as the value of real resources transferred. The problems involved in designing an equitable tax system are discussed in the next chapter. There are two concepts of equity which must be distinguished: *Horizontal equity* and *vertical equity*. A tax is said to be horizontally equitable if it treats equals equally. That is, if two persons have equal welfare before the tax is imposed, they would have equal welfare after as well. To apply the criterion of horizontal equity to a tax system, one must be able to ascertain objectively when two persons have equal welfare levels. The vertical equity criterion is concerned with how the tax system treats persons of differing welfare levels. In order to judge the degree to which the tax system is vertically equitable, one must be prepared to make a judgment about the appropriate way to treat people at different utility levels. That is, what should be the relative reductions in utility imposed upon persons with different utilities? The answer to that question requires making an interpersonal utility comparison, which is a value judgment.

In assessing the equity of the tax system, we should also be concerned with the distribution of the benefits of public expenditures that the taxes finance. This has often been neglected in discussions of equity, presumably because the distribution of these benefits is difficult, if not impossible, to measure. The problem is partially circumvented by comparing various tax systems which yield the same amount of resources to the government. Nonetheless, that is not a completely satisfactory way of dealing with the problem. A tax system which appears to be horizontally equitable may not be, if persons who otherwise appear equal achieve different benefits from public expenditures. Similarly, judgments as to the vertical equity of a tax system may be invalidated by the neglect of differing benefits achieved from public expenditures.

Although efficiency and equity are the two main criteria that economists writing in the theory of public finance have considered in analyzing taxes, policymakers have, in addition, been concerned with other properties of taxes. For one thing, the administrative costs and the ease of implementation and enforcement of various taxes may be important. For example, taxing an individual according to income received may or may not be easier than taxing him on total expenditures from an accounting point of view. We shall discuss this issue in Chapter 10. Similarly, choosing an individual's wealth as a tax base may be costly because of the difficulties in measuring such forms of wealth as human capital (or human wealth). Also, there may be difficulties in preventing tax evasion on wealth held as liquid assets. Often a sales tax may be levied on sales made at the wholesale level rather than the retail level, because fewer tax-paying units are involved so the costs of collection are lower.

Another criterion often valued by policymakers is the flexibility of the tax's revenue with the level of economic activity. If the revenue of a tax rises and falls with economic activity, it will function as an automatic stabilizer for fiscal policy purposes.

Finally, some taxes are levied simply because they raise a lot of revenue easily. The corporate income tax is difficult to defend on equity grounds, as will become obvious later. Yet, because of the magnitude of its base (i.e. corporation profits) and its potentially non-distorting nature, it is a good revenue raiser. Taxes on tobacco and alcohol are also reliable revenue sources, since the demands for these commodities do not change very much with price changes. This latter property, as it turns out, also makes those taxes very efficient, even though that may not have been what motivated the policymakers to levy them. The importance of these other criteria for the choice of actual taxes will become apparent in Chapter 13 when we discuss the United States tax system.

Governments in practice rely upon a wide variety of tax sources, partly in an attempt to secure the right trade-off between equity and efficiency. The spectrum of taxes levied includes taxes on the income of households (personal income tax, payroll tax), taxes on the income of firms (corporate income tax), taxes on property and wealth (local property tax), taxes on the purchases by households and firms (general sales tax, specific excise taxes), taxes on imports (tariffs), and taxes on bequests or inheritances. For the purposes of the analysis that follows, it is often convenient to classify taxes according to how they impinge upon the household budget. The budget might be considered to consist of a *source* (or income) side and a *use* (or expenditure) side.

Taxes on the source side include all taxes that are levied on factor incomes. They may be *partial factor taxes*, which are taxes of a factor used in some, but not all, industries. A corporate income tax is a partial factor tax on capital income in the corporate sector of the economy. A *general factor tax* is a tax levied on a factor income, no matter where it is used. The payroll tax on labor income is an example of this. Finally, a *general income tax* is a tax on all factor incomes, regardless of where they are generated. The personal income tax is of this sort.

Taxes on the use side are taxes levied on the purchase of commodities. They may be *selective commodity taxes*, those levied on the purchase of particular items. Examples of this are the excise taxes levied on alcohol and tobacco. Use taxes may be *general commodity taxes* levied on all purchases of commodities regardless of type. Retail sales taxes are of this sort.

Finally, we may distinguish between *ad valorem* and *per-unit* taxes, and between *personal* and *in rem* taxes. An *ad valorem* tax is one whose rate is given as a proportion of the selling price and therefore as a proportion of the value of a sale. Sales taxes are generally of this sort. A per-unit tax is one that is levied as a fixed amount per quantity sold. Tobacco and alcohol taxes are frequently of this sort. Personal taxes are taxes levied on a specific individual, such as the personal income tax. They can be made to vary in rate from individual to individual as with a progressive income tax. An *in rem* tax is one that is imposed on an impersonal transaction such as a sale of a commodity. *In rem* taxes do not discriminate among individuals and so will apply at the same rate to all.

THE EFFICIENCY OF TAXES

9–2   Early analysis of the efficiency of taxes in the literature concentrated on determining which of two taxes is the most efficient tool for raising a given amount of revenue from a single consumer and from society as a whole, a selective excise tax or a proportional income tax. We begin with an analysis of that case and gradually add further complications, ending up with a discussion of the most efficient structure of taxes.

When dealing with the economy as a whole, we want to avoid dealing with issues of distribution and equity. To do this, we adopt the analytical device of a single consumer economy. It is assumed that all consumers can be aggregated into a single "representative" consumer. The circumstances under which one can do this are actually quite restrictive. Either it must be assumed, following Samuelson (1950), that the government is continually redistributing income optimally, or that the government simply does not care about redistribution and that the preferences of consumers are simply aggregated into a single set of preferences. Neither of these is particularly satisfactory. The former assumes rather unrealistic behavior by the government, while the latter requires quite restrictive assumptions about household preferences in order for the aggregation to be possible. (Basically, preferences must be identical and homothetic.) The single consumer economy does, however, allow us to concentrate on issues of efficiency. The question of distributive equity will be returned to in the next chapter.

Income vs. Excise Taxation: The Two-Good Case

Consider the case of a single consumer with a given income, and the choice of spending that income on two commodities, X and Y.[1] Suppose that a given amount of revenue must be raised from this individual, using either an excise tax on X or an income tax. In the context of this model, where there is no saving, an income tax is equivalent to a general consumption tax at the appropriate rate.[2] The question to be answered is which one of the taxes imposes the least excess burden.

Figure 9–1 can be used to illustrate that the income tax is unambiguously more efficient here. In the absence of the tax the consumer's budget constraint is AB. The imposition of the income tax moves the budget line parallel inwards to CD, where AC is the amount of revenue raised in terms of good Y. The individual selects point II on indifference curve U_2. The burden of the resource transfer is the difference in utility in going from U_1 to U_2. Measured as the amount of income in terms of good Y which is equivalent to the loss of utility from the tax, the burden of tax payments is AC, the exact amount of resources transferred.[3] There is therefore no excess burden or deadweight loss with the income tax. This is to be expected since the income tax does not distort the relative prices of X and Y, so the efficiency conditions are not upset. The income tax in this model is referred to as a *lump-sum tax* since it is a tax levied on an item which is fixed in quantity.

To raise the same amount of revenue with the excise tax on X, the price of X to the consumer must rise until the consumer achieves an equilibrium along the line CD. The line CD represents the locus of all points which yield the amount of revenue AC. The excise tax on X yielding the amount of revenue AC will be that which leaves the consumer at point III on indifference curve U_3. The budget line AE will have a slope of $p_X(1 + t_X)/p_Y$, the relative prices faced by the consumer, where t_X is the tax rate on X. The increase in the relative price of X due to the tax increases the slope of the budget line and ensures that the point III will be on a lower indifference curve than the point II. Therefore, in this model, an excise tax is definitely inferior to an income tax, and obviously this holds for more than two goods as well as more than one individual. The excise tax, in effect, imposes an *excess burden* or deadweight loss of $U_2 - U_3$ or CF in terms of good Y evaluated at the old prices.

This analysis is a partial equilibrium analysis for a single individual facing fixed relative prices from the market. The same analysis can be extended to the entire economy by substituting a production possibility curve for a budget line, and a social indifference map for an individual one as in Little (1951) and Friedman (1952). Figure 9–1 can be reinterpreted as a single consumer, two-good economy with fixed supply prices and fixed factor supplies. The budget line AB is the production possibility curve for the economy as a whole. The budget line CD attained under an income tax can also be viewed as the production possibility curve remaining to the private sector after the government has removed the equivalent of AC units of resources in terms of Y from the private sector. With an excise tax, the budget line facing the consumer is AE, and the equilibrium must lie along the production possibility curve CD.

The reason why the excise tax is inferior to the income tax can be put in different terms. The excise tax violates the overall conditions for a Pareto

Figure 9–1

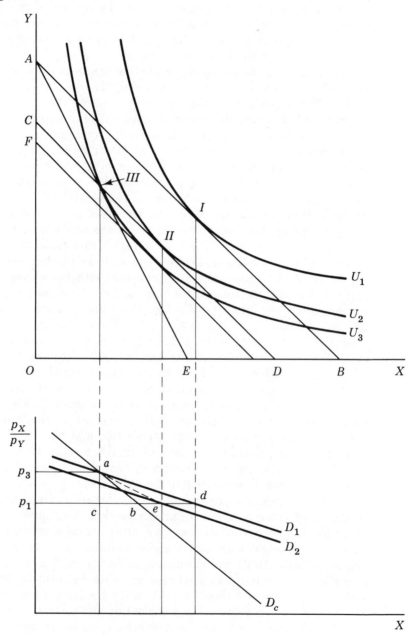

optimum as discussed in Chapter 2. Here, $MRS_{XY} = p_X(1 + t_X)/p_Y$; while $MRT_{XY} = p_X/p_Y$. Therefore, $MRT_{XY} \neq MRS_{XY}$. In the case of the income tax, the overall efficiency conditions are satisfied, since at the equilibrium the consumer's indifference curve is tangential to the production possibility curve (so $MRS = MRT$).

The same conclusion emerges if producer prices are variable. In Fig. 9–2, PP represents society's aggregate production possibility curve (again assuming factors to be fixed in supply). In the absence of government, the individual would choose the combination of X and Y represented by the point A on PP. This would be a Pareto-optimal allocation of resources since $MRS_{XY} = MRT_{XY}$. Suppose now that the government wants to acquire some resources for public services. After having the requisite resources removed, the private sector is assumed to have the production possibility curve $P'P'$ remaining, showing the quantities of X and Y now available for private use. That is, each point on the curve $P'P'$ corresponds to a point on PP with a given amount of X and Y removed. Point C corresponds to point D on PP and has the same MRT. The same applies for B and E. The consumer's indifference map will also have shifted due to the benefits of public expenditures affecting the relative preferences between X and Y. In other words, the indifference map is actually three-dimensional in the two goods and public expenditures. The curves depicted are cross-sectional views of the indifference map for a given level of public expenditures. The indifference curves U' and U'' represent indifference curves taken from the new map.

Suppose we compare two alternative ways of removing the resources by taxation—an income tax and an excise tax on X. In the context of the present model an income tax will not impose any distortions on the economy. True, there will be a difference between the labor and capital income paid to the individual by firms and that received by the individual after the tax. But, because we have assumed fixed factor supplies this will be of no consequence for the efficiency of the allocation of resources. The only prices which are important in determining resource allocation in this economy are the relative prices of X and Y. Under an income tax these relative prices are the same for consumers as for firms, so the overall efficiency condition for private goods continues to hold and the private sector achieves a Pareto optimum at the point B. The income tax in this simple economy is completely efficient. Note that a tax on either labor or capital income individually would also be efficient, since labor and capital are fixed in supply in this particular example. So also would a general consumption tax be efficient.

An excise tax levied on purchases of good X will, however, cause a distortion between the relative price facing the individual (MRS_{XY}) and the relative price facing producers (MRT_{XY}). If the latter is p_X/p_Y, the former will be $p_X(1 + t_X)/p_Y$ where t_X is the tax. The point C represents the equilibrium that would be achieved when the government imposes an excise tax on X to finance its purchases of resources for public expenditures.

Figure 9–2

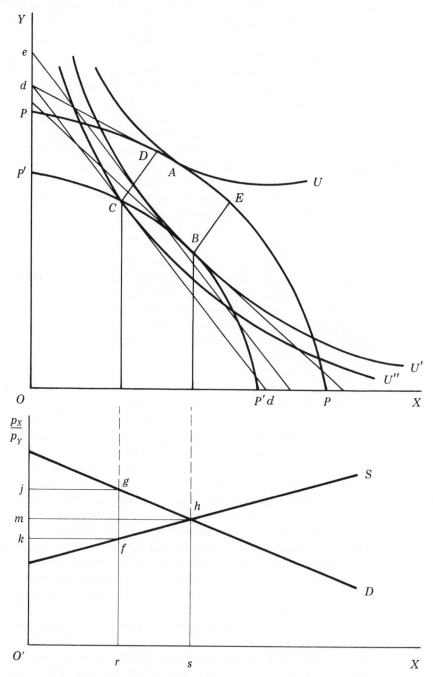

At this equilibrium, the budget line facing the community will be dd. Its slope will be $p_X(1 + t_X)/p_Y$, and its intercept, Od, will be the income or gross national expenditure for the consumers in the economy measured in terms of good Y. The consumers will choose the point C on the private goods' production possibility curve $P'P'$. This will correspond to the point D on society's overall production possibility curve PP. The slope at D is the marginal rate of transformation or relative price to producers p_X/p_Y. The intercept Od will be the gross national product at factor cost to society. The equilibrium will be such that gross national product equals gross national income, Od. In this situation, the individual reaches the indifference level U'', which is necessarily lower than that reached with an income tax yielding the same real revenue to the government, U'. The loss in utility $U' - U''$ is again the deadweight loss or excess burden of the tax system.

Since we cannot measure utility, however, we cannot measure the deadweight loss directly. An alternative way to portray the deadweight loss, which is measured in monetary terms, can be developed using demand and supply curves. In the lower panel of Fig. 9–2, curves D and S show the demand for and supply of good X, which depend on the relative price of X in terms of Y, p_X/p_Y. With lump-sum taxation, the equilibrium relative price of X is $O'm$, given by the common slope of the production possibility and indifference curves at their tangency point B in the upper panel. Under lump-sum taxation, the equilibrium quantity of good X will be $O's$. Now, when an excise tax is imposed on X, at the rate of t_X, a new equilibrium will be attained at a gross-of-tax price $p_X(1 + t_x) = rg$ for consumers and a net-of-tax price $p_X = rf$ for producers, with an equilibrium quantity, $O'r$. The higher price rg faced by consumers in this equilibrium corresponds with the more steeply-sloped budget line dd in the upper panel of Fig. 9–2, and the lower price rf received by producers corresponds to the flatter slope of the production possibility curve $P'P'$ at point C. According to the principles of consumers' and producers' surplus analysis presented in Chapter 2, the deadweight loss is approximately the area fgh.

In moving from B to C, the loss in consumer's surplus is $jghm$ and the loss in producer's surplus is $mhfk$. These losses are partly offset by the gain in tax revenue $jgfk$ which can now be used to reduce the income tax, leaving a net loss of fgh. The same area may be arrived at more directly by subtracting the total loss to consumers, $rghs$, minus the reduction in the total cost to society, $rfhs$.

The close correspondence between the upper and lower panels of Fig. 9–2 suggests that there may be a close linkage between the deadweight loss from excise taxation as represented by the loss in utility from U' to U'', and as represented alternatively by the loss in consumers' surplus fgh. This is in fact the case, although the precise nature of the connection between the two is slightly technical. In the Appendix to this chapter, we discuss in greater detail the general relationship between consumers' and producers' surplus and the underlying preferences of consumers.

It should be noted that some excise taxes may actually reduce, rather than increase, the deadweight losses in the economy. This will be the case when a tax is levied to correct distortions arising out of the workings of the market economy. When some activity emits external diseconomies, an excise tax levied on that activity will improve the allocation of resources. The nature of the efficiency gain was fully discussed in Chapter 5 and need not be repeated here. Several taxes might be said to fall into this category, including taxes on alcohol, tobacco, and gasoline. The first two may correct for the external costs involved in drinking and smoking, whereas the last may be considered a levy paid for automobile pollution. The tax rates on these commodities may well be in excess of the external costs generated, inasmuch as they are good sources of revenue. Unfortunately, the potential for raising revenue through externality-correcting taxes is limited and, therefore, other distorting taxes may have to be used.

Also, some taxes are really in the nature of user prices, such as road tolls. These taxes are performing an allocative function and, to the extent that they are correctly levied, do not impose any inefficiencies on the economy.

This analysis generalizes to the case of more than two goods. As long as income remains fixed, an income tax is a lump-sum tax and generates no deadweight loss. Any excise tax on a single commodity or on a group of commodities will distort relative prices and impose a deadweight loss. Of course, a proportional tax on all commodities will be equivalent to an income tax and will not be distortionary. Since it raises all prices to consumers proportionately, it will not distort relative prices. While the superiority of the income tax remains intact, we are not yet in a position to judge among excise taxes imposed on different commodities or groups of commodities.

Income vs. Excise Taxation: Variable Income

As Little (1951) showed, the superiority of the income tax over an excise tax is no longer assured when income is variable, because the supplies of factors of production can vary. Suppose, for simplicity, that the consumer derives all his income from the supply of labor (L) at a fixed wage rate (w) and spends it on either X or Y as before. In the absence of taxation, his budget constraint may be written:

$$p_X X + p_Y Y = wL. \tag{9-1}$$

The individual's marginal rate of substitution between X and Y is p_X/p_Y, the same as society's marginal rate of transformation. Now the individual can substitute each of the goods for labor at the rates w/p_X and w/p_Y. Since the individual is presumed to get disutility from additional supplies of labor, the marginal rate of substitution between each commodity and labor is the negative of these ratios. The ratios $-w/p_X$ and $-w/p_Y$ also represent the marginal rate of transformation between labor and each commodity, i.e. the amount of labor that must be given up in order to obtain more of the commodity. In a competitive economy, the ratio w/p_X will equal the marginal product of labor in producing X. A Pareto optimum requires that the marginal rate of substitution equal the marginal rate of transformation between all pairs of X, Y, and L. In a competitive economy, these conditions will be satisfied as follows when no taxes are present:

$$MRS_{XY} = \frac{p_X}{p_Y} = MRT_{XY}$$

$$MRS_{LX} = \frac{-w}{p_X} = MRT_{LX}$$

$$MRS_{LY} = \frac{-w}{p_Y} = MRT_{LY}. \tag{9–2}$$

An alternative way to view the optimality conditions is to define the leisure (Z) taken by an individual as the total number of hours available (H, e.g., 24 hours per day) less the amount of labor taken; or, $Z = H - L$. Since H is fixed, any increase in labor will represent a corresponding decrease in leisure and vice versa. By the same token, an increase in labor will represent the same decrease in utility as will a decrease in leisure. Therefore, the marginal utility of leisure can be defined as the negative of the marginal utility of labor. Correspondingly, the MRS between leisure and any good will be the negative of the MRS between labor and that good,[4] that is, $MRS_{ZX} = w/p_X$ and $MRS_{ZY} = w/p_Y$. By analogous reasoning on the production side, we may define the MRT between leisure and any good as the negative of the MRT between labor and the good, so $MRT_{ZX} = w/p_X$ and $MRT_{ZY} = w/p_Y$. We may also rewrite the consumer's budget constraint equation (9–1) by substituting in the definition of Z to give:

$$p_X X + p_Y Y + w Z = wH. \tag{9–3}$$

We can then interpret leisure as being a good like X and Y. The budget constraint says that the total value of the commodities X, Y, and Z consumed must equal the value of the total time available to the consumer evaluated at the wage rate.

Consider now the imposition of various sorts of excise and income taxes. An excise tax will distort the price of the commodity on which it is levied relative to all other prices. An income tax is again equivalent to proportional taxation on both commodities. It will distort the prices of both goods relative to the wage rate. The following summarizes the relationships that hold among relative prices, marginal rates of transformation, and marginal rates of substitution under each of the taxes, where the taxes are assumed to be *ad valorem:*

Excise tax on X(t_X)

$$MRS_{XY} = p_X(1 + t_X)/p_Y \neq MRT_{XY}$$

$$MRS_{XZ} = p_X(1 + t_X)/w \neq MRT_{XZ}$$

$$MRS_{YZ} = p_Y/w = MRT_{YZ} \tag{9-4}$$

Excise tax on Y(t_Y)

$$MRS_{XY} = p_X/p_Y(1 + t_Y) \neq MRT_{XY}$$

$$MRS_{XZ} = p_X/w = MRT_{XZ}$$

$$MRS_{YZ} = p_Y(1 + t_Y)/w \neq MRT_{YZ} \tag{9-5}$$

Income tax (t)

$$MRS_{XY} = p_X/p_Y = MRT_{XY}$$

$$MRS_{XZ} = p_X/w(1 - t) \neq MRT_{XZ}$$

$$MRS_{YZ} = p_Y/w(1 - t) \neq MRT_{YZ} \tag{9-6}$$

Each of the taxes imposes a distortion on two of the three markets, and we cannot say *a priori* which tax is best. This point may be illustrated geometrically using the three-dimensional diagram, adopted from Little (1951), shown in Fig. 9–3. For simplicity of presentation we assume that prices p_X, p_Y, and w are fixed, although this is not necessary.[5]

The three-dimensional plane *ABC* represents the net-of-tax production possibility surface for the economy, the analog of $P'P'$ in Fig. 9–2. The X- and Z-axes are in the plane of the page, while the Y-axis can be imagined coming out of the page perpendicular to O. The points on the plane *ABC* represent the various combinations of X, Y, and Z available to the private sector after the government demand for resources has been met. The slope of any point on *ABC* in the direction of the plane formed by any pair of the axes represents the marginal rate of transformation between that pair of goods. Since *ABC* is flat, the *MRT*'s are the same everywhere. Thus, the slope of *AC* in the plane of the page is MRT_{ZX}. The slope of *BC* in the YZ-plane is MRT_{YZ}, and the slope of *AB* in the XY-plane is MRT_{XY}.

Figure 9–3

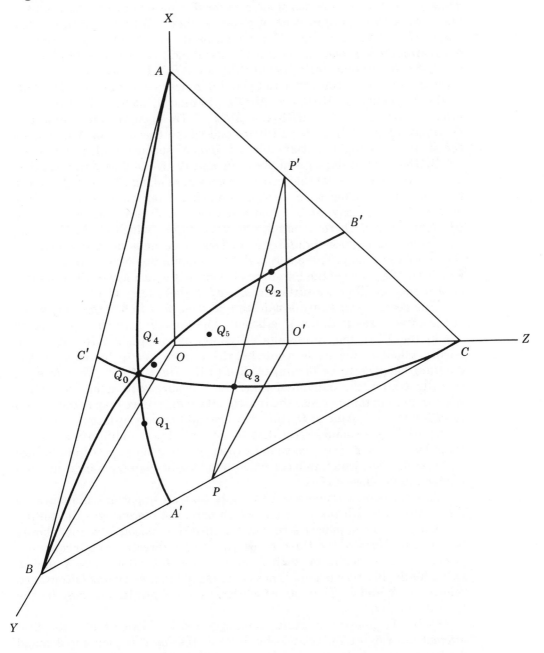

One can then imagine a three-dimensional social indifference map (not drawn) composed of a series of saucers moving outward from the origin O and convex to the origin. One of those saucers will be tangential to the plane ABC at the point Q_0. That would be the Pareto-optimal allocation of resources corresponding to the given social indifference map. At all other points the indifference surfaces cut the plane ABC. The locus of points AA' represents all those points where the indifference map is tangential to ABC in the YZ plane, or $MRS_{ZY} = MRT_{ZY}$. Similarly, along BB', $MRS_{XZ} = MRT_{XZ}$; and, along CC', $MRS_{XY} = MRT_{XY}$. These curves all intersect at Q_0 where $MRS = MRT$ for all pairs and where the slope of ABC equals the slope of the highest attainable indifference surface in all directions.

By the relationships given above in Eqs. (9–4)–(9–6), we can see that an income tax will leave the economy somewhere along CC', say Q_3 (where more leisure is taken than at Q_0). Similarly, a tax on X will leave the economy on AA' (say, at Q_1), and a tax on Y will leave the economy on BB' (say, at Q_2). There is nothing to say, *a priori*, which of Q_1, Q_2, or Q_3 will be on the highest indifference surface. It depends upon the shape of the indifference map. There may well be a combination of the various taxes which satisfies none of the Pareto conditions, but which leaves the economy on a higher indifference surface than any of these (e.g., Q_4).

This geometrical analysis can lead us some way in determining which of the three taxes is the most efficient. The line PP', which is parallel to AB in the XY-plane, represents all points on the plane ABC at which leisure taken is the same as under the income tax (point Q_3). As the diagram happens to be drawn, Q_2 lies to the right of PP'. Therefore, in this illustration the individual takes more leisure with a tax on Y than with an income tax. Because the individual's indifference map is tangential to PP' in the XY-plane at Q_3, and because indifference surfaces are convex to the origin, we would expect that Q_2 lies on a lower indifference surface than does Q_3. Similarly, we would expect by the geometry of indifference surfaces that Q_1, which induces much less leisure than Q_3, would lie on a higher indifference surface.

This conjecture would seem to imply that an important influence on the matter of which tax is best is which one most discourages the taking of leisure. There is indeed a convincing intuitive reason why this should be the case. None of the three taxes hits leisure directly. The income tax is equivalent to a tax on both X and Y, and the others tax X and Y individually. Because leisure is not being taxed, its use is being encouraged relative to X and Y. That tax which least encourages its use may be the least distorting.

While the above conjecture was suggested by Little (1951), the first attempt to formalize the relationship between the "best" tax and the demand for leisure was by Corlett and Hague (1953–4). Their analysis did not go so far as to determine which tax, or combination of taxes, was best. Rather, their procedure was as follows: Suppose we already have an income tax in existence, so we are at the point Q_3. Recall that the income tax is equivalent to a proportional tax on both goods. If we were to increase marginally the tax on one good and decrease it on the other so as to raise the same total revenue, would the representative consumer be better off? The answer turned out to be that the consumer would be better off if the marginal change induced him to take less leisure, thus confirming the conjecture stated above. Furthermore, the marginal change would induce less leisure if the good whose rate was increased was the one which was most complementary to leisure. This would be then like an indirect tax on leisure (which cannot be taxed directly).

The proof of the Corlett and Hague result requires the use of some calculus and is omitted here. The intuitive reasoning behind it can be established geometrically using Fig. 9–4, which shows the demand and supply curves for labor. Because of our assumption of fixed production prices, the demand curve for labor is perfectly elastic at the wage rate w. With the income tax in existence at the rate t, the demand price for labor, w, exceeds the price received by suppliers, $w(1 - t)$. As this is the only tax in existence, the deadweight loss of the tax system is the area abc.

Consider now a *marginal* change in the tax system. If the change causes the supply curve to shift to the right, say, to S', the efficiency of the economy is improved. The increase in labor supplied is valued at the margin at w, while the opportunity cost of supplying the labor is only $w(1 - t)$. The

Figure 9–4

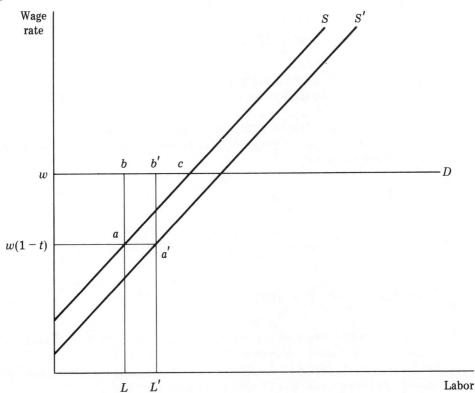

gain to society from the marginal increase in labor supplied, LL', is the area $abb'a'$. As this is the only distorted market, it is the only source of welfare gain from a marginal change. Conversely, any reduction in labor supplied from a tax change would make society worse off. A tax increase on the commodity more complementary with leisure will increase the price of that commodity, reduce the demand for both it and leisure, and therefore cause the supply of labor curve to shift right as in Fig. 9–4. Society's welfare will be improved.

It is useful to cast this analysis in an intertemporal context. The commodities X and Y can be thought of as present and future consumption in a two-period context, and Z is leisure as before. To be fully consistent, it would probably be better to distinguish between present leisure and future leisure (e.g. retirement). However, for present purposes to facilitate comparison with the previous three-good case, we simply treat leisure as a single good without identifying it with a period. Recall from Chapter 2 that in an intertemporal context the budget constraint says that the present value of consumption expenditures must equal the present value of income. In terms of the budget constraint of Eq. (9–3), that means we can interpret p_X as the price of X in the present period, and p_Y as the price of Y in the future period discounted to the present period at the consumer's discount rate. Thus, if r is the interest rate in the absence of taxes, and if the future price of Y is q_Y, then $p_Y = q_Y/(1 + r)$ so the consumer's budget constraint becomes

$$p_X X + \frac{q_Y Y}{(1 + r)} + wZ = wH \qquad (9\text{–}7)$$

where we assume labor is supplied in the first period, and where H is the total number of hours available in the first period, either for leisure or labor.

In the absence of taxes, applying the same reasoning as before, equality between the marginal rates of substitution and transformation for the three pairs of goods yields:

$$MRS_{XY} = \frac{p_X(1 + r)}{q_Y} = MRT_{XY}$$

$$MRS_{XZ} = \frac{p_X}{w} = MRT_{XZ}$$

$$MRS_{YZ} = \frac{q_Y}{w(1 + r)} = MRT_{YZ}. \qquad (9\text{–}8)$$

The interpretation of an income tax is now slightly different in an intertemporal context. A proportional income tax at the rate t applies both to the wage rate w and to the interest rate r, as discussed before. Therefore, under an income tax, the budget constraint becomes:

$$p_X X + \frac{q_Y Y}{(1 + r[1 - t])} + w(1 - t)Z = w(1 - t)H \tag{9-9}$$

or, equivalently,

$$p_X(1 + s)X + \frac{q_Y(1 + s)Y}{(1 + r[1 - t])} + wZ = wH \tag{9-10}$$

where $(1 + s) = 1/(1 - t)$. The income tax is therefore like a proportional consumption tax in each period at the rate s plus a tax on interest income. It can readily be seen that the income tax distorts all three marginal conditions. In particular,

$$MRS_{XY} = \frac{p_X(1 + r[1 - t])}{q_Y} \neq MRT_{XY}$$

$$MRS_{XZ} = \frac{p_X(1 + s)}{w} \neq MRT_{XZ}$$

$$MRS_{YZ} = \frac{q_Y(1 + s)}{w(1 + r[1 - t])} \neq MRT_{YZ}. \tag{9-11}$$

The income tax increases the relative price of future versus present consumption because of its effect on the discount rate, and it increases the price of both goods relative to leisure.

On the other hand, a proportional consumption or expenditure tax raises the prices of present and future consumption in the same proportion, and so does not distort their relative price. The budget constraint in this case is:

$$p_X(1 + s)X + \frac{q_Y(1 + s)Y}{(1 + r)} + wZ = wH \tag{9-12}$$

where s is the rate of tax. As mentioned earlier, this is equivalent to a tax on income with interest income exempt, or, in terms of the simple case being considered here, a tax on labor income. The relationships between the marginal rates of substitution and transformation under an expenditure tax are:

$$MRS_{XY} = \frac{p_X(1 + r)}{q_Y} = MRT_{XY}$$

$$MRS_{XZ} = \frac{p_X(1 + s)}{w} \neq MRT_{XZ}$$

$$MRS_{YZ} = \frac{q_Y(1 + s)}{w(1 + r)} \neq MRT_{YZ}. \tag{9-13}$$

The tax increases the prices of present and future consumption relative to leisure, but does not distort the relative prices of present versus future consumption.

Even though the expenditure tax distorts only two margins while the income tax distorts all three, one cannot say *a priori* that the consumer reaches a higher level of indifference under one than under the other. In terms of Fig. 9–3, the expenditure tax leaves the consumer at a point such as Q_3, while the income tax might be at a point such as Q_5, where none of the marginal conditions are being satisfied. Since the income tax lowers the price of present consumption X relative to future consumption, we might expect Q_5 to lie above the line CC' as shown.

The application of the Corlett and Hague result to this case can provide some insight into the sorts of circumstances that might lead to a preference for expenditure taxation rather than income taxation on efficiency grounds. In this case, starting with a proportional tax on X and Y is equivalent to starting with a proportional expenditure tax. As before, this can be viewed as a proportional subsidy on leisure. The Corlett and Hague exercise is to change tax rates marginally, raising the rate on one good and reducing it on the other, so as to maintain the same tax revenue. If the tax change reduces the demand for leisure, the consumer is better off. Suppose we increase the tax on Y (future consumption) and reduce it on X (present consumption). This is like moving the tax system in the direction of an income tax. If the consumer responds by taking more leisure, welfare will have decreased; therefore we can say that a consumer is better off under expenditure taxation than income taxation. This will be the case if present consumption is more complementary with leisure than is future consumption. If present and future consumption are equally as complementary (or substitutable) for leisure, point Q_3 will be optimal, since a marginal change in either direction will not affect leisure. However, if future consumption is more complementary with leisure than is present consumption, society's welfare will improve if the tax rate on future consumption is raised, and that on present consumption reduced.

Whether or not the system should move so far in that direction as to become a full income tax system, or whether an income tax is actually better than an expenditure tax if both are non-optimal, is a question which the Corlett and Hague analysis alone is unable to answer. All we can say is that in order to prefer an income tax on efficiency grounds, future consumption should be relatively more complementary with leisure. Empirically, it is not unrealistic to think that this might be the case. To the extent that we view leisure as retirement, it is quite plausible to imagine that future consumption is a closer complement for leisure than is present consumption.

The Optimal Tax Mix

The Corlett and Hague proposition was only proven for marginal changes about Q_3 in Fig. 9–3. Suppose we are interested in establishing the best point on the surface ABC that can be attained by a mixture of excise and/or income taxes. We may first note the important point that the Pareto-optimal allocation Q_0 cannot be attained by any mix of these taxes. At Q_0, $MRS = MRT$ between all three pair-wise combinations of X, Y, and Z. Suppose a proportional tax t is levied on each of the goods X and Y. Then,

$$MRS_{XY} = \frac{p_X(1+t)}{p_Y(1+t)} = \frac{p_X}{p_Y} = MRT_{XY}. \tag{9-14}$$

In order for the Pareto optimality condition (9–14) to hold, we need an equal tax rate on X and Y. By the same token, in order that the same condition hold between leisure and each of the two goods, we require the following to hold:

$$MRS_{ZX} = \frac{w(1+t)}{p_X(1+t)} = \frac{w}{p_X} = MRT_{ZX}. \tag{9-15}$$

A similar equation must hold between Y and Z. However, increasing the price of leisure to $w(1+t)$ to the individual involves *subsidizing* labor at the rate t. It is easy to see that this would generate no revenue for the government. The individual's budget constraint is:

$$p_X(1+t)X + p_Y(1+t)Y = w(1+t)L. \tag{9-16}$$

Since the value of inputs to producers must equal the value of outputs, the budget constraint equation (9–1) must hold for the economy. Combining Eqs. (9–1) and (9–16) yields:

$$tp_XX + tp_YY = twL. \tag{9-17}$$

In words, the revenue generated by the tax on X and Y will just be used up to subsidize L. Any income and excise tax system that satisfies the Pareto-optimal conditions will yield no revenue.[6]

Since we cannot reach the Pareto-optimal point Q_0 with a combination of income or excise taxes, some set of distorting taxes must be imposed. The best we can do is to impose the set of distorting taxes which raises the required tax revenue, but at the same time minimizes the deadweight loss. The minimization of deadweight loss is equivalent to the maximization of utility of the representative consumer. Such a set of taxes is conventionally called the *optimal tax system*. Unfortunately there is no simple way to characterize the properties of the optimal tax system geometrically in Fig. 9–3. We can summarize the main results generated by the optimal tax analysis.[7]

(a) The Inverse Elasticity Rule The rules that govern the rates at which taxes ought to be levied on various commodities dictate that the tax rate on a particular commodity will depend in general upon the characteristics of the demand function for that commodity, including all the complementarity

or substitutability relations it has with other commodities. If we ignore all these latter relations, or cross-price effects in demand, and assume that the dominant argument in the demand function is the good's own price, the optimal tax rules simplify considerably. The set of optimal taxes is then inversely proportional to the corresponding elasticities of demand, the factor of proportionality being determined by the amount of revenue that must be raised. Those commodities with the least elastic demands should have the highest tax rates. In the extreme, if a commodity has a completely inelastic demand, all tax revenues should be derived from the taxation of that commodity, and there would be no deadweight loss. In this case, the tax would be equivalent to a lump-sum tax.

We can make some sense of this rule geometrically by using demand curves. Figure 9–5, adopted from Baumol and Bradford (1970), illustrates the importance of the elasticity of demand as a determinant of the least deadweight loss tax system. Consider a commodity, Q, whose price and output in the absence of taxation are p_1 and Q_1. We consider two alternative demand curves: an elastic one, D_e, and an inelastic one, D_i. Suppose now

Figure 9–5

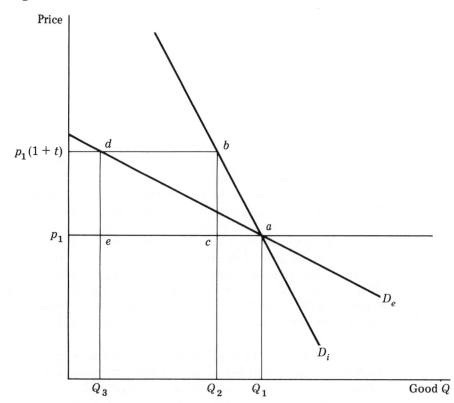

that an *ad valorem* tax at the rate t is imposed so that the price rises to $p_1(1 + t)$. If the demand curve were elastic, the demand would fall to Q_3, tax revenue raised would be $p_1(1 + t)dep_1$, and the deadweight loss would be *dae*. In the inelastic case, the output would be Q_2, tax revenue would be $p_1(1 + t)bcp_1$, and the deadweight loss would be *bac*. Comparing the two cases, it is easily seen that the deadweight loss per dollar of tax revenue raised is lower for the inelastic case $(bac/p_1(1 + t)bcp_1)$ than for the elastic case $(dae/p_1(1 + t)dep_1)$. Therefore, we ought to impose a higher tax the lower is the elasticity of demand.

When the taxes are levied optimally, the deadweight loss per dollar of tax revenue will be the same for both commodities. For the commodity with the elastic demand, this may be written as follows, assuming linear demand curves:

$$\frac{dae}{p_1(1 + t_e)dep_1} = \frac{-\frac{1}{2}(\Delta Q_e \cdot t_e p_1)}{t_e p_1 \cdot Q_e} \tag{9-18}$$

where t_e is the tax rate on this commodity, Q_e is the demand after the tax, and ΔQ_e is the change in demand due to the tax, which is negative. The product $t_e p_1$ is the change in price due to the tax. Suppose we denote the (arc) elasticity of demand as η_e. Then, it can be approximately defined by:

$$\eta_e \cong -\frac{\Delta Q_e \cdot p_1}{Q_e \cdot t_e p_1}. \tag{9-19}$$

By substituting Eq. (9–19) into Eq. (9–18), the deadweight loss per unit of tax revenue is approximately $\frac{1}{2}\eta_e t_e$. Doing the same for commodity i, the deadweight loss per unit of tax revenue is approximately $\frac{1}{2}\eta_i t_i$. Since these two must be equal under the optimal tax scheme:

$$\frac{t_e}{t_i} = \frac{\eta_i}{\eta_e}. \tag{9-20}$$

That is, commodity tax rates should be inversely proportional to the elasticity of demand.

This demonstration is actually somewhat misleading, since the tax system that has least deadweight loss will be the one for which the loss from *marginal* tax changes are equated. In the diagram, it is *average* deadweight losses which are being equated. However, for the case of linear demand curves, the tax system which minimizes average deadweight losses is also the one which minimizes marginal deadweight losses. For non-linear demand curves, Eq. (9–20) will be exact for marginal changes, and will characterize the optimal tax structure.

(b) Ramsey's Proportionate Reduction Rule   The so-called Ramsey rule, named after one of the earliest contributors to the theory of optimal taxation (Ramsey [1927]), says that the optimal set of taxes is that which approximately

reduces the demand for all commodities in the same proportion (including leisure). We say "approximately" because the rule was only proven for the levying of an infinitesimally small amount of tax. The intuitive sense of the Ramsey rule is closely related to the inverse elasticity rule given above. Equation (9–18) for the deadweight loss per unit of tax revenue reduces immediately to $-\frac{1}{2}\Delta Q_e/Q_e$. Under the optimal tax system, this amount must be the same for all commodities, or:

$$\frac{\Delta Q_e}{Q_e} = \frac{\Delta Q_i}{Q_i}. \tag{9–21}$$

Of course, this proof offers an interpretation only in the case in which cross-price effects may be ignored. The Ramsey rule holds in the more general case as well, as is shown in Diamond and Mirrlees (1971).

(c) Directly Additive Utility Functions If the individual's utility function can be written in the directly additive form, the optimal tax rate on each commodity will be inversely proportional to the income elasticity of demand. That is, necessities would bear higher tax rates than luxuries. This result was originally a conjecture by Little (1951), formed on the basis of his geometric analysis. It was later proven formally by Atkinson and Stiglitz (1972). The directly additive form of the utility function is as follows:

$$U = U_1(X_1) + U_2(X_2) + \cdots + U_n(X_n) + U_L(L). \tag{9–22}$$

Utility functions of this form have the property that the marginal rate of substitution between any pair of commodities is independent of the quantity consumed of any other commodity. While in practice utility functions may not exhibit direct additivity, this result does bring into sharp focus the likelihood of a conflict between efficiency and equity considerations. A tax system which tends to tax heavily those commodities with low income elasticities of demand will conflict with equity if the latter requires that the tax system be redistributive, since commodities with low income elasticities of demand form a larger proportion of the expenditures of low income persons.

(d) The Optimality of the Income Tax In an economy with many goods and one factor, say, labor, an income tax or a general consumption tax at the same rate on all commodities will be optimal under a particular set of circumstances. The circumstances required are fairly stringent, and are derived by Atkinson and Stiglitz (1972). First, the income elasticity of demand for all the goods must be unity;[8] and, second, the consumer's preferences must be separable as between labor and all goods. That is, changes in L must not affect the marginal rate of substitution between any pair of the goods. Since we know from observation that different commodities have differing income elasticities of demand, we can infer that

relying solely upon the proportional income tax will not be optimal (except if factors of production are in completely inelastic supply). This result can be extended to an intertemporal context by treating consumption in different periods as different goods. The consumer's income must be interpreted now as lifetime wealth, or the present value of the stream of future income. In this case, if the demands in each period have a unitary elasticity of demand with respect to lifetime wealth, and if preferences are separable between labor and consumption in all periods, uniform taxation is desirable. In this case, uniform taxation involves a proportional consumption or expenditure tax, rather than a proportional income tax.

One should not attach too much weight to these results, since they are derived under highly restrictive circumstances. In particular, the tax instruments available are limited to taxes on commodity demands. The only choice is the rate of tax for each commodity, and only a single consumer is considered. Once less restrictive assumptions are adopted, a less restrictive set of results will occur. Consider some examples: First, if a lump-sum tax could be levied on the single consumer, it would obviously dominate commodity taxation. In a single-consumer context, it is not apparent why lump-sum taxation would not be feasible. Second, taxes are levied in a many-consumer setting, and it would be interesting to know the conditions under which income (or expenditure) taxation remains the optimal form of taxation in this setting; that is, when taxes on individual commodities at differential rates can be dispensed with. The analysis of this question is rather complex, since the introduction of many consumers into the problem inevitably introduces equity as well as efficiency considerations. We shall be content simply to state the results here. A fuller analysis may be found in Atkinson and Stiglitz (1980). Two main results have been derived. In a many-consumer economy, if the government is able to levy any set of distorting commodity taxes and to collect an identical lump-sum tax (or give an identical lump-sum subsidy) to all persons, the optimal set of commodity tax distortions would be a uniform rate applied to all commodities if consumer preferences were identical and gave rise to the so-called *linear expenditure system*. With such preferences, households have, for each good, a constant marginal propensity to consume with respect to income. In this case, a uniform set of commodity taxes with an identical lump-sum tax or subsidy for all is equivalent to the linear progressive income tax discussed in Chapter 11, or to a linear progressive expenditure tax in an intertemporal context. Second, if the government is allowed to levy both a set of distorting commodity taxes and a general progressive income tax (not necessarily linear), the commodity taxes can be dispensed with entirely if labor is weakly separable from commodities in each consumer's utility function; that is, if the marginal rate of substitution between goods is independent of the amount of labor supplied. Once again, in an intertemporal context where the goods are differentiated by time of consumption, this result refers to a general progressive expenditure tax.

APPENDIX TO CHAPTER 9:
A CLOSER LOOK AT CONSUMER'S
AND PRODUCER'S SURPLUS

As we saw in Section 9–2's discussion of the deadweight loss from taxation, we can consider changes in economic welfare either from the perspective of consumer's and producer's surplus, or in terms of changes in utility levels. In this appendix, we shall relate those two approaches. First we consider the effect on a single consumer of a change in the price of some good. Then we examine, in a quite symmetrical fashion, the effect of a change in the price of a factor supplied by a consumer, such as labor.

(a) Consumer's Surplus, Indifference Curves, and Demand Curves

The upper panel of Fig. 9–6 depicts an individual's choice between a good, X, and a composite good, M, representing all other goods or expenditures measured in monetary terms.[9] The quantity $O\overline{M}$ is the individual's total income which may be spent on good X or on other goods, and U_1 and U_2 are two representative indifference curves for the individual. Initially, the budget line facing the individual is the line $\overline{M}Y$. It has a slope of p_1 where p_1 is the rate at which income can be converted into X; in other words, p_1 is the price of X in monetary units. At this price, and with income $O\overline{M}$, the individual chooses to consume an amount X_1 of the good, and to spend ON on other commodities. He attains a utility level of U_1. Suppose there is a *ceteris paribus* fall in the price of X to p_2 resulting in a rotation of the budget line to $\overline{M}Z$. The individual's consumption of the good rises to X_3 and he reaches the higher utility level U_2.

The purpose of the notion of consumer's surplus is to "measure" the increase in utility in going from U_1 to U_2. This would seem to be an insuperable task, since in constructing utility curves we only assume that indifference curves give preference orderings and not utility measures. Instead of measuring utility directly, the consumer's surplus attempts to measure the *monetary equivalent* of utility changes. That is, it measures the change in the level of money income that would be required to raise the individual from indifference curve U_1 to indifference curve U_2. One such measure is derived by breaking up the move from X_1 to X_3 into a substitution effect and an income effect. The substitution effect of the price reduction moves the individual along the indifference curve U_1 from the quantity X_1 to X_2. This "compensated" price change involves no change in utility. The income effect is a movement from X_2 on U_1 to X_3 on U_2 without changing the price p_2. The income or money transfer hypothetically involved in the income effect is the amount $M^*\overline{M}$ and is called the *compensating variation*.[10] It is the maximum amount that the individual would be willing to pay to secure the price reduction. The compensating variation will be used as the monetary measure of welfare change.

Figure 9–6

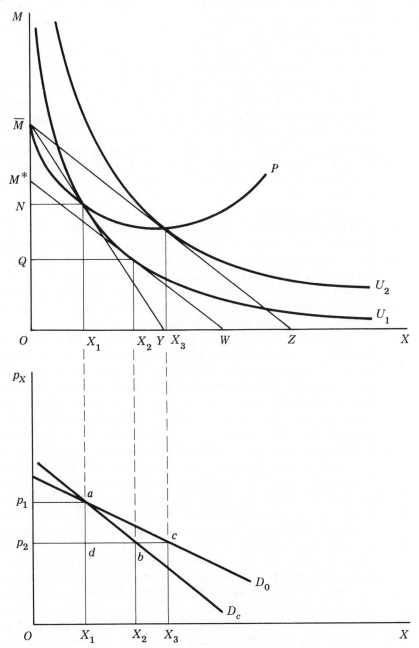

There is a close relationship between the compensating variation $M^*\overline{M}$ and the conventional consumer's surplus generated from the demand curves for the individual. In order to show it, it is first necessary to distinguish between the two types of demand curves shown in the lower part of Fig. 9–6. The curve D_o is the *ordinary demand curve*, and is constructed by taking the combinations of price and quantity of X at all points along the price-consumption line $\overline{M}P$ associated with the income level $O\overline{M}$. Two such points are (p_1, X_1) and (p_2, X_3). The curve D_c is the *compensated demand curve* constructed by taking the quantities of X demanded at various prices while compensating the individual via income transfers to remain on the indifference curve U_1. It is simply the quantity and the slope at each point along U_1. Since D_c includes changes in X due to substitution effects alone, it differs from D_o by the income effect. Two points on D_c shown are (p_1, X_1) and (p_2, X_2).

Several properties of these demand curves are worth noting. First, if X is a normal good so it has a positive income effect $(X_3 > X_2)$, D_o will be flatter than D_c, and vice versa for inferior goods. If income effects are zero, the two curves coincide. A different compensated demand curve can be constructed for each level of utility. For normal goods, D_c will be further to the right for higher levels of utility. Finally, changes in income $O\overline{M}$ will cause a shift in the ordinary demand curve. A rise in income will cause D_o to shift right for normal goods.

It can be shown that the compensating variation $M^*\overline{M}$, our monetary measure of welfare change, is equal to the area p_1abp_2 in the lower part of Fig. 9–6. An algebraic demonstration may be found in Burns (1973). Here, we shall show it geometrically. To do so, note first that $\overline{M}N$ is the income used to purchase X_1 at the price p_1. It is equal to Op_1aX_1 in the lower part of the figure. Similarly, M^*Q is the income that would be required to purchase X_2 at a price p_2. It is equal to Op_2bX_2 in the lower part of Fig. 9–6. Finally, the area X_1abX_2 can be shown to equal NQ by the following line of reasoning: Imagine starting on the indifference curve U_1 with a consumption X_1 of X and ON of other goods, and moving to X_2 of X but extracting from the consumer the maximum income that he would pay to go from X_1 to X_2. That amount is NQ, since the points (X_1, N) and (X_2, Q) are on U_1. That is, the consumer would pay as much as NQ to increase consumption of X from X_1 to X_2. Any more would reduce the level of utility below U_1. Now imagine the move from X_1 to X_2 taking place in gradual steps, each of which involves the consumer in paying the maximum for the incremental increase in X. This hypothetical breaking up of the move from X_1 to X_2 is depicted in Fig. 9–7, which reproduces the same indifference curve as U_1 in Fig. 9–6. To secure the initial incremental increase in X_1 to f, the consumer gives up Nr in income. The income given up per unit of output gained, Nr/X_1f, is approximately the *MRS* of X for income at that point in the indifference curve. Similarly, the amount given up in the next incremental increase, rs/fg, is approximately the *MRS* of X for income at the output f on U_1, and so on. As one increases X from X_1 to X_2, the

Figure 9–7

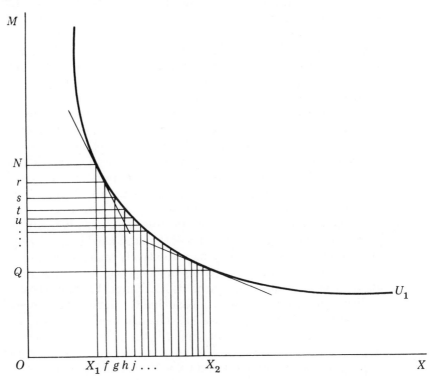

individual gives up for each unit increase in X an amount of income given by his MRS at that point. Therefore, the total amount of income given up in going from X_1 to X_2 is the sum of the MRS's paid on each increment. Since the curve D_c in Fig. 9–6 is a curve of MRS at each output along U_1, the area beneath that curve between X_1 and X_2, or X_1abX_2, is the sum of the amounts given up to secure the increase. Therefore, $X_1abX_2 = NQ$. Since we have now established that $\overline{MN} = Op_1aX_1$, $M^*Q = Op_2bX_2$, and $NQ = X_1abX_2$, combining these three we obtain:

$$\overline{MN} + NQ - M^*Q = Op_1aX_1 + X_1abX_2 - Op_2bX_2 \tag{9-23}$$

or

$$\overline{MM^*} = p_1abp_2. \tag{9-24}$$

The area p_1abp_2 corresponds to what we normally call consumer's surplus and has a rough intuitive interpretation. The amount of money the individual spent on X_1 before the price change was p_1aX_1O. When the price is reduced to p_2, the individual's consumption would rise to X_2, and his expenditures on X would be p_2bX_2O if his income were compensated to keep him on U_1.

He saves $p_1 ad p_2$ in expenditures on the first X_1 units of consumption, since the price has fallen, and is better off in monetary terms to that extent. On the last $X_1 X_2$ units of consumption he would have been willing to pay $X_1 ab X_2$, the sum of all the marginal values he attaches to each unit of X from X_1 to X_2. Since he only has to pay $X_1 db X_2$ for these units, he gets a surplus of value over expenditures of abd. His total benefit net of expenditures from the price fall is therefore $p_1 ab p_2$, the compensating variation that must be taken from him to keep him at utility level U_1.

In practice we might only observe points on the ordinary demand curve D_o rather than points on D_c. Therefore, for most applied purposes, the measure of consumers' surplus from a price change is taken to be $p_1 ac p_2$, the relevant area beneath the ordinary demand curve. It is worth noting here that this area is only an approximation to the "true" consumer's surplus. For normal goods, it is an overestimate of the difference between the maximum the consumer would pay and what is actually paid for a quantity of output. Conversely, for inferior goods, it is an underestimate. However, given the inaccuracies of the data used in most empirical studies of welfare change, this may be a relatively small source of error.[11]

The compensating variation or consumer's surplus measure derived above is not a unique measure of utility change. We have chosen to "measure" utility in monetary terms by measuring the vertical distance between, say, U_1 and U_2 in Fig. 9–6. However, that distance depends upon the slope of the budget line used. For example, if the slope p_1 had been used instead of p_2, the vertical shift of $\overline{MY}$ up to tangency with U_2 would in general require a different amount of income than $M^* \overline{M}$.[12] Indeed, one can conceive of a great many other measures of the distance between U_1 and U_2 using constructs other than vertical shifts of budget lines. This problem of the nonuniqueness of monetary measures of utility change is an unresolved problem which plagues all applications of welfare economics. We shall assume that the differences between the various measures are not great enough to pose serious problems, and shall consistently use the compensating variation, as approximated by the appropriate area beneath the ordinary demand curve, as a measure of welfare change.

(b) Producer's Surplus and Supply Curves

The concept of producer's surplus is defined in a way analogous to that of consumer's surplus. Consider an individual supplying a factor of production, say, labor (L) whose price changes. Figure 9–8 illustrates this case: The indifference map relating labor and money income (or other expenditures) M is drawn to reflect the fact that supplying labor causes disutility to the individual. Initially, the individual's budget line is EB_1, where OE is income from nonlabor sources and the slope of EB_1 is the wage rate, w_1. Under these circumstances the individual will supply L_1 units of labor to the market. When the price of labor rises to w_2, the individual's budget line

Figure 9–8

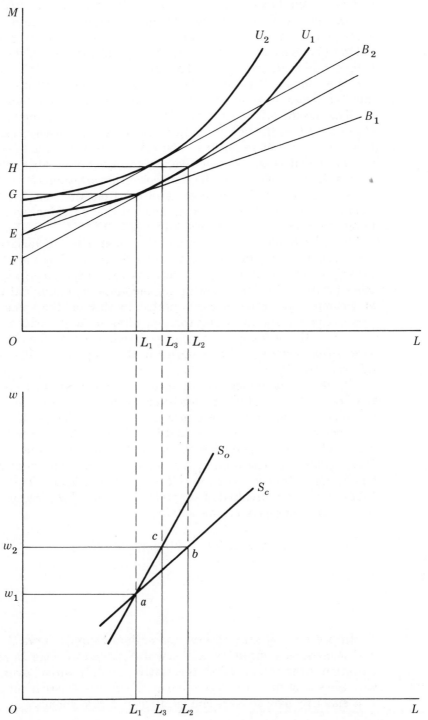

rotates to EB_2 with the steeper slope of w_2. The amount of labor supplied is now L_3. We have drawn L_3 to be greater than L_1, but it need not be.

The effects of the wage rate change can be separated into a substitution effect and an income effect. The substitution effect involves a move along the indifference curve U_1 to L_2, at which point the slope of the compensated budget line is tangent to U_1. The individual will supply L_2 units of labor and the compensating variation will be EF, the amount of income that must be taken away in order to keep the individual on indifference curve U_1. The income effect is the movement from U_1 to U_2, due to the payment of income EF at the new wage rate. If leisure is a normal good, the income rise will induce more leisure to be taken, and thus less labor. Therefore, the income effect will be negative and the amount of labor selected L_3 will be less than L_2. We define the compensating variation EF as the monetary measure of the welfare change resulting from the rise in the wage rate from w_1 to w_2. It is the maximum amount the individual would be willing to pay in order to have the rise in wage rate.

In order to obtain a measure of this compensating variation, we must construct the individual's supply curves for labor. These are shown in the lower part of Fig. 9–8. The curve S_c is the *compensated supply curve* of labor for the individual, showing the amounts the individual would supply at various wage rates if compensated to stay on the same indifference curve. The one shown is that corresponding to indifference curve U_1. The curve S_o is the *ordinary supply curve* of labor, showing the changes in labor supply from *ceteris paribus* changes in the wage rate while other income, OE, remains fixed.

By reasoning analogous to that of subsection (a), it can be shown that the area w_2baw_1, called the *producer's surplus,* equals the compensating variation EF and therefore is a measure of welfare change. The total receipts for labor at the original wage and income, Ow_1aL_1, equals EG. The total receipts for labor at point b with income OF and wage rate w_2 are Ow_2bL_2. That equals FH. The minimum amount that the individual would accept for the move from L_1 to L_2 is GH or the area abL_2L_1. This is called the *total cost* to the individual of supplying the labor L_1L_2. Summing up these three areas appropriately we obtain

$$Ow_2bL_2 - Ow_1aL_1 - abL_2L_1 = FH - EG - GH \qquad (9\text{–}25)$$

or

$$w_2baw_1 = EF. \qquad (9\text{–}26)$$

In practice, we may observe the ordinary supply curve S_o rather than S_c. The producer's surplus associated with S_o underestimates the compensating variation if the income effect is negative, and if positive, overestimates it, with the size of the error depending on the income elasticity of labor supply. This elasticity may be large and negative; in fact, economists have sometimes concluded that the ordinary labor supply curve is backward-bending, because the income effect of higher wages induces workers to enjoy more leisure, and this more than offsets the substitution effect which induces workers to take less leisure. Whether this is the true situation or not, it is clear that income effects may not be negligible in the analysis of labor supply, and we should therefore be particularly careful about the interpretation of labor supply schedules when using them for welfare analysis. In our applications, we shall assume that the difference is negligible, and treat the welfare change measure as being the producer's surplus associated with either supply curve.

CHAPTER NOTES

1. The classic analysis of this case was presented by Hotelling (1938) in his famous article about marginal cost pricing. He proved algebraically that an income tax would be superior to an excise tax when factor supplies were fixed.

2. This is most easily seen algebraically as follows. Suppose a consumer has an income of I. Then, his budget constraint in the absence of a tax will be:

$$I = p_X X + p_Y Y$$

where X and Y are the two goods. Consider now an income tax levied at the rate t on income I. The after-tax budget constraint becomes:

$$I(1 - t) = p_X X + p_Y Y.$$

If a proportional excise tax at the rate s is levied on X and Y, the after-tax budget constraint is:

$$I = (1 + s)p_X X + (1 + s)p_Y Y.$$

The two budget constraints can be seen to be equivalent if $(1 + s) = 1/(1 - t)$; that is, if $s = t/(1 - t)$.

3. This measure ignores the benefits derived from the use of the tax revenue by assuming it does not affect the indifference curves as drawn. The amount, AC, is what is referred to as the compensating variation measure of welfare change. See the discussion in the Appendix to this chapter.

4. This is so because the MRS is the ratio of marginal utilities. Therefore,

$$MRS_{LX} = MU_L/MU_X = -w/p_X$$

and

$$MRS_{ZX} = MU_Z/MU_X$$
$$= -MU_L/MU_X = w/p_X.$$

The same holds for MRS_{ZY}.

5. In a general equilibrium interpretation of this analysis, if labor is the only variable factor of production and if there is no unearned income, all production processes must exhibit constant returns-to-scale in labor and the production

surface must be flat. If the production surface were not flat, so some industries produced with decreasing or increasing returns to labor, there must be some pure profits or rent being earned; this would show up in the consumer's budget constraint. Therefore, a flat production possibility surface is the only one consistent with the analysis provided, if that analysis is intended to be applicable to the economy as a whole rather than to a particular individual.

6. Only lump-sum taxes will yield tax revenue without upsetting the Pareto efficiency conditions. They may be so-called head or poll taxes levied on each individual at the same rate. Lump-sum taxes may also be taxes on factors of production fixed in supply, or on pure rent. They can yield an amount of tax revenue equal to fixed-factor income or rent in the economy. In the model with which we are working here, these possible sources of nondistorting taxes have been assumed away (or completely exploited already).

7. In this section we are dealing only with rules for efficient taxation and are neglecting equity considerations. These results have been derived in many different places. See, for example, Diamond and Mirrlees (1971), Atkinson and Stiglitz (1972), and Sandmo (1976).

8. That is, the consumer's preferences must have the property of homotheticity. Homothetic indifference curves have the same slope (MRS) along any ray from the origin.

9. Provided the relative prices of all other goods do not change, we may represent them as a single commodity. This is referred to as the "composite commodity theorem" and is attributed to Hicks (1946). For a discussion of the problem see Green (1971).

10. For a thorough discussion of the notion of compensating variation, see Hicks (1956). The relationship between compensating variation and consumer's surplus is developed in detail in Patinkin (1963).

11. See, however, footnote 10 in Chapter 2.

12. The amount of income required at the prices p_1 is called the *equivalent variation*. It is the minimum amount of money the individual would have been willing to accept in order to forego the price change. The various monetary measures of utility change were first discussed by Hicks (1943). For a recent restatement of the problem, see Burns (1973).

10

The Normative Analysis of Taxation: Equity Aspects

INTRODUCTION

10–1   The results of Section 9–2 indicate that the set of commodity taxes which imposes the least deadweight loss is not likely to be a very equitable set. The problem arises because, as we discussed in Part I, the efficiency criterion treats one dollar as being of equal social value no matter to whom it accrues. The use of the efficiency criterion has been justified mainly on two grounds: First, one may simply assume that the goals of efficiency and distribution are separable, and that somewhere in the background the government is tending to redistributive matters in the appropriate way. Second, one might subscribe to the hypothetical compensation criterion of welfare economics and assume that any move which yields a positive net efficiency gain when all dollar gains and losses are aggregated will satisfy the compensation test. In the case of designing a tax system, these justifications for ignoring equity do not seem satisfactory, inasmuch as the tax system itself is the prime tool with which the government pursues distributive or equity goals. Therefore, one ought to take both equity and efficiency into account in judging a tax system. In other words, in comparing two alternative tax arrangements, one should put the appropriate social weights on gains and losses (under one tax system as compared with another) that accrue to various groups of persons.

   As discussed in Chapter 9, it is useful to separate equity considerations into horizontal and vertical equity. We begin with a detailed discussion of these concepts and their implications for the choice of a tax base. We conclude with some consideration of the optimal degree of progressivity of the tax system, given the conflict that may exist between equity and efficiency.

HORIZONTAL EQUITY

10–2   The conventional idea of horizontal equity, as discussed for example in Feldstein (1976a) and Musgrave (1976), supposes that if two persons have equal welfare before a tax is imposed, they should enjoy equal welfare after the tax. That is, "equals should be treated equally." The notion of horizontal equity is not itself based upon economic analysis; it is a principle of justice the acceptance of which involves a value judgment. Economists have been prepared to assume that this principle of horizontal equity is one that most, if not all, persons in society would accept. Nonetheless, the principle is not easily made operational. To judge the horizontal equity of a tax system, one must be able to say when two persons are equally well off. To do the latter requires an interpersonal comparison of welfare levels which economists are reluctant to make.

To illustrate some of the problems involved, consider two persons who have exactly the same indifference maps, and these maps show their orderings of various commodity bundles. That is, faced with exactly the same set of income and prices, they would choose the same bundle of commodities. Suppose they have the same budget lines, or incomes, and so consume the same amounts of all commodities. Are we to judge them to be equal for tax purposes? On purely objective grounds, to do so would not be warranted. The assumption of identical indifference maps carries no implications about the relative utility levels attained by the two individuals on the "same" indifference curve. Indifference curves are orderings, and are not cardinal measures of utility. The two persons might differ in their capacity to enjoy the same bundles of commodities. If so, a tax system which treated the two as if they were alike would be horizontally inequitable. By the same token, if the two were judged to be equally well-off, any tax which did not discriminate between them would be horizontally equitable. This includes income taxes, excise taxes, and almost all other taxes actually in use.

Income tax systems, in practice, attempt to take into account the fact that people with the same budget lines may have differing abilities to enjoy the fruits of their consumption. Thus, deductions from income are given for medical expenditures and certain educational expenses. Deductions are given according to the number of persons who must be supported out of the income. Deductions are also allowed for certain obvious handicaps, such as blindness or old age. All of these deductions from income for tax purposes can be considered to be measures that attempt to make the income tax system more horizontally equitable. Since no equivalent deductions are given for other types of taxes (such as excise or property taxes), these other taxes do not satisfy the horizontal equity criterion when persons differ in their capacities to enjoy a given bundle of goods.

Things get even more complicated when differences in taste are allowed for, that is, when indifference maps themselves differ. For example, suppose one person has a relatively strong preference for leisure compared with another person and, as a result, takes relatively more leisure than income. If the two attain equal welfare levels in the absence of any taxes, an income tax will be horizontally inequitable. It will discriminate against the individual with the less strong preference for leisure. Similarly, excise taxes will discriminate against individuals with relatively strong preferences for the commodities being taxed.

Yet another way in which horizontal inequity can arise occurs when differences in the perceived advantages or disadvantages of particular types of work exist, and when these differences are reflected in different incomes. An income tax will be inequitable, since it will discriminate against those employed in jobs which compensate for the disadvantages and risks associated with that line of work.

The arguments above are not intended to imply that horizontal equity is not a desirable goal, but merely to show that it is difficult to attain. Rules-of-thumb are typically used to judge the horizontal equity of taxes. As mentioned earlier, if the principle of horizontal equity is taken in its most complete sense, the relative benefits of public expenditures should be included in determining when two persons are equally well-off. This is extremely difficult to do, since the benefits of public expenditures to different persons are not revealed in any market price. The practical application of the principle of horizontal equity will be observed in our survey of the United States tax system in Chapter 13.

VERTICAL EQUITY AND THE CHOICE OF A TAX BASE

10–3   The problem of vertical equity is one stage more complex than that of horizontal equity. Not only must we be able to judge when two persons are equally well-off (horizontal equity), but also we must have some scale according to which the well-being of different persons might be measured. Several constructs have been suggested in the literature for measuring the well-being or *ability-to-pay* for tax purposes; the most commonly cited is the *comprehensive income base,* whose origin is attributed to Haig (1921) and Simons (1938). The comprehensive income base includes all income of an individual, regardless of either its source or its use. It can be defined as the sum of current consumption plus net accretions to wealth (both physical and human). It includes on an equal basis such things as labor income, income from the ownership of capital (dividends, interest, rents), accrued capital gains (increases in the value of owned capital), gifts received, and bequests received.

As noted earlier, an income tax levied on the comprehensive income base will generally not be horizontally equitable if individuals do not have the same tastes, especially regarding work or leisure, or regarding the relative disadvantages of doing different types of work. In addition, the comprehensive income base treats as equals two persons who have the same income, despite the fact that the sources of that income may vary. One may obtain income largely from labor, whereas the other may obtain unearned income from one source or another. This may well be considered horizontally inequitable since the latter attains more real income in the form of leisure time.

Historically, most authors (e.g. Musgrave [1959], Simons [1938], Feldstein [1976a]), have assumed that the comprehensive income base is the best available measure of the overall well-bein of individuals after allowing for certain deductions such as the cost of earning income, medical expenses, deductions for dependents, and the like. Even so, there are certain conceptual problems in implementing the comprehensive income base for tax purposes. We shall discuss four of these: capital gains, inflation, fluctuating incomes, and imputed income. Then we shall consider as alternative tax bases the expenditure tax and the wealth tax. Finally, the use of a social welfare function for actually making vertical equity comparisons is discussed.

Capital Gains

Capital gains are legitimately included in the comprehensive income base since they represent additions to net worth. However, their measurement is not without problems. For one thing, individuals may not realize their capital gains in the same period in which they accrue. The capital gains accrue as the value of assets rises, but these gains are only realized when the assets are converted into money through selling them. The comprehensive income base as defined above should include accrued capital gains as income, since they represent additions to net worth. For many types of assets, including accrued capital gains in the income base would involve valuing each individual's holdings of assets periodically, since market values may not be established. For widely traded homogeneous assets such as some stocks and bonds, this represents no real problem since they have well-defined market prices. On the other hand, for many physical assets, such a procedure would be costly and, to some extent, arbitrary, since no market prices may exist. For this reason, capital gains are normally included as income only when realized.

Apart from administrative convenience, taxing capital gains on a re-alization, rather than accrual, basis has both desirable and undesirable consequences. As to the latter, an incentive is built in to postpone realization, since this would postpone the payment of taxes. The holders of an asset whose value has increased will benefit from what amounts to an interest-free loan of the tax payment. This incentive to postpone realization is called the *lock-in effect*. Discussions of the lock-in effect may be found in Holt and Shelton (1962), David (1968), Diamond (1975), and Green and Sheshinsky (1978). Indeed, if the capital gain is not realized until death, the taxpayer can avoid paying a capital gains tax entirely. The capital asset becomes a bequest to the owner's heirs. For this reason, some countries treat asset transfers at death as if they were realized and subject them to capital gains tax (e.g., Canada). In any case, the lock-in effect, by discouraging the realization of capital gains, impedes the otherwise smooth functioning of capital markets.

A problem related to the lock-in effect, but one which applies to both dividends and capital gains, is the incentive that may exist to postpone taxation at the personal level by accumulating funds in a corporation. Since corporations are owned by households, profits earned by corporations represent capital income earned on behalf of the shareholders. To the extent that these profits are paid out as dividends, they will enter the personal income tax base and be taxed. However, if they are retained by the corporation as a source of finance for capital investment, they will give rise to increases in share prices to the firm's owners that reflect the ability of the firm to pay out higher dividends in the future. Since accrued capital gains are not taxed, taxes on current capital income can be postponed in this manner. This incentive to postpone taxes on profits by retaining earnings is part of the rationale for the corporate income tax. By taxing profits earned at source this tax could be seen as a withholding device, in which case taxpayers should be credited for the corporate tax paid on their behalf via an integration device (e.g. a dividend tax credit, as is done in some countries). The use of the corporate tax as a withholding device in the U.S. is discussed further in Chapter 13.

The treatment of owner-occupied housing is also problematic when capital gains taxation is on a realization basis. An individual might be inhibited from selling his house in order to buy another one elsewhere if a capital gains tax must be paid on the sale of the former. For example, he may have purchased a house for $30,000 and sold it for $40,000. If the applicable tax rate were 25 percent, he would be required to pay $2,500 tax on the realized gain of $10,000 and, therefore, would only have $37,500 with which to buy a new house. That is, he would not have enough left after tax to buy an equivalent-quality house to the one he now occupies. He would be discouraged from undertaking the transaction because of this special type of lock-in effect. In society as a whole, labor mobility would be impeded. For this reason, owner-occupied residences are often excluded from the capital gains tax.

There are also advantages to be had from taxing capital gains on realization rather than accrual. First, taxation on accrual might force asset owners to sell assets prematurely in order to obtain the money to pay the tax. (Such liquidity problems would not arise with perfectly functioning capital markets, since the asset owner would then be able to borrow against the gain in asset value.) Second, taxing capital gains on a realization basis allows the income-earner to have some control over the timing of his receipts of income over a period of years. The importance of evening out income fluctuations is discussed under *Fluctuating Incomes* on p. 264.

Inflation

The existence of inflation—an increase in the general price level—gives rise to two sorts of problems, both of which provide a rationale for some sort of indexation of the tax system. One problem arises from the presence of illusory capital gains, and the other out of the progressivity of the tax structure in nominal terms. To indicate the nature of these problems, consider the following way of accounting for taxable income in the absence of inflation: If we ignore gifts and bequests, and think of all income from the ownership of property as capital income, taxable income, defined as *comprehensive income,* is the sum of labor and capital income. If we define Y to be income, W to be wage payments, A to be the value of assets held, and r to be the rate of return received on the holding of assets (e.g. interest, dividends, etc.), taxable income over a given period is defined to be:

$$Y = W + rA + \Delta A \tag{10-1}$$

where ΔA is the (accrued) capital gain or loss on assets held over the period. This would be a suitable base for the comprehensive income tax.

Consider now the situation in the presence of inflation. The comprehensive income base should be defined in real terms. If P is the index of general prices (e.g. the consumer price index), real comprehensive income would be:

$$\frac{Y}{P} = \frac{W}{P} + \frac{rA}{P} + \Delta\left(\frac{A}{P}\right) \tag{10-2}$$

where $\Delta(A/P)$ is the change in the real value of assets held over the period and r is now understood to be the *nominal* rate of interest. The relation between inflation and the interest rate was discussed in Chapter 8. This last term in (10-2) can be shown to be approximately equal to $\Delta A/P - A(\Delta P/P^2)$.[1] Therefore, (10-2) may be written:

$$\frac{Y}{P} = \frac{W}{P} + \frac{rA}{P} + \frac{\Delta A}{P} - \frac{\Delta P}{P} \cdot \frac{A}{P}. \tag{10-3}$$

If (10-3) were the tax base used, inflation would pose no problem other than the administrative problems of measuring each term on the right hand side. However, tax accounting is usually done in nominal terms. The measure of nominal income which is consistent with this definition of real income is obtained by multiplying (10–3) through by the price level P to give:

$$Y = W + rA + \Delta A - \pi A \tag{10–4}$$

where π is $\Delta P/P$, the annual rate of inflation.

As mentioned, accounting for taxable income in nominal terms gives rise to two problems: One concerns the fact that if the tax base is defined in nominal terms, if the tax rate structure is also defined in nominal terms, and if the rate structure is progressive, inflation will itself cause an increase in real tax revenues being collected. That is, a 10 percent rise in a person's nominal income will cause the person to move into a tax bracket with a higher tax rate, and will cause tax payments to rise by more than 10 percent. To avoid this, the rate structure itself should be indexed. That is, personal exemptions and deductions should increase annually at the rate of inflation, and so should the tax brackets.

The other problem arises from the last term in Eq. (10–4). According to (10–4), the tax base should be nominal labor income (W) plus nominal capital income ($rA + \Delta A$) less πA, the loss in the real asset value due to inflation. This last term πA could be subtracted out, or it could be accounted for indirectly in the following way: For assets which earn interest or dividends, the rA and πA terms could be combined to yield $(r - \pi)A$. Thus, if capital income of this sort were included in the tax base in real terms, the loss in real asset values would automatically be accounted for. On the other hand, if the capital income in question takes the form of a nominal capital gain (ΔA), ΔA ought to be reduced by the inflationary part of the gain, πA. In summary, the tax system should tax labor income in nominal terms, but *index* all capital income. Interest, dividends, and rent ought to be taxed in real terms, and nominal capital gains ought to be purged of purely inflationary gains, πA.[2]

A numerical example might help to illustrate the treatment of inflationary capital gains: Consider the simple example illustrated in Table 10–1, comparing the effects of a general inflation on two sources of income, wage

Table 10–1

	Zero Inflation	10% Inflation (Tax on Money Income)	10% Inflation (Inflationary Capital Gains Exempt)
Wages	$10,000	$11,000	$11,000
Asset value	10,000	11,000	11,000
Income tax at 20%	2000	2200	2200
Capital gains tax at 20%	—	200	—
Real tax paid	2000	2182	2000

income and capital gains. An individual who earns $10,000 in wage income and has assets worth $10,000 in the absence of inflation will pay $2000 in tax, assuming the tax rate to be 20 percent and assuming the asset value does not change. The individual's comprehensive income will be $10,000 before tax, and $8000 after tax.

If the inflation rate is 10 percent so all prices and incomes rise by 10 percent, wage income is $11,000 and the asset value is $11,000. The individual, before tax, is no better off, nor is he worse off, than before. Suppose, however, the tax is based upon comprehensive income defined in money terms. The individual will be required to pay $2200 in tax on his wage income and $200 in tax on the capital gain, for a total tax payment of $2400. Since the real value of this tax payment is $2400/1.1 = $2182, which exceeds the $2000 paid in the absence of inflation, the individual is worse off because of the inflation. The reason for the anomaly is that the apparent capital gain of $1000 is illusory, since it does not add to purchasing power. The third column of Table 10–1 shows that, when the inflationary capital gain is exempt from tax, the same amount of real tax is paid.

Fluctuating Incomes

Problems of horizontal equity under the comprehensive income base also arise when incomes fluctuate from year to year, and when marginal tax rates vary with income. The *marginal tax rate* is defined as the proportion of income paid in taxes on the last increment of income, or:

$$m = \frac{\Delta T}{\Delta Y} \tag{10–5}$$

where m is the marginal tax rate, T is the total tax paid, and Y is taxable income. Suppose marginal tax rates rise as incomes rise ($\Delta m/\Delta Y > 0$). Under these circumstances, a person who receives a steady income will pay less in taxes over a given period of years than a person who receives the same cumulative income over those years, but whose annual income fluctuates.[3]

A numerical example will serve to illustrate the problem. Suppose the tax system imposes a flat 10 percent rate on the first $10,000 of taxable income, but the rate increases by 1 percent on each $1000 increment beyond that. Thus, 11 percent is paid on the first $1000 after $10,000, 12 percent on the next $1000, and so on. In other words, the marginal tax rate rises in steps of 1 percent on each $1000 after $10,000. In Table 10–2, the streams of income over five years, and the taxes paid, are shown for two persons. Person 1 earns a constant $15,000 per year for a total of $75,000 over five years. Person 2 earns the same amount over the five years, but in varying amounts each year. As can be seen by the numbers, person 2 pays $1000 more in taxes than person 1 simply because of the fluctuating incomes. Because of the increasing marginal tax rates, the increase in tax payments

Table 10–2

Year	Person 1		Person 2	
	Income	*Tax*	*Income*	*Tax*
1	$15,000	$1650	$20,000	$2550
2	15,000	1650	10,000	1000
3	15,000	1650	25,000	3700
4	15,000	1650	10,000	1000
5	15,000	1650	10,000	1000
Total	75,000	8250	75,000	9250

in high-income years more than offsets the reduction in tax payments in low-income years. Yet, on equity grounds, one presumably would want to treat the two as being more or less identical. This is a particularly important problem for athletes and performers, who may have a small number of years of very high income and several years with much lower income.

The obvious way out of this difficulty is to allow some method of averaging income over a period of years. The classic discussion of this may be found in Vickrey (1947). With the ability to computerize tax accounting, it is a fairly straightforward matter for the taxing authorities to maintain a record of the stream of taxable income for an individual over the years, and apply some averaging formula to that stream. The averaging formula may even include the foregone interest earnings on taxes paid on high incomes early on. An open question is over how long a period the averaging formula should apply. From a horizontal equity point of view, one might be tempted to say, the longer the better. In the limit, lifetime averaging might be advocated. In fact, some implicit forms of lifetime income averaging exist in tax systems that allow a deduction from taxable income for pension contribution and retirement savings, then collect a tax on their proceeds during retirement. However, the general principle of lifetime averaging may not be equitable, since many things change over the course of a number of years that affect the well-being of individuals. For example, tax schedules change from time to time. Over a long period they may change quite dramatically, and one is unclear as to which set of rates should be used for lifetime averaging. In recent years, tax rates have increased, but so has the level of provision of public services. The benefits of these services are borne unevenly by persons of different ages. In practice, most countries that apply income averaging do so over a much more limited period of time, such as five years.

Imputed Income

One final problem in applying the notion of a comprehensive income base is that of imputed income, or real income obtained which does not pass through the market. For example, a farmer who grows vegetables for his own consumption bypasses the market mechanism. He is in a position identical to someone who grows vegetables, sells them for "income," and uses the income to make consumption purchases. Because such types of income do not pass through the market mechanism, they are difficult to record as income for tax purposes, although it is clear that on equity grounds they ought to be.

There are many sorts of imputed income that ought to be included in the comprehensive income base but which may not be because of administrative difficulty. We shall cite some of the more important categories here.

(i) *Leisure*   One can consider the taking of leisure to be a form of real income which an individual has chosen instead of money income. The inclusion of leisure value in comprehensive income would partly remove the implicit inequity in the income tax mentioned above in favor of leisure-lovers. It would also eliminate a source of distortion in the income tax already discussed in Chapter 9 and considered further in Chapter 11.

(ii) *Household Services*   Another form of imputed income which would be extremely difficult to tabulate is the value of, say, a home-maker's services in the home. Some of the services performed have a market value attached to them, and some attempts have been made to compute the value of a home-maker's services from these market values.

(iii) *Imputed Rent*   Another significant source of imputed income accrues to individuals who own their own homes. On horizontal equity grounds, an owner-occupier of a $40,000 home is in the same position as the owner of a $40,000 home who rents the latter for, say, $4000 per year and, in turn, pays $4000 rent per year in the house he occupies. Just as the $4000 received in rent by the latter person is included in his income tax base, so should the equivalent rent that the owner-occupier "pays to himself" be included in the income tax base. Otherwise, the owner-occupier is favored by the tax system.

Consumption or Expenditure Taxation

Despite the difficulties mentioned above, the Haig-Simons comprehensive income base, with appropriate deductions, is perhaps the most widely accepted measure of a taxpayer's level of well-being. Yet it has not been the only one advocated. Two other measures have been suggested as indices upon which to base an equitable tax system: They are the total consumption expenditures of an individual and that individual's wealth. Let us consider these in turn.

The case for a consumption, or expenditure, tax was articulated some time ago by Kaldor (1955), and more recently by the United States Treasury *Blueprints for Basic Tax Reform* (1977), and the report of the Meade Committee (1978) in the United Kingdom, the so-called Meade Report. The normative arguments for aggregate consumption as the tax base are twofold: First, it is consumption that generates utility for the taxpayer, rather than income. Second, as Kaldor argued, consumption represents how much the taxpayer "takes out of the social pot," rather than how much he "puts in" in income earned.

While these equity arguments form the main justification for a consumption tax base, there are efficiency implications as well. Although these were discussed in Chapter 9 and will be taken up in more detail in the next chapter, the nature of the efficiency effects can be reviewed here. The main difference between income and consumption from an efficiency point of view is that the former distorts the savings decision while the latter does not. That is, since an income tax is levied on capital income (e.g. interest and dividends), the rate of return to savers is less than the gross return that savings yield when invested in productive capital. A tax on consumption expenditures does not have this property since it is equivalent to an income tax with capital income exempt. On the other hand, the distortion that the income tax imposes on the labor supply decision also exists under the consumption tax. We cannot say *a priori* whether the consumption tax is more or less efficient than the income tax, since both impose distortions.

The design of the consumption tax raises some interesting issues. Consider first the case where all consumer expenditures are for current consumption; that is, there are no durables such as housing and automobiles. In this case, consumption can be measured in one of two ways—first, by directly measuring consumer expenditures, and second, indirectly by subtracting savings from income. The latter method is much simpler to administer and is the one we concentrate on here. It should be noted that savings can be either positive or negative, and the tax system should treat them symmetrically. That is, if the taxpayer runs down his assets or borrows to consume, this reduction in net wealth must be *added* to income to yield consumption. In addition, any gifts or inheritances received ought to be included as income. In the case of non-durables, consumption and consumer expenditures are one and the same, so we can refer to the tax equivalently as a consumption tax or an expenditure tax.[4]

It might appear as if the expenditure tax is more difficult to administer than the income tax, since income must be calculated and asset accumulation and decumulation must be kept track of as well. However, there are two advantages to an expenditure tax. First, income need only be calculated on a realization basis, rather than on an accrued basis; that is, capital gains should only be included when actually realized. This is because the tax base is actual current expenditures, and can be computed by subtracting from realized income that part which is saved. Accrued capital gains which are not realized are automatically saved. The second advantage is that there is no need to index the capital income part of the tax base. Once again, what is required is nominal current expenditure, which is nominal income less nominal savings. If the taxpayer wishes to avoid paying taxes on inflationary income, he can simply save the inflationary gains and keep his real wealth intact.

One main difficulty of the expenditure tax concerns the time profile of the tax base. Individuals typically have high levels of expenditures early in life when income is at its lowest. To impose an expenditure tax could impose severe liquidity problems on young individuals who are already entering into debt to purchase consumer durables. If capital markets are not perfect, the tax payments will have to come out of reduced spending, and that may be very distortionary. Income tax payments, on the other hand, will be heaviest in years of high income when individuals are in a better position to pay them without recourse to borrowing. One way out of this difficulty is to choose a tax base that is equivalent to the expenditure tax in present value terms, but which has a more desirable time profile. One possibility is a tax that simply exempts capital income. It can be shown that such a tax base is equivalent to a tax base that exempts savings.[5]

The other major difficulty with designing the consumption tax occurs when some consumer expenditures are on durable goods. In this case there will be a distinction between consumer expenditures and the services of consumption *per se*. Presumably, the latter represents the appropriate measure of consumption to be included in the tax base. However, the inclusion in the tax base of consumption services from durables raises measurement problems. Consider the purchase of a house. To arrive at a measure of consumption services in the tax base, one should ideally treat the purchase of the house as the acquisition of wealth and make it deductible from the tax base. Then, the imputed services of living in the house ought to be added to the tax base. Since the latter are difficult to measure, it is usual to treat housing and other durables on a *cash flow* basis, rather than on an imputed consumption basis. To do this, the housing purchase is no longer made deductible and the imputed consumption taxes are not taxable. The tax base becomes *expenditures* rather than consumption.

An expenditure tax designed this way will yield a very uneven tax base over time, since it is particularly large at times of large consumer durable purchases. (Recall that any debt acquired to purchase the durable will show up in the tax base as negative savings). There are two difficulties with this. The first is the liquidity problem that may result as the taxpayer incurs high taxes at a time when earned income is not particularly high. The second is that the uneven tax base will give rise to averaging problems, as discussed earlier. One way out of this problem is to have a comprehensive tax base averaging system. The other is to treat the financial assets used to acquire durables as if the tax base were income-net-of-capital. That is, the acquisition of the funds by borrowing would not be considered income, but the interest payments on the borrowed funds would not be tax deductible.

All in all, the case for consumption or expenditure taxation is not clear cut. It depends upon one's judgment concerning the various pros and cons outlined above. From a purely administrative point of view, the expenditure tax is, if anything, easier to administer than a comprehensive income tax, since there is no need for indexation or for taxing capital gains on accrual. There are liquidity problems if capital markets are imperfect, and there is certainly a need for averaging because of the "lumpiness" of expenditures. However, an expenditure tax would certainly be workable. Whether or not it is actually desirable depends on the equity and efficiency issues to be discussed in later chapters. An account of some of the issues may be found in Pechman (1980) and Mieszkowski (1980).

Wealth Taxation

The other alternative to the comprehensive income base is to use the total wealth of an individual as a basis for equitable taxation. The total wealth of an individual represents the stock of purchasing power that an individual has accumulated. In principle, an individual's wealth is the present value of his future income stream. Therefore, a tax on wealth (once-over or periodically) is equivalent to a tax on an individual's future income and, to that extent, is the same as an income tax.

The case against a wealth tax is primarily the difficulty involved with administering it. A wealth tax is a tax on a stock rather than a flow, and that stock must be evaluated each time the tax is collected (e.g. annually). Not only does this involve the administrative costs of collecting and recording asset values for the myriad of asset forms held by individuals, it also involves difficult valuation problems, since many assets do not have market prices. Of specific importance is the difficulty in evaluating human wealth, that is, the present value of future labor income. These difficulties overwhelm whatever slight advantages there may be for wealth, as opposed to income, as a basis for taxation. Not surprisingly, income is universally preferred to wealth as a tax base.

THE CHOICE OF A
SOCIAL WELFARE FUNCTION

10–4   Deciding upon the appropriate index with which to measure the well-being of an individual is only the first part of the problem. Vertical equity requires one to make a value judgment as to how the burden of taxation ought to fall on different persons at relatively different positions on the scale of the index, say, income. Ultimately, this involves an implicit choice of a social welfare function that attaches different social weights on income received by various people. We shall provide a brief overview here of the issues that arise, and the implications of various value judgments for choosing a social welfare function.

Just as an individual utility function is a representation of the preference-ordering of an individual over alternative bundles of goods, so a social welfare function is a representation of the preference-ordering for society over alternative resource allocations. By an allocation of resources we mean both a combination of commodities produced, and a distribution of those commodities over consumers. In other words, each allocation of resources will yield a particular combination of utility levels reached by the members of society.[6] Up to this point, we have considered ways of attaching monetary measures to the utility levels reached by an individual. The task now is to discuss how these might be aggregated into an index of social welfare so that alternative allocations might be compared, including allocations that are not comparable using the Pareto criterion.

We are already implicitly assuming that the social welfare function or the social ordering should reflect individual utilities attained in different situations; that is, it should be some aggregate of individual utilities. This, of course, already involves a value judgment, but one which is often imposed in the literature. The social welfare function is said to be *individualistic,* since it reflects the preferences of individuals in the society. The classic work in this area, and the one upon which most of the literature builds, is by Arrow (1951b). We begin by outlining what is known as *Arrow's Possibility Theorem,* and then we consider some implications and extensions of it.

Arrow was interested in knowing whether or not a social welfare function could be obtained from aggregating individual preference orderings when the only information available was the individual preference orderings themselves. In particular, individual utility levels are taken to be neither measurable nor comparable among individuals. Only the raw indifference maps are available. He found that, indeed, a social welfare function could be constructed, but if one wished it to satisfy certain basic desirable properties, the only admissible social welfare function would be an unattractive one, i.e., a dictatorship. The properties or value judgments Arrow set down as being ones that a reasonable social welfare function should satisfy at a minimum were the following:

Pareto Principle: If all individuals prefer one allocation to another, society should do the same.

Unrestricted Domain: The same social welfare function should apply regardless of the particular preference orderings of individuals. That is, all possible individual preference orderings are permissible.

Independence of Irrelevant Alternatives: The social ordering of any two allocations should not depend upon the preferences or availability of any other allocation. This means, effectively, that the social welfare function reflects all possible pair-wise comparisons.

Using an elegant series of logical arguments, Arrow proved that, given only the preference orderings of individuals, the only social welfare function that would simultaneously satisfy the Pareto principle, unrestricted domain, and the independence of irrelevant alternatives, would be a dictatorship form. That is, the social preference ordering would reflect exactly the preference orderings over allocations of some arbitrarily-named individual. This is known as the Arrow possibility theorem and the proof is omitted here.[7] (It is available in many sources in the literature, such as Mueller [1979] and Ng [1980]). It should also be pointed out that Arrow assumed that the social welfare ordering had to be transitive. That is, if society prefers A to B and B to C, it has to prefer A to C. It is quite possible to have an intransitive social ordering that is consistent with the above properties and is not a dictatorship. For example, the method of majority voting is a way of ordering social states that is consistent with these properties but which, as we have seen in Chapter 6, leads to intransitive results (the problem of cyclical majorities). We saw there that this could only be avoided by imposing restrictions on preferences, thus violating unrestricted domain.

Perhaps some intuitive insight into the proof can be gained by looking at it in the following way. What we desire is a social welfare function that aggregates individual utility functions by some function $W(U^1, U^2, \ldots, U^i, \ldots, U^n)$ where U^i is the utility function of individual i. The utility function U^i is an ordering; that is, it is a function reflecting any arbitrary way of numbering indifference levels in an increasing way. Since all we know is the individual's preference *ordering*, any other way of numbering indifference levels in an increasing way would do as well. In other words, there are an indefinite number of utility functions which can be used to represent individual i's preference ordering. Mathematically speaking, all these utility functions will represent the same underlying preference ordering and will be increasing functions of one another. More generally, suppose a utility function U^i is found which represents the preferences of an individual satisfactorily; that is, $U^i(Y^0) \geqq U^i(Y^1)$ for two outcomes, Y^0 and Y^1, whenever Y^0 is preferred, indifferent, or not preferred to Y^1. Then any increasing function of U^i will serve just as well as a representation of the preferences (e.g. U^{i2}, log U^i, $a + bU^i$, etc.). That is what is meant by saying they are ordinal utility functions. Now, since utility levels are not comparable between persons, U^i need bear no particular relationship to U^j. Therefore, the choice of utility index for persons i and j can be done independently. Moreover, the utility functions U^i and U^j can be transformed independently, and this should not affect the social ordering of alternative outcomes. Thus, the social ordering given by $W(U^1, \ldots, U^i, U^j, \ldots, U^n)$ should be the same as that given by $W(U^1, \ldots, U^{i2}, \log U^j, \ldots, U^n)$, for example. The proof of the Arrow theorem proceeds by showing that the only social welfare function that yields an invariant ordering of alternative outcomes when individual utility functions are transformed independently is the dictatorship.

Clearly this is an unsatisfactory result, since dictatorship is a highly restrictive form of social welfare function. There are two potential ways out of the impasse. One is to weaken the conditions that the social welfare function is required to satisfy. Although there is a considerable literature on this (see Sen [1970] in particular), it is not a completely satisfactory way to proceed, since the conditions themselves are all fairly innocuous.

The other way to proceed is to increase the information available. As mentioned, the only information is a set of ordinal, non-comparable, individual utility functions. There are two ways that the information base can be increased. One is to make the utility functions "more measurable," and the other is to admit interpersonal comparisons of utility. Basically, what happens is that as more and more information about the measurability and comparability of utility is made available, the scope of possible social welfare functions is widened. A comprehensive survey may be found in Sen (1977a) and in Boadway and Bruce (1984). We can do no more than indicate the nature of the results here.

As far as measurability is concerned, it is possible to think of various degrees of it. The least restrictive form of measurability is ordinal measurability, which is what we have assumed so far. Next, one may have *cardinal* measurability of utility levels. Cardinal measurability is familiar as being the way in which temperature, height, weight, etc. are measured. In addition to ordering utility levels, cardinal measurement allows one to compare changes in utility between alternative pairs of utility levels. The analogy with temperature is useful. We can say that a change from 10° Celsius to 15° Celsius is equivalent to the change from 15° Celsius to 20° Celsius since in each case the difference is five degrees Celsius. The Celsius scale is not unique, though, since temperature can be measured by, say, the Fahrenheit scale. The important thing to notice is that the two scales are related by the positive linear transform, degrees *Fahrenheit = (9/5) degrees Celsius + 32*. Thus, the above comparison is between the change from 50° Fahrenheit to 59° Fahrenheit and from 59° Fahrenheit to 68° Fahrenheit, in both cases 9° Fahrenheit. As can be seen by this example, the changes in utility between any alternate pairs of situations can always be compared under cardinal measurability. One can move further up the scale of measurability by making utility *fully measurable*.

There are also various notions of interpersonal comparability. Three concepts of measurability found in the literature are the following: level comparability, unit comparability, and full comparability. Level comparability implies that one can always say that one person is better off, or worse off, or equally as well off, as another person for a given allocation. Level comparability is permissible with only ordinal utility functions; however, now the method of ordering utility levels among individuals must be consistent with the level comparisons that are made. This means that if two individuals are judged equally well off in a given situation, they must have identical numbers attached to their utility levels. Technically, this implies that utility functions cannot be transformed independently. If an increasing transform is made of one person's utility function (e.g. U^i is transformed to log U^i), the same transform must be applied to all persons' utility functions. Unit comparability implies that changes in utility can be compared over individuals, so one could say one person's utility increases by more than another's in going from one situation to another. Unit comparability makes sense only if utilities are at least cardinally measurable. Finally, full comparability implies that one person's utility function can be fully compared with another's.

As mentioned, the more information available, the wider the range of social welfare functions possible. Some examples of social welfare functions possible under alternative informational assumptions are as follows;

(i) *Cardinal Non-comparable Utility Functions*   If we make utility functions cardinally measurable but retain non-comparability, the Arrow possibility theorem still applies. Only dictatorship forms are possible (see Sen [1970]).

(ii) *Cardinal Unit Comparable Utility Functions*   If changes in utility levels can be compared, that is information that can be used in constructing a social welfare function of the *general utilitarian form* $W = \Sigma\, a_i\, U^i$, where a_i are arbitrary positive constants. In comparing two social states, welfare has increased if $\Delta W = \Sigma\, a_i\, \Delta U^i > 0$. Since we can compare ΔU^i over individuals, this is permissible. A special case of this is where all a_i are the same, say, unity; then $W = \Sigma\, U^i$, the *utilitarian* social welfare function.

(iii) *Level Comparable Utility Functions*   If levels are comparable, it does not matter what measurability is allowed. The additional information allows levels to be comparable, and social welfare functions that rely only on this can be used. An example is the *maximin* form, which says that social outcomes should be ordered according to the utility level attained by the individual having the lowest level of utility in each outcome.

(iv) *Level and Unit Comparability*   If both levels and units are comparable, either of the above social welfare functions are possible.

(v) *Full Comparability and Measurability*   In this case any functional form for the social welfare function $W(U^1, \ldots, U^n)$ is permitted (including those listed above), provided only that the value of the function increases with an increase in all utility levels (so the Pareto principle is satisfied). This general case is what is sometimes referred to as the Bergson-Samuelson social welfare function. It can be seen that it requires more information than the previous forms.

The above discussion shows that as one allows more information to be made available, the scope of permissible social welfare functions widens. Each of the above-mentioned social welfare functions have certain properties that have led to them being introduced into the literature in their own right. Let us conclude this section with a consideration of the genesis and properties of some of them.

By far the most well-known and widely advocated social welfare function is that which results from the principle of utilitarianism. It is associated with the works of Bentham (1907) and Mill (1921). This principle states that society should aim to maximize the sum of the utilities of all individuals;

that is, $W = \sum_{i=1}^{n} U^i$.

The appeal of utilitarianism to many presumably arises out of the fact that, under certain conditions, it implies an equal distribution of income.

Suppose that utility levels depend upon an individual's income, that all individuals have identical utility functions, and that those utility functions have the property of diminishing marginal utility of income. Then, if there is a fixed amount of income to be divided among all members of the society, the same amount should go to each. This is so because that will make the marginal utility of all the same, and so total utility will be maximized.

In a two-person economy, this principle may be illustrated with Fig. 10–1, which was used by Sen (1973) for the same purpose. The distance $O_A O_B$ represents the total amount of income available for two persons, A and B. A's curve of marginal utility (MU^A) is drawn from the origin O_A as the line aa. B's marginal utility (MU^B) is drawn in the quadrant northwest from O_B as bb, and is identical to aa. The distribution of income which maximizes total utility (the areas beneath MU^A and MU^B) is shown as $\overline{Y}$ where $MU^A = MU^B$. At this distribution, both individuals have the same income, $Y_A = Y_B$.

Unfortunately, the assumptions upon which the equality of incomes result is based are very restrictive. For one thing, if the marginal utility of income was constant, the distribution of income would be irrelevant. One distribution would be as good as another. If the marginal utility of income rose, the utilitarian principle would call for all the income to go to one individual. For another thing, persons may not obtain equal utilities from the same amount of income. Suppose that B needs more income to

Figure 10–1

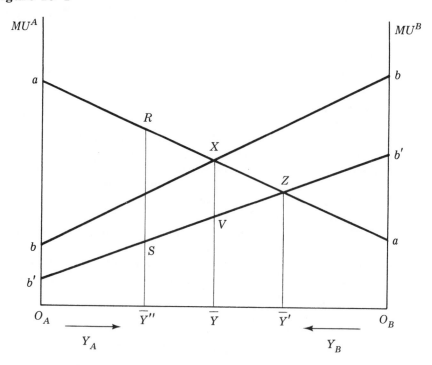

obtain the same level of utility as *A*, say, because of a physical handicap. *B*'s marginal utility function may appear as *b'b'*. At an equal distribution of income, $\overline{Y}$, *A* will be receiving more total utility than *B* and will also have a higher marginal utility. The principle of utilitarianism will call for increasing *A*'s utility even further, by increasing his income until the marginal utilities are equal again at *Z* where $Y_A > Y_B$. In this case, not only is the utilitarian principle inegalitarian in terms of income, it is even more unequal in terms of utility. Therefore, those who support utilitarianism because of its presumed tendency towards equality will be disappointed under these circumstances. The difficulty arises because utilitarianism advocates maximizing the sum of utilities, regardless of how those utilities are distributed. If one person's lower utility is more than made up for by another person's higher utility, society is assumed to be made better off.

This problem can be avoided only by having a social welfare function that puts a weight on equality of utilities *per se*. Figure 10–2 depicts graphically the form of various social welfare functions in the two-person

Figure 10–2

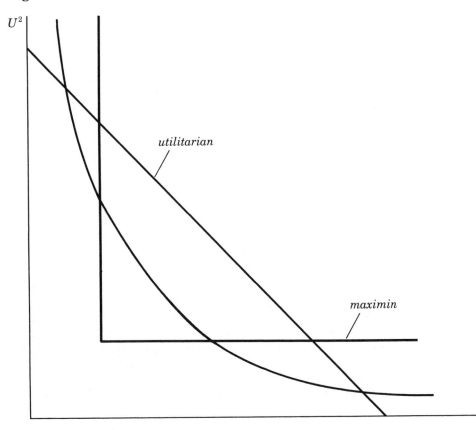

case, $W(U^1, U^2)$. For each of three cases, a single social indifference curve has been chosen that represents the utility combinations that will lead to a given level of social welfare, W. The utilitarian case is a straight line with slope of -1. At the opposite case is maximin, which gives maximum weight to equality of utilities. In between is a convex indifferent curve that gives some weight to equality of utilities but not as much as in the maximin case. Note that while the utilitarian form would distribute income in favor of persons such as type A, who gets more utility per dollar of income, the maximin form would do just the opposite. It would give relatively more income towards those least able to obtain total utility from income. The smoothly concave indifference curve would admit of intermediate cases.

The equal-income result may be resurrected, as Lerner (1944) showed, even if persons have different utility schedules, if it is unknown which utility schedule attaches to whom. For example, suppose that in Fig. 10–1 *aa* and *b'b'* are two possible utility schedules but, as we cannot observe utility directly, we do not know which utility schedule any particular individual has. Suppose we assume that there is an equal probability of each person having either of the schedules. Then it will be the case that the distribution of income which maximizes expected total utility is an equal distribution. To show this, imagine starting at an equal distribution of income, $\overline{Y}$. A redistribution of income to $\overline{Y}'$ causes total utility to rise by XZV. A symmetrically opposite redistribution from $\overline{Y}$ to $\overline{Y}''$ causes total utility to decline by $RXVS$. The difficulty is that, when undertaking a given redistribution, because one does not know which individual has which utility function, one does not know whether total utility will rise or fall. However, because $RXVS$ exceeds XZV, the probable fall exceeds the probable gain, and the highest expected utility is generated by an equal distribution of income. This same result generalizes to more than two persons and to any arbitrary possible utility schedule, provided that they exhibit diminishing marginal utility of income.

An alternative way to avoid the inherent tendency of utilitarianism towards inequality is to postulate a social welfare function that specifically places more weight on individuals with lower utility levels. For example, instead of simply adding individual utilities together, one might weight individual utilities according to some measure of the ability to enjoy. In this case, the social welfare function is the generalized utilitarian form, $W = \Sigma \, a_i U^i$, where a_i are weights reflecting the marginal contribution of individual i's utility to social welfare. One must, of course, make a value judgment in order to specify the a_i's. Harsanyi (1955) showed that if all individuals were uncertain about their future utility, and if they behaved so as to maximize expected utility, a social welfare function respecting individual preferences would be of this form. Unfortunately, such a procedure does not determine the weights to use.

Recently, Rawls (1971) has presented a detailed argument in favor of a maximin form of social welfare function. Rawls attempted to infer what distributive value judgment would be made by a rational, self-interested man who is completely uncertain about his future position in society. The person is imagined to be in an "original position," in which he knows nothing about his tastes, income, abilities, etc. when he joins society. Conceptually, it is as if a giant lottery were to be conducted in which every person is given a number, the numbers are all collected and then redistributed at random. Each individual has an equal chance of being any other. Rawls argues that under these circumstances, an individual would choose a social welfare function which satisfied the following properties:

(i) Each person has a prior right to the same amount of basic liberty.
(ii) Social and economic inequalities should be arranged to maximize the well-being of the least well-off and to ensure equality of opportunity.

These principles are then considered to be rational, normative rules of justice. The presumption that individuals will opt unanimously for the maximin criterion is itself not a logical deduction, but must be based on an assumption that individuals will be extreme risk-averters in the decision under consideration.

Utilitarianism and the Rawlsian maximin principle are but two of the many possible criteria upon which vertical equity might be based. In analyzing the effects of actual tax systems, there is no requirement for us to preselect a specific value judgment about the ideal income distribution. The economist may proceed by analyzing the economic effects of various redistributive measures, and then allowing the policymaker to decide among them. However, in our discussion of taxes we shall frequently be working under a presumption that, on equity grounds, a tax system should operate to make income distribution more, rather than less, equal as compared with what it would be in the absence of taxes. This presumption can be regarded as much a reflection of empirical fact as a value judgment. Governments do, in fact, attempt through their tax policies to make the distribution of income (and utility) more equal.

The example of Fig. 10–1 is based upon yet another important assumption, the failure of which critically affects the amount of income redistribution that is carried out, regardless of the nature of the social welfare function one has in mind. The total amount of income available for redistribution is assumed to be fixed.

Let us now turn to the implications of explicitly introducing the equity-efficiency trade-off into the choice of a tax system.

EQUITY CONSIDERATIONS IN
THE CHOICE OF A TAX SYSTEM

10–5   Two main difficulties arise in attempting to integrate equity with efficiency in the theoretical design of a tax system. First, as we have stressed throughout this book, the application of the criterion of equity requires one to make explicit value judgments of the nature of interpersonal comparisons of utility. Formally, this may be done with the aid of a social welfare function. Second, from a technical point of view the analytical derivation of optimal tax rules that incorporate both equity and efficiency is rather involved mathematically and beyond the scope of this book. We shall simply indicate the manner in which the literature has developed thus far, and the qualitative nature of the results that have been obtained. The reader seeking more detailed discussion is referred to Diamond and Mirrlees (1971), Atkinson and Stiglitz (1976), Mirrlees (1971), Stern (1976), and Atkinson (1977).

There are two separate strands to the literature. The first, and least interesting from a policy point of view, is the attempt to introduce equity considerations into the choice of optimal commodity taxes. This is typically done by postulating a general individualistic social welfare function and finding the set of commodity taxes that yields the appropriate revenue to the government and maximizes the social welfare function. The general tenor of the results is as follows. The optimal set of taxes depends upon two sorts of things: First, relative tax rates depend upon the relative dead-weight losses from taxing various commodities, as in the pure efficiency case. All other things being equal, the less elastic is its demand, the higher will be the tax on a commodity.

Second, the set of relative taxes depends upon vertical equity considerations in the following manner: Different commodities will be consumed in different proportions by different income or utility groups. For example, some commodities will be luxuries, and some necessities. Two taxes will differ in the way in which they affect the relative prices of luxuries and necessities, and therefore will affect relative utility levels. A tax on a luxury good will tend to reduce real incomes relatively more for high-income persons compared with low-income persons than a tax on a necessity good. This is because luxuries form a relatively larger proportion of the budget of high-income persons than of low-income persons, and a tax on a luxury will tend to raise the relative price of the luxury good. If, at the margin, one can place a value on the marginal social utility of incomes of different income groups, one can evaluate the relative effects on social welfare of marginal changes in taxes via their effects on real incomes of different income groups. (Formally, one can compare the relative effects on social welfare of price changes in various commodities by the use of what Feldstein [1972b] has called a *distribution characteristic* of a good.[8] The distribution characteristic of good X_i is defined as the weighted average of marginal social utilities of income of all persons in the economy, weighted by the proportion of total output of the commodity.) We might call this the "equity" or "distributive" effect of a tax change.[9] The determination of the equity effect of an increase in the price of a good requires knowledge of two things: the proportions in which different income groups consume it, and the value judgment one makes about the marginal social utility of incomes of various persons. If one assumes that the marginal social utility of income diminishes as income rises, the equity weight attached to changes in the price of necessities will exceed that attached to changes in the price of luxuries. A rise in the price of a necessity good (say, due to a tax rise) will reduce social welfare more than a rise in the price of a luxury good. *Ceteris paribus,* the tax rate on luxuries would be higher than that on necessities due to the influence of these equity rates.

When one commodity tax is substituted at the margin for another, there will be both efficiency effects (changes in deadweight loss) and equity effects (changes in the level of social welfare due to changes in real incomes of various groups). The optimal set of commodity taxes depends upon both equity and efficiency considerations, according to a fairly complicated and not too intuitively meaningful rule. Since in many cases the equity effect will counter the efficiency effect for a tax on a particular good, the optimal tax structure may differ considerably from the one which minimizes deadweight loss.

As mentioned above, this method of integrating equity and efficiency, though instructive for the theoretical development of the optimal taxation literature, is not too interesting from a policy point of view. Commodity taxes, being *in rem,* are limited in their ability to redistribute income since they cannot be given progressive rate structures. Governments rely mainly on the progressive income tax to pursue the goal of equity. Much of the interesting analysis of optimal tax systems for equity has been concerned with how progressive the income tax should be. Because of the complexity of the analysis, models of the "optimal income tax" typically ignore the possibility of levying commodity taxes by assuming that there is only one consumption good and one factor of production (e.g. labor).[10] We shall adopt that convention in the following discussion.

The determination of the progressivity of the income tax involves weighing two conflicting tendencies, equity and efficiency. In the simple one-good, one-factor model, inefficiencies arise solely due to the distortion of the marginal rate of transformation between leisure and consumption. This distortion will differ for different income groups. The more progressive is the income tax, the greater will be the marginal distortion levied upon higher income groups. In these models, higher income groups are those endowed with more ability to supply labor value per hour (or "efficiency units" of labor); therefore, under a progressive income tax system, the most "efficient" suppliers of output-producing labor will be the most strongly affected at the margin. As the tax becomes more progressive, the output loss to the economy rises, and this is the prime source of limitation on progressivity. The less elastic is the labor supply, the less is the loss in efficiency from a given rate of progression.

On the equity side, it is usually presumed that the appropriate social welfare function will be individualistic. If this function were to exhibit diminishing marginal utility of income, there would be a tendency to want to make incomes more equal, assuming that the same utility functions are applicable to individuals of all income groups. Depending upon the rate at which the marginal social utility of income diminishes as incomes rise, and upon the efficiency losses from progression as determined by the elasticity of the supply of labor, the tax will be more or less progressive. In order to get more specific results, one must make more specific assumptions about the properties of social welfare functions, as well as about the elasticity of the labor supply. Some of the results for particular models are as follows:

(i) *Invariable Labor Supply* We have already discussed this case above, so we need only summarize the results here. With a completely inelastic labor supply (or other factor supply if there are other sources of income) equity considerations alone will determine progressivity. If all individuals have identical utility functions, and if the marginal social utility of income declines as income rises, utilitarianism[11] would call for perfect equality of incomes, or 100 percent progressivity. Indeed, so would more general individualistic social welfare functions having the property of diminishing marginal social utility of incomes. If the marginal utility of income were constant, utilitarianism would call for no redistribution. More general social welfare functions with diminishing marginal social utility would still call for complete equality.

On the other hand, if utility functions differ among individuals, an application of the utilitarian principle would call for redistribution of income towards those most able to derive utility from it. Whether this requires progressive or regressive taxation depends upon whether or not persons with the most "ability to enjoy" income had the highest or lowest incomes before tax. If they tended to have lower incomes, the tax system would have to redistribute incomes heavily towards them. With different utility functions, one would also get different results from social welfare functions other than utilitarianism. For example, if the social welfare function weighted low-utility persons relatively more heavily, the tax system would give them more income (come closer to equality) than utilitarianism. The extreme case of this is the social welfare function that is concerned only with the utility level of the lowest utility person, the so-called maximin, or Rawlsian, social welfare function.

(ii) *Variable Labor Supply* Once the supply of labor is variable, the case for making incomes more equal is no longer clearcut. Consider, for example, the case in which lump-sum taxation can be imposed on individuals so that income can be redistributed costlessly. For simplicity, consider a two-person economy in which both persons have identical preferences, but one person has higher skills and therefore a higher wage rate. The government must raise a fixed amount of revenue from taxing these two persons. To simplify the analysis further, assume that the government is using the maximin criterion. This will imply that utilities of the two individuals should be equalized.

The situation is diagrammed in Fig. 10–3, where Y is income, L is labor, and K is the maximum hours of time available. The budget line before tax for the high-income person is OA, and for the low-income person is OB. Lump-sum taxation will shift these budget lines parallel inwards.

Figure 10–3

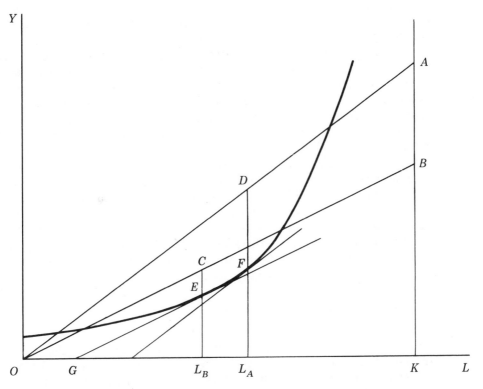

The optimal tax scheme will remove revenue in such a way as to leave the individuals on the same indifference curve such as the one illustrated. The high-income person will end up supplying L_A of labor, making a gross income of DL_A and paying taxes of DF. The low-income person will supply L_B of labor, receive income CL_B, and pay taxes of CE. A priori, one cannot say whether the average tax rate is higher or lower for the high-income person. That is, DF/DL_A can be larger or smaller than CE/CL_B.[12]

When utilitarianism is the criterion used, equality of utility is no longer desired even when lump-sum taxes are possible, for in this case, the optimum requires the marginal utility of income to be the same for all, and there is no reason why, at points E and F, the marginal utilities of income should be the same.

In practice, lump-sum taxes are not used to redistribute income. Instead, progressive income taxes are used. In this case, there is yet another reason why social welfare will not be maximized by equalizing incomes. Increasing the marginal tax rates on high-income groups will reduce the real income of this group. This reduced real income can be divided into two parts: the revenue generated for the government, and the deadweight loss of the tax.

Only the former can be transferred to low-income persons.[13] Therefore, since the gain in monetary terms to low-income persons is less than the loss to high-income persons by the deadweight loss of the tax, in order that the change in utility to the two be equal at the margin, high-income persons must be left with higher incomes than low-income persons when the optimal degree of progressivity is attained. The amount of progressivity desired under utiltarianism will depend upon the elasticity of supply of labor, and upon the rate at which the marginal utility of income diminishes. The greater either of these factors is, the less progressive taxation will be.

When factor supplies were fixed, all individualistic social welfare functions exhibiting diminishing marginal social utility of incomes and treating all persons symmetrically (including utilitarianism and maximin) gave identical results when individuals had the same utility functions, complete equality of incomes. With variable factor supplies, this is no longer the case. The greater the weight given to low-income persons, the more progressive the tax will be.

To see this, suppose we think of an abstract economy consisting of two sorts of persons, the rich R and the poor P. The criterion for the optimal progressivity of the income tax may be stated as follows:[14]

$$MSU_P = -MSU_R \tag{10--6}$$

where MSU_P is the change in social utility attributable to the income of the poor from an increase in rate of progressivity of the tax, and MSU_R is the change in the social utility of the income accruing to the rich from the same tax change. Under a regime of utilitarianism this criterion becomes simply:

$$MU_P = -MU_R. \tag{10--7}$$

That is, the contributions of individual utility changes to social welfare are the same no matter who receives them ($MU_R = MSU_R$; $MU_P = MSU_P$). With variable factor supplies, $-MU_R$ will result from the real resource transfer from R to P, and from the extra deadweight loss due to the higher marginal tax rate, while MU_P will be the result of the transfer to P (ignoring for simplicity any deadweight loss involved in the transfer to P, the existence of which only serves to strengthen the conclusions). If utility functions have diminishing marginal utilities of income, then condition (10--7) will dictate that R-type persons will have higher incomes than P-type persons at the optimum, and full equality will not result as mentioned above. That is, the marginal utility of income to P must exceed the marginal utility of income to R in order that the money income transferred to P will raise P's utility by enough to cover both the reduction in money income of R and the deadweight loss of the tax increase.

Consider now a general social welfare function that attributes larger social weight to increases of utility of low-income persons than of high-income persons. The optimal progressivity is attained when equation (10–6) applies, and we may separate the two sides of it to give:

$$\frac{\Delta SW}{\Delta U_P} \cdot MU_P = \frac{\Delta SW}{\Delta U_R} \cdot MU_R \tag{10–8}$$

where $\Delta SW/\Delta U_P$ is the marginal change in social welfare from a change in utility of the poor and $\Delta SW/\Delta U_R$ is defined similarly for the rich. Under the assumed circumstances, $\Delta SW/\Delta U_P > \Delta SW/\Delta U_R$. The tax system which satisfied Eq. (10–7) will not satisfy Eq. (10–8); the left-hand side of the latter will exceed the right-hand side. Therefore, greater progressivity will be required to bring the two into equality.

The degree of progressivity will depend upon three things: the relative weight given to the utility of low-income persons in the social welfare function, the rate at which individual marginal utility of income declines, and the elasticity of factor supply. The most extreme case of the former is the Rawlsian maximin social welfare function already encountered. According to this criterion, a tax system is judged solely by the maximization of the utility level of the lowest utility person. In the two-group example given above this occurs when

$$MSU_P = 0. \tag{10–9}$$

The progression of the income tax is carried to the point at which further increases in progression do not yield any increases in real income to the poor group. Clearly, this will result in a more progressive tax system than that of Eq. (10–8) discussed above.

The above results are merely suggestive of the sorts of influences at work in determining the optimal degree of progressivity of the income tax. In order to put them into operation, one must be able to make cardinal measures of individual utility levels as well as interpersonal comparisons of such measures, both of which economists are no better equipped to do than anyone else. Matters become even more complicated if utility functions or tastes differ among individuals, as discussed in Allingham (1975), and Atkinson and Stiglitz (1976). In practice, the choice regarding the progressivity of the income tax is taken through the political process.[15]

In the above discussion, the main factor limiting the progressivity of the income tax from an efficiency point of view was the deadweight loss resulting from increasing the rate of progression. It has been pointed out, for example, by Kesselman (1976), that the progressive income tax is not the most efficient way of redistributing income. The progressive income tax is a tax levied upon total earnings and does not discriminate between the contributions of hours worked and the wage rate upon gross earnings.

Kesselman has suggested the use of an instrument called the *graduated earnings tax*. Unlike the income tax, the graduated earnings tax discriminates between the wage rate and the number of hours worked. Taxes depend negatively on time worked and positively on earnings.[16] Kesselman undertook a number of simulations of simple economies using various social welfare functions and elasticity of labor supply assumptions. He found, in comparing the linear progressive income tax with the graduated earnings tax, that the latter allowed society to attain a higher level of social welfare, and promoted more equality than the former. Although the simulations were performed for simple economies in which all members had identical utility functions, and in which abilities bore a one-to-one relationship to wage rates,[17] the approach is suggestive of the fact that there are alternatives available to government that may be superior to the progressive income tax for pursuing equity goals.

CHAPTER NOTES

1. This expression is exact for differential changes. To see this, carry out the differentiation as follows:

$$\frac{d\left(\frac{A}{P}\right)}{dt} = \frac{dA}{dt}\cdot\frac{1}{P} - \frac{A}{p^2}\frac{dP}{dt} = \frac{\dot{A}}{P} - \frac{A}{P}\frac{\dot{P}}{P}$$

where the dot refers to the time differentiation and $\dot{P}/P$ is the rate of inflation. In the discrete change case, the exact expression is:

$$\Delta\left(\frac{A}{P}\right) = \frac{\Delta A}{P} - A\frac{\Delta p}{p^2} - \frac{\Delta A \Delta P}{p^2}.$$

The latter term is neglected in Eq. (10–3).

2. For suggestions as to how this might be done in practice, see Helliwell (1969) and Diamond (1975).

3. The comparison should really be between the present values of taxes paid by the two individuals rather than the simple sum of taxes paid. However, for simplicity, we shall ignore the complication of discounting tax revenues over time since it does not affect the point at issue.

4. One should not confuse commodity taxes with expenditure taxes. The former are levied on commodity purchases and do not discriminate among individuals. Expenditure taxes are taxes levied upon the total expenditures of an individual and may be levied at progressive rates.

5. In the case of the consumption tax, capital income is included in the tax base, but wealth accumulation is excluded. Thus, for a bond worth B, the interest rB is included in the base, but the acquisition of the bond B is deductible. Under an income tax system with capital income exempt, B is not deductible

and rB is not taxable. When the discount rate is r, the present value of these bases is the same.

6. More generally, the literature refers to a social welfare function as a way of ordering alternative "social states," where a social state can refer to more than simply the outcomes of the economy. Extensive surveys of the topic may be found in Sen (1970, 1977b). The use of the concept of a social welfare function is generally attributed to Bergson (1938).

7. Arrow's theorem is often referred to as an impossibility theorem, rather than a possibility theorem. This is because we can state the result in the following alternative way: It is impossible to have a social welfare function that satisfies the Pareto principle, unrestricted domain, the independence of irrelevant alternatives, and which is, nevertheless, not a dictatorship.

8. The distribution characteristic of good X_i is defined as a weighted average of marginal social utilities of income of all persons where the weights are the proportions of total output consumed by each person. Thus, if β^j is the marginal social utility of income of person j, the distribution characteristic of good X_i is defined by:

$$R_i = \Sigma \frac{\beta^j X_i^j}{j X_i}.$$

9. A comparison of distribution characteristics between two goods indicates the relative reduction in social utility occurring from marginal price increases of those two goods.

10. Atkinson and Stiglitz (1976) have shown that one can dispense with commodity taxation and rely solely on progressive income taxation when all income is earned by labor and when the utility function is weakly separable between labor and all consumption goods. That is, if the utility function may be written in the form:

$$U = U[V(X_1, \ldots, X_n), H]$$

where X_i are commodities and H is labor. This function has the property that the marginal rate of substitution between any pair of commodities is independent of H. The assumption of a single factor of production requires that we ignore possible complementarity/substitutability in production between, say, different types of labor (e.g. white collar and blue collar). Recent studies have stressed the restrictiveness of this assumption.

11. Recall that utilitarianism treats utility gains symmetrically no matter who receives them. That is, the social welfare function may be written in the special form:

$$W = \Sigma U^j.$$

It has the property that the marginal social utility of income is simply the marginal utility of income of the individual to whom the income accrues. In social welfare functions of the more general form, $W(U^1, \ldots, U^s)$, there is a difference between the marginal social utility of income and the marginal utility of an individual's income. This is elaborated below in the subsection on variable labor supply.

12. It has been proven algebraically by Sadka (1976) that the tax will be progressive (average tax rate will rise with income) if the elasticity of the indifference curve rises with L. A geometric proof of this is as follows. The average tax rate may be written:

$$\frac{CE}{CL_B} = \frac{OG}{OL_B} = \frac{OL_B - GL_B}{OL_B} = 1 - \frac{GL_B}{OL_B}.$$

The elasticity of the indifference curve at point E is:

$$\eta = \frac{EL_B}{GL_B} \cdot \frac{OL_B}{EL_B} = \frac{OL_B}{GL_B}.$$

Therefore

$$\frac{CE}{CL_B} = 1 - \frac{1}{\eta} = \text{Average tax rate.}$$

If η rises as one moves up the indifference curve, the average tax rate will rise and the tax will be progressive under the maximin criterion.

13. There may also be a deadweight loss involved in transferring income to low-income persons by the income tax system. The nature of this deadweight loss may be seen in the discussion of negative income taxation in Chapter 14.

14. This condition follows directly as the condition of maximization of a social welfare function.

15. For an analysis of the rate of progression of a linear progressive income tax that would be chosen by a process of simple majority rule, see Romer (1975).

16. Note that an even better scheme for redistributing income would be to apply the rate not on earnings but on the actual wage rate. That is, one could have a lump-sum tax based on the wage rate. To the extent that wages reflected abilities, one would have an ability tax as discussed by Allingham (1975).

17. With nonidentical utility functions, the graduated earnings tax would fail to meet the criterion of horizontal equity for much the same reasons as the comprehensive income tax does. Also, to assume that wage rates are exogenously determined by given abilities may be ignoring important dynamic effects of progressive taxation on the structure of wages (e.g. through the accumulation of human capital through education).

11

The Incentive Effects of Taxation

INTRODUCTION

11–1   This chapter and the following one constitute what might be termed the positive analysis of taxation, that is, the analysis of how taxes impinge upon the output of the economy as determined by household and firm decision-making, and how taxes influence the relative prices of goods and factors and hence affect the welfare of different individuals or income groups. This latter, called the incidence problem, is discussed in the following chapter.

The analysis and empirical study of the effects of taxation have developed for the most part in a partial equilibrium setting. That is, the influence of a particular tax, say, an income tax, on a particular market, say, the labor market, has been conducted under the *ceteris paribus* assumption that no other relevant variables change. In many contexts this may be a valid procedure for obtaining the primary effects of the tax, and in this chapter we shall for the most part follow the partial equilibrium approach. However, there are some taxes whose effects are so pervasive over different sectors of the economy that they are better treated using a general equilibrium approach. For example, a tax which falls on a broad group of industries of the economy, such as the corporate tax falling on the corporate sector, may require a general equilibrium approach. In the next chapter, we develop a commonly used neoclassical general equilibrium model for the analysis of tax incidence. For obvious heuristic reasons, the general equilibrium analysis of the resource allocation effects of taxes is presented there rather than in this chapter.

The following sections by no means present an exhaustive survey of the effects of taxation on economic choice. Rather, they include those effects which have drawn the most attention from public finance scholars in the past, presumably reflecting a judgment that these are among the most important effects. Most attention has been devoted to the influence of taxes on the markets for factors of production—labor, capital, and risk-taking— since it is these which ultimately determine the ability of the economy to produce output. Consequently, the taxes that fall directly on payments to factors of production, such as the personal income tax and the corporation tax, have been much more fully analyzed than those falling on purchases of output. The following sections, beginning with the effect of taxes on labor supply, will tend to reflect that bias.

LABOR SUPPLY

11–2   Income taxes are taxes on the payments to all factors of production, including labor. Since they reduce the return to the individual household from supplying labor, we might expect that they would influence the choice as to how much labor to supply. In analyzing this question, however, we must recognize the complexity of the concept of a "supply of labor." Of course, a household's labor supply is partly determined by the number of hours spent at work rather than at leisure. Thus, as a first attempt to investigate the effect of income taxation on household supply of labor, part (a) of this section utilizes a very simple model in which an individual faced with a given wage rate is assumed to allocate his time between leisure and income-earning activities according to preferences represented by an indifference map. Then, in part (b), we build from this analysis of the individual to an analysis of the market, showing how an income tax affects equilibrium wage rates and generates an excess burden.

One additional way in which taxes and other government policies can influence labor supply is by changing the incentives for labor force participation. Households may be induced to enter the labor force, on a full or part-time basis, or to leave the labor force altogether. This appears to be a more important phenomenon for some types of individuals than others. Much has been written, for example, about the labor-force participation of married women and about the retirement decisions of the elderly. In part (b) we briefly analyze the participation decision. Since the possibility of induced retirement has been the focus of some controversy in the evaluation of old age security systems, we discuss this issue further in Chapter 14.

(a) Taxes and Hours of Work: The Individual

Let us consider the behavior of an individual who enjoys both leisure and income (or more precisely, the things that income can buy). Figure 11–1 shows some indifference curves representing the individual's preferences for these "goods." The household is constrained by the fact that income is

Figure 11–1

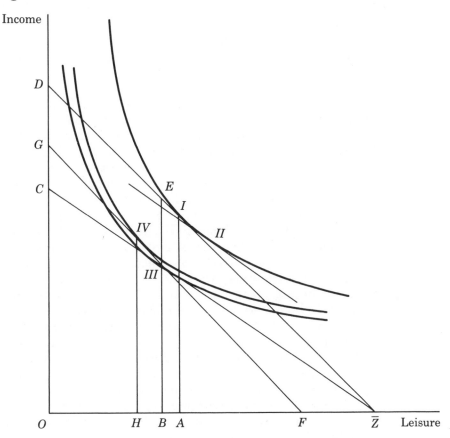

obtained by working, which means not consuming leisure. In the absence of an income tax, this constraint is shown by the budget line $D\overline{Z}$, whose slope is simply the given wage rate, since that represents the amount of income that may be earned by giving up additional units of leisure. The quantity $\overline{Z}$ is the maximum amount of leisure the individual could take, that is, when no work is done. Since we assume that all income is derived from wage payments, the individual has no income if he takes the maximum amount of leisure. With the indifference map of the individual containing the indifference curves as shown, the point of maximum utility is I, at which point OA units of leisure are taken (per period of time). Since work is leisure not taken, this represents a quantity of labor supplied equal to $A\overline{Z}$.

Suppose now a *proportional* income tax at rate t is imposed on all income earned with no exemptions. We define a proportional tax to mean one with the property that the ratio of tax liabilities to income is the same at all income levels. In keeping with our partial equilibrium analysis, assume the wage rate remains fixed at w. The budget line now rotates inward to $C\overline{Z}$ with slope $w(1 - t)$. As the diagram is drawn, the individual selects point *III*, which represents a greater supply of labor, $\overline{Z}B$. However, the preferences of the individual could as easily have been such that B lies to the right of A so less labor is supplied. Therefore, we cannot predict *a priori* whether a proportional income tax would yield more or less labor supply.

Further insight into the problem can be gained by dissecting the move from *I* to *III* into a substitution and an income effect. The substitution effect involves a move along the original indifference curve to the point *II* with the slope $w(1 - t)$. It represents the effect of a "pure" price change. Since the price of leisure has fallen, the substitution effect always tends to induce the individual to take more leisure (supply less labor). The income effect moves the individual from *II* to *III*. It is equivalent to reducing the individual's income without changing prices. If leisure is a normal good, the income effect will tend to reduce leisure (increase labor). With a lower real income, the individual works harder to try to recover part of his lost income. Depending on the relative strengths of the income and substitution effects, the individual may work more or less. Of course, if leisure is an inferior commodity, both income and substitution effects will induce the individual to take more leisure or supply less labor.

This analysis of the effects on labor supply of imposing an income tax on an individual is not particularly interesting, since it ignores the use to which the tax revenue is put. It assumes that the tax revenues raised by the income tax are either taken out of the economy or are used in such a way that the indifference map of the individual, as drawn in Fig. 11–1, is not affected. This is clearly an unacceptable procedure for analyzing the impact of income taxation on labor supply in the real world. Still, we would like to be able to avoid analyzing the effects on labor supply of the use of the tax revenues raised by the tax. One way to do this is to compare the proportional income tax with another tax yielding the same tax revenues. Our comparison would be between two taxes yielding a given amount of revenue, assuming that the revenue were to be used in the same way under the two taxes.

In Fig. 11–1 we compare the effect on labor supply of a proportional income tax and a pure lump-sum tax yielding the same revenue. $D\overline{Z}$ is the budget line gross-of-tax. A proportional tax at the rate DC/OD causes the budget line to rotate to $C\overline{Z}$. The individual selects the point *III*, takes OB units of leisure, and supplies $B\overline{Z}$ units of labor. The tax revenue generated at the point *III* is the distance between the pretax and after-tax budget lines, or $EIII$. A lump-sum tax will cause the budget line to move inward without changing its slope, the relative price of leisure. The lump-sum tax yielding the revenue $EIII$ will result in the budget line GF. Along the budget line GF the individual will select point *IV*, taking OH units of leisure and supplying $H\overline{Z}$ units of labor.

In comparing the effects of a proportional income tax with those of a lump-sum tax, we need only be concerned with the points reached under the two taxes, *III* and *IV*. The point of equilibrium on the pretax budget line, *I*, is not relevant and need not even be comparable with *III* and *IV*. That is because the use of the tax revenues under the two taxes might be expected to influence the individual's indifference map relating income and leisure. Points *III* and *IV* come from the same indifference map, since the use of the tax revenues are the same. Point *I* need not come from the same map.

Because of the geometric properties of indifference curves, the point *IV* must always lie to the left of the point *III*, on a higher indifference curve. This is because at the point *III*, the slope of the budget line under lump-sum taxation (w) exceeds the slope under proportional income taxation [$w(1 - t)$]. Therefore, we have the result that proportional income taxation causes labor supply to be lower than an equal-yield lump-sum tax.

Suppose now the individual is faced with a progressive income tax. By progressive we mean that the *average tax rate* (total taxes divided by income) rises as income rises. The simplest form of progressive tax is the *linear progressive income tax* which has a *constant* marginal tax rate. Algebraically, a linear progressive income tax schedule is characterized by:

$$T = t(Y - E) \tag{11-1}$$

where T = Total taxes paid

t = Marginal tax rate (constant)

Y = Before-tax income

E = Fixed exemption level.

The average tax paid is seen from Eq. (11–1) to be:

$$\frac{T}{Y} = t\left(1 - \frac{E}{Y}\right). \tag{11-2}$$

As income Y rises, the average tax rate T/Y rises. Such a tax schedule is depicted in Fig. 11–2. As above, $Y\overline{Z}$ represents the before-tax budget line. The budget line under a linear progressive tax is shown as $CA\overline{Z}$. Notice that the amount of tax paid equals the vertical distance between the budget lines before and after tax. For example, if Z_1 "hours" of leisure are taken, before-tax income is Z_1x, after-tax income is Z_1y, and tax paid is xy.

The linear progressive tax schedule of Eq. (11–1) is equivalent to what has become popularly known as the *flat rate tax*. The simplest flat rate tax would be characterized by an exemption level, possibly varying with personal

Figure 11–2

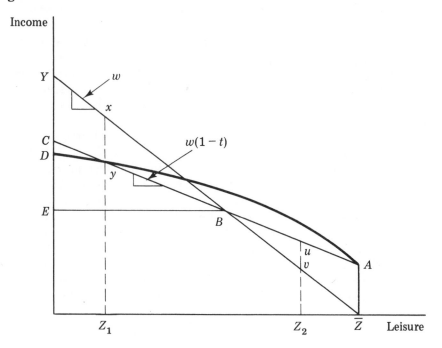

circumstances, and a single marginal tax rate. For example, the proposal in the U.S. Congress from Senator Helms and Representative Crane would be for a personal exemption level of $2000 and a single tax rate of 10 percent. Another proposal from Senator De Concini would have a higher tax rate (20 percent) but higher exemptions ($3000 for a single taxpayer, $5000 for a married couple, $4500 for a head of household, and $600 per dependent). Slightly more complicated versions eliminate some, but not all, deductions and may have a higher tax rate at higher income levels. The latter is sometimes referred to as a *dual flat rate tax* system. It is similar to the income tax rate structure in the United Kingdom, which has a constant basic marginal tax rate, but which imposes a special surtax at higher income levels. The proposal of Senator Bradley is similar to this. He would have a flat tax rate of 14 percent for single taxpayers with incomes up to $25,000 and married taxpayers up to $40,000. Beyond that, a progressive surtax would be imposed varying from 6 percent to 14 percent, depending on income level.

Flat rate taxation has been advocated as a replacement for the personal income tax on two main grounds. First, because of its simplicity, it would be much easier to administer for both taxpayers and tax authorities alike. This is because in its simplest form the flat rate tax would dispense with all forms of exclusions, deductions, and credits. That is, the base of the tax would be broadened so as to include all forms of income indiscriminately.

This would remove the incentive for taxpayers and their accountants to spend the time and effort required to earn as much of the income as possible in an untaxed or sheltered form.

Second, since most flat rate taxes lower the marginal tax rate (and raise the exemption level) it is argued that there will be a greater incentive to work, save, and take risks, and less incentive to place funds in forms of activity which are sheltered from tax by deductions or other special treatment. Indeed, it is argued by some (the so-called "supply-side economists") that these incentive effects would be so strong that a lowering of marginal tax rates by itself would generate an increase in tax revenues through the induced increase in economic activity. This view that tax revenues would rise with a fall in income tax rates is a cornerstone of what is referred to as "Reaganomics." At the moment, the magnitude of these incentive effects is an unanswered, empirical question. It is the purpose of this chapter to analyze the various influences at work on the incentives of taxpayers from various sorts of taxes, including the linear progressive tax.

It is, however, worth being a bit cautious at the outset, since the simultaneous broadening of the tax base, lowering of the marginal tax rates, and increasing the exemption level is likely to have a differential impact on households by income group. Many studies (e.g. Slemrod and Yitzhaki [1983] in the U.S. and Walker [1983] in Canada) find that the introduction of a simple flat rate tax would reduce the tax burden for upper income classes and possibly for the lowest ones, and increase it for the middle ones. In addition to the equity consequences of this, this change in relative tax burdens will itself affect incentives through income effects. This question will be given more consideration later in this section.

A special case exists when leisure taken is Z_2 in Fig. 11–2, so after-tax income $Z_2 u$ exceeds before-tax income $Z_2 v$. In this case, the linear progressive income tax schedule in Eq. (11–1) dictates a negative tax (i.e. a subsidy) of uv, since income Y is less than exemptions E. The point B is called the breakeven level of income, since at that point $Y = E$ and no tax is paid. Tax systems which give a subsidy on incomes earned less than the exemption level are called *negative income tax* systems. We shall analyze them in more detail in Chapter 14. A linear progressive tax system that does not give negative taxes on low incomes would show an after-tax budget line $CB\overline{Z}$. The locus $DA\overline{Z}$ in Fig. 11–2 also depicts a *non-linear* progressive tax system, one with an *increasing* marginal tax rate. Here, the slope of the budget line falls as income rises.

An interesting exercise is to compare a progressive and proportional income tax yielding the same revenue to the government. This is done in Fig. 11–3. As before, $Y\overline{Z}$ represents the before-tax budget line, and $CA\overline{Z}$ that with a linear progressive income tax. The individual selects the quantity of leisure, Z_1, and pays taxes equal to xy. In order to find a proportional income tax that yields the same revenue, xy, we construct the locus of all points yielding that tax revenue, TT (parallel to $Y\overline{Z}$ at a distance xy). Any proportional tax which leaves the individual on TT will yield the same

Figure 11–3

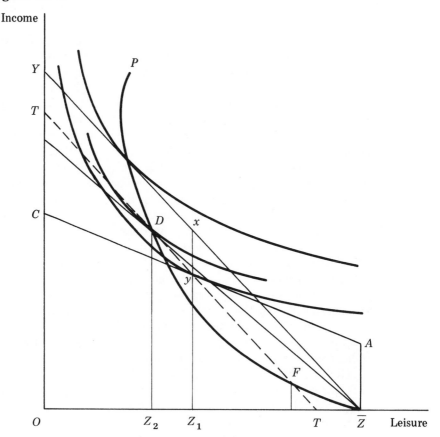

revenue. The price-consumption line $P\overline{Z}$ gives the combination of income and leisure that would be obtained from various proportional taxes. That is, it is the locus of points chosen by the individual as the budget line is rotated about the point $\overline{Z}$. At point D with Z_2 of leisure, equal tax revenue would be generated as at Z_1 under the linear progressive tax. Note that, due to the shape of indifference curves, Z_2 will lie to the left of Z_1; that is, more labor would be supplied under the proportional tax than under the progressive tax.

Point D is not the only point of equal tax revenues. Another exists at point F, with a much higher marginal tax rate than at y or D (and a much lower level of utility).[1] However, one might be justified in ruling out F as being so obviously inferior to D that the government would not levy it. They can obtain the same revenue at D with a much lower rate. Then we could conclude that a proportional tax yielding the same tax revenue as a linear progressive tax would induce a greater supply of labor. The same can be seen to hold true for more general progressive tax structures such as $DA\overline{Z}$ in Fig. 11–2. If two taxes yield the same total revenue but one has a higher marginal rate than the other, more labor will be supplied under the latter.

While that proposition holds for an individual, it is not sufficient for analyzing the effects on aggregate labor supply when one substitutes a progressive tax for a proportional one, since the tax revenue obtained from each individual will generally change. Indeed, the purpose of the substitution is presumably to obtain more income tax from those with higher incomes, and less from those with lower incomes. The analysis is somewhat suggestive, though. Consider the simple case of a linear progressive income tax with the same marginal rate for all. If we want to generate the same aggregate tax revenue using this tax as would be generated using a proportional tax, we would expect the marginal tax rate to be higher under the former (since the introduction of an exemption level reduces tax revenues). Everyone faces the higher marginal tax rate, but higher-income persons pay higher total taxes and lower-income persons pay lower total taxes.[2] If leisure is a normal good, we would expect the lower total taxes to tend to reduce labor supply for low-income persons via the income effect. When combined with the higher marginal tax rate, the substitution of a linear progressive for a proportional income tax would tend unambiguously to reduce the labor supply of low-income persons. For high-income persons, the effect is ambiguous, since higher total taxes tend to increase labor supply by the income effect, while higher marginal tax rates tend to reduce it.

A similar sort of analysis can be done for the substitution of a linear progressive tax (or flat rate tax) for a progressive tax with increasing marginal tax rates, such as the present one. As mentioned earlier, higher-income persons are likely to face lower marginal tax rates and to pay lower total taxes. The lower marginal tax rate will tend to encourage more work effort due to the substitution effect, but the lower total taxes will discourage work effort by the income effect if leisure is a normal good. Thus, we cannot say *a priori* whether work effort will rise or fall for high income persons. Low income persons face higher marginal tax rates (thus inducing less work effort), and also lower total taxes (thus also inducing less work effort by an income effect). Overall, low income persons will actually be induced to work less by the flat rate tax. For middle-income persons, the effect on work effort will likely be ambiguous. The fact that they pay higher taxes will induce more effort by the income effect. For those who face lower marginal tax rates, more effort should be forthcoming; but for those with higher marginal tax rates, the net effect is ambiguous. Which taxpayers fall into what category depends on the exact form the tax structure takes. We conclude that not just the magnitude of the effect on work effort from introducing a flat rate tax is uncertain; even the direction is. One estimate has been made by Hausman (1981b). He estimated that aggregate labor supply would increase by from 5 percent to 10 percent if a flat rate tax were introduced in the United States. However, he assumed quite low marginal tax rates (between 14.6 percent and 20.7 percent).

Other sorts of tax considerations might be analyzed within the framework of the above model. Suppose, for example, the individual has a source of nonlabor income, say, capital income. His before-tax budget line might then look like $YO\overline{Z}$ in Fig. 11–4, where $O\overline{Z}$ is capital income before tax. With a proportional income tax at the rate t falling on both capital and labor income, the budget line shifts to $BC\overline{Z}$, where $C\overline{Z} = (1 - t)O\overline{Z}$ and the slope of BC is $(1 - t)w$. Once again, the effect of the proportional tax on labor supply is unpredictable. However, the existence of capital income and its taxation provide income effects on the supply of labor in addition to the influences noted earlier. If leisure is a normal good, the existence of unearned income will tend to encourage the individual to supply less labor than otherwise. The taxing of that income will induce an increase of labor supply over and above what would occur if only labor income were taxed.

Of course, other taxes influence the individual's choice of leisure as well. We have abstracted from these by assuming that the individual's choice can be simplified to that of income vs. leisure. This allows us to

Figure 11–4

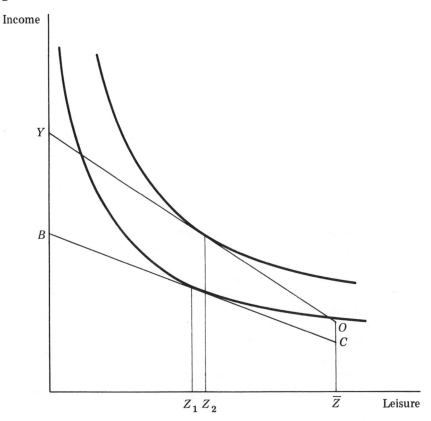

analyze the effects of a tax on income, but not a tax on a commodity or group of commodities. A specific tax on commodity X, for example, affects the price of X relative to all other commodities as well as relative to leisure. There is thus a substitution effect working in favor of all other commodities and leisure. To analyze this case geometrically we require a three-dimensional diagram. Such an analysis was presented in Chapter 9. Suffice it to recall for now that specific taxes on different commodities will induce a greater supply of labor the more complementary is the commodity with leisure. This result turns out to be of special importance in the normative analysis of taxation, that is, in the choice of an optimal set of taxes.

(b) Taxes and Hours of Work: The Market

The analysis of the income tax on household choice, as presented above, makes the unrealistic assumption that the gross-of-tax wage rate does not change as the tax is imposed. Since the income tax applies to all households supplying labor, it affects the aggregate supply of labor, and thus might be expected to influence the market wage rate. Simple demand and supply curve analysis will suffice to illustrate the effects of a variable wage determined on the market for labor. To take the simplest case, let us assume that the labor whose market wage we are analyzing is a homogeneous factor of production, and consider the application of a proportional income tax. In Fig. 11–5, the demand and supply curves for labor are labeled D and S. For the moment, we interpret the supply curve S as the aggregate of all household supply curves, based on price-consumption curves derived from individual indifference maps. As it is drawn, S is upward-sloping, indicating that the substitution effect dominates the income effect. The demand for labor, D, shows the quantities of labor that all firms in the economy would be willing to purchase at different wage rates. The downward slope is due to the diminishing marginal product of labor in production processes. As with all supply and demand curves, these are drawn under the *ceteris paribus* assumption that all other prices and incomes are fixed. For example, the price of capital is assumed fixed. A change in the price of capital would cause the D curve to shift.[3] The general equilibrium analysis of the next chapter takes into account these "secondary" price and income changes.

A proportional income tax at the rate t levied on the gross wage w is now imposed. With a gross wage of w, the net wage received by labor would be $w(1 - t)$ and the supply curve S would reflect the quantity of labor supplied at various net wages. Since the demand curve is in terms of gross wage rates, in order to make the two curves comparable, we redraw the supply curve in terms of gross wage rates by raising S in the proportion $1/(1 - t)$. The curve $S/(1 - t)$ then represents the quantities of labor that would be supplied at each gross wage rate, given that labor would only receive $(1 - t)$ of the gross wage. Market equilibrium is determined at the

Figure 11–5

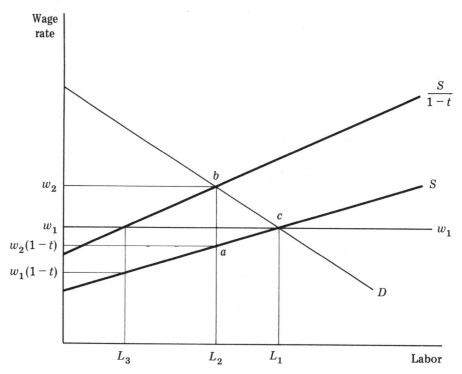

point b with the lower labor supply L_2, the gross wage rate w_2, and the net wage rate $w_2(1 - t)$. Notice that taking into consideration the variability of the wage rate tempers the overall influence of the tax on labor supply. With a constant wage w_1, we would predict a reduction in the labor supply to L_3 rather than L_2. In general, the reduction of the labor supply from L_1 will be greater the flatter (more elastic) are the D and S curves.

Finally, we can depict the excess burden of income taxation in Fig. 11–5. For that purpose, one should, strictly speaking, use a compensated rather than uncompensated labor supply schedule, for reasons noted in the Appendix to Chapter 9. Although for many goods the compensated/uncompensated distinction can be safely ignored, it has been argued that there is a quantitatively significant difference between the two in the case of labor supply (see the discussion below). Therefore, let us now interpret the curve S as a compensated, rather than ordinary, labor supply curve. Then, in the move from L_1 to L_2, the demanders lose w_2bcw_1 of consumers' surplus, and the suppliers lose $w_1caw_2(1 - t)$ of producers' surplus. The total loss in economic surplus is therefore $w_2bcaw_2(1 - t)$. Of this, $w_2baw_2(1 - t)$ is recouped by the government in the form of tax revenue. The remaining abc is lost to the economy and is the deadweight loss or excess burden. It will be more fully discussed in Chapter 12.

The choice model we have been using, while suggestive, is quite un-realistic as a representation of the household labor supply decision, at least in the short run. Individuals are not able to vary their hours of work continuously, either because of institutionally imposed rigidities (e.g. unions) or indivisibilities (eight-hour day). It is true that there is some ability to decide on overtime work, moonlighting, or self-employment. But that only holds for a small portion of the labor force. For the others, the short-run choice may be between working a fixed period of time or not working. We can depict this diagramatically as well, but the results are inconclusive.

In Fig. 11–6 we retain the assumption that the individual has continuous preferences, but we assume he has only a limited choice of leisure-income combinations. Basically, he can choose to work $Z_1\overline{Z}$ hours or not at all. If he works $Z_1\overline{Z}$ hours, he earns the income Z_1A calculated at the wage rate w. Notice that he can no longer set w equal to his MRS, as can be seen by the slope of the hypothetical budget line through A. If he chooses not

Figure 11–6

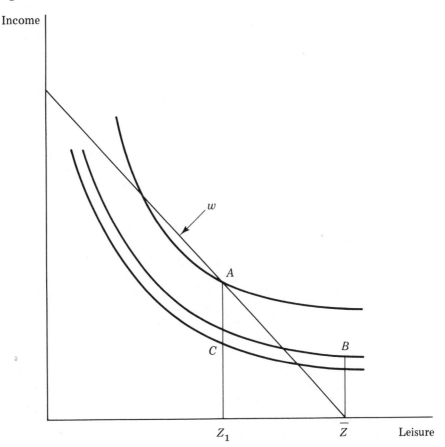

to work, he receives $\overline{Z}$ leisure and income $\overline{Z}B$ from, say, welfare or unemployment insurance. If an income tax is now imposed on his earned
income, he will receive only Z_1C from working $Z_1\overline{Z}$ hours. As the diagram
is drawn, he will choose not to work, but will accept the income $\overline{Z}B$ and
not work. We have absolutely no principles to guide us as to whether C
is on a higher or lower indifference curve than B for any particular person
although, for the population as a whole, at least some persons would cease
working.

The theoretical discussion presented so far provides an invaluable
framework for the systematic analysis of the effects of taxes on labor supply
in its hours of work dimension. Of course, no theoretical model can determine
the quantitative response of workers in real economies to changes in tax
policy. For this information, one must resort to empirical study. While this
subject is large (we cannot hope to survey it here; for an overview of earlier
work, see Break [1974]), it is useful to discuss rather briefly some of the
relevant research that has been done. Three sorts of studies may be identified:
surveys of specific groups, experiments conducted on specific groups (like
the New Jersey Income Maintenance Experiment), and econometric estimates
of labor supply curves. The survey and experimental studies have tended
to concentrate on the groups of income-earners who are most able to vary
their work effort. One of the earliest surveys was a study by Break (1957),
later repeated by the Fields and Stanbury surveys (1970), of English accountants and solicitors. The upshot of these studies was that between 13
and 19 percent of those interviewed felt that the progressive tax system
gave them a definite disincentive to work. Similar results were obtained
in survey samples of American business executives by Holland (1970) and
of over-$18,000 income-earners by Barlow, Brazer, and Morgan (1966).

All these studies found that work effort fell as marginal tax rates rose.
The results of econometric studies have been more mixed, however. First
of all, with respect to the elasticity of the ordinary labor supply curve,
most studies recognize, as noted above, that the income and substitution
effects of a change in the after-tax wage rate may, and presumably do,
work in opposite directions (since leisure is presumably a normal good). A
number of analyses find that these effects are of comparable magnitude,
so that the ordinary labor supply schedule has only a small elasticity. Some
even find that the income effect outweighs the substitution effect so that
the labor supply schedule is slightly backward-bending (Kosters [1969],
Owens [1971]). This latter conclusion, of course, is consistent with the long-
run observed tendency for the work week to fall as wages rise. On the
other hand, it appears that elasticities of labor supply vary significantly
for different subgroups of the population. For example, a recent study by
Hausman (1981b) finds a nearly vertical labor supply schedule for a sample
of United States husbands, while the elasticity of labor supply for wives
is on the order of 0.9. Thus, it may be seriously misleading to talk about
"the" elasticity of labor supply; a better approach is to recognize the differences
in labor supply behavior of different classes of workers.

Although the elasticity of the ordinary labor supply schedule is of interest for some purposes, it is the compensated elasticity that is crucial for estimating the excess burden of an income tax. Even if we accept the more or less conventional finding that the overall ordinary elasticity of labor supply is fairly small, or possibly even negative, it does not necessarily follow that the compensated elasticity, which reflects only the substitution effect of a change in the net wage rate, is small. In fact, Hausman estimates that the small, ordinary, elasticity of labor supply for prime-age males is the result of offsetting income and substitution effects, each of substantial size. (It is possible to infer a compensated wage elasticity for prime-age males of roughly 0.5 from the estimates reported in that study.) For other groups as well, the compensated elasticity is substantially higher than the ordinary elasticity. Hausman estimates the excess burden per dollar of tax revenue collected to be 22 percent for husbands and 58 percent for wives, under the existing progressive United States tax structure. This illustrates quite clearly the possible quantitative importance of the distinction between ordinary and compensated labor supply curves.

Unfortunately, these estimates, though certainly suggestive, must be regarded as rather tentative. Estimation of labor supply behavior presents many fascinating, but difficult, theoretical and econometric problems that have been the focus of substantial amounts of recent research. For an accessible discussion with further references see Deaton and Muellbauer (1980, Ch. 11). The possibility of obtaining a better understanding of the effects of tax policy on labor supply provides an important justification for this research.

THE SUPPLY OF SAVINGS

11–3   By foregoing current consumption, society frees up resources that can be used for the production of capital goods that increase the economy's productive capacity. Higher production in future periods, i.e. economic growth, then becomes possible. Of course, the accumulation of capital (by which we mean non-human capital) is not the only source of economic growth. Technological change, improvements in health and education, and many other factors, are clearly at work. Capital accumulation has always played a central role in the analysis of economic growth, however, and properly so. Both for this reason, and because the ownership and accumulation of capital have fundamental equity implications, the possible effects of tax policy on savings and capital formation have been the subject of intense scrutiny in both policy debates and economic analysis. In this section, we will review in broad outline some of the theoretical and empirical approaches that have been taken in the area of savings. The mechanism of capital accumulation is very complex, however, so not all of the relevant questions can be dealt with here. Thus, the effects of tax policy on business investment are discussed below in Section 11–5, and general equilibrium effects in a dynamic economy are taken up in the next chapter.

The main focus of our discussion here will be household saving, since this is a chief means by which resources are made available for capital formation. There are, of course, many forms that household saving may take, including the direct purchase of corporate equity (stocks) and debt (bonds), the deposit of funds in thrift institutions and mutual funds, contributions to pension funds, the purchase of durable goods (especially housing), and the purchase of government debt. For the most part we shall assume that all assets earn the same risk-free rate of return, so that all forms of saving are equivalent to one another. This is a very useful simplification when one wishes to focus on the household's intertemporal decision-making in its purest form.

But, even accepting this simplification, one should recognize that not all saving is carried out directly by households. Businesses, for example, save by retaining part of their earnings to finance new investment or to retire debt. Governments also save to the extent that revenues from taxes exceed expenditures. In the case of the federal government, this saving has often been negative, taking the form of government borrowing to finance deficits. It can be argued, though, that business saving is really just a different form of household saving, since households—specifically, the owners of businesses—are the ultimate claimants to business assets, and are made wealthier by increases in the net worth of corporations. This effectively permits one to ignore business saving as something separate from household saving, a simplification which we shall exploit in most of this section. For evidence that households adjust their personal saving in response to changes in corporate saving, see Feldstein (1973a). Whether one can argue that households see government saving (or dissaving) as an extension of their personal account is much more debatable, however, and we give a somewhat more detailed discussion of this issue.

To start with, let us recall the simple two-period model of intertemporal behavior presented in Chapter 2. The essential features of that model are that a consumer has preferences over present and future consumption, C_p and C_f, and chooses the consumption pattern which best satisfies these preferences, subject to a budget constraint. (For simplicity, we ignore here the possibility of bequests.) Taxes influence this intertemporal choice by changing the budget constraint. We shall consider various combinations of three different taxes, namely, a tax at rate t_p on wage income in the present period; a tax at rate t_f on wage income in the future; and a tax at rate t_r on interest income. With a proportional tax on all income at the same rate in both periods, we have simply $t_p = t_f = t_r$. With a proportional tax on wage income only, again at the same rate in both periods, we have $t_p = t_f$ and $t_r = 0$. (The equivalence between a proportional wage income tax and a consumption or expenditure tax is discussed later.) By distinguishing these rates, we can thus allow for several possible tax structures.

As in Chapter 2, we denote present and future wage income by Y_p and Y_f respectively, and let r be the before-tax rate of interest at which the household can borrow or lend as much as desired. Throughout this section we shall treat Y_p, Y_f, and r as fixed, thus ignoring the possible variability of labor supply, wage rates, and the interest rate. To derive the household's budget constraint in the presence of taxes, note that after-tax earnings in the present amount to $(1 - t_p)Y_p$. Savings therefore equal $(1 - t_p)Y_p - C_p$, where C_p is current consumption. Before-tax interest income is r times savings, but only $(1 - t_r)$ of this is left to the household after paying the interest income tax. Thus, future consumption, C_f, allowing for future after-tax earnings, the return of principal, and after-tax interest income from savings, must be given by

$$C_f = (1 - t_f)Y_f + [(1 - t_p)Y_p - C_p][1 + r(1 - t_r)] \tag{11-3}$$

or, letting Y_p^*, Y_f^*, and r^* denote after-tax earnings and the net-of-tax interest rate, respectively,

$$C_f = Y_f^* + (Y_p^* - C_p)(1 + r^*). \tag{11-4}$$

This expression is identical in form to Eq. (2–23) in Chapter 2, and can likewise be put into the form of Eq. (2–24):

$$C_p + \frac{C_f}{1 + r^*} = Y_p^* + \frac{Y_f^*}{1 + r^*}. \tag{11-5}$$

The interpretation of Eq. (11–5) can be given in terms quite similar to Eq. (2–24). On the left-hand side is the present value of lifetime consumption, discounted at the net interest rate r^*. On the right is the household's (after-tax) lifetime wealth, namely the present value of after-tax wage income, again discounted at the net interest rate r^*. Thus, taxes change the household's budget constraint in two basic ways: (a) Taxes on wage income reduce effective earnings, and thus reduce lifetime wealth; and (b) a tax on interest reduces the rate at which the future is discounted, because $r^* < r$. This latter has two important effects: On the one hand, the present value of any given amount of future consumption is increased; or, put another way, its cost to the consumer, in terms of current consumption foregone, is increased. On the other hand, the present value of future earnings increases, and to this extent lifetime wealth increases. Of course, a tax on *all* income has all of these effects simultaneously.

The effect of interest rates on lifetime wealth, referred to by Summers (1981) as the "human wealth effect," deserves special emphasis. In many applications of the simple two-period life cycle model, the first period ("present") is taken to be the working lifetime of an individual, while the second period ("future") is the retirement period. As Summers notes, this specification implies that $Y_f^* = 0$ and interest rates can therefore have no effect on lifetime wealth. By contrast, in a more realistic multi-period model (e.g. one in which each period of time refers to a year or a decade), the working lifetime would extend over several periods, and the human wealth effect would therefore be operative. By neglecting the human wealth effect, the simple two-period model gives a misleading estimate of the effect of interest rate changes on savings: Because an interest rate increase lowers human wealth, C_p will tend to fall if (as is reasonably assumed) it is a normal good. Savings, the difference between current income and consumption, will therefore tend to be higher because of the human wealth effect. The conventional two-period model with $Y_f^* = 0$ ignores this effect, and results in underestimates of the interest-elasticity of savings.

Let us now examine the effects of taxation diagrammatically. Since the conventional life cycle model with $Y_f^* = 0$ is slightly easier to analyze, we shall begin with that. The reader need only keep in mind that human wealth effects are being set aside, and that they can be brought into the analysis, with implications of the sort just noted, at the expense of some added complexity.

In Fig. 11–7, the line AB shows the budget line in the absence of taxes, with $OA = Y_p$ the household's first-period earnings, and with slope of $AB = -(1 + r)^{-1}$ showing the price of future consumption relative to present consumption. The household chooses to consume at point I, where the marginal rate of substitution of present for future consumption MRS_{fp} is equated to the relative price ratio $(1 + r)^{-1}$. The household's savings are $Y_p - C_p = FA$. As discussed in Chapter 2, point I corresponds to an efficient intertemporal allocation of resources if $(1 + r)^{-1}$ is also equal to the marginal rate of transformation MRT_{fp} of future into present consumption.

Now if a tax on wage income alone is introduced at rate t_p, the household's first-period income (i.e. lifetime wealth) is reduced to $(1 - t_p)Y_p = OC$, shifting the budget line AB to CD without changing its slope. If consumption in each period is a normal good, as one would expect, this reduction in lifetime wealth reduces both C_p and C_f, as shown by the move to point II. Because C_f has fallen from OG to OJ, savings have also fallen from FA to HC. The government collects tax revenue of CA in the first period. Note that because the wage income tax has not reduced the net return on savings, the relative price of future consumption is still $(1 + r)^{-1}$, and the post-tax consumption point II still corresponds to an intertemporally efficient allocation of resources at which $MRS_{fp} = MRT_{fp}$.

Next consider a tax on both wage and interest income at rates $t_p = t_r$. The household's first-period net income and lifetime wealth still drops to OC because of the tax on earnings, but the tax on interest also changes the slope of the budget line, rotating it about the point C to CE. This reflects the increase in the relative price of future consumption mentioned earlier, and both the income and substitution effect of this price increase work to reduce C_f if C_f is normal. If so, we can certainly expect the new household equilibrium at point III to be to the left of II. On the other hand,

Figure 11–7

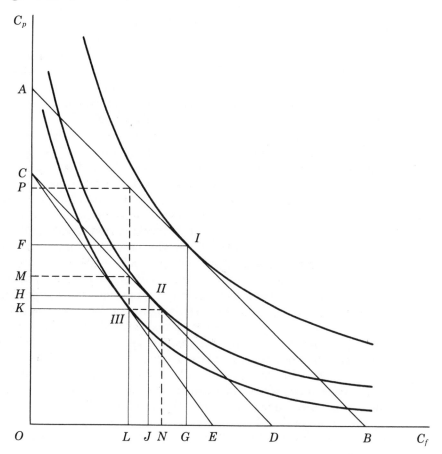

the effect on C_p is ambiguous, since a lower real income tends to reduce present consumption, but the substitution effect of a higher relative price of future consumption tends to increase it. As drawn, the new equilibrium at *III* lies below *II* so that, compared to the pure earnings tax previously considered, savings are slightly higher (by the amount $KH = KC - HC$). The change in savings between these cases, however, could have been negative, that is, the addition of a tax on interest income could cause savings to fall. But whether savings go up or down, it is essential to realize that the tax destroys the equality between the MRS_{fp} and MRT_{fp} at the post-tax equilibrium point *III*, since at that point $MRS_{fp} = (1 + r^*)^{-1} > (1 + r)^{-1} = MRT_{fp}$. That is, *regardless of the effect on savings, interest income taxation disturbs the efficiency of intertemporal resource allocation.* This may seem counter-intuitive, since it is often argued that such a tax creates inefficiencies only to the extent that it discourages saving. It has also been argued, though this is now more widely debated, that the amount of saving is in fact quite insensitive to the net rate of return earned by savers. It would appear to follow that a tax on the return to saving therefore generates very little inefficiency. We can see from the above discussion, however, that even if we accept the purported empirical fact that saving is little affected by taxation, it is a *non sequitur* to conclude that taxes do not interfere with efficient resource allocation. What matters is whether MRS_{fp} is equated to MRT_{fp}, and this condition will not obtain, regardless of what happens to the magnitude of savings, under interest income taxes. For further discussion, see Feldstein (1977a, 1978a).

To some extent, a comparison of wage income taxation ($t_p > 0 = t_r$), with taxation of all income ($t_p = t_r > 0$), in Fig. 11–7 is hampered by the fact that the present value of tax revenues collected is higher in the second case. To see this, note that earnings taxation under the income tax yields CA of revenue in the first period, just as in the case of wage income taxation alone. The tax on all income, however, yields additional revenue of LN in the future when interest income is realized and taxed, and this revenue has a present value of KM.[4] Thus, the present value of taxation of both wage and interest income is $KM + CA = KM + MP = KP > CA$. However, it is easy to analyze a pure wage income tax that generates the same present value of revenue. Figure 11–8 reproduces the budget lines AB and CE from Fig. 11–7, and point *III* is again the equilibrium point with the tax on all income, yielding KP of tax revenue. Clearly, the budget line corresponding to a wage income tax with the same present value of revenue must be QR, obtained by rotating CE around *III* until its slope is again $(1 + r)^{-1}$, parallel to AB, since $KP = QA$. Let us refer to this as an *equal-yield* wage income tax. The consumer's new equilibrium with the equal-yield wage income tax is at point *IV*, which must necessarily lie below and to the right of *III*. This means that present consumption is lower, and future consumption higher, than with the tax on both wage and interest income. One cannot, however, be certain that the household's saving has been increased, since one may have $KC \gtrless SQ$. Note also that the household attains a higher level of utility with the earnings tax. This is because the equilibrium at *IV* is efficient, with $MRS_{fp} = MRT_{fp}$, in contrast to *III*.

While it is not possible to say whether household saving increases or decreases under the equal-yield wage income tax, it is possible to reach a definite conclusion about the rate of capital accumulation in the economy, by taking into account government saving. Let us assume, in comparing the tax on wage and interest income with its equal-yield wage income tax, that the government uses the tax revenue to carry out a given pattern of expenditure in each period, regardless of the tax system being used. We have not specified what that pattern is, and if it involves heavy expenditure in the future, it might require saving a large part of the tax revenue generated in the present; whereas if the expenditure occurs mainly in the present it might, in the income tax case, require government borrowing to be paid back out of future interest income tax revenues. But whatever this pattern may be, we can say how the amount of government saving

Figure 11–8

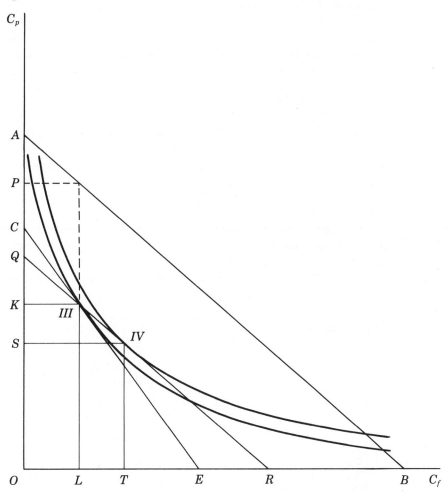

changes as we shift from the income tax to the equal-yield earnings tax. Tax revenues occur earlier in the second case, and to use them to finance the same expenditure necessitates an increase in saving, or a reduction in borrowing, compared to the initial situation with both wage and interest income taxes. In fact, present tax revenues are higher by $QA - CA = QC$ in the wage income tax case, and this is the net change in government saving that must result from the change in tax policy. The change in total *national* saving from the change to the equal-yield wage income tax is thus $SQ - KC$ (the change in household saving) $+ QC = SK > 0$, which is unambiguously positive, and is exactly the reduction in current consumption as the household moves from *III* to *IV*. Thus, there is no doubt that, by discouraging current consumption, the shift away from a tax on income inclusive of interest encourages capital formation and economic growth in the form of higher future output and consumption.

The effects of changes in the timing of tax collections on household vs. national saving can be brought out even more clearly if we relax the assumption that $Y_f = 0$. In Fig. 11–9 the budget line AB shows a household's consumption possibilities, in the absence of any taxes, with earnings of $Y_p = OE$ in the present, and $Y_f = OF$ in the future, as shown by the point P. The slope of AB is $(1 + r)^{-1}$ as before. Now suppose an earnings tax at the uniform rate $t_p = t_f$ is imposed. This shifts the budget line to CD, determined by the point Q on the ray OP, at which net present income is $(1 - t_p)Y_p = OG$ and net future income is $(1 - t_f)Y_f = OH$. The present value of taxes collected is $GE + HF(1 + r)^{-1} = CA$, which is also the reduction in the household's lifetime wealth. Suppose that the household chooses to consume at point I in the post-tax situation, so that household savings equals $(1 - t_p)Y_p - C_p = OG - OL = LG$.

Consider now the effect of a tax cut in the present, to be offset by higher future taxes that leave the present value of government revenue unchanged, such as represented by a shift from Q to R. Since tax collections are postponed, the government must save less or borrow more, in the

Figure 11–9

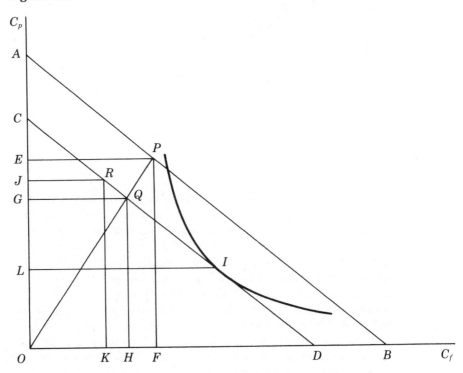

amount *GJ*, in order to finance the same pattern of government expenditure over time. On this account, national saving declines. The consumer's lifetime wealth is unchanged at *OC*, however, and so the consumer still faces the budget line *CD*. The consumption point chosen is thus still at *I*, even though present after-tax income has increased from *OG* to *OJ*. To achieve *I*, the household must save more to offset the higher taxes due in the future, and in fact household savings will rise by *GJ* to *LJ* in total. The net change in national saving, resulting from a decrease of *GJ* by the government and an increase of *GJ* by the household, is therefore zero.

This is a perfectly reasonable conclusion, given the framework within which the tax policy change is being analyzed. A tax cut in the present increases government indebtedness by an equal amount. This extra government debt is perceived as the present value of higher future taxes by households, and thus leaves their lifetime wealth and desired life cycle consumption unchanged. They therefore respond to government borrowing by additional saving of exactly the same amount; the real intertemporal allocation of resources, including present and future consumption and real capital formation, is entirely unchanged. On the other hand, this conclusion differs strikingly from the views expressed in much of the literature of conventional macro-economics, where it is hypothesized that current consumption depends heavily on current disposable income. If that were the true situation, then the present tax cut followed by the future tax increase would have real effects on the economy: Current consumption would rise, future consumption would fall, government savings would fall, and household savings would increase only by the marginal propensity to save multiplied by the reduction in present taxes. On balance, national saving and capital accumulation would fall.

These contrasting results reveal that the two-period life cycle model as we have used it is somehow incompatible with the notions underlying simple Keynesian consumption functions, and it is clearly important to try to ascertain the underlying cause(s) of this incompatibility. There are several possibilities.

First, households may simply not be intertemporal optimizers. Out of habit, ignorance, or otherwise, they may follow a rule of thumb in making savings decisions, such as: spend the fraction *MPC* < 1 of each additional dollar of disposable income. This is a fundamentally different view of household behavior than that of the life cycle model, one which denies that households attempt to do any intertemporal planning at all.

Second, our life cycle analysis has assumed that households confronted with a present tax cut know that future taxes will rise by just enough to keep the present value of tax revenues constant. In the real world, it is not obvious that households would fully perceive the true burden of future taxes resulting from a present tax cut, even if this were an explicitly-announced policy. To the extent that they lack perfect foresight, they may fail to anticipate future tax liabilities, and incorrectly perceive an increase in lifetime wealth. This induces an increase in present consumption, as a simple consumption function would predict. (Conversely, a tax increase would diminish current consumption.)

Third, households may believe that future taxes will rise, but only after their death. If a household does not plan to leave any bequests, then tax cuts in the present need not be offset by higher taxes in the "future" relevant to that household, namely later in the household's own lifetime. Quite similarly to the preceding point, the tax cut will then increase lifetime wealth and lead to higher present consumption. By contrast, the conclusion (that there are no real effects from a tax cut followed by tax increases of equal present value in the perhaps distant future) is restored when households are altruistic towards their children and engage in sophisticated bequest planning, as discussed in Chapter 2. The reason, of course, is that the multi-generational analogue of lifetime wealth is not changed by the tax policy change, and so the government dissaving is exactly offset by extra household saving, including higher bequests, that leaves the time paths of real consumption and capital accumulation unchanged. There is a lively controversy about how much foresight households really have, and the extent to which future tax increases, either within one's own lifetime or beyond it, are anticipated. See Barro (1974, 1976), Feldstein (1976c), and Buchanan (1976) for some discussion of these issues.

Fourth, households may not be able to borrow as much as desired at the going interest rate, as the simple life cycle model assumes. An example might be a household that expects rapidly rising earnings over the life cycle, and that would like to smooth the path of life-cycle consumption by having present consumption in excess of present income. In the absence of previously-accumulated wealth that could be drawn down, the household may not be able to consume as much as desired, because lenders may not be prepared to let the household go into debt with no other security than the prospect of higher future earnings. Another example might be a young individual in a wealthy family who expects to receive a large inheritance in the future, but whose current income is relatively low. Such an individual would also like to smooth life-cycle consumption by going into debt now and paying back the debt when the inheritance is received, but might not find any willing lenders. For these credit-constrained consumers, present consumption C_p is limited by their disposable current income $(1 - t_p)Y_p$, making them "reactors" (in the suggestive terminology of Blinder [1976]), rather than life-cycle "planners" of the type we have analyzed in our standard two-period model. That is, they will respond to changes in their present circumstances as if they were not planning for the future at all; in response to a present tax cut followed by future tax increases, they will increase current consumption, just as a simple consumption function would predict, because credit constraints have thwarted their attempt to increase current consumption. For reactors, government borrowing can substitute for desired but unachievable household borrowing, and thus can increase present consumption, and reduce national saving and capital accumulation.

Each of these four points questions the simple two-period life cycle model (and of course its multi-period and multi-generational extensions as well) in a different way. Clearly it is of great importance for the analysis of the effects of tax policy on savings to try to address these questions, and to see which views of household behavior, expectations formation, and capital market structure are most relevant to the real world. Given the evident complexity of this task, however, it is hardly surprising that these issues remain open and are the subject of debate. We shall review below some of the empirical research that focuses on these issues. In Chapter 14, when we discuss social security programs, many of these questions about intertemporal behavior will become important again.

Before turning to the empirical evidence, let us briefly consider two further issues: the choice between wage income and consumption (or expenditure) taxation, and the effect of taxes on business saving. The disincentive effect of an income tax on savings has been a principal consideration in the debate over the adoption of an expenditure tax, as discussed in Chapter 10. We shall pursue this argument further by considering the relative effects of wage and consumption (or expenditure) taxation on savings.

The budget constraint Eq. (11–5) allows for labor and interest income taxes, but must be modified if we wish to allow for taxes, at rates s_p and s_f, on present and future consumption. If we let C_p continue to represent the real consumption enjoyed by a household in the present, then the outlay required to achieve that consumption will rise, in the presence of the tax, to $(1 + s_p)C_p$. That is, the consumption or expenditure tax increases the effective price of consumption. Diagrammatically, the effect of s_p is to shift down the vertical intercept of the budget line in, e.g., Fig. 11–7, while the effect of the tax on future consumption s_f is to shift leftward the horizontal intercept. Clearly, a tax on consumption in all periods at a uniform rate of $s = s_p = s_f$ will shift the budget line inward just parallel to the pretax budget line, and thus, with perfect capital markets, is equivalent in its effects to a tax on wage income alone, or a tax on income with interest income exempt.[5] It should be noted, however, that labor income taxes are paid earlier in the life cycle than consumption taxes, so that the switch from a labor income to an expenditure tax would be similar in its effects as to a present tax cut/future tax increase, illustrated by the move from Q to R in Fig. 11–9. Following the previous discussion, one can see that a switch between labor income and expenditure taxation can have various real effects if capital market imperfections, or the other qualifications mentioned, arise. In the absence of those qualifications, however, it is clear that an expenditure tax does not reduce the net return on saving, does not distort intertemporal resource allocation, and would result in higher national saving and capital accumulation than an equal yield tax on all income. This result is often cited in support of consumption taxation.

As noted at the beginning of this section, one part of national saving is the saving carried out by businesses through retention of earnings. In Section 11–5, the effects of taxes on the underlying determinants of retained earnings (such as dividend payouts, borrowing, etc.) are discussed in some detail. Here it remains to assess the extent to which the simple model of household saving discussed earlier may need to be modified to allow for business saving.

According to one argument, there are significant differences between the savings behavior of households and those of firms organized as corporations. (In the case of sole proprietorships and partnerships, businesses are treated as extensions of households for tax purposes, and the economic distinction between the two also becomes less clear.) The argument might be put this way: A large part of capital formation is accounted for by business investment, and much business investment is financed by retained earnings. If retained earnings are reduced by one dollar and paid out as a dividend to the households that own the firm, the household's disposable income, and hence current consumption, is likely to increase, while business investment will fall. The net effect of the reallocation of the dollar from the business to the household sector is thus to reduce national saving (as business saving falls by one dollar and household saving increases only by the marginal propensity to save times one dollar). This argument is used to support policies that discourage dividend payouts by corporations, and encourage retention of earnings, on the grounds that this enhances capital formation and economic growth.

A counter argument can be given, however. It begins with the recognition that the net worth of a corporation in some sense contributes to the net worth of its owners. If a corporation pays out a dollar rather than investing it, both the value of its physical assets and its net worth for accounting purposes will be lower by one dollar. In a simple world without taxes, standard theories of stock valuation suggest that competitively traded shares would then fall in value, also by one dollar. The owners, then, receive a one dollar dividend but suffer a one dollar capital loss. Evidently, the effect of the payout is to leave their wealth, and hence desired consumption, unchanged. But with unchanged consumption, what happens to the one dollar of extra current income? The owners save it in order to offset the capital loss, leaving their net worth intact and permitting future consumption to proceed as planned. National saving is unchanged, since business saving is down by one dollar and household saving up by one dollar. In a world such as this, households "see through the corporate veil," and realize that corporate net worth is really just part of their personal net worth in some consolidated, private-sector balance sheet. There is little advantage to encouraging retention of profits by special tax incentives in this situation, since increases in corporate saving will be offset by household dissaving, leaving national saving and capital accumulation unaffected.[6]

Which of these views of corporate saving is more appropriate cannot be answered definitively. The simple life cycle model used above is fully compatible with the second view, perhaps incompatible with the first. Fundamentally, however, there is no way to resolve the issue by theoretical argument. Only careful empirical testing of competing hypotheses can hope to settle the matter. Efforts along these lines have been made by Bhatia (1979), Feldstein (1973a), and von Furstenberg (1981), among others.

Let us now briefly review some of the recent empirical literature that examines the effect of taxes on saving. In one sense, a large part of applied macroeconomics, that branch that analyzes consumption functions, deals with this topic. An important conclusion, supported in many studies, is that current disposable income positively affects consumption. This is what a textbook Keynesian consumption function leads one to expect, of course. Unfortunately for present purposes, models in this literature are usually constructed with objectives (namely, short-run macro-forecasting) other than those we have in mind here, and often exclude the possible effects of some of the variables which the theoretical analysis above suggests may be important. One should also note here, however, that lifetime wealth, the variable that one would perhaps most like to include in a consumption function from the viewpoint of a life-cycle savings model, is not directly observable. This is the present discounted value of a household's earnings (plus any initial wealth that it may have); future earnings streams, as well as the future interest rates that are used to discount them, are inherently unobservable. This is an important example (and unfortunately not the only one) of the problems of unobserved or unobservable variables that arise in much of the empirical literature dealing with intertemporal behavior. Given this problem, it may be that the inclusion of current (and lagged) disposable personal income in an estimated consumption function is as close as one can get to a proxy for lifetime wealth.

The role of wealth and/or income is central to all studies of consumption and savings behavior. A further issue of particular concern for tax analysis, and the issue that has received perhaps the greatest amount of attention lately, is the extent to which savings depends on the interest rate. Recall that interest rate changes have a theoretically ambiguous effect on saving because of offsetting income and substitution effects. A large number of early studies concluded that, indeed, interest rates seem to have little effect on savings, suggesting that these effects roughly offset one another.

However, if we are attempting to test the hypothesis that households act as life-cycle savers in the spirit of our standard model, it is crucial that one recognize that the relevant variable to which savings might respond is not the before-tax nominal interest rate. Rather, one should seek to analyze the effect of changes in the *expected real after-tax* rate of return, that is, the real terms at which households expect to be able to transform present into future consumption. Unfortunately, this variable is unobservable; one must resort to various ingenious efforts (such as estimating the anticipated rate of inflation in order to derive real rates from nominal ones) even to approximate it. This path is strewn with pitfalls, however. Boskin (1978) argues that the interest elasticity of saving is on the order of 0.4, in contrast to earlier works, such as those by Wright (1969), Weber (1970), and David and Scadding (1974), that found savings to be insensitive to interest rates. Howrey and Hymans, (1978), on the other hand, find little support for a strong interest elasticity of saving. Von Furstenberg (1981) concludes that reliable estimates are almost impossible to obtain because of the unob-servability of the expected real net rate of return. It seems necessary to conclude that there is substantial uncertainty about the responsiveness of saving to interest rates, and thus, in particular, to changes in tax rates on interest income. Perhaps future research will help to settle this issue. (We should note again, however, that even if the interest elasticity of savings is zero, it remains true that an interest income tax results in an inefficient intertemporal allocation of resources by lowering national saving relative to an equal-yield labor income tax.)

Another question about savings behavior, touched on in the theoretical discussion, concerns the extent and nature of saving for bequests. This is particularly relevant for any issue of government tax or transfer policy where the policy is likely to have effects extending beyond the lifetimes of some, or all, of the people alive at the time the policy is undertaken. This would be true of changes in tax policy that change the timing of tax revenue flows, as discussed above. It is also important in the analysis of social security programs, discussed later in Chapter 14, where more empirical work is also reviewed. Bequest behavior has attracted a substantial amount of attention in recent research by, among others, Brittain (1978), Menchik (1979, 1980), Kotlikoff and Summers (1981), and Tomes (1981). Very little is known yet about behavioral responses to exogenous changes, however. Empirical work has been plagued by an absence of good-quality data on the size and distribution of intergenerational transfers, especially in relation to all of the parent and child characteristics that are likely determinants of such transfers. Kotlikoff and Summers argue, however, that a substantial amount of household saving is eventually transferred to heirs, suggesting that bequests are empirically important in the process of capital accumulation. The crucial, and as yet unanswered, question is what motivates such saving, and how is it influenced by changes in government policy. It is probably safe to say that the simple two-period life cycle model, which does not allow for bequests at all, is inadequate. It is not clear if it should be amended to allow for some rule-of-thumb saving for bequests; or for sophisticated intergenerational utility maximization; or for the possibility that people are uncertain about the length of their lives, and might therefore preserve some of their wealth in old age in case they should need resources for future consumption; or if still other plausible hypotheses are more appropriate. Unfortunately, the answers to many policy questions will remain in doubt until these issues are resolved.

THE EFFECT OF TAXATION ON RISK-TAKING

11–4   The decision to invest current resources for future income often involves a choice among investments of varying risk, or chances of loss. If we assume that individuals (as savers or owners of firms) are risk-averse, some com-pensation must be afforded for the taking of a risk. A high-risk investment will only be undertaken if its expected yield exceeds the expected yield that may be obtained on safe assets (e.g. government bonds) by enough to compensate for the taking of the risk. This "risk premium" may be regarded as the payment for the opportunity cost of bearing the risk. The imposition of taxes on the returns from investment (e.g. corporate or personal income taxes) may influence the decision to invest in risky assets by reducing the rate of return, since the tax will impinge upon the risk premium as well as upon the normal rate of return. There may therefore be an incentive to change the amount of investment allocated to risky projects, as well as to influence the aggregate amount of investment forthcoming. Indeed, one of the arguments popularly voiced against the capital gains tax is its supposed detrimental effect on risk-taking. In this section we shall present a simple analysis of the effects of income taxation on risk-taking in a partial equilibrium, two-period model. This analysis, though unrealistic in some respects, will suffice to illustrate the main influences of taxation on risk-taking, some of which might seem rather surprising to a noneconomist.

Suppose we consider an individual[7] who has a given quantity of assets or wealth, A, which he wants to allocate among investments of varying degrees of risk. To make matters simple, suppose the individual can purchase varying amounts of a completely riskless asset with zero yield (e.g. cash in a noninflationary world) or an asset with a risky yield. Our problem is to ascertain, first, how the portfolio of asset size A would be allocated between the riskless and the risky asset, and, second, to see how the allocation changes when taxes are imposed. In order to perform the analysis we require a model which depicts the individual's choice process. In the simple model we use, it is assumed that the relevant properties of an asset that influence the utility an individual derives from the asset can be summarized in two parameters: the *yield* and the *risk*. It is assumed that there are n possible rates of return on the asset $X_i(i = 1, \ldots, n)$. Let p_i be the probability of return X_i occurring, as estimated by the investor. The yield y is the expected return of the asset defined by:

$$y = \Sigma\, p_i X_i \tag{11-6}$$

where $\Sigma\, p_i = 1$. Of course, some of the X_i may be negative reflecting a loss.

The definition of the risk of the asset is somewhat more arbitrary, since many alternatives are possible, all of which focus on the probabilities of getting other than the expected or mean return, y. One of the earliest notions of risk used was that employed by Domar and Musgrave (1944) in their pioneering study of the effects of taxation on risk-taking. They defined risk to be the expected loss of an asset:

$$r = -\Sigma\, q_i L_i \tag{11-7}$$

where L_i are the outcomes X_i such that $X_i < 0$ and q_i are the probabilities of those outcomes. Another candidate for the measure of risk is the standard deviation of the returns X_i, denoted σ^8 since it reflects the amount of dispersion of returns about the mean, y. Neither of these measures captures all the important properties of probability distributions except in very special cases. We shall return to that problem below. Regardless of which of the above measures of risk we use, the same qualitative results are obtained in our simple model. For simplicity, we use r, the expected loss.

Figure 11–10 depicts the decision-making process of the individual under consideration. The individual's tastes are given by a set of indifference curves such as U_1, U_2, and U_3. The shape of these indifference curves reflect the fact that the taking of risk is a "bad." More risk must be compensated for by an increased yield. Therefore, indifference curves are positively sloped. At the same time, there is an increasing marginal rate of substitution of risk for yield reflected in the decreasing steepness of each indifference curve as one moves northeast.

The combinations of risk and yield available to the individual on the market are reflected in the opportunity line OP. The point P gives the risk and yield that would be obtained if the portfolio consisted entirely of the risky asset. The origin is the risk and yield of the riskless asset. The various combinations of riskless and risky assets are then given by all points along OP. As one moves from O to P, the share of the portfolio held as the risky

Figure 11–10

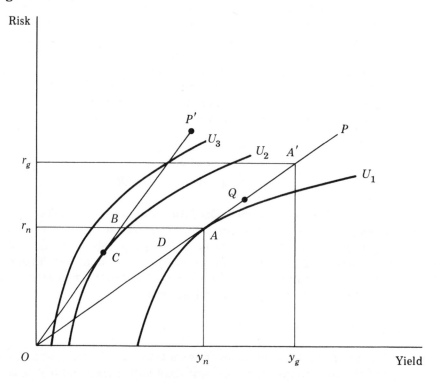

asset increases in proportion. In the absence of taxation, the individual selects the point A at which OA/OP of his portfolio is held in the risky asset.

Consider now the imposition of a proportional income tax on the returns, X_i, and assume that the tax treats losses symmetrically with gains. The analysis is equally applicable to a linear progressive or flat rate income tax, since what is important is that the marginal tax rate be fixed. The tax payment due on a return X_i is tX_i, which is negative for losses, indicating that a tax rebate or credit is received. Such a system is said to allow *full loss offset*. In practice, this may be done either by allowing losses on one source of income to be deducted from gains elsewhere; or, if losses exceed gains, by giving a subsidy in the current period or allowing losses to be carried forward or backward to other years. Most tax systems will have at least partial provision for loss-offsetting, if not complete loss-offsetting provisions. With full loss-offset, the yield of the risky asset is reduced to:

$$y_n = \Sigma \, p_i X_i (1 - t) = (1 - t)y \tag{11-8}$$

and the risk is reduced to:

$$r_n = -\Sigma \, q_i L_i (1 - t) = (1 - t)r. \tag{11-9}$$

Since risk and yield are reduced in proportion, the point P on the risk–yield opportunity line moves in to the origin in the proportion $(1 - t)$ to the point Q. The new opportunity line is therefore OQ.

To the individual, the budget line appears not to have changed. He can still attain the point A, which affords him exactly the same yield at the same risk. But the point A now reflects a different portfolio, since now OA/OQ of the portfolio consists of the risky asset. In other words, the point A corresponds to the point A' on the pretax opportunity line, and the individual has been induced to hold more of the risky asset. From society's point of view, the taking of risk has increased even though the individual does not perceive it to have increased. The reason is that the government is now assuming part of the risk. The expected tax revenue to the government will be $y_n \, y_g$, and its risk will be $r_n \, r_g$. The government, by sharing symmetrically in both gains and losses, shares in both the return and risk of the portfolio.

The question remains, is society better off as a result of the increased share of resources devoted to risky investment? The answer to that question depends upon how one assesses the opportunity cost to society of the risk taken by the government. If the costs of risk-taking by the government were evaluated exactly as the individual had evaluated them, society would be worse off, since the individual is worse off at A' than at A. However, the cost to society of risks taken by the government may be lower than if the individual had taken the same risk. This is so if the government is able to diversify its assets more than the individual, or if the government can spread its risk over many individuals. The principles of risk-pooling and risk-spreading apply here exactly as they did earlier in Chapter 8. If stock markets are functioning well, the government may only have a limited advantage over the individual in this regard. The net benefits to society from the increased risk-taking are less to the degree that individuals are able to pool and spread risk through stock markets.

The prediction that taxation must increase risk-taking falls down once we relax some of the assumptions of the model. For example, suppose the tax system allows less than full loss-offset. Figure 11–10 also depicts the case of *zero loss-offset*. In this case, the tax reduces all positive yields of the portfolio without affecting negative yields. The point P therefore moves horizontally left to P', and the new opportunity locus is OP'. Point B on OP' represents the same portfolio as A on OP. Depending on the shape of the individual's indifference curves, his new utility-maximizing point C may be either above or below B. This depends upon the relative strength of income and substitution effects. If the taking of risk has a positive income elasticity of demand, both the income and substitution effects will tend to reduce the amount of risk taken. It is clear, in this case, that the effect on risk depends critically upon whether or not full loss-offset is given, since with full loss-offset risk increases, but with zero loss-offset it decreases.

Figure 11–11

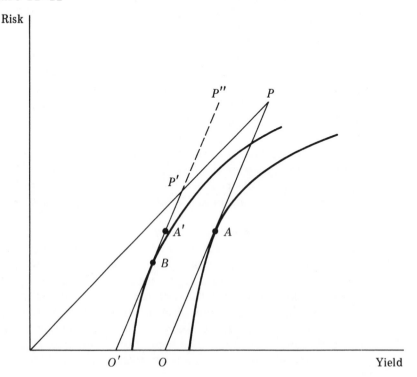

With partial loss-offset, the opportunity will lie somewhere between *OP'*
and *OP*. It is apparent that the more loss-offset is given, the more likely
it is that risk-taking will increase.

Another obvious extension to the model is to allow the riskless asset
to have a positive yield, as in Fig. 11–11. Now the tax falls on both the
risky and the riskless asset. With full loss-offset, the opportunity locus
moves from *OP* to *O'P'* under taxation at the rate *P'P"/O'P"*. There are
now two potentially opposing influences on the individual. The taxation of
the risky asset *per se* provides an incentive to increase the share held of
the risky asset as before. However, now the taxation of the riskless asset
reduces the yield of the portfolio without changing the risk. This income
effect will tend to reduce the holding of the risky asset if the taking of
risk has a positive income elasticity of demand. The overall outcome is
unpredictable *a priori*. The point *B* on *O'P'* may or may not represent a
larger share of the risky asset than point *A* on *OP*. The smaller the income
elasticity of demand for risk, the more likely it is that risk-taking will
increase.

Similar results are obtained if the individual's portfolio consists of many
independent assets rather than just two. In this case the opportunity locus
will no longer necessarily be a straight line. Rather, it may well take the
shape of *OP* in Fig. 11–12. As one moves from *O* to *P*, the yield initially

Figure 11–12

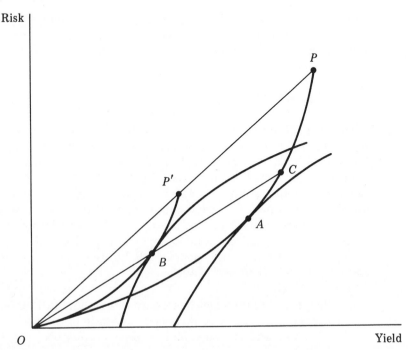

increases more rapidly than the risk, due to the principle of portfolio diversification.[9] Risk increases more rapidly as more and more is held in the form of fewer and fewer risky assets. Even with a zero return on the riskless asset, a tax with full loss-offset need not necessarily increase the taking of risk. Since all gains and losses are reduced in the same proportion, a tax with full loss-offset causes each point on OP to move toward the origin in the proportion $(1 - t)$ since all gains and losses are reduced in the same proportion. The posttax opportunity locus is OP'. The individual will situate his portfolio at a point such as B, which corresponds to point C on OP. Although there may be some presumption that C represents a more risky portfolio than A, as in the case illustrated, this is not necessarily the case, since consumer preferences may be such that C lies below A on OP.

Although the above results were derived using a very naive model of choice under risk, the results are basically the same when a more sophisticated model is used. The main deficiency in the above model is that it assumes that risk can be characterized by a single characteristic of the probability distribution of returns. It neglects, for example, the fact that the skew of the distribution may be important, as well as other moments.

A more general approach to decision-making under risk is the so-called expected utility hypothesis encountered already in Chapter 3 and Chapter 8. According to that hypothesis, the individual will choose that asset combination which maximizes expected utility defined as:

$$EU = \Sigma \, p_i U(Y_i) \tag{11-10}$$

where Y_i is the wealth that the portfolio would generate with a probability p_i.[10] In the simple case of a risky asset yielding a return of X_i, and a riskless asset yielding no return, the wealth in the presence of an income tax is:

$$Y_i = A + (1 - t)ax_i \tag{11-11}$$

where a is the amount of initial wealth A held as the risky asset, t is the tax rate, and x_i is the rate of return on A dollar's-worth of the risky asset (i.e. $x_i = X_i/A$). The individual's problem is to choose the value of a which maximizes expected utility given by Eq. (11-10) subject to the wealth constraint equation Eq. (11-11). One can then deduce from the properties of the utility function U what might happen to a as t is increased.

The analysis involves the use of calculus and is not presented here. Instead, we summarize the most important results that have been derived using the expected utility model,[11] all limited to the choice between two assets, one risky and one riskless.

(i) When the riskless asset has a zero return, and full loss-offset is given, increasing the tax rate increases the share of the portfolio held as the risky asset, and the individual's expected utility does not change (exactly as above).

(ii) When the risky asset has a positive return, an increase in the tax rate will increase the share of portfolio held as a risky asset if the individual has "increasing relative risk-aversion." The properties of increasing relative risk-aversion mean that the elasticity of a with respect to changes in initial wealth A is less than one. In other words, as wealth rises, the proportion held as risky asset falls.

(iii) From the definition of relative risk-aversion, a tax on wealth will increase the share held as a risky asset if the individual has increasing relative risk-aversion.

(iv) With no loss-offset, no simple predictable results are obtained.

The above propositions on risk appear to be fairly inconclusive and have yet to be tested empirically. Nonetheless, the intuitively appealing popular argument that capital gains taxes reduce risk-taking does not appear to have much theoretical support. The theory would, if anything, lean the other way. The analysis as presented is deficient in that the aggregate size of the portfolio is taken as fixed. Yet capital income taxation may well affect the size of the portfolio if it affects the yield to be attained.[12] We have also neglected to analyze the effects of progressive taxes. It ought to be obvious that if marginal tax rates are progressive, loss-offsets will be less than complete and, to that extent, risk-taking would likely be retarded. This constitutes one of the arguments in favor of a flat rate tax. Relative to a tax with increasing marginal rates, it would induce more risk-taking. However, the magnitude of the effect can only be conjectured at this time.

THE EFFECT OF TAXATION ON THE INVESTMENT AND FINANCIAL DECISIONS OF FIRMS

11-5   Firms purchase or hire factors of production and materials to produce output in order to make a profit.[13] The amount of each input they choose to use in production processes will depend upon the value of output that additional increments of the input will produce for the firm (the *marginal revenue product*), and the incremental cost involved in using additional amounts of the input, including any costs of financing. Taxes impinge upon the input decision to the extent that they influence the marginal benefit or revenue product and the marginal cost of each input. We shall be primarily concerned here with the demand for capital assets of the firm, or the investment decision, although similar considerations could be brought to bear on the demand for current inputs, such as labor or materials. Most types of taxes will influence the investment decision, but we shall concentrate upon the corporate income tax and the personal income tax, since most of the analysis in the literature centers on these. We shall also concentrate primarily upon one particular type of capital asset, *depreciable capital* (e.g. machinery and structures). As discussed later on, similar principles apply to other sorts of capital assets, such as land, inventories, and depletable resources.

The analysis that follows is called a *partial equilibrium analysis,* and concentrates upon the influence of taxation on decision-making at the firm level. This means that we take as given parameters such items as factor prices and rates of interest. Obviously, since corporate and personal taxes are broad-based taxes, they will have *general equilibrium effects* in the economy as a whole. That is, they will have an influence on market prices, including factor prices and interest rates, that the individual firm takes as given. These general equilibrium effects will be analyzed in the next chapter, where we will study the effect of taxes on the allocation of capital across industries, and not simply the effect on the demand for capital by a particular firm. The partial equilibrium analysis we present here is, however, an important building block for the general equilibrium analysis.

At the outset it is worth asking if we need a corporate tax at' all. The question is relevant, since all private sector corporations are ultimately owned by households; why not then tax the households directly? There are three reasons why one may wish to levy a corporate tax. The first is that it is capable of raising large amounts of revenue at low administrative cost to the government, and since it already exists, there would be significant transitional problems with abandoning it. Though not an economic argument, it is one which economists have taken seriously (e.g. Meade [1978]), because the effects of the existing tax system have been "capitalized" into the stock market values of firms. To abandon it would introduce windfall gains and losses. The second reason is that, if properly designed, the corporate tax has the potential to be an ideal tax from an efficiency point of view. If the tax base is defined to be pure economic profits (or its equivalent), the tax will take a portion of these pure profits or rents, and business investment decisions will not be distorted. If a firm is maximizing profits in the absence of the tax, taxing a share of the profits earned will not affect the output and input choices of the firm. This is a fact we discuss in more detail in this section. The third reason why corporate taxes exist is to tax, at source, capital income that would otherwise escape taxation altogether, or for which taxation could be postponed. The corporate tax is said to be a *withholding device.* There are two circumstances in which withholding may be desirable. One is to withhold against capital income earned by foreign-owned corporations which would otherwise escape taxation altogether. The other is to withhold against earnings retained in corporations. In this case, personal taxation is postponed until the shareholders take out the retained earnings either as dividends or as capital gains. Since a corporate tax has already been withheld, under the ideal tax system it ought to be refunded when the capital income becomes taxable in the hands of shareholders. This provides the rationale for the integration of the personal and corporate tax systems, as discussed in the *Blueprints for Basic Tax Reform* of the United States Treasury (1977). If the system of tax crediting at the personal level were ideal, so that exact credit would be given for the previously-paid corporate tax, the corporate tax itself would be inconsequential.

As a prelude to describing in detail exactly how taxes influence the decisions of firms, it is worthwhile to provide an overview of the way firms are assumed to decide on the purchase of capital assets, and the ways in which taxes enter that decision. Looking at the investment decision at a basic level, the firm acquires and installs capital goods during one period of time, and uses them in conjunction with other variable inputs to produce output in the future. Since cash must be expended now to produce revenue in the future, some financing is required, and it might come from three sources. The first is debt issued (on which interest must be paid); the second is retained earnings from current or past profits; and the third is new equity issues. (A fourth source of finance could be that obtained from the government in the form of investment tax credits, special loans, etc.). The retained earnings yield a future return to existing shareholders in the form of dividends and capital gains, while new equity issues yield dividends and capital gains to new shareholders.

The business is assumed to maximize profits so that inputs are acquired until the marginal benefit equals the marginal cost for each type of input. Firms are continually making investment decisions either to acquire additional capital or to replace depreciating capital, so their capital stock changes from period to period. In each period they will endeavor to adjust their capital assets so that the marginal benefit of having an additional increment of capital exactly equals the marginal cost of having an additional increment of capital on hand. The marginal benefit is the marginal revenue product; in the case of a competitive firm, this is also the value of the marginal product after tax. The marginal cost of a capital asset used to produce the output during that period is a somewhat more subtle concept, since the asset, once acquired, will last for several periods. What we need to do is to impute to each period a cost associated with holding and using the asset. If an asset is used for one period, there are four components that make up the imputed cost. First, there is the *cost of financing* the asset, including the interest paid on debt, plus the imputed return paid to shareholders (existing and new). The latter is included because equity funds tied up in financing the capital could have yielded a return elsewhere for the shareholders. Second, the asset will *depreciate* due to wear and tear. At the end of the period it will not be able to produce as much output as at the beginning and will therefore be worth less in dollar value. Third, the dollar value of the capital may change due to obsolescence, changes in relative prices, or inflation. That is, there will be a *capital loss (or gain)* on the asset. Finally, the holding of the capital asset may give rise to some *tax savings*, to the extent that capital costs are deductible from the tax base. These four components of the cost of holding an additional unit of capital can be aggregated to arrive at the marginal cost, or what is referred to as the *user cost of capital*. Firms will wish to invest until the marginal revenue product of capital just equals the user cost of capital.[14] If the user cost of capital increases, the incentive to invest will fall, and vice versa. Our task is to specify the exact formulation for the user cost of capital so we can show how taxes and inflation influence both the user cost and the investment decision of the firm. We begin with a case in which no taxes exist, then add corporate taxes, personal taxes, and inflation in sequence. In what follows, firms will be assumed to be perfectly competitive, taking prices as given.

(a) The No-Tax Case

In the absence of taxes and inflation, the mathematical expression for the user cost of capital is appealingly simple. Suppose that the purchase price of one unit of capital is q. It will vary from period to period, but we omit time subscripts for simplicity. The capital is assumed to depreciate proportionately at the rate δ in each period. Then, $q\delta$ will be the depreciation incurred during the period on a unit of capital worth q dollars. The cost of financing the asset is assumed to be r dollars per dollar of financing, or qr dollars per unit of capital. The capital loss on the asset will be $-\Delta q$ over the period. The user cost of capital, denoted c, is the sum of these, or:

$$c = q(r + \delta - g) \tag{11-12}$$

where $g = \Delta q/q$ is the rate of price change of capital goods.

The firm will invest until the user cost of capital equals the value of its marginal product, or

$$p\,MP_k = q(r + \delta - g) \tag{11-13}$$

where p is the output price, and MP_k is the marginal product of capital. We presume that as the firm acquires more capital, the marginal product of capital falls. It continues to acquire capital until Eq. (11–13) is satisfied.[15]

The cost of finance, r, is the rate the firm has to pay its creditors to finance its cash requirements for marginal funds. Since its marginal financing can come either from debt or equity, the cost of each of those sources of funds must be known. In the case of debt, the cost of financing is the interest rate the firm has to pay on its debt at the margin, say, i. This is a one-period interest rate, and we ignore the fact that it may vary according to the maturity of the debt. For equity, the cost of finance is exactly that which is required to compensate shareholders (new or existing) to provide more equity funds. Call the cost of equity ρ. One might expect ρ to equal the return that the shareholders could obtain on the funds elsewhere in the economy, plus any risk premium associated with funds held in this firm. If β is the proportion of marginal funds obtained from debt, and $(1 - \beta)$ from equity, the cost of finance to the firm will be:

$$r = Bi + (1 - \beta)\rho. \tag{11-14}$$

This is the value of r that would appear in the user cost expression Eq. (11–13).

This formulation for the cost of finance leaves some questions unanswered. In particular, what exactly determines β, the ratio of debt to total financing? No clear answer to that question exists in the literature, although several phenomena have been discussed that influence the choice of financial structure. One extreme view is that expressed by Modigliani and Miller (1958), in a celebrated article. The essence of the article is that the choice of β is irrelevant to the shareholders of the firm. Note first of all that as β rises, the variability of returns to equity holders rises. That is because the actual returns the firm receives on its investment are uncertain, and the part that must be paid out to debt-holders is fixed in amount. As Modigliani and Miller pointed out, in a world of perfectly functioning stock markets and no bankruptcy, the choice of β is irrelevant. If firms change their debt-to-equity ratio, and thereby change the variability of returns to equity holders, this can be exactly offset by the equity holders if they change the debt-equity ratios in their personal portfolios in opposite directions. For example, suppose a firm issues one dollar of new debt *ceteris paribus*. The debt will give the firm an additional one dollar, which can be paid out as dividends, and which creates a future interest liability of i per period. The debt-equity ratio of the firm will have risen, and the shareholders appear to have been put in a riskier position. However, if the shareholder uses his one dollar of new dividends to purchase a bond bearing an interest rate, i, he will receive interest equal to what the firm has to pay out. The effect of the firm's actions has been cancelled out, and the additional one dollar of borrowing done by the firm is exactly met by the one dollar savings by the shareholder. The purchase of debt by the firm is therefore irrelevant to the shareholder, so β is irrelevant. Once the possibility of costly bankruptcy, imperfect capital markets, or taxes are introduced, it can be shown that the Modigliani-Miller result no longer holds, and the debt-equity ratio is no longer irrelevant. For example, increasing the debt-equity ratio will increase the probability of bankruptcy, which bears a real cost, and this cannot be offset by the shareholder.

Another way to view the problem has been presented by Baumol and Malkiel (1967). They have suggested one rough-and-ready way of imagining the firm choosing its debt-equity ratio. First, the rate of return required on equity, ρ, might be thought of as rising with the debt-equity ratio of the firm, since the greater the debt-equity ratio, the more variable are the returns to equity. There is an assumption that this cannot be fully undone by personal transactions. Second, the interest rate the firm must pay might also rise with the debt-equity ratio, since the probability of bankruptcy rises. If both i and ρ are increasing functions of β, the cost of capital, r, itself will be a function of β. The firm might then be viewed as choosing the level of β which minimizes the cost of finance.

We need not be concerned with exactly how the financial structure of the firm is determined. For the most part, we may take that as given. Once taxes are introduced, to the extent that they treat debt differently from equity, they will induce the firm to substitute one for the other. This will, in turn, influence the cost of finance and the investment decision of the firm. One of the purposes of this section will be to explain the direction that those incentives take. The magnitude is a matter for empirical investigation.

This no-tax case serves as a useful benchmark against which to judge the effects of taxes and inflation. One can think of the user cost in Eq. (11–13) as being the "neutral" user cost of capital. A tax would then be neutral, *vis-à-vis* the investment decision, if it did not change the expression for the user cost of capital to the firm.

(b) Corporate Taxes

Suppose we now introduce a simple corporate tax system with a fairly conventional structure. The tax base consists of revenue, less current costs (wages, materials, fuels, etc.), less deductions for the costs of using capital. The latter consists of a depreciation allowance for tax purposes and any interest costs paid. The user cost-of-capital formula Eq. (11–12), the cost of finance Eq. (11–14), and the profit-maximizing condition Eq. (11–13), can be amended to take this into account. The tax will reduce the marginal benefit from investing, since the revenues generated by marginal investments will be taxed. However, the marginal cost of investing will also be reduced, since tax savings will result from the deductions of depreciation and interest costs.

To see exactly how the incentive to invest is effected, let the corporate tax rate be u, and let depreciation for tax purposes be at the *declining balance* rate of α. In fact, other depreciation schedules may be used (such as *straight-line* or *sum-of-the-years-digits* methods), and our formula could readily be amended to take them into account. Note that α is not necessarily set equal to the true depreciation rate, δ. For convenience, let us simply ignore the capital gain term g, or, equivalently, assume it to be incorporated into the depreciation rate δ so that δ can be thought of as the true economic depreciation rate, incorporating both wear and tear and relative price changes.[16] Then, as will be explained, the marginal condition satisfied when the firm has chosen its optimal capital stock is (see Auerbach [1979]):

$$(1 - u)p\, MP_k = q(r + \delta)\left(1 - \frac{u\alpha}{r + \alpha}\right) \tag{11–15}$$

where $r = Bi(1 - u) + (1 - \beta)\rho$. The left-hand side, the marginal benefit, has been reduced by $(1 - u)$, since the revenues generated by the sale of output are taxed at the rate u. On the right-hand side, the imputed cost of finance, r, has changed, since interest costs are tax deductible; therefore, the cost to the firm of borrowing is $i(1 - u)$. The term in the last brackets in Eq. (11–15) represents the effect of the write-off for depreciation. It can be interpreted as follows: The purchase price on the market of a unit of capital is q dollars. However, once purchased, that unit of capital gives rise to a stream of depreciation write-offs at the declining balance rate, α. It can be shown that the present value to the firm of future depreciation write-offs on a dollar's worth of capital is $\alpha/(r + \alpha)$.[17] Therefore, the present value of the tax savings on one dollar's worth of capital is $u\alpha/(r + \alpha)$. We can think of the effective purchase price of a unit of capital as being the actual purchase price, q, net of the present value of future tax savings from depreciation deductions; that is, $q(1 - u\alpha/[r + \alpha])$. Then, the right-hand side can be interpreted as the user cost of a unit of capital, bearing an effective price of $q(1 - u\alpha/[r + \alpha])$.[18]

The firm will desire the quantity of capital such that the marginal condition Eq. (11–15) is satisfied. In order to compare it with the no-tax result, it is useful to rewrite it in the following way:

$$p \, MP_k = q \frac{(r + \delta)}{(1 - u)} \left(1 - \frac{u\alpha}{r + \alpha} \right). \tag{11–16}$$

The incentive effect of the tax on investment can be obtained by comparing the right-hand side of Eq. (11–16) with the neutral case $q(r + \delta)$. If the former has been increased by the tax, investment is discouraged, and if decreased by the tax, investment is encouraged. *A priori* it is not obvious whether or not the tax retards or induces investment. It depends upon the magnitudes of α and β. In general, however, a tax of this form will not be neutral.

In addition, the tax will distort the financing decision of the firm. By allowing interest deductibility, but not equity cost deductibility, the tax reduces the relative price of debt financing and induces the firm to increase its debt-equity ratio, or, as the finance literature puts it, to become more highly *leveraged* (or highly geared). For the tax to be truly neutral, it must be neutral as regards both the financial structure of the firm and the investment decision, given the financial structure.

The above discussion is for depreciable capital. Similar analyses apply to other sorts. For example, with non-depreciable capital, $\delta = 0$ and $\alpha = 0$, so the marginal condition becomes $pMP_k = qr/(1 - u)$. A similar expression could be derived for inventory capital. In the absence of price changes, the cost of holding inventory capital equals the cost of financing. The treatment of inventory capital becomes considerably more complicated when the prices of goods in inventory are changing. This is because the costing of goods taken out of inventory may not be written off at current or replacement values. For a fuller discussion of the user cost of holding inventories, see Boadway, Bruce and Mintz (1982).

It is interesting to investigate what sorts of corporate tax structures will be neutral. There are three cases that may be distinguished.

(i) *True economic depreciation and full cost of finance deductibility.* The first case to consider is that in which the depreciation rate for tax purposes equals the true depreciation rate ($\alpha = \delta$), and both interest costs, i, and equity costs, ρ, of holding capital are tax deductible. The cost of finance to the firm will now be $r = Bi(1 - u) + (1 - \beta)\rho(1 - u)$, so neither debt nor equity is favored, and Eq. (11–16) can be written:

$$pMP_k = q\frac{(r + \delta)}{1 - u}\left(1 - \frac{u\delta}{r + \delta}\right)$$

$$= q\frac{(r + \delta)}{1 - u}\left(\frac{r + \delta - u\delta}{r + \delta}\right)$$

$$= \frac{q(r + \delta[1 - u])}{1 - u}$$

$$= q(\text{Bi} + [1 - \beta]\rho + \delta) \qquad\qquad (11\text{--}17)$$

which is the same as the neutral case. This tax scheme, though ideal, is difficult to implement, since the tax authorities must know both the true rate of depreciation, δ, and the imputed cost of equity finance, ρ. Since neither of these is directly observable, it is unlikely that the tax base could be properly defined.

(ii) *Cash Flow Taxation.* The second case is the case of cash flow taxation, or immediate expensing, originally advocated by Smith (1963), and more recently analyzed in Meade (1978), and Boadway, Bruce and Mintz (1983). If capital expenditures are written off when made and no other capital deductions are allowed, including interest, Eq. (11–16) can be shown to reduce to the neutral case. To see this, notice first that the cost of finance becomes $Bi + (1 - \beta)\rho$, since interest is no longer deductible. Also, with immediate write-off, the depreciation rate α equals ∞. The last bracket in Eq. (11–16) can be rewritten as $(1 - u/[1 + r/\alpha])$, which becomes $(1 - u)$ when $\alpha = \infty$. In this case the $(1 - u)$ terms cancel out, and Eq. (11–16) reduces to the no-tax case. This type of tax structure is particularly appealing from an administrative point of view, since under it the authorities do not need to know the true depreciation rate or the cost of finance to the firm, as under the previous case.

Notice also the implicit assumption in the above that the tax rate u applies symmetrically to years in which losses are made. For neutrality, the firm must receive a subsidy in these years, or a full loss-offset against its income elsewhere. In practice, firms may not be allowed to claim subsidies in losing years, but may instead be allowed to carry forward losses to future years. The carry-forward of losses to future years is not a perfect substitute for full loss-offset or subsidy treatment, since it means that the implicit subsidy on losses is postponed until the future, when positive profits are earned. This imposes on the firm a cost equal to the foregone interest on the amount of the subsidy. A system of immediate write-off would increase the likelihood of the firm's incurring losses in early years, since its deductions will be high when capital is being accumulated. To preserve the neutrality of such a scheme, full loss-offset provisions must be in force. This means that the revenues generated for the government by a firm's investment are postponed until later, and may be negative in years of high investment.

(iii) *Present value of capital cost write-offs equals the purchase price of capital.* The previous two cases are actually special cases of a more general neutrality rule. Consider a tax which allows a depreciation write-off at the declining balance rate, α, as before. Under such a scheme, the book value of undepreciated capital on an initial investment of one dollar will decline in the proportion $(1 - \alpha)$ each year. Thus, if one dollar is purchased in year zero, $(1 - \alpha)$ will be left undepreciated in year 1, $(1 - \alpha)^2$ in year 2, and so on to $(1 - \alpha)^t$ in year t. The depreciation write-off in year t is $\alpha(1 - \alpha)^t$. Now suppose we allow a cost of finance write-off of r times the amount of undepreciated capital, so that in year t, the cost of finance write-off is $r(1 - \alpha)^t$. The cost of finance, r, will be the actual cost the firm must pay for debt and equity, $Bi + (1 - \beta)\rho$. Under such a scheme, the cost of finance write-off is similar to the depreciation write-off, and can be viewed as giving rise to a future stream of tax saving, or equivalently reducing the effective purchase price of capital goods. The effective purchase price of a unit of capital will be $q(1 - u\alpha/[r + \alpha] - ur/[r + \alpha]$ or $q(1 - u)$. This is exactly the same as the effective purchase price under immediate write-off. The marginal condition (11–16) becomes

$$pMP_k = q\frac{(r + \delta)}{(1 - u)}(1 - u) = q(r + \delta) \tag{11–18}$$

where $r = Bi + (1 - \beta)\rho$. Thus, the tax is neutral. Furthermore, it will be neutral regardless of the depreciation rate α chosen (see Boadway and Bruce [1979]). If $\alpha = \delta$, we have case (i) above, while if $\alpha = \infty$, we have case (ii), as the reader can readily verify. Indeed, it will more generally apply for depreciation schedules that do not follow the declining balance method, such as straightline depreciation. Provided the cost of finance write-off is based on the undepreciated value of the capital of the firm, however calculated, the tax will be neutral. In principle, the firm could be allowed to choose its own depreciation structure as it wished, and neutrality could still result. Of course, the cost of finance write-off must not be restricted to interest payments only, or the firm will be induced to substitute debt for equity artificially, and neutrality will be lost.

All the above tax schemes are neutral as regards the investment decision of the firm. That is, they do not affect the marginal decision to invest. This does not mean that they do not yield tax revenues, only that they yield no tax revenues on projects which are marginal to society. On infra-marginal projects, the tax captures part of the pure profits or rents. In that sense, a neutral tax is an ideal, efficient tax, since it collects revenue without imposing any distortions or deadweight loss on the economy. It would be particularly effective as a tax on industries generating significant rents, such as resource industries.

The corporate tax is often amended to incorporate investment incentives of various sorts. Let us complete this part of the discussion by indicating how investment incentives can influence the marginal investment decision of the firm. There are alternative forms that an investment incentive can take. One common form is an *investment tax credit,* which gives firms a tax credit of, say, ϕ for each dollar of investment undertaken. Investment tax credits may be of two kinds: those that are given over and above depreciation allowances, and those that reduce the amount of capital subject to the depreciation allowance. Under the former, the effective price of purchasing a unit of capital will be q, less the investment tax credit, less the tax saving due to depreciation (which is the same size as before). Then, the marginal condition determining the desired capital for the firm is:

$$pMP_k = q\frac{(r + \delta)}{(1 - u)}\left(1 - \phi - \frac{u\alpha}{r + \alpha}\right). \tag{11–19}$$

If the tax credit reduces the depreciation base for the firm, only $q(1 - \phi)$ may be depreciated in the future. In this case, the marginal condition is:

$$pMP_k = q\frac{(r + \delta)}{(1 - u)}(1 - \phi)\left(1 - \frac{u\alpha}{r + \alpha}\right). \tag{11–20}$$

In either of these cases, the investment incentive reduces the marginal cost of capital to the firm (the right-hand side of the marginal condition) and so encourages the firm to invest more. There are other ways in which investment incentives may be instituted, such as investment tax credits that apply to net investment only (rather than gross investment), or deductions from corporate taxable income which depend upon the level of investment (sometimes referred to as investment allowances). Another example is accelerated depreciation, which involves increasing α. In these other cases, the specific way in which the marginal condition is amended depends upon the specific measure under consideration. In fact, investment allowances have the same effect on the user cost of capital as a tax credit. One represents a reduction in taxable income in proportion to investment, and the other a reduction in taxes payable in proportion to investment. With a 50 percent tax rate, an investment allowance of 20 percent would have the same effect as a tax credit of 10 percent. In all cases, the effect is to reduce the marginal cost of investment.

It might also be noted that, in addition to influencing the amount of capital a firm chooses to employ, investment incentives can also influence the *choice of technique* of production. By reducing the user cost of capital relative to the cost of employing other inputs such as labor, the firm will be persuaded to increase the capital intensity of its technique of production. In the case in which the other input is labor, investment incentives will cause the firm to increase its capital-labor ratio.

Similarly, investment incentives can influence the desired durability of the capital stock held by the firm. For instance, it can be shown that the investment tax credit leads firms to use short-lived rather than long-lived capital (see Bradford [1980] and Harberger [1980]). A simple example will illustrate why. Suppose we compare two investments, both yielding a 10 percent rate of return in the absence of an investment tax credit, but having differing depreciation rates. To take extreme cases, suppose one investment has no depreciation at all and yields a perpetual stream of output, while the other depreciates entirely after one period and has to be replaced each period. If we imagine an initial investment of $1000, then the non-depreciating capital will yield a steady stream of output and revenue of $100 per period, in perpetuity. An investment tax credit of, say, 10 percent will reduce the effective purchase price of the investment to $900, but will leave unaffected the revenue stream. On the other hand, for the one-period investment yielding the same rate of return, the $1000 investment must yield $1100 of gross return, of which $1000 covers depreciation. The $1000 is reinvested, leaving the same net return of $100. The same happens in each period in the future. An investment tax credit of 10 percent now reduces not only the initial purchase price of capital to $900, but also, since it applies to replacement investment as well, it reduces the purchase price of the replacement investment, done each period, to $900 as well. This means that the net stream of return has been increased to $200 per period, much higher than in the no-depreciation case. Thus, the investment tax credit favors short-lived capital, since it applies to replacement as well as to new investment.

The magnitude of the influence of investment incentives, and the corporate tax structure in general, on the investment decision of a firm is a matter for empirical investigation. In a seminal piece on the topic, Hall and Jorgenson (1967) estimated that the 7 percent investment tax credit introduced in the United States in 1962 had a dramatic effect on investment. For example, 40.9 percent of net investment in manufacturing equipment in 1963 could be attributed to the tax credit. The adoption of accelerated depreciation methods in 1954 (e.g. sum-of-years-digits), and the reduction of service lives in 1962, also had a substantial impact on investment. These studies, and the neo-classical theory of investment on which they are based, are not without their critics. For good surveys of the approach and its shortcomings, see Helliwell (1976), and Brechling (1975).

(c) Personal Taxes

Personal income taxes indirectly influence the investment decision of a firm through their impact upon the cost of finance to the firm. They also introduce a further distortion on capital markets by driving a wedge between the cost of finance to the firm, and the net (after-tax) return received by households on their savings.

Suppose, as before, that i is the interest rate paid by firms on the market for debt, and ρ is the marginal return that shareholders must receive on their equity held in the firm. Suppose that m is the personal tax rate paid by households in the economy, and assume it to be constant over households so as to avoid the complications arising from the progressivity of the rate structure. Also, let θ be the tax rate payable on equity income received by shareholders. We assume that θ is the same for both capital gains and dividend income, thereby avoiding considerable complications arising from the preferential treatment of capital gains.[19] The cost of debt to the firm will be $i(1 - u)$, assuming interest deductibility under the corporate tax. In the case of equity, in order to provide shareholders with a rate of return of ρ after tax, the before-tax return on equity must be $\rho/(1 - \theta)$. Therefore, the weighted cost of finance to the firm must be:

$$r = Bi(1 - u) + (1 - \beta)\rho/(1 - \theta). \tag{11-21}$$

The marginal condition facing the firm will be the same as Eq. (11-15) above.

The cost of finance to the economy will be the after-tax return required to compensate savers for their savings. In the case of debt, it will be $i(1 - m)$, and for equity, ρ. Therefore, the net cost of finance from a social point of view, denoted r^*, will be:

$$r^* = Bi(1 - m) + (1 - \beta)\rho. \tag{11-22}$$

In addition to the distortion imposed on the financial structure of the firm by the interest deductibility provision of the corporate tax, the personal tax may also influence the relative costs of debt and equity finance. If interest is taxed more heavily under the personal tax than are dividends and capital gains, the relative cost of debt finance to the firm will rise, thereby inducing lower leverage in contrast to the corporate tax.

Now, even if the corporate tax is neutral, the tax system itself will impose a distortion on capital markets, because the personal tax applies to capital income. One way to see this is through the concept of an *effective tax rate* on capital markets defined as follows: Since pMP_k is the marginal gross return generated by a unit of capital, pMP_k/q will be the gross rate of return on a dollar's worth of capital. The net rate of return, or the rate of return on capital net of depreciation, will be $pMP_k/q - \delta$, denoted σ. Using Eq. (11-16), it will be given by:

$$\sigma = pMP_k/q - \delta = \frac{(r + \delta)}{(1 - u)}\left(1 - \frac{u\alpha}{r + \alpha}\right) - \delta. \tag{11-23}$$

Assuming that the net return to capital, σ, falls with the rate of investment, we can depict an investment demand schedule as in Fig. 11-13, showing investment as a function of the net rate of return to capital.[20] Note that if the corporate tax structure were neutral, as discussed above, then Eq. (11–23) would reduce to $\sigma = r$.

Similarly, if the net return to savers is r^* from Eq. (11–22), we can think of savings increasing with the value of r^*. Figure 11–13 shows an upward sloping savings supply function $S(r^*)$. In the presence of taxes, r and r^* will generally differ, as can be seen by inspecting Eqs. (11–21) and (11–22).

If there were no taxes, inspection of Eqs. (11–21), (11–22), and (11–23) will show that $\sigma = r = r^*$, so the net return on capital equals the net return to savings. In this case, the investment and savings in the economy would be given by I^0 and there would be no distortion. However, in the presence of taxes, $\sigma \neq r^*$ so I^0 is not achieved. The diagram depicts the case in which the tax system causes the return on capital to exceed the return to savings, $\sigma > r^*$, although this need not necessarily be the case.

Figure 11–13

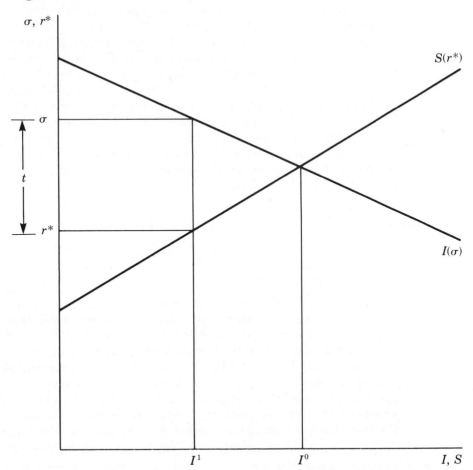

The difference between σ and r^* is called the *effective tax rate on capital markets* and is shown as t. It combines the distorting influences of both the corporate and personal taxes.

If the corporate tax were neutral, say, due to a cash flow tax system, the effective tax would reflect only the distortion imposed by the personal tax on capital income. In this case $\sigma = r = Bi + (1 - \beta)\rho/(1 - \theta)$; however r will exceed r^* because of the personal tax. That is, the cost of finance to the firm will exceed the return on savings to households, so capital markets will be distorted. On the other hand, if there were no personal tax on capital income (as under an expenditure tax system), the effective tax distortion would be due entirely to the corporate tax. In this case r^* would be the cost of finance the firm must buy on the market, but $\sigma \neq r^*$ from Eq. (11–23). As we have seen, the corporate tax could either retard investment (so $\sigma > r^*$) or stimulate investment (so $\sigma < r^*$).

(d) Inflation

So far we have ignored inflation. The purpose of this final part of the section will be to incorporate inflation into the above analysis of the effect of taxes on the investment decision of the firm. Inflation interacts with the tax system in several ways and can influence the size of the distortion on the capital market. As a benchmark, consider the introduction of inflation into the no-tax case discussed earlier. Now we must distinguish between *real* and *nominal* variables. Nominal prices are the prices that actually exist in each period, what we have called p and q for output and capital goods prices. Real prices are nominal prices deflated by some price index. Thus, for example, if the inflation rate is π per period, and if p_t and q_t are the nominal prices in period t, the real prices measured in terms of period zero dollars will be defined by:

$$\overline{p}_t = \frac{p_t}{(1 + \pi)^t}$$

$$\overline{q}_t = \frac{q_t}{(1 + \pi)^t}. \tag{11–24}$$

Here, the rate of inflation, π, is the rate of increase in some suitable price index, such as the consumer price index. We also distinguish between real and nominal interest rates and rates of return. In the absence of taxes, we would expect interest rates and rates of return to rise by the rate of inflation, as suggested by Fisher (1930). This is because, if inflation is at the rate π, creditors who lend x dollars on the market must receive $x(1 + \pi)$ at the end of the period to compensate them for the loss in real value of the amount of the loan. In addition, they must receive the usual interest on the loan that they would have received in the absence of inflation. By the same token, creditors would be willing to pay back a principal $x(1 + \pi)$

plus the real interest, and be equally as well off as they were in the absence of inflation. Thus, inflation will cause nominal interest rates to rise by π, so[21]:

$$i = \bar{i} + \pi$$

$$\rho = \bar{\rho} + \pi$$

$$r = \bar{r} + \pi \qquad (11\text{–}25)$$

where $\bar{i}$ is the real rate of interest, i is the nominal rate of interest, and so on. The inflation rate π is the expected rate of inflation.

The equilibrium condition determining the choice of capital by the firm is now $pMP_k = q(r + \delta - g)$, as before. The term g is the rate of nominal price increase of q; it will be the inflation rate π plus any change in the real price of capital goods. If we assume the real price of capital goods to be unchanged (or incorporate them into δ as before), the equilibrium condition can be written as:

$$\frac{pMP_k}{q} = \frac{\overline{pMP_k}}{\bar{q}} = \bar{r} + \delta. \qquad (11\text{–}26)$$

If inflation causes nominal interest rates to rise by the rate of inflation, then the real cost of finance, $\bar{r}$, will be unchanged by inflation. The solution to Eq. (11–26) for the optimal capital stock will be the same as the solution to Eq. (11–13), and inflation will be neutral.

Suppose corporate and personal taxes exist now. If these tax systems were not designed to account for inflation, the presence of inflation would influence the effective tax imposed by the tax system. In the case of the corporate tax, this happens for two reasons. First, depreciation deductions may be based upon the original nominal value of the capital being depreciated, or the *historic cost.*[22] Thus, the real value of the depreciation deduction falls with inflation. Second, firms are allowed to deduct nominal, rather than real, interest payments. In other words, they are allowed to deduct as costs the fall in real value of principal due to inflation. Inflation thus increases the value of interest deductions. In the case of personal taxes, as discussed in Chapter 10, the tax base is nominal capital income (interest, dividends, and capital gains). This means that households are being taxed partly on nominal returns, which represent only a maintenance of their real asset values, as well as on real interest payments.

The implications of the lack of inflation accounting of the corporate and personal tax systems can be seen by amending the marginal condition for the firm Eq. (11–16), the expressions for the cost of finance Eq. (11–21), and the return to savers Eq. (11–22) to incorporate inflation. In the case of the former, the present value of the depreciation allowances using the rate α based on historic cost will be $\alpha/(r + \alpha)$ or $\alpha/(\bar{r} + \pi + \alpha)$.[23] Therefore, Eq. (11–16) can be written:

$$\frac{pMP_k}{q} = \frac{(\bar{r} + \delta)}{(1 - u)} \left(1 - \frac{u\alpha}{\bar{r} + \pi + \alpha}\right). \tag{11--27}$$

The real cost of finance, $\bar{r}$, appears in the first term on the right-hand side since, as above, it incorporates the nominal cost of finance, r, less the inflationary increase in the price of capital goods (that part of g which reflects inflation). As before, we can define the (real) net return on capital σ as $pMP_k/q - \delta$. As for the cost of finance to the firm, it will now be given by:

$$\bar{r} = Bi(1 - u) + (1 - \beta)\rho/(1 - \theta) - \pi. \tag{11--28}$$

This expression reflects the nominal interest deductibility of the firm, since now the nominal cost of debt is $i(1 - u)$. It also reflects the nominal taxability of equity returns at the personal level, since now it is the nominal return on equity, ρ, that must be grossed up at the tax rate θ. Finally, the net return to savers in real terms may be written:

$$\bar{r}^* = Bi(1 - m) + (1 - \beta)\rho - \pi. \tag{11--29}$$

Notice that the nominal interest rate, i, is also subject to the personal tax.

The effective tax rate on capital markets is now defined to be $t = \sigma - \bar{r}^*$, the difference between the real rate of return on investment and the real rate of return on savings. In general, changes in the rate of inflation will influence the size of the effective tax distortion. This can be avoided if the corporate and personal tax structures are indexed for inflation. In the case of the personal tax, only real capital income should be taxed. We have discussed how this might be done in the previous chapter. The corporate tax requires two amendments to be made. First, depreciation write-offs should be based upon the replacement value of capital, rather than the historic value. One way to do this is to increase the book value of undepreciated capital by the rate of inflation each year. Second, real, rather than nominal, interest write-offs should be allowed.

In order to make the tax structure fully neutral (that is, make the effective tax rate zero), similar prescriptions to those discussed earlier should be applied. At the personal level, capital income should escape taxation altogether. At the corporate level, a system of cash flow taxation would be neutral. Equivalently, any combination of cost of finance write-offs and depreciation deductions, such that the present value of the deductions equalled the purchase price of capital, would still be neutral.

Effective tax rates indicate only the magnitude of tax distortions on capital markets, not the quantitative impact of taxes and inflation on the level of investment and savings. They are, however, of interest for tax reform. Effective tax rates have been calculated for the tax structures of several countries including the United States, United Kingdom, Germany, and Sweden by King *et al.* (1983), and Canada by Boadway, Bruce and Mintz (1982). Naturally, the tax rates vary across countries, but they are of substantial size. For example, effective tax rates in the United States on depreciable capital are found to be on the order of 40 percent to 45 percent of the return to capital, while for Canada they are about 30 percent for machinery and 45 percent for buildings. These represent significant distortions on the capital markets of these countries. Increases in the rate of inflation also had differential affects on the effective tax rates. In the United States, it has been found that inflation moderately increases the effective tax rate, while in Canada inflation slightly reduces the effective tax rate.

OTHER DISINCENTIVE EFFECTS OF THE TAX SYSTEM

11–6   Each of the types of taxes that might be levied imposes specific types of incentive on decision-making because of the way in which its tax base is defined. We shall enumerate some of the more important of these distorting effects by considering each of the types of taxes in turn.

(a) Personal Income Tax

The practical definition of the tax base for income tax purposes causes a number of difficulties which give rise to distorting influences. We saw in the last chapter some of the problems involved in defining an equitable comprehensive income tax base: the inability to measure imputed income, the desire to deduct the cost of earning income, and the treatment of capital gains. The methods for dealing with each of these problems often, in practice, give rise to distorting influences on taxpayers' decision-making.

The inability to tax imputed income is particularly important for the case of owner-occupied housing which yields real income in the form of imputed rent. The treatment of imputed rent, relative to income generated by renting housing rather than owning it, may influence an individual's decisions regarding the purchase of a house. If the individual buys a house, the return to that asset in the form of imputed rent is not taxable. On the other hand, if he were to buy a financial asset yielding a monetary rate of interest, and at the same time rent a house, he would be subject to additional income tax on the return to the asset if interest income were taxable. Thus, he is financially better off owning a home.[24] The decision is subject to an even greater distortion if, in addition to not including imputed rent in his tax base, the individual homeowner is allowed a deduction for property taxes and mortgage interest paid against his taxable income. A similar argument applies to all consumer durables that yield an imputed rent in use. Housing is obviously the most important of these, since for most other consumer durables rental is not a realistic option.

Tax systems may also allow interest payments on personal loans to be deductible from taxable income, on the principle that they represent a cost of earning income, e.g. other interest income. While this may be true for loans taken out to purchase financial assets, it is not true of loans for consumer durables, since the return to the latter is not taxed. Therefore, interest payment deductions favor those who purchase consumer durables.

We have already mentioned the fact that capital gains for tax purposes must realistically be included as taxable income only when realized, rather than when accrued. This gives an incentive for individuals to postpone realization in order to put off paying taxes, thus impairing the free operation of the capital market. This "lock-in" effect is particularly strong if the capital asset can be bequeathed to heirs without being subject to capital gains tax. In this case, the latter can be avoided entirely, although an estate tax may be payable on it. However, estate taxes are typically lower than capital gains taxes.

The tax treatment of capital gains gives rise to another problem. Capital gains are often treated preferentially in the tax base. For example, they may be subject to lower rates. The reasons for this may be either that capital gains often represent risky investments and the government may want to encourage that,[25] or to compensate for the fact that part of the gain may be illusory in times of inflation and ought not to be taxed. In any case, this preferential treatment gives individuals an incentive to take their income in the form of capital gains rather than ordinary income, and considerable resources may be devoted to finding ways of doing this. This preferential treatment of capital gains may also give firms an incentive to retain earnings rather than pay out dividends, thus encouraging investment.

There may also be distortionary influences arising from the relative treatment of married vs. single persons which could conceivably, however unlikely, influence the decision to marry. One such influence is the practice of income-splitting that allows husband and wife to pool their income and be taxed as if each obtained one-half the family income. Whenever the incomes of husband and wife differ significantly, there will be a tax saving from income-splitting, as compared with taxing each one individually, if the tax system has a progressive marginal rate of tax. Thus, there is a tax advantage to being married that may be substantial. The fact that the tax system does not tax the imputed income of the care of the home provides a further benefit to marriage, since marriage will often enable one spouse to cease working outside the home and devote his or her nonleisure time to untaxed housekeeping. On the other hand, if the tax system does not allow income-splitting, but taxes returns jointly according to a uniform schedule, tax liabilities will rise with marriage because of progression. The tax system which does not allow income-splitting may mitigate the effects on marriage by establishing a separate rate schedule. These tax advantages to marriage are not likely to be of more than marginal significance in the decision to marry. The appropriate treatment of the family unit poses problems mostly of equity. We shall return to this in Chapter 13.

The income tax system may also offer various deductions as an attempt to encourage certain types of activities, say, because they are of a public-good nature. For example, donations to charity may be tax-deductible, as may be educational expenditures. While such deductions may, in fact, succeed in giving an incentive to partake of these types of expenditure,[26] it is not clear that they are the most efficient or equitable way of doing so. A deduction from taxable income represents a progressive subsidy, since the value of a deduction depends upon the marginal tax rate of the recipient. A $1000 deduction from taxable income is worth $500 in reduced taxes to someone in the 50 percent tax bracket, but only $200 to someone in the 20 percent bracket. Thus, high-income persons are given much more incentive to make these expenditures than are low-income persons. It is quite possible, especially if these activities have high income elasticities of demand, that a proportional subsidy, costing the government as much as the deduction in lost revenue, would give rise to more expenditures on these items. A proportional subsidy could be given through the income tax system by allowing a credit, against taxes payable, of a certain percentage of the expenditures, that is, a tax credit rather than a deduction from taxable income.

State and even local governments may have their own income taxes. The existence of various income taxes paid to different levels of government gives rise to another sort of problem. If the tax rates differ in different states, and if these differences do not reflect the net benefit of government services, workers may have an incentive to move from one location to another with a different tax-benefit mix. These sorts of problems, which arise in all federal types of governments, are discussed in Part IV.

(b) Commodity Taxation

Commodity taxes may be specific (on one commodity or group of commodities) or general. Specific excise taxes, of course, are a disincentive to purchase the commodities on which they are levied. The amount by which the tax reduces purchases will depend upon the elasticity of demand for the commodity in question. The less elastic is the demand and the supply, the less will the demand be reduced.[27]

The decision to levy specific excise taxes, and therefore to strike particular markets, may be taken for various reasons. The use of the commodity in question may emit an external diseconomy that is not captured in the price system. Examples of this would be the consumption of alcohol, tobacco products, and gasoline. The use of these products gives rise to social costs of pollution, injury, or death; and a tax, rather than imposing a distortion, may offset one. Specific taxes may be levied as user charges or benefit taxes. Toll roads are an example of this, as are license fees and the gasoline tax. These may be user costs for the use of roads, and therefore be part of the "price" of using them. The levying of specific taxes on commodities in inelastic demand may also be justified, because they impose very little deadweight loss as a proportion of revenue raised. This was discussed fully in Chapter 9.

General commodity taxes may be of various sorts. A proportional commodity tax on all transactions is equivalent to a proportional income tax that exempts interest income if capital markets are perfect. If capital markets are not perfect (so individuals cannot borrow and lend at a given interest rate against future earnings) the two will not be identical, since their time streams differ. Empirically, consumption expenditures in the early and late periods of life tend to be relatively high compared with income. Without perfect capital markets, a general consumption tax would reduce consumption much more in early years relative to the income tax, since individuals could not easily borrow to pay the tax. The general consumption tax might also give specific exemptions on necessity purchases which the income tax could not do.

On the other hand, income taxes, being taxes on individuals, can easily be made progressive. Consumption taxes might also be made progressive if they were levied on the consumption expenditure of individuals. The latter type of tax, an expenditure tax, has been advocated from time to time by those who favor expenditures as a more equitable tax base than income. As we saw in Chapter 9, two difficulties arise with expenditure taxation. One is the administrative difficulty involved in applying it—a record is needed of each individual's total expenditures every year. The other is that without perfect capital markets, an expenditure tax would impose a liquidity problem in periods of heavy dissaving, and retard expenditures significantly. A system of averaging would help alleviate the problem, but not entirely solve it.

A general commodity tax may also be levied at one of various stages of production, such as retail, wholesale, or manufacturing levels. Taxes levied at the latter two stages are easier to administer because there are fewer firms from which to collect them; at the same time, they have certain drawbacks. For one thing, taxes levied before the retail stage may be subject to a phenomenon called *pyramiding*. That is, if a fixed mark-up is applied at each stage of production, the mark-up will apply to the tax-inclusive price when the tax is levied at an earlier stage. Also, a tax levied at an early stage may not capture such items as the sale of services (restaurants, etc.). Finally, it may be more difficult to exempt certain goods from the tax if the tax is applied at an earlier stage. Retail-level taxes avoid many of these problems.

Commodity taxes may be simultaneously imposed at several stages of production, rather than simply one. Two types of multi-stage taxes have been in use at various times, mainly in Europe: A *turnover tax* and a *value-added tax*. A turnover tax imposes a fixed rate of tax on all transactions at whatever stage. Despite the fact that very low rates can be used to gather large amounts of revenue, the turnover tax has some obvious disadvantages. First, it strikes relatively heavily at commodities that pass through many stages of production (e.g. services, as opposed to manufactured goods). In addition to the distorting effect on relative prices, there is an incentive to integrate vertically so as to reduce the number of stages through which interfirm transactions take place. Another disadvantage of the turnover tax is the difficulty of exempting specific commodities from the tax. To do so, one must know the cumulation of taxes that have been paid on the prior stages of production and marketing.

The value-added tax avoids many of the problems of the turnover tax, since it takes only the value added at each stage of production and not the entire value. Therefore its base is ultimately the final value of the product. As such, it is exactly equivalent to a proportional tax on factor incomes. However, value-added taxes may exempt purchases of capital goods, thus reducing the tax base to the value of consumer purchases only. If so, it is equal in its economic effects to a general consumption tax. The value-added tax suffers from higher administrative costs compared to income or consumption taxes. Many of these costs are incurred by firms rather than the government. Value-added taxes do have the advantage that they can be constructed to provide a built-in check on evasion. Each firm is taxed on the total value of its sales and is allowed to deduct taxes paid at prior stages; each firm therefore has an incentive to report the tax due from upstream suppliers, which makes it difficult for the upstream suppliers to falsify their tax assessments. Moreover, value-added taxes can be rebated on exports. For that reason some countries have proposed replacing corporation taxes with them. Overall, these taxes do not appear to have significant advantages over general consumption or income taxes.

(c) Property Taxation

Property taxes are taxes levied periodically (say, annually) on the value of certain types of real capital. Inasmuch as the value of a stock of capital represents the present value of the stream of income generated by it, it is similar to a tax on the return to capital. If all capital (including land) were included in its base and taxed at the same rate, the tax would be equivalent to a general tax on the factor of production capital, and its effect would depend upon the elasticity of supply and demand for capital. If the capital stock were fixed, the tax would be borne entirely out of capital's income and no distortion would be imposed on its use. The next chapter considers general factor taxes in more detail.

Property taxes are not general taxes, however. Because they are local, they are levied at different rates in different cities. Cities with relatively high tax rates will discourage the formation of capital, and may cause the emigration of labor if the high rates are not offset by benefits from public services. Property taxes also may discriminate against various types of property. Residential property may bear different tax rates than commercial and industrial property, and this will influence the allocation of capital among these uses. The property tax may treat the site value of land differently from the value of structures or the value of equipment. Often, residential home improvements are discouraged if they are subject to the property tax. Finally, the methods of assessment of property values are to some extent arbitrary, since market values have not always been established at a time near enough to the assessment date. Methods of assessment may vary from place to place, and this may introduce further distortions into the system.

(d) Estate and Gift Taxes

While estate taxes levied on the value of an estate at the owner's death, or gift taxes levied on the giving of large gifts, are imposed mainly for equity reasons, they may in addition distort resource allocation decisions. To the extent that individuals save for purposes of providing wealth for their heirs, the taxation of estates serves to increase the price of such saving. As with any other price change, there is an income effect and a substitution effect, and one cannot predict *a priori* whether saving will be reduced on that account. If such savings have a positive income elasticity, they would be reduced, but the magnitude of such effects have not adequately been tested. At the same time, estate taxes help to offset the lock-in effect of capital gains taxation by taxing the transfer of capital between generations. The usefulness of this is reduced, however, if the rate of taxation is lower than capital gains tax rates.

There are some provisions of estate taxation that may influence the manner in which savings are accumulated for bequest or donation, and these affect the allocation of capital within the economy. If family businesses or farms are exempt from the tax, there will be an incentive to accumulate capital in these forms. Charitable donations or the creation of charitable foundations may be exempt from the estate tax, in which case there is an incentive to give part of the estate to such organizations.[28] To the extent that charitable organizations provide services of a public-good nature, the subsidization of bequests to them may repair a distortion in resource allocation, rather than create one. The tax system may also allow for the creation of trusts. The sum of money put into a trust can be used to provide a stream of income for the lifetime of the immediate heirs of the donor. A bequest used for a trust fund is subject to an estate tax when the trust is created, but then not again until the trust has been dissolved two, or possibly three, generations later. The advantage of creating a trust is to avoid the payment of estate tax by the next one or two generations. Funds put into trust are managed so as to give an income to the heirs. It has been argued that such funds are managed conservatively, thereby reducing the supply of funds available for more risky investments.

(e) Payroll Taxes

Payroll taxes are proportionate taxes on labor income used to finance social security (pensions) and unemployment insurance. Such taxes are general factor taxes whose effects will be more fully discussed in the following chapter. As with general capital taxes, they will be borne entirely by labor, if labor is inelastic in supply.

However, it is often argued that payroll taxes may have a significant influence on personal savings because of the nature of the benefits that they finance. These payroll contributions are used to pay for retirement income, and for income in the event of unemployment. To the extent that individuals might save specifically for these eventualities, the social security and unemployment insurance programs provide a substitute. Individuals may treat these payroll taxes as savings and cut back their personal savings proportionately (or at least partly). However, the revenues from payroll taxes may not be used as private savings might have been. They may be used to pay current pensions of the retired generation, rather than saved and used for pensions of those who contributed. In this case, the existence of public social security schemes may retard savings and economic growth. We discuss these issues further in Chapter 14.

CHAPTER NOTES

1. The analysis presented here is similar to that found in Musgrave (1959), Ch. 11. The possibility of there being two points of equal tax revenue was pointed out in a comment on the Musgrave analysis by Barlow and Sparks (1964). For a further discussion of the issue, see Head (1966), and Barlow and Sparks (1966).

2. Under a proportional tax system, total taxes paid are $T = tY$ where t is the tax rate and Y is income. Under a linear progressive tax with exemption level E and tax rate t', an individual with income Y would pay total taxes of $T' = t'(Y - E)$. Comparing these, we see that

$$T' \gtrless T \text{ if } t'(Y - E) \gtrless tY$$

or $\quad Y \gtrless t' \dfrac{E}{(t' - t)}.$

Since $(t' - t) > 0$ when total revenues are the same under the two tax systems, individuals with $Y < t'E/(t' - t)$ will pay less tax under the progressive system and those with $Y > t'E/(t' - t)$ will pay more.

3. If labor and capital are substitutes in the production process, as is usually assumed, a rise in the price of capital will give firms an incentive to substitute labor for capital. That is, the demand curve for labor will shift to the right.

4. To see this, note that $-KM$ is the vertical displacement along the line CD associated with the horizontal displacement of LN. The ratio of the two, $-KM/LN$, must equal the slope of that line, which we know is $-(1 + r)^{-1}$. Therefore, $KM/LN = (1 + r)^{-1}$ or $KM = LN/(1 + r)$, so that KM is indeed the present value of the interest income taxes collected.

   It should perhaps be emphasized that the present value of tax revenue is computed using the before-tax rate of interest, r, not the after-tax rate, r^*, at which households discount the future. To see that the government's expenditure over time is limited by the present value of tax revenues computed at the interest rate, r, let G_p and G_f be government "consumption," or real expenditure in the present and future, respectively. Assuming that interest on government debt is subject to taxation at the same rate t_r as interest on private debt, the government must pay an interest rate of r in order to offer the same net return to lenders as private borrowing does. In the future, the government will have to repay principal and interest on its first-period borrowing, which will cost $(1 + r)(G_p - t_pY_p)$. It will receive revenues from current wage taxation and from the tax on interest income. Thus the budget constraint in the future requires that

$$(1 + r)(G_p - t_pY_p) + G_f = t_fY_f + t_r\, r[(1 - t_p)Y_p - C_p].$$

Dividing through by $1 + r$ confirms that the present value of real government expenditure, $G_p + (1 + r)^{-1}G_f$, equals the present value of present and future tax revenue

$$t_pY_p + \frac{t_fY_f + t_r r[(1 - t_p)Y_p - G_p]}{1 + r},$$

discounted at rate r. One can easily check that the same result holds true if government interest payments are tax exempt.

5. The budget constraint with consumption taxes becomes

$$(1 + s_p)C_p + \frac{(1 + s_f)C_f}{1 + r} = Y_p + \frac{Y_f}{1 + r}.$$

If the tax rate is the same in both periods, $s = s_p = s_f$, one can divide through by $1 + s$ to see that the effect of the tax is equivalent to a reduction of Y_p and Y_f by the proportion $1/(1 + s)$. This corresponds to a labor income tax at a rate t such that $1 - t = 1/(1 + s)$, or $t = 1 - 1/(1 + s)$. Note, however, that a progressive consumption tax, or one with tax rates that vary over time, is *not* equivalent to a labor income tax. If the tax is progressive, the rate s_p would be higher than s_f if, say, present consumption were higher than future. But if the tax rate is higher in the present, the price of future relative to present consumption falls. These relative price effects arise whenever the tax rate on consumption is not the same at all times, but obviously do not occur under a wage income tax.

6. The real world is somewhat more complicated than this discussion has allowed, because the tax system in practice treats capital gains and dividends differentially (as discussed in Section 11–5 below). As Auerbach (1979) and others have shown, the simple stock-valuation formula (that predicts a one dollar drop in share value associated with a one dollar increase in dividend payouts) must be modified accordingly. The basic conclusion that household wealth is increased by business saving remains valid in slightly altered form, however.

7. One might also think of the behavior of a firm acting on behalf of its individual shareholders.

8. The formula for the standard deviation of the returns is given by:

$$\sigma = \sqrt{\Sigma p_i(X_i - y)^2}.$$

9. The principle of portfolio diversification operates as follows: Suppose one holds a portfolio of several assets, each of which has its own expected return and

standard deviation. If the returns on the various assets are less than perfectly correlated, the standard deviation of the portfolio will be less than the sum of the standard deviations of the component assets. This is due to the tendency of low gains on some assets to be offset by positive gains on others. For a full analytical discussion of the principle, see Markowitz (1959).

10. It can be shown that the maximization of expected utility is equivalent to maximizing a utility function whose arguments are the mean and the standard deviation when one of two circumstances prevail: The utility function may be written in the quadratic form, or the probability distribution of returns is a normal distribution (which can be characterized entirely by the mean and standard deviation). For a discussion of this, see Richter (1960).

11. These results appeared simultaneously in the literature in Mossin (1968), and Stiglitz (1969). The reader is referred there for algebraic proofs of them.

12. For an analysis of the effects of income taxation on both the size of portfolio and the share held as a risky asset in a two-period asset model, see Ahsan (1976).

13. Firms also buy and sell financial assets for profit, thereby acting as financial intermediaries. For simplicity, we ignore these activities and concentrate on the sale of goods and services.

14. If there are installation costs, or adjustment costs to investing such as the disruption of production, the firm will invest until the marginal revenue product, net of adjustment costs, equals the user cost of capital. See Lucas (1967) and Gould (1968).

15. Equation (11–13) can be derived formally as the first-order condition to an optimization problem of the firm. For a firm hiring labor and capital only, the problem is to choose a stream of capital, K_t, and labor, L_t, so as to maximize $\Sigma(1 + r)^{-t}(pF(K_t, L_t) - wL_t - q_t(K_{t+1} - K_t + \delta K_t))$ where $F(K_t, L_t)$ is the production function. This problem yields Eq. (11–13) as the first-order condition on K_t. See Jorgenson (1967) or Sandmo (1974).

16. The term "true economic depreciation" is that used by Samuelson (1964) in a similar context. He defined it to include both physical depreciation and changes in the price of capital goods.

17. This can be proven as follows: With a declining balance method of depreciation, a proportion α is depreciated each period, leaving $(1 - \alpha)$ of the original dollar's worth of capital at the end of period 1, $(1 - \alpha)^2$ at the end of period 2, and $(1 - \alpha)^t$ at the end of period t. Depreciation in period t is $\alpha(1 - \alpha)^t$. Discounting the stream of depreciation deductions at the rate r, we obtain

$$\sum_{t=1}^{\infty} \alpha(1+r)^{-t}(1 - \alpha)^t = \alpha/(r + \alpha).$$

18. The marginal condition Eq. (11–15) can readily be derived as the first-order condition of a maximization problem of a competitive firm. This is a problem which allows the firm to choose its stream of future capital purchases so as to maximize the present value of the future stream of cash flow of the firm, discounted at the rate r. (See, for example, Auerbach [1979], and Boadway and Bruce [1979]).

19. If dividends and capital gains are taxed at different personal rates, the cost to the firm of equity financing by retained earnings differs from that of new equity

issues. In particular, if capital gains are taxed at lower rates, financing by retained earnings is favored. This is because substituting a dollar of retained earnings for a dollar of new issues to finance the same capital implies a dollar's dividends paid out, and the capital gain from one dollar of retained earnings created. Since dividends are taxed at a rate exceeding capital gains, shareholders will incur less tax liability by substituting retained earnings for new issues. Since the incentives in the personal tax system seem to favor financing by retentions rather than new issues, and the corporate tax favors debt financing to either type of equity financing, it has been a puzzle in the literature as to why firms ever resort to new equity issues. For a full discussion of this see King (1977).

20. Strictly speaking, the marginal condition Eq. (11–23) determines the demand for capital, and there is no reason why the firm should not instantaneously adjust its capital stock to the optimal amount. The demand for a flow of investment would not be defined. To obtain an investment flow over time, one must assume that firms cannot get to their optimal capital stock instantaneously, due to adjustment costs, delivery lags, etc. (See Jorgenson [1963], Brechling [1975].) Figure (11–13) assumes this to be the case.

21. Actually, as Fisher (1930) pointed out, the correct relation between nominal and real rates in a discrete time model is given by $(1 + i) = (1 + \bar{i})(1 + \pi) = (1 + \bar{i} + \pi + \bar{i}\pi)$. This implies $i = \bar{i} + \pi + \bar{i}\pi$. We ignore the term $\bar{i}\pi$, since it will normally be of negligible size. The same holds for ρ and r.

22. In the case of inventories, a similar problem arises if inventory use is written off according to first-in-first-out (FIFO) accounting practices, which is similar to historic cost accounting. The problem is circumvented if last-in-first-out (LIFO) accounting is used for tax purposes.

23. The demonstration of this is the same as before. A one dollar investment is written off in the amount α in the first period, $\alpha(1 - \alpha)$ in the second, $\alpha(1 - \alpha)^t$ in period t-1, etc. Discounting the stream of write-offs at the nominal cost of finance, r, yields $\alpha(r + \alpha)$ as the present value of the future streams of historic cost-based depreciation.

24. A simple numerical example will suffice to illustrate the bias in favor of home ownership, as opposed to rental of housing. Consider a person who purchases a $50,000 house. Suppose that this house would have yielded an annual rate of return of 10 percent if rented. If the individual concerned is indifferent between renting and owning, his imputed rent will be $5000 annually. Because this imputed rent is not taxable, the individual does not add the $5000 to taxable income. Suppose the individual were to rent a house instead, and use the $50,000 to yield a return on the capital market. Assuming the return to capital in general is the same as the return on housing, 10 percent, the individual can earn $5000 in capital income on the investment, but will have to pay rent of $5000. Since, however, the capital income of $5000 will be taxable, the individual is worse off by the tax paid on $5000. There are two alternative corrections to this distortion of the individual's choice. One is to exclude all interest (capital) income from the tax base. This would be an efficient solution, since it would eliminate the distortion imposed on the decision to save as discussed in Section 11–3 above. A solution which respects the notion of the

comprehensive tax base would be to include imputed rent as well as capital income in the income tax base.

25. Recall that in Section 11–4 we saw that the taxation of capital gains may not, in fact, reduce risk-taking, but may have the opposite effect. Therefore, a policy of giving preferential treatment to capital gains may not have the intended effect.

26. For example, Feldstein and Clotfelter (1976) estimated that the elasticity of charitable donations with respect to the price of giving them is slightly greater than unity. The price of making donations is the amount of after-tax income foregone per dollar of donations at the margin. For persons itemizing deductions (see Chapter 13), this price will be one minus the marginal tax rate.

27. The importance of the elasticities of demand and supply in determining the price and output changes resulting from the imposition of the tax is discussed in the following chapter. See, for example, Fig. 12–1 and the discussion of it.

28. Boskin (1976) estimates the effect of the charitable bequest deduction on the magnitude of charitable bequests given. He finds that the elasticity of charitable bequests, with respect to the price of giving them, is greater than one except for exceptionally large estates. The price of giving charitable bequests is $(1 - t)$ where t is the marginal tax rate applicable to the estate. These results imply that the charitable deduction results in a greater quantity of additional bequests than tax revenue foregone by the government. In that sense, it is more efficient than the government simply supporting charitable foundations with tax revenues.

12

Tax Incidence

INTRODUCTION

12–1 The study of tax incidence attempts to determine who in the economy bears the "burden" of taxation. That is, who in the private sector sacrifices the resources transferred to the public sector by taxation, and how is the distribution of this sacrifice different under one tax as opposed to another. As with much of economic analysis, the exercises are counterfactual, in the sense that one is trying to find out how resources would have been allocated, and incomes or welfare distributed, in the absence of the tax. Since we cannot perform laboratory experiments in the economy, the predictions we make about the incidence of various taxes depends heavily upon how we assume the economy operates. On this latter, there is still substantial controversy among economists, and progress in the study of tax incidence is only as advanced as the economic theory behind it. Consequently, the analysis of this chapter must be viewed as a survey of tax incidence theory as it has advanced thus far, rather than as a definitive statement. The study of tax incidence is a matter of ongoing concern for public finance specialists, both from a theoretical and an empirical point of view.

Because the levying of taxes affects relative prices in the economy, and therefore sets up forces causing changes in resource allocation and prices, it is apparent that the party (household or firm) which legally must pay the tax is not necessarily the one who bears the burden of the tax. The tax may be shifted to other households or firms in the economy via price changes. For example, a corporation must legally pay the corporation income tax, and so is said to bear the *legal* or *statutory incidence*. Yet, the entire burden of the transfer of resources will not fall on the corporation if it can recoup part of the tax revenue in the form of higher prices for its output.

The corporation is said to have *shifted* part of the tax to consumers so the true economic incidence is borne both by consumers and the corporation. This is referred to as *forward shifting*. At the same time, the corporation may shift part of the tax *backward* to labor or other inputs by paying them a lower price.

This chapter analyzes various mechanisms for shifting the burden of taxes among different households of the economy. The typical household in the economy "owns" a certain quantity of factors of production which it sells for the going factor prices; it then uses the proceeds to buy goods at the going goods prices. Any tendency for the tax to cause factor prices to fall or goods prices to rise will make it worse off. In practice, some goods prices may rise and others fall, so that whether or not the household is better off or worse off depends upon the relative weights or expenditure shares of various goods in its consumption bundle. A given tax change, whether it be on a good or on a factor, may induce changes in both goods and factor prices through the workings of the price system. An analysis which attempts to take into consideration the effect of a tax change on all prices in the economy is called a *general equilibrium analysis*.

It often may be sufficient to consider only the effect of a tax change in the market in which it is imposed, if the changes induced elsewhere are small. An analysis which limits itself to the initial or impact effect of tax changes on immediate markets is called a *partial equilibrium analysis*. While it has the virtue of simplicity, it may provide misleading results for broadly based taxes. The next two sections present partial equilibrium and general equilibrium tax incidence analyses respectively.

At the outset, it should be recognized that much of tax incidence theory limits itself to analyzing the effects of taxes on relative prices of goods and factors (incidence on the *use* side and on the *source* side of income respectively). What we are ultimately interested in is the impact on relative welfare or utility levels of different persons or income groups. Such effects on the personal distribution of income depend upon how the ownership of factors of production (such as capital, labor skills, etc.) are distributed among individuals, and how tastes are distributed among individuals. In order to determine the personal incidence of taxes, it is necessary to know first how various relative prices are affected, and almost all tax incidence theory has concentrated on this question. Going from the change in relative prices of goods and factors to the change in relative utility of different persons requires knowledge of how important are the various goods and factors in each household's budget. For example, a tax change which raises the price of capital and reduces the price of labor will help persons who own relatively large amounts of capital as compared with labor. Or, a relative rise in the price of a good with a high income elasticity of demand (a luxury good), compared with that of a good with low income elasticity of demand (a necessity good), hurts high-income persons relative to low-income persons. Those attempts which have been made to extend tax incidence analysis to personal welfare distribution have tended to use income as the measuring rod of utility. Taxes are then classified as more progressive if their incidence falls on higher-income groups.

In conducting the incidence exercises below, it is important to bear in mind how the overall government budget is changing, especially in the general equilibrium analysis. The tax revenue raised when a tax is imposed must be used for something, and there are several possibilities. The tax revenue may represent an expansion in the government budget, and may be spent on public sector goods. If so, one should take these public expenditures (or transfer payments) directly into account in the incidence study. The study of the combined effects of tax increases and government spending of the tax revenues is called *balanced-budget incidence*. Alternatively, one can avoid taking expenditures into account by analyzing the incidence effects of replacing one tax with another that yields exactly the same revenue (including a lump-sum tax). Such studies are called *differential incidence* studies.[1] One of the deficiencies of a partial equilibrium analysis is that it ignores the question of how the tax revenue is used, and concentrates simply on the initial impact of raising the revenue.

PARTIAL EQUILIBRIUM ANALYSIS

12-2   Partial equilibrium tax incidence is deceptively simple, and one could argue that that is because all the interesting problems have been assumed away. We shall present partial equilibrium analyses of taxation on various competitive and noncompetitive markets, and then point out the deficiencies of such analyses.

Consider first the case of a proportional tax imposed on a perfectly competitive market. It may be a market for either goods or factors of production, with many buyers and sellers. If it is a market for a good, the tax would be a selective commodity tax falling only on this good as, for example, a tax on gasoline or tobacco. If it is a factor market, the tax is a general factor tax on all uses of that factor. An example of this would be a payroll tax on labor income alone. A general income tax would not fit this description, since it includes a tax on capital—a separate factor of production whose price is determined on a separate market.

The partial equilibrium incidence of such a tax is depicted in Fig. 12–1, where X is the output and p the price. The initial equilibrium output is X_1, with the price p_1. Suppose now an *ad valorem* tax on X at the rate t is imposed where t is calculated on the net price.[2] Since the demand curve D is drawn to show the quantities that would be demanded at various gross prices $p(1 + t)$(prices inclusive of tax), but the supply curve S is drawn to show the quantities supplied at various net prices $p,$ the two are not directly comparable. Therefore, we convert S to a curve showing the amount that would be supplied at various gross prices by raising it vertically by the amount of tax paid at each point (i.e. multiply it by $[1 + t]$). The new market equilibrium output is X_2, with the net price p_2 and gross price

Figure 12–1

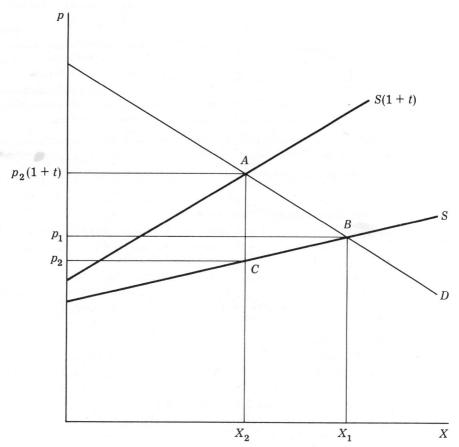

$p_2(1 + t)$. The sellers of the product have had to absorb a price fall from p_1 to p_2, and are therefore worse off. However, the net price has not fallen by the full amount of the tax, since the gross price to demanders has risen from p_1 to $p_2(1 + t)$. Thus, if the sellers bear the legal incidence of the tax, they have shifted part of the burden to the buyers. The same result would have been achieved had we shifted D downward by the amount of the tax (e.g. divided by $1 + t$) rather than shift S upward.

In this partial equilibrium case we can go further than simply cataloging the price changes. In Fig. 12–1, we can also measure the burden borne by each of the parties involved. The demanders lose an amount of consumers' surplus equal to the area $p_2(1 + t)ABp_1$, and the suppliers lose producers' surplus equal to p_1BCp_2, for a total loss of $p_2(1 + t)ABCp_2$. This exceeds the gain in government tax revenue $p_2(1 + t)ACp_2$ by the triangle ABC which is the deadweight loss of the tax. Section 12–8 will present a fuller analysis of the deadweight loss of taxation.

The distribution of the burden of taxation (as well as the magnitude of the deadweight loss relative to tax revenue generated) depends upon the slopes of the demand and supply curves. For example, if the supply curve were vertical so that supply is completely inelastic, the tax will not change the quantity supplied, the gross price will not change [$p_1 = p_2(1 + t)$], and the entire burden of the tax would be borne by the supplier. Moreover, no deadweight loss would be generated. The suppliers will also bear the full burden of the tax if demand is perfectly elastic, although in this case there is a substantial deadweight loss included in the burden. Conversely, with perfectly elastic supply, the demanders bear the burden of the tax, including the deadweight loss. Finally, if demand is perfectly inelastic, the demanders will bear the entire burden, and no deadweight loss will result. In general, we may say that demanders will bear relatively more of the burden the more elastic is supply, and the less elastic is demand. One can show that the ratio of the deadweight loss borne by consumers to that borne by firms is η_s/η_D, the ratio of the supply and demand elasticities (since the ratio of the deadweight losses is $\frac{1}{2}(\Delta p_D \Delta X) \div \frac{1}{2}(\Delta p_S \Delta X)$, where p_D and p_S are demand and supply prices).

As a complete theory of tax incidence, the above partial equilibrium analysis is insufficient; it ignores a number of changes in relative prices that are likely to take place in other markets, and which will influence relative utility levels. If the market being taxed is a market for a factor of production, the decrease in supply of that factor (as a result of the imposition of the tax) will cause a relative scarcity of that factor compared to others, and will tend to reduce the gross-of-tax relative price of other factors. The strength of this effect on other factor prices will depend upon how substitutable one factor is for the other in production processes, and upon the share of the taxed factor in the cost of producing output. While it is true that the demand curve drawn for the factor of production being taxed implicitly takes into consideration these influences in determining its shape,[3] the analysis fails to show explicitly how other factor prices are influenced; this latter is an important part of incidence analysis. In analyzing, say, a tax on labor income, we are interested not only in what happens to the price of labor, but also to the price of capital, since we would like to know how the tax bears on the owners of various factors of production. Similarly, but to a more limited extent, we would expect the tax on a factor of production to affect households on the use side of their income through changes in relative goods prices. Thus, a tax on labor income, by increasing the gross-of-tax price of labor relative to capital, will cause the prices of commodities produced with labor-intensive techniques of production to rise relative to other commodities. The same sorts of problems arise if we are analyzing a tax on a specific commodity output. A partial equilibrium analysis can only tell us what happens to the price of that commodity. The tax is also likely to cause other commodity prices to change, as well as relative factor prices. If the commodity being taxed represents a small share of total consumer expenditures, this will not be as important a drawback to the partial equilibrium approach as in the case of factor taxes.

Another problem with the above analysis is that it is extremely limited in the types of taxes it can properly handle, that is, those taxes which apply to a specific market. In particular, it can neither handle partial factor taxes, or general income or commodity taxes. Partial factor taxes, or taxes on a limited number of uses of a factor of production (for example, the corporate income tax, to the extent that it is a tax on the return to corporate sector capital), bears only on part of the market for that factor, even though they will influence the economy-wide factor price. Demand and supply curves will obviously not suffice, since only part of the demand and supply is being taxed. A general income tax can be viewed as a tax on all factors of production; thus it simultaneously hits several markets at once, so the analysis of a single market is insufficient. The same problems arise when commodity taxes are levied on several commodities at the same time, as is the case with general commodity taxes. Even if all commodities or factors are taxed at the same rate, their relative prices may change if they have different elasticities of demand or supply. A single aggregate demand and supply curve analysis will not pick up these relative price changes.

A final problem with partial equilibrium analysis is that it ignores the use to which the government revenue is put.[4] This is a particularly important problem when one wants to do a differential incidence analysis to compare two taxes. All these problems are explicitly taken into consideration in the general equilibrium analysis of taxes presented below. That is not to say that the partial equilibrium analysis is without value. It does present the primary or initial effects of the taxes and, in certain circumstances, these may be the most important.[5]

The above partial equilibrium analysis is applicable only to perfectly competitive markets. In practice, markets which are subject to a tax might be less than perfectly competitive. Let us consider the extreme case in which the industry is a monopoly and is subject to a specific commodity tax on its output. Figure 12–2 illustrates the case of an *ad valorem* tax at rate t imposed on commodity X. Before the tax, the monopolist selects an output X_1, where marginal revenue (MR_1) equals marginal cost (MC). The price at output X_1 is p_1, as determined by the average revenue curve (AR_1).

Now an *ad valorem* excise tax is imposed. Whatever output the firm sells, its net price is now reduced by the tax. The amount by which the net price diverges from the gross price depends upon the output level chosen, since the tax is based upon the price. The higher the price, the higher the tax. The average revenue curve to the firm becomes AR_2, where $AR_1 = AR_2(1 + t)$. As a result, the marginal revenue curve facing the firm is MR_2. The profit-maximizing output of the firm is now X_2, with a net price of p_2 and a gross price to consumers of $p_2(1 + t)$. As expected, output has fallen and the price to consumers has risen, reflecting the partial shifting of the tax to the consumers. The share of the burden imposed upon

Figure 12–2

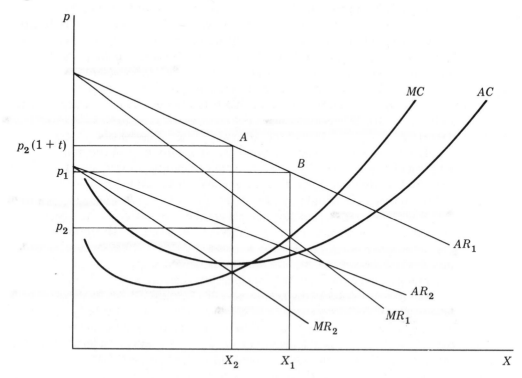

consumers $[p_2(1 + t)ABp_1]$ will be greater the less elastic is the demand curve and the flatter is the *MC* curve of the firm.[6] This result is similar to that obtained in the competitive case above. Once again, however, the partial equilibrium view may be insufficient if the tax applies to more commodities than one.

In practice, many industries are neither perfectly competitive nor monopolistic, but fall into the oligopolistic range between the two. The partial equilibrium analysis of the effects of taxing an oligopolistic industry is virtually undeveloped at this stage, mainly because of the absence of a complete theory as to what behavioral rules govern oligopoly industries. Some conjectures may, however, be made. If firms practice mark-up pricing or average cost pricing, any tax which is considered by firms to be a cost will be shifted. In an oligopoly industry, where firms hesitate to raise prices if they feel competitors will not follow, firms may shift taxes forward, since this is a cost increase that all competitors face. They may therefore feel that all firms will follow a price rise. Or, firms in an oligopoly industry may pursue a policy of defensive pricing. That is, they may set their prices only so high as to preclude the entry of other, possibly higher-cost, firms into the industry. If a tax increase affects the costs of all potential entrants as well as those already in the industry, it will likely be shifted. On the other hand, if the tax is a tax on profits, and if potential entrants have only marginal profits while those already in the industry have larger profits, the tax cannot be passed on without encouraging some entry.

Finally, firms may, instead of maximizing profits, maximize sales or total revenues (net of tax). In this case, the effect of a tax on the output of a firm would depend upon whether the firm treated the tax as an addition to cost or a subtraction from revenues. Taxes on factor inputs may well be treated as increased costs, in which case the firm would not change its output or price, and would absorb all the tax. By contrast, a *per unit* commodity tax would cause the firm to reduce its output and raise its price, thus shifting part of the tax forward, while price and output would be unchanged, implying no forward shifting, under an *ad valorem* tax. This difference arises because under an *ad valorem* tax, marginal revenue equals zero (the maximum revenue point) at the same output level X_0, as Fig. 12–3 shows. *AR* and *MR* are the average and marginal revenue curves before the tax, and *AR'* and *MR'* are those after. On the other hand, a per-unit tax would cause a parallel, leftward, shift of both *MR* and *AR*, leading to a lower output and higher price. Unfortunately, this analysis

Figure 12–3

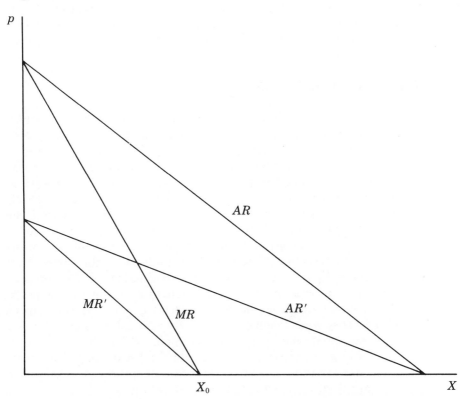

remains rather speculative, and is hardly enough upon which to base a theory of tax incidence. The analysis of tax incidence with imperfect markets awaits further research, in both partial and general equilibrium models.

As far as evidence of the shifting of particular taxes in partial equilibrium models is concerned, such evidence as exists is mainly for the corporation profits tax. In a celebrated contribution, Krzyzaniak and Musgrave (1964) studied the relationship between corporate tax changes on the one hand, and rates of return to capital, profit margins, and the share of capital on the other, using time series data for the United States. They found that the rate of return on capital and the profit margin tended to rise to cover increases in the corporate tax fully. This would indicate 100 percent shifting. On the other hand, the factor share accruing to capital did not rise by as much as would be required by 100 percent shifting, indicating that other nontax factors may have been at work. The full shifting results of this study have been criticized by other authors on the econometric grounds that the relationship between rates of return and tax rates cannot be accounted for solely by the shifting of taxes. Tax rate increases may be accompanied by other phenomena which contribute to higher rates of return on capital (e.g. excess aggregate demand in the economy, government spending, etc.). See Cragg, Harberger, and Mieszkowski (1967, 1970) and Krzyzaniak and Musgrave (1970). Other more recent econometric studies of corporate tax shifting include Gordon (1967), Oakland (1972a), and Dusansky (1972). As yet, no empirical consensus has been arrived at regarding whether the corporate tax is fully shifted, not shifted, or partially shifted.

GENERAL EQUILIBRIUM ANALYSIS

12–3   The general equilibrium analysis of a tax change explicitly takes into consideration the changes in price and quantity that occur on all markets (for both goods and factors) as a result of the change. In the real world, this would be a mammoth task, due to the large number of markets that actually exist. For the purposes of analysis, we must therefore abstract from the real world by assuming that the economy consists of a manageable number of markets for goods and factors. It turns out that considerable insight can be obtained into the general equilibrium incidence of tax changes if we restrict ourselves to an economy consisting of two goods and two factors of production.[7] The model we shall use is the same as that used in Chapter 2 in our discussion of the optimality of the competitive price system.[8] This section will be devoted to a geometrical exposition of the theory of tax incidence in the two-sector general equilibrium model. (See also Krause and Johnson [1972]). Appendix I presents the conventional algebraic treatment of the same problem. Although the algebraic analysis provides some additional insight into the parameters determining the incidence of taxation, it may be skipped without loss of continuity by readers who are ill-at-ease with mathematical analysis.

It is useful to catalog the specific assumptions made in the two-sector model, and to add those used here for the purposes of tax incidence analysis. They are as follows:

1. The economy has available two factors of production: labor (L) and capital (K). The services of these factors may be purchased at prices w (wage rate) and r (rental rate), as determined on competitive markets. In the presence of taxes these factor prices may vary from use to use as explained below.
2. The factors L and K are used in the production of two commodities, X and Y. Firms in each of these industries operate competitively, with production technologies exhibiting some substitutability between L and K, as illustrated by smooth isoquants such as those in Fig. 12–4. Competitive behavior in the factor markets means that firms will equate the marginal rate of technical substitution (the slope of the isoquants) to the wage-rental ratio (w/r) (the slope of the isocost lines).
3. The technology of production in each industry is assumed to exhibit *constant returns-to-scale,* or, mathematically, each industry's production function is said to be *linearly homogeneous.*[9] This means that a proportionate increase in both inputs (for instance, a doubling of L and K)

Figure 12–4

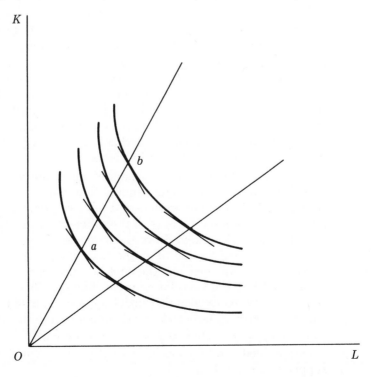

results in an increase in output of exactly the same proportion (output also doubles). As illustrated in Fig. 12–4, constant returns implies that the slopes of all isoquants are constant along any ray from the origin. Since each ray from the origin is associated with a particular capital–labor ratio (i.e. K/L = slope of a ray), the $MRTS$ between labor and capital, and therefore the wage-rental ratio, will be uniquely associated with a given capital–labor ratio regardless of the level of output produced. In particular, as the capital–labor ratio rises, the wage–rental ratio rises as well. The curvature of the isoquants determines the amount of the wage–rental ratio changes in response to a change in K/L, or vice versa, and is characterized quantitatively by the *elasticity of substitution* which we define below.

4. The two industries X and Y may have differently curved isoquants and may exhibit different capital–labor ratios at the same wage–rental ratio. That industry that has the higher K/L at any given wage–rental ratio is said to be the capital-intensive one. The other industry is then the labor-intensive one.[10]

5. Both labor and capital are fully employed and completely mobile between industries. We shall assume, unless otherwise stated, that the supplies of labor and capital are fixed to the economy. This implies that we may represent the production possibilities of the economy in an Edgeworth box diagram as in Fig. 2–4. From the contract curve of the Edgeworth box we may derive the production possibility curve of Fig. 2–5.

6. All exercises involve the substitution of one tax for another, yielding the same resource transfer to the public sector. If the tax being substituted for is a lump-sum tax, the exercise can be equivalently thought of as the raising of revenues by a tax and returning the proceeds to the consumer in a lump-sum. In all instances, it is assumed that the government has acquired a given quantity of labor and capital. We are concerned with how the remaining L and K are allocated by the price mechanism, and how that allocation changes when the type of tax used to finance the government's purchases is changed. In other words, the analysis is of differential tax incidence.

7. On the demand side, the simplest version of the model aggregates the entire economy into a single demand function in which the demand for each good depends upon income and relative product prices. The income term is often ignored because of the differential-incidence nature of the tax changes undertaken. Since the same resources are available to the private sector before and after the tax change, after-tax income is approximately unchanged, and the analysis may concentrate on the changes in demand induced by relative price changes alone, and ignore income changes.[11] In more general models, more than one income group is admitted, with different demand functions for the two goods, one of which may be a luxury and the other a necessity.

8. Prices of goods and factors of production are such that demand equals supply on all markets.

As mentioned above, the degree of curvature of isoquants can be described by the elasticity of substitution between labor and capital, which we define as the percentage change of the capital–labor ratio divided by the percentage change in the rental–wage ratio:[12]

$$\sigma = -\frac{\Delta(K/L)}{K/L} \div \frac{\Delta(r/w)}{r/w}. \tag{12-1}$$

The flatter is the isoquant (i.e. the less curvature it has), the higher is σ. The latter takes on a value of infinity if isoquants are straight lines, and zero if isoquants permit no substitution and so are right-angled. In general, σ may take on different values at various points on an isoquant but, for simplification, it is sometimes assumed to be constant throughout the isoquant map. If so, the production function is of the constant-elasticity-of-substitution type (CES).[13]

As will become clear, the reason that the elasticity of substitution is important for tax incidence analysis is that it allows one to characterize the response of relative factor prices to tax-induced changes in factor supplies, whether in a particular sector or in the economy as a whole. With a low σ, an increase in the capital–labor ratio will give rise to a large increase in the wage–rental ratio, while the opposite is true for high values of σ. If $\sigma < 1$, a 1 percent increase in the capital–labor ratio will be accompanied by a more-than-one-percent increase in (w/r), with the result that the ratio of wage income to capital income (wL/rK) rises. Thus, it is clear that σ also governs the behavior of relative factor incomes, a key topic of interest in incidence analysis, as the economy is disturbed by changes in tax policy.

We now put the above model to work in the study of the incidence of four types of taxes: specific commodity tax, general consumption or income tax,[14] general factor tax, and partial factor tax. We shall proceed by analyzing insofar as possible the general equilibrium incidence of these taxes using geometrical techniques.

(a) Specific Commodity Tax

Suppose we consider the simple case in which factor supplies are fixed. Then the substitution of a tax on good X for an equal-yield lump-sum tax may be analyzed using the production possibility curve PP of Fig. 12–5. The curve PP shows the combinations of X and Y available for use in the private sector after the public sector has met its given requirements. When lump-sum taxation is used, the economy reaches a point such as A where $MRT_{XY} = MRS_{XY}$. Assume for the moment that all individuals have identical tastes and incomes, so that the indifference curves drawn have the same properties as those of individual consumers. When lump-sum taxation, bearing equally on all individuals, is replaced by a tax on good X at rate t_X, the economy moves to point B, at which the relative price of X to

Figure 12–5

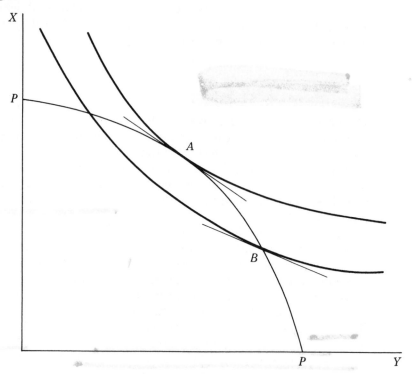

consumers has risen and that to producers has fallen such that

$$MRS_{XY} = \frac{p_X\,(1 + t_X)}{p_Y} = (1 + t_X)MRT_{XY}. \tag{12–2}$$

To determine the influence of the reduction in MRT_{XY} on relative factor prices we use the Edgeworth box diagram in Fig. 12–6. Recall from Chapter 2 that each point on the contract curve in Figure 12–6 corresponds to a point on the production possibility curve PP in Fig. 12–5. The same two points, A and B, on PP are shown on the contract curve joining O_X and O_Y. At the point A, the rental-wage ratio is given by the common slope of the isoquants of X and Y. It is denoted $(r/w)_A$. Notice that at A, the ratio of labor to capital employed in X, L_X/K_X is the slope of the line O_XA. Similarly, the ratio L_Y/K_Y is the slope of the line O_YA taken from the origin O_Y. As the diagram is drawn, $L_X/K_X > L_Y/K_Y$ at A and at all other points along the contract curve. Industry X is therefore labor-intensive and industry Y is capital-intensive. Had the contract curve been a diagonal line, the factor intensities in X and Y would have been equal ($L_X/K_X = L_Y/K_Y$). Had the contract curve been southeast of the diagonal, Y would have been labor-intensive and X capital-intensive.

Figure 12–6

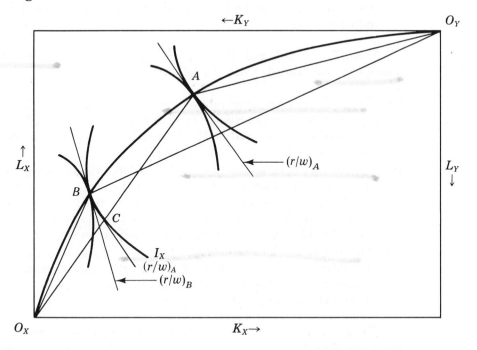

After the tax is imposed on X, the economy's production is reallocated from point A to point B. The important thing to notice about this change is that the labor-capital ratio has risen in *both* industries. As labor and capital are released from the X industry, which employs relatively more labor per unit of capital than the Y industry, the labor-capital ratio must be increased in both industries in order to employ all factors. As the labor-capital ratio rises in both industries, so does $MRTS_{KL}$ or r/w. The relative rise in the price of capital compared with labor induces firms to economize on capital by raising their ratio of labor to capital. Therefore, in the move from A to B, the ratio r/w must rise until all labor and capital are fully employed. Thus, $(r/w)_B > (r/w)_A$. To prove this geometrically, note that the slope of the isoquant I_X at point C along the ray $O_X A$ must be equal to $-(r/w)_A$, because of constant returns to scale in industry X. Since the new tangency of isoquants at point B must lie northwest of C because the labor-capital ratio rises in industry X (and in Y as well, of course), this tangency must occur at a point where I_X is more steeply sloped than at C, confirming the above conclusion that $(r/w)_B > (r/w)_A$.

This demonstrates that a tax imposed on the X industry will cause r/w to rise if the X industry is relatively labor-intensive. A similar analysis would show that r/w would fall if the X industry were relatively capital-intensive. More generally, this result may be stated as follows:

A tax imposed on the output of an industry will cause a reduction in the relative price of the factor used relatively intensively in the taxed industry.

From Figs. 12–5 and 12–6 we can infer that the magnitude of the change in r/w depends upon the following:

(i) The difference in factor proportions. The greater the difference in L/K, the more it must change in each industry in moving from A to B, and so the greater will be the change in r/w. (If L/K is identical in both industries, r/w will not change.)

(ii) The elasticity of demand for X. The greater the elasticity of demand for X (or the elasticity of substitution in demand of X for Y), the greater will be the reallocation of demand from X to Y, and so the greater will be the change in r/w. (If the elasticity of demand or substitution in demand is zero, there will be no change in r/w.)

(iii) The elasticity of substitution in X and Y. The smaller the elasticities of substitution of L for K in X and Y, the more curvature will the isoquants have, and the greater will be the change in r/w resulting from a change in factor ratios.

The above analysis shows how the relative goods and factor prices might be expected to change as a result of the tax on X in an economy consisting of identical individuals. We now assume there are many different individuals in the economy, each of whom has different preferences for X and Y, and each of whom owns differing amounts of labor and capital. The tax will still divert demand from X to Y as compared with, say, a nondistorting tax levied on all income. The effect of that shift in demand on relative factor prices will be as analyzed above. As compared with a proportional income tax, the excise tax will hurt those individuals who get proportionately large amounts of income from the factor used intensively in the taxed industry (since its relative reward will fall). Conversely, individuals obtaining a large share of their income from the factor used intensively in the untaxed industry will be better off after the tax change.

On the use side of the budget, individuals will consume differing proportions of the two goods. The tax will be borne relatively more heavily by those individuals for which X takes up a larger share of their budget. For example, if X is a luxury good with an income elasticity of demand above unity, the tax would be borne more by high-income persons than would an equal-yield income tax.

Finally, we might briefly inquire into the implications of having a variable, rather than a fixed, factor supply. Suppose, for example, that the labor supply varies with the wage rate. If X is a labor-intensive industry, a tax on X tends to cause the wage rate to fall. The fall in the wage rate is tempered by the reduction in the supply of labor forthcoming. The economy-wide K/L ratio falls, and the impact of the tax on r/w is reduced. By the same token, if X is capital-intensive, the tax would tend to reduce r/w, thus causing the labor supply to rise. The additional supply of labor raises L/K in the economy, thus reducing the fall in r/w. In either case the beneficial or detrimental impact of the tax change on the return to labor is reduced because of the variability of the labor supply.

(b) General Consumption Tax

Consider now a tax imposed on X and Y at the same rate. In an economy with fixed labor and capital supplies, such a tax is a lump-sum tax, since it is equivalent to a tax on fixed-factor incomes. It is borne in proportion to the income (or consumption) of each member of the economy. In a single-consumer economy or one with several identical consumers, the substitution of a general consumption tax for a general income tax would not affect relative prices, resource allocation, or utility levels.

In an economy with individuals of differing tastes or incomes, that is no longer the case. For example, imagine substituting a general income tax (which is nondistorting here) for a lump-sum tax levied in equal amounts on all persons, or a *head tax*. Both taxes are efficient, but the income tax will increase the incomes of low-income persons and reduce the incomes of high-income persons compared with a head tax of equal yield. If the preferences of high- and low-income persons differ, this pure income redistribution will cause a reallocation of resources. If X has a higher income elasticity than does Y, the tax change will reduce the demand for X and increase that for Y. The relative factor price of the factor used intensively in the production of X will fall exactly as in (a) above.

If factor supplies are variable, a general tax on income or consumption will no longer be neutral. The tax would reduce the return from supplying factors of production, and therefore the supplies would change. For example, if the labor supply varies positively with the wage rate, but capital is fixed, a general income tax would reduce the supply of labor, reduce the economy's L/K ratio, and thereby reduce r/w. Labor-owners would have succeeded in shifting part of their tax burden to capital owners. If capital were variable, the opposite would hold.

(c) General Factor Tax

Consider now the imposition of a general factor tax on, say, the incomes of labor (a payroll tax). In a one-consumer economy with fixed factor supplies, the analysis is once again straightforward. Since it is a lump-sum tax, the tax on the fixed factor labor will be completely absorbed out of labor income. There would be no change in resource allocation or relative prices.

In an economy with many nonidentical consumers, the substitution of a tax on labor income for another lump-sum tax of equal yield would represent a pure redistribution of income against the owners of labor. The commodity most strongly preferred by earners of labor income would suffer a decline in demand. Resources would be reallocated away from it, and the factor used relatively intensively in its production would receive a lower relative reward.

A general factor tax is no longer a lump-sum tax when the factor upon which it is imposed is variable in supply. For example, a payroll tax on labor income will reduce the net wage received from supplying labor and cause the supply of labor to fall. This causes the economy-wide K/L ratio to fall, and induces a rise in w/r paid by firms. In effect, labor owners have been able partially to avoid the tax by reducing their supply of labor. In so doing, they have shifted part of the tax to capital. On the use side of the household budget, the tax on labor income will cause the relative price of the good that is produced in the labor-intensive industry to rise. This is so because labor costs are a relatively larger proportion of the total costs of production in the labor-intensive industry than in the capital-intensive one. Thus, not only will labor owners shift part of the tax to capital owners by reducing L/K, but also they will shift part of the burden of the tax to those for whom the labor-intensive commodity is a more important item in the budget.

The ability of labor-owners to shift the tax will depend upon the following:

(i)   The elasticity of supply of labor. The more elastic the supply, the greater will be the shifting.
(ii) The elasticity of substitution in X and Y. The lower the elasticity of substitution, the greater will be the change in w/r for a given change in L/K.
(iii) The lower the elasticity of demand for the labor-intensive good, the more will the tax be borne by the demanders of it.

(d) Partial Factor Tax

A tax on the use of a factor in one industry is the most complex of the taxes to analyze, since it causes production inefficiency in the economy so that it is operating below the production possibility curve. Consider, for example, a tax on capital in the X industry at the rate of t_{KX}. This might be thought of as the corporation income tax, where X is the corporate sector and Y is the unincorporated sector of the economy. To facilitate geometric analysis, we shall assume that factor supplies are fixed. This enables us to use the Edgeworth box diagram of Fig. 12–7 to illustrate the possible allocations of the given stocks of labor and capital between the two industries.

Under lump-sum taxation, the economy will operate with full efficiency. A point such as A will be reached along the contract curve representing the outputs of X and Y, at which $MRT_{XY} = MRS_{XY}$. At A, the rental–wage ratio $(r/w)_A$ equals $MRTS_{KL}$ in both industries. Imagine now the substitution of a tax on capital in X for the lump-sum tax. We would predict that two things would happen. First, since the input of one of the factors

Figure 12–7

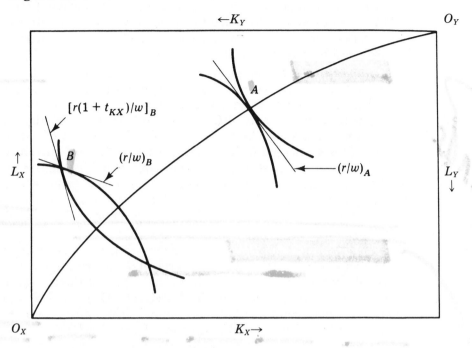

in X is being taxed, the price of X would rise relative to Y. This would cause demand to shift from X to Y, and resources would be reallocated from industry X to industry Y.

Second, the tax on K_X violates the production efficiency conditions discussed in Chapter 2 since

$$MRTS^Y_{KL} = \frac{r}{w}; \quad MRTS^X_{KL} = \frac{r(1 + t_{KX})}{w}. \tag{12–3}$$

This is so since the net-of-tax return to capital must be the same in both industries; otherwise, owners of capital would have an incentive to reallocate capital to the industry yielding the higher return. Thus, r, the return to capital in Y, must also be the net-of-tax return in X so $r(1 + t_{KX})$ is the gross-of-tax return, or the value of the marginal product. Since the $MRTS_{KL}$ differs in X and Y, the allocation of L and K will be off the contract curve. Suppose B is the new equilibrium production point attained under the partial factor tax. At B, X is producing less, and Y is producing more than at A, and production is inefficient.

In analyzing the incidence of the partial capital tax it is useful to distinguish conceptually between the reallocation of output from X to Y

due to the change in relative prices and the movement off the contract curve due to the induced inefficiency. Using the terminology of Mieszkowski (1967), the former will be called the *output effect*, and the latter the *factor substitution effect*. Let us consider how each of these effects bears upon the relative prices of labor and capital (r/w).

Output Effect   The output effect is concerned with the effect on r/w of a reallocation of resources from X to Y, but ignores the production inefficiency. It is identical to the effects of reallocating resources under a specific commodity tax discussed in (a) above. If X is labor-intensive (as in Fig. 12–7), the reallocation of L and K from X to Y tends to cause r/w to rise, since the ratio of L to K released in X exceeds the ratio of L to K currently used in Y. Labor becomes less scarce relative to capital, and its relative price falls. If the taxed industry X were capital-intensive, the opposite would hold; the output effect would produce a tendency for r/w to fall. Therefore, the output effect of imposing a tax on K_X can work for or against capital owners, according to whether X is labor or capital intensive.[15]

Factor Substitution Effect   The factor substitution effect is concerned with the movement off the contract curve to B, as a result of the distortion imposed upon the market for capital. The impact of the tax *initially* is to reduce the return to capital in the X industry. Owners of capital will be induced to move capital out of X and into Y. This causes the L/K ratio to rise in X and fall in Y, so $MRTS_{KL}^Y$ will fall and $MRTS_{KL}^X$ will rise. The movement of capital will continue until the economy-wide r/w falls by enough so that $MRTS_{KL}^X = r(1 + t_{KX})/w$ and $MRTS_{KL}^Y = r/w$. Unlike the output effect, the factor substitution effect has an unambiguous influence on r/w. It causes r/w to fall, thereby tending to harm capital owners relative to labor owners.

The overall impact of the tax on r/w depends upon the combined strengths of the output and factor substitution effects. There are several possibilities. If the X industry is capital-intensive, both effects will cause r/w to fall.[16] Compared with, say, a lump-sum tax on all factor incomes, capital owners would be worse off and labor owners better off. If the output effect were strong enough, r/w could fall by more than rt_{KX} and capital owners would be worse off than under a general factor tax on capital income (which is borne fully by capital).

If the X industry is labor-intensive, the output and factor substitution effects work in opposite directions. One cannot predict the effect of the tax on r/w a priori. It depends upon the relative strengths of the two effects. If they just offset one another, r/w will not change, and the incidence of t_{KX} will be the same as that of a general income tax on all capital and labor income. In effect, capital will have succeeded in shifting a share of the tax burden to labor. It is even possible that r/w will rise when the tax is imposed. This could occur if the X industry were strongly labor-intensive and the output effect were large. Capital owners would be better off under a tax on capital in X than under a general tax on all income.

The magnitude of the change in r/w will depend upon the characteristics of demand and production in the economy. The following summarizes the influence of various parameters on the change in r/w:

(i) The larger the elasticity of demand for X, the greater will be the magnitude of the output effect on r/w. This is so because the greater will be the reallocation of resources from X to Y.

(ii) The larger the difference in K/L in X and Y, the larger will be the output effect.

(iii) The larger capital's share in the cost of producing X, the greater will be the output effect, since the change in p_X/p_Y will be greater.

(iv) The smaller the elasticities of substitution in X and Y, the larger will be the output effects. This is so since r/w will change more for a given change in L/K in each industry.

(v) The larger the elasticity of substitution in X, the larger will be the factor substitution effect. If L and K are very substitutable in X, $MRTS_{KL}^X$ will not change much when L_X/K_X changes, so that the brunt of the tax will be felt in a reduction in r/w, rather than a rise in $r(1 + t_{KX})/w$.

These tendencies are all made explicit in the algebraic treatment of tax incidence in Appendix I.

The above discussion dealing with incidence on the source side is independent of whether or not there are many consumers in the economy. With many consumers, incidence on the use side will be important as well. The tax will cause p_X/p_Y to rise, thereby bearing more heavily on those for whom good X is an important budget item.

With variable factor supplies the analysis would be somewhat more complicated, since the change in factor rewards would induce a change in factor supplies. For example, suppose labor is variable in supply. A tax on capital in X which caused r/w to fall would cause the labor supply to rise. This would temper the fall in r/w, and would reduce the extent to which capital-owners bore the tax. In addition, if capital were variable in supply, a fall in r/w would reduce the supply of capital and lessen the fall in r/w. Thus, variability of factor supply here, as earlier, tends to reduce the magnitude of changes in r/w due to the tax change.

As can be seen, even in this simplified static model of the economy, the incidence of a partial factor tax cannot be predicted deductively. It depends upon such key parameters as the elasticities of substitution in both production and consumption, and the relative factor intensities in the two sectors. Unfortunately, we do not have reliable-enough empirical estimates of the parameters involved to be able to state with any certainty the incidence of, say, the corporate tax. Nonetheless, one can simulate the effects of tax changes in static two-sector models by using best-guess estimates of the elasticity parameters, and by using observed capital-labor ratios aggregated over two broad industrial groupings of the economy that roughly correspond to corporate and unincorporated sectors. (The correspondence can only be rough, since in many industries, such as agriculture and retail trade, some firms are incorporated and some are not.) The classic study is that of Harberger (1962). He found, using 1953–59 data, that when elasticities of substitution in production and demand did not differ much from unity, the corporate tax was borne on the source side almost entirely by capital owners (in both sectors). The actual equation he used to estimate this is Eq. (12–49) in Appendix I to this chapter, and is based on a linear approximation to the changes that would occur in response to the substitution of a corporate tax for a lump-sum tax. These results were confirmed by Shoven and Whalley (1972), who calculated the change in r/w exactly by solving the general equilibrium system explicitly. Similar results were obtained for Canada by Boadway and Treddenick (1978). Their sensitivity analysis indicated that changes in the elasticities had relatively little impact on the results. Instead, the results tended to be largely determined by relative factor intensities and relative outputs of the two sectors, both of which could be observed.

These "empirical" results stand in sharp contrast with the results of the statistical time series analysis of Krzyzaniak and Musgrave (1964), reported earlier. It will be recalled that these authors found that gross returns to capital rose with increases in the corporate tax rate over time, thus indicating full shifting of the tax. The differences may lie partly in the fact that the Krzyzaniak-Musgrave analysis incorporates a dynamic element into the study, while the Harberger analysis explicitly does not. We shall return later to the theoretical implications of allowing the capital stock to respond to changes in its rate of return over time. What is obvious is that no empirical consensus exists, at this point in time, on the incidence of the corporate tax.

EXTENSIONS AND LIMITATIONS
OF THE SIMPLE MODEL

12–4   Many authors have utilized the static, neoclassical general equilibrium model to analyze situations other than those we have pointed out above. Since we do not have space to deal with each completely, we can only summarize the various extensions here and their relation to the simple model.

(i) *Factor Immobility*   The model assumes that both labor and capital are mobile between industries, and in equilibrium always locate so that the net return to a factor is the same everywhere. While such an assumption may be reasonable for, say, unskilled labor, it may not be for land, or industry-specific factors of production. It is a straightforward matter to amend the above model to allow for complete immobility of one of the factors. If capital is immobile, its return may diverge in its various uses. A partial factor tax on capital then becomes a tax on a fixed factor, and is borne entirely by that factor. A tax on the output of the industry will, however, cause a reallocation of resources, with the mobile factor moving and reducing its return elsewhere. The return to the fixed factor in the untaxed industry will increase. One would also like to introduce imperfect factor mobility into the analysis, by making factor movements depend upon relative differentials, or introducing transport costs.

(ii) *Property Tax*   Property taxation is the main source of own-revenues for local governments in many countries, including the United States and Canada. Because it is a local tax, property tax rates and the details of the administration of the tax vary considerably. Essentially, the tax is an annual levy on the *assessed value* of real property, *real* property referring to land and the structures built on land (as distinct from *personal* property, which includes property such as automobiles, furniture, etc., for households; and vehicles, inventories, machinery, etc., for firms). Assessed values are determined by tax assessors according to practices that vary from locality to locality, but generally, they are meant to reflect market values. The correspondence between market and assessed value is far from exact, however, for several reasons. First, whereas properties are often reassessed infrequently, actual property values may fluctuate substantially, perhaps because of changes in the character of individual properties (due to improvements or neighborhood changes, for example), or because of general market fluctuations, especially during periods of inflation. Deviations between true and assessed values also arise because some classes of property are deliberately assessed differentially. For example, single family dwellings or residential property in general are oftentimes assessed at only a proportion (such as fifty percent) of market value, while commercial or industrial property is assessed at higher rates that are determined by local policy.

For the sake of simplicity, however, let us initially abstract from the problem of assessment other than at market value. As a further simplification, let us recognize that, although it is a tax on property value, that is, on the *price* of property considered as an asset, the fundamental effects of the property tax are equivalent to those of a tax on the *returns* to the asset. For example, if a property earning a before-tax return of 10 percent (whether in terms of actual rental income, or in terms of imputed returns to owner-occupied property) is subjected to a 3 percent tax on market value, the net return on the property is lowered to 7 percent. This has the same effects as a tax at a 30 percent rate on the income derived from the property.[17]

We may now present the traditional partial equilibrium analysis of property tax incidence. One begins by recognizing that property consists of both land and structures, and that the property tax lowers the net return on each. To the extent that the tax lowers the net return on land, it will be borne entirely by landowners, because land is limited in supply. To the extent that the tax lowers the net return on structures, it may be shifted, at least in the long run. The reason is that capital is held to be perfectly elastically supplied to any *one* locality, so that a local tax cannot depress its rate of return below what can be earned elsewhere. The tax on residential structures would therefore be shifted forward to consumers of property services. In the case of rental property, this means the tax falls on renters rather than on landlords. In the case of commercial property, the tax on structures tends to lower the cost of labor relative to capital as a factor of production, encouraging the substitution of labor for capital, which would lower labor productivity and thus wages. If, however, labor is perfectly elastically supplied to any *one* locality, it is impossible to depress wages and thus shift the burden of the tax to labor. It has been argued, therefore, that the property tax simply increases the cost of production in the locality, and is shifted forward to consumers in the form of higher prices.

This analysis has been used to conclude that a tax on land is an ideal tax, since it imposes no deadweight loss and since it is borne by landowners who, on average, have relatively high incomes. It has also been argued that the part of the property tax that falls on structures—and this would be the bulk of the tax, since structures are a larger component of property value than is land—is a regressive tax. This is because it falls on the consumption of housing services or on consumption goods in general; housing consumption in particular and consumption in general both decline as a proportion of income as income rises. The overall regressivity of the tax is exacerbated, some contend, because of assessment practices that tend to impose higher burdens on rental relative to owner-occupied housing, and on lower-income housing generally.

This view of the property tax as a regressive tax has been challenged in recent years, however (see Mieszkowski [1972], Musgrave [1974], Aaron [1974, 1975], and McLure [1977]). The partial equilibrium analysis given above focuses on the elasticity of supply of capital to any *one* locality. But consider the general equilibrium effects of thousands of property taxes in thousands of localities. Though rates and administrative practices differ, their combined effect in some average sense is to tax capital, at least capital in the form of structures, throughout the economy as a whole. If the supply of capital to the economy as a whole is inelastic, then the overall effect of a *system* of property taxation by all local governments is to lower the net return to capital. Since capital ownership is distributed progressively relative to income, the overall incidence of the tax is also progressive.

There are some qualifications that one should make to this argument, however. First, the underlying premise that capital is inelastically supplied may be inappropriate, as suggested in the discussion of Section 11–3. If the supply of capital in the economy as a whole is depressed by the property tax, the productivity of labor will fall, the productivity of capital will rise (as it becomes increasingly scarce), and the burden of the tax will be shifted to some extent to labor. The magnitude of the change in factor prices will depend on factor supply elasticities, and on the elasticity of substitution in production. Second, the tax is not a uniform tax on all capital at the nationwide average rate. As noted above, it is levied at higher rates in some localities than in others, and some types of capital are taxed more heavily than others. This will tend to drive capital out of some jurisdictions or uses, and into others, with corresponding effects on factor and output prices. For instance, if capital leaves a high-tax jurisdiction, it will tend to depress land prices there and, if labor is not mobile, wages as well. In addition, the associated inflow of capital to a low-tax jurisdiction will tend to have effects working in the opposite direction: Other factor prices will rise, and goods prices will fall. These effects, arising out of the variations in property tax rates across jurisdictions or uses of capital, need not, however, overturn the judgment that the system of property taxation, taken as a whole, is progressive.

The above analysis identifies certain empirical issues that must be resolved to determine the incidence of property taxes. The elasticity of supply of capital must be determined, and if it is not zero, the elasticity of labor supply and the elasticity of substitution in production must all be known in order to determine the overall incidence of property taxes. In addition, there is much more detailed information that one would need in order to quantify the effect of all of the deviations in effective property tax rates from the average, both by locality and sector. Needless to say, this detailed information will not be easy to obtain. At the economy-wide level, the evidence on the elasticity of supply of capital is a matter of some controversy. However, it would be hard to escape the conclusion that the tax does, at least to some degree, depress the net rate of return to capital. Thus, the new view and relevant empirical evidence do suggest that the tax falls partly, if not wholly, on capital, undermining the traditional view that the property tax is one of the more regressive components of the overall tax system.

Finally, let us note that, while the new view of property tax incidence emphasizes the effect of the tax on the net return to capital, the traditional view of the incidence of the part of the tax that lowers the net return on land is also open to question. First, note that a tax on land depresses land values. If a parcel of land is expected to return R per year in rent forever, and if the rate of interest used to discount future returns is i, then in the absence of taxes, the parcel will have a market value of R/i. If the land is now subjected to a tax of T per year, the net return falls to $(R\text{-}T)$ and the value of the property falls to $(R\text{-}T)/i$. The loss in value is (T/i), the present discounted value of tax payments. When the market value of an asset, such as land, falls in anticipation of a stream of future taxes, the taxes are said to be *capitalized* in the asset's price.

Land tax capitalization can be important in the incidence of a land tax for the following reason: If households are life-cycle savers, a tax on land lowers household wealth *ceteris paribus*, and therefore lowers household consumption in the later stages of the life cycle. To preserve future consumption, households may attempt to save more, thereby accumulating more capital. This in turn will drive down the return on capital, and increase the gross returns to land and labor: In the above notation, R would rise. The *net* return on land therefore does not fall by as much as it would otherwise, and the land tax is thus partially shifted to capital, despite the inelastic supply of land. While this conclusion is sensitive to one's assumption about the nature of savings behavior, it at least shows quite clearly the importance of analyzing the incidence of a land tax in an explicitly inter-temporal setting. For further discussion of this issue, see Section 12–6 below.

(iii) *Trade Unions* An alternative way of defining the two (or more) sectors of the economy would be to distinguish between unionized and non-unionized sectors (Johnson and Mieszkowski [1970]; Diewert [1974]). One might then view unions as a device distorting relative prices, analogous to a partial factor distortion. The benefits of unionization may not accrue entirely to unionized labor, but might be shifted to other factors via the general equilibrium system. Thus, a rise in w_X will cause p_X to rise and will shift demand to Y. Depending on the relative capital intensities, labor may gain or lose over and above the initial or impact benefits of unionization.

(iv) *Household Sector*   Yet another way to define the two sectors is to distinguish between a market and a nonmarket sector, as in Boskin (1975). In the nonmarket sector, labor is largely untaxed household labor, and capital is the imputed return on consumer durables and owner-occupied housing. Boskin assumes that, because these items do not enter as taxable income, and because the return to capital and labor are taxed in market activities, there is preferential treatment of household capital and labor. This differential tax treatment serves to distort the economy in favor of the household or nonmarket sector. Both capital and labor are reallocated to household uses from the market.

(v) *Many Sectors, Factors, Households; Discrete vs. Infinitesimal Tax Changes* The standard tax incidence model assumes only two factors of production and two outputs, whereas some tax incidence questions may require that one recognize the existence of many factors and goods. This would be true, for instance, if one wished to take into account the special tax treatment of, say, the extractive or real estate industries, as distinguished from other corporate and non-corporate businesses. In fact, it might be desirable to separate the economy into many sectors, with many factors of production. A basic problem with doing so is that the structure of the economic model to be used for tax analysis becomes so complicated as to be very unwieldy, or even useless. The same might be said of allowing for the existence of many different types of households in the economy. Such an extension would be most interesting if one wished to find out the effects of tax policy changes on, say, the size distribution of income. Indeed, it is impossible to analyze such important issues as the implications of tax rate progressivity in a model that does not distinguish different income classes. Again, the problem with making the desired extension is that the model becomes hopelessly complex.

Recent years, however, have seen promising new developments that suggest that some of the most limiting features of the standard two-sector model can successfully be overcome. Following work by Scarf (1969), Shoven and Whalley (1972), and many others, methods have been developed for analyzing the effects of taxes in more complex models by using computers to determine the economy's general equilibrium response to policy changes. One can, for instance, separate an economy into ten or twenty industries, with technologies described by production functions of certain types, while allowing for several types of consumers with particular endowments of factors and particular preferences. One can compute the equilibrium prices and quantities for all goods and factors under any given tax policy, and thus compare equilibria with different policies. This computational approach has another advantage over the standard two-sector analysis. As one can see by studying Appendix I, the usual two-sector approach permits one to study only the effects of small, or, strictly speaking, infinitesimal, changes in tax policy. Of course, marginal analysis pervades economics, and is not necessarily more troublesome here than elsewhere. On the other hand, if one wishes to analyze the effects of big discrete changes in policy, such as an abolition of a corporate income tax with a tax rate of about 50 percent, it is clearly less than fully satisfactory to proceed within a framework that requires extrapolation from the analysis of changes on the order of 1 percent. The computational approach is, at least in principle, completely free of this limitation.

Unfortunately (though not surprisingly), the implementation of dis-aggregated computational techniques requires a great deal of empirical information. One needs to be able to describe quantitatively the structure of technology, and preferences for every industry and consumer in the economy. In the absence of detailed information of this type, one is compelled to fall back on more or less plausible assumptions about various parameters, and the results of the analysis of tax policy thus depend on these assumptions. Perhaps detailed econometric studies will gradually improve this situation.

(vi) *The Methodology of Comparative Statics* The basic spirit of the analysis of tax policy, using either the standard two-sector model or the multi-sector computational approach, is that one is comparing two static economies, each with a different tax policy, but one with the same supplies of factors of production, which are assumed to be perfectly mobile in the hypothetical movement from one equilibrium to the next, and with unchanged technologies.

There are two potential ways one might interpret the comparative static exercise. First, one may want to interpret it as an analysis of what would happen in the economy if tax rates actually did change by the prescribed amounts, and the economy were given enough time to adjust to the new equilibrium. The difficulty with this interpretation is that the time it would take for economies to adjust from one equilibrium to another would be very long indeed, given that capital, once bolted down, is not mobile. At best, it can be simultaneously accumulated in one industry and run down (de-preciated) elsewhere. However, during the process of transition from one equilibrium to another, many things would change, including technology, tastes, and the supplies of factors of production. As an analysis of the process of change from one equilibrium to another, the neoclassical comparative static approach might not be too useful, except for indicating general tendencies.

The other interpretation of the comparative static approach might be that one is not looking at the beginning and endpoints of a transition from one equilibrium to another, but one is comparing two separate, competitive economies. One is the economy as it now exists (assuming it to be perfectly competitive); the other is the economy as it would hypothetically have looked, had some tax not been in existence while the same factors of production had been accumulated and used with the same technique of production. While this latter interpretation may accord closely with what the comparative static analysis purports to do, it does not provide us with an analysis of the process of tax incidence over time. In fact it does not analyze a process at all, but compares two coterminous equilibria; the existing one and a hypothetical one.

There are several ways that one might attempt to deal more explicitly with the issues glossed over by the comparative statics approach. One way, discussed in Section 12–6, is to attempt an explicitly intertemporal analysis of tax incidence. An alternative, discussed for example by McLure (1974, 1975a), is to assume the immobility of some factors of production, this immobility characterizing the situation in the short run. Still a third alternative, presented by Asimakopolos and Burbidge (1974), focuses on the short-run process of tax incidence in a Keynesian framework. Since the results differ substantially from those obtained under neoclassical assumptions, an outline of a simple version of their model is presented next.

AN ALTERNATIVE VIEW OF TAX INCIDENCE: THE KEYNESIAN SHORT-RUN MODEL

12–5   In the Asimakopolos-Burbidge model, as in standard Keynesian analysis, the short run is defined by the fact that the stock of capital or plant is given both in the aggregate and in individual plants. For simplicity, the stock of labor is also fixed, but may be varied between plants. In the model we analyze below, we assume that full employment of both plant and labor is maintained. In addition, technology is assumed to be of the fixed proportions sort, with each plant having a reversed L-shaped supply curve. These two assumptions assure that each plant operates on the vertical part of its supply curve, and that labor does not change plants when the economy changes. With an L-shaped supply curve and a given distribution of labor among firms, output for the economy as a whole is given by an equation of the form:

$$O = aL \tag{12–4}$$

where O is gross output, L is the labor supply, and a is the economy-wide output-to-labor ratio. O is an aggregate index of output of different types.

With full employment maintained, O is given. Output may be used for either consumption (C), gross investment (I), or government expenditures (G), so:

$$O = C + I + G. \tag{12-5}$$

The key assumption of the Keynesian (or Kaleckian; see Kalecki [1937]), short-run analysis is that investment is fixed. With O and G fixed, that implies, from Eq. (12-5), that aggregate consumption is also fixed. The analysis then turns on how aggregate consumption is divided among the different "classes" in society, of which we consider two: The rentiers and the workers. The workers' money income is derived from a fixed money wage. In the simple case in which workers are assumed to consume all their income, their real income depends upon the price of the output of the economy.

Pricing is assumed to be of the markup sort. Prices are marked up a certain percentage over average variable costs, λ, such that:

$$p = (1 + \lambda)\frac{w}{a}. \tag{12-6}$$

Both w and a are fixed, but λ adjusts so as to ensure the basic market-clearing equality of the system, savings equals investment $(S = pI)$. The rentiers' income is derived from the markup over wages in each firm. When a consumption tax is imposed, the consumer prices are given by:

$$p' = (1 + t_c)p. \tag{12-7}$$

Money GNP can be written either as the sum of the values of outputs, or as the sum of the payments to factors of production. Therefore, we may derive:

$$p'C + pI + pG = wL + \pi + t_c pC + pD \tag{12-8}$$

where π represents profits (gross-of-tax, but net-of-depreciation) and D denotes real depreciation expenditures (which are fixed). By substituting Eqs. (12-4) through (12-7) into Eq. (12-8), we obtain an equation relating the required markup λ to the level of real profits π/p:

$$\left[\frac{\lambda}{1 + \lambda}\right] aL = \frac{\pi}{p} + D. \tag{12-9}$$

The higher the markup, the higher will be real profits, since a, L, and D are fixed.

The exercise to be performed is one of differential incidence. Suppose the level of government expenditure is fixed, and we are interested in the effect of substituting one tax for another so as to raise the same amount of real revenue. The government's budget constraint is:

$$pG = t_w wL + t_f \pi + t_r(1 - t_f) \beta\pi + t_c pC \qquad (12\text{--}10)$$

where t_w is the tax on labor income, t_f is the tax on profits, t_r is the tax on rentiers' income, and β is the share of profits distributed to rentiers. No personal tax is levied on retained earnings.

The fundamental equilibrium condition to be satisfied in this Keynesian model is the savings-investment equality. Since investment is fixed, the system operates by adjusting the markup so as to generate the correct amount of profits to finance the given investment. Savings for gross investment comes from three sources: depreciation, retained earnings of firms, and rentiers' savings, according to the following equation:

$$S = pI = (1 - t_f)\pi[(1 - \beta) + s(1 - t_r)\beta] + pD \qquad (12\text{--}11)$$

where s is the average propensity to save out of rentiers' income. (Recall that workers do not save.) Since D and I are fixed, it is easy to see from Eq. (12–9) that the basic equilibrating mechanism in the economy is the level of real profits π/p which, from Eq. (12–9) is related to the markup λ. Rewriting Eq. (12–11) by dividing through by p, and rearranging gives:

$$(1 - t_f)\frac{\pi}{p}[(1 - \beta) + s(1 - t_r)\beta] = I - D. \qquad (12\text{--}12)$$

The two equations (12–9) and (12–12) are sufficient to determine the markup λ and the level of real profits π/p. In addition, they allow us to make the following inferences about differential tax incidence:

(i)   Suppose we increase t_f (profits tax) and reduce t_w (wage or payroll tax) so as to maintain the same level of G. From Eq. (12–12), $(1 - t_f) \pi/p$ must remain unchanged whenever t_r is unchanged. Therefore, rentiers' real income $(1 - t_f) (\pi/p)\beta$ is unchanged, and so is their consumption. Thus, workers' consumption is unchanged, implying that the profits tax and wage tax are equivalent ways of raising revenue. What has happened is that as t_f rose, π/p rose, therefore λ rose. The higher markup means higher prices to the workers, but this is offset by their lower tax rate t_w. The interest in this result lies in the fact that the results generated are very different from those of the neoclassical model. In the fixed-factor version of the latter, a general factor tax is borne entirely by the factor. Substituting a profits tax for an equal-yield payroll tax would make labor better off by the full amount of the tax.

(ii) When any tax is substituted for t_r, workers are worse off and rentiers are better off. Such a change always generates an increase in rentiers' consumption.[18]

(iii) A balanced budget increase in G and all taxes will make workers worse off.[19] It reduces the aggregate amount of C available, including that available for workers.

This simple example illustrates how drastically the incidence results can change as the assumptions of the model change.[20] The results of the Keynesian model presented depended critically upon the assumption of a fixed level of investment, and a fixed payout ratio. One might well wish to entertain other assumptions regarding the workings of the economy. Ultimately, it is an empirical question as to what model best describes reality.

DYNAMIC TAX INCIDENCE

12–6 All the discussion of tax incidence so far has been in a static or one-period setting. Factors of production were taken to be either fixed in supply, or more or less elastically supplied in response to changes in factor prices. The technology of production was taken as given, and prices and resource allocations were determined through the clearing of markets in general equilibrium. The analysis of tax incidence involved determining how the prices would have differed in equilibrium, had certain taxes been present. The real world consists of more than one period. Economies are growing over time at varying rates, due to the growth in factors of production and to technological change. Since some of these changes, particularly the accumulation of capital stocks, are endogenous to the workings of the market economy, tax changes may influence the growth of factor supplies and therefore have a long-run impact on the returns to factors of production.

The analysis of the development of economies over time is rather complicated technically, even in the simplest of models. Much of the dynamic tax incidence analysis that has been conducted has utilized the single-sector, neoclassical growth model, and has compared the steady-state paths generated under various tax regimes. The workings of such a model are presented in Appendix II. Here we shall present a more intuitive discussion of the major forces at work. In the latter part of this section, we will investigate some of the consequences of introducing overlapping generations into the economy.

The basic ideas can be illustrated if we work at a highly aggregated level. Suppose we think of the economy as producing a single aggregate output (or gross national product), using as inputs the available stocks of primary factors of production, labor, L, and capital, K. The technology of the economy is captured in an aggregate production function in the form $Y = F(L,K)$, where Y is output, and the production function $F(L,K)$ has the usual properties of positive but diminishing marginal products of labor and capital. In addition, we will assume that the production function exhibits constant returns-to-scale. As discussed in Section 12–3, the property of constant returns-to-scale implies two things. First, it implies that if inputs are increased by a given proportion, output will increase in the same proportion. Second, relative factor prices will depend only on the ratio of capital to labor in the economy. As in Fig. 12–4, the wage-rental ratio will equal the marginal rate of technical substitution which, for a constant returns-to-scale production function, is uniquely determined by the ratio of capital to labor (the slope of a ray through the origin). Changes in the capital–labor ratio will change the wage–rental ratio by an amount that depends inversely on the elasticity of substitution.

Next, let us imagine the economy evolving through time. To make matters simple, suppose that growth in output arises solely from the growth in factor supplies (L and K). That is, technological change is ignored. (In principle, this source of growth could be added. However, it is inappropriate for our purposes here unless the rate of technological progress itself is dependent on tax rates.) The labor force is assumed to grow at a given proportional rate of n per period. The growth of the capital stock is, however, endogenously determined. The increment added to the capital stock in each period depends upon the amount of income that is saved, since current savings is assumed to equal current investment. For a given tax regime, the proportion of national income saved can be taken as given to begin with.

It is useful to describe first an economy which is growing in the *steady state*. In the steady state, by definition, both labor and capital are growing at the same rate, n. Because the production function has constant returns, output will also grow at the same rate, n. Thus, all inputs and outputs are growing at the same rate. Also, relative prices in this economy will be unchanging along the steady state path. Since K and L are growing at the same rate, the ratio K/L will be constant. This implies that the wage-rental ratio is constant. Thus, the share of output going to capital and labor will also be constant, and each person's income and consumption will be constant over time. In principle, there can be a great number of different steady states, each one corresponding to a different ratio of capital to labor. In each of these steady states, the growth rate will be the same (n), but the amount of capital and the wage–rental ratio will differ. Long-run tax incidence analysis is concerned with analyzing how the steady-state growth path is influenced by different tax regimes.

The steady-state growth path is obviously fictitious, since economies are continually subject to exogenous changes and are not in a steady state. Nonetheless, it is frequently used as a vehicle for dynamic tax incidence for several reasons. For one, it is relatively easy to handle analytically. More important, the impact of tax changes in the steady state is a useful way of looking at the *long-run* effect of taxes since, in the simple models we are dealing with here, the steady state is the growth path to which the economy tends in the long run. To see this, imagine that the economy is out of the steady state, say, because the capital stock is growing at a rate higher than n, the rate of growth of labor. Due to the constant returns-to-scale of the production function, output will be growing at a rate somewhere between n and the growth rate of the capital stock. Since savings is a fixed proportion of output, and output is growing at a rate less than the capital stock, savings cannot support a continued higher rate in growth of the latter, so the rate of growth of the capital stock must fall. It will continue to fall gradually over time until it converges to the same rate of growth as the labor supply, n; that is, until the steady state is reached. The steady state that is reached will be the one which is appropriate for the given savings rate. It will have a particular value of K/L, and therefore a particular value of w/r. Notice that if the capital stock is growing faster than the labor force, as in the above experiment, the capital-labor ratio will continually be rising, as will the wage-rental ratio, as the economy converges to the steady state. It will only cease to rise when the rate of growth of capital equals n. Analogous, but opposite, results are obtained if the capital stock is initially growing less rapidly than the labor force. In this case, a steady state will be approached as the capital-labor ratio and wage-rental ratio fall.

It can be shown that the higher the savings ratio, the higher will be the steady state, K/L, and the higher will be w/r. The simplest way to see this is to imagine the economy in a steady state for a particular savings ratio, and to let that savings ratio rise. The instantaneous effect of this will be to increase the rate of growth of capital above that of labor. By the same process as above, the economy will converge to a new steady state, but it will be one with a higher capital-labor ratio than otherwise would have been the case (since the path of labor growth is unchanged, but the capital stock has risen above its previous path).

Consider now the impact of taxes in such a setting, concentrating on factor taxes. Specifically, consider the substitution of a tax on capital income for an equal-yield tax on labor income. Note first that in the static, one-period equivalent of the model we are using here, a factor tax will be borne entirely by the factor on which it is imposed, since the factor supply is fixed. That means that substituting a capital income tax for a labor income tax will relocate the entire burden of the tax from wage earners to capital owners, and will have no effect on resource allocation. Once the economy is made dynamic, the possibility of tax shifting by factor suppliers is introduced.

To see this, assume now that the propensity to save out of capital income is higher than the propensity to save from labor income. Suppose that the economy is initially in a steady state, with a given set of tax rates on capital and labor; and that the government reduces the tax rate on labor and increases it on capital so as to generate the same tax revenues. In the short run, labor is better off, since it pays less of its income in taxes, and capital is worse off. However, since labor owners save less of their income than capital owners, the proportion of national income saved falls. Following the same line of reasoning as before, the economy will move towards a new steady state, with a lower capital-labor ratio and a lower wage-rental ratio. That is, part of the initial tax burden on capital will be shifted to labor, over time, through a reduction in the accumulation of capital.

The magnitude of long-run shifting will depend upon the difference between the savings out of capital and labor income. If the same proportion of each were saved, there would be no capital accumulation effect. However, the greater the saving out of capital income relative to labor income, the more will be the shifting. The amount of shifting will also depend upon the elasticity of substitution of the production function. The lower the elasticity of substitution, the greater will be the response of w/r to changes in K/L, and so the greater will be the shifting. Labor could actually end up being worse off in the long run, despite the fact that its tax rate has fallen and the tax levied on capital income has risen. If labor's wage-fall more than offsets the reduction in its tax rate, this would be the case as shown by Feldstein (1974a). Thus, the one-period effect of tax changes could be very different from the long-run effect.

Concentrating on the long-run effects of the tax change could be misleading, however, since it could take the economy a considerable period of time to go from one steady state to another. If we were to investigate the path of response of the economy to the above tax change, we might find that it takes a long time for capital to shift the tax on itself to labor. (See Boadway [1979]). When the tax is initially changed, labor is immediately better off, since it pays less tax. Only gradually is the capital-labor ratio, and thus the wage-rental ratio, reduced, and it may be some time before the fall in the wage rate overcomes the reduction in tax payments by labor. Thus, even though labor may eventually be worse off by the tax change, it may nonetheless prefer the exchange, since there could be a long period of time over which it is better off. This is obviously an empirical question.

The above analysis, and that presented in Appendix II, is obviously done for a very simple model. One could extend it to more complicated models of the economy, but the analysis immediately becomes fairly complex. Examples in the literature include the introduction of variable labor supply by Feldstein (1974b) and the separation of the economy into two sectors by Ballantine (1978). The former allows one to investigate the consequences of variability of labor supply in each period, while the latter allows for the analysis of partial factor taxes. One of the interesting results obtained is that variability of factor supply has no effect on the steady state growth path, in the sense that it does not affect the ratios K/L or w/r attained in equilibrium. Nonetheless, a variable labor supply is not unimportant. For one thing, it will influence the transition paths between steady states. For another, although the steady-state capital-labor and wage-rental ratios are independent of the elasticity of labor supply, and thus output per unit of labor is independent as well, output per person will vary with the elasticity of labor supply, since the labor supplied per person will vary. This implies that the underlying welfare effects of tax changes will depend upon the elasticity of labor supply, even if the production characteristics in the steady state do not.

The next example of dynamic tax incidence that we will study concerns the implications of taxing an asset which is fixed in supply, such as land, but which serves as a store of wealth for life-cycle savers, and which earns a rate of return in competition with other assets that are variable in supply. Traditional partial equilibrium arguments suggest that a tax on land can never be shifted, because land is inelastically supplied. Feldstein (1977b) has questioned this view, however, on several grounds. Most importantly, he has emphasized that the gross and net of tax returns on land depend on the quantities of other factors used in production along with land, especially the amount of capital. It follows, then, that if a land tax somehow disturbs the process of capital accumulation, the before-tax return on land will change; its net of tax return will therefore not fall by precisely the amount of the tax; and some shifting of the tax will occur.

To pursue this line of thought further, one needs to specify how the stock of capital in the economy is determined, and how it is influenced by a land tax. As we have already seen, there are several competing views among economists about how savings decisions are made; one might expect the analysis of land taxation in an intertemporal economy to depend upon which of these views one adopts. This actually is the case, for reasons that we explain on an intuitive basis in this subsection. A somewhat more detailed, but still informal, treatment of land taxation is presented in Appendix II.

To begin with, we assume with Feldstein that households are life-cycle savers who do not leave or receive bequests. To see how Feldstein arrives at the conclusion that a land rent tax is shifted, we begin by noting that at any moment of time, society possesses a stock of wealth consisting of capital and land. If output, consumption, and capital are measured in homogeneous units (as in the one-sector growth model previously discussed), and if p is the price of land in terms of these homogeneous goods, the value of the stock of wealth is $K + pT$, where K is the capital stock and T is the fixed stock of land. Each generation of households, when young, acquires society's wealth from its older owners by saving a portion of its earnings. When old, it then sells the wealth to finance consumption. When a land tax is imposed, p falls, due to capitalization of the tax, so that the value of the stock of wealth falls. *Ceteris paribus*, this reduces the value of assets carried into old age by the current young generation, and thus reduces old-age consumption. Clearly the way for the current young households to avoid this is to increase the stock of capital in the economy so as to restore, at least partially, the total value of wealth. This increase in K increases the marginal product and gross rent of land, so that the net return on land falls by less than the amount of the tax, while the productivity and returns of time over which it is better off. This is obviously an empirical question.

By contrast, Calvo, Kotlikoff and Rodriguez (1979) consider an economy where each generation cares about the utility of its children, and therefore leaves bequests. In this intergenerational utility maximization setting, the Feldstein result is overturned. The capital stock is unaffected by the land rent tax, the productivity of land is unchanged, and the net return on land is therefore reduced by precisely the amount of the tax. In other words, the classical, non-shifting, conclusion is preserved.

This result applies because the land tax is capitalized in the price of land, just as in the Feldstein model with no bequests. In this case, however, households respond by lowering the amount bequeathed by exactly the reduction in land value, say $(p - p')T$ if p and p' are the before- and after-tax prices of land. When this occurs, each young household's current income will be smaller by $(p - p')T$, because the bequest that it receives from the older generation has fallen by this amount. Thus, for a given amount of earnings and consumption when young, savings will fall by $(p - p')T$. The value of the stock of wealth falls by precisely this amount as well, because of the capitalization of the tax. The upshot is that current savings fall by the same amount as the value of wealth, and the current young savers will be able to satisfy their demand for assets by holding the same pre-tax amount of capital, K, plus the new lower-valued stock of land. There is therefore no tendency for K to change, and therefore no shifting of the tax.

The contrast in results between Feldstein, and Calvo, Kotlikoff, and Rodriguez hinges on their differing assumptions about household savings behavior. This supports a general conclusion that one might draw about the analysis of tax policy in an intertemporal economy, namely, that the results of the analysis will be sensitive to the precise nature of savings behavior. This conclusion underlines the importance of attempting to determine empirically which hypothesis about savings behavior is most appropriate.

ESTIMATES OF THE INCIDENCE
OF THE UNITED STATES TAX SYSTEM
BY INCOME GROUP

12–7   Our analysis so far has centered mainly on the incidence of taxes on the *functional distribution of income* (the relative factor rewards). Ultimately, we are interested in how taxes affect the *personal distribution of income*, that is, how their burden is allocated across income groups. Given that existing theoretical and empirical analysis has left us with few concrete predictions concerning the impact of various taxes on the rewards to factors of production, any attempt to go the next step, and try to estimate the incidence of taxes by income group, must be approached with some caution. Nonetheless, several attempts have been made to estimate the distributive impact of individual taxes and groups of taxes. To do so involves making an assumption about what other changes would occur if these taxes were eliminated. As discussed in Section 12–1, one must recognize that government expenditures would have to fall, or other taxes would have to increase, or both, if any given tax or taxes were to be eliminated. When one is discussing the overall incidence of an entire system of taxation, the first approach, based on the concept of balanced-budget incidence, has little appeal, since the elimination of all government expenditure would be associated with all sorts of drastic economic effects that one does not wish to consider. On the other hand, the differential incidence approach, which involves analyzing the reduction of some taxes and the increase of others, is also problematic. If one is conceptually eliminating all existing taxes, what substitute tax, yielding the same revenue, will replace them? The outcome of the overall tax incidence analysis will be dependent on the substitute tax chosen. This is not an issue that has been effectively resolved in existing studies of the overall incidence of taxation. Perhaps the best way to interpret existing studies is to imagine, as suggested by Thurow (1975), that they are comparing the incidence impact of eliminating existing taxes and replacing them with a tax whose burden is distributed proportionally with income.

There is another difficulty that arises in assessing overall tax incidence, namely that one must often rely on crude *assumptions* about the shifting pattern of the tax or taxes involved. For example, suppose one wants to estimate the incidence of the excise taxes on gasoline. Assume that some fraction is shifted forward to consumers, and the rest is borne by the owners of firms. That part which is shifted forward to consumers is borne by various income groups according to how much each one spends upon gasoline. The part that is not shifted is borne by income groups according to the share of the firms they own. In general, one must have data on the use of income by income groups, and on the source (labor, capital, etc.). Since these studies are based upon assumptions about the shifting patterns, rather than upon empirical studies, they cannot be regarded as definitive. Nonetheless, they do give some idea of the broad incidence pattern of taxes, and are interesting for that reason. As many of the studies give broadly similar results, we shall not provide an exhaustive survey. Rather, some representative studies will be briefly discussed.

(a) The Overall Tax Structure

Several attempts have been made to estimate the pattern of incidence of the entire tax structure, including not only federal taxes, but also state and local taxes. Broadly speaking, the results do not differ a great deal. A typical study is that done by Gillespie (1965) for the United States tax structure of 1960. He did a similar study for Canada in Gillespie (1976) and obtained similar results. In Table 12–1, the incidence of each type of tax as a percentage of gross income is shown for seven different income groups. Gross income is defined to include money income received from factors of production; imputed income, such as capital gains and retained earnings; and nonmoney income, such as imputed rent, and food grown and consumed on farms. It does not include government transfer payments. That is, it is intended to be income in the absence of government. The allocation of total tax payments to each income group was computed by

Table 12–1   Taxes Paid as a Percentage of Gross Income, by Income Bracket, 1960 (Estimated)

Tax Source	Family Money Income							
	Under $2000	$2000– 2999	$3000– 3999	$4000– 4999	$5000– 7499	$7500– 9999	$10,000– Over	Total
Federal taxes								
1. Individual income	3.9	7.0	7.9	6.6	6.7	8.1	15.6	10.4
2. Estate and gift	—	—	—	—	—	—	1.2	0.4
3. Corporation profits	11.4	10.8	6.5	5.3	3.5	2.3	7.4	5.3
4. Excises and customs	9.6	9.9	7.1	7.2	4.8	2.0	1.1	3.3
5. Social Security	12.9	14.3	12.0	9.0	5.7	3.4	1.4	4.4
6. Total Federal	37.8	42.0	33.6	28.1	20.8	15.7	26.6	23.9
State and local taxes								
7. Individual income	0.2	0.2	0.5	0.6	0.6	0.6	0.8	0.6
8. Estate and gift	—	—	—	—	—	—	0.3	0.1
9. Corporation profits	0.6	0.6	0.4	0.3	0.2	0.1	0.4	0.3
10. Sales and excise	11.2	11.7	8.6	8.7	5.8	2.5	1.4	4.0
11. Property	12.7	10.8	7.0	6.7	5.0	3.1	2.0	4.0
12. Social security	1.6	1.8	1.6	1.1	0.8	0.8	0.4	0.8
13. Total state & local	26.2	25.1	18.0	17.4	12.4	7.1	5.3	9.8
14. Total taxes	64.1	67.2	51.6	45.5	33.2	22.8	31.9	33.7

Source: W. Irwin Gillespie, "Effect of Public Expenditures on the Distribution of Income," in *Essays in Fiscal Federalism,* ed. Richard A. Musgrave (Washington: The Brookings Institution, 1965), 122–86, Table 3. Used by permission.

making the following assumptions about the shifting of the taxes:

- *Personal income tax:* Borne by individual income earners
- *Corporate profits tax:* Two-thirds borne by owners and one-third shifted to consumers
- *Consumption taxes (selective and general):* Shifted to consumers
- *Payroll taxes:* Employee's share borne by employee; employer's share half borne by employee and half shifted to consumers
- *Property taxes:* half shifted to consumers and half borne by homeowners and renters
- *Estate and gift taxes:* Borne by highest income bracket

Using these shifting assumptions, the total taxes paid are allocated among income groups according to their share of consumption, labor income, expenditures on housing, or share of corporate ownership, as the case may be. Since figures are not directly available on the shares of corporate ownership held by different income groups, they must be estimated in some other way. In practice, this is done by assuming that the shares of dividend earnings by income class reflect the shares of corporate ownership.

One critical assumption in this study, and in others of the same sort, is that income before taxes (gross income) is unaffected by the tax system. In practice, this is unlikely to be true. Not only will the tax system influence GNP by affecting the quantities of factors of production forthcoming, it will also influence relative factor prices and the share of income going to various groups. The analysis implicitly assumes that all factors of production are in fixed supply, and ignores the general equilibrium effects on factor prices considered earlier in this chapter. This is unfortunate, but necessary, due to the lack of empirical knowledge of the production and demand parameters of the general equilibrium system.

As can be seen from Table 12–1, the tax system as a whole exhibits progressivity up to an income of about $3000, then is regressive up to incomes of $10,000, and progressive thereafter. The extremely high effective tax rates in the lower income classes are mitigated considerably when one includes government transfers-less-taxes as part of the income base (see Gillespie [1965], Table 4, p. 136). Nonetheless, the same broad pattern emerges. The tax system shows progressivity up to incomes of $5000, regressivity to $10,000, and progressivity elsewhere. Most low-income persons continue to have effective tax rates above the economy-wide average.

Somewhat similar results were obtained in a more recent study of Musgrave, Case, and Leonard (1974). They found the tax structure to be (for the most part) proportional, with some progression in incomes below $5700 and above $35,000. These results, and others of the same sort, tend to indicate that, at least on the tax side of the government budget, less income redistribution may be taking place than one might expect. Gillespie also attempts to allocate the benefits of the expenditure side of the budget to income groups. He finds that the regressiveness of the tax system is more than offset by the pattern of benefits accruing to different income groups. Combining both expenditures and taxes, the middle income brackets ($4000–$10,000) are subject to almost no redistribution. Their tax payments are roughly offset by their benefits from expenditures. Redistribution does occur from the high-income groups to the low. While these results are suggestive, they are derived from a model that requires fairly strong assumptions about the benefits obtained from different types of government expenditures.

Several other studies have been done of the incidence of individual taxes over income groups. The results obtained are broadly consistent with those of Gillespie shown in Table 12–1. The following indicates some of the incidence patterns found elsewhere for particular taxes.

(b) Personal Income Tax

Pechman (1977) estimated the effective tax rate by income group by taking into consideration all preference items and deductions under the 1969 Tax

Reform Act provisions. His figures indicate the federal income tax paid as a percentage of adjusted gross income. Assuming that the tax is borne entirely by income earners, these rates would indicate the rate of progressivity (or otherwise) of the tax structure. His results show that the tax rates are much less progressive than statutory rates, rising to a maximum average rate of 17 percent on incomes of \$25,000–\$50,000, and 34 percent at incomes above \$1,000,000. This mild progressivity is reflected throughout the income scale. Similar results were obtained by Musgrave, Case, and Leonard (1974).

(c) Payroll Taxes

A study by Pechman, Aaron, and Taussig (1968) estimated the incidence by income group of a payroll tax levied at the rate of 10 percent on labor income, under varying shifting assumptions. When the employee is assumed to bear the entire tax, the tax appears to be progressive up to incomes of \$7000 or \$8000 (where effective rates approach 10 percent of total income) and regressive thereafter. When one-half the tax is assumed to be shifted forward to consumers as higher prices, and one-half borne by employees, the tax is regressive throughout the range, being nearly proportional at the low end of the scale. Once again, similar results were obtained by Musgrave, Case, and Leonard (1974).

(d) Consumption Taxes

Musgrave (1955) estimated that the federal excise taxes levied in 1954 were mildly regressive throughout the income range, beginning at 5 percent of income, and gradually falling throughout. This assumes that the taxes are borne by consumers. The incidence pattern of a 2 percent retail sales tax in 1965 was studied by the Advisory Committee on Intergovernmental Relations (1967). The tax was found to be very mildly regressive over the income range.

(e) Property Taxes

Pechman and Okner (1974) estimated the incidence of property taxation under alternative assumptions for 1966. If the property tax were borne entirely by property owners, it appeared to be progressive, beginning at 2.5 percent of income at the bottom end, and rising to about 10 percent at the top. However, if consumers were assumed to bear the property tax *except* for that falling on land, the pattern reverses itself. Tax rates decline from 6.5 percent at the low end of the income scale to less than 1 percent at the upper end. This is obviously because the purchase of housing services is a necessity with a fairly low income elasticity of demand. This example indicates how sensitive some of these incidence results might be to the shifting assumption.

(f) Corporation Income Taxes

This tax is particularly difficult to estimate with confidence, because of the uncertainty of shifting as well as the difficulty of attributing corporate profits to various income groups. The latter can be approximated by dividend receipts. Assuming that one-half the tax is shifted to consumers and the remainder borne by the capital owners, Musgrave, Case, and Leonard (1974) found that the tax did not differ greatly from proportionality. It appeared mildly regressive at the lower end, and mildly progressive thereafter. As with the property tax, when the shifting assumptions are changed, so is the incidence pattern. The less the tax is shifted, the more progressive it appears to be.

THE MEASUREMENT OF THE DEADWEIGHT LOSS OF TAXATION

12–8   As discussed in Chapters 9 and 10, the choice of a tax system involves trading off the conflicting considerations of equity and efficiency. The incidence analysis of this chapter forms the basis for evaluating the equity effects of various taxes. Let us conclude by discussing the principles involved in measuring the efficiency effects of taxes.

As we have noted, the deadweight loss or excess burden of the tax system consists of the reduction in utility that the tax distortions introduce, over and above the reduction in utility that would occur from the same resource transfer under lump-sum taxation. Various techniques have been devised for measuring this excess burden in monetary terms, and a limited number of attempts have been made to estimate the excess burden arising from individual taxes. In this section we shall briefly describe the techniques advocated by Harberger (1964) for measuring excess burden.

A convenient place to begin is with the simple model of Section 9–2 above, in which the only source of distortion is an excise tax on one good, as illustrated in Fig. 9–1. Assume that this diagram refers to the entire economy, so that relative production prices are fixed; that is, society's production possibility curve, AB, is linear. The measurement of the excess burden of this excise tax on X is shown in the lower part of Fig. 9–1. The excess burden will be measured in units of Y, so one may think of Y as being all other expenditures in money terms. The curve, D_1, is the ordinary demand curve generated by the price-consumption curve (not shown) through points III and I, and D_c is the compensated demand curve along the indifference curve, U_3.

The loss in utility to the consumer measured, in terms of Y at the original prices (before tax), is the "compensating variation" AF. It is the amount of money the consumer would be willing to pay in order not to have the excise tax levied. (See the Appendix to Chapter 9). It is composed of the real resource transfer AC and the excess burden CF. As we showed in the Appendix to Chapter 9, the distance AF corresponds to the area to the left of the compensated demand curve D_c, or p_3abp_1, the consumer's surplus. Since the tax revenue generated is p_3acp_1, this means the excess burden can be measured by the triangular area abc. We cannot observe the compensated demand curve, D_c, or even the point b on the market. At best, we may only observe the ordinary demand curve, D_1. We may approximate the excess burden by the area adc, but the two will only be identical when D_1 and D_c are identical; that is, when income effects are negligible.

A closer approximation is obtained when we perform the differential incidence experiment of substituting the excise tax on X for an equal-yield income tax. This is equivalent to comparing points II and III in Fig. 9–1. Point II is the same as e on the ordinary demand curve D_2 in the lower part of Fig. 9–1. It includes all the income effect of the excise tax removed except for that associated with the excess burden (CF). The triangular area aec is a close approximation to the deadweight loss abc.

We can obtain an approximate measure of the excess burden abc if we assume that the demand curves are linear. Denoting the excess burden by W, we obtain:

$$W \cong \frac{1}{2}(ac)(ce) = -\frac{1}{2}\Delta p_X \Delta X$$

$$= \frac{1}{2}t_X^2 \eta_X p_X X \tag{12–13}$$

where t_X is the *ad valorem* tax rate on $X(= \Delta p_X/p_X)$, and η_X is the elasticity of demand along the constant revenue demand curve $ae[= -(\Delta X/X)/(\Delta p_X/p_X)]$. Therefore, the deadweight loss is proportional to the elasticity of demand and the square of the tax rate. If the supply curve is upward sloping, there will be some producer's surplus, as well as consumer's surplus, in the deadweight loss "triangle." The deadweight loss will then involve both demand and supply elasticities, and will be approximated by:

$$\frac{1}{2}t^2 \frac{p_X X}{(1/\eta) + (1/\varepsilon)} \tag{12–14}$$

where ε is the elasticity of supply. A more complete analysis of this case may be found in Bishop (1968).

A similar analysis applies for estimating the burden of a proportional income tax in an economy in which the labor supply is variable and no other taxes are in existence. This case is shown in Fig. 12–8, where it is again assumed that relative producer prices (marginal costs) are fixed so that the wage rate is fixed. The supply curve S is again considered to be the supply curve generated by substituting an income tax for a lump-sum tax of equal yield. The loss in producers' surplus to the suppliers of labor, due to the income tax at rate t, is the area $wcbw(1 - t)$. This is partly

Figure 12–8

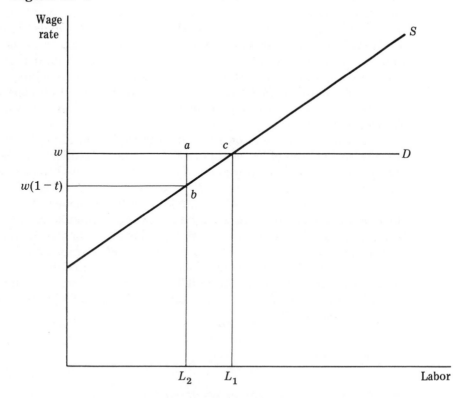

offset by the gain in government revenue of $wabw(1 - t)$, leaving a deadweight loss of acb. Assuming the supply curve to be approximately linear, this area is given by:

$$abc = \frac{1}{2} \Delta w \, \Delta L$$

$$= \frac{1}{2} t^2 \, \varepsilon w L \tag{12–15}$$

where ε is the elasticity of supply of labor evaluated when the tax revenue replaces a lump-sum tax to the supplier of labor. In one of the early applications of deadweight loss measurement, Harberger (1964) estimated, using this formula, that the excess burden of the United States tax system in 1961 was about $1 billion per year out of $42 billion in personal income tax revenues.

A similar methodology has been used to estimate the excess burden arising from partial factor taxation, once again neglecting any other taxes that may be in existence. Consider the case of taxation of capital in a particular sector of the economy, say, X. Figure 12–9 illustrates the excess burden of a tax on K_X in an economy in which the aggregate supply of capital is fixed. The curves D_{KX} and D_{KY} reflect the derived demand curves for capital in each of the two sectors. The downward slope reflects the fact that as the price of capital services r falls and more capital is used, the value of the marginal product of capital falls due to the diminishing marginal product of capital. Before the tax is imposed, the rental on capital is established at r_1, where the aggregate demand for capital ($K_{X_1} + K_{Y_1}$) equals the aggregate supply.

A tax is now imposed on the return to capital in X at the rate t. As we saw earlier, the effect of this tax is to cause a reallocation of capital out of X and into Y, until the net-of-tax rate of return is the same in the two industries. This occurs at a net return of $r_2(1 - t)$ in Fig. 12–9, where $(K_{X_1} - K_{X_2}) = (K_{Y_2} - K_{Y_1})$, so all capital is fully employed. As a result of the reduction in capital used in X, the total value of production attributable to K_X is reduced by the area $K_{X_2} ab K_{X_1}$. However, the additional capital in Y generates a total value of output of $K_{Y_1} de K_{Y_2}$. Since $K_{X_2}K_{X_1}$ equals $K_{Y_1}K_{Y_2}$, the area $K_{X_2} cg K_{X_1}$ equals $K_{Y_1} de K_{Y_2}$, the gain in output in Y. Therefore, the net loss in output value to society is the area $abgc$. Once again assuming the demand curves for capital to be linear, this area may be approximated as follows:

$$abgc = \frac{1}{2} \Delta K_X t r_2. \tag{12–16}$$

In Appendix I to this chapter we derive an expression for ΔK_X.

Figure 12–9

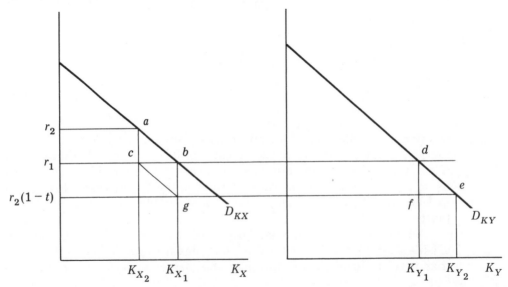

Harberger (1962) estimated, using the above model and assuming that the entire corporate income tax reflected a tax on the return to capital in the corporate sector, that the excess burden of the tax in the years 1953–59 was between 2.4 and 7.0 percent of corporate tax revenues. An alternative calculation was done by Shoven and Whalley (1972), using the Harberger model but, instead of relying on a linear approximation of the demand for capital services, they explicitly solved the general equilibrium system for the pre- and post-tax allocations. Using the same parameter values for the economy as Harberger, their results suggested that the excess burden was between 2.2 and 11.7 percent of tax revenues.

These estimates of the excess burden of the corporate tax treat the full amount of the tax revenues collected as being distortionary. In calculating the tax rate t, Harberger (1962) used the ratio of corporate tax collected divided by total payments to capital in the corporate sector. That is, he used the *average* corporate tax rate to measure the marginal distortion of the corporate tax. This average tax rate may be a significant overestimate of the marginal distortion of the corporate tax. As we have already seen in the preceding chapter, the magnitude of the marginal distortion imposed by the corporate tax depends upon the generosity of the deductions for depreciation and interest, and any investment tax credit. If the present value of these deductions equals the original cost of capital purchases, there will be no marginal tax distortion. Nonetheless, the average tax would be positive, since there would be tax revenues obtained from infra-marginal profits. In this case, the excess burden of the corporate tax would be minimal, and the Harberger estimates would represent a significant overestimate. The impact on the Harberger estimates of taking deductions fully into account is analyzed in more detail in Ballantine and McLure (1980).

The above examples all neglect the fact that distortions exist elsewhere in the economy, as well as that of the tax whose excess burden is being estimated. As a result, there may be welfare changes induced in the excess burdens of these other distorted markets when the tax in question is changed. The argument is analogous to the theory of second best as discussed in Chapter 7. It may be illustrated with a simple example of an economy in which good Y is subject to a given tax, and one wishes to determine the effects of introducing a tax on X. Figure 12–10, similar to one used by Harberger (1964), depicts this case. For simplicity we assume that producer prices are fixed. The demand curve for X is D_X, and that for Y, before the tax on X is imposed, is D_Y. There is a tax in existence on commodity Y at the per-unit rate t_Y. We want to estimate the change in social welfare from imposing a tax on X given the tax on Y.

Suppose we levy a tax on X that raises the price of X by an amount t_X per unit of output. (There is no need to distinguish between *ad valorem* and per-unit excise taxes here, since, with producer prices fixed, they are equivalent.) The demand for X is reduced from X_1 to X_2, thereby reducing total benefits by X_2bcX_1. Since there is also a saving in resource costs of X_2acX_1, the net change in excess burden on the market for X is abc. At the same time, the change in the price of X will induce changes in the

Figure 12–10

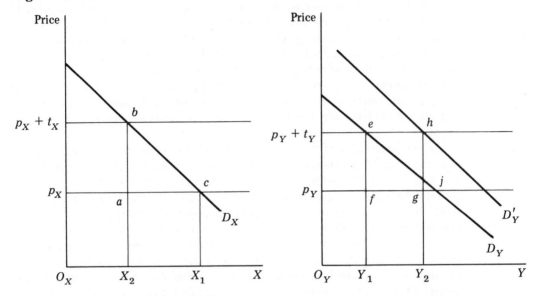

demand for Y if the two are related. If X and Y are substitutes, the demand curve for Y will shift to the right to D_Y' as in Fig. 12–10. This causes the demand for Y to rise from Y_1 to Y_2, and total benefits to increase by Y_1ehY_2. The additional resource costs of producing the extra Y are Y_1fgY_2, leaving a net benefit of *ehgf*. Adding these two changes together, we find that the net change in welfare from the imposition of the tax on X is:

$$- abc + ehgf \cong \frac{1}{2} t_X \Delta X + t_Y \Delta Y. \tag{12–17}$$

This change may, of course, be either positive or negative.

We may also evaluate the aggregate deadweight loss of the two taxes combined as follows. Imagine the taxes to be imposed in sequence, and measure the change in welfare as each tax is imposed. First a tax of t_Y per unit is imposed on Y. The deadweight loss incurred is *efj*, following the usual method of measurement. Next, a tax on X of t_X per unit is imposed with the tax on Y already in place. The additional change in welfare is given by the preceding equation. The aggregate deadweight loss of the tax is therefore $-efj - abc + ehgf$, or

$$\frac{1}{2} t_Y \left. \frac{\Delta Y}{\Delta t_Y} \right|_{t_X=0} \Delta t_Y + \frac{1}{2} t_X \left. \frac{\Delta X}{\Delta t_X} \right|_{t_Y=t_Y} \Delta t_X + t_Y \left. \frac{\Delta Y}{\Delta t_X} \right|_{t_Y=t_Y} \Delta t_X \tag{12–18}$$

where $\Delta Y/\Delta t_Y$ is the change in the demand for Y induced by a change in

t_Y, etc., and these changes are evaluated with the values of the other tax given as shown.

The same method may be expanded to the case of many taxes. The additional excess burden added to the economy when a tax is imposed on X_n at the per-unit rate t_n, when per-unit taxes exist on goods $(X_1, ..., X_{n-1})$, is approximately as follows:

$$\frac{1}{2} t_n \, \Delta X_n + \sum_{i=1}^{n-1} t_i \, \Delta X_i. \tag{12–19}$$

The first term is equivalent to the usual deadweight loss triangle. The second is the sum of rectangular areas, such as *ehgf* in Fig. 12–10, for all distorted commodities. The aggregate deadweight loss of the tax system as a whole is then computed by imagining each tax to be imposed in some arbitrary order. To the extent that taxes offset one another, the estimate of the excess burden arising from any one of them will be misleadingly high. At the same time, because excess burden varies with the square of the tax rate, different taxes that impose cumulative distortions on the same transaction cause the deadweight loss to rise sharply. For example, corporate taxes and property taxes may cause the effective rate of tax on corporate capital to be very high. The estimate of the deadweight loss imposed by one of them in isolation will be a significant underestimate.

Applications of the above methodology to measure the excess burden of actual tax systems have been few. Boskin (1975) utilized the approach to estimate the excess burden that resulted from the differential tax treatment of labor and capital employed in the household and market sectors. This model was discussed earlier in this chapter. With no tax on household labor, but varying tax rates on market labor (personal income and payroll taxes), household capital (property taxes), and market capital (corporate income and property taxes), the welfare cost was estimated to be between 6 and 13 percent of tax revenues. This measure ignores any distortions that occur within the market sector. The deadweight loss of the Canadian commodity tax, tariff, and corporate tax systems has been estimated by Boadway and Treddenick (1978) to be in the neighborhood of one percent of gross national product. The method used was to compute the allocation of resources in the presence and absence of the various tax distortions, using a general equilibrium computational method. The change in welfare was then estimated directly, using index number comparisons.

The theory of deadweight losses from taxation also has important applications to the evaluation of public expenditures. As discussed at some length in Chapter 8, proper assessment of the economic effects of a public expenditure program requires that one take into account the full range of costs and benefits of the program. A main part of these costs will be the value of the resources transferred from the private to the public sector, via the tax system, for the financing of the public expenditure. We have seen, however, that the true economic cost of a dollar's worth of taxation generally exceeds a dollar because of the distortions or inefficiencies generated by taxes. One should expect, therefore, that the true cost of some additional public expenditure must include the extra or marginal deadweight loss entailed by extra distortionary taxation.

This possibility was first discussed by Pigou (1951), and has been studied subsequently by Atkinson and Stern (1974), Browning (1976), Wildasin (1979a, 1984), Usher (1983), and others. The essence of the problem can most easily be seen by supposing that the only tax in the economy is a tax on labor at rate t, and that the before-tax wage rate of labor is fixed at w. The net wage rate is therefore $w(1-t)$, and Fig. 12–11 portrays an initial equilibrium with a tax rate of t_0 and a labor supply of L_0. Suppose now that some additional public expenditure is undertaken that necessitates an increase in the tax rate from t_0 to t_1, so that the net wage falls to $w(1-t_1)$ and the equilibrium labor supply falls to L_1. The tax increase causes a loss of producers' surplus equal to $w(1-t_0)$ de $w(1-t_1)$, which, for our present purpose, may be approximated by the rectangle $w(1-t_0)$ ce $w(1-t_1)$. The increase in revenue resulting from the tax increase, which equals the extra expenditure being undertaken, is $w(1-t_0)$ ce $w(1-t_1)$ − $abcd$. Therefore, the social cost of the public expenditure per dollar of expenditure is the ratio of these magnitudes, or

$$SMC = \frac{w(1-t_0) \ ce \ w(1-t_1)}{w(1-t_0) \ ce \ w(1-t_1) \ - \ abcd}$$

$$= \frac{1}{1 - \dfrac{abcd}{w(1-t_0) \ ce \ w(1-t_1)}}. \tag{12–20}$$

Now $abcd$ is equal to $wt_0(L_0 - L_1) = -wt_0 \Delta L$, if $\Delta L = L_1 - L_0$ represents the change in the amount of labor supplied when the tax increases. On the other hand, $w(1-t_0)$ ce $w(1-t_1)$ is equal to minus the change in the net wage times L_1, i.e. $[w(1-t_0) - w(1-t_1)] L_1 = -L_1 \Delta w(1-t)$. Thus,

$$\frac{abcd}{w(1-t_0) \ ce \ w(1-t_1)} = \frac{-wt_0 \, \Delta L}{-L_1 \, \Delta \, w(1-t)} \cong \frac{t_0}{1-t_0} \varepsilon, \tag{12–21}$$

where ε is the elasticity of labor supply, defined to be $(\Delta LW)/(\Delta WL)$. Therefore

$$SMC = \frac{1}{1 - \dfrac{t_0}{1-t_0} \varepsilon}. \tag{12–22}$$

This result establishes that the social marginal cost of a dollar of public expenditure exceeds one dollar, provided that the tax rate is initially non-zero, and that the elasticity of labor supply is positive. Intuitively, the higher the initial tax distortion, the more costly is some further distortion; and the greater the elasticity of supply, the greater the marginal deadweight

Figure 12–11

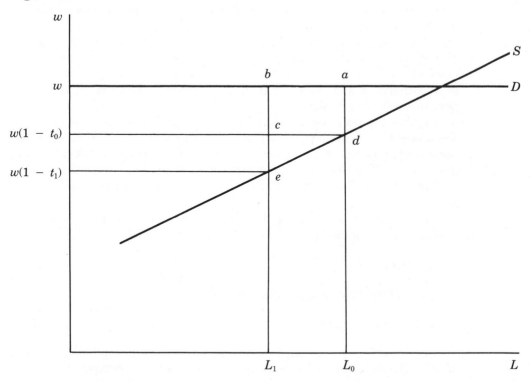

loss from this extra distortion. Estimates of the marginal social cost of a dollar's worth of income tax revenues in the United States have been made by several authors. They range widely, however, from close to $1.00 to $2.00 or more (Usher [1983], Wildasin [1984]).

When there is more than one tax distortion in the economy, this analysis must be extended to take into account simultaneous tax rate changes and their general equilibrium effects on interrelated markets. In addition, we have ignored the possible effects of the government expenditure program on the (compensated) supply curve for the taxed commodity, and the equity complications that arise in a many-consumer economy. These complications can seriously affect the estimated *SMC* in practice, and detailed calculations reflecting them have not yet been made.

APPENDIX I: ALGEBRAIC TREATMENT OF THE TWO-SECTOR MODEL

Here we present an algebraic treatment of the two-sector general equilibrium model. Although a small amount of calculus is used, the algebraic sense of the model can be obtained by substituting discrete changes Δ for differential changes denoted by d.

The analysis to be presented here will be based upon that of Mieszkowski (1967) which, in turn, is a refinement and generalization of the earlier tax incidence analysis of Harberger (1962). We present the simplest case of a fixed-factor economy, with a single aggregate demand function incorporating all consumers as well as the government. Following the above authors, the government is assumed to spend the tax revenues in exactly the same way as consumers would have. This is the same as assuming that the tax revenues are given back to the consumers as lump-sum transfers, or, equivalently, that the tax revenues simply replace equal lump-sum tax revenues. We proceed by presenting the equations of the general equilibrium system according to the following classifications: supply, demand, market clearing, and pricing. The analysis is a comparative static one, and all equations will be presented in terms of differential changes rather than absolute values.

(i) *Supply* The basic supply relationship is the production function. For industry X it reads:

$$X = f(L_X, K_X). \tag{12-23}$$

Totally differentiating this equation yields:

$$dX = f_L \, dL_X + f_K \, dK_X \tag{12-24}$$

where f_L and f_K are the marginal products of labor and capital, $\partial f/\partial L_X$ and $\partial f/\partial K_X$. By the competitive assumption, factor payments equal the values of marginal products (e.g. $w_X = p_X f_L$). Using this relationship and dividing by X converts Eq. (12–24) into:

$$\hat{X} = \theta_{LX}\hat{L}_X + \theta_{KX}\hat{K}_X \tag{12-25}$$

where the caret represents a proportionate change ($\hat{X} = dX/X$), θ_{LX} is labor's share in the cost of producing X($\theta_{LX} = w_X L_X / p_X X$), and θ_{KX} is capital's share ($\theta_{KX} = r_X K_X / p_X X$). Since we assume that production functions are linear homogeneous, factor payments just exhaust the product value, so $\theta_{LX} + \theta_{KX} = 1$.[21] While we could derive an equation analogous to (12–25) for industry Y, it turns out that we have no need of it in the system.[22]

The other supply relationships of interest to us are the elasticities of substitution σ_X and σ_Y. The point of value of σ_X is defined as:

$$\sigma_X = -\frac{d(K_X/L_X)/(K_X/L_X)}{d(r_X/w_X)/(r_X/w_X)} \tag{12-26}$$

where r_X and w_X are the gross returns to capital and labor in X. Carrying out the differentiations in numerator and denominator, the expression becomes:

$$\hat{K}_X - \hat{L}_X = -\sigma_X(\hat{r}_X - \hat{w}_X). \tag{12-27}$$

Similarly, the expression for σ_Y becomes:

$$\hat{K}_Y - \hat{L}_Y = -\sigma_Y(\hat{r}_Y - \hat{w}_Y). \tag{12-28}$$

(ii) *Demand* The basic demand equation for X would, in general, be of the form:

$$X = X(I, p_X, p_Y) \tag{12-29}$$

where I is income. Since demand functions are homogeneous of degree zero in all prices and income, only relative prices are important. Furthermore, since income changes can safely be ignored (because the government spends the tax revenues in the same way as the consumers would), this demand equation is usually simply written as:

$$X = X(p_X/p_Y). \tag{12-30}$$

Differentiating Eq. (12–30), and converting it to a rate of change by dividing through by X, the demand for X in proportional change terms becomes:

$$\hat{X} = E(\hat{p}_X - \hat{p}_Y) \tag{12-31}$$

where E is approximately the compensated relative price elasticity of demand for X. The term "approximately" is inserted because the assuming away of income effects ignores the deadweight loss of welfare that occurs due to the tax.

To see this, consider the case of an excise tax on X depicted in Fig. 12–12. Before the tax is imposed, the economy is at point A with an output of X_1. The excise tax on X with the proceeds distributed lump-sum moves the economy along the production possibility curve to point B, with an output of X_2, and a new set of relative prices p_X/p_Y. The compensated elasticity of demand would indicate the change in X that would be demanded from the change in p_X/p_Y if the consumer stayed on the same indifference curve. In this case, the consumer would go to point C and would consume X_3. Due to the deadweight loss of the tax, the consumer's utility is reduced and, at the new relative prices, he can only attain point B with a demand of X_2. Only if indifference curves are parallel in a vertical direction are X_2 and X_3 the same. Therefore, the appropriate elasticity E for inclusion in Eq. (12–31) is really the elasticity of demand for X with respect to p_X/p_Y along the production possibility curve,[23] and not the compensated elasticity. In the case of partial factor taxes, the analysis is complicated further by the fact that the post-tax point B lies within the production possibility curve. We assume in the following analysis that the correct interpretation of E is being used. As before, we do not need a corresponding demand equation for Y, since Y is implicitly solved when the remainder of the model is solved.

Figure 12–12

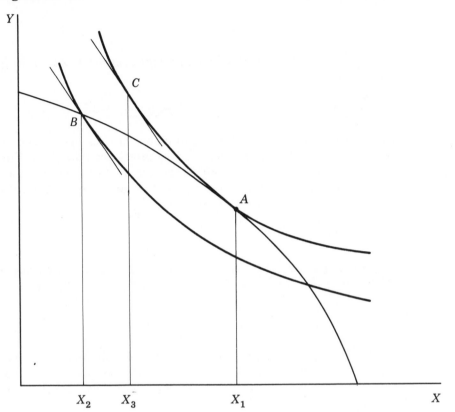

(iii) *Market Clearing Conditions*   The model assumes that all factors are fully employed, so that the given supply of each must be used up in the two industries. Market clearing conditions for K and L are:

$$K_X + K_Y = \overline{K} \tag{12-32}$$

$$L_X + L_Y = \overline{L} \tag{12-33}$$

where $\overline{K}$ and $\overline{L}$ are the given supplies of the factors. Totally differentiating these market clearing conditions gives:

$$dK_X = -dK_Y \tag{12-34}$$

$$dL_X = -dL_Y. \tag{12-35}$$

The market clearing conditions for X are already implicitly included in the analysis, since the same quantity X is used in both supply and demand relationships in Eqs. (12–25) and (12–31).

(iv) *Pricing Equations*   The pricing equation for p_X is derived from the equality between the value of inputs and outputs:

$$p_X X = w_X L_X + r_X K_X. \tag{12-36}$$

Total differentiation of this equation gives:

$$p_X dX + X\, dp_X = w_X\, dL_X + r_X\, dK_X + L_X\, dw_X + K_X\, dr_X. \tag{12-37}$$

However, from the total differential of the production function for X, Eq. (12-23), we know:[24]

$$p_X\, dX = w_X\, dL_X + r_X\, dK_X. \tag{12-38}$$

Therefore, subtracting this from the above equation we get:

$$X\, dp_X = L_X\, dw_X + K_X\, dr_X \tag{12-39}$$

or, rewriting this in proportionate change terms,

$$\hat{p}_X = \theta_{LX}\hat{w}_X + \theta_{KX}\hat{r}_X. \tag{12-40}$$

Here, $\hat{w}_X$ and $\hat{r}_X$ are the changes in gross factor payments in industry X.

Suppose we consider for illustrative purposes the imposition of a tax on capital in X at the *ad valorem* rate T_{KX}. Then the net return to capital in the economy, r, is related to r_X as follows:

$$r = r_Y = r_X(1 - T_{KX}). \tag{12-41}$$

If we differentiate this expression and assume that $dT_{KX} = T_{KX}$ so that the tax is zero at the start,[25] we obtain:

$$\hat{r} = \hat{r}_X - T_{KX}. \tag{12-42}$$

With no tax on either L_X or X the pricing equation is:

$$\hat{p}_X = \theta_{LX}\hat{w} + \theta_{KX}(\hat{r} + T_{KX}). \tag{12-43}$$

Similarly, for $\hat{p}_Y$ if we assume no taxes on the Y industry, we obtain:

$$\hat{p}_Y = \theta_{LY}\hat{w} + \theta_{KY}\hat{r}. \tag{12-44}$$

So far we have eight equations (12-25, 12-27, 12-28, 12-31, 12-34, 12-35, 12-43, 12-44) in nine unknowns (X, $\hat{p}_X$, $\hat{p}_Y$, $\hat{r}$, $\hat{w}$, $\hat{K}_X$, $\hat{L}_X$, $\hat{K}_Y$, $\hat{L}_Y$) so the system cannot yet be solved. However, we can eliminate one of the variables by noting that the system can only be solved for relative prices. Technically, the system is homogeneous of degree zero in prices, so that doubling all prices (p_X, p_Y, w, r) would have absolutely no effect on the allocation of resources. Therefore, the price *level* can be arbitrarily chosen, and the simplest way to do that is to arbitrarily set one of the prices to unity. We set $w = 1$, so $\hat{w} = 0$; that is, labor is the numeraire and all prices are measured in terms of labor units. That eliminates $\hat{w}$ from the set of unknowns and leaves us with eight equations in eight unknowns. Since all equations are linear, we may solve for each of the unknowns in terms of the exogenous variables in the model (θ's, E, σ_X, σ_Y, and T_{KX}) using the methods of matrix algebra.

To illustrate the nature of the solution, we present the solution for $\hat{r}$ which, because labor is the numeraire, is the proportionate change in the rental-wage ratio. By manipulating the above equation, as shown for example in Mieszkowski (1967), or Shoven and Whalley (1972), the solution for $\hat{r}$ becomes:

$$\hat{r} = \frac{E\theta_{KX}(K_X/K_Y - L_X/L_Y) - \sigma_X(\theta_{LX}K_X/K_Y + \theta_{KX}L_X/L_Y)}{E(\theta_{KY} - \theta_{KX})(K_X/K_Y - L_X/L_Y) + \sigma_Y + \sigma_X(\theta_{LX}K_X/K_Y + \theta_{KX}L_X/L_Y)}T_{KX}.$$

$$(12\text{--}45)$$

Suppose we rewrite Eq. (12–45) as follows:

$$\hat{r} = \frac{\theta_{KX}A + B}{D}T_{KX}. \qquad (12\text{--}46)$$

To interpret these results, note first that the denominator D is always positive.[26] The first term in the numerator is positive if $K_X/L_X < K_Y/L_Y$ (if X is labor-intensive), and negative if $K_X/L_X > K_Y/L_Y$ (if X is capital-intensive). This first term is just the output effect referred to in the main text. The release of factors from X will be detrimental to capital if X is a capital-intensive industry. Notice that the output effect is stronger the greater the absolute value of E, the elasticity of demand for X. This reflects the fact that the greater this elasticity, the more resources will be transferred from X to Y as a result of the tax.

The second term in Eq. (12–46), denoted B, is always negative (since $\sigma_X > 0$). It corresponds to the factor substitution effect. It will have a greater depressing effect on r the larger is the elasticity of substitution in X. In that case, capital is less able to shift the tax by substitution out of the X industry.

If $\hat{r} = 0$, the economy-wide rental-wage ratio remains unchanged when the tax is imposed. The burden of the tax falls on each factor income in proportion to the factor's contribution to GNP. This means capital has succeeded in shifting to labor a share of the burden. If $\hat{r} < 0$, capital bears a larger share of the burden than its proportional contribution to GNP, and vice versa. From Eq. (12–46) the effect of T_{KX} on $\hat{r}$ is ambiguous unless X is capital-intensive. If so, $\hat{r} < 0$ and capital will bear a greater share of the tax than its share of GNP; that is, a greater share than it would bear under a general income tax.

By proceeding as above, a partial factor tax on labor in X at the rate T_{LX} can be shown to affect $\hat{r}$ as follows:

$$\hat{r} = \frac{\theta_{LX}A - B}{D} T_{XL}. \tag{12-47}$$

The terms A, B, and D are exactly as defined above. Here, the tax unambiguously falls on capital in less than its share ($\hat{r} > 0$) if X is labor-intensive.

By combining the two partial factor taxes at equal rate ($T_{XL} = T_{KL}$) simultaneously, we have the equivalent of a specific commodity tax on X. From Eqs. (12–46) and (12–47)

$$\hat{r} = \frac{A}{D} T_X. \tag{12-48}$$

No factor substitution effect occurs, and capital's share of the burden exceeds its contribution to GNP when X is capital-intensive ($A > 0$), and vice versa.

From the same equations above, we could also solve for relative goods price changes ($\hat{p}_X$, $\hat{p}_Y$) and resource reallocation ($\hat{X}$, $\hat{K}_X$, $\hat{K}_Y$, $\hat{L}_X$, $\hat{L}_Y$). These are, however, of relatively limited interest to us for incidence questions. In Section 12–8 we presented a method for estimating the deadweight loss of, say, T_{KX}. The deadweight loss turned out to depend directly upon the change in capital in X. Solving the above system for $\hat{K}_X$ we obtain:

$$\hat{K}_X = \frac{\sigma_X[E(\theta_{KY} - \theta_{KX})\,L_X/L_Y - \sigma_Y\theta_{LX}] + [E\theta_{KX}(\sigma_Y + \sigma + (L_X/L_Y)]}{D} \tag{12-49}$$

where D is defined as in Eq. (12–46).

Finally, while we have considered the simplest version of the two-sector incidence model here, we could have complicated the analysis by allowing factor supplies to vary, or by allowing for more than one type of demand. The above analysis does, however, serve to illustrate the methodological approach of neoclassical general equilibrium tax incidence analysis.

APPENDIX II: DYNAMIC TAX INCIDENCE: A MORE FORMAL TREATMENT

In this Appendix we elaborate on the discussion of dynamic tax incidence in Section 12–6. The first subsection deals with the analysis of tax incidence in a simple one-sector growth model. This subsection uses a modest amount of simple differential calculus. However, the basic ideas of the analysis can be grasped by substituting discrete changes (e.g. ΔX) for differential changes $(dX, \partial X)$. The second subsection discusses the incidence of land rent taxation, using only simple algebra.

(a) The Incidence of a Capital Income Tax in a Neoclassical Growth Model

As we have seen in the discussion in Section 12–6 and as shown in analyses by Sato (1967), Feldstein (1974a), Grieson (1975), and others, the basic new element that a dynamic analysis adds to tax incidence is the ability to shift taxes through time by changes in the accumulation of factors of production. Thus, a tax which strikes capital income may, in the short run, be borne by capital owners. However, in the long run, if the accumulation of capital is reduced relative to that of labor, the economy's capital-labor ratio will fall, causing the wage-rental ratio to fall as well. Through time, part of the tax is shifted to labor by the change in factor proportions.

Consider the single-sector, neoclassical economy with an aggregate production function of the form:

$$Y = F(K, L) \tag{12–50}$$

where Y is output, K is capital, and L is labor. We assume no technical progress, so (12–50) holds over time. The sole source of growth is changes in K and L. Assume that the production function F is linear homogeneous, so that multiplying K and L by the factor λ causes Y to increase by λ as well. If λ is $1/L$, Eq. (12–50) can be written as:

$$y = F(k, 1) = f(k) \tag{12–51}$$

where $y = Y/L$ and $k = K/L$ are now in per capita terms. In this economy, output is used either for consumption, capital accumulation, or government expenditures. The latter is assumed to be fixed in per capita terms, and is financed either by a tax on capital income, t_r, or a tax on labor income, t_w, or both. Thus, government expenditure per capita, g, is equated to tax revenue per capita:

$$g = t_w w + t_r rk \tag{12–52}$$

where w is the wage rate net-of-tax, and r the rental on capital net-of-tax.

Investment in capital accumulation is financed by savings out of capital and labor incomes. We make the assumption that the propensities to save out of these sources of income, s_r and s_w, differ and, in particular, $s_r > s_w$. Per capita savings, s, is therefore:

$$s = s_r rk + s_w w. \tag{12–53}$$

Gross investment equals aggregate savings. For simplicity, we assume there is no depreciation of capital, so gross investment also equals capital accumulation,

$$dK = S, \quad \text{or} \quad \frac{dK}{L} = s.$$

Since $d(K/L) = dK/L - K\,dL/L^2$, we can write:[27]

$$s = dk + k\frac{dL}{L}. \tag{12–54}$$

Let us assume that labor grows at a constant exponential rate n, so $dL/L = n$. Thus, from Eqs. (12–53) and (12–54), we get the following basic equation on the change of the capital-labor ratio k:

$$dk = s_r rk + s_w w - nk. \tag{12–55}$$

In this analysis, we consider only steady states.[28] When the economy is in the steady state, capital, labor, and output all grow at the same rate n. The capital-labor ratio k is fixed so $dk = 0$ in the steady state.

In Eq. (12–55) there are three variables, r, w, and k. However, r and w are both related to k through the production technology. In particular, w and r are the net-of-tax marginal products of labor and capital. In per capita terms, these marginal products may be written:[29]

$$w(1 + t_w) = f(k) - kf'(k) \tag{12–56}$$

and

$$r(1 + t_r) = f'(k) \tag{12–57}$$

where

$$f'(k) = \frac{df(k)}{dk}. \tag{12–58}$$

Substituting Eqs. (12–56) and (12–57) into (12–55), and assuming a steady state so $dk = 0$, we obtain:

$$0 = \frac{s_r\,kf'(k)}{1 + t_r} + \frac{s_w[f(k) - kf'(k)]}{1 + t_w} - nk. \tag{12–59}$$

Given the propensities to save s_r and s_w, the growth rate of labor n, and the tax rates t_r and t_w, Eq. (12–59) may be solved for the steady-state value of the capital-labor ratio k. From k all other variables may be derived including the payments to labor and capital.

The values that t_w and t_r may take are limited by the requirement to satisfy the government budget constraint (12–52). We may use this latter constraint to eliminate t_w from Eq. (12–59). From Eq. (12–52), $t_w = (g - t_r rk)/w$. Substitution into Eq. (12–59) gives:

$$0 = s_w[f(k) - g] + \frac{(s_r - s_w)\, kf'(k)}{1 + t_r} - nk. \tag{12–60}$$

Equation (12–60) now contains two variables, an endogenous one, k, and an exogenous one, t_r. Since the equation is nonlinear, we cannot easily solve for k as a function of t_r. Instead, by totally differentiating it, we can solve for dk as a function of dt_r as follows:

$$\frac{dk}{dt_r} = \frac{(s_r - s_w)kf'(k)/(1 + t_r)^2}{s_w f'(k) + (s_r - s_w)[f'(k) + kf''(k)]/(1 + t_r) - n}. \tag{12–61}$$

This gives the change in k that will result from an incremental increase in t_r and fall in t_w, which yields the same steady-state revenue to the government.

Equation (12–61) is a complicated expression indeed. Yet, we can make some qualitative statements regarding the effect of substituting a capital tax for a labor tax so as to raise the same revenue.

(i) The right-hand side of Eq. (12–61) will be negative as long as $s_r > s_w$. The numerator is positive by inspection. The denominator represents the derivative of the right-hand side of Eq. (12–55) with respect to k. It must be negative if the dynamic system is to be stable.[30] This result is intuitively plausible. If savings out of capital incomes exceed that out of wage incomes, increasing the tax on the former and reducing the tax on the latter will reduce the overall savings rate and reduce capital formation. The new steady-state equilibrium will have a lower wage-rental ratio, and part of the tax burden will have been shifted to labor income.

(ii) To get some idea of the parameters that are important in determining the amount of dynamic shifting that takes place, we note the following definition of the elasticity of substitution:

$$\sigma = -\frac{\alpha f'(k)}{kf''(k)} \tag{12–62}$$

where α is labor's gross-of-tax share of output in GNP.[31] Using this definition and Eq. (12–57), Eq. (12–61) can be written:

$$\frac{dk}{dt_r} = \frac{(s_r - s_w)\, r/(1 + t_r)}{s_w r(1 + t_r) + (s_r - s_w)r[1 + (\alpha/\sigma)] - n}. \tag{12–63}$$

dk/dt_r will be larger the larger is the difference between s_r and s_w, the larger is the elasticity of substitution σ, and the smaller is labor's share α.

The analysis can, of course, be complicated by adding more sectors or more taxes, and by making the savings rates dependent upon the rates of return. Not much more insight is gained into the problem by so doing. Perhaps the greatest drawback to the above analysis is that it is confined to steady states. The same sort of conceptual question arises as in the comparative static case. How are we to interpret the exercise? As an analysis of the process of movement from one steady-state equilibrium to another, it is not too useful, since it may take considerable time to go from one steady state to the other. During this time, many other things will have changed. On the other hand, it could be considered a hypothetical comparison between an economy growing under one sort of tax regime with what the economy might have looked like under an alternative set of taxes. If this latter interpretation is used, as would seem to be plausible, we still lack a dynamic analysis of the process of tax shifting in a growing economy.

(b) Land Rent Taxation in an Intertemporal Economy

Let us now develop somewhat more formally the analysis of land rent taxation in an intertemporal economy. While we shall not present a complete analysis of the problem here, it is fairly straightforward to sketch a framework within which the source of the differences between the Feldstein, and Calvo, Kotlikoff and Rodriguez analyses (discussed earlier) can be identified. We begin with a description of an economy with no land taxes, and then consider the imposition of a tax on land rents.

First, we assume the total population of the economy is constant over time, that a new generation is born each period, and that each generation lives for two periods. In the first period of life, each household enjoys c_1 units of consumption, and supplies L units of labor. In the second period, the household consumes c_2. The amount of labor supplied per capita is assumed constant, and the amount of land per capita, also constant, is denoted by T. The amount of capital per capita, K, is measured in the same units as the consumption good, and is determined according to the consumption/savings decisions of households. Per capita production in the economy is a function of L, T, and K, say, $F(L, T, K)$, and if factors are hired competitively, each will be paid according to its marginal product, denoted F_L, F_T, and F_K respectively. Note that since capital is the only variable factor, these marginal products will vary only with K. In particular, we assume that F_L and F_T increase, and F_K decreases, with increases in K. It is precisely through these relationships that a land tax, by changing K, can change factor prices and thus be shifted.

Each household attempts to maximize its lifetime utility, which depends on c_1, c_2, and, possibly, the utility of its children. In fact, let us consider the intergenerational utility-maximizing model first, for convenience. The household's choices are constrained as follows: In the second period of its life, the household expends resources on consumption c_2 and, if desired, on a bequest, b. The household has no earnings, however, and so these expenditures can be financed only by drawing down savings, plus interest on savings, from the first period in life. The interest rate will equal the marginal product of capital, F_K, since this is the price producers would be willing to pay for the use of a unit of capital for one period, so that if s is the amount saved when young, the second-period budget constraint is

$$c_2 + b = s(1 + F_K), \tag{12–64}$$

or

$$\frac{c_2}{1 + F_K} + \frac{b}{1 + F_K} = s. \tag{12–65}$$

When a household leaves a bequest, that bequest is received by a household (the child) in the first period of life. For simplicity, let us confine all of our discussion to *steady states* of the economy, that is, situations where the amount of capital, factor prices, and hence all household decisions, are the same from period to period. In particular, the amount of bequest received by a household when young is equal to the amount it eventually pays when old, namely, b. Each household's income when young, therefore, is $F_L L + b$, its wage income plus the bequest it receives. Its savings, s, is equal to this income less consumption c_1. Substituting into (12–65), we have the household's lifetime budget constraint:

$$c_1 + \frac{c_2}{1 + F_K} + \frac{b}{1 + F_K} = F_L L + b. \tag{12–66}$$

This is actually the form of the budget constraint in an economy with no bequests as well, the only difference being that $b = 0$ on each side. In either case, the interpretation is that the present value of expenditures over the life cycle equals the present value of receipts.

We must now specify exactly how saving takes place in the economy. All saving is carried out by the young, who use their savings to purchase assets that they can sell in old age. One asset is capital, the other is land. Let the price of land relative to capital and consumption be p. (In a steady state, p is constant over time.) Then, at the beginning of a period of time, the households who have just become old own the amount, K, of capital per capita, and land worth pT per capita, which they wish to sell, while the new young generation, with savings of $s = F_L L + b - c$, per capita, wishes to buy assets. In equilibrium, the demand for assets must equal the supply, or

$$F_L L + b - c_1 = K + pT. \tag{12-67}$$

Of course, households are willing to hold both land and capital as assets only if the rates of return from holding each are equal. The return per dollar's worth of capital is F_K, while a unit of land returns F_T to its owner at a cost of p. Thus, in equilibrium, we must have $F_T/p = F_K$, or

$$p = \frac{F_T}{F_K}. \tag{12-68}$$

Note that p is exactly the present value of the perpetual rent stream F_T, discounted at the interest rate F_K.

Let us now examine the effect of a land rent tax in this economy, at a rate t. We suppose that the tax proceeds are disposed of by paying them out to old households, although the conclusions would be unaffected if the tax revenues were paid to the young.

To analyze the effect of the tax, let us suppose at first that the capital stock, and hence all factor prices, remains unchanged. We can follow through the implications of this assumption, and if all of the conditions for equilibrium in the economy can still be satisfied, we can conclude that the supposition is correct.

With K fixed, the first point to observe is that the price of land must fall by the present value of future tax payments. This follows from the equilibrium condition of equal net returns on land and capital, $(1 - t) F_T/p' = F_K$ or

$$p' = \frac{(1 - t)F_T}{F_K} = \frac{F_T}{F_K} - \frac{tF_T}{F_K} \tag{12-69}$$

where p' is the new equilibrium price of land.

Next, observe that the household budget constraint in the presence of the tax becomes

$$c_1 + \frac{c_2}{1 + F_K} + \frac{b}{1 + F_K} = F_L L + b + \frac{tF_T T}{1 + F_K} \tag{12-70}$$

due to the receipt of the government's revenue of $tF_T T$ in old age. Clearly, if b is unchanged, this will increase lifetime wealth and cause an increase in consumption in each period (assuming c_1 and c_2 are normal goods). Suppose, however, that b changes to $b' = b - tF_T T/F_K$ when the tax is imposed. This means that the left-hand side of (12–70) falls by

$$\frac{tF_T T}{F_K(1 + F_K)} \tag{12-71}$$

because of the reduction in future bequest payouts. The right-hand side of (12–70) falls by

$$\frac{tF_T T}{F_K} - \frac{tF_T T}{1 + F_K} \tag{12-72}$$

because of a reduction in bequests received when young, coupled with an increase in future income. Finding a common denominator of $F_K(1 + F_K)$ for the terms in (12–72), we see that the expressions in (12–71) and (12–72) are equal, that is, if bequests fall to b' when the tax is imposed, the opportunity set for lifetime consumption c_1 and c_2 will be unchanged. Since preferences are the same before and after the tax, the choice of c_1 and c_2, and hence lifetime utility, will be unaffected for every generation.

Finally, consider what happens to the asset market equilibrium. If bequests fall to b', then with K and c_1 unchanged, the amount of saving by the young will fall by $tF_T T/F_K$. The total value of assets being sold by the old falls by the same amount because, by (12–69), the price of land has fallen. Each side of (12–67), therefore, falls by the same amount, so that asset markets remain in equilibrium.

In sum, we have shown that all of the conditions for equilibrium in the economy continue to hold, once a land tax is imposed, if (a) land values fall by the capitalized value of future taxes; (b) bequests fall by the same amount; and (c) all other variables in the economy—consumption, the capital stock, and all factor prices—remain unchanged. It follows that the tax is not shifted, the conclusion reached by Calvo, Kotlikoff, and Rodriguez.

It is now easy to see how the contrary conclusion could be reached by Feldstein, in a world with no intergenerational transfers. Again, we suppose provisionally that the capital stock remains fixed after the land tax is imposed.

First, according to the household budget constraint (12–70), with $b = 0$, lifetime wealth rises by $tF_T T(1 + F_K)$. First-period consumption therefore rises by $\Delta c_1/\Delta y$ times this amount, if we let $\Delta c_1/\Delta y$ denote the extra period 1 consumption carried out per dollar increase in lifetime wealth. Note that this did not occur in the model with bequests.

Now consider the asset-market equilibrium conditions. Again, the price of land must fall to p', as shown in (12–69), in order to preserve equal net rates of return on land and capital. The effect of the tax is therefore to disturb the equilibrium condition (12–67) in two ways (recalling that now $b = 0$). Because lifetime wealth has risen, the demand for assets falls by $(tF_T T/[1 + F_K]) (\Delta c_1/\Delta y)$. Because the price of land falls, the value of assets supplied falls by $tF_T T/F_K$. Both because $F_K < 1 + F_K$, and because $\Delta c_1/\Delta y < 1$ (if c_2 is normal), the first of these expressions is smaller than the second; that is, the reduction in asset value is greater than the reduction in savings. The asset market therefore cannot be in equilibrium at the pre-tax value of K: Households will wish to save more, which can only be done by increasing the stock of capital. But this, as we have already discussed, lowers the net return on capital, and causes the net return on land to fall by less than the amount of the tax. This establishes Feldstein's conclusion that the tax is shifted.

CHAPTER NOTES

1. See Musgrave (1959), Ch. 12, for a fuller discussion of the concepts of balanced-budget and differential incidence.

2. Typically, selective excise taxes on goods are levied upon the net price of the goods if they are *ad valorem* taxes. Payroll or factor taxes are usually levied on the gross price (i.e. deducted from wages by applying the tax rate to the pretax wage). From an analytical point of view, it makes no difference whether the tax is based upon the gross price or the net price, since they are ultimately equivalent. To see this, suppose p_n is the net price and p_g is the gross price. If the tax is based on the net price at the rate t_n:

$$p_n(1 + t_n) = p_g.$$

If the tax is based on the gross price at the rate t_g:

$$p_n = p_g(1 - t_g).$$

Comparing these two expressions, the same divergence between p_n and p_g will occur under the two taxes if $1 - t_g = 1/(1 + t_n)$, or $t_g = t_n/(1 + t_n)$.

3. For example, the more substitutable are other factors for the taxed factor, the more elastic will be the demand for the taxed factor, and the greater will be the burden of the tax on suppliers.

4. One might argue that the demand and supply curves have been drawn to take the use of the tax revenues into account. Nonetheless, the use of the tax revenues is also likely to influence prices on other markets.

5. For example, with perfectly inelastic factor supplies, the partial equilibrium analysis of a general factor or income tax is completely correct. In this case the factor being taxed bears the entire burden of the tax, as would be predicted from a partial equilibrium analysis with inelastic supply.

6. It can be shown that a per-unit tax imposed on a monopoly industry will result in a higher price than an *ad valorem* tax yielding the same revenue. This is the same thing as saying that a per-unit tax that results in the same output and price (inclusive of the tax) as an *ad valorem* tax will result in lower tax revenues. Under competitive conditions, *ad valorem* and per-unit taxes are equivalent. Proofs of these propositions may be found in Musgrave (1959), pp. 287–311. For a comparison of the welfare effects of the two taxes, see Bishop (1968).

7. This approach to tax incidence theory was pioneered by Harberger (1962). Its full implications have been drawn out by Mieszkowski (1967). Some useful survey articles of the general equilibrium theory of tax incidence are Mieszkowski (1969), Break (1974), and McLure (1975a).

8. Analytical descriptions of the two-sector static neoclassical general equilibrium model may be found in Jones (1965), Johnson (1971), and Caves and Jones (1973).

9. Production functions of this sort have the important property that, in competitive conditions, when all factors of production are receiving the value of their marginal products as payments, the total product is just exhausted, so no pure profits exist. The production functions are industry production functions. The constant returns-to-scale property may be taken to imply that identical firms within an industry can be replicated. An industry's output may be doubled by doubling the number of firms. Even though individual firms may have U-shaped cost curves, the industry as a whole will have horizontal cost curves. Competition ensures that each firm will produce at the minimum point on its average cost curve.

10. Even though an industry X is capital-intensive at one value of r/w, it need not be capital-intensive at all values of r/w. That is, so-called "factor-intensity reversals" may take place if the elasticities of substitution differ between the two industries. Such a phenomenon has played an important role in the theory of international trade, but we may safely neglect it here. For a discussion of it, see Minhas (1962).

11. Income effects are not entirely washed out by this assumption, due to the fact that there is a deadweight loss in real income involved in levying the tax. The exact nature of the approximation involved in ignoring income effects on demand is discussed in Appendix I.

12. The point elasticity of substitution is given in differential terms by:

$$\sigma = -\frac{d(K/L)}{K/L} \div \frac{d(r/w)}{r/w}.$$

13. For a full description of the CES production function, see Arrow, Chenery, Minhas, and Solow (1961). A special case of the CES production function occurs when $\sigma = 1$. That is the Cobb-Douglas production function which may be written:

$$X = AL^{\alpha}K^{1-\alpha}$$

where A is a scale parameter, and α is a constant less than one. In fact one can show that α is the share of labor in output and $(1 - \alpha)$ is the share of capital. With an elasticity of substitution of unity, these shares are constant since rK/wL is constant when $\sigma = 1$ from Eq. 12–1.

14. In this model with no savings, a general commodity tax is identical to a general income tax, since all income is spent on consumption goods.

15. This output effect is equivalent to the so-called Stolper-Samuelson (1941) theorem in international trade. This theorem says that when a tariff is imposed on imports in the two-sector neoclassical model, the price of the factor used intensively in the import-competing industry rises, and the price of the other factor falls.

16. One might expect the corporate sector to be more capital-intensive than the unincorporated sector, in which case both the output and factor substitution effects would make capital owners worse off.

17. Strictly speaking, this equivalence is valid only if property owners cannot change the time pattern of investment in property. As Bentick (1979) and others have shown, there is an incentive to accelerate the timing of property development under a tax on current market value, whereas this is not so for a tax on the current income from property.

18. From Eq. (12–12), a fall in t_r must be accompanied by a rise in $(1 - t_f)\pi/p$. Therefore, rentiers' real income, $(1 - t_f)(\pi/p)\beta$, must rise and so must their consumption.

19. This neglects any benefits that might accrue to workers from the increase in government expenditures.

20. Asimakopulos and Burbidge also consider a model in which unemployment is allowed to exist.

21. That is, $p_X X = w_X L_X + r_X K_x$. Dividing through by $p_X X$ yields $\theta_{LX} + \theta_{KX} = 1$.

22. The technical reason for this is as follows: By Walras' law, if all budget constraints in a general equilibrium system are satisfied, and if all markets clear (supply equals demand) except for one, then necessarily the last market must also clear. This means that in analyzing the equilibrium, or changes in the equilibrium, in such a system, we can dispense with one of the market clearing conditions. In our system, we shall dispense with market clearing for Y, so we need not worry about its demand or supply conditions. If the markets for X, L, and K all clear, the market for Y must necessarily clear by Walras' law. For an exposition of Walras' law in simple general equilibrium models, see Henderson and Quandt (1980).

23. For a discussion of the notion of a demand curve constrained by the economy's production possibility curve, see Bailey (1954).

24. Total differentiation of Eq. (12–23) gives:

$$dX = f_L\, dL_X + f_K\, dK_X.$$

Multiply through by p_X to get:

$$p_X\, dX = p_X f_L\, dL_X + p_X f_K\, dK_X.$$

From the marginal productivity conditions of profit maximization,

$$p_X\, dX = w_X\, dL_X + r_X\, dK_X.$$

25. If taxes exist at the start of the comparative static exercise, the algebra complicates considerably. For an analysis of this case, see Vandendorpe and Friedlaender (1976).

26. This is because E is always negative. As well, $\theta_{KY} - \theta_{KX}$ always has an opposite sign to $K_X/K_Y - L_X/L_Y$ starting at the no-tax situation. This follows directly from the definitions of θ_{KX} and θ_{LX}.

27. In the discrete change case, $\Delta(K/L) = \Delta K/L - K\,\Delta L/L^2 - \Delta K \Delta L/L^2$, so that Eq. (12–54) reads $s = \Delta K + K\,\Delta L/L - \Delta K \Delta L/L^2$. The latter term involving second-order changes is neglected when one uses the differential analysis to estimate discrete changes, or when one interprets differential changes as discrete ones.

28. See the classic article by Solow (1956) for an analysis of the steady state and its stability properties.

29. These expressions are obtained as follows. The marginal productivity conditions imply the following:

$$r(1 + t_r) = \partial F/\partial K$$
$$w(1 + t_W) = \partial F/\partial L$$

Since $f = F/L$, $\partial F/\partial K = \partial(Lf)/\partial K = L\, \partial f/\partial k \cdot \partial k/\partial K = \partial f/\partial k = f'$. Therefore, Eq. (12–57) follows. Similarly, $\partial F/\partial L = \partial(Lf)/\partial L = f + L\partial f/\partial k \cdot \partial k/\partial L = f - k\, \partial f/\partial k$. This is just Eq. (12–56).

30. This was proven in Solow (1956). Stability requires that any increase in k above the steady-state value automatically sets forces in motion to reduce it; and any reduction in k below the steady-state value causes k to rise. Equation (12–55) is the equation determining changes in the value of k. In the steady state, the left-hand side $dk = 0$. If k rises slightly, stability requires that dk be negative. In other words, the differential of the right-hand side of Eq. (12–55) must be negative.

31. The elasticity of substitution may be written:

$$\sigma = -\frac{dk}{d(r/w)} \cdot \frac{r}{wk}$$

where $k = K/L$ as above. From footnote 29, we know that $r = f'(k)$ and $w = f(k) - kf'(k)$. Using these, we derive:

$$d\frac{r}{w} = d\left[\frac{f'(k)}{f(k) - kf'(k)}\right] = \frac{f(k)f''(k)\,dk}{w^2}.$$

Substituting this for $d(r/w)$ in the expression for σ, we obtain:

$$\sigma = -\frac{dk\,w^2}{f(k)f''(k)\,dk} \cdot \frac{r}{wk} = -\frac{\alpha f'(k)}{kf''(k)}$$

where $\alpha = w/f(k)$ is the share of labor in outputs.

13

The United States Tax Structure

INTRODUCTION

13–1 In the United States, taxes are levied by various levels of government and on various sources. While we cannot hope to go into the full details of the provisions applicable to each type of tax,[1] we shall survey the most important economic characteristics of the taxes. Each of these characteristics will have implications for the equity or economic efficiency of the tax system, or both. The main taxes that will be discussed here include the personal income tax, corporation tax, consumption taxes of various sorts, property taxes, and estate and gift taxes. No attempt will be made to discuss export and import tariffs (or customs duties), or minor sources of revenue such as license fees. The payroll tax is discussed in Chapter 14 in connection with social security.

Different levels of government rely on different sources of tax revenues. The federal government generates the bulk of its revenue from personal and corporate income taxes, and payroll taxes, with lesser amounts from specific excise taxes, and estate and gift taxes. States use mainly income taxes and general retail sales taxes to varying degrees, and local governments rely heavily on property taxation. Table 13–1 shows the proportions of total tax revenues generated by each type of tax for each level of government.

THE PERSONAL INCOME TAX

13–2 The personal income tax is the largest source of revenue to the federal government, presumably because it is perceived as being the tax that can be made to conform most closely to widely held notions of horizontal and

Table 13-1   Revenue from Own Sources, by Source and Level of Government 1981–82

Source	Federal Amount ($ Millions)	Federal % of Total	State Amount ($ Millions)	State % of Total	Local Amount ($ Millions)	Local % of Total
Individual Income Tax	298,111	43.5	45,708	17.5	5,078	2.6
Corporation Income Tax	49,207	7.2	14,006	5.4	1,027	0.5
Property Tax	—	—	3,113	1.2	78,805	40.0
General Sales Tax	—	—	50,343	19.2	10,240	5.2
Custom Duties	8,917	1.3	—	—	—	—
Selective Excise Taxes and Liquor Store Revenue	36,758	5.4	31,312	12.0	5,086	2.6
Motor Vehicle and Operator Licenses	—	—	6,051	2.3	409	0.2
Utility Revenue	—	—	2,085	0.8	28,182	14.3
Charges and Miscellaneous General Revenue	90,896	13.3	43,338	16.6	59,599	30.2
Death and Gift Taxes	7,991	1.2	2,350	0.9	—	—
Insurance Trust Revenue (Payroll Tax)	189,814	27.7	50,848	19.4	5,257	2.7
Other Taxes	4,141	0.6	12,630	4.8	3,487	1.8
Total Own-Source Revenue	685,835		261,784		197,168	

Source: United States Department of Commerce (1983a), Table 4, p. 19.

vertical equity. Yet there are several provisions of the tax that have been enacted for other reasons, mainly to give an incentive to taxpayers to make certain types of expenditures. In assessing the personal income tax, we shall attempt to indicate how the structure of the tax relates to the characteristics of an equitable tax, as discussed in Chapter 10, as well as to indicate the distortions it introduces.

The overall computation of individual income tax payments proceeds in the following steps: First, the individual totals up money income receipts from various defined sources to arrive at a figure called *adjusted gross income,* or AGI. Next the individual is allowed to reduce the AGI by the amount of *personal exemptions* and *deductions* that reflect family circumstances or that allow for a variety of personal expenditures deemed, for one reason or another, to be untaxable. The sum resulting after making these subtractions from AGI is called *taxable income.* The tax payable is calculated by applying the *rate structure* to taxable income. In arriving at the final tax liability, certain tax credits can then be applied. Each of these steps is discussed in turn.

(a) Adjusted Gross Income

The concept of AGI, although it includes the flow of income from a variety of sources, is much less broadly defined than the comprehensive income base discussed in Chapter 10. The latter included all additions to net worth plus current consumption. AGI, on the other hand, omits several items which are part of the comprehensive income base, and therefore violates the criterion of horizontal equity as defined by the latter. The following summarizes the main ways in which AGI differs from the comprehensive income base.

(i) *Imputed Income*   Imputed income is generally excluded from AGI, presumably due to the difficulties of measurement. This is especially important in the case of imputed rent on owner-occupied housing.

(ii) *Transfers*   Gifts and inheritances received, although additions to net worth are not included as part of AGI. The fact that the donor may have been taxed upon giving them is not relevant from the point of view of the equitable treatment of recipients. Transfer payments, such as social security benefits, are not currently included in AGI. Unemployment insurance (UI) benefits are, however, partially taxable. For a married couple filing a joint return, one-half of the excess, over $18,000, of other AGI plus unemployment benefits is subject to taxation, up to the amount of unemployment benefits received. For a married individual filing a separate return, one-half of all UI benefits are taxable; for single and other taxpayers, one-half of the excess of other AGI and UI benefits over $12,000 is included in taxable income. Again, in both of these latter cases, the total amount added to AGI on account of UI benefits is limited to the total amount of benefits received. (Beginning in 1984, social security benefits will be treated similarly to UI: one-half of benefits will be taxable, if benefits and other income exceed a specified minimum.)

Since employee contributions to these social insurance plans are not tax deductible, it could be argued that it would be equitable not to tax the benefits from them. Employer contributions on behalf of employees are, however, deducted from tax (not included in AGI), so, to that extent at least, receipts should be included. Moreover, there is an efficiency issue involved. If one is concerned that the social security system creates undesirable incentives for early retirement, or if UI benefits encourage workers to remain unemployed, failure to tax these benefits strengthens these adverse incentive effects (see Feldstein [1973b], for example, on unemployment insurance). For this reason as well, it has been argued that such transfer payments should be taxed like ordinary income.

(iii) *Capital Gains*   Capital gains are not fully included in AGI. Forty percent of realized capital gains on assets held over 12 months are added to AGI, as well as the full capital gain on those held for shorter periods.[2]

One-half of long-term capital losses may be deducted from current income up to $3000, and amounts in excess of that may be carried forward. Also, the tax due on the capital gain from the sale of a home is deferred if a new home is purchased with the proceeds within two years; and if the taxpayer is age 55 or older, up to $125,000 of the gain from the sale of a house is completely exempt from taxation.

The inclusion of capital gains when realized rather than accrued is done out of administrative convenience. We have already seen that this produces a "lock-in" effect, discouraging the realization of such gains. The preferential rate treatment given to capital gains has been justified on several grounds. It may be regarded as a rough adjustment for the fact that a portion of capital gains will be illusory in times of inflation, and therefore should not be taxed. Or, it may reflect a recognition that capital gains are one form in which corporate profits accrue to the owners of corporations. Since these profits have already been taxed at the corporate level, preferential treatment at the personal level mitigates the effects of double taxation. This is discussed more fully in Section 13–3, below. Finally, preferential treatment of capital gains is often justified on the basis of avoiding giving a disincentive to risky investments. As we saw in Chapter 11, the theoretical case for this view has yet to be made.

(iv) *Dividends*   The first $100 ($200 for married taxpayers filing joint returns) of dividends received is also excluded.[3] This exclusion might be justified on grounds of administrative convenience, to save the taxpayers and government the trouble of keeping track of relatively small sums. Alternatively, it can be argued, as in (iii) above, that dividends originate with corporate profits that are already heavily taxed. The exemption of dividends, although limited in size, benefits high-income earners relative to low. Since the value of a reduction in taxable income to the taxpayer is the resulting tax saving, and that depends on the individual's marginal tax rate, persons in higher tax brackets obtain more relief than do those in lower tax brackets. Therefore, this remedy is not equitable as a means of avoiding double taxation; nor is the capital gains exclusion equitable, for that matter. A more equitable solution to the double taxation problem might be to allow tax credits on the excess taxes paid.[4]

(v) *Interest on State and Local Bonds*   One of the most important exclusions from AGI is interest payments received on state and local bonds. Once again, this provision is of much more benefit to those in higher tax brackets than those in lower ones. In addition, the provision diverts funds from more risky investments to financing state and local borrowing, and encourages the financing of state and local public expenditures by debt.[5] One justification for it is that it facilitates the transfer of federal funds into the hands of state and local governments.[6] It is, however, a very inefficient way of doing so. To the extent that interest rates on these bonds do not fall by the full amount of the tax reduction, part of the benefits go to taxpayers who own such bonds (especially those in the high tax brackets), rather than to the state or local government. An outright transfer of public funds would be both more efficient and more equitable.

(vi) *Pension and IRA Contributions and Distributions*   Employer contributions to pension funds are not included in the AGI of employees, while employee contributions are included. When a worker retires, pension benefits equal to the employee's contributions are excluded from AGI, while other benefits are included. The interest on funds accumulating over the working years is not taxable as it accrues, but it is taxable when paid out as retirement benefits. In addition, workers may establish Individual Retirement Accounts (IRAs), under which up to $2000 of earnings annually (up to $2000 each, if both husband and wife work, or up to $2250 if one spouse is non-working and married, filing jointly) may be excluded from AGI and deposited into an interest-bearing account. These funds may accumulate interest tax-free until age seventy, but cannot be withdrawn prior to age sixty without penalty. When the funds are paid out (distributions must begin no later than age seventy), they are then subject to taxation. Thus, employer pension contributions and IRA contributions are subject to special tax treatment in two respects: First, the funds in the pension or IRA accounts can compound at the before-tax rate of interest; second, since earnings-plus-interest are only taxable upon retirement, the taxes are deferred, and are generally taxable at lower rates because taxable income tends to be lower during retirement. Such provisions tend to move the tax system in the direction of a consumption or expenditure tax, and give rise to the efficiency and equity effects already discussed in Chapters 9 and 10. From the perspective of comprehensive income taxation, these special provisions are inequitable, but a consumption tax advocate would argue the opposite. If IRA provisions continue to be liberalized, as they have been in recent years, the movement toward an expenditure tax may become, *de facto,* quite substantial.

(b) Exemptions and Deductions

To arrive at taxable income, a taxpayer is permitted certain exemptions and deductions from AGI. A fixed, per capita, exemption of $1000 is allowed for the taxpayer, for the spouse if a joint return is filed, and for each dependent. Additional $1000 exemptions are available for taxpayers who are over age 65 or blind, and similarly for spouses, if filing jointly. The rationale for such exemptions could be, in part, that they raise the progressivity of the average tax rate structure, as we saw in Section 11–2. Exemptions are also sometimes justified on ability-to-pay grounds, as discussed in part c(iv), *The Family Unit,* below.

In addition to exemptions, further deductions are allowed on certain categories of expenditure. To claim these deductions, a taxpayer must itemize them on the income tax return, and itemizations must exceed the zero tax rate income bracket limits discussed below. These amounts are $2300 for single taxpayers and heads of household (unmarried taxpayers with dependents), $3400 for married taxpayers filing joint returns, and $1700 for married taxpayers filing separate returns. There are four main categories of itemized deductions.

(i) *Medical Expenses*   In general, medical and dental expenses in excess of 5 percent of AGI are deductible. For medicines and drugs, only expenditures in excess of 1 percent of AGI can be added in to determine total medical expenditures. (The 1 percent limitation has been eliminated for tax years after 1983.) Health and dental insurance premiums are deductible, and other expenses such as physicians' fees, the cost of hospital services, etc., are deductible except insofar as they are covered by insurance. The rationale for these deductions is that ability to pay should be defined net of major health expenditures, so that equity dictates that special allowances be given to taxpayers who incur such expenditures.

(ii) *Interest Expense*   Interest payments of all sorts by taxpayers are deductible from their AGI. This may be justified to the extent that such deductions represent the cost of earning capital income elsewhere, and the latter is taxed. However, many interest payments are on consumer loans used to purchase houses or other consumer durables. Since the latter yield a return in the form of imputed income, which is not included in the tax base, there is no justification on equity grounds for deductions on interest paid to finance them. As well as being inequitable, it gives an incentive to become a homeowner rather than a renter.

(iii) *State and Local Taxes*   Deductions are given for taxes paid to state and local governments, including income taxes, property taxes, and general sales taxes. Various justifications have been advanced for this deduction. For example, the taxes might be regarded as a cost of earning income. However, to the extent that the taxes yield offsetting benefits in the form of local public goods, it is hard to justify on equity grounds. Another possible rationale is that it makes it easier for state and local governments to raise taxes, and reflects an implicit transfer of federal funds to local governments. While this may be true, it is not clear that it is the most efficient or equitable way of making intergovernmental transfers. The states and localities with the highest tax rates benefit most. We shall return to the problem of the appropriate form of intergovernmental transfers in Chapter 15.

(iv) *Charitable Donations*   Charitable donations to religious, educational, and other nonprofit organizations are fully tax-deductible for those who itemize their deductions, and are partially deductible for non-itemizers. The grounds for this deduction is presumably that of efficiency. To the extent that these organizations provide services of the nature of a public good, or emit significant external economies, some subsidy is required to provide an incentive to support them financially. Note, however, that the implicit subsidy depends on the taxpayer's marginal tax rate t: A one dollar contribution costs $(1 - t)$ net, which equals as little as fifty cents for a high tax-bracket taxpayer, but rises to eighty-nine cents for low-bracket individuals. (Non-itemizers may deduct 25 percent of the first $100 of contributions. For them, the cost of the contribution is a full dollar for contributions in excess of $100.) There seems to be no efficiency basis for the difference in subsidy rates, since there does not seem to be any reason to believe that the rate at which external benefits are generated from donations of higher-income persons exceeds that at which they are generated from donations of low-income persons. If not, a tax credit or subsidy method would be more efficient. It is of course possible that donations by different income groups could go systematically to different organizations that yield different external benefits. If this were so, efficiency would call for different rates of subsidy to different income groups. But that case has yet to be made empirically.

(c) The Rate Structure and Tax Credits

After the various exemptions and deductions are eliminated from AGI, the resulting *taxable income* forms the basis for computing tax payable, using the appropriate structure of tax rates. There are a number of noteworthy properties of the rate structure applicable in the United States which are discussed below.

(i) *Progression* The structure of income tax rates is progressive in terms of both marginal and average tax rates, although the rate structures differ by type of taxpayer, as seen in Table 13–2. Each type of taxpayer has a zero-rate bracket, showing the amount of taxable income that is not actually taxed. This amount is $2300 for single taxpayers and heads of household, $3400 for married taxpayers filing jointly, and $1700 for married taxpayers filing separately. The next income bracket in each case is subject to taxation at an 11 percent rate, and the rates rise gradually thereafter until a maximum rate of 50 percent is achieved. Over the same range of incomes, average rates vary from zero to 35.4 percent of taxable income. Including exemptions makes the average tax rate structure appear even more progressive, at least beyond the zero-rate brackets. For single taxpayers, for instance, the average tax rate relative to AGI ranges from zero percent at AGI = $2300, to .32 percent at AGI = $3400, to 2.8 percent at AGI = $4400, eventually approaching the average tax rate on taxable income at the top of the scale. This latter calculation is somewhat misleading, however, since it neglects the fact that higher-income taxpayers are often better able to take advantage of the deductions that tend to lower taxable income, and hence lower the average tax rate as a proportion of AGI, at the higher income levels.

A problem arises in a system of progressive tax rates during periods of inflation. Since both tax rates and exemption levels are denominated in money income terms, their value in real terms changes during periods of inflation. Exemptions are worth less, and increases in money income put taxpayers into higher marginal tax brackets, even if their real incomes

Table 13–2 Federal Marginal and Average Income Tax Rates 1983, For Single and Married Taxpayers

Single Taxpayers		
Taxable Income ($)	*Marginal Rate (%)**	*Average Rate (%)†*
0– 2,300	0	0
2,300– 3,400	11	0
3,400– 4,400	13	3.6
4,400– 8,500	15	5.7
8,500–10,800	17	10.2
10,800–12,900	19	11.6
12,900–15,000	21	12.8
15,000–18,200	24	14.0
18,200–23,500	28	15.7
23,500–28,800	32	18.5
28,800–34,100	36	21.0
34,100–41,500	40	23.3
41,500–55,300	45	26.3
55,300–	50	31.0

Married Taxpayers Filing Jointly		
Taxable Income ($)	*Marginal Rate (%)**	*Average Rate (%)†*
0– 3,400	0	0
3,400– 5,500	11	0
5,500– 7,600	13	4.2
7,600– 11,900	15	6.6
11,900– 16,000	17	9.7
16,000– 20,200	19	11.5
20,200– 24,600	23	13.1
24,600– 29,900	26	14.9
29,900– 35,200	30	16.8
35,200– 45,800	35	18.8
45,800– 60,000	40	22.6
60,000– 85,600	44	26.7
85,600–109,400	48	31.9
109,400–	50	35.4

† Calculated as taxes paid per unit of taxable income at lower boundary of each bracket.
* Source: Internal Revenue Code.

have not changed. The net effect is a windfall transfer of real tax revenues to the government. Some governments (e.g. Canada) have eliminated this problem by indexing both the exemption levels and the rate structure (the tax brackets) to the rate of inflation. In this way, the tax structure is denominated in real terms rather than in money terms. Reforms of this sort have been the subject of recent debate in the United States, and indexing of tax brackets and exemptions is currently scheduled for implementation in 1985. It has been suggested, however, that tax indexing should be postponed or cancelled, and it is unclear at this writing what the final decision will be.

(ii) *Minimum Tax*   The goal of the *alternative minimum tax* is to extract more tax from those individuals who have succeeded in reducing their taxable income substantially by the use of various tax preferences. This tax is assessed on *alternative minimum taxable income,* and is equal to 20 percent of alternative minimum taxable income over $40,000 for married taxpayers filing jointly ($30,000 for single taxpayers), to the extent that this exceeds the regular income tax. Alternative minimum taxable income is essentially AGI plus various tax preference items, including the 60 percent long-term capital gains deduction, accelerated depreciation of real and personal property, excess depletion and drilling expenses, and certain stock options, the value of which is excluded from AGI, less deductions for charitable contributions, medical expenses, interest expense, and a few lesser items. The purpose of these minimum taxes is to close some of the loopholes that make the tax system inequitable.

(iii) *Income Averaging*   A tax system with progressive marginal tax rates discriminates unfairly against taxpayers whose income fluctuates from one year to the next.[7] The extra tax paid in high-income years is not offset by the tax saving in low-income years, since the latter is determined using a lower marginal rate than the former. To remedy this inequity, a limited amount of income averaging is allowed. Averaging is permitted if *averageable income,* the excess of taxable income in a given year over 120 percent of average taxable income of the previous four years, exceeds $3000. If so, an amount is computed that we may here call "averaged income," equal to the average of current income and 120 percent of the previous four years' incomes. If this averaged income had been realized in the previous four years, taxes then would have been higher; thus, four times the excess of the tax on averaged income, less the tax on 120 percent of average income of the previous four years, is assessed. In addition, in place of the tax on current income, the taxpayer pays a tax on the averaged income itself. Thus, the high current income is spread more evenly over five years, which reduces the extra tax imposed on the variable income, due to progressivity.

There are several deficiencies in this system, from both equity and efficiency viewpoints. First, since "averaged income" exceeds true average income, the amount of averaging is artificially limited for no apparent reason. Perhaps more important is the fact that, while increases in income can be averaged, decreases cannot be. Furthermore, the benefits of averaging do not accrue to low-income persons, due to the lower limit of $3000. Finally, a minor defect is that the system does not take into account tax rate changes that may have occurred in the meantime.

(iv) *The Family Unit* The tax system differentiates between families according to size and marital status. As noted above, $1,000 exemptions are available for taxpayers, spouses, and dependents. There is also a zero bracket, which varies by type of taxpaying unit, that excludes a certain amount of income from taxation. These features of the system can be justified on the grounds that a certain minimum amount of income, depending on family circumstances, is needed for "subsistence," or necessary expenditures, and that this minimum does not really provide any ability to pay taxes. One might question, however, whether a fixed per-capita exemption is appropriate, or whether dependents other than the spouse should be granted lower exemptions on the principle that there are certain economies of jointly-consumed goods enjoyed by a family unit.[8] On the other hand, dependents may necessitate extraordinary expenses for, say, education, which would add to the subsistence level of expenditures. It would seem that although existing provisions are unlikely to reflect subsistence expenditures very precisely, it is hard to say in which direction and by what amounts they should be modified. Indeed, the very concept of "subsistence" or "necessary" expenditure is quite problematic.

A second important question is how to treat married versus single taxpayers. Certain unavoidable conflicts arise between various desiderata, given a progressive tax system. (a) It might be desirable for a married couple to be treated as a taxpaying unit, with a tax levied on the unit independent of the division of income between husband and wife. (b) It might be desirable that all taxpaying units, whether they consist of single individuals or married couples, should be taxed identically; that is, the tax depends only on the unit's income, regardless of the family structure of the unit. (c) It might be desirable for the tax system to treat a couple identically, whether or not they are married; that is, a change in marital status should not be penalized or rewarded by the tax system. Unfortunately, (a), (b), and (c) are mutually incompatible if the tax system is progressive. To see this, note that the tax $T(Y)$ assessed on a given income is to depend only on Y, not on the family status of the unit earning this income, according to (b). By (a), the tax on husband and wife should depend only on their total income, $Y_H + Y_W$. By (c), the tax on H and W should be the same if they are taxed as a family or singly. Thus, we should have $T(Y_H + Y_W) = T(Y_H) + T(Y_W)$ for whatever incomes Y_H and Y_W the couple might earn. Only a linear, i.e. *proportional,* tax function $T(Y)$ can satisfy this equation, however. If $T(Y)$ is progressive, then one will obviously find that $T(Y_H + Y_W) > T(Y_H) + T(Y_W)$. That is, the tax is greater on the combined income than on the incomes taxed separately, provided that both spouses have some income.

Existing tax policy strikes a compromise among these goals by not achieving any of them. Since married couples are taxed as a unit, one can see, by comparing parts A and B of Table 13–2, that condition (b) is not satisfied. A given amount of income is taxed more favorably if it accrues to a married couple than if it accrues to a single individual. On the other hand, if two individuals with roughly equal incomes marry, it is clear that they will pay higher taxes as a result. The favorable tax treatment of the married unit is not sufficiently favorable to offset the progressivity of the system. Condition (c) is thus violated. This effect is mitigated, however, by a special deduction for couples, both of whom work. In computing AGI, a deduction of 10 percent of the lesser of $30,000 or the earnings of the spouse with lower earnings is permitted. This has two effects: On the one hand, it lowers the extra tax burden borne by a couple on account of their married status; on the other hand, it lowers by 10 percent the effective marginal rate of tax on the secondary earner, and this, in turn, has a substitution effect at the labor/leisure margin. This relief is not equivalent to full income-splitting, and couples with roughly equal earnings will still find it disadvantageous to be treated as married; thus (c) is still violated. On the other hand, by allowing this deduction, condition (a) is violated: A couple with a given total income will be treated more favorably if that income is earned in part by each spouse, than if it is earned only by one. Whether this system is the most satisfactory, feasible one is obviously open to question. As an additional complication, one may note that married couples, especially those with a sole earner, may enjoy the exclusion from taxation of imputed income from household work, and married couples in general may enjoy certain economies from living together. Ultimately, however, a trade-off among the three desiderata is simply unavoidable, and it is hard to see how to resolve the trade-off, other than by a judgment among conflicting values.[9]

(v) *Tax Credits*   There are a variety of tax credits, introduced for a variety of purposes, that are available to taxpayers. Here we discuss a few of the more important ones.

The *residential energy credit,* which is 15 percent of the first $2000 of expenditure on home insulation and other energy-saving items in the tax-payer's residence, has clearly been designed to serve as an incentive for energy-saving behavior. Note that the effective reduction in price is 15 percent for all home-owning taxpayers, in contrast to what the situation would be if a deduction were allowed. In the latter case, the amount of subsidy would be one minus the taxpayer's marginal tax rate for itemizers, and zero for non-itemizers.

The *credit for child and dependent care* is available for taxpayers who incur expenses for housekeeping or child care because they are working outside their homes. The credit is equal to a certain percentage of such expenses, up to a limit of $2400 for a single dependent, or $4800 for two or more. The taxpayer is credited with 30 percent of the expenses if AGI is $10,000 or less, with the percentage falling by one point for each $2000 of AGI above $10,000 until it reaches 20 percent at an AGI of $28,000. For taxpayers with AGI in excess of $28,000, the percentage remains at 20 percent. Such credits obviously increase the net return to market employment for secondary earners in families with children; this credit also works to some extent to reduce the extra tax imposed on two-earner married couples, although this is obviously true only for married couples with dependents. If the elasticity of labor supply of secondary workers is relatively high, an argument could be made for this credit on efficiency grounds.

An *earned income credit* is given to low-income workers with dependent children. The tax credit is equal to 10 percent of earned income up to $5000, provided that AGI is less than $6000. As AGI rises, however, the credit is limited to $500 minus 12.5 percent of AGI above $6000. This implies that the credit shrinks to zero at an AGI of $10,000. A rationale for this credit is that it increases the progressivity of the tax system, although one should observe that only low-income households that actually *earn* income and that have children are entitled to the credit, so that it is not available to many low-income households. Alternatively, the credit can be seen as a subsidy to encourage work by low-income earners. For instance, a married worker with dependent children, a non-working spouse, and earnings of $3000 with no additional income, obtains $1.10 after tax for every additional dollar of earnings (since the marginal tax rate is zero for such a taxpayer). On the other hand, the credit raises the effective tax rate at higher points in the scale: If the same worker earns $8000, the marginal tax rate is 15 percent, so that an extra dollar of earnings returns only $(1-.15-.125) = $.725, after one takes into account the loss of the earned income credit, for an effective marginal tax rate of almost 30 percent—a tax rate that is not otherwise attained until an income of nearly $30,000 is achieved. In other words, the credit lowers the effective marginal tax by 10 percent for very low income workers, but raises it by 12.5 percent for workers with incomes between $6000 and $10,000. The efficiency effects of this restructuring of incentives are obviously ambiguous. It is, however, relevant to observe that the higher marginal tax rate would apply to many more workers than the lower rate, since relatively few workers have AGI below $6000.

Finally, we mention a *tax credit for the elderly*. A credit is given to taxpayers over 65 equal to 15 percent of up to $2500 ($3750 for married, filing jointly). The 15 percent is only applied, however, to the excess of the $2500 ($3750) over social security benefits, and one-half of AGI in excess of $7500 (or $10,000 if married, filing jointly). Thus, a single taxpayer with social security income of $1500 would find the credit reduced by 7.5 percent for each dollar of AGI above $7500, until, with an AGI of $9500, the credit would drop to zero. Obviously this credit helps low-income elderly persons, especially those without much social security coverage, and this might be considered ethically desirable. Of course, as with all income-conditioned tax relief, there is an added distortion, in this case a marginal tax rate that is higher by 7.5 percent for taxpayers with AGIs from $7500 ($10,000 if married, filing jointly) up to perhaps $12,500 ($17,500), depending on the amount of social security benefits.

In conclusion, we should note that not only the federal government uses a personal income tax. In addition, almost all states also levy their own income taxes. For the most part, their provisions are very similar to the federal income tax, varying from state to state in minor ways. For example, some states allow deductions for interest earnings on federal securities. Also, as the federal tax allows a deduction for state and local taxes, some states allow deductions of federal taxes paid. Tax rates are also considerably lower than the federal rates, and personal exemptions higher, reflecting the lower amount of tax revenue involved from this source for states as compared with the federal government.

THE CORPORATION INCOME TAX

13–3   The corporation income tax is basically a tax on the accounting profits of corporations. As such, as we have seen in Section 11–5, it includes elements of a tax on the pure economic profits of firms, as well as a tax on imputed costs of firms such as risk and entrepreneurship. It may also be, partly, a tax on the normal returns to capital of a firm, to the extent that the firm is not able to fully deduct its true costs of capital, including depreciation and imputed interest. On efficiency grounds, the tax is an ideal tax to the extent that it falls upon pure profits. However, to the extent that it falls upon the returns to capital, risk, or entrepreneurship, it distorts the markets for these factors and possibly reduces their supply. The overall distorting effect on the economy is tempered by the fact that there is also a tax on labor, the payroll tax, which we discuss in Chapter 14. There remains a great deal of dispute among economists as to the magnitude of the distorting effects of the corporation income tax.

The equity effects of the tax are also under dispute. The base of the tax is corporation profits, which eventually show up as capital income (dividends or capital gains) of the owners of the corporation. Since this capital income is taxed by the corporation tax, and then again by the personal income tax on the owners, it has been argued that this constitutes a double taxation of capital income from corporate sources. If one wished to treat all sources of income alike, this might appear to violate the notion of horizontal equity. On the other hand, it may contribute to vertical equity to the extent that capital income is received relatively more by high-income persons, and one wishes to redistribute income. It is an imperfect way of achieving vertical equity, since the corporation tax rate applicable to capital income is the same, regardless of who is to receive it. Furthermore, this double taxation argument relies upon the assumption that the incidence of the tax is upon the recipients of capital income, and is not shifted to consumers or other factors of production. As we saw in Chapter 12, it is by no means certain that this will be the case. Nonetheless, there has been considerable interest in proposals to integrate the corporate and personal income taxes, and we shall return to them in (d) below.

First, we shall provide a general overview of the main provisions of the corporation income tax. The tax base will be discussed, followed by some of the more important deductions, and, finally, the rate structure.

(a) The Tax Base

The corporation income tax is not levied upon all income from capital. Rather, it is levied only on capital income earned by corporations. Income earned by unincorporated business is treated as personal income of the owners of the business, with full allowance for deductions of business expenses similar to those given under the corporation income tax. Businesses which do incorporate are subject to the corporation income tax, and their owners are also subject to the personal income tax on capital income earned through a corporation. Despite the apparent tax disadvantages of incorporating a firm, the latter is often done because of the substantial advantages of incorporating, including limited liability, and access to equity markets for financing.

The corporation income tax does not fall on all corporations. Those with thirty-five or fewer shareholders may elect to be treated as partnerships. That means that all corporate income is treated as personal income of the owners, and is taxed as such upon receipt. Financial institutions such as banks, insurance companies, and savings and loan associations are subject to the corporation tax, but they are given special treatment. Since financial institutions use part of their revenues to build up reserves for bad debts, the earnings they use to build up reserves are exempt from the tax. In general, these provisions have been very generous, and have allowed a deduction for build-up of reserves much in excess of actual loss experience. Savings banks are allowed to deduct up to 40 percent of taxable income. Commercial banks were allowed to deduct up to 1 percent of outstanding loans for reserve build-up in 1982. This has recently been reduced to 0.6 percent. In 1988, the amount deductible for reserves will be based upon the actual loss experience of the bank for the previous five years.

Also exempt from the tax are religious, education, and charitable organizations; fraternal organizations; trade associations; and labor unions. They are, however, taxed on unrelated business income, in order to prevent abuse and unfair competition. In addition, they must pay a tax of 2 percent on all net investment incomes. As a proportion of the tax base, these tax-exempt organizations are very small.

For those corporations that are subject to the tax, the tax base is their total revenue less certain allowable deductions, including current operating expenses and certain capital expenses. The next subsection discusses the nature of these expenses allowed, as well as other deductions, or preferential treatment of certain types of expenses or income.

(b) Deductions and Preferential Treatment

Taxable income of a corporation is simply total revenue less total allowable costs. Since some revenues and costs are given preferential treatment, and some cost items are difficult to measure, the computation of taxable income is not as straightforward as it appears. Some of the more important provisions are as follows.

(i) *Current Expenses* Current expenses include the costs of currently used inputs, such as labor, and intermediate inputs purchased elsewhere. This category of costs is relatively straightforward, except for a few ambiguous cases. For example, it is not clear how employee expense accounts ought to be treated—as a business cost, or as an element of the employee's wage or salary income. Currently, they tend to be treated as the former and, therefore, are not subject to tax. One could argue that they should be treated as part of the imputed income of the employee and subject to the personal income tax. Failing that, it could be argued that they ought not to be an allowable expense, on the grounds that to treat them as such is to subsidize the payment of imputed and untaxed personal income.

There are also some imputed costs that the firm cannot deduct, such as the cost involved in on-the-job training. This would be very difficult to measure in practice.

(ii) *Capital Expenses* Capital expenses consist of so-called *capital consumption allowances* and interest costs. Interest costs include all interest payments on interest-bearing debt issued by the corporation. Imputed interest on equity capital used is not allowed as a deduction. We have discussed the implications of this for investment in Section 11–5.

Capital consumption allowances consist of depreciation on capital and investment tax credits. When a corporation purchases new machinery or equipment, this equipment is generally assigned a 3- or 5-year service lifetime, according to rules in place since 1981, and discussed below. Essentially, vehicles such as automobiles and light trucks fall into the first category, with most other equipment treated as 5-year property. For 5-year property, a corporation is allowed a 10 percent investment tax credit in the year of purchase, and is permitted a 6 percent credit for 3-year property. No credit is allowed for investment in structures or real estate. This credit can be applied to a large portion of the corporation's current tax liabilities (the first $25,000 in tax liabilities plus 85 percent of tax liabilities over $25,000). Any credit beyond this can be carried back to the three prior tax years and carried forward for 15 years. Note that, like all tax credits, the investment tax credit reduces tax liabilities dollar for dollar, unlike deductions that reduce only taxable income. In order to obtain a reduction in tax paid equal to 10 percent of investment via deductions, a corporation in the 46 percent tax bracket would have to be allowed to deduct $10/46 \cong 22$ percent of the purchase price. This credit obviously provides a substantial incentive for firms to undertake new investment.

Corporations have also been allowed to depreciate the cost of capital assets, that is, to deduct from taxable income, over a series of years, the purchase price of the assets. Beginning in 1983, however, the cost to be depreciated is the purchase price less half of the investment tax credit claimed by the corporation. Alternatively, the corporation will be allowed to depreciate the entire cost if it claims an investment tax credit 2 percent less than otherwise obtainable.

The rates of depreciation on capital assets, and the lifetimes over which depreciation takes place, have recently been the subject of major changes in the tax law. Previously, a corporation would have to determine the *service lifetime* of an asset in accordance with guidelines provided by the Internal Revenue Service (IRS), and would then choose one of several accounting methods to determine the portion of the asset's cost that could be deducted each year. The simplest such method is *straight-line* depreciation, according to which the original cost, C, of an asset with a service life of T years would be deducted at the rate C/T per year for T years. Other methods, which would allow for larger deductions in early years and smaller ones later on, were also available. Such *accelerated depreciation* techniques would be advantageous to a firm, since they allow current taxes to be reduced at the expense of higher future taxes; given that corporations face positive interest rates, they clearly could gain from such tax deferrals.

An example of an accelerated depreciation method is the 150 percent declining balance method, where 150 percent of the straight line rate, $1/T$, is applied to the current undepreciated balance of the original cost of the asset (so each year, the deduction is $1.5/T$ times that part of the original cost of the asset that has not previously been deducted). Thus, the stream of depreciation allowed is:

$$\frac{1.5C}{T}, \left(C - \frac{1.5C}{T}\right)\frac{1.5}{T}, \left(C - \frac{1.5C}{T} - \left[C - \frac{1.5C}{T}\right]\frac{1.5}{T}\right)\frac{1.5}{T} \text{ etc.,} \qquad (13\text{--}1)$$

which obviously increases the amount of deductions in early years compared to the straight-line depreciation of C/T. The corporation would be allowed, at any time, to switch over to straight-line depreciation on the remaining undepreciated balance. This would allow the firm to choose somewhat faster write-offs in the later years of the asset's service life than it could under continued application of the declining balance method.

Partly because the previous system involved making difficult and disputable judgments about service lives, depreciation methods for assets placed in service beginning in 1981 were drastically simplified. The Accelerated Cost Recovery System (ACRS) requires that all assets be placed in one of only a few categories of property. Each category specifies both the period of time over which the asset will be depreciated, and the rate at which it will be depreciated. *Three-year property* includes automobiles, light trucks, and other assets that had been determined, according to previous IRS rules, to have a service life of four years or less. *Five-year property* includes most other machinery and equipment, while *15-year property* includes real estate. (There are special categories for public utility property and low-income rental housing, but we ignore them here.) The depreciation rates for the first two cases, and for a 15-year asset placed in service in the first month

Table 13–3 ACRS Depreciation Schedules

	Percentage of Asset Depreciated per Year		
Year	3-Year Property	5-Year Property	15-Year Property*
1	25	15	12
2	38	22	10
3	37	21	9
4		21	8
5		21	7
6			6
7			6
8			6
9			6
10–15			5

* Assuming asset placed in service in first month of tax year.
Source: Internal Revenue Code.

of a taxable year (the rates in this case depending on the month the asset is placed in service), are shown in Table 13–3. These rates reflect accelerated declining-balance depreciation at a 150 percent rate in the case of 3- and 5-year property, and at 175 percent in the case of 15-year property, with a switchover to straight-line depreciation later in the asset's life. This is not immediately apparent in the first two cases because of a half-year convention, according to which the allowable depreciation for the first year is only half of what a full 150 percent declining balance would yield. It is as if the asset were purchased at mid-year and the depreciation for that year pro-rated accordingly. The amount of first-year depreciation does not depend on when the asset is actually purchased, however, which encourages corporations to cluster asset purchases toward the end of the taxable year. It should be noted that the schedules shown in Table 13–3 are the only ones that can be used, unless the corporation elects to use straight-line depreciation over the asset's entire lifetime.

While the amount of acceleration reflected in the schedules of Table 13–3 is less in some cases than permitted under previous rules (for example, 200 percent declining balance could sometimes be used under the old rules), the ACRS significantly accelerates depreciation, relative to the earlier system, by shortening the lifetime over which depreciation is taken. The amount by which the ACRS lifetime falls short of the true economic lifetime is, of course, variable, because economic lifetimes vary by asset. Clearly, these new rules can create non-neutralities by changing the relative treatment of longer-lived vs. shorter-lived assets within each class. This was true of the previous system as well, for which service lifetimes varied by narrowly defined type of asset, but not necessarily in accordance with true economic lifetimes (for instance, machinery used in manufacture of motor vehicles had an allowed lifetime of 5–7 years; assets used in the manufacture of aerospace products had lifetimes of 8–12 years, etc.). Still, it is possible that the old system, with its diverse treatment of many assets, reflected true underlying economic diversity more than the new three-class system. To this extent, the new policy may result in greater intersectoral non-neutralities than the old. Moreover, it has been argued that the new system gives much more substantial deductions for 3- and 5-year property (machinery and equipment), than for structures (Auerbach [1982a,b]). This is true partly because the investment tax credit is available for the former but not the latter, although the reduction in the depreciable cost by half of the investment tax credit, a law that took effect in 1983, mitigates this problem to some extent.

While the desire to simplify the tax system may have motivated the introduction of the ACRS, it may also have been designed to provide a tax incentive for investment that would partly offset the disincentives created by high inflation. Depreciation is based on the original purchase price of assets, their historical cost, rather than their current market or replacement values. As noted in Chapter 11, historic cost depreciation lowers the real value of depreciation deductions during inflation, and this raises the user cost of capital. Obviously, the more generous depreciation methods allowed under ACRS provide an incentive in the opposite direction, and so may provide a crude offset against the effects of inflation. But restructuring the whole depreciation system is a crude way to deal with this problem, since the extra investment incentive provided is not linked to the inflation rate. It will therefore be too small in a highly inflationary economy, and too large in an economy with relatively stable prices.

(iii) *Inventories* Most corporations maintain inventories of raw materials, goods purchased for resale, etc., and these inventories will generally fluctuate from year to year. The change in the value of inventories over the year is included in corporate taxable income. Thus, a decline in the value of inventories over the course of the year indicates net using up of costly items and reduces taxable income like other costs. On the other hand, an increase in the value of inventories adds to corporate net worth, and increases taxable income.

A difficulty arises in the tax treatment of inventories when the prices of inventory goods fluctuate over time. In an inflationary economy, for example, the prices of goods held in inventory will generally rise over time. One must then determine the prices to be used for evaluating the change in inventories.

Under existing tax policy, there are two main methods by which inventories are valued. According to the first-in, first-out (FIFO) method, it is supposed that units of inventory are used up in the order in which they were purchased, that is, that "old" units of inventory are used up first. This method can give rise to spurious taxable income, as can easily be seen in the case of a corporation that begins and ends the year with no net change in the physical quantity of inventories held. Such a firm, under FIFO, would be treated as having increased the value of its inventories, since the items used up would be worth less at their old, and hence lower, prices than their newer, higher-priced replacements.

Firms need not use FIFO as an inventory valuation method, however. They may also use the last-in, first-out (LIFO) system, which treats inventories as if the most recently purchased units are the first to be used up. This means that the units of inventory used are valued at higher, more recent prices. This causes the year-end closing inventory to be valued at a lower amount, and so reduces the measured change in the value of inventories. This system therefore results in lower taxable income and tax liabilities in an inflationary economy than does FIFO, and the choice between FIFO and LIFO is thus of economic importance. Surprisingly, many firms have continued to use FIFO during recent periods of relatively high inflation, for reasons that are not entirely clear. It has been argued that one reason for preferring FIFO arises from the IRS regulation requiring that firms using LIFO for tax purposes must also use it for computing corporate income for corporate financial statements, stockholder reports, etc. If the current management of the firm believes that its performance is judged by current accounting net income, it will have an incentive to select FIFO in order to "blow up" current income. However, this argument assumes that stockholders and others fail to see through these accounting devices, and are tricked into rewarding managers for making decisions that increase accounting income at the expense of the higher real returns that are sacrificed by the choice of FIFO. Many economists would be loathe to accept this argument, because it seems to contradict the widely-used behavioral hypothesis that firms make decisions in order to make their owners as well off as possible. No very persuasive alternative explanation for the use of FIFO, rather than LIFO, seems to be available at present, however.

(iv) *Research and Development* Expenditures on research and development are treated as current costs, and may be written off in the year in which they accrue. This is obviously desirable to prevent a disincentive for such activities.

(v) *Loss-offset Provisions* Firms may offset losses against income of the previous three years. If this does not cover the losses, they may be carried forward for fifteen years. These loss-offset provisions are complete except for two things. First, interest on tax payments paid in the past, or tax reductions carried forward, are foregone. Second, losses may not be fully recovered in the fifteen-year period. Nonetheless, the provisions are substantial enough so as to have almost the effect of full loss-offsetting.

(vi) *Capital Gains* Capital gains earned by assets held over twelve months are taxed at a lower rate (28 percent) than ordinary income. Capital losses may be offset against other capital gains, but not against ordinary income. Net capital losses may be carried back three years, and forward five, to offset past or future capital gains. This preferential capital gains treatment presumably is thought to provide an incentive to supply risk capital although, as we argued in Section 11–4, the theoretical justification for this is far from clear.

(vii) *Intercorporate Dividends*   Firms can deduct 85 percent of dividends received from other corporations, and 100 percent of dividends received from affiliates. This is to prevent the same capital income from being taxed twice.

(viii) *Foreign Income*   The tax base of a corporation includes dividends repatriated to the United States. Credit is given for tax paid on these dividends to foreign governments. Since only repatriated dividends are included in the tax base, corporations can postpone payment of tax on earnings retained in foreign subsidiaries, and this can be beneficial if the foreign country involved has lower corporation tax rates than the United States. This leads to some abuses by corporations who set up subsidiaries in low-tax countries, or tax havens, and arrange to take their profits in these tax havens. Some attempt has been made to deal with specific tax havens by including their income in the United States firm's tax base.

(ix) *Mining Depletion Allowances*   In addition to being able to deduct the ordinary depreciation allowances on their capital equipment, mining industries have been allowed an immediate write-off of exploration and certain development costs, and a *depletion allowance* meant to reflect the "using up" of a mineral deposit.

Under *cost depletion,* a corporation can deduct the proportion of the estimated mineral deposits extracted each year, multiplied by that part of the cost of the mineral-bearing property attributable to the presence of the mineral deposit. The total deductions taken over the extraction period cannot exceed the original cost of the mineral rights in the property. By contrast, under *percentage depletion,* the firm is allowed to deduct a fixed percentage of gross sales each year, regardless of the original cost of the property. Percentage depletion rates for various minerals vary from 5 to 22 percent.

The overall effect of the percentage depletion allowance, combined with immediate deduction of exploration costs, is that deductions greatly exceed costs incurred. In effect, two deductions are being allowed for the costs of acquiring a deposit, thus unduly benefiting the mineral industries. The presumed justification for this favorable treatment is to encourage the undertaking of risky ventures, and to assist in the financing of the strategic mineral industries. However, given the size of the corporations generally involved, their access to capital markets, and their ability to diversify risks, it is not clear that such preferential treatment is warranted on efficiency grounds.

Table 13-4 Corporate Income Tax Rates, 1983

Income ($)	Tax Rate (%)
0–25,000	15
25,000–50,000	18
50,000–75,000	30
75,000–100,000	40
100,000+	46

Source: Commerce Clearing House, *1984 U.S. Master Tax Guide* (Chicago, 1983).

(c) The Rate Structure

The rate structure applied to taxable income of a corporation is very simple. As shown in Table 13–4, the rate increases from 15 percent on the first $25,000 of income to 46 percent on income over $100,000. Well over 90 percent of corporate income is subject to the higher rate. The lower rates are justified as a means of giving assistance to small businesses, presumably for non-economic reasons. However, the system of multiple rates provides an incentive for larger firms to split up into many corporations, thereby taking advantage of the lower rates on the first $100,000 earned in each. Firms are effectively prevented from so doing by limiting affiliated groups of corporations to lower rates on only the first $100,000 of combined income.

As with the personal income tax, the corporation income tax also has a 15 percent minimum tax on preference items. Preference income includes the value of preferential deductions from the tax base. It includes 18/46 of capital gains, accelerated depreciation on real property placed in service before 1981 (and thus not covered by ACRS), reserve build-ups of financial institutions in excess of bad debt losses, and depletion allowances in excess of the cost incurred in obtaining mineral deposits. The 15 percent tax is applied to all preference income in excess of tax paid or $10,000, whichever is larger.

(d) Integration of Personal and Corporate Taxation

To the extent that the corporation income tax is not shifted, the capital income of corporation owners will be subject to double taxation as mentioned above. This may be regarded as both inequitable and inefficient, although that judgment must be tempered to the extent that the tax is shifted, and to the extent that the payroll tax on labor income offsets it. Nonetheless, alternative methods of providing relief from any double taxation merit consideration, since they have played a prominent role in the literature, and since the tax system does include some provisions with that intent. Since the problem is one of double taxation, the obvious remedy is to remove one or other sources of the double taxation. Some of the possible methods, discussed further in McLure (1978), are as follows.

(i) *Eliminate Corporate Taxation*   If the corporate tax were eliminated, and all capital income were taxed fully as personal income, there would be no double taxation. Capital gains would have to be fully taxed and, in order to avoid postponement of tax payments on retained earnings, capital gains on corporate stock would have to be taxed as they accrued. While in principle this remedy would seem equitable, the elimination of the corporate tax would also eliminate a large revenue source, which may be very efficient to the extent that it falls on pure profits.

(ii) *Exempt Dividends*   Dividends could be exempted from corporate taxation either by deducting them from the corporate tax base or, in a more complicated way, by giving dividend recipients full credit for corporate taxes paid on their behalf. The latter could be accomplished as follows. Suppose the corporate tax rate were 50 percent and an individual earned dividends of $100. That implies that the corporation must have earned profits of $100/0.5 = $200, paid a tax of $100, and distributed the remaining $100. The dividend recipient would add the "grossed-up" dividends before tax of $200 to his income, calculate his taxes, and deduct $100 from taxes paid, since that was the sum paid by the corporation on his behalf. This method does not deal adequately with profits that go into retained earnings and presumably show up as capital gains. Unless some tax relief is given on the capital gains earned, there will be double taxation of that part of capital income.

(iii) *The Partnership Method*   The partnership method treats the corporation tax paid on all profits, whether distributed or retained, as a withholding tax paid on behalf of its shareholders. All profits would be regarded as the capital income of the shareholders, and pro-rated among them. With dividends, there is no problem, since they are in fact distributed to shareholders. With retained earnings, shareholders would be assumed to be the earners of retained profits, say, according to the proportion of the equity they owned. For each shareholder, his pro-rated share of the corporation's profits (both distributed and retained) would be grossed-up as in (ii) by adding the tax paid on those profits by the corporation. This grossed-up capital income would be added to the individual's taxable personal income, the tax payable calculated, and full tax credit given for the tax paid by the firm on his behalf. Although a partnership method of this sort was recommended for Canada by the Royal Commission on Taxation (1966), it has never been implemented. For one thing, the administrative costs of such a complex system may be high. For another, the pro-rating of retained earnings becomes problematic when shares change hands frequently over the tax year.

(iv) *Partial Methods*   Most tax systems allow only partial integration of corporate and personal taxes. This may, in part, reflect the uncertainty as to who actually bears the burden of corporate taxation. It may also reflect the fact that any steps taken toward integration imply a reduction in tax revenues, which must then be made up elsewhere, possibly at a greater cost in terms of economic efficiency. Partial credit is often given for corporate taxes paid on retained earnings by affording preferential tax treatment to capital gains. This is not an exact method, since the preferential treatment of capital gains may well be of relatively more benefit to those in higher tax brackets. If capital gains to be included in taxable income are reduced to a fraction of the total realized by an individual, the tax saving to the individual will be higher, the higher is his marginal tax bracket.

Two methods of giving relief to dividend-earners have been used. One is to give as a tax credit a proportion of the dividends received by an individual. The other is to give as a deduction from taxable income a proportion of dividends received. Although neither would exactly compensate for the tax paid on behalf of that individual by the corporation, the former method has merit in that it gives the same amount of benefit to all dividend earners, regardless of their tax bracket. The latter method benefits those with higher incomes relatively more, because the benefit received from a deduction from income increases with the marginal tax rate.

In some very rough sense, the special tax treatment of dividends and capital gains, discussed earlier in Section 13–2, approximates such a partial integration system. The amount of tax relief for corporate-source income stops short, however, of what would be required under a more consistent and thoroughgoing integration system.

CONSUMPTION TAXES

13–4   Taxes levied on consumption purchases play a relatively minor role in the federal tax system, but continue to be a significant source of revenue for state governments. We shall consider each of these in turn.

(a) Federal Taxes

All consumption taxes levied at the federal level are selective excise taxes levied on specific groups of commodities. The most important of these are the per-unit specific taxes levied on liquor products (spirits, wines, beer), tobacco (cigars, cigarettes, tobacco, and snuff), and gasoline. A less significant *ad valorem* tax is levied upon telephone services, and there are a multitude of other minor excise taxes.

Presumably, one reason for the low reliance on consumption taxes is their inequitable nature if levied *in rem,* rather than on individuals *per se.* (Consumption taxes could be levied on a personal basis in the form of a proportional or progressive expenditure tax, however, as discussed in Chapter 10.)

Consumption taxes levied on a general or selective basis tend to be inequitable according to traditional ability-to-pay criteria, since consumption expenditures tend to fall as a proportion of income, as income rises. Therefore, they are regressive taxes relative to income. Selective excises have the additional disadvantage of being horizontally inequitable, since they fall relatively heavily upon the persons who prefer taxed commodities. This, of course, assumes that these taxes are not shifted. Since the commodities upon which they fall tend to have fairly inelastic demands and elastic supplies, that is probably a reasonable assumption.

Taxes on inelastically demanded commodities such as liquor, alcohol, and gasoline, are likely to be very efficient taxes despite their inequity. They impose very little deadweight loss per dollar of revenue raised. At the same time, because the use of these commodities tends to emit external costs to the rest of society (pollution, health care, etc.), they could be justified as an attempt to price the commodities more nearly to cover marginal social costs.

The federal government does not levy a general consumption tax. Indeed, such a tax might be considered redundant, inasmuch as such a tax is nearly equivalent to a proportional income tax with interest exempt. Adding a proportional income tax to the progressive one already existing would not add anything except administrative costs.

(b) State Taxes

States rely heavily on consumption taxes. Almost all have retail sales taxes at various rates, as well as specific excise taxes on liquor, tobacco, gasoline, and vehicle licenses. The principles applicable to the selective excises are similar to those discussed in (a) above.

The retail sales tax is a general consumption tax levied at the retail level. It is not a very equitable tax, being slightly regressive at best. State governments presumably rely heavily on it so as to avoid making greater use of the income tax. One reason for that is that states having higher income tax rates might tend to lose citizens via migration to low tax states. In addition, the retail sales tax, being a tax on use rather than source, falls partly on nonresidents who happen to make purchases in the state.

The retail sales tax, being very general, may be fairly efficient at raising revenue. As we saw in Chapter 9, it discriminates against labor and in favor of leisure. To the extent that the labor supply is inelastic, there will be little deadweight loss incurred.

Some countries levy general taxes at stages other than the retail stage; for example, at the wholesale or manufacturing stages. Levying the tax at these stages has the advantage that there are fewer firms, and therefore fewer collection units, involved. However, there are also several disadvantages, as we saw in Chapter 9. First, to the extent that markup pricing is practiced, taxes imposed at an early stage will be pyramided in size by the time they reach the retail stage. Second, intrafirm transactions at earlier stages may be hard to value and prone to evasion. Finally, taxing at an early stage makes it difficult, if not impossible, to include services in the tax base. In addition, taxing at the retail level makes it easier to exclude such items as food and children's clothing, if desired, on equity grounds. Therefore the retail level would seem to be superior.

PROPERTY TAXES

13-5   Property taxes generate a large proportion of the tax revenues of local governments (municipalities, townships, counties, school districts, etc.). This is because the property tax base is probably the least mobile of the potential tax bases available to local governments. Local income taxes, although a minor source of tax to some larger cities, can be avoided by migration. Local consumption taxes, also used by some cities, can be avoided by purchasing outside the jurisdiction. Local governments do have available other sources of nontax revenues, such as user fees for local services and automobile licensing. But the property tax is likely to remain a major source of local revenue for the foreseeable future.

The administration of property taxes, including both the assessing of property values and the setting of rates, is decentralized to the local governments themselves. While this decentralization is desirable to the extent that different communities have different revenue needs, it also gives rise to various inequities and distortions. The tax itself is an annual tax on the values of certain types of property, mainly real estate, business fixed capital, and inventories. It taxes both the site value of land, and the improvements or capital added to the land at a uniform rate. The procedure followed is to assess the value of all property within a jurisdiction, and then select the tax rate that will yield the amount of revenue required. Tax rates tend to average between 1 and 3 percent of the true value of property.

Because the valuation procedure is decentralized, and because it is to some extent arbitrary (since well-defined market values do not exist for all property), anomalies of valuation can occur both within jurisdictions and between jurisdictions. Different properties may be valued relatively differently compared to their true values within a locality. The same types of properties may be valued differently between localities. To avoid some of these problems, particularly the latter, it has been suggested that the valuation task should be centralized at the state level.

Different localities may also impose different tax rates on the same type of property. This may or may not be offset by benefits provided to the two types of property by local expenditures. If not, this can give rise to both inequity and inefficiency.

Due to these differences of valuation procedure, and of tax rates over different types of property and different localities, the property tax imposes certain distorting influences upon the allocation of capital among localities. In addition, depending upon the incidence of the tax, there may be an influence upon the aggregate amount of capital accumulation. We shall briefly outline the incidence and efficiency effects of the tax.

(a) Incidence

As mentioned above, the tax is assessed equally on site values and improvements. However, the ability to shift taxes on these two bases may vary considerably. Since land sites are relatively fixed, one might expect that the part of the tax falling on them would be absorbed by the site owners. Improvements, however, are not fixed. In the aggregate, improvements are additions to the economy's capital stock. To the extent that the aggregate capital stock is variable, property taxes in general may be shifted forward to consumers, or backward to labor. This is especially true for the case of housing, which may be expected to be in relatively inelastic demand. To the extent that the tax is shifted forward, it may turn out to be regressive, especially the housing component of the tax. One group that may be especially hard hit are the elderly, since they tend as a group to be owner-occupiers of their homes. Many states now give tax credits for property taxes paid (in part or in entirety) by the elderly against state income taxes. The alleged regressivity of the property tax depends upon its being shifted forward. If the supply of capital were relatively fixed, capital owners might be expected to bear the tax, and it would be much more progressive.

A complicating factor making the incidence pattern difficult to gauge is the difference in rates across jurisdictions. If capital is mobile among jurisdictions, it can shift the burden onto other factors and consumers by moving out of that jurisdiction into one with lower rates. As yet, the evidence on the incidence of the property tax is inconclusive.

(b) Efficiency Effects

There are a number of ways in which the property tax distorts resource allocation in the economy. Because it includes in its base both site values and improvements, it discourages investment in residential and commercial/industrial structures. For this reason, it has been advocated that site values should be taxed separately from, and at higher rates than, improvements. By the same reasoning, it may discourage business capital formation, to the extent that it is a general tax on capital.

Important distortions also arise from the differential treatment across jurisdictions. The location decisions of firms may be affected by relative property tax rates (less local benefits) across jurisdictions. Moreover, the location of labor might similarly be affected. It is often the case, for example, that property tax rates in the inner city may be higher than those in the suburbs, causing individuals and families to relocate.

Localities may well recognize that their taxing decisions have an influence on, say, industrial location, and will attempt to induce industries to move in by offering preferential tax treatment. If all localities engage in this same activity, the resultant "tax competition" may be beneficial to none of them. We shall discuss in more detail in Chapter 15 some of the problems that arise in multijurisdiction nations with mobile factors of production. The only way many of them can be avoided is by making the administration of the property tax more centralized at the state level, or to metropolitan governments. The opportunity cost of so doing is likely to be a reduction in diversity of local government tax-benefit mixes to suit local tastes.

ESTATE AND GIFT TAXES

13–6 A relatively minor source of revenue to the federal and state governments is the taxation of certain transfers of wealth. The federal government imposes an *estate tax*, which taxes the donor on transfers of wealth (bequests) upon death. The federal government also imposes a tax upon transfers of wealth before death in the form of a *gift tax*. Most state governments impose *inheritance taxes* on the recipients of inheritances, although some use estate taxes. A few states also impose gift taxes.

Taxes on the transfer of wealth might be regarded as potentially useful taxes for the purposes of redistributing wealth. However, they have never been used to their full potential in the United States due to public resistance. On equity grounds, one would expect that both inheritances and gifts received ought to be included in the comprehensive income base of recipients, since they represent additions to net worth. Yet, at the federal level it is the donor, or more accurately the donor's estate, which is taxed progressively. No differentiation is drawn according to who receives the estate (except in the case of the spouse as discussed below). Perhaps the reason for this is that it would be considered inequitable to tax the receipt of an estate entirely in the year in which it was received. Still, some form of averaging could be introduced.

The federal estate and gift taxes were integrated in the Tax Reform Act of 1976. The gift tax is a tax on persons who make gifts during their lifetime. It is complementary to the estate tax, in the sense that it prevents people from disposing of their wealth before death in order to avoid the estate tax. Since gifts can be given gradually, rather than all at once, the gift tax base is the cumulative value of gifts made by an individual in the past. Each year, the tax payable on that year's gift is calculated by applying the marginal tax rate applicable to the total value of gifts given up to that year. Rates rise progressively from 18 percent gradually up to 60 percent, depending on the cumulative value of gifts given. (The top marginal rate is reached on cumulative transfers of more than \$3.5 million. By 1985 the top rate is scheduled to be scaled down to 50 percent on cumulative transfers over \$2.5 million.) However, a single donor can make gifts of up to \$10,000, tax-free, every year, and married couples may give up to \$20,000. In addition, gifts to spouses are exempt from taxation.

Once the tax payable on gifts is calculated, a taxpayer can reduce it by applying a lifetime tax credit. (This will rise from \$79,300 in 1983 to \$192,800 in 1987.) If the tax credit is not completely used up in this way, the amount left over may be used as a tax credit against estate taxes. This method of tax credits replaced a lifetime exemption system used prior to 1976, according to which a given amount of transfers was exempt from gift and estate taxation. The current tax credit of \$79,300 offsets the tax that would be collected on transfers of \$275,000, and is thus equivalent to an exemption of that amount. The scheduled credit for 1987 and beyond is equivalent to an exemption of \$600,000.

The base of the estate tax is straightforward to calculate. First, the total value of all property in the estate, called the *gross estate,* is computed. Next, several *deductions* are allowed. All funeral and estate expenses are deducted, as well as outstanding debt. All charitable bequests are also deducted. Finally, a *marital deduction* from the estate is allowed for all bequests to the surviving spouse. The tax rate is then obtained from a tax base calculated by adding cumulative lifetime gifts given (after the appropriate deduction) and the estate after deductions. The appropriate marginal tax rate is applied to the tax base to arrive at taxes due. Finally, any of the above-mentioned tax credit that has not been applied to gift taxes can be used to reduce estate taxes to arrive at a figure for taxes payable. While the marginal rates of taxation appear to be quite steep, the overall redistributive impact of the tax is considerably mitigated by the size of the deductions and exemptions allowed.

The effective rate of estate taxation is further lowered by the availability of a number of (sometimes) rather arcane methods for transferring wealth across generations, without its being subject to taxation. (For detailed discussion of many of these, see Cooper [1980].) One of the simpler and more widely-used techniques is the generation-skipping trust, which permits avoidance of estate taxation for a generation. When a person dies, part of the estate may be used to establish a trust for the remaining spouse and the children. The trust provides a stream of income to the spouse (called a *life tenant* of trust) and upon the spouse's death, to the children for the remainder of their lives. When the children die, the property in the trust goes into the hands of some third party called the remainderman (often children or grandchildren of the trust recipients, sometimes even charitable organizations). Estate tax is paid initially when the originator of the trust dies, and not again until the remainderman dies. No estate tax is paid on the death of the spouse, or on the death of the children. In that way, payment of the estate tax skips one or more generations. On equity grounds, it would seem desirable to impose an estate tax on the value of the trust as each successive life tenant dies.

While the estate tax could potentially be important for the distribution of income and wealth, and for the accumulation of capital in the economy as a whole, it currently yields so little revenue and offers so many opportunities for avoidance that any efficiency and equity effects that it may have are likely to be relatively small. Recent changes in the tax law have generally liberalized the system by permitting larger tax credits, and by exempting inter-spousal transfers that previously had been subject to tax, so that the role of the estate tax appears, if anything, to be diminishing over time.

CHAPTER NOTES

1. A comprehensive survey of the taxes levied in the United States may be found in Pechman (1983). Equivalent surveys may be found for Canada in Boadway and Kitchen (1984), and for the United Kingdom in Kay and King (1978).

2. The tax saving due to this special treatment of capital gains is partly offset by the minimum tax discussed below. Capital gains not included as full income are treated as preferential income, and are subject to the minimum tax.

3. In addition, $750 ($1500 on joint returns) of dividends paid in the form of stock by a public utility may be excluded if the dividends are reinvested. Since the stock thus obtained is subject, when sold, to capital gains taxation on its full value, this special exclusion effectively permits investors to convert dividend income, otherwise taxable at ordinary rates, to preferentially-treated capital gains income. To the extent that utilities pay out dividends in excess of the amount desired by particular shareholders (as opposed to retaining them), these shareholders will find the special exclusion advantageous. Currently, this special exclusion, which took effect in 1982, is scheduled to terminate in 1985.

4. For example, in the Canadian tax system, a tax credit is given to all taxpayers equal to 50 percent of dividends received. This is only a partially equitable remedy for the double taxation problem, since capital gains are treated much like in the United States—one-half is deducted from taxable income. In addition, 150 percent of dividends are included as taxable income. A fuller discussion of the double taxation of corporate profits is presented in the discussion of the corporation income tax in Section 13–3.

5. This bias towards local debt finance is to some extent offset by the fact that state and local taxes paid are also deductible from income. See subsection (b) below.

6. It has also been argued that the Constitution precludes federal government taxation of interest on state and local government securities. The legal status of this position seems unclear; presumably the issue can be resolved only if the federal government actually attempts to tax such interest, so that the tax could then be challenged and the case brought before the courts.

7. See Chapter 10 for a fuller discussion of the equity problems encountered with fluctuating incomes in a tax system with progressive marginal tax rates.

8. For example, in the Canadian tax system, the exemption for children and other dependents is much lower than the exemption for a spouse.

9. It may also be noted that separate tax schedules are available for single heads of families and for married couples filing separately. The rates applicable for the former are about midway between the rates for single persons and for joint returns. For the latter, the same rate schedule is used as for married couples filing joint returns. However, since the rates are applied to half the income of the joint return, the width of brackets is twice as great under joint returns.

IV

Interpersonal and Intergovernmental Transfers

IV

14

Transfers to Individuals and Social Insurance

INTRODUCTION

14–1   Not all revenues of the government are used for expenditures on goods and services. Some are used for transfer payments of various sorts, including the provision of social insurance. In turn, transfer payments can be made to households, to firms, and to other levels of governments. These final two chapters are concerned with transfers to households and to governments respectively. These are by far the most significant forms of transfer, both in terms of the sums involved, and in terms of the economic literature devoted to them.

Transfer payments to households can take several forms and may be instituted for many different motives. Two fundamental reasons are to redistribute income in favor of those less well off, and to provide a form of social insurance. In a sense, transfers to low-income persons are just like negative taxes. One might therefore expect that their analysis would be similar to that of other taxes, as discussed in the preceding chapters. While this is true to a certain extent, there are certain unique issues that arise in conjunction with transfers. The next section discusses some of these, focusing especially on two issues: The first is the design of various types of transfer and their relative impact on the incentive of recipients to work; the other is the distinction between cash and in-kind transfers.

The final three sections consider each of three separate types of social insurance schemes: social security, unemployment insurance, and medical insurance. Each of these schemes has some redistributive effects, but their primary function is the insuring of households against falls in utility. The first two involve insuring against falls in income. In the case of social security, the fall in income is due to retirement, while for unemployment insurance, the fall in income is due to job loss. The third scheme insures against increases in expenditures due to ill health. For each of these forms of social insurance we shall say something about the extent of, and rationale for, public sector involvement, and the economic effects.

INCOME REDISTRIBUTION

14–2   Redistribution of income is a major governmental function in modern economies. In this section we discuss programs which redistribute in favor of low-income households. This is by no means the total extent of government redistributive activity: Tariffs and quotas on imports, certain regulatory policies, and agricultural price supports, to name only a few examples, are policies which have redistribution (in these cases, from consumers and/or taxpayers to protected industries) as a major effect. But redistribution to the poor is a large and important government activity, worth careful attention.

Some statistics describing the magnitude of several important transfer programs are displayed in Table 14–1.[1] The largest program, in terms of *cash* benefits paid out, is Aid to Families with Dependent Children (AFDC), which provides benefits to low-income families with children under eighteen.[2] AFDC is what is popularly known as "welfare," and it has grown substantially in size over the past two decades. Supplemental Security Income (SSI) provides cash benefits to the poor who are aged, blind, and disabled; only the payments to the elderly poor are shown in the table. In addition to these cash transfer programs, Table 14–1 also records assistance to low-income households from two programs that provide benefits in kind. Medicaid makes payments for health care provided to qualifying low-income households. (These payments are made to the suppliers of the medical care, such as doctors, hospitals, etc., rather than to the individuals.) The Food Stamp program provides low-income households with coupons redeemable for food. These programs have also grown quickly. Indeed, their importance relative to AFDC has increased greatly. Medicaid and the Food Stamp programs now provide benefits two and one-half times the size of AFDC. Altogether, the programs shown in Table 14–1 paid out total benefits worth $46 billion in 1980, amounting to 2.1 percent of personal income.

Redistribution to the poor is, of course, a controversial subject. It is partly a debate about value judgments: Some people have stronger preferences for redistribution than others. Persuasive ethical arguments can be brought to bear on both sides. On the one hand, egalitarian principles of justice favor substantial redistribution. On the other hand, fairness criteria that emphasize reward in proportion to productive contributions, or the values of individual freedom and government non-intervention in the affairs of its citizens, argue against income redistribution. This ethical debate transcends economics and cannot be resolved here. (A useful recent review of

Table 14–1 Benefit Payments Under Selected Transfer Programs, 1950–1981, Selected Years

Year	Aid to Families with Dependent Children ($ Thousands)	(% of PI)*	Supplemental Security Income† ($ Thousands)	(% of PI)	Medicaid ($ Thousands)	(% of PI)	Food Stamps ($ Thousands)	(% of PI)	Total ($ Thousands)	(% of PI)
1950	551,653	.24	—	—	—	—	—	—	551,653	.24
1955	617,841	.20	—	—	—	—	—	—	617,841	.20
1960	1,000,784	.25	—	—	—	—	—	—	1,000,784	.25
1965	1,660,186	.31	—	—	—	—	32,494	.00	1,692,680	.31
1970	4,852,964	.60	—	—	—	—	550,806	.07	5,403,770	.67
1975	9,210,995	.73	1,842,980	.14	12,292,000	.97	4,386,144	.35	27,732,119	2.19
1980	12,475,245	.68	1,860,194	.09	23,301,000	1.08	8,685,521	.40	46,321,960	2.14
1981	NA	NA	1,967,015	.08	NA	NA	10,615,964	.44	NA	NA

* Personal Income

† Excludes payments to Blind and Disabled

NA: Not available

Sources: United States Department of Health and Human Services (1982), Tables 24 (p. 78), 150 (p. 220), 158 (p. 225), and 188 (p. 247).

these ethical issues can be found in Gordon [1980].) A large part of the debate about income redistribution, however, turns on matters about which economics does have something to say. For example, there is great concern about the extent to which income-maintenance programs may induce recipients to work less, or to avoid working altogether. The tools of economic analysis clearly can be brought to bear on this phenomenon. In principle, at least, theoretical and empirical economics should make it possible to ascertain the nature and magnitude of such effects, and to assess the consequences of proposed policy reforms. Thus, our goal here will be to study some of the important policy issues concerning redistribution programs on which economic analysis can shed some light. First, we shall discuss how incentive problems can occur under different redistributive programs, and how changes in policy may alter household labor supply. Then we examine the question of whether or not there are economically important differences between cash transfer programs like AFDC and in-kind transfers such as food stamps, and try to determine what rationale might be offered for in-kind, as opposed to cash, redistribution.

(a) Incentive Effects of Transfer Programs

Income redistribution programs inherently give rise to incentive problems, because the amount of income transferred to a household must diminish as a household's income rises. This reduces the benefit to the household of getting extra income, and thus reduces the incentive to extra effort, savings, etc.

The incentive problem is most plainly visible in what would probably be the simplest kind of anti-poverty program, one providing a *guaranteed annual income*. Suppose that the goal of the government is to ensure that each household receives at least a certain minimum level of income, say $M per year. Then one possible policy is to pay a cash transfer to each household with an income of less than the minimum, equal to the difference between M and the household's actual income, say, Y. Such a program would have certain advantages: It would ensure that no household would have less than the minimum income, thus achieving the program's redistributive objective; and that no government funds would be transferred to households with above-minimum income, thus keeping down the cost of the program. However, this scheme has one overwhelming drawback: Consider a household with less than the minimum income, say $Y < M$. Suppose a household member has an opportunity to work some extra hours, or to take a new (or first) job, that would increase family income by some amount, say, ΔY. Suppose, in addition (though this is not really essential to the main conclusion), that the household would still be earning less than M even if it took this opportunity, that is, that $Y + \Delta Y < M$. What, then, is the net gain to the household if it earns the extra ΔY? Previously, it received a transfer of $M - Y$, whereas it would now receive $M - Y -$

ΔY, which is smaller by ΔY. Its total income with transfers was initially $Y + (M - Y) = M$, whereas if it earned ΔY more it would be $Y + \Delta Y + (M - Y - \Delta Y) = M$! That is, it receives a *zero* net increase in total income when it earns more. In effect, the household faces an implicit tax under this system, with a marginal tax rate of 100 percent. It is natural to expect that if the extra earnings opportunity requires any extra effort at all, it will not be chosen by the household.

Systems like this have actually been used in the United States in the past. Beginning in 1967, however, the AFDC program was amended so that one-third of monthly earnings is "disregarded" in determining the amount to be paid to a given household. That is, each additional dollar of earnings only reduces the benefit received by 67 percent. This is a much lower marginal tax rate than 100 percent, but it is interesting to note that the highest marginal tax rate on earnings under the individual income tax—attained only at quite high income levels (see Chapter 13)—is 50 percent. Thus welfare recipients still face quite high marginal tax rates. Should the rates be lower? If so, the marginal return per hour worked would be higher. But there are drawbacks. For a given minimum income guarantee M, as marginal tax rates fall, the higher must be a household's income before it finally stops receiving any transfers. This may make the program more costly, and may result in transfers to households with incomes that are not low enough to warrant them.

To see this last point more clearly, let us sketch the general structure of income redistribution programs of this type, often referred to as negative income tax (NIT) plans. (The concept of a NIT was first articulated by Friedman [1964], and was further discussed by Green [1967], and Tobin [1969].) In the case where the marginal tax rate is constant (the same for all households), the program can be completely described with just two numbers: The marginal tax rate, t, and the maximum transfer, or minimum net income, M. Households with zero income from own sources receive M, while each dollar increase in earnings reduces the amount of transfer received by $\$t$. Eventually, as earnings increase, the transfer will have been reduced by M, at which point the amount received is zero. The level of income at which this occurs, say Y_B, is known as the *break-even* level of income, and is determined by the condition that

$$tY_B = M \tag{14-1}$$

or

$$Y_B = \frac{M}{t}. \tag{14-2}$$

To illustrate, in Fig. 14–1 we consider a hypothetical NIT, in which a household with zero income receives a transfer of M equal to $\$4000$. We also hypothesize a marginal tax rate of t equal to .5. The line AB shows

Figure 14–1

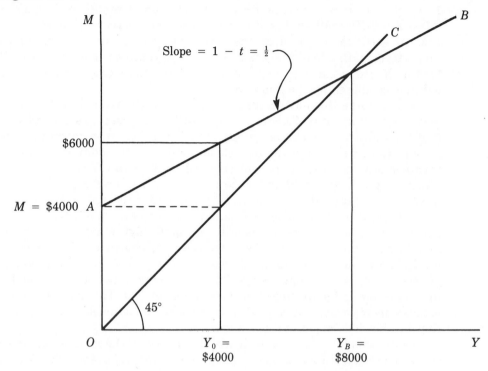

the income inclusive of transfer that a household would receive at each level of income Y. If the household earns nothing, it receives the full amount of transfer, $4000. As its own income rises, say to $4000, the amount of transfer falls by 50 percent, or $2000. This is shown by the vertical distance between the line AB and the 45° line OC. The height of AB at $Y = 4000 shows that the total transfer-inclusive income received is $6000. By the time income reaches $8000, the amount transferred has fallen to zero. The slope of the line AB is one minus the marginal tax rate, one-half, showing that each $2000 increase in earnings increases net income by $1000. (Beyond the break-even income of $8000, the household would begin paying positive taxes. If the marginal tax rate were to remain at one-half, the segment of AB beyond the break-even point would illustrate how the household's after-tax income rises with earnings.) The point A is given by the amount M, the maximum transfer. Clearly, the intersection point of AB with the 45° line OC, which determines the break-even level of income Y_B, will lie further to the right as M increases (this shifts AB upward), and as t decreases (this increases the slope of AB). As the marginal tax rate approaches zero, the break-even level rises without limit. These properties of the system are revealed in Eqs. (14–1) and (14–2).

The dilemma for policy design is now evident: (1) To insure satisfactory living standards for households with no or very little income, the maximum transfer, M, should not be too small. (2) To preserve a reward for earning extra income, the marginal tax rate, t, should be relatively low. (3) To keep the total cost of the program under control, to limit the number of transfer recipients (and thus the number of households facing work disincentives), and to avoid transferring income to households with incomes that are already adequate, the break-even level of income Y_B should be fairly low. Unfortunately, as Eq. (14–2) and Fig. 14–1 show, these objectives are fundamentally incompatible, and some trade-off among them must be made.

Under a guaranteed annual income system, one which makes transfers just sufficient to raise income to the minimum "adequate" level M, and which allows no transfers to households with higher incomes, the break-even level is exactly M, thus satisfying objectives (1) and (3) above. However, for households with earned incomes of less than M, the marginal tax rate, t, is 100 percent, so that objective (2) is sacrificed. If one then lowers the tax rate t, say to 67 percent, either objective (1), or (3), or both must be compromised. This may be worthwhile, however, in order to provide some work incentives for transfer recipients. Clearly, in order to decide whether this trade-off is advantageous, it is of major importance to know how the supply of effort responds to changes in incentives. Of course, this is not the only reason to be concerned with the incentive effects of income maintenance programs. Encouraging low-income households to work may in itself be seen as a policy goal. For both of these reasons, we now turn to a detailed analysis of the incentive effects of a NIT.

In Fig. 14–2, we depict an individual who must make a labor/leisure tradeoff. In the absence of an income maintenance plan, the individual faces a budget line, $Y\overline{Z}$, with a slope equal to the wage, w. He chooses Z_1 units of leisure, working $\overline{Z} - Z_1$ hours and earning an income of CZ_1. Now suppose a NIT scheme is introduced, offering a minimum income of $B\overline{Z}$ and a break-even income of HO. By Eq. 14–1, this corresponds to a marginal tax rate of $t = B\overline{Z}/HO$. Under this scheme, assuming that the individual may vary his hours of work continuously, the budget line shifts from $Y\overline{Z}$ to AB. The individual then chooses to work Z_2 hours, and receives a transfer-inclusive income of DZ_2, FZ_2 of which is earned, and DF of which is received as a cash transfer.

Recall that a worker's labor-supply response to an income tax, as discussed in Chapter 11, is theoretically ambiguous, because of income and substitution effects working in opposite directions. This ambiguity does not arise under a NIT, as long as leisure is normal. As in the income tax case, the substitution effect encourages the individual to take more leisure, as shown by the move from C to E. This is so, because the relative price of leisure (in terms of income) has fallen from w to $w(1-t)$. The income effect, unlike the income tax case, is equivalent to an increase in income moving the individual from E to D. If leisure is a normal good, the income effect of

Figure 14–2

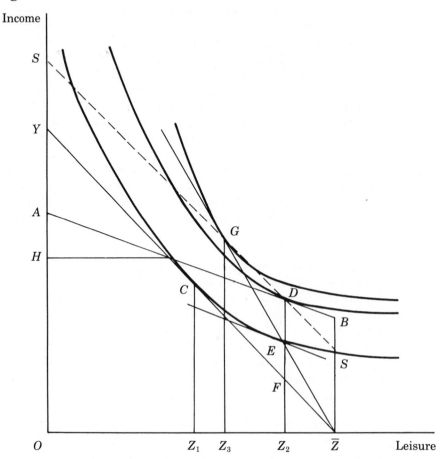

the NIT, in addition to the substitution effect, causes the individual to take more leisure, or supply less labor. Therefore, the effect is unambiguous.

It is interesting to note that a NIT may not succeed in its aim of increasing the income of the poor. It is quite possible that the after-tax income under a NIT, DZ_2, could be less than income before the scheme was introduced, CZ_1. The individual could decide to take the bulk of his increase in real income as leisure. This is especially true if t is high: For example, in the extreme case of a guaranteed annual income, t is equal to unity for all individuals earning less than the guaranteed level, and the household would consume $\overline{Z}$ units of leisure. It may also be true if the individual is not free to vary his work effort, and so must either select C or B.

As a matter of policy, public decision-makers may value schemes more highly that induce low-income persons to take less leisure and obtain higher money incomes. The income effects of schemes favoring the poor are always going to induce more leisure if the latter is normal, so alternative schemes must rely on avoiding the adverse substitution effect of the NIT. One such scheme is the *wage subsidy*, sometimes called a *negative wage tax*. (Such programs have been discussed by Zeckhauser [1971], Browning [1973], and Kesselman [1973].) Under such a scheme, individuals in low-wage jobs would receive an *ad valorem* subsidy on their wage rates.

Let us consider the wage subsidy scheme with no exemptions, having the same cost to the government as the above NIT. In Fig. 14–2, the line *SS* represents the locus of all points of after-tax income for the individual, such that the government would pay an equivalent amount as under the NIT (*DF*). The wage subsidy scheme which leaves the individual on *SS* is that shown by the budget line $\overline{Z}G$, whose slope is $w(1 + s)$ where s is the wage subsidy rate. Since the point G is always to the left of D, a wage subsidy scheme will always result in more work effort and more income, as compared with an equal-cost NIT. In that sense, it is preferable to the NIT. (Of course, Z_3 may be greater or less than Z_1, depending on the relative strengths of income and substitution effects.) The reason for this result is simply that since the price of leisure is now higher $[w(1 + s)]$, the substitution effect tends to cause more work and less leisure. Finally, note that we cannot predict *a priori* which scheme the recipients would prefer. The point G may lie on a higher or lower indifference curve than D, depending upon the shape of the indifference curves.

Wage subsidies have the further property that their rates may be varied according to the wage rates. For example, the wage subsidy might be determined by a formula such as:

$$s = c(w_s - w) \tag{14–3}$$

where c is some constant, and w_s is some "break-even wage rate," above which the wage subsidy is zero. Thus, the higher the wage rate, the lower the subsidy. There are, however, some problems with sole reliance on the wage subsidy as a means of treating low-income earners. For one, the wage subsidy assists only those who are working. Those who are unable to work, or who are involuntarily unemployed, receive no assistance. For that reason, the scheme would have to be supplemented by some other program assisting the latter groups. Also, since the wage subsidy scheme subsidizes labor income only, it does not satisfy the horizontal equity criterion. Two workers earning the same wage rate may have different nonlabor incomes. This may not be an extremely great problem in practice. In any case, it is mitigated by the existence of the personal income tax alongside wage subsidy schemes.

Empirical research on negative income tax schemes to assist low-income families have tended to confirm the adverse influence of such plans on work incentives. However, the magnitude of such effects is under dispute. A three-year experiment was conducted on families in some urban areas of New Jersey and Pennsylvania to attempt to estimate the effects on work effort of NIT type schemes. The results showed that for a NIT with marginal rate of 50 percent, work hours were reduced by 7–9 percent by husbands, but much more for wives, especially white wives (United States Department of Health, Education, and Welfare [1973]). It is hard to know how much of the effect was due to the temporary nature of the plan. Econometric studies of labor supply response to such plans have typically found much higher disincentives to work. Both hours worked and labor participation rates were found to be significantly affected in a study by Kalachek and Raines (1970). Boskin (1972) also found large disincentive effects on the basis of a labor supply estimation.

(b) Cash vs. In-Kind Transfers

Given that redistribution in favor of low-income households is to be carried out, there is the question of what form it should take. In particular, what can be said about the effects of in-kind transfer programs that provide benefits in units of specific commodities such as food, housing, or health care? Compared with cash transfers of equal dollar value, do such in-kind transfers increase the amount of food, housing, or health care consumed by low-income households? This is evidently the rationale for such programs.

To see whether this rationale is valid, consider a household that, in the absence of transfers of any kind, is able to buy the combinations of food and other goods shown by the budget line *AB* in Fig. 14–3. For simplicity, let us measure the units of food and other goods in dollars'

Figure 14–3

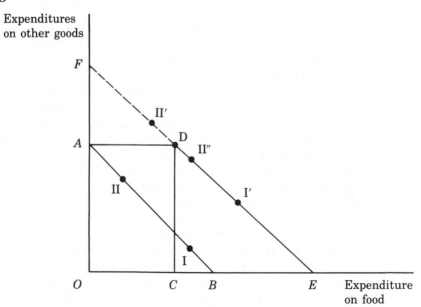

worth of expenditures, so that AB has a slope of -1, and the household's pre-transfer income is $OA = OB$. Now suppose that the household is given food stamps worth OC, redeemable only in food. How does this change the opportunity set facing the household?

First, the household can, if it wishes, spend all of its own cash income on other goods, using only food stamps for food. This would allow it to consume along the line segment AD. The household might wish to consume more than OC units of food, however, in which case it could sacrifice some expenditure on other goods. It is obvious, but essential, to note that each extra dollar of food expenditure requires the household to give up a dollar's worth of expenditure on other goods; that is, the relative price of units of food in excess of OC is no lower than before the food stamp program. Thus, the budget line extends from D to E, parallel to AB with a slope of -1.

Compare this with the effect of a pure cash transfer of equal dollar amount. A transfer of OC dollars shifts the budget line rightward or upward by OC parallel to AB. This results in a new budget line FE, which differs from the budget line with the in-kind transfer only in that it includes the dashed segment FD.

To see how the household's consumption bundle would change as a result of either of these transfers, we would need to know the household's indifference map. Without actually drawing in the indifference map, the various possibilities can easily be indicated. Suppose first that the household, in the absence of any transfers, consumes more than OC units of food. For instance, the household's initial equilibrium might be at point I on AB. If both food and other goods are normal, the household's response to either food stamps or the cash transfer would be to locate somewhere northeast of I on the budget lines ADE or FE, such as at point I'. At I' the household consumes more food, but the extra food consumption is the same whether the transfer is in cash or in-kind. Moreover, food consumption does not rise by the full amount of the transfer, OC. Rather, it rises by OC times the marginal propensity to spend on food. If this propensity is, say, one-third, then food consumption would only rise by one-third of OC, even if the transfer takes the form of food stamps. The reason this can happen, of course, is that the household receiving food stamps can reduce the cash it had previously been spending on food, for example by spending $\$.67$ less on food for each dollar's worth of food stamps received. (In fact, it would be *possible* for the household to reduce its food expenditures by one dollar for every dollar in food stamps, in effect converting the entire food stamp transfer into expenditure on other goods, and moving directly north from point I in Fig. 14–3. It would not actually choose to keep food consumption constant, however, provided that food is a normal good.) But, however much food consumption increases, the most important point is that it will increase just as much under a cash transfer as under food stamps. The real impact of the food stamp transfer on the household is thus identical to that under a cash transfer of equal dollar value, so that there can be no economic rationale for favoring in-kind transfers in this case.

All of this assumes that the household initially consumes more than *OC* units of food. This would not necessarily be the case, however, especially if *OC* is a large amount. Suppose instead that the household initially consumes at point *II* with less than *OC* units of food. If it receives a cash transfer of *OC*, it will locate at the tangency of an indifference curve to the budget line *FE*, either in the segment *FD*, as point *II'*, or along *DE*, as at point *II"*. Which of these locations would occur obviously depends on how income-elastic the demand for food is, and how large *OC* is. Now, contrast this with a transfer of food stamps of *OC*. If the household's indifference map is such that a tangency occurs at point *II"*, then, just as in the preceding case, the household's consumption bundle changes exactly as it would under a cash transfer, and there is no difference between cash and in-kind transfers in terms of their real economic effects. On the other hand, if the household has a tangency at point *II'* on *FE*, the two programs differ. The point *II'* is not attainable under the food stamp program, and the best that the household can do is to locate at point *D*. There are two important ways that this outcome differs from that attained with cash transfers. First, the household consumes more food, exactly *OC*, under a food stamp program. It reduces its cash expenditures on food to zero, but is unable to carry any further the conversion of food units into units of other goods, and so remains at *D*. Second, and quite importantly, the household is worse off under food stamps than it would be under a cash transfer, at least according to its own value system, as reflected in its indifference map.

This second fact is of interest both positively and normatively. To begin with, from a positive viewpoint, if the household would like to consume less than *OC* units of food, in order to move toward a point like *I'*, what can it do? One thing that it can do is to use its food stamps to obtain food for someone else, which it then sells to them. If the household is able to do this—and it would obviously be fairly difficult to prevent it from doing so—then the budget line under food stamps essentially opens up to all of *FE*, just as under a cash transfer. Actually, this is not quite right, because it takes effort to arrange these special transactions. The food stamp recipient might have to offer the food at something less than its cash value, for instance, in order to make it worthwhile for others to trade in this way. The costs of such trades, in other words, give rise to a feasible consumption set for the recipient, lying above *AD* but falling somewhat short of *FD*. In these circumstances, one would expect institutions to arise which would help to economize on such transaction costs, and, in fact, black markets for food stamps have come into existence. Such markets allow the household to approximate the cash-transfer budget line *FE* even more closely, making it better off (in terms of its own indifference map).

Secondly, consider the normative issue. If effective black markets do not come into existence, is it good or bad for transfer recipients to be restricted to consuming at point *D*, when they would prefer points like *I'*? After all, it is no more costly to taxpayers to transfer *OC* in cash, so they would presumably be no worse off under a cash transfer system, while those beneficiaries desiring to consume less than OC dollar's worth of food would be better off. In other words, cash transfers would appear to Pareto-dominate in-kind transfers. Similar reasoning indicates that if black markets arise that effectively convert the in-kind transfers into cash transfers, they will result in a Pareto improvement. This argument assumes, however, that taxpayers only care about the cost of the program, that is, the total dollar outlay. Such an assumption may be invalid because, as observed by Tobin (1970), taxpayers might not care about how well-off the poor are in terms of their (the poor's) own perceptions of economic well-being, but they might care whether the poor achieve certain standards of consumption of certain specific goods. To use the terminology of Chapter 5, this is a case of *consumption externality*, where the donors obtain utility from the consumption of particular goods by the poor. If taxpayers are made worse off when the poor economize on their food consumption, and increase their consumption of other goods by moving from D to II', then that move is, of course, no longer Pareto-improving. This, perhaps, gets to the heart of the cash vs. in-kind transfers question, and may explain why the latter are used so extensively.

Recall again, however, that an effective distinction arises between cash and in-kind transfers only when the amount of the good transferred is greater than the recipient would wish to consume. Undoubtedly this is not the situation for most food-stamp recipients, who are observed to spend not just food stamps, but cash as well, to carry out their desired food expenditures. With other kinds of in-kind transfers, however, the minimum-consumption constraint may be more likely to be binding, and the prospects for black-market evasion of the minimum-consumption constraint may also be smaller. This might be the case, for example, with respect to Medicaid. It would be quite difficult to transfer (sell) the rights to health care obtained by Medicaid beneficiaries, and the program may well provide more health care than low-income households would willingly buy if they could receive cash benefits of equal value instead. In this case, in-kind transfers may result in better health for low-income households than would be obtained with cash transfers; this may be a desirable consequence of such a policy. Certainly, if taxpayer-donors paternalistically place a higher value on a dollar's worth of health care for the poor than on a dollar's worth of other goods, they (the donors) would be better off under this program.[3] This may make such redistribution politically more attractive than cash transfers, and may help to explain why such forms of redistribution have grown so rapidly in recent years. It should be noted, however, that if the consumption of food, for example, by low-income households actually does generate external benefits for society, the lump-sum in-kind transfer, as a general rule, is not a Pareto-efficient redistributive mechanism. Rather, as the externality theory discussed in Chapter 5 would suggest, the appropriate policy is to lower the relative price of the externality-generating consumption goods, thereby subsidizing such consumption at the margin. A food stamp program does not have this feature. On the other hand, rent subsidy programs, under which the government pays a specified percentage of the monthly rent for low-income households, do encourage substitution of housing for other goods at the margin. In principle, a subsidy rate could be chosen that correctly internalizes the external benefit of housing consumption to higher-income households, thus bringing about a Pareto-efficient outcome.

SOCIAL SECURITY

14–3   The social security system, by which is meant the Old Age, Survivors, Disability and Health Insurance (OASDHI) program, is by far the largest social insurance/transfer program in the United States today. As its name suggests, it has several functions, chief among which is the provision of monthly cash benefit payments to retired workers and their families and, upon the death of the worker, to surviving family members. It also pays benefits to disabled workers, and provides medical benefits to the elderly. In 1981, these programs paid out benefits of $184 billion, of which $124 billion (about two-thirds) was paid under the old age and survivors insurance (OASI) component of the program, $18 billion under disability insurance, and $43 billion under medical insurance (a program known as Medicare). As might be expected with a program of this size, social security has been the subject of a great deal of popular and academic controversy. In this section, we focus on the economic effects of the main component of the social security system, that is, the OASI program. We examine its role as an insurance program, its distributional impact, and the incentives or disincentives that it creates for private saving and capital accumulation, early retirement, and labor supply prior to retirement. Section 14–5 discusses public health insurance programs, such as Medicare.

While the OASI program is fairly complex, a broad outline of its main features is necessary in order to understand the major economic issues that it raises. Some of the more detailed aspects of OASI are discussed later in this section.

First, the program is financed by a special tax on earnings, a *payroll tax*, the proceeds of which are earmarked for the social security trust funds from which benefits are paid. Over the years, the system has required "contributions" to the system by each covered worker equal to a fixed percentage of earnings up to a maximum amount. In addition, the employer has been required to contribute an equal percentage of the same taxable earnings. Both the percentage rate and the maximum taxable earnings have increased over time; for 1983, the employee and employer rates are 6.7 percent each, or 13.4 percent in total, on earnings up to $35,700. (The combined contribution, or tax rate, is currently scheduled to increase until 1990, at which time it will reach 15.3 percent.) Second, the benefits paid out under the program are in the nature of an *annuity*, that is, payments are made on a regular basis, beginning at retirement, for the lifetime of the beneficiary. For a single worker, this means that benefits are received until death; for a married worker, the surviving spouse continues to receive benefits, after the death of the worker, for the remainder of her or his lifetime. Third, the benefits paid to a worker are not directly tied to the contributions (or taxes) paid into the system, either by the individual worker or by the worker's generation or age cohort. This is so for two reasons: To begin with, all insured workers are eligible for a certain minimum social security payment. (The minimum was $182.90 per month in 1982.) Beyond this, the monthly benefit payable to a particular worker is equal to a specified percentage of that worker's average monthly earnings in the pre-retirement years. This percentage varies inversely with the worker's average monthly earnings, so that benefits are relatively greater for workers with lower earnings and contributions. Moreover, the benefit rates applicable to any particular age group or cohort of retirees may be set, relatively generously or not, as a matter of legislative discretion, and are not auto-matically fixed in relation to past contributions. Historically, retired workers have received benefits that are quite large in relation to their lifetime contributions. Fourth, benefits become payable to a limited degree at age sixty-two, and are fully payable at age sixty-five. If retirement is deferred to after age sixty-five, slightly higher benefits can be obtained. Once benefits are being collected, however, an individual who continues to work finds that benefits are reduced by 50 percent of earnings above a certain amount; in 1982, this amount was $4440 for workers aged sixty-two to sixty-four, and $6000 for workers aged sixty-five to seventy-two. (Workers above age seventy-two suffer no reduction in benefits.)

With this basic outline in mind, let us examine the economic effects of social security.

(a) Social Security Insurance

There are two main kinds of risk or uncertainty for which social security provides insurance. The first arises from the fact that individuals have lifetimes of uncertain length. A worker who has accumulated a given amount of wealth as of retirement faces the problem of deciding how quickly to consume all, or part of, that wealth in retirement. To be certain of having some consumption through the remaining years of life, the individual would have to consume at a low rate, planning to preserve some wealth even beyond age eighty or ninety. Of course, the chance of living to age ninety or 100 is fairly small for any individual (though of all individuals currently aged sixty-five, there are predictable proportions that will survive to those ages). Therefore, a conservative consumption strategy makes it almost certain that the individual will die with some wealth left unconsumed, wealth which he would have consumed if the date of death had been known. To avoid this outcome, the individual can choose a less conservative strategy, for example, by consuming at a rate that is expected to exhaust the stock of wealth by age seventy-five. For those individuals who end up dying at or before age seventy-five, this plan yields a better outcome. Of course there are some individuals who will live to an older age, and who will then have little or no wealth with which to sustain themselves. Individuals who follow less than completely conservative consumption plans—and this would undoubtedly constitute a large proportion of the aged—therefore expose themselves to the risk of destitution in old age.[4]

Individuals have opportunities to protect themselves from these risks, however. First, they can build up a stock of wealth during their working years and, upon retirement, purchase an annuity, that is, a stream of income from retirement until death (or until the death of a spouse). Life insurance companies, for example, often offer policies that require regular premium payments up to a specified age, at which time the policyholder can select from one of several benefit plans. Such individual insurance arrangements are often costly, however, both in terms of marketing and administrative costs on the part of the insurance company, and in terms of the costs of making an informed decision on the part of the individual. Pension plans, which are organized on a group basis for the workers in particular firms or industries, provide the same type of insurance: Workers contribute a portion of their earnings (or the employer makes such contributions as part of the workers' overall compensation package) during the working years, and then draw annuity benefits at retirement. Group insurance of this sort is often less costly than individual insurance. Aside from marketing and administrative costs, however, both individual and group insurance plans will pay benefits which are *actuarially fair*, that is, they provide a stream of annuity payments to each worker over the remaining years of life, which will equal, on average, the contributions paid during the working years (plus accumulated interest). This is characteristic of private insurance plans because they are generally required to be *fully funded*, that is, benefits are legally allowed to be paid to retirees only to the extent of their actual contributions. In particular, current benefits cannot be paid out from current contributions into the program; they must be paid from accumulated past contributions.

Social security provides insurance against the risk of an uncertain lifetime, because benefits are annuitized. However, as noted above, social security benefits are not linked to the actual contributions paid into the program, and in practice, the program has generally financed benefits to retirees from the contributions of those currently working. Such a system is referred to as *unfunded*, or is said to be financed on a *pay-as-you-go* basis. With unfunded systems, it is possible for workers to receive more or less than actuarially fair returns. This constitutes a major difference between private and public insurance plans, one which has important implications that we will discuss below. In any case, the fact that social security benefits are annuitized means that they provide protection against an uncertain date of death.

A second risk facing individuals is uncertainty about the age of retirement. While one's age of retirement is partly a matter of discretion and conscious decision, it is undoubtedly influenced by uncontrolled and uncertain factors as well. The most obvious example is health, which may fail because of chance illnesses or accidents, and induce an individual to stop working at an early age.[5] But other, more subtle, risks influence the age of retirement as well. For different individuals, vigor, stamina, and mental capability seem to decline with age at widely varying rates, for reasons that are, at least in part, beyond individual control. If the age of retirement is uncertain for any given individual, lifetime earnings and consumption must also be uncertain. Those unfortunate enough to have to retire at an early age will be worse off than someone who can retire at a later age.

Social security offers some protection against this risk. It does so by making the receipt of benefits conditional on retirement. However, like many forms of insurance, this one is subject to the problem of moral hazard (Diamond and Mirrlees [1978]). As noted, the insured-against event, retirement, is only partly determined by uncontrollable and uncertain factors. It also depends on individual choice, and it is obviously more likely to be chosen if it is well insured. Put in plainer language, social security may create incentives for workers to retire earlier, since benefit payments, which can only be received on retirement, make retirement more attractive.

We discuss the effect of social security on retirement in greater detail below, but we may note here that there is no fully satisfactory way to deal with this moral hazard problem. One can, of course, try to determine whether the individual is retiring on account of external events, such as illness or injury, and make the payment of benefits conditional on such events. This is, in effect, what the Disability Insurance component of OASDHI does for younger workers. But such methods are costly to administer, and make it impossible to insure against relatively unobservable random causes of retirement, such as general weakness or fatigue. And, of course, outright disability itself is not easily defined: How severe, for instance, must arthritis become before a worker is disabled? Thus, the current system, which simply makes benefits conditional on the act of retirement, is not necessarily inferior to feasible alternatives. A further possibility of reducing the moral hazard problem is to offer higher benefits to workers who defer retirement. This, however, can defeat the purpose of insuring against the risk of early retirement if carried very far.

If social security does offer insurance against the risks of uncertain lifetime or early retirement, so, too, do private retirement plans. What, then, is the rationale for public provision of such insurance? One rationale, and perhaps the most important one, is based on paternalism: People may be unwise, short-sighted, or ill-informed. When they are young, they may fail to save adequately for old age, either because they are thoughtless, or because they do not understand (or are not aware of) the opportunities provided in the marketplace for such saving. A difficulty that always arises with paternalistic arguments of this sort, of course, is that it presupposes that some external agent—the government, in this case—understands what is in an individual's own interest better than the individual himself. For decisions that are relatively complex, such as the problem of life-cycle planning, this paternalistic view may be more appealing than usual; nonetheless, it is always debatable. Diamond (1977) presents evidence that a significant minority of people arrive at old age with "inadequate" wealth, that is, wealth less than that necessary to sustain consumption at a rate of (say) half of that achieved in the working years. Even if most households do plan in some "reasonable" way for old age (and a number of empirical studies of saving behavior, cited in Chapter 11, suggest that this may be the case), it might still be desirable to have some compulsory insurance/savings plan that would require *all* households to make some provision for old age. Society would then be able to prevent some workers from acting contrary to their own best interests. (Alternatively, of course, it might be possible to establish an income maintenance program for the indigent aged.)

Does the argument for compulsory savings mean that a public program like social security is called for? It would seem possible simply to require that individuals contribute to some private plan of their choice and achieve on their own the basic insurance coverage now provided by social security. While private insurance plans are subject to moral hazard and administrative costs, these problems certainly arise under public programs as well. It is possible, however, that a public program economizes on decision-making costs (since the burden of choice is lifted from the individual), and that a huge public program allows for lower administrative costs than do many private plans. These considerations aside, however, paternalistic arguments do not specifically seem to call for *public provision* of old-age insurance, even though they may justify compulsory coverage for all households. Of course, public social security has achieved certain other results, which have nothing to do with insurance against an uncertain lifetime or age of retirement, that private plans could not achieve. We now discuss some of these.

(b) Social Security as a Redistributive Mechanism

The social security system redistributes income in two major ways. First, it redistributes among the members of any *given* generation; this intragenerational redistribution is a result of the benefit structure of the program relative to contributions. Second, the program redistributes *across* generations. The intergenerational redistribution results from the fact that the system is financed on a pay-as-you-go basis. We discuss each of these forms of redistribution in turn.

As noted earlier, the benefits received by an insured worker are calculated as a declining percentage of average monthly earnings, except that benefits must equal a certain minimum.[6] In contrast to a program where benefits, like contributions, are strictly proportional to earnings, the system tends to redistribute in favor of those with relatively low wage income. Although there would be certain exceptions, such redistribution clearly tends to equalize both the post-retirement and lifetime incomes within a given age group. It is important to note that private-sector retirement plans generally do not have such equalizing features; indeed, an *adverse selection* problem would arise if they attempted to do so. A strongly redistributive program would look unattractive to high-earnings workers, who would attempt to save through programs that exclude low-earnings workers, while low-wage earners would be attracted to the redistributive program. With many low-income and few high-income workers, the redistributive program would obviously fail. Thus, like most redistributive programs, redistribution through pension plans must be carried out publicly, and public intervention in the old-age security "industry" may be appropriate to the extent that this sort of redistribution is desired. Of course, there may be other ways of meeting the same (or similar) redistributive objectives. If, for example, one's goal is to aid the elderly poor, this might be achieved more effectively by providing special benefits to the elderly poor at the expense of high income individuals generally. Indeed, the Supplemental Security Income (SSI) program, which paid benefits of $2.7 billion in 1981, does exactly this.[7] It is financed from general revenues, rather than from the payroll tax, and benefits are paid to those elderly individuals with low current income (and wealth). In contrast to social security, a person's average earnings during the working years is irrelevant in computing benefits. Given the feasibility of programs like SSI, which aim directly at the elderly poor, the role of a redistributive benefit structure in the OASI program is open to question.

This redistributive feature of the social security system alters labor supply incentives in important ways. In contrast to a program that would pay benefits strictly in proportion to earnings, individuals with very low earnings can expect no increase in social security benefits until they reach a level of earnings at which they surpass the minimum. Beyond this point, higher earnings at first bring large increases in benefits, until the percentage increase of benefits with higher earnings drops off. The overall quantitative impact of the labor supply incentives set up by these redistributive features of the social security program is theoretically ambiguous, since they create potentially offsetting income and substitution effects. Some empirical evidence on labor supply is discussed later.

The social security system also redistributes among the members of a given generation according to marital status, family size, and labor force participation by spouses. When a worker retires, benefits are increased by 50 percent if the worker has a spouse aged sixty-five or older. (There are reduced benefits for spouses aged sixty-two to sixty-five.) Benefits are also higher when children under eighteen are present. In addition, when a worker dies, a surviving spouse continues to receive benefits, usually equal to the full benefit to which the worker alone would have been entitled. Thus, the total benefits paid out on behalf of a worker with given average monthly earnings will be higher if that worker is married and has children than otherwise. On the other hand, when both spouses work, family benefits are not equal to the sum of the benefits attainable separately by either spouse, since there is an overall limit on benefits paid to any one family. This tends to work against two-earner couples.

These forms of redistribution raise issues not unlike those arising in the analysis of the tax treatment of the family. Clearly, they result in the treatment of individuals in a way that is dependent on family status, and in ways that would not occur under a private insurance program. The rationale for such redistribution, like certain features of the tax system, is presumably that the family, rather than the individual, should be treated as the basic participating unit. However, this creates conflicts with the opposite perspective. Which viewpoint is the correct one seems to be a matter of value judgment.

The second major form of redistribution caused by the social security system is a redistribution across generations. This has occurred because the system has operated largely on an unfunded basis, with the beneficiaries at any point in time receiving benefits financed primarily by the contributions of those currently working. The nature of this redistribution can be best appreciated by comparing the present unfunded system with a funded one. Under the latter, the members of each generation are required to finance their own benefits by making contributions to a fund during their working years. The money in this fund would be invested, presumably in government bonds, and would earn the going rate of return, say, r. By the time the members of the generation reach retirement age, a stock of wealth, comprising both contributions and interest, will have been built up. Benefits would then be paid, according to actuarial principles, at a rate which would exactly exhaust the accumulated stock at the time that the last surviving members of the generation die. This program would make the covered generation neither better off nor worse off in an overall sense, provided that its members would have saved for old age anyway. They are simply saving in a different form, and earning the same market rate of return on their savings that they would have earned had they saved privately.[8] In addition, this program would involve no redistribution to or from any other generation.

With unfunded social security, the situation is quite different. Suppose, for instance, that a program were set up whereby the members of any given generation would contribute a fixed amount, per capita, to a fund that would immediately pay out its receipts to the current elderly population. When such a program begins, say in period 1, it will provide a windfall gain to those who are elderly at that time; they begin to receive benefits without ever having contributed to the system. They enjoy this windfall at the expense of the initial group of contributing workers, whose payments into the system are financing the initial beneficiaries. If the program were stopped after this initial period, period 2's workers would not have to make any contributions, period 1's workers, now retired, would not receive any benefits, and the net impact of the program would have been a one-time, intergenerational transfer. But suppose that the program continues beyond the first period, and suppose also that the population is growing. Then, in period 2, the newly-retired population would receive benefits financed by the now more-numerous working population. This would not only make it possible for the new retirees to recoup their own earlier contributions; they would actually receive more than they contributed, because the number of workers contributing to the system had grown. In effect, the new retirees are compensated for their transfers to an earlier generation by a second intergenerational transfer, from period 2's workers, of which the retirees are the beneficiaries.

This program could be maintained indefinitely, with each generation aiding its predecessor, and being aided in turn by its successor. As long as the population continues to grow, each generation earns a "return" on its contributions, in that it will receive benefits in excess of its contributions. The rate of this return is, in fact, exactly equal to the rate of population growth. Provided that the system never terminates, no generation ends up having contributed to the support of its elders without receiving support in its turn.

So far, we have been discussing the impact of an unfunded system where the contributions made are a fixed amount per capita. Suppose instead that contributions are made through a payroll tax, and equal a fixed percentage of earnings. Then contributions and benefits would grow over time, not only because of population growth (and thus a growth of earnings resulting from a larger work force), but also because earnings per capita increase over time as a result of technical progress and capital accumulation. The rate of return on an unfunded social security program financed in this way would therefore be the growth rate of total earnings or, essentially, the growth rate of GNP, say, g.

How does this compare with a fully-funded system? Obviously, an unfunded program works much more to the benefit of those who retire during the start-up period than does a funded system. These individuals are the beneficiaries of the initial intergenerational transfer, which they receive without having had to make contributions themselves. Such windfalls vanish when the system moves into a long-run equilibrium, since each generation is not only a recipient of intergenerational transfers, but also a donor. On balance, each generation will "gain," in the sense that benefits will exceed contributions, providing a return, g, equal to the growth rate of GNP. However, this rate-of-return need not be as great, or greater than, the return on private savings, r; in fact, it will ordinarily be lower than r. In this sense, succeeding generations do not fare as well as if their contributions had been invested and had yielded the private sector (gross or before-tax) rate of return, as would be the case under a fully-funded program. Finally, if an unfunded system ever terminates, the last contributing generation suffers a windfall loss, just as the initial beneficiaries enjoyed a windfall gain. The final participating generation makes contributions to the system to finance the benefits enjoyed by its elders, but never receives any benefits in return. Under a fully-funded system, a termination of the program does not hurt the last participants, whose contributions enable the government to pay them their own benefits, with no transfer to a preceding generation.

In view of these general principles, the United States experience with an unfunded social security system is easily understood. Contributions to the system have increased rapidly over time, for several reasons. Population increase has played an important part, as has growth in earnings-per-worker. In addition, the payroll tax earmarked for OASI has increased, from 2 percent in the early years of the program to over 9 percent at present. Finally, the number of covered workers has increased. When the program began in 1937, all workers employed in commerce and industry were covered. In 1950, regularly-employed farm and domestic workers, and many self-employed workers, were required to participate in the program. In 1954, self-employed farmers and others were added. At present, virtually the entire workforce, with the notable exception of many government employees, is required to participate in the social security program. All of these factors have added to the growth of contributions to the system, and, since the program is operated on an unfunded basis, benefits have also increased. Consequently, workers who have retired have benefited considerably from social security.

Of course, we have seen that such high benefits in relation to contributions cannot be a long-run feature of an unfunded system; indeed, the prospects for the social security system indicate less favorable returns for future beneficiaries. There is no longer substantial room for growth in social security coverage; current demographic trends point to a much reduced (or zero) population growth rate in the future as the "baby boom" gives way to the "baby bust." If, in addition, contribution rates do not rise much more, total contributions to the system will increase in the future mainly from the growth of earnings-per-worker. In real terms, this may only amount to 1 or 2 percent per year. This is a much lower rate of return than retirees covered by social security have enjoyed in the past, and a rate that is also well below the (gross) rate of return on private savings. It is, therefore, reasonable to surmise that the initial windfall gains generated by the unfunded social security system will soon be coming to an end.[9]

Whether or not the intergenerational transfers inherent in a pay-as-you-go social security system are desirable is largely an ethical question. The answer depends on the relative neediness of younger and older households. In an economy experiencing rising real incomes over time, younger generations will, on average, be better off than older ones, so that intergenerational transfers will, on average, redistribute in an equalizing fashion. Note, however, that some young workers who are poor and have low earnings will contribute to the program, while some beneficiaries are rich. If a major goal of social security is to redistribute from the young rich to the elderly poor, therefore, there may be some question as to the appropriateness of the existing program design.

Intergenerational redistribution has undoubtedly been one of the major effects of the social security program. However, it has given rise to unintended incentive effects that may have had undesirable consequences. We now turn to this issue.

(c) Social Security and Saving

It has been argued, quite forcefully by some economists, that the social security system has reduced private saving to a significant extent. Feldstein (1974c, 1982), for example, argues that social security has reduced personal savings by approximately 40 percent. This is clearly an effect of great importance if the estimate is even roughly correct. Some analysts would dispute this conclusion, however, and at present there is considerable controversy about this issue. In order to understand how social security might depress savings, and why the actual magnitude of the effect on savings is difficult to ascertain and is the subject of dispute, let us turn to a theoretical analysis of social security in a simple life-cycle savings model.

We begin by assuming individuals intend to leave no bequests and that a household's lifetime can be divided into two periods. In the first period of life, the household works, earning an income of Y, of which T is taxed away by the social security payroll tax. The net-of-tax earnings of $(Y - T)$ is then either consumed, with C_1 the amount of consumption, or saved. In the second period of life, the worker is retired and has no earnings. For the moment, let us assume that retirement age is fixed. Second period consumption, denoted by C_2, is financed from social security benefits and by drawing down savings accumulated earlier in life. If B is the social security benefit level, and r is the (net) rate-of-return on first-period savings, C_2 is given by

$$C_2 = (Y - T - C_1)(1 + r) + B, \tag{14--4}$$

or, dividing by $(1 + r)$ and rearranging,

$$C_1 + \frac{C_2}{1 + r} = Y - T + \frac{B}{1 + r}. \tag{14--5}$$

This budget constraint is interpreted in the usual way: The present value of lifetime consumption, shown on the left-hand side of Eq. (14–5), is equal to lifetime wealth. In the absence of social security, this lifetime wealth would be Y. With social security, lifetime wealth changes by the present value of benefits minus contributions. This lifetime wealth effect is of crucial importance.

Now consider a social security system that is operated on a fully-funded basis, like private pension plans. Then the worker's contributions of T would earn a normal rate of return, r, so that benefits B would equal $(1 + r)T$. In this case, the social security program forces savings of T when young, but does not change lifetime wealth, as Eq. (14–5) shows. With an unchanged lifetime wealth, the household would find it optimal to maintain the same planned consumption over the life cycle. What happens, then, is that disposable income when young falls by T, consumption, C_1, remains unchanged, and *private* saving when young therefore falls by the full amount, T. *Public* saving, on the other hand, rises by T. Then, in retirement, the worker is able to carry out exactly the same consumption, C_2, as in the absence of social security, financing this consumption from lower private wealth and from exactly compensating social security benefits. In effect, with a fully-funded system, each dollar of public saving in the form of contributions displaces a dollar of private saving, leaving total national saving unchanged. The reduction in private saving resulting from social security is referred to as the "asset substitution effect."

With unfunded social security, however, lifetime wealth will no longer be unaffected; depending on the circumstances, the present value of benefits can exceed, or fall short of, contributions. The change in lifetime wealth resulting from social security, $B/(1 + r) - T$, is called (net) *social security wealth*, and will certainly be positive for those who retire during the start-up phase of the program. For them, T is zero or small, while B is positive and substantial, giving rise to the windfall gains described in subsection (b). For reasons described there, workers in the United States who have already retired have generally been in this position. On the other hand, as the system matures and moves toward a long-run equilibrium, the return on contributions to the system is limited by the growth of population and earnings per worker or, essentially, the growth rate of GNP, g. In the long run, whether social security wealth is positive or negative depends on the relationship between g and the rate of return on private savings, r. Since $B = (1 + g)T$, social security wealth is equal to

$$\frac{B}{1 + r} - T = \left(\frac{1 + g}{1 + r} - 1\right)T, \tag{14-6}$$

which will be greater or less than zero, depending on whether g is greater or less than r. In actual experience, it has generally been true that g is less than r. As a result, one would expect to find negative social security wealth in the long run. Finally, if the system were ever to terminate, social security wealth would become strongly negative, since workers would still have to make contributions as the system was phased out $(T > O)$, but would receive no benefits $(B = O)$.

Because an unfunded system can change lifetime wealth, it will generally change a household's lifetime consumption plan as well. A simple way to see this is to consider the situation facing a worker who retires just as the program begins. The worker thus enjoys retirement benefits, but does not have to pay payroll taxes to support the system. Before the program is introduced, the household faces a lifetime budget constraint, allowing the choice of a consumption plan on the budget line EF in Fig. 14–4. Here OE represents earnings when young, which in the simple two-period model are equal to lifetime wealth. The household, under these circumstances,

Figure 14–4

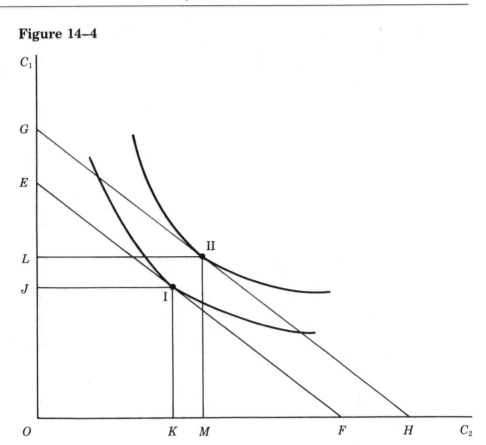

would choose the lifetime consumption plan represented by point I, with consumption of OJ in the first period, and OK in the second. Savings in the first period (income minus consumption) equal EJ. Now, suppose that a social security program is introduced that will pay retirement benefits equal to $B/(1 + r) = EG$, say, but which will not require any contributions by this household. Provided that the household correctly anticipates these benefits, it enjoys positive social security wealth of EG, which shifts out the budget line to GH, parallel to EF. The program thus expands the lifetime opportunity set, and if consumption in each period of life is a normal good, the household will move to a point such as II, with higher consumption in both periods. Notice what happens to savings: While earnings are still equal to OE, consumption has risen to OL, and savings therefore fall by JL. Thus, because of the creation of positive social security wealth, the household is induced to save less when young. Social security thus displaces private saving, that is, there is an asset substitution effect. Unlike the case of a funded social security program, however, with an unfunded system there is no offsetting increase in public saving. As a result, national (private plus public) saving is reduced.

The depressant effect of social security on saving is most obvious when one considers a worker retiring just as the program gets underway. However, it should be clear that lifetime consumption increases for all households who enjoy an increase in lifetime wealth from the social security system, even if they make some contributions when young. Since social security wealth has been positive for most or all generations up to the present time (for the reasons discussed above), one would expect that aggregate consumption has been higher since the program's inception. But if aggregate consumption has been higher because of social security, aggregate saving must have been smaller and, as a result, society's accumulation of capital must have been slowed. This is the theoretical explanation that has been offered for the estimated depressant effect of social security on savings and capital accumulation discussed above.

While the asset substitution effect provides a plausible explanation for a reduction in savings as a result of social security, it has been derived within the framework of a very simple model. As Feldstein (1974c) has stressed, social security can also influence the retirement decision. This possibility should be taken into account, because it can influence savings behavior indirectly. First, note that if leisure in old age is a normal good, an increase in lifetime wealth resulting from the introduction of a social security program will result in a lower supply of labor later in life, possibly in the form of earlier retirement. Second, since social security benefits are reduced by 50 percent for every dollar of earnings above a certain minimum, earnings for workers over age sixty-five (and to a lesser extent, for workers aged sixty-two to sixty-five) are, in effect, subject to a substantial implicit tax. This, too, can induce earlier retirement, or a reduction in earnings when old. If workers do retire earlier, for either or both of these reasons, they may be motivated to save at a higher rate when young. The reason for this is two-fold. First, with fewer working years, assets must be accumulated at a higher rate in order to build up any desired stock of wealth by the date of retirement. Second, the worker will wish to enter retirement with a larger stock of wealth, since past accumulation will have to finance more years of old-age consumption. (This effect is partly offset by the availability of social security benefits in old age, of course.) On both counts, the worker may be induced to save more for old age. This has been called the "induced retirement effect" of social security.

Since the asset substitution and induced retirement effects of social security work in different directions, the total effect on savings is theoretically ambiguous. The issue must then be resolved by empirical analysis. Feldstein (1974c), in a famous study, calculated social security wealth for members of different generations, added it up to find total social security wealth in each year since the beginning of the social security program, and tried to determine whether higher social security wealth was associated with higher aggregate consumption. The relationship estimated by Feldstein indicated that social security wealth has indeed increased consumption substantially, implying that the asset-substitution effect has been quite powerful. Related work by Munnell (1974) and Darby (1979) has found much smaller effects of social security on savings, however. While the asset-substitution effect, taken by itself, may be substantial, these studies find that the induced retirement effect has also been very strong, so that the net impact on savings is quite small—on the order of a 0–10 percent reduction, as compared with Feldstein's estimate of nearly 40 percent.

There is therefore some doubt about the actual size of the effect on savings by social security. This doubt is compounded by the fact that analysis of the asset-substitution effect requires a prior estimate of the amount of social security wealth. Social security wealth is not in itself observable. As the theoretical discussion above has made clear, what really matters to a young saver's plan of lifetime consumption is the *expected* social security benefits and contributions (and the rate of interest used to determine the present value of each). If, for instance, we wish to compute the social security wealth of a worker aged twenty in 1950, we would have to determine that worker's expectation of social security contributions through the year 1995 (assuming retirement at age sixty-five), and of benefits through (roughly) the year 2020. The benefits would have to be weighted in an appropriate way by the chances of the worker receiving (or having his or her surviving spouse receive) benefits for up to twenty-five years or more after retirement. But of course we cannot directly observe what a worker expects, and it is certainly not clear how a worker would form expectations for such a long time into the future. Contribution rates and maximum taxable earnings have varied substantially over the years, as have benefits. Table 14–2 shows that the combined (employer plus employee) contribution rate to OASI has risen from 2 percent on earnings of $3000 or less, to 9.15 percent in 1982 on earnings up to $32,400. Benefits, as a proportion of personal income, have increased from a negligible amount in the 1940s to over 5 percent at present. How much of this change would have been correctly anticipated by a worker in 1950? How much of whatever changes the next forty years will bring will be correctly anticipated? This is obviously a somewhat speculative matter. Yet, if a social security wealth measure is to be constructed, such problems must be resolved by making some definite assumption about expected contributions and benefits.

Presumably, the way to deal with this problem is to choose a variety of more or less plausible assumptions about the formation of expectations, and to see whether estimated social security wealth, and especially the estimated effect of the social security system on consumption and savings, are about the same in each case. Unfortunately, the contrary outcome results: Under different assumptions, it is quite possible for the estimated effect of social security on consumption to be insignificant (see Leimer and Lesnoy [1982]). This of course does not *prove* that the effect is negligible, but it does indicate that the estimated effect in any particular case depends heavily on whether or not the expectational assumption made is a valid

Table 14–2   OASI Contributions and Benefits 1940–1982, Selected Years

Year	Combined Contribution Rate (percent)	Maximum Taxable Earnings	Total Cash Benefits (millions of $)	Total Cash Benefits as Percentage of Personal Income
1940	2.0	$ 3,000	35	.04
1945	2.0	3,000	274	.16
1950	3.0	3,000	961	.43
1955	4.0	4,200	4,968	1.61
1960	5.5	4,800	10,677	2.67
1965	6.75	4,800	16,737	3.12
1970	7.3	7,800	28,796	3.55
1975	8.75	14,100	58,509	4.63
1980	9.04	25,900	105,074	4.86
1981	9.4	29,700	123,796	5.15
1982	9.15	32,400	NA	NA

Source: United States Department of Health and Human Services (1982), p. 29 and Table 46, p. 101.

one. Since there is no easy way to check this, it is likely that there will be considerable uncertainty and controversy about the impact of social security on savings for some time to come.

The empirical work just cited is based on a simple life-cycle savings model, with perfect capital markets and no bequests. As we saw in Chapter 11, however, the effects of tax policy in an intertemporal setting can depend in important ways on the nature of capital markets and household savings behavior. The same is also true in the case of social security. Suppose, for instance, that some young workers face borrowing constraints in the capital market: They wish to borrow to finance current consumption, but are unable to do so. Since they are saving nothing and consuming their entire disposable incomes, the required contributions under social security reduce their disposable income still further, causing a *decrease* in consumption. To the extent that workers face borrowing constraints, the decline in savings associated with the asset-substitution effect will be mitigated or eliminated. Of course, not all households are credit-constrained, and, in fact, most are not. But borrowing constraints might still affect a significant proportion of workers, and thus have a noticeable effect on the response of savings to social security.

Similarly, let us consider the effect of social security when households are intergenerational optimizers who leave bequests for their children out of altruistic feelings for them. A pay-as-you-go system sets up a series of intergenerational transfers from young to old, as discussed above. Suppose that these transfers are correctly anticipated by all households. Then, in effect, the social security system is creating a series of forced negative bequests across generations. However, the stream of income extending into the indefinite future, which determines the wealth of a sequence of generations, does not change because of the program, and so the intergenerational budget set—that is, the possible paths of consumption across generations, is left unchanged. Intuitively, then, one would expect the chosen path of consumption to be unaffected by the program, and that the path of national saving, or income minus consumption, would be unaffected as well. This means, as Barro (1974) has argued, that the asset-substitution effect of social security would be completely nullified.

To see in more detail how this can occur, let us write down the budget constraints facing parents and their children under a pay-as-you-go social security program that only lasts for one generation. (That is, the children are taxed to provide for the parents.) It will become clear that the argument extends to a many-period program as well.

Suppose a parent lives for two periods, earning income of Y_1 in the first period of life, and spending the second period in retirement. Let parental consumption in these two periods be written C_1^P and C_2^P, let B be the social security benefits received when old, and let I^P be the bequest left to the children at the end of the second period of life. Then, if r is the rate of return on first-period savings of $Y_1 - C_1^P$, the amount of bequest must satisfy

$$I^P = B + (Y_1 - C_1^P)(1 + r) - C_2^P, \tag{14–7}$$

since the bequest must equal second-period wealth minus second-period consumption.

Similarly, if the children earn income of Y_2 by working in period 2, consume C_2^C and C_3^C in their two periods of life, leave a bequest to their children of I^C, and pay payroll taxes of B to support the benefits paid out to their parents, the bequest that they make to their own children must be

$$I^C = (Y_2 + I^P - B - C_2^C)(1 + r) - C_3^C. \tag{14–8}$$

This equation reflects the fact that the parental bequest is received when young, that is, in the first period of life.

Consider now how the presence of the social security system has affected the choices open to each generation. Parents, receiving benefits of B when old, can now leave a bequest that is higher by exactly that amount, if they leave their own consumption unchanged, as shown by Eq. (14–7). Children, in order to be no worse off because of the taxes they pay into the system, would need to receive a bequest that is higher by exactly B. If they do, the higher bequest would offset the taxes they pay, and their feasible consumption choices and bequests would be unchanged, as shown by Eq. (14–8). In fact, substituting into Eq. (14–8) from Eq. (14–7) to eliminate I^P, dividing by $(1 + r)^2$, and rearranging, we see that the overall constraint limiting the consumption of these two generations, and their bequest to the third generation, is

$$C_1^P + \frac{C_2^P + C_2^C}{1 + r} + \frac{C_3^C}{(1 + r)^2} + \frac{I^C}{(1 + r)^2} = Y_1 + \frac{Y_2}{1 + r}, \tag{14–9}$$

that is, the present value of consumption plus the bequest to the third generation is equal to the present value of income. Since the size of the social security program, B, does not appear in Eq. (14–9), it is clear that the constraint, and therefore the consumption choices by these individuals, is unaffected by the program. When the program forces transfers from young to old, the old simply respond by increasing their bequest to the young in an exactly offsetting fashion, leaving total private savings unchanged.

Thus, the expected impact of an unfunded social security program on savings and capital accumulation is dramatically different in an economy with intergenerational or dynastic utility maximizers, as compared with the simple life-cycle savings economy with no bequests. Unfortunately, it is not by any means obvious which of these views of the world is closer to reality, and no decisive tests that would resolve the matter have been conducted to date. Further research will be needed to resolve this issue.

In conclusion, it should be emphasized that the possible reduction in savings resulting from social security in the simple life-cycle framework results only from the fact that the system is financed on a pay-as-you-go basis. This is what creates positive social security wealth and an increase in consumption. By contrast, a fully-funded system builds up a reserve to pay for retirement benefits, with public saving substituting for private saving. Total national saving and capital accumulation are left unchanged. Thus, a reduction in savings is not a necessary consequence of all types of social security systems. It would be difficult for the United States to change to a funded system at present, however: Contribution rates would have to increase substantially, enough to continue to finance benefits for current retirees, and to build up a reserve for the current working population. (This is assuming that the government does not refuse benefits to those who are retired, or about to retire.) As already noted, demographic trends indicate that contribution rates will have to rise in the future if they are to continue to finance benefits on an unfunded basis. The transition to a fully funded system might therefore be awkward. In effect, whenever an unfunded system is phased out, a loss is suffered by the last contributing generation, and it is difficult to know when such a loss should be imposed.

(d) Social Security and Retirement

Because the social security system is intended to provide benefits to retirees, benefits are sharply reduced for older workers who continue to earn income. As noted earlier, benefits are reduced by 50 percent for earnings above a certain amount (currently $6000 dollars per year), which means that for most workers, continued full-time employment after age sixty-five leads to a complete loss of social security benefits.

This implicit tax on earnings for workers over sixty-five might be expected to lead to an increase in the number of individuals retiring at that age. Indeed, as Table 14–3 shows, labor force participation by men in this age bracket has definitely fallen. Whether this can be attributed to the social security program is not clear, however. During a time of rising income and wealth, earlier retirement would be expected if the income elasticity of demand for leisure in old age is high, as it might well be; thus some reduction in labor force participation would presumably have occurred even in the absence of social security. On the other hand, a gradual improvement in the health of older people could postpone retirement. And, of course, rising real wages encourage a substitution effect in favor of more work and less leisure. This, to some degree, offsets the income effect and therefore favors delayed retirement.

The determination of the effect of social security on retirement thus presents a difficult empirical problem. Some studies (such as Boskin [1977]) find that social security has indeed contributed to earlier retirement. On the other hand, the 50 percent reduction in benefits is only one of the ways the social security system affects the labor supply incentives facing older

Table 14–3 Labor Force Participation by Males Age 65 and Over, 1900–1982, Selected Years

Year	Labor Force Participation Rate (Percent)
1900	63.1
1920	55.6
1930	54.0
1940	41.8
1945	48.7
1950	45.8
1955	39.6
1960	33.1
1965	27.9
1970	26.8
1975	21.7
1980	19.1
1981	18.4
1982	17.8

Source: 1900–1970: United States Department of Commerce (1975), pp. 131–132. 1975–1981: United States Department of Commerce (1983b) p. 377. 1982: United States Department of Labor (1983), Table 4, p. 144.

workers. For workers who take early retirement, that is, retirement between ages sixty-two and sixty-five, monthly social security benefits are reduced in an actuarial fashion to reflect the longer expected period of retirement for such individuals. For workers who postpone retirement beyond age sixty-five, monthly benefits are slightly increased. Moreover, it is important to remember that monthly benefits are based on average monthly earnings. At age sixty-two or older, a worker may be earning at a wage rate higher than that obtained in previous years, since wages generally increase over the working lifetime, and this can result in an increase in average earnings, and thus in benefits. While it is true that one more year of work may only increase average earnings by a small amount, the increase in average earnings will raise benefits for the entire retirement period, so that this effect can be important. In fact, a study by Blinder, Gordon, and Wise (1980) found that the actuarial increases, together with the increases in average earnings resulting from an additional year's work, combined to more than offset the 50 percent earnings tax for many workers aged sixty-two to sixty-five, and to offset to a large degree the 50 percent tax for workers aged sixty-five and slightly older.

Thus, workers retiring at age sixty-five may have little or no special incentive to do so on account of social security. On the other hand, workers who would have retired between ages sixty-two and sixty-five may actually postpone retirement until age sixty-five because of social security. Of course, workers may not be sufficiently aware of the details of the benefit structure to be influenced by these incentives. Nevertheless, these considerations do weaken the theoretical presumption that social security has created powerful incentives for early retirement. Ultimately, more empirical research will be necessary to resolve the issue. While it is likely that the social security system has contributed to earlier retirement for some categories of workers, especially those who would have retired at relatively older ages, the quantitative size of this effect is not easily determined, and remains the subject of investigation.

(e) Incidence of the Payroll Tax

Since payroll taxes cover most of the labor force, the tax may be considered a general proportional tax on labor income. From an economic point of view, it should not be relevant whether the employer or the employee pays it. In either case a wedge, equal to the *combined* tax rates on employees and employers, is driven between a worker's net-of-tax wage and the firm's gross wage payment. Since the tax is general, it can only be avoided or shifted by varying the supply of labor. If the supply of labor is relatively inelastic, the incidence of the tax would fall mainly on labor income. Or, if the wage-earner views the tax as being a payment towards retirement security, then the tax will not be regarded as a reduction in real income, and there will be no incentive to change behavior. There may be some rationale for this, to the extent that future benefits received reflect current earnings. There is no conclusive evidence as to the incidence of the payroll tax, but most discussion has assumed that it is largely borne by labor income. Brittain (1972), for example, found that the evidence would not support the hypothesis that the gross-of-tax wage increased when social security tax rates increased. This is consistent with the view that the tax is absorbed by the wage or salary earner. On the other hand, Beach and Balfour (1983) find that only about 60 percent of the tax on employers falls on male workers (who have highly inelastic labor supply curves), and even less falls on female workers (who have much more elastic labor supply curves). Beach and Balfour attribute this partial shifting of the payroll tax on employers to labor market rigidities and imperfections.

To the extent that the tax is borne by labor income, it would be expected to be a regressive tax. For one thing, since it applies only to labor income, and since capital income as a proportion of total income rises as income rises, the payroll tax as a proportion of total income falls as income rises. This regressivity is further strengthened by the upper limit on payroll tax payments mentioned above. On the other hand, for those at the very low end of the income scale, the tax may be progressive, since these groups receive proportionately more of their income as transfers, rather than wage income. Pechman (1977) has estimated that in 1964, payroll taxes were progressive up to incomes of $7000 or $8000, and regressive beyond that. The regressivity is mitigated to the extent that the benefits are not regressive. In fact, they are probably progressive for much the same reason as the tax payments are regressive.

Given that these social insurance schemes are not operated on a true insurance basis, a good case can be made for separating the taxing from the expenditures side, and financing such schemes out of general revenues. If that were the case, a payroll tax would have to stand on its own as an element of the overall tax system. Under these circumstances, if the payroll tax were kept at all, it would be hard to make a case for an upper limit on contributions. It might even be preferable, on equity grounds, to eliminate the payroll tax altogether, and rely on the more general personal income tax.

UNEMPLOYMENT INSURANCE

14–4   The major reason for social insurance programs is to reduce the risk associated with unpredictable fluctuations in household utility levels. One can think of these fluctuations as having two major sources: First, the income received by the household may be uncertain. Second, even if income is fixed, the household may be faced with uncertainty in the amount of expenditures required to attain a given utility level. In this section, we investigate uncertainty on the income side, in particular, uncertainty arising from the possibility of unemployment. In the following section, uncertainty on the expenditure side is considered, using the specific example of the possibility of heavy expenses incurred because of ill health.

In both instances, in the absence of insurance, households would face a significant "cost of risk" similar to that discussed in Chapter 8. In the case of income fluctuations, households would be willing to take a reduction in *expected* income in return for a reduction in the *variability* of their income. Thus, households could be made better off if an insurer were to offer to even out the fluctuations in their income, in return for some given premium. The premium a household would be willing to pay would be at least as great as the expected value of the insurance payments it would receive in the uncertain future.

For such an insurance scheme to be viable, some insurer must be willing to take on the risk associated with the variability of household income, the same variability that the household wished to avoid. Why should an insurer be willing to do this? There are two reasons why an insurer might be willing to take on such income fluctuations. First, the insurer might simply be less averse to risk than the household. That is, the cost of risk for given income fluctuations might be less for the insurer than for the household being insured. Second, and presumably far more important, is the fact that insurers can reduce the variability of their returns by "pooling their risks." That is, if several households are insured by the same insurer, and if the income fluctuations of those households are not perfectly correlated, then the variability of the portfolio of insurance policies to the insured will be less than the variability experienced by each household being insured. If there are an indefinitely large number of households, and if their income fluctuations are completely uncorrelated, then the portfolio of their aggregate incomes will be perfectly certain. (This phenomenon of risk-pooling is similar to that occurring in stock markets where, for example, mutual funds hold diversified portfolios of many stocks, thus creating a portfolio with less variability per dollar than the stocks themselves.) In the context of insurance, the presence of risk-pooling means that the risk facing insurers is less than that facing individual households, so the provision of insurance can be mutually beneficial.

Unemployment insurance can be viewed as a particular type of insurance against income fluctuations, except that in this case, the insurance is provided publicly. Instead of the insurance being a voluntary contract between the insurers and the insured, it is compulsory. All eligible workers must be part of the scheme. While the general structure of the unemployment insurance system in the United States is similar to that of other countries, unemployment insurance is mainly a state, rather than a federal, responsibility, so that no uniform set of provisions apply across the nation. Therefore, we cannot be too specific about the details of the system. Nevertheless, the broad outlines can be described.

(a) Eligibility

Almost all wage and salary workers are covered by unemployment insurance. The exceptions are some workers in small firms, farms, private households, and non-profit organizations. In order to qualify for benefits, workers in covered unemployment must also satisfy some qualification requirements. These requirements are intended to include only those who have a substantial recent attachment to the work force. The criteria for satisfying the attachment conditions are defined either by a minimum number of weeks of employment, or a minimum level of earnings in the past fifty-two weeks, or both, depending upon the state.

(b) Benefits

Assuming that an unemployed worker is entitled to unemployment insurance benefits, the amount of the benefits depends upon the wage of the worker when employed. Roughly speaking, the weekly benefit is usually at least 50 percent of weekly wages, up to a maximum weekly wage. The maximum insured earnings are defined as a proportion of the average covered wage in the state, and are usually from one-half to two-thirds of that wage. It turns out that about 40 percent of claimants obtain the maximum. The value of the benefits also depends upon the duration over which payments are made. Although this once again varies by state, the duration is usually twenty-six weeks. Less than twenty-six weeks of benefits may be awarded if previous weeks of insured work or insured wages are low. Alternatively, benefits may be extended for longer durations if aggregate unemployment is high. It should also be noted that workers may be disqualified from receiving benefits if they are deemed not to be involuntarily unemployed.

There are three reasons for disqualification. First, workers may voluntarily quit without good cause. Second, workers may be discharged for misconduct. Third, workers may refuse suitable employment without good reason. Determining which of these reasons is sufficient to warrant disqualification is an administrative decision that may be more or less severe, depending upon the jurisdiction involved. Disqualification for one of these reasons often carries a suspension of benefits for a limited period, usually up to six weeks. Finally, benefits in the hands of the recipients are partially taxable. The proportion of benefits included in the personal tax base rises with income, as discussed in Chapter 13.

(c) Financing

The financing of unemployment insurance benefits comes from funds accumulated through a payroll tax levied on employers. The payroll tax is levied at a flat rate on each worker's wages up to a maximum taxable wage base. The rate varies from state to state. In addition, the rate may vary from firm to firm, on the basis of experience. This *experience rating* varies from state to state, and is usually only partial in those states using it. The basic method of experience rating is to make the payroll tax rate vary inversely with the ratio of cumulative past contributions to cumulative past benefit payments, up to a maximum rate. For those firms at the maximum rate, which includes a substantial proportion of all businesses, the experience rating will be ineffective, since further layoffs will not affect payroll tax rates. For those firms below the maximum, the experience rating is only partial, since the payroll tax rate does not rise to cover the full amount of the additional benefit payments induced by a layoff at the margin. This will be important in analyzing the effect of the unemployment insurance on the behavior of the firm, as we do below.

As a prelude to evaluating the effects of unemployment insurance on the allocation of resources in the economy, it is useful to consider what an "ideal" unemployment insurance scheme might look like. Suppose we view unemployment insurance as a scheme for insuring workers against temporary loss of income through unemployment. A typical worker, in the absence of insurance, would face the uncertainty of either being employed at his going wage rate or being unemployed and receiving no income. Given the probabilities of his being employed and unemployed, it would be possible to design an *actuarially fair* insurance policy for this worker, where, as with social security, "actuarially fair" means that the premium paid per dollar of insurance exactly equals the expected cost of benefit payouts by the insurer. If the insurer were risk-neutral, or could pool risks fully, an actuarially fair policy would be appropriate, since there would be no need to compensate the insurer for risk. The worker would then be permitted to purchase whatever amount of insurance he wished. Under certain circumstances, it can be shown that the worker would fully insure himself, that is, purchase enough insurance so that the benefits received when unemployed equalled the wage received when employed.[10] Note the important property of the ideal insurance scheme, that different types of workers would pay different premiums if they faced different probabilities of being unemployed.

One does not observe the ideal unemployment insurance scheme, or anything near to it, being provided by the private sector. Why is that the case? There are two sorts of institutions in the private sector that might, in principle, be willing to insure a worker, the insurance industry and the worker's employer. There are several reasons why the insurance industry is precluded from providing voluntary unemployment insurance in the same way as it provides, say, life insurance or automobile insurance. For one thing, there is likely to be a significant moral hazard problem, since the loss of employment is not an altogether random event. The worker may be able to exploit the system, and will have an incentive to do so, by increasing both his rate of job turnover and the duration of his unemployment. If the insurance company is unable to monitor the cause of unemployment, a moral hazard problem will exist. What could make the moral hazard more difficult to detect is that the employer might, with the implicit agreement of the worker, exploit the system by increasing temporary lay-offs. This is a problem with publicly, as well as privately, provided unemployment insurance schemes, and we shall return to it below.

In addition to the moral hazard problem, there is likely to be an adverse selection problem facing private insurers. Different workers face different probabilities of being unemployed; therefore they should, in principle, have different unemployment insurance premiums. If the insurance companies are unable to distinguish workers by level of risk, the same insurance policies may have to be offered to all workers. In that case, the optimal insurance scheme cannot be set for each type of worker and, as Rothschild and Stiglitz (1976) have shown, there may be no equilibrium possible in the market for insurance.

Finally, the private insurance industry may not be able to insure workers against the risk of unemployment, even in the absence of moral hazard and adverse selection, because the risk of unemployment may not be an "insurable risk." That is, it may not be possible for insurance companies to pool the risks of various workers being unemployed. This will be the case to the extent that the probabilities of various workers being unemployed are correlated. If the probabilities of unemployment are related closely to the aggregate level of economic activity, the probabilities of unemployment would be correlated, and the insurers could not generally eliminate its risk by pooling. Nonetheless, unemployment insurance might be viewed as socially desirable on distributive grounds, that is, as a way of redistributing income to those unfortunate enough to be unemployed. In this case, the term unemployment *insurance* is a misnomer; the program's goal would be redistribution, which, as we have seen repeatedly, is a function that generally must be carried out through the public sector. For these various reasons, unemployment insurance is not likely to be provided by the private insurance market.

Another potential source of unemployment insurance for workers is through the employer itself. This possibility comes out most forcefully when workers are thought of as having a permanent attachment to a firm. This is the view taken in the so-called *implicit contract* literature, on which the following discussion is based (see especially Baily [1974], Feldstein [1976b] and Azariadis [1975]). According to this literature, when workers take employment at a firm, the terms of that employment are much broader than simply an agreed-upon wage rate. In addition to an explicitly-set wage-rate-plus-fringe benefits package, the worker and employer implicitly agree on the lay-off policy of the firm. The lay-off policy defines the extent to which the firm will respond to a downturn by laying off workers (or reducing hours worked), as opposed to keeping workers on to produce at a loss or to build up inventories. From the worker's point of view, the layoff policy of the firm is reflected in the probability of unemployment. Since businesses have to attract permanent employees from other firms bidding for the same pool of workers, they will be induced to offer their employees the most attractive combination of benefits and layoff probabilities that are consistent with earning a normal or competitive return on capital.

To see the implications of this, consider the following example of a competitive firm operating in a cyclical industry, such as fishing or agriculture. For a proportion π of the year, the firm receives a price p for its output. During the remaining $(1 - \pi)$ it receives only αp, where $\alpha < 1$. Both the firm and the workers know the value of all these variables. Suppose there is no unemployment insurance. The business must decide upon a wage rate in each period, as well as the number of workers to employ in peak and off-peak periods. The difference in these two numbers is the number laid off in the off-peak period. It is assumed that those laid off are randomly drawn from the firm's workers. Each worker views his "implicit contract" with the firm as consisting of a wage rate in each period of employment, and the probability of being laid off in the off-peak period and receiving no income. This probability will be equal to the proportion of the work force laid off. From this package the worker will obtain a certain expected utility given by:

$$EU = \pi u(w_1) + (1 - \pi) \left[\frac{N_2}{N_1} u(w_2) + \left(1 - \frac{N_2}{N_1}\right) u(0) \right] \qquad (14\text{--}10)$$

where $u(w_1)$ is the utility obtained from working at a wage of w_1, $u(w_2)$ is the same for w_2, and $u(0)$ is the utility from being laid off with no wage, but enjoying leisure. There are N_1 workers hired, and N_2 are kept on in the off-peak period. Therefore, N_2/N_1 is the probability of each worker being employed in the off-peak period.

The firm selects both a wage policy (w_1, w_2) and a hiring policy (N_1, N_2) so as to maximize profits, given that it must provide a level of expected utility for its workers equivalent to what they could obtain elsewhere. Without going into the formal derivation of the equilibrium wage-lay-off policy, we shall simply state the outcome and provide an intuitive interpretation.[11] The nature of the problem ensures that the conditions of employment offered are those which allow the firm to attract workers at a minimum labor cost to itself. The implicit contract arrived at is characterized as follows:

(a) Wage Policy

The wage rate will be the same in both peak and off-peak periods. This removes the risk of income fluctuation between the two periods, when the worker is employed. It is beneficial for the firm to remove this risk, since it no longer has to compensate the worker for the risk of this income fluctuation. Thus, workers can be attracted to the firm at a lower total compensation than otherwise. Notice that since we have only assumed wage payments to be made if the worker is employed, there will still be a risk of income fluctuation arising from the possibility of being laid off. We return to that below.

(b) Lay-off Policy

The number of workers laid off in the off-peak period is such that the value of the marginal product to the firm of hiring one more worker is equal to the value of leisure to the worker if laid off. Since the wage rate paid in the two periods presumably exceeds the value of leisure, this implies that the wage rate exceeds the value of the marginal product of labor in the off-peak period, so the firm operates at a loss. Correspondingly, the wage rate is less than the value of the marginal product of labor during the peak period, so that the firm can earn enough to offset its off-peak losses.

Given the restrictions we have imposed on the firm, in particular the assumption that no wage payments are made to the laid-off workers, the above contractual arrangements are optimal, both privately and from a social point of view. However, the worker still bears the risk associated with the possibility of being laid off. Some of this cost to the workers can be reduced if we allow the firm to make payments to workers who are laid off. We can think of this as being a firm-specific unemployment insurance scheme. If we retain the previous assumptions, especially the assumption that workers are attached to the firm for the entire cycle, but now allow the firm to make payments to its laid-off workers, we would find that it would be in the mutual interest of firm and workers for these wage payments to be positive. Indeed, under certain circumstances, exactly the same wage would be paid to both employed and unemployed workers.[12] The intuitive reason for this is that wage payments to the unemployed will reduce the degree of utility fluctuations in employed and unemployed states, and will therefore reduce the risk. With less risk to bear, the total compensation that must be paid to workers on average over the cycle will be lower, and therefore the firm will make more profit.

Thus, according to the implicit contract view of wage policy, firms would have an incentive to establish their own "unemployment insurance" schemes. These schemes would be self-financed by each firm, or, to use a common term, they would be *fully experience-rated*. A scheme which is fully experience-rated for each firm generally refers to a scheme under which the marginal cost of laying off a worker is the full amount of unemployment compensation required.[13] Under full experience-rating, it can be shown that the implicit contract between firm and worker would contain a lay-off policy in which the value of the product of the marginal worker in the off-peak period equals the value of foregone leisure, as before. This, in turn, is the socially optimal lay-off policy.

Businesses do not offer their workers fully experience-rated unemployment insurance schemes as described above. This is not to say that they do not offer any insurance at all. There are implicit ways in which firms insure their workers, such as by severance pay arrangements, seniority rules, or simply by hoarding labor in off-peak periods. However, full un-employment insurance is not offered, presumably because the implicit contract view abstracts from the real world in a variety of ways. Workers may not be as closely attached to the firm as the theory assumes; firms may not be able to pool the risks of unemployment for the reasons discussed earlier; and firms may not be able to fully distinguish temporary falls in their fortunes from more permanent ones. Nonetheless, the incentives analyzed in the implicit contract literature have proven to be valuable benchmarks in judging the effects of publicly provided unemployment insurance schemes, to which we now turn.

The existing unemployment insurance scheme is neither actuarially fair by type of worker, nor fully experience-rated by firm or industry. These design characteristics account for many of the resource allocation effects of the scheme. We consider four of these in turn.

(i) *Temporary Layoffs* By affecting the opportunity cost of the layoff, unemployment insurance influences the decision by the firm to lay off workers in times of low demand. We have seen above, in the context of the implicit contract model, that a fully experience-rated unemployment insurance scheme is ideal from the point of view of the layoff decision. When the firm is required to bear the full cost of payments received by workers laid off, they will be induced to lay off workers efficiently, that is, until the foregone output of the laid-off worker equals the value of leisure time acquired. Furthermore, workers would willingly acquiesce in this decision.

Relative to this ideal situation, an unemployment insurance scheme that is less than fully experience-rated will induce firms to lay off excessive workers during the downturn as opposed to, say, reducing hours of work or accumulating inventories. As Feldstein (1976b) has pointed out, the unemployment insurance scheme will effectively subsidize the layoff decision by the firm. This is because the marginal payment of benefits to a laid-off worker exceeds the marginal cost incurred by the firm in payroll tax payments. The latter are only partly, if at all, related to the firm's layoff experience. From the point of view of the firm and its workers, the marginal benefit of a layoff is the excess of the unemployment insurance benefit received by the laid-off workers over the additional premiums incurred by the firm.[14]

Two further points ought to be made about the implications of a less than fully experience-rated system. The first is that the above analysis compares the existing system with the ideal alternative. If, instead, the existing system were compared with what might exist in the absence of public unemployment insurance, the impact on layoffs might be beneficial. For example, in the absence of unemployment insurance, too few layoffs might occur, since the firm may resist using layoffs because of the adverse risk imposed on workers. Second, the case for full experience-rating is based on a model in which workers are permanently attached to one firm, and in which the only source of unemployment is the temporary layoff. In fact, unemployment occurs for other reasons, such as structural changes in the economy, or workers changing jobs in order to seek a better "match" between skills and jobs. One would presumably not want the latter type of unemployment to be insured by a scheme experience-rated to a particular firm. Since it is not administratively feasible to design a scheme that separates the temporarily laid-off from the rest of the unemployed, such a scheme, designed to cope only with the temporarily unemployed, would not be desirable. For example, it might influence the firm's decision to hire permanent workers, or to lay off others permanently.

Nonetheless, the effect of unemployment insurance on layoffs remains an important empirical question, and some work has been done in this area. Using microdata for March 1971, from the monthly Department of Labor survey of 60,000 households, Feldstein (1978b) investigated the statistical relation between the proportion of workers on temporary layoff, and an unemployment insurance variable and some industry and demographic characteristics. The unemployment insurance variable used was the so-called *benefit-replacement ratio*, that is, the ratio of unemployment benefits received by the average worker to foregone earnings net-of-tax. Feldstein found that the unemployment insurance scheme accounted for almost one-half of temporary unemployment. Unfortunately, this study did not test the implications of experience-rating for temporary layoffs, since the only unemployment insurance variable used was the benefit-replacement ratio.

(ii) *Turnover and Duration of Unemployment*   As mentioned above, not all unemployment consists of temporary layoffs of persons who are then recalled by the same firm. Workers lose their jobs as the longer-term fortunes of firms and industries decline due to structural changes in the economy, such as relative price changes or technological improvements. Also, workers may leave jobs for which they are not well suited to find others more suitable. These sources of unemployment may be encompassed under the term *job turnover*. The greater the rate of job turnover, the higher is the observed rate of unemployment at any given point in time. In addition, the longer the time between leaving one job and taking another, known as the *duration* of the unemployment spell, the greater is the measured rate of unemployment. The exposure to the risk of job turnover is one which might well be insured.

Three difficulties arise in insuring against the risk of job turnover. The first is the simple informational problem of knowing the appropriate probabilities of turnover for groups of workers in order to set the appropriate premium, that is, the actuarially appropriate premium. Since such information is hard to come by, unemployment insurance schemes are uniformly applied.

The second problem is that an unemployment insurance scheme designed to insure against risk of temporary layoff should be different from one designed to deal with structural change and job turnover. For example, while experience-rating may be appropriate for the former, it will not be for the latter. The difficulty is that it is hard for the insurer to distinguish between temporary unemployment and permanent unemployment. As a result, the same scheme usually applies to both. That is one reason why full experience-rating may not be appropriate.

The third difficulty is one of moral hazard. Workers themselves may have some influence on the turnover decision, and they may have an influence on the duration of the unemployment. Just as unemployment insurance subsidizes temporary layoffs, so too it subsidizes the costs of the job-search activities that are incurred when workers leave one job and attempt to find another. Since benefits received have no implications for future premiums to be paid, workers will treat the benefits they receive as a marginal subsidy to job-search activity. They will be willing to change jobs more frequently, on average, and to spend more time searching. There is a benefit to this, in that in the long run, workers may be better matched to jobs. Against this must be set the extra social costs of the search activity. It is an empirical question whether or not the benefits will outweigh the costs.

(iii) *Supply of Labor*   Unemployment insurance benefits may influence the supply of labor, especially the participation rate, for two reasons: First, the reduction in the financial risks associated with unemployment makes working relatively more attractive than otherwise. Second, the absence of actuarial fairness in the scheme means that some groups of workers will obtain net benefits from it, and others net losses. Those who will be net beneficiaries will enter the labor force. This may include the so-called "secondary workers," those with less attachment to the labor force. For example, second income-earners in a family might enter the labor force temporarily in the expectation of receiving benefits in excess of their contributions.

The fact that unemployment insurance is not actuarially fair has equity implications as well. Some groups will receive positive expected net benefits from the scheme, and others negative net benefits. The effect of this is, of course, lessened to the extent that benefits received are taxable sources of income. However, the inequities cannot be fully eliminated.

(iv) *General Equilibrium Effects*   Finally, as Topel and Welch (1980) have pointed out, the lack of actuarial fairness and experience-rating in the unemployment insurance scheme will bring about inter-industry re-allocations of the labor force. There is likely to be a systematic difference, over industries, of unemployment experience. Some will be inherently more cyclical and riskier than others. Workers in these more volatile industries will be net beneficiaries from unemployment insurance in the actuarial sense, and workers will reallocate towards those industries in response to the unemployment insurance scheme. The situation is not unlike that of the general equilibrium reallocation of capital due to the corporate income tax. In this case, the unemployment insurance scheme effectively subsidizes the hiring of labor in volatile industries, since the net benefit of the unemployment insurance scheme to these workers is a form of compensation comparable to a wage payment.

The overall assessment of the existing unemployment scheme would involve weighing all these various factors. It is still very much an open question, and the topic of ongoing research.

MEDICAL INSURANCE

14–5   In the previous section, we considered the insurance of uncertain utility arising out of the possibility of income fluctuation. In this section we look at an example of utility uncertainty caused by the possibility of incurring medical expenditures in the event of ill health. The method of providing medical insurance varies from country to country. In some countries, such as Canada and Great Britain, full medical and hospital insurance is provided on a compulsory basis through the public sector. In the United States, the role of government is somewhat more limited, though certainly present. As was mentioned in Section 14–3, persons eligible for social security are covered under Medicare for medical expenses incurred. As with old age security, this is funded through the payroll tax. In addition, low-income persons are eligible for medical expense coverage under the Medicaid program, funded out of general revenues. Persons not eligible for either of these forms of medical insurance are responsible for their own coverage. Many are covered by private insurance plans, often organized through their employers.

Even here the government plays a role by implicitly subsidizing expenditures on medical care. This is done in two ways. First, and most important, health insurance premiums incurred by employers on behalf of their employees (which is the way most private health insurance is financed) are untaxed benefits to employees. They are deductible as costs to the employer, but are neither included as taxable income for the employee, nor as part of the payroll tax. The marginal subsidy is thus the marginal tax rate of the worker plus the social security tax rate. Second, for an individual who acquires his own insurance, premiums may be deducted if medical expenses are itemized. Thus, privately provided health insurance is subsidized significantly.[15]

Perhaps the first question we should ask is why the public sector should be involved in medical insurance provision at all. Why not leave it entirely to the private sector, as is done with, say, home insurance? There is a long history of debates over this question in the political forum, and there continues to be some dispute. It is probably fair to say that, even among economists, no conclusive agreement has been reached about the appropriate role of government in the provision of medical care. What we can do is summarize some of the arguments that have been advanced by economists concerning the sorts of market failures that can arise in this industry. Many of these are to be found in the seminal contribution by Arrow (1963). The arguments are as follows:

(a) Externalities

The provision of medical care to an individual may yield external benefits to other persons in the economy, and may therefore be justifiably encouraged. This will be the case for the prevention and treatment of communicable diseases, whose spread may be reduced. As with external benefits more generally, individuals acting in response to private market prices will not have enough incentive to undertake the socially optimal level of medical expenditures. The externality argument also applies if utility functions are interdependent. An individual may be altruistic, in the sense that improvements in the health of others improve his utility. If so, it would be efficient to provide medical care over and above what private markets would provide. Of course, the magnitude of these external effects remains purely speculative.

(b) Restrictive Practices in the Provision of Medical Care

It is sometimes alleged that the cost of medical care to an individual is excessive, due to various monopoly-like practices by the suppliers of medical care. These include the ability of medical professions to regulate themselves by licensing or influencing the numbers admitted to training programs, and by restrictions imposed on imperfect substitutes for medical services. Whether or not these practices actually lead to an underprovision of medical services is not obvious, since there are other influences working in the opposite direction. One of these is the observed tendency for doctors to price-discriminate by income group. Another is the fact that the suppliers of medical services have a significant influence on the quantities of services demanded. For example, doctors prescribe drugs and recommend treatment.

(c) Redistributive Arguments

It might be argued that medical care should be publicly provided on redistributive grounds (other than those resulting from interdependent utility functions already discussed). The argument might go as follows: By nature, different persons are randomly endowed with different susceptibilities to medical problems. Those unfortunate enough to be born with a high risk of disease or disability could only obtain insurance from private insurers at higher premiums than low-risk persons, if at all. The uniform provision of medical insurance to all might therefore be viewed as society insuring persons against the risks of nature. Unlike other insurance, this type of medical insurance would be provided on identical terms to persons of all risk classes, even though the risk class to which various persons belong could be well known. That is, it is not actuarially fair. This is why the medical insurance must be compulsory. If it were not, low-risk persons would opt out.

As with other redistributive arguments for public sector activity, this one implies a value judgment, or an equity judgment, that the other efficiency arguments for medical insurance do not require. It will therefore not be accepted by all, and probably lies at the root of much disagreement over the pros and cons of public medical insurance. One interesting way to view the value judgment underlying this argument for public medical insurance is in terms of the so-called *contractarian* view of social welfare used by Harsanyi (1955) and Rawls (1971). They argue that an appropriate way for an individual to form a judgment about equity and redistribution is to abstract from his personal circumstances altogether by imagining himself to be "behind a veil of ignorance," or "in an original position." In this original position, each person is assumed to have no objective information about his income, wealth, etc. For the purposes of health insurance, it is imagined that the person does not know what health characteristics nature has endowed him with. In this original position, before the riskiness of each person has been revealed, all persons would be equally insurable. If one accepted this contractarian view of equity, medical insurance would be provided to all persons on the same terms, even though their riskiness is, in fact, fully known, and they would not be uniformly insured by an efficiently-operating insurance system.

(d) Moral Hazard and the Imperfection of Insurance Markets

One of the main reasons for insurance against medical expenditures is to reduce the risk faced by individuals. As we stated in the previous section, it will always be efficient to insure individuals against risks if someone else in society is willing to take on the individual's risk for a price not greater than the cost of the risk to the individual (the amount that would be paid to avoid the risk). This can be the case if insurers are able to pool risks more efficiently than individuals. A prerequisite to the efficient provision of insurance is that the insurers can monitor the events that are being insured against. If not, insurance markets may be subject to moral hazard, which will preclude the optimal insurance from being provided. That is, persons being insured may be able to take actions that influence the observable things being insured against, and they exploit this to their advantage in a socially inefficient way.

In the context of medical insurance, the events that the insurer would like to insure against are various states of ill health. If those states could themselves be monitored by insurers, medical insurance policies could be designed that allowed persons insured to purchase as much insurance as they wished, where the premium would be related to the probability of ill health for the person in question,[16] and where the full amount of the insurance purchased against a particular state of health would be paid out in the event the state occurred. This is not the way medical insurance is actually implemented, however. States of ill health are not directly monitored by insurers. Instead, they are only indirectly and imperfectly inferred from the actual amount of medical *expenditures* undertaken. The presumption is that the medical expenditures undertaken are directly related to the state of ill health. Unfortunately, for any given state of health, medical expenditures can be influenced by the persons being insured. In the presence of medical insurance, individuals will be induced to undertake inefficiently large amounts of expenditures on medical care, and this will preclude insurers from offering the socially optimal amount of insurance.

This can be illustrated geometrically using a simplified version of an analysis due to Pauly (1968). Consider the case shown in Fig. 14–5, in which there can be only two states of health, a good state and a bad state.

Figure 14–5

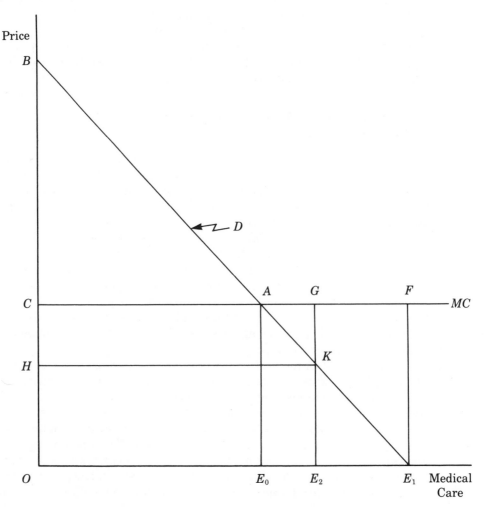

In the good state, no medical expenses are required. In the bad state, there will be a demand for medical care, shown by the downward sloping demand curve labelled D. The implication is that the more medical care provided, the better off an ill person will be; but, as with other goods, the marginal benefit of medical care will diminish as more is administered. For simplicity, it is assumed that medical care can be provided at constant marginal cost, MC. If there were no insurance, in the event of ill health the person would purchase E_0 units of medical care at a total cost of $MC \cdot E_0$, since at that quantity marginal benefit would equal marginal cost.

In the absence of insurance the person would be exposed to a risk, the risk being reflected in the possibility of having to incur expenses of $MC \cdot E_0$ in the event of ill health, as well as having to suffer the disutility of any remaining effects of the ill health. If the probability of ill health is π, then the person's expected medical expenditures would be $\pi \cdot MC \cdot E_0$. An ideal insurance scheme would insure against these expenditures. If an insurance contract could be written that paid the individual an amount, $MC \cdot E_0$, in the event of ill health, this risk could be eliminated, and the socially optimal amount of medical expenditures E_0 would be undertaken. If the insurance could be offered at actuarially fair terms, the premium paid for the E_0 units of medical care would be $\pi \cdot MC \cdot E_0$. Individuals would receive the medical care E_0 but their expenditures (premiums) would be independent of the state of their health.

The ideal scheme requires the insurer to know E_0, the socially optimal medical care for the state of ill health. In practice, it will not know this. Instead, the insurance scheme will provide insurance for whatever expenditures are undertaken in the ill state. Consider an insurance scheme that did that. If the ill state occurred, and if persons were fully insured against medical expenditures, they would demand the quantity E_1 of medical care at a social cost (and cost to the insurer) of $MC \cdot E_1$. In order for such an insurance scheme to be actuarially fair, the premium paid would have to be $\pi \cdot MC \cdot E_1$, the expected medical expenditure of the insured person. Several remarks can be made about this "market" solution. As long as $E_1 > E_0$, a socially inefficient amount of medical care would be provided. As is apparent, the expenditures will be more excessive the more elastic is the demand for medical care. Of course, there are many things which affect the elasticity of demand, including the influence of the suppliers of medical care themselves. If demand were completely inelastic, E_0 would coincide with E_1, and the insurance would be socially optimal. If demand is elastic enough, the premium, $\pi \cdot MC \cdot E_1$, might be so large that it might not be worthwhile for the individual to buy insurance at all. The extra cost of the insurance outweighs the value of reduction of risk to the individual. The risk is said to be *uninsurable*. Whether or not this occurs also depends upon how risk-averse the person is, and how variable the outcomes are (i.e. how far right the demand curve, D, is). To summarize, the possibility of uninsurability rises the more elastic the demand for medical care is, the less risk-averse is the person, and the less variable the expenditures on states of health. For example, catastrophic illness may well be more insurable than preventive medicine.

The efficiency cost associated with the moral hazard can be shown in Fig. 14–5 as well. Since the marginal cost of medical care is the curve MC, and the marginal benefit is the curve D, every unit of medical care above E_0 gives rise to an excess of cost over benefit equal to the vertical difference between those two curves. Summing these up for all units of care between E_0 and E_1, the excess of costs over benefits in the event of ill health is the area AFE_1. It will be greater as the demand for medical care becomes more elastic. The expected welfare loss is therefore $\pi \cdot AFE_1$. If this welfare loss exceeds the gain from risk reduction, the risk will not be insurable.

In the above examples, we assumed that all expenditures were fully insured. There are ways of partially insuring against illness that may reduce the welfare cost of moral hazard, and may turn uninsurable risks under full insurance into insurable risks under partial insurance. One form of partial insurance is *coinsurance,* according to which the insurer agrees to pay a fraction of medical expenditures incurred.[17] In Fig. 14–5, if the insurer agrees to pay a proportion, CH/HO, of medical expenditures in the event of illness, the person insured will face a private cost of OH per unit of care, and will consume E_2 units. In this case, the expected cost to the insurance company is $\pi \cdot CH \cdot E_2$, and this would be the actuarially fair premium. The welfare cost of the moral hazard would be reduced to $\pi \cdot AGK$; at the same time, the risk facing the individual would not be entirely eliminated, since he would be liable for the share $OHKE_2$ of medical costs during illness. The particular amount of coinsurance that would be appropriate for each individual would depend upon his riskiness, his preferences for medical care (his demand curve), and his aversion to risk. (See Zeckhauser [1970] for a more detailed analysis of optimal medical insurance under moral hazard.)

So far we have concentrated on one particular type of moral hazard, that arising from the ability of the insured person to influence medical expenditures. There is another form of moral hazard that may make it difficult for insurers to provide insurance optimally. Individuals may be able to influence the probability of insured-against events by taking certain actions, such as preventive expenditures or other precautions. If the actions of persons cannot be directly monitored, insurance may encourage these persons to undertake socially inefficient amounts of such actions. The problems that arise are similar to those considered above. A fuller analysis may be found in Pauly (1974) and Marshall (1976), and the reader is referred there for the details.

Although we have been discussing the failure of insurance markets to provide the socially optimal level of insurance, we have been careful not to identify who the insurers might be. The reason for this precaution is that there is no reason to believe that the public sector will have no more access to the additional information required to provide the optimal amount of insurance than will the private sector. Recall that the problem has arisen from the inability of the insurer, whoever it may be, to monitor fully the underlying states of nature being insured against, and the actions of the insured. Since that is the case, the existence of moral hazard is not a strong argument for public-versus-private provision of insurance. Instead it is a problem which leads to an inefficient system of insurance, no matter who provides it.

CHAPTER NOTES

1. These are not the only redistribution programs favoring the poor. Later in this chapter we discuss the social security system, some elements of which have worked to favor the elderly poor. In addition, redistribution in favor of the poor takes place through some housing programs (urban renewal, public housing, rent subsidies), school-lunch programs, special educational opportunities to disadvantaged children such as Head Start, job training programs such as those funded under the Comprehensive Employment and Training Act (CETA), and so on. The total dollar amounts involved in such programs are great, but it is a bit more difficult in some cases to determine how much of the program expenditures represent net benefits to the poor.

2. To be eligible for AFDC, a family must either have only one parent present or, if both are present, the one that is the principal income earner must be unemployed.

3. It is not altogether clear how strong the case is for redistribution programs that favor the interests of the donors over the interests of the recipients. Of course, the crux of the issue is that the poor may not know their own best interests, so that society should paternalistically protect them by limiting their consumption opportunities in certain ways.

4. It is interesting to note that the presumption that the aged consume at a rate that eventually depletes their wealth, a presumption on which much of this discussion is based, may in fact be invalid. Mirer (1979), for instance, studied the relationship between wealth and age among the aged, and found that, on average, wealth tends to *increase* with age. This need not be true of all individuals, and, for some, the above description of steadily declining wealth in old age may be accurate. Nonetheless, evidence like that presented by Mirer indicates that this may not be the typical case.

5. Of course, accidents and illnesses may do more than just encourage workers to retire earlier. They may also strike early in life, making it impossible to engage in normal employment. The Disability Insurance (DI) component of the social security system is designed to insure workers against such risks.

6. More specifically, under current law, each fully-insured worker is entitled to a *primary insurance amount* (PIA) which, for workers retiring after 1978, is calculated from the *average indexed monthly earnings* (AIME), an average of monthly earnings that is adjusted to take inflation into account. The precise benefit schedule varies from year to year because it is automatically linked to the inflation rate. For workers retiring in 1982, the minimum monthly benefit

was $182.90. The PIA was computed to be: 90 percent of the first $230 of AIME, plus 32 percent of the next $1,158, plus 15 percent of any AIME above $1,388.

7. SSI also pays benefits to the blind and disabled. These benefits amounted to $5.6 billion in 1981.

8. This is correct except insofar as the tax treatment of interest might differ between saving on personal account and saving under social security. If the former were taxed and the latter were not, it would obviously be advantageous for the members of a given generation to save through social security, although they and other taxpayers would have to pay higher taxes on other income to make up the treasury's loss from this exemption.

9. The social security "crisis" has been much discussed in recent years, and it is appropriate to digress for a moment to relate it to our present discussion. (See also Stein [1980] and Feldstein [1977c] for more discussion.) At least until the passage of the Social Security Amendments of 1983, it was argued that there were two main problems: a short-run difficulty in meeting the program's commitments to existing retirees, and a longer-term problem resulting from the above-mentioned demographic changes and from the "maturing" of the system as it moves out of its protracted start-up phase. Of the two, the first is probably the least serious. Although the social security trust fund has been reduced to a low level, as benefit expenditures have exceeded revenue inflows, the recent and scheduled future payroll tax rate and base increases mentioned earlier, together with some other, comparatively minor, adjustments introduced in the 1983 amendments, should ensure the near-term solvency of the system. In the longer term, unfavorable demographic changes are expected to present substantial difficulties. Of course, no one really knows what future fertility rates, and hence population size, will be, nor can future labor force participation rates, wage rates, and so on, be known with certainty. As a result, the government actuaries who prepare projections of future social security benefits consider a range of assumptions for the future values of crucial variables, ranging from optimistic, to mid-range, to pessimistic.

One key indicator of social security's prospects that is computed in these projections (see Board of Trustees of the Federal Old-Age and Survivors Insurance and Disability Insurance Trust Funds [1983]) is benefit expenditures in future years, expressed as a percentage of total taxable payrolls. Currently this percentage is about 12 percent. Under the mid-range projections, it will fall to about 9.5 percent around the year 2000. After that date, however, expenditures will increase relative to payrolls as the aging of the "baby boom" generation, and the subsequent fall in fertility, make their presence felt in the form of an expanding population of retired beneficiaries and a declining pool of contributing workers. By 2025, the benefit/payroll percentage will be at about 13.5 percent under the mid-range projection (10.7 percent and 17.4 percent under the optimistic and pessimistic assumptions, respectively), and the mid-range projections for 2050 are about 15 percent (10.1 percent and 23.8 percent under the optimistic and pessimistic cases). These same demographic trends show up in the projected ratio of workers covered by the payroll tax to social security beneficiaries. In 1945, there were 41.9 covered workers per beneficiary, in 1950, 16.5. By 1970, the ratio had dropped to 3.6, and it reached 3.2 in 1980. Under the mid-range projections, this ratio will stand at about 3.3 in the year 2000, falling to about 2.2 by the year 2025, and finally declining to 2.0 by 2050. While the optimistic forecast puts the ratio at about 2.6 in 2025 and 2050, pessimistic assumptions suggest that it will have fallen to 1.9 in 2025, and will drop still further, to 1.4, by 2050.

These are sobering numbers, and their message is clear. For the social security system to remain solvent, taxes will have to be increased in the long run, and/or benefits will have to be cut. As we have seen, substantial tax increases are scheduled to take effect in the next few years. In addition, the 1983 amendments seek to alleviate the long-term funding problem by an increase in the normal retirement age from 65 to 67, to be phased in between 2000 and 2022, by larger reductions in benefits for those retiring early and greater increases in benefits for those who postpone retirement, by requiring all newly hired federal government employees to participate in the program, and by various other provisions. With these amendments in place, it is projected that the system will remain financially viable, except under pessimistic assumptions, for the next 75 years. Obviously, these changes mean that the implicit "rate of return" on social security will be considerably lower for today's young workers than that received by today's beneficiaries. Unfortunately, as we have seen, this could not be avoided under an unfunded system, especially given the demographic changes to which the system must adjust.

10. This will be the case when the worker's utility from income is independent of his utility from leisure. This is discussed in Sargent (1979). The reason for this result is as follows: When the worker insures himself against income risks, he equates the marginal utility of income in all states of the world (in this case, employment and unemployment). If the marginal utility of income is independent of leisure, this implies that income should be the same, whether employed or not.

11. The algebraic statement of the firm's problem is as follows: Choose w_1, w_2, N_1, N_2 so as to

    Max $\pi(p_1 F(N_1) - w_1 N_1) + (1 - \pi)(p_2 F(N_2) - w_2 N2)$
    subject to $EU = \bar{u}$

    where p_1 and p_2 are the firm's selling price in the peak and off-peak periods, EU is given by Eq. (14–10), $F(N)$ is the firm's production function, and u is the level of utility workers can obtain elsewhere in the economy. The complete analysis may be found in Baily (1974) and Azariadis (1975).

12. These circumstances are the same as discussed above in footnote 10, viz., that the utility obtained from income be independent of the amount of leisure taken.

13. We use the term "experience-rating" to apply to the fact that the premium paid by each firm depends on its layoff experience. Alternatively, experience-rating could be applied to industries as a whole, or to firms aggregated into risk classes.

14. The magnitude of the implicit subsidy to layoffs will depend upon the tax treatment of premiums and benefits. If premiums are tax deductible (as in the United States), the subsidy is lower than otherwise, since the premium saving is lower. Similarly, if benefits are taxable, the subsidy is reduced, since part of the benefit to workers is taxed away. Thus, bringing unemployment insurance benefits fully into the tax system would reduce the implicit subsidy to lay off workers temporarily.

15. Feldstein and Friedman (1977) have estimated the impact of this subsidy on the aggregate demand for health insurance for 1970. They found that the

inefficiency or welfare loss arising from this subsidy was extremely large indeed, on the order of $8 billion for that year. In addition, they found that the subsidy went disproportionately to higher-income families.

16. Indeed, with actuarially fair insurance, the premium per dollar of insurance would be equal to the probability of a claim. That is because the probability of a claim is the same thing as the expected payment on one dollar's worth of insurance.

17. Another form of partial insurance is insurance with deductibility. The analysis of this may be found in Pauly (1968).

15

The Theory of
Fiscal Federalism

INTRODUCTION

15-1   In most countries, the public sector is stratified into more than one level
of government, each one having a different set of expenditure responsibilities
and taxing powers. In the United States, the main levels of government
are the federal government, the state governments, and the various local
governments (municipalities and townships). Each of these strata of government tends to be responsible for a particular set of public sector functions,
whether that responsibility be vested in them by the Constitution, or whether
the responsibility be delegated from a higher authority (as with many local
government functions). The federal government provides for such things
as national defense, justice, and foreign affairs; the state governments for
highways, education, social welfare, and health; and local governments for
local services such as fire protection, police, water and sewage, and garbage
disposal. In addition, each level of government has assumed responsibility
for a particular set of transfer payments. These include not only transfer
payments to individuals, as with social security, welfare, and unemployment
insurance, but also transfer payments from one level of government to
another (lower) level. This chapter will analyze the economics of multilevel
or federal systems of government.[1]

   The obvious first question that arises is what is the economic rationale
for having a federal division of public sector functions? In other words,
why not rely solely upon the national government to perform such economic
functions as must be done collectively? Recall from Chapter 3 that governments may be involved in the public provision of goods and services,

in the provision of incentives to various activities (taxes, subsidies, regulations), or in the redistribution of income. The primary justification for the public provision of goods and services was the existence of public goods (pure or impure, final or intermediate). Because of the property of joint consumption and possibly non-excludability, these goods could not be efficiently provided by private markets, thereby establishing an *a priori* case for considering public provision. However, not all public goods may be jointly consumed on a nation-wide basis. Some have the property that their benefits are restricted to a particular geographical area. Public goods whose benefits are so restricted are called *local* public goods. The optimal allocation of local public goods is determined by the usual Samuelson condition that the sum of the marginal benefits generated equals the marginal cost. In the case of local public goods, marginal benefits accrue only to those living in the appropriate geographical area.

From a normative point of view, it does not matter who decides on the level of output of a local public good, provided they take into account all the appropriate benefits and costs. From a positive point of view, however, it is more likely that the benefits and costs of the local public good are registered correctly if the decision regarding its provision is taken collectively by those living in the area that the local public good serves. In this way, each locality will be able to provide the level and mix of local public goods that tend to be preferred by those who live in the locality. There is no reason why different localities should consume the same amounts of local public goods, as might occur if a single higher level of government were responsible for choosing them. Therein lies the primary economic rationale for a federal system of government.

Although much of the role of public sector activities is involved with the provision of goods and services, local or national, the public sector is also often involved with interfering with the operation of the private market in other ways. For example, as we saw in Chapter 5, the existence of externalities may provide a justification for either taxing or subsidizing various activities, depending upon whether the activity emits an external diseconomy or economy. In this case, as in the public good case, one can distinguish "local" externalities from national ones. Air pollution within an urban area might be considered to be an externality that primarily influences persons in that area. The responsibility for correcting it might therefore be assigned to a state or local government, rather than the national government. By the same token, the pollution of a river that crosses state boundaries may require federal action for efficiency. In the following sections, we shall present our analysis primarily in terms of local public goods. This is for purely expositional reasons. The same arguments that apply to local, as opposed to national, public goods also apply to local, as opposed to national, externalities. Only the remedy may differ: in the one case, it is public provision, while in the other it is taxation, subsidization, or regulation, as the case may be. The same may be said to be true of the problem of increasing-returns industries. To the extent that such industries operate on national markets (e.g. railways), they might best be dealt with by the national government. At the same time, one could justify giving responsibility over increasing-returns industries, which service only local residents, to local levels of government (e.g. local transportation and utility services).

The following section discusses in more detail the economic principles involved in assigning different public sector functions (both expenditure and tax-transfer functions) to different levels of government. This discussion will make clear the importance of the mobility of labor and capital among localities in the assignment of responsibilities. The implications of inter-jurisdictional mobility are discussed in Section 15–3 . Finally, it will become evident that intergovernmental grants have an important role to play, from both an efficiency and an equity point of view, in federal economic structures. The theory of intergovernmental grants will be presented in Section 15–4. Section 15–5 discusses the United States experience with intergovernmental transfers.

THE ASSIGNMENT OF FUNCTIONS TO THE APPROPRIATE LEVEL OF GOVERNMENT

15–2   In discussing the economic theory of fiscal federalism, it is generally presumed that the method of taking collective decisions is predetermined, and that it is relatively efficient. That is, governments, due to the incentives of vote-maximizing or whatever, tend to take resource allocation decisions according to the collective preferences of their constituents.[2] In this way, the distinction between the positive theory of fiscal federalism and the normative theory tends to become blurred, since governments are treated as if they behave optimally. We shall follow that convention here.

The economic decisions taken by governments can be viewed as serving two purposes: First, there are those that are intended to influence the allocation of resources, such as the provision of public goods and services. This class of decisions can be referred to as the *allocative role* of government. Second, some decisions of government are designed to redistribute income. This is the *distributive* role of government. We shall consider the assignment of each of these roles in turn.

Assignment of the Allocative Role

Assuming that governments behave in the interests of their constituents, the general case for *decentralizing* some of the allocative functions to lower levels of governments is straightforward. To the extent that the benefits of a particular public sector decision, such as the provision of a local public good, accrue only to a particular group in the population, only the tastes of that group need be taken into consideration when deciding on that output. Those tastes can be more accurately reflected in the output chosen if the collective decision is taken by a government representing only those affected. In a society in which the central government assumes responsibility for the provision of local public goods to various localities, there would be a tendency to provide a uniform quantity of such goods for all localities. Decentralizing such decisions allows different localities to provide different quantities of various local public goods according to their different collective tastes. Therefore, there is something to be said for matching the provision of local public goods with a level of government whose jurisdiction includes only those who benefit from the particular good.

The benefits from decentralizing local public goods can be seen using Fig. 15–1 for the case of two localities, A and B. For a particular local public good, G, the sum of the benefits to residents in A for various levels of local public good G^A provided there is shown as the curve ΣMRS^A. The marginal cost of providing G^A, assumed to be constant and the same for both localities, is MRT. The optimal amount of G^A is G_0^A where $\Sigma MRS^A = MRT$. Similarly, for locality B, the optimal level of G^B is G_0^B, drawn here as larger than G_0^A. Suppose the central government decides to provide a uniform amount of local public good in each locality. It might do this by providing the level appropriate to the average locality. In Fig. 15–1, the curve $\Sigma\overline{MRS}$ shows the average of the aggregate marginal benefits in the two localities. The central government would provide the level $\overline{G}_0$ in each locality. Since this is less than the optimum in B, and more than the optimum in A, the economy is not as well off as it would be under decentralized provision. In particular, the deadweight loss of uniform provision is the sum of the areas xyz in B, and uzv in A.

In many cases, the number of persons who can share in the consumption of a local public good is variable, as we saw in Chapter 4. There is a definite

Figure 15–1

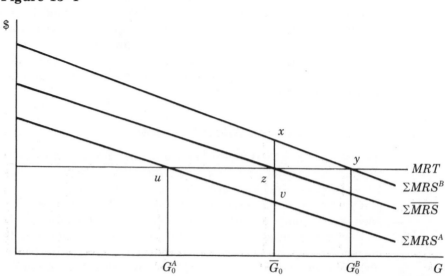

benefit to be had from increasing the number of sharers. The more persons sharing in the use of the public good, the lower is the cost share borne by each. However, these so-called economies of scale in the consumption of a public good must be weighed against the disadvantages of having more users. These include the congestion costs imposed by admitting additional users to the use of the public good, and the locational disadvantages to users of being further away from the source of the public good the larger the area it covers. In principle, for any local public good there will be an optimal number of users, which will constitute the optimal jurisdiction from the point of view of collective decision-making.

Since each local public good has an optimal number of users, or covers an optimal geographic area, one can imagine in theory an *optimal constitution,* or perfect mapping of functions as Breton (1965) has called it, that assigns responsibility for provision of such public goods to the appropriate level of government representing only those persons affected. Local public goods would be provided by the appropriate form of local government, national public goods would be provided federally, and all those in between would be appropriately provided for. There are a number of reasons why actual mappings will not be perfect in this sense, and why the provision of particular public goods are either more or less centralized than the above would require. Some of the more important reasons, discussed in detail in Oates (1972), are as follows.

(a) Costs of Decision-making

If the Constitution had to allow for a separate level of government for each function, the number of jurisdictions would tend to be large, jurisdictions would tend to be overlapping geographically, and the size of decision units would have to change as population patterns changed. If one supposes there is a fixed cost involved in administering each jurisdiction, the costs of having so many centers of collective decision-making would be immense. Furthermore, a large number of overlapping jurisdictions, each one responsible for a particular function of government, would be confusing for the individual citizen, and might cause informational problems that would prevent efficient decisions from being taken. Typically, therefore, constitutions limit collective decision-making to a small number of jurisdictions, organized hierarchically and in such a way that jurisdictions at a given level (for example, states) do not overlap in terms of the composition of their constituents. Moreover, the size of jurisdictions is fairly unchanging over time.

(b) Interregional Externalities

Frequently the main beneficiaries of a local public expenditure are the local citizens, but benefits of a lesser amount may spread further away to other areas. This may be the case for such things as local transportation facilities (highways), education, or health services. Each of these items benefits those in whose region they are supplied, in addition to "spilling out" into surrounding regions. At the same time, similar expenditures in other regions will provide benefits which "spill in" to this region. In other words, there will be reciprocal externalities generated among the various regions. The principle of perfect mapping, outlined above, might suggest that these externality-generating local public expenditures should be undertaken by the central government, since they provide benefits to persons throughout the nation. However, a case can be made for decentralizing these functions, even though doing so would result in interjurisdictional externalities that local jurisdictions would have no incentive to weigh when choosing output levels. The main beneficiaries of these local expenditures are local residents. Since residents of different areas might have different preferences for the levels of such goods provided locally, efficiency requires that different levels be provided in each region. Central provision of such goods to each region will not likely discriminate properly among the tastes of various regions, and will tend to provide the same amount to each region. Such an outcome would be nonoptimal.

The choice of an appropriate level of government for the provision of such goods will involve trading off the diversity of tastes and the relative size of the external effects of spillovers generated. The more diverse are tastes and the smaller the size of externalities, the greater will be the case for decentralizing the provision of these goods. In practice, many of the functions that are granted to state and local governments, such as education, highways, etc., yield spillover benefits to residents of surrounding jurisdictions. In the absence of federally-imposed incentives, an inefficient amount of such services would tend to be provided by the lower levels of government, since they would neglect the benefits generated for nonresidents. In particular, the neglect of spillover benefits would tend to cause local governments to provide too little of these public goods. The problem of how the federal government might correct for these spillovers is discussed in Section 15–4.

While the existence of spillover benefits from state and local public services tends to cause these governments to spend too little, another source of interregional externality might have the opposite effect. That is the phenomenon of *tax exporting*. A jurisdiction is said to export its taxes when a part of their incidence is borne by non-residents. This can occur in a variety of ways. State sales taxes may be borne by non-residents when they make purchases in the state levying the tax. State taxes on corporate income may be borne by non-resident capital owners. State severance taxes on resource properties may be borne by non-resident owners of resources. Local property taxes may be borne by non-resident property owners, and so on. In all of these cases, the cost to residents of an additional dollar of tax revenue may be less than one dollar, so the marginal cost of financing an additional dollar of expenditure will be less than a dollar. In this case, the tax exporting jurisdiction may overexpand its public sector. Across the entire country, tax exporting will be reciprocal among states; each will be able to export some of its taxes to the other. The net effect is that all states will have an incentive to overexpand.

The existence of tax exporting can support the case for centralizing some tax revenue sources, for example, taxes such as resource taxes and corporate taxes, which are not levied on households on the basis of place of residence. The centralization may involve the central government having to transfer tax revenues to lower levels of government appropriately. The form these transfers might take is discussed below in Section 15–4. Alternatively, it may simply involve the centralized coordination of federal, state, and local tax collections (as is done in Canada, for example).

Tax exporting can also occur between levels of government. If state and local taxes are deductible from federal tax payments, as they are in the United States, part of the tax collections by local governments are effectively being subsidized by the federal government. This, too, would provide an incentive for local jurisdictions to overexpand their public sectors.

(c) Mobility of Labor and Capital

To the extent that labor and capital are mobile, they may respond to collective decisions taken by local governments. As Tiebout (1956) suggested, and as we shall analyze more carefully in Section 15–3, there will be an incentive for individuals to move to the jurisdiction offering the set of public goods and taxes that best reflects their tastes. At the same time, capital may move in response to tax and public expenditure decisions that affect the rate of return on capital. In one sense, the existence of mobility of factors, especially labor, enhances the case for the decentralized provision of local public goods. Different localities will be able to provide a mix of public goods and taxes that suits the tastes of its residents. This will induce persons of similar preferences to congregate together in localities, thereby improving the efficiency of the economy.

However, the existence of mobility is a mixed blessing, and may give rise to certain inefficiencies of decentralized public sector decision-making. Depending on the types of taxes levied by lower level jurisdictions, and on the degree of publicness of the goods and services they provide, perfect mobility of labor may not lead to the efficient allocation of resources envisaged by Tiebout. As discussed more fully in the following section, the market signals that potential migrants respond to, which include the benefits from local public services and the differences in taxes incurred across jurisdictions, may not be the socially correct ones. Such tax/expenditure decisions of local jurisdictions are said to induce *fiscal externalities,* which cause labor to allocate itself inefficiently across jurisdictions. The extent of the fiscal externality depends upon how "public" or "private" are local public goods and services, and the extent to which local taxes are *residence-based* or *source-based.* A tax is residence-based if its payment by a household is contingent upon residency, that is, if the household can avoid it by migrating. The personal income tax is residence-based in this sense, while the corporate tax is not. Source-based taxes are levied on income generated within a locality, and must be paid regardless of the residency of the owner. As is shown in the next section, there are two extreme cases. If all local expenditures are on pure public goods, then to the extent that they are financed by residence-based taxes, there will be a tendency for inefficient labor migration. At the other extreme, if all local public expenditures are on private-type goods, inefficiency will be induced whenever taxes are source-based. In between, if some public expenditures are on pure public goods, some are on pure private goods, and some are on impure or congested public goods, some mixture of residence- and source-based taxes is called for. Thus the appropriate *mix* of local taxes depends upon the nature of local public services. It is apparent that no constitutional assignment of particular types of taxes is called for in this case. Instead, the induced inefficiency of migration resulting from the wrong mix of local taxes can be dealt with by approriate intergovernmental transfers, as discussed below in Section 15–4.

Inefficiencies can also arise from the local taxation of mobile factors of production other than labor, in particular, capital.[3] For one thing, any differential taxation of capital by local jurisdictions will give rise to inefficiencies in the allocation of capital across jurisdictions. In addition, local jurisdictions might feel constrained to set low tax rates on capital to avoid discouraging capital accumulation in their localities. Indeed, they may, as a matter of policy, specifically attempt to attract capital by low tax rates, or even subsidies. If several jurisdictions follow these policies, they are said to be engaging in *tax competition*.[4] If all jursidictions compete to attract capital via their taxes, the collective result will be self-defeating. All will end up with lower tax rates (or larger subsidies), but the allocation of capital across jurisdictions will be little affected. They will all have lower tax revenues from capital income as a result of the competition, and therefore they must either rely on other tax sources or reduce their level of public services. Neither alternative will be optimal. Once again, it is not obvious what implications this should have for the constitutional assignment of tax power between levels of government. What it does mean is that, *de facto,* central governments are better able to collect certain taxes efficiently than are local governments.

These problems suggest that higher levels of government should have greater taxing powers than lower levels, despite the fact that the diversity of tastes would suggest matching taxing levels to local expenditure decisions. This is a trade-off that is ultimately reached by compromising the advantages and disadvantages of tax collection decentralization. In practice, it is typically the case that the ability of local and state governments to levy taxes falls short of the revenues required to finance their desired level of public goods. Because the central government has a greater power to levy taxes, there is a case for having it levy at least some taxes on behalf of local governments, and transferring the tax resources to them. Intergovernmental transfers arising for this reason will be discussed in Section 15–4, below.

Assignment of the Distributive Role

Our discussion thus far has centered upon the assignment of various public expenditure and taxing functions to appropriate levels of government. Governments are also concerned with the redistribution of income through the tax-transfer process, and the question arises as to which level of government ought to assume responsibility for the distribution functions of the public sector. Some authors have argued forcefully that the central government should be given the ultimate role of determining the distribution of income. (See Musgrave (1959), p. 181 and Oates (1972), pp. 6–8). The main reason for this concerns the mobility of individuals among jurisdictions. If one jurisdiction attempted to undertake stronger redistributive policy than others, there would be an incentive for the poor to migrate into that jurisdiction, and the wealthy to migrate out. The policy would be ultimately self-defeating. Local jurisdictions would be reluctant to undertake the desired amounts of redistribution. Not only would too little redistribution be undertaken, but also that which was undertaken by some localities would tend to cause a misallocation of population. Therefore, it is argued that only the central government can efficiently undertake the function of income redistribution.

Perhaps more striking is the fact that even if all local jurisdictions pursued the same redistributive policy, the presence of local government redistribution would itself induce migration from one area to another. This point, first noted by Buchanan (1950), can be illustrated with a simple numerical example. Consider two states, called A and B, that differ in their mix of high- and low-income people. In state A, the richer state, there are two persons with incomes of $30,000 per year for every one person with an income of $10,000. The poorer state, B, has one person with income of $30,000 for every two persons with incomes of $10,000. Suppose now that each state levies a proportional income tax of 20 percent, and uses the proceeds to provide public services of a purely private-good kind in equal amounts to all citizens. The overall impact of this budget package will be redistributive, since all persons receive the same benefits from public expenditures, but tax payments rise with income.

Table 15–1 illustrates the impact of the state budgets on the real income of the two types of persons, where the real income is market income amended to incorporate the net benefits of public sector activities (per capita expenditures − taxes paid). As the table indicates, while persons of a given income pay the same taxes in each state, they receive different benefits because of the population mix. Those in the richer state receive more than those in the poorer state. The last row of the table gives the *net fiscal benefit* accruing to each type of person as a result of the activities of the state government. It corresponds to what Buchanan (1950) has called the

Table 15–1   The Impact of State Budgets on Real Income

	State A		State B	
	Person with $30,000 income	*Person with $10,000 income*	*Person with $30,000 income*	*Person with $10,000 income*
Tax Payment	6,000	2,000	6,000	2,000
Per capita public expenditures	4,667	4,667	3,333	3,333
Net fiscal benefit	−1,333	2,667	−2,667	1,333

fiscal residuum. In this particular example, all persons, regardless of income, have a fiscal residuum which is $1,333 higher in state A than in state B. There will thus be an incentive to migrate from state B to state A for all persons, purely on account of the state's redistributive activities.

Although this point was illustrated for a particular example, it can be shown as generally true that whenever local government budgets are redistributive, there will be higher fiscal residua in higher income states. (This is discussed in detail in Boadway and Flatters [1982]). By the same token, if local government budgets are regressive, there will be a tendency to migrate to low-income localities. Only if the budgets are distributionally neutral will there be no incentives to migrate. The reader can readily verify this for the above example.

From an economic efficiency point of view, then, it might seem desirable to centralize the redistributive function. Unfortunately, this is virtually impossible to do by constitutional assignment of powers. Almost any taxing or expenditure decision of local governments will have distributive implications; it cannot be avoided. Nonetheless, there are certain things the central government can do to overcome some of the differences in distributive policies across states, or to counter the discrepancies in fiscal residua caused by state redistributive budgets *per se.*

First, the federal tax system may collect the bulk of the taxes, make the bulk of the transfers, and legislate a tax system which attempts to achieve horizontal and vertical equity nationwide. The same progressive tax system may apply to all individuals, regardless of where they reside. Also, credit may be given for taxes paid to lower levels of government by individuals residing in various regions. In this way, the degree of redistribution of income through the tax-transfer process will be fairly uniform over all regions.

Finally, as we have seen, even if state redistributive policies were uniform across states, inefficient migration would be induced by differences in fiscal residua. These differences between fiscal residua across jurisdictions from state redistributive policies arise from differences in the size of per capita tax bases. One way to alleviate this problem, advocated by Buchanan (1950), is to set up a system of equalizing transfers among jurisdictions to reduce the inequalities in state tax bases. The appropriate form that these intergovernmental transfers might take is discussed more fully in Section 15–4.

The above arguments in favor of giving the central government responsibility for income (or utility) redistribution, though strong, are not completely clear-cut. Pauly (1973) has presented an analysis in which a case is made for giving some redistributive function to local governments. This parallels the case for decentralizing the provision of local public goods based upon differences in taste. We shall present the main arguments advanced by Pauly, using a truncated version of his analysis. The general notion is as follows: Suppose income redistribution is of the Pareto-optimal or efficient sort; that is, it is motivated out of utility interdependencies, as discussed in Chapters 3 and 5. Income transfers from the rich to the poor are undertaken because the rich obtain utility increases from increases in the level of income of the poor. In other words, income redistribution is of the nature of a pure public good undertaken collectively by the public sector. Furthermore, assume that income redistribution benefits are of the nature of a local public good. That is, the rich get more benefits from income increases to the poor in their community than to the poor living elsewhere. Benefits may decrease with distance, either because the perception of the poor falls off, or because some of the disadvantages associated with poverty (e.g. crime) fall off as the poor are further away. In any case, if redistribution is more a local public good (with or without interregional spillovers) than a national one, differences in tastes and incomes over regions may dictate a differing amount of redistribution in each. In this case, as in the case of other local public goods, a *prima facie* case exists for considering decentralization of its provision.

Following Pauly, we shall develop a very simple model to illustrate the point, beginning with one that makes the case for decentralization as strongly as possible. The economy consists of two regions, A and B, each containing a number of poor or welfare recipients, and a number of taxpayers, all with given incomes. There are P^A and P^B poor in the two regions, each of whom has an income of Y_P. The taxpayers have incomes denoted Y^i, of which some will be used to pay for transfers to the poor. The utility function of a typical taxpayer in either region will generally be written:

$$U^i = U^i(Y^i, W^A, P^A, W^B, P^B) \tag{15–1}$$

where Y^i is after-tax income of taxpayer i, and W^A and W^B are the levels of income to which the poor in the two regions are raised. This utility function has the property that utility U^i will increase (or remain the same) for increases in Y^i, W^A and W^B; and it will fall (or remain the same) for increases in P^A and P^B.[5] In order to make the extreme case for decentralization the following strong assumptions are made initially:

(i) All taxpayers and welfare recipients are immobile, regardless of taxes or transfers made.

(ii) Taxpayers in A get benefits from transfers to P^A only; similarly for taxpayers in B. That is, there are no spillovers of redistributive benefits from one region to the other.

(iii) All redistribution that takes place is of the Pareto-optimal sort, and all collective decisions are taken efficiently.

Under these assumptions, the utility functions for residents of the two regions are:

$$U^i = U^i(Y^i, W^A, P^A) \quad i \text{ in } A \tag{15-2}$$

$$U^j = U^j(Y^j, W^B, P^B) \quad j \text{ in } B. \tag{15-3}$$

The Samuelson conditions for the optimal redistribution can be applied as follows: The benefit from increasing W^A at the margin is $\sum_{i \text{ in } A} MB^i_{W^A}$ where $MB^i_{W^A}$ is the marginal benefit of W^A to person i. Since there are P^A persons, the marginal cost of increasing welfare payments to them is P^A dollars. Therefore, at the optimum,

$$\sum_{i \text{ in } A} MB^i_{W^A} = P^A. \tag{15-4}$$

By analogous reasoning, the optimal redistribution to the poor in B is determined by:

$$\sum_{j \text{ in } B} MB^j_{W^B} = P^B. \tag{15-5}$$

In general, there is no reason why W^A and W^B as determined by Eqs. (15-4) and (15-5) should be the same.[6] There are many reasons why they could differ. The tastes of taxpayers in the two regions may differ, causing one to prefer more redistribution than the other. Even with identical tastes, income differences in the region may cause different desired levels of W^A and W^B. If income redistribution has a positive income elasticity of demand, the wealthier region would prefer more than the less wealthy region. It is also clear that, in these circumstances, decentralization of the redistributive function to the regions A and B would result in the optimal outcome.

Income redistribution, if left to the central government, will be inefficient if the central government is intent upon providing a uniform amount of redistribution over both regions. The level of incomes of welfare recipients chosen by the central government, denoted $W(= W^A = W^B)$, will be determined by applying the Samuelson conditions over the nation as a whole, or:

$$\sum_{i \text{ in } A} MB^i_{WA} + \sum_{j \text{ in } B} MB^j_{WB} = P^A + P^B \tag{15-6}$$

where $W^A = W^B$. In general, satisfaction of Eq. (15–6) will not ensure satisfaction of Eqs. (15–4) and (15–5) and the central government will provide an inefficient amount of redistribution, as in Fig. 15–1 earlier.

This one-sided case for decentralization breaks down when any of the three assumptions listed above are not satisfied. Then the assignment of the redistributive function becomes ambiguous, and a perfect mapping may not be possible. Consider, for example, what happens when the second assumption is relaxed, and spillovers between A and B regions occur. Taxpayers in A obtain benefits from increases in W^B (though smaller than the benefits they receive from increases in W^A) and vice versa. The optimality conditions governing the extent of redistribution carried out in the two regions are now:

$$\sum_{i \text{ in } A} MB^i_{WA} + \sum_{j \text{ in } B} MB^j_{WA} = P^A \tag{15-7}$$

$$\sum_{i \text{ in } A} MB^i_{WB} + \sum_{j \text{ in } B} MB^j_{WB} = P^B. \tag{15-8}$$

In this case both decentralized and centralized provision would be inefficient. If A and B regions were given responsibility for redistribution they would set income levels for the poor dictated by Eqs. (15–4) and (15–5). The spillover benefits of welfare provision to residents outside the region would be neglected, and one might expect a lower-than-optimal level of redistribution to be undertaken. Centralized provision of a uniform level across jurisdictions would not be optimal either, since Eqs. (15–7) and (15–8) would, in general, require different levels of W^A and W^B in the two regions. In principle, the correct provision of W^A and W^B could be attained by a system of decentralized provision of redistribution, combined with an appropriate federal subsidy to each region to correct the spillover externality. The use of intergovernmental subsidies to correct spillovers of this and other sorts is discussed in Section 15–4.

The above analysis has assumed that all individuals were fixed in location. Suppose, by contrast, that the poor are mobile between the two regions, in response to differentials in the welfare levels provided in each. Then, even though the total number of poor in the nation is fixed, their distribution over the two areas will vary, depending upon the levels of minimum income set in the two regions. Consider the case in which there are no spillovers of redistributional benefits between the two regions. Then the appropriate utility functions are Eqs. (15–2) and (15–3). The additional difficulty that arises here is that changes in the welfare provision in A,

W^A, will affect the distribution of poor over the two regions, P^A and P^B, as well as the costs of providing the welfare. Presumably a *ceteris paribus* increase in W^A will cause P^A to rise and P^B to fall. This induced migration of the poor causes a reduction in utility in A and a rise in B. The problem is that the latter will not be properly taken into consideration in a decentralized system of income redistribution.

The level of W^A chosen under a decentralized system will be that at which the marginal benefit equals the marginal costs of welfare payment to taxpayers in A. This condition may be written as follows:

$$\sum_{i \text{ in } A} MB^i_{W^A} + \sum_{i \text{ in } A} MB^i_{P^A} \cdot \frac{\Delta P^A}{\Delta W^A} = P^A + (W^A - Y_p)\frac{\Delta P^A}{\Delta W^A}. \qquad (15\text{--}9)$$

In this expression, $MB^i_{P^A}$ is the marginal benefit to a resident in A from an increase in the number of poor in A, and $\Delta P^A/\Delta W^A$ is the increase in the number of poor in A resulting from a change in W^A (given the level of W^B prevailing in B). Since we have assumed $MB^i_{P^A}$ to be negative, the additional term on the left-hand side is negative. In other words, the mobility of the poor reduces the benefits that residents in A obtain from increases in W^A because of the effect it has on attracting welfare recipients. At the same time, the cost of increasing the level of W^A is higher than before. The term $(W^A - Y_P)\Delta P^A/\Delta W^A$ represents the additional costs to the residents of A from increases in W^A due to the need to make welfare payments to the migrants. Therefore, both on the cost side and on the benefit side, welfare payments will tend to be reduced by mobility of the poor.

The behavior of jurisdiction A, according to Eq. (15–9), is not optimal, since it neglects the changes in benefits and costs accruing to residents of B from changes in W^A. The same migration of welfare recipients from B, which reduces the benefits and increases the costs to A residents, at the same time increases benefits and reduces costs in B for the same reasons. The increase in P^A represents an equal decline in P^B, which raises utility levels of taxpayers in B. The decline in P^B also reduces tax payments required to support the poor in B. Taking these effects into account, the appropriate optimality condition which should be satisfied in determining W^A is:

$$\sum_{i \text{ in } A} MB^i_{W^A} + \left[\sum_{i \text{ in } A} MB^i_{P^A} - \sum_{j \text{ in } B} MB^j_{P^B} \right] \Delta P^A/\Delta W^A$$

$$= P^A + [(W^A - Y_P) - (W^B - Y_P)] \, \Delta P^A/\Delta W^A. \qquad (15\text{--}10)$$

An analogous expression holds for the optimal provison of W^B.

Once again, neither a decentralized nor a centralized system of redistribution would be efficient. The decentralized system would provide too low a level of redistribution due to the mutual neglect of spillover benefits caused by migration. The centralized system, in which a uniform level of redistribution is instituted in both regions, is not optimal, since the level of W^A satisfying Eq. (15–10) and the corresponding level for W^B will not be the same. Taste and income differences will often cause them to differ. In principle, the efficient solution can be attained either by bargaining among the local levels of government, if feasible, or by a system of grants from the central government, as discussed below in Section 15–4.

One might relax other assumptions of the above model and obtain other sources of inefficiency, of either local or central responsibility, for redistribution. For example, Pauly considers the case in which taxpayers are mobile. A similar case of the inefficiency of taxpayer mobility is considered in Section 15–3. In addition, he considers the case in which collective decisions are not taken optimally, but according to a direct-democracy, majority-rule system of voting on each issue. The point is that the solution of the assignment problem for the redistributive function remains vague. The case for decentralization is strongest the less mobile are individuals, the more dissimilar are tastes for redistribution over regions, and the more redistribution can be considered to be of the Pareto-optimal sort, and specific to the preferences of local residents. In practice, there does seem to be some decentralization of the redistributive function in the United States. State and local governments do assume responsibility for welfare payments, and do levy progressive income taxes. Thus, redistribution may vary from state to state. At the same time, the federal government undertakes some nationally uniform redistributive measures.

THE TIEBOUT MODEL AND THE EFFICIENCY OF FREE MOBILITY AMONG REGIONS

15–3   In addition to providing an economic rationale for federal systems of government, the existence of local public goods adds an important spatial dimension to the problem of the efficiency of resource allocation in decentralized market economies. This was first exploited in a celebrated paper by Tiebout (1956). The so-called Tiebout model purported to show that in a nation consisting of a large number of communities, each deciding upon its own mix of local public goods and local taxes according to the desires of its residents, and with perfect (costless) mobility of individuals, not only would the optimal level of local public goods be provided in each locality, but also the nation's residents would locate themselves in an efficient manner. Tiebout assumed that all residents were fully informed, that the number of communities was large enough that the individual had a virtually continuous spectrum of public goods—tax mixes from which to choose— and that each person's income was independent of where he chose to locate. Tiebout's reasoning was very informal and, in retrospect, clearly incomplete. However, the claim that household mobility allows for some decentralized, quasi-market solution to the problem of preference revelation, and that it leads to efficient local public good provision, is a most provocative one. It has stimulated a large amount of research, much of it within the last decade. In this section, we review the intuition behind the Tiebout argument, and discuss some of its limitations. Then we turn to the separate, but closely related, problem of efficient locational choice by mobile households.

(a) Preference Revelation for Local Public Goods

Tiebout's study immediately followed, and was clearly motivated by, Samuelson's famous 1954 paper on public goods. Samuelson concluded that individuals generally have no incentive to reveal their true "preferences"— their marginal rates of substitution or marginal benefits—for public goods. Indeed, they would have every incentive to conceal them if their taxes were to be based on their revealed preferences, as would be true under a system of benefit or Lindahl pricing. Therefore, no market-type mechanism could be relied upon to allocate resources optimally to public goods. The Tiebout model offered an alternative mechanism for preference revelation, at least for the case of local public goods. If consumers are mobile among communities, they can "shop" for the community that offers a mix of local public goods and taxes best suited to their tastes. By this locational choice process, sometimes called "voting with the feet," consumers reveal their preferences for local public goods. They would tend to migrate to communities with expenditure-tax mixes according closely with their preferences, so that the residents living in a particular locality would tend to have similar preferences for the local public good. Tiebout claimed that the problem of preference revelation could thus be solved, and that there was no obstacle to the efficient provision of local public goods, provided that there were enough communities offering a wide-enough variety of local public goods.

Unfortunately, the precise basis for this claim was not made very explicit by Tiebout. For instance, Tiebout did not make clear the mechanism by which expenditure levels in each community would be set, and the way that this mechanism would exploit the information on preferences that is supposedly revealed by voting with the feet. Indeed, it is not really clear what is meant by "similar" preferences, or by "revelation" of preferences. Similar preferences could mean identical indifference maps or utility functions, identical marginal benefit schedules for local public goods, or identical "demands" for local public goods, in the sense of most-preferred levels of provision. In general, these three meanings need not coincide. Revelation of preferences is likewise somewhat ambiguous. Does this mean simply that households have a most-preferred community, and that they move to it? Or does it mean something stronger? For example, can one ascertain a household's marginal benefit for the local public good at a given level of provision, or, even more, its entire marginal benefit schedule, once it decides to live in a particular locality? Presumably one of the latter would have to be true, if voting with the feet is to resolve the problem raised by

Samuelson: If revealed information on preferences is used to determine levels of local public good provision, that information must include ΣMB.

The extent to which preferences for local public goods are revealed by mobile households, the sense in which residents in particular communities have similar tastes for such goods, and the implications of this process of sorting by locational choice for the determination of efficient local public expenditure, are the subject of ongoing research. As yet, there seem to be many negative results. But the Tiebout intuition is persuasive, and has motivated considerable empirical research.

A study by Oates (1969) attempted to test the "Tiebout hypothesis" by examining the influence of local public expenditures and taxes on property values in a sample of communities in New Jersey. Oates argued that if the quality and quantity of local public goods and the level of property taxes were determinants of residential choice for consumers, local property values ought to be influenced by them. Communities that had high levels of local public services would tend to attract residents, all other things being equal. The increased demand to locate there would drive up local property values, since the quantity of property was presumably relatively fixed. An equilibrium would be established in which part, or all, of the value of local public services was "capitalized" into local property values. The amount of capitalization would depend upon the mobility of consumers, and the elasticity of supply of local property. On the other hand, local property taxes would have the opposite effect. If one community was identical to another except for the level of property taxes,[7] the mobility of residents would cause property values to be lower in the high-tax region. Among communities, local property values would differ, due to variability in the level of public services and taxes, as well as for other reasons.

Oates attempted to estimate the extent to which local property values capitalized the level of public services and property taxes. Using a cross-section of fifty-three communities in northeastern New Jersey in 1960, he ran a regression of the median home value of the community against the effective property tax rate,[8] the level of educational expenditures per pupil, and a number of other variables expected to have an influence on local property values.[9] The level of educational expenditures per pupil was taken to be a proxy measure of the level of local public services. The regression showed a significant, positive association between the level of per pupil expenditures and local property values, and a negative association between the tax rate and local property values.[10] That is, both expenditure levels and tax rates appear to be capitalized to some extent, thus lending support to the Tiebout hypothesis of intercommunity mobility.

The implications of the empirical results of Oates for the explanatory power of the Tiebout model have been disputed in the literature, for example, in a paper by Edel and Sclar (1974). (See also Hamilton [1976] and Pauly [1976].) They argue that in a world in which the Tiebout mechanism is operating perfectly, no capitalization of taxes and expenditures would be expected to occur. It is true that if two communities had persons with the *same* preferences, but different levels of public goods and expenditures, tax capitalization would occur. However, if the Tiebout mechanism were working, communities with persons having identical demands for expenditures and taxes would provide identical levels of them, while communities with persons of different tastes would provide appropriately different levels and mixes of expenditures and taxes. Like persons would congregate together, and these homogeneous communities would differ from one another in taxes and expenditures, but not property values.[11] Therefore, the fact that tax and expenditure capitalization does occur may indicate a disequilibrium situation in which the Tiebout model has not fully adjusted. They argue that a more appropriate test of the Tiebout hypothesis is to see whether capitalization falls over time as communities adjust. Unfortunately, as Pauly (1976) points out, if the situation is one of disequilibrium, one cannot make any inferences about whether or not it is moving towards equilibrium from such an analysis.

Subsequent to Edel and Sclar, Meadows (1976) has attempted to resurrect the Oates analysis of the Tiebout mechanism by estimating a full simultaneous equation model for determining property values. As in the Oates model, property values are assumed to be determined by tax rates and expenditure levels,[12] as well as a number of other variables. At the same time, the tax rates themselves are endogenously determined by expenditures and a number of other variables, including fiscal capacity and the level of state aid; and, expenditure levels are dependent upon tax rates and other variables. The effect of increased tax rates on property values is much more complicated than was implied in the Oates model, since tax rate changes will themselves cause expenditure levels to change, and therefore property values. Meadows' estimation of the simultaneous equation system (using the same data as Oates) allows him to include not only the direct impact of the increased tax rate on property values, but also the indirect or induced effect of changes in expenditure levels on property values. Meadows found that, by taking all these indirect effects into account, the overall impact of both tax changes and expenditure levels on property values is much lower than that obtained by Oates. This would tend to indicate that the sample of municipalities used might have been much closer to a Tiebout equilibrium than Oates' analysis would suggest. Research into this question is still very much an ongoing concern, with many theoretical and empirical issues remaining to be resolved. Recent studies include Brueckner (1979), Epple, Zelenitz, and Visscher (1978), Sonstelie and Portney (1978, 1980), Wildasin (1979b), and many others.

(b) Optimal Spatial Allocation of Resources

If a fully efficient allocation of resources is to be achieved in a federal system with freely mobile households, efficient levels of local public good provision must be achieved. In addition, households must be efficiently assigned to localities: There must not exist an alternative distribution of households across locations that makes at least one household better off and none worse off. One cannot be certain that efficiency will be attained, however. As has been argued in a series of studies by Buchanan and Wagner (1970), Buchanan and Goetz (1972), Flatters, Henderson, and Mieszkowski (1974), Stiglitz (1977), Wildasin (1980) and others, individual migration among communities in a decentralized federal system may generate externalities which result in inefficient outcomes. Only if local taxes are correctly designed will efficiency be attainable.

To analyze the question of efficient locational choice, let us consider an economy consisting of a number of regions, each one providing local public goods financed by levying some form of taxes upon local residents and/or local goods or factors. The local public goods benefit only residents of the region in which they are provided; there are no spillovers. The population of the nation, which makes up the labor force, is perfectly mobile across localities, and moves to the locality that maximizes individual utility. As we know from our discussion of public goods in Chapter 4, there are economies of scale in the use of public goods. The more persons that use them, the lower is the tax price for each. Therefore, there is a benefit to be had from increasing the population of each region. In order to prevent the entire population from settling in one region, some offsetting disadvantge must be had from increasing a region's population.

There are two obvious ways that this occurs in the real world. First, regions or localities are endowed with fixed amounts of certain factors of production that are immobile among regions; land is one main example. As households migrate from one region to another in this Ricardian world, wage rates will tend to rise in regions that lose population, and fall in regions that gain population, due to the diminishing marginal product of labor. Or, if the fixed factor is used in the production of locally-consumed goods, as, for instance, land is used in the production of residential housing, locally-consumed goods will have rising supply curves, so that the price of the consumer good will fall as households leave a region or locality, and be driven up as they enter. Whether wage rates fall, or housing prices rise, or both, what is important is that real income or utilty will tend to fall as the population in a region increases, because of the increasing relative scarcity of fixed factors, and this will work to limit population size. A second factor that offsets the benefits of larger population results from the impurity of local public goods. If the addition of more persons to the public service or facility reduces the benefits to those already consuming it, this rivalry or congestion effect will tend to decrease the attractiveness of the community as population rises, thus helping to limit population size.

Let us begin by abstracting from congestion effects, assuming instead that local public goods are purely public, so that the only limit to increased population is the diminishing marginal product of labor, and/or the rising price of consumption goods. If no public goods existed, households would migrate until real incomes were equated everywhere. This would be an efficient outcome, for if real income were higher in one location than the other, it would be Pareto-improving to move one household from the low-income to the high-income location.

When there are local public goods, however, the equilibrium location assignment may not be optimal. Consider the marginal household which, in equilibrium, is indifferent between locations A and B. Suppose the total utility or benefit from locating in A is TB^A, which is determined by real private goods consumption, and by the quantity of local public goods provided. Real private goods consumption depends on wage income, on the price of locally-produced private goods, and on local taxes. If TB^B similarly represents the total benefit from locating in B, then the condition for locational equilibrium is

$$TB^A = TB^B. \tag{15-11}$$

This may or may not correspond to an efficient allocation of households across regions, depending on the nature of local taxes. Suppose, for example, that region A imposes a residence-based tax, such as a head or income tax, so that the marginal household would have to pay T^A on locating there. Then the social benefit of having the household locate in A is not just the value of the private and public goods that he gets to consume, as measured by TB^A. In addition, by contributing T^A in local taxes, the individual will reduce the amount that the rest of the residents would have to pay to finance the local public goods. This will increase their private good consumption, in total, by T^A. Therefore, the social benefit from having the household locate in A is $TB^A + T^A$, and similarly for B. Efficiency requires that the social marginal benefit from relocating a household between A and B must be equal, or

$$TB^A + T^A = TB^B + T^B. \tag{15-12}$$

Clearly, the efficient allocation described by Eq. (15–12) will be achieved in equilibrium only if $T^A = T^B$, for then the efficiency condition Eq. (15–12) and the equilibrium condition Eq. (15–11) coincide. In theory, there is no necessity for this to be the case. The region endowed with the most land will typically have the largest population at the equilibrium, the largest quantity of public goods, and the lowest tax price per unit of public good. However, *a priori* there is no reason why the tax bill per person (the tax price times the quantity of public goods) should be the same in both regions.[13] It could be higher in either region.

All of this discussion is based on the assumption that each locality uses a residence-based tax to finance its public good expenditures. Suppose, by contrast, that localities tax the ownership or returns to the locationally-fixed factors, such as land. In this case, all local tax burdens fall on landowners, regardless of where they might reside, and no household will bear a higher tax on account of its entry into a locality. (This is true even if the migrant buys land upon entering the locality and pays taxes thereafter, because the real burden of the tax will have been capitalized into the purchase price of the land, and will remain with the original owner.) Consequently, an immigrant generates no external benefit for existing residents in a locality, and the social benefit from having a household enter locality A will be just TB^A, and similarly for B. The equilibrium condition Eq. (15–11) therefore also describes the efficient allocation of households across regions, and the equilibrium will be efficient. Thus, an efficient outcome is possible if localities tax locationally fixed factors to finance pure local public goods.

Efficient locational choices are also achieved under other forms of source-based taxes, such as a tax on capital income *originating* in the locality The amount of revenue flowing from such taxes does not change when a household enters a locality, and the household's locational choice does not therefore result in a fiscal externality. Of course, some source-based taxes can result in other types of inefficiency. For example, local taxes on capital income might interfere with efficient allocation of capital across regions as capital is driven from high- to low-tax locations. This problem obviously cannot arise with taxes on locationally fixed factors such as land, and taxes on immobile factors therefore result in fully efficient outcomes.

If local public goods are impure, another source of inefficiency arises. When a household enters a community, it will impose congestion costs on the users of the local public good there. Let MCC^A be the marginal congestion cost of adding one more household to locality A, and similarly define MCC^B. Then if T^A and T^B represent the amount of residence-based taxes levied in A and B, the efficiency condition becomes

$$TB^A + T^A - MCC^A = TB^B + T^B - MCC^B. \qquad \text{(15–13)}$$

This condition reflects the fact that an entrant to a community imposes two sorts of externalities: lower taxes for existing residents (T^A) and congestion (MCC^A). Clearly, the equilibrium distribution of households across regions, at which Eq. (15–11) holds, need not satisfy the efficiency condition Eq. (15–13). Notice also that if localities use source-based taxes (such as a tax on fixed factors), so that $T^A = T^B = 0$, the equilibrium will again not be efficient unless MCC^A happens to equal MCC^B, an outcome that would be fortuitous.

It is possible, however, to ensure an efficient outcome by a proper mix of residence-based and source-based taxes, say, a head tax and a tax on fixed factors. Each locality could choose a head tax that would equal the marginal congestion cost in that locality, so that for locality A, $T^A = MCC^A$, and likewise for B. Each locality would collect a certain amount in taxes this way. These generally would not equal local public expenditures, as for instance would be true if congestion effects were small. Then any remaining revenue needs could be met from taxation of fixed factors, which, we recall, does not result in migration externalities. Then each locality could collect its required revenue and, at the same time, the efficiency condition Eq. (15–13) would reduce to the equilibrium condition Eq. (15–11). That is, the equilibrium would then be efficient.

Of course, implementing such a tax system might be difficult, since it involves choosing the proper mix between fixed-factor taxes and taxes on mobile households. An important special case arises, however, when local public goods are completely rivalrous (like private goods) so that the cost of providing the public good in, say, locality A is C^A dollars per capita times the number N^A of households located in the community. Then if one more household enters, the marginal cost of servicing it with the public good is $MCC^A = C^A$, where we assume that the marginal cost is constant and equal to the average cost. An income or head tax set at the rate $T^A = MCC^A$ will thus yield $N^A T^A = N^A MC^A = N^A C^A$ dollars in revenue, precisely the total amount of public expenditure. Thus, when local public goods are competely rivalrous, no source-based tax is required, and all revenue should be raised via residence-based taxes. In this case, like the pure public good case, the efficient tax system involves only one type of tax.

It might be recalled from our discussion in Chapter 6 that empirical estimates of the demand for local public services have typically found these services to be completely rivalrous or private in nature. (See Borcherding and Deacon [1972], Bergstrom and Goodman [1973], and the survey by Romer and Rosenthal [1979a].) This would lend support to the case for residence-based taxation by local jurisdictions.

THE THEORY OF INTERGOVERNMENTAL GRANTS

15–4   Grants from higher to lower levels of government are facts of life in multi-level systems of government. They may be given either for efficiency or equity reasons. They may be given to encourage particular types of expenditures by lower levels of government, or simply to increase their purchasing power. Grants are of two broad types, *unconditional* and *conditional*. Unconditional grants are lump-sum transfers of purchasing power from one level of government to another. Conditional grants are grants that are tied in some way to the behavior of the recipient government. They may, for example, be given on the condition that the recipient government match a certain proportion of them with their own expenditures. Furthermore, they may be tied to specific types of expenditures (health, education, etc.) rather than being available for general expenditures.[14] As we shall see in Section 15–5, matching grants that are specific to particular sorts of expenditures are common in the United States. Conditional grants may also be closed-ended. That is, there may be an upper limit on the amount of funds that the upper level of government may provide. Finally, the magnitude of either conditional or unconditional grants may be related to some characteristic of the recipient government. For example, it may be related to the "fiscal capacity" of a jurisdiction as measured by, say, per capita income, or the per capita magnitude of various tax bases. Or, the amount of the transfer (or the matching formula) may be related to the "needs" of the jurisdiction, where the measure of the need may depend upon the type of grant being given. It may be the cost per capita of providing a particular level of service in the jurisdiction.

The purpose of this section is to discuss the rationale for intergovernmental transfers, and to briefly analyze the economic effects of such transfers. We shall discuss four theoretical justifications for transfers from one jurisdiction to another, and consider the appropriate form the transfer should take in each case.

(a) Interjurisdictional Spillovers

As discussed in Section 15–2, expenditures by lower levels of governments may provide benefits to nonresidents. Yet, there is no incentive for these spillover benefits to be taken into consideration by the government when deciding upon how much to produce. The case is analogous to that of an externality between two parties, discussed in Chapter 5. If region A is undertaking a public expenditure that benefits the residents of region B, the efficient level of output of the expenditure will be that at which:

$$MB_A + MB_B = MC \tag{15-14}$$

where MB_A is the collective benefit to residents of A, MB_B is that to residents of B, and MC is the marginal cost of the activity.

If the government in A is behaving efficiently on behalf of its own constituents, as we shall assume, it will select the level of expenditures at which

$$MB_A = MC. \tag{15-15}$$

It is clear that in order to induce A to spend the correct amount on the activity, a subsidy should be granted at the per-unit rate of MB_B.[15] Then the marginal cost to A of expanding the activity would be $MC - MB_B$, and it would behave so as to satisfy Eq. (15–14). Equivalently, A could be induced to behave optimally if a matching grant were instituted at the rate $MB_B/(MB_A + MB_B)$. The marginal cost of expansion of the activity to A would be $MC[1 - MB_B/(MB_A + MB_B)]$. A would expand the activity until:

$$MB_A = MC \left[1 - \frac{MB_B}{MB_A + MB_B} \right] = MC \cdot \frac{MB_A}{MB_A + MB_B}. \tag{15-16}$$

Since Eq. (15–16) reduces to Eq. (15–14), A would be undertaking the optimal level of the activity.

If, at the same time, B emits a spillover on A, exactly the same principle will apply. B must be given a matching grant at the appropriate rate, not necessarily the rate given to A.[16] The rate of subsidy should be related solely to the amount of spillover generated. There is no apparent reason why it should either be related to need or capacity or be closed-ended.

Matching grants are not the only way to induce the region to provide the efficient level of expenditures on a spillover-generating activity. An unconditional grant could be used as well, but it is easy to show that it would be an inefficient way to do so. Consider Fig. 15–2, which depicts the collective choice of residents in A for spillover-generating activity X vis-a-vis all other expenditures (private and public). In the absence of the transfer, the budget constraint facing residents of A is CD. They select point I, the point which maximizes their collective preferences as indicated by the social indifference curves. A matching grant is now given at the

Figure 15–2

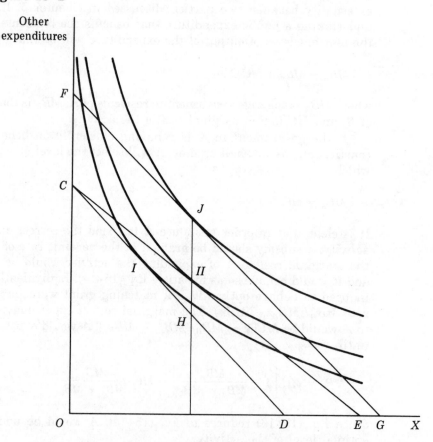

rate DE/OE. The demand for X rises to that given by the point II, at which point the total grant given in dollar terms amounts to IIH. In order to induce the same expenditures on X, an unconditional grant of HJ, which shifts the budget line out to FG, would have to be given.

Not only is it more costly to the central government, but it is inefficient as well. The unconditional grant is purely an income-changing phenomenon. Since it does not change relative prices, A will continue to behave according to Eq. (15–15) and select an inefficient mix of expenditures.

(b) Fiscal Imbalance

Because of the interjurisdictional mobility of the tax base, it may be efficient to assign to the central government taxing powers that are relatively large compared with expenditure responsibilities, and the opposite for lower levels of government. In this case, it will be efficient for the central government to collect more tax revenues than it needs, and transfer the excess to lower jurisdictions who are collecting less than they need. This procedure is known as *revenue sharing*. Presumably, the transfer to a lower unit ought to be of the sort that makes the lower level as well off as possible. It can be shown that the form of the transfer that achieves this is the unconditional grant.

This is illustrated in Fig. 15–3, showing once again the choice of residents of A between any particular public expenditure X and all other expenditures.[17] In the absence of a subsidy, they will choose the point I on the budget line CD. An unconditional grant in the amount CF will raise the budget line to FG, and result in a choice of point II on indifference curve U_3. The matching grant, which results in the same total transfer, will be that at the rate DE/OE. Under it, taxpayers would select the point III on indifference curve U_2. Of necessity, U_2 must be below U_3. Therefore, an unconditional grant will be superior to a matching one from the point of view of benefiting the recipient most.

One way to accomplish the goal of closing the fiscal gap between revenue sources and expenditure responsibilities is simply to have a federal-state agreement, whereby the federal government collects tax revenues on behalf of the states, and turns them back to each state. (This is done in Canada for the income tax.) Such a tax collection arrangement, if negotiated with all states, has the advantage that a uniform tax base is being applied nationwide. However, to rely on it solely implies that there is no need for the federal government to redistribute tax revenues among states. As the following two subsections suggest, there are likely to be efficiency and equity reasons why the central government might wish to transfer revenues to state governments according to a criterion other than that of just returning tax revenues to the states in which they were collected. It may be sensible to take into account the fiscal (tax-raising) capacity of the state, as well.

Figure 15–3

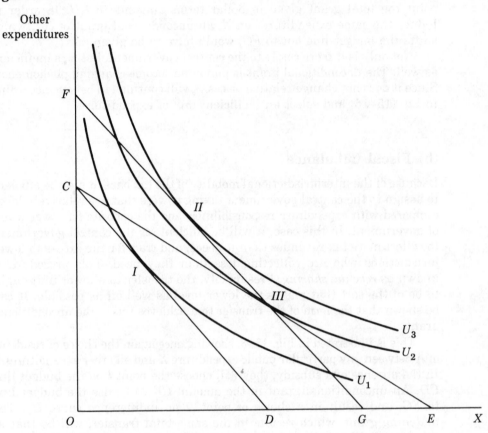

(c) Inefficiencies of Labor Mobility

As we saw in Sections 15–2 and 15–3, the fiscal actions of lower level governments can introduce incentives, which are inefficient from a social point of view, for individuals to migrate between jurisdictions. These inefficiencies can arise for two reasons. As discussed in Section 15–3, when residence-based taxes do not exactly reflect the marginal congestion cost or opportunity cost imposed on existing residents from a potential migrant, inefficient migration will be induced. There will be an incentive for too much migration from jurisdictions with relatively high residence-based taxes (or too little migration into these jurisdictions), and vice versa. The other source of inefficient incentives to migrate, discussed in Section 15–2, arises when lower-level jurisdictions have redistributive budgets. Even if all jurisdictions follow the same redistributive patterns, there will be an incentive for labor to migrate to higher-income areas because of the differences in fiscal residua from redistribution. The importance of the inefficiency in labor allocation induced by lower-level budgets depends upon the degree of mobility of labor.

One way to correct this inefficiency, in principle, is to arrange for a system of interjurisdictional transfers. The transfers should go from those jurisdictions that are more fiscally attractive to those that are less so. The transfer should eliminate the inefficient incentives. To be more specific, we can characterize in each jurisdiction the fiscally-induced incentive to migrate per capita as the sum of the difference between residence-based tax liabilities and marginal congestion costs per person ($T^i - MCC^i$), plus the fiscal residuum from redistribution. The appropriate interjurisdictional transfer would eliminate this difference.

The operation of such a scheme can best be illustrated using a specific example. Consider a federation consisting of states A and B. Suppose that these states provide, through their public sectors, purely private goods in equal, per capita amounts, to each of their citizens. Let A be a resource-rich state, in the sense that the value of resources per capita exceeds that in state B. In fact, suppose state A obtains a great deal of tax revenue from resource taxes, R^A, while state B obtains none. If L^A is the population of state A, and L^B of state B, then R^A/L^A is the per capita amount of public services provided through resource tax revenues. If all other public services are financed by distributionally-neutral residence-based taxes, the inefficiencies of migration can be illustrated, as in Fig. 15–4, where migration is assumed to be costless. The diagram depicts the curve of wage payments in state A, W_A, drawn from origin O_A and that of state B, W_B, drawn from origin O_B. Both curves decline, due to the existence of fixed factors in A and B. In the absence of the tax on resource rents, workers would allocate themselves over the two states until $W_A = W_B$. The resulting allocation, L^o, would be the efficient allocation.

When the per capita benefits of resource taxes can be obtained by migration, workers will allocate themselves over the two regions until $W_A + R^A/L^A = W_B$. This is shown in the diagram as the inefficient allocation, L^e, characterized by an excess of workers in state A. This inefficiency can be eliminated by a set of interjurisdictional transfers that "equalizes" per capita resource tax collections. In this case, one half of R^A/L^A would have to be transferred from state A to state B. The example continues to hold if state B collects resource revenues as well. Whenever per capita resource tax collections differ in the two states, so $R^A/L^A \neq R^B/L^B$, inefficiency of migration will be induced. This source of inefficiency would be eliminated if per capita resource tax revenues were equalized over states.

The remedy of equalizing resource revenues over states is a difficult one to implement. If the federal government tried to institute a scheme of interjurisdictional transfers that reallocated actual state tax collections from a particular source among states, this would introduce a severe disincentive on states to raise revenues from this source. The scheme would be, in effect, a 100 percent tax on marginal state tax collections. To use the terminology of Musgrave (1961), the scheme would discourage *tax effort* by the states. The scheme could only work if the redistribution did not

Figure 15–4

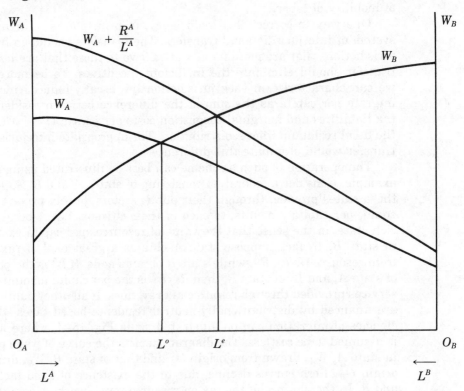

penalize tax effort so strongly. For example, the federal government might attempt to equalize the ability of states to raise tax revenues from various sources, or their *tax capacity*, instead of actual tax collections. One way to do this, the way used in Canada, would be as follows: Suppose the federal government wanted to bring the revenue-raising capability of each of the states below the national average up to the national average standard. For each state revenue source, the nationwide base of the tax, and the national average tax rate (total state tax revenue from that source divided by the base), could be calculated, as could the nationwide per capita tax collected by the states. By applying the national average tax rate to a state's tax base, one could find the amount of revenue that state would collect at national average tax rates from its own tax base, and convert it to per capita terms. The difference between the national average per capita tax collections from that state revenue source, and the amount collected by applying the national average rate to the state tax base, would give the per capita grant required to bring up to the national average the revenue-raising capacity from that revenue source. The same calculation would be done for all revenue sources. For states above the national average, the formula could be used to determine the amount to be taken away.

The above result depends on the special assumptions we have made. In particular, the assumption that resource tax revenues are spent on private-type public services is critical. If the revenues were spent entirely on pure public goods, no inefficiency would result, as we have seen earlier, so no transfers would be required. If the revenues were spent on congested public goods, partial equalization would be efficient. Thus, the degree of equalization of resource tax revenues depends on the empirical question of how private are the services provided by state governments. The result applies, however, more generally than to just resource tax revenues. It applies to any tax that is not residence-based (such as state corporate taxes).

Next, let us add the possibility of redistributive residence-based taxes. These give rise to inefficiencies similar to those discussed above, and call for similar interjurisdictional transfers. As we have seen, the redistributive actions of local governments create fiscal residua, which will be systematically higher in high-income states relative to low-income states. The different fiscal residua will induce migration until the fiscal residuum differences for each type of labor are offset by market wage differences. Thus, Fig. 15–4 can be interpreted as applying to a particular type (e.g. income level) of labor, and the per capita resource tax differential is replaced by the fiscal residuum differential. Efficiency can be restored by eliminating the fiscal residuum differentials by a set of interjurisdictional transfers.

For example, consider the case of Table 15–1, in which residence-based taxes are proportional to income, and benefits are equal, per capita, private-type public services. In this case, the fiscal residuum differential is equal to the difference in average per capita income tax collections across the two states. Thus, efficiency would call for the complete equalization of residence-based tax collections.[18] This result depends upon the specifics of the example used. For example, as discussed in Boadway and Flatters (1982), it can be shown that if state budgets are less redistributive than the above, less than full equalization of residence-based tax revenues is called for; while if they are more redistributive, more than full equalization is called for.

This example assumes that both state governments pursue the same redistributive policies. If they do not, no scheme of intergovernmental transfers can completely eliminate fiscal residuum differences for all persons. Such transfers can only eliminate such differences on average. Inefficiencies arising from different distributional policies cannot be eliminated by transfers, and simply have to be accepted as one of the costs of decentralized federal systems of government.

(d) Equal Treatment of Equals

The efficiency arguments for intergovernmental transfers apply whenever there is labor mobility across jurisdictions. However, the more costly is migration, the less mobile is labor, and the less will be the importance of fiscally induced migration inefficiencies. However, similar arguments may be made that inefficiencies of migration also give rise to horizontal inequities across jurisdictions when mobility is less than perfect. Let us consider the extreme case in which labor is completely immobile across jurisdictions.

Recall, from Chapter 10, the concept of horizontal equity. The public sector is said to be horizontally equitable if any two individuals who are equally well-off in the absence of it, are also equally well-off in its presence; that is, if equals are treated equally. Suppose we wish the principle of horizontal equity to be satisfied in a federal system of government. Any two equally well-off persons in the federation should be treated equally by the federal public sector, regardless of where they reside. Buchanan (1950) has used the term *fiscal equity* to refer to horizontal equity across the federation. The difficulty in applying the principle of horizontal equity in a federal system of government is that the independent actions of lower levels of government will typically cause otherwise identical persons, residing in two separate jurisdictions, to be treated differently. That is because they are likely to obtain different *net fiscal benefits* (or fiscal residua) from the budgetary actions of their particular government.

Differences in net fiscal benefits accruing to individuals in different states can arise for the same reasons as inefficient migration. The same fiscal residuum differentials that arise from the redistributive actions of local governments, causing inefficient migration, will also cause horizontal inequities in the absence of migration. Individuals of a given income level, residing in a high-income state, will obtain a larger net benefit from the state fiscal activities than will a similar person residing in a different state. This source of horizontal inequity in the treatment of identical individuals in different states can be removed by a set of interstate transfers that equalize the fiscal residua across states. Thus, exactly the same remedy applies on equity grounds as applies on efficiency grounds. It is one of those rare occasions in economic policy when efficiency and equity arguments coincide.

As with the efficiency case, horizontal inequities can arise from the allocative function of state (and local) governments as well as from the redistributive function. The net fiscal benefit an individual obtains from residing in a particular state is the difference between the value of public services, and the taxes ultimately paid by the household. For an otherwise identical person, this can differ from state to state for several reasons. For one thing, if populations differ and if public goods are being provided, an individual would *ceteris paribus* be better off in the state with the higher population, because of economies of scale in the consumption of public goods. For another, if different states rely on different taxes, otherwise identical persons would be treated differently in the two states. This will be the case if states can export their taxes in different proportions. Thus, if one state can tax resource rents that are not owned by residents of the state, while the other cannot, differences in net fiscal benefits will occur. In principle, these could be eliminated by interjurisdictional transfers.

The transfers required in this case will generally differ from those appropriate to the efficiency of migration. For example, net fiscal benefit differences, arising from the local provision of pure public goods financed by non-resident-based taxes, should not be equalized from an efficiency point of view. However, although they are difficult to measure, they should be equalized from a horizontal equity point of view.

There is one special case in which equity and efficiency would call for the same equalizing transfers. It is similar to the example considered in the sub-section dealing with equity. Suppose the state government provides private-type public services, and finances them with source-based taxation. We saw earlier that, on efficiency grounds, full equalization is called for. If the source-based taxes are not incident on residents, full equalization would also be called for on equity grounds. This would be the case for resource rents, which would in any case be publicly owned.

These equity and efficiency arguments call for interstate transfers that require no federal financing. However, they could implicitly be affected by the federal government in the design of its revenue-sharing transfers. If the federal government collects more taxes than it needs, and transfers the surplus to the states, the revenue-sharing formula could incorporate differences in fiscal capacity of the states so as to achieve the efficiency and/or equity goals outlined above.

To summarize the arguments thus far, the appropriate type of grant from a higher level of government to a lower level will depend upon the purpose for which the grant is being given. If the purpose is to encourage a particular type of public expenditure by the recipient government, a subsidy or conditional matching grant on that expenditure would be appropriate. This would be applicable if the central government were attempting to internalize the interjurisdictional spillover or externality from a local government expenditure. The rate of subsidy (the matching formula) should depend upon the magnitude of the marginal spillover, although in practice the central government is unlikely to know the exact magnitude.

On the other hand, if the purpose of the intergovernmental transfer is simply to transfer purchasing power from a higher level of government to a lower one, an unconditional grant is appropriate. This is so because, given the amount that is being transferred, an unconditional grant leaves the recipient best off.

The United States government makes use of both conditional matching and unconditional grants in transferring funds to state and local governments, and these can be justified according to the above criteria. However, the formulas used for a variety of conditional grants do not conform to the above, theoretically-justified, types. In particular, the matching grants are frequently closed-ended, in the sense that there is a maximum amount of grant the recipient may receive. The properties of closed-end matching grants are worth pursuing, and are depicted in Fig. 15–5. (See also Thurow

Figure 15–5

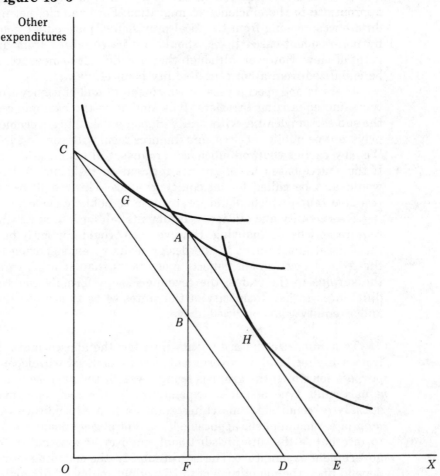

[1966] and Wilde [1968].) In this diagram, *CD* is the budget line of the recipient jurisdiction, showing the combinations of *A* and other expenditures that could be purchased in the absence of a grant.

Consider the imposition of a matching conditional grant, which rotates *CD* outward, but which stipulates that the maximum that can be obtained by the recipient is *AB* dollars. After *AB* dollars has been provided as matching funds, any further expenditures must come entirely from the budget of the recipient jurisdiction. The budget line effectively facing the recipient in the presence of the grant is given by *CAE*. The price of *X* until *OF* is purchased is the slope of *CA*. Purchases beyond *OF* may be obtained at a price given by the slope of *AE* (which equals the slope of *CD*).

Depending upon the preferences of the recipient jurisdiction, three types of outcomes can occur illustrated by the three indifference curves shown in Fig. 15–5. If preferences are such that the point G is chosen, the amount of the transfer received is less than the maximum, and the closing of the grant is irrelevant. The grant has the same effects as an open-ended grant, and would be an efficient way to correct for intergenerational spillovers.

Suppose, however, that the jurisdiction had such strong preferences for X so as to choose the point H beyond the upper limit of the grant. In this case, the grant is exactly equivalent to a lump-sum transfer and is an inefficient way of internalizing the externality. Alternatively, the recipient might choose the point A, at which point all the grant is used. This case is equivalent to neither a matching grant nor a lump-sum grant.

One could always infer from actual expenditures which of these three circumstances existed for a particular grant. If more than OF of X were being purchased, the matching formula would be serving no purpose, since the grant would be equivalent to an unconditional transfer. On the other hand, if less than OF were being purchased, the closing of the grant would make no difference. If the purpose of the grant were to internalize inter-jurisdictional spillovers, it is clear that an open-ended matching grant would be more appropriate.

(e) Behavioral Modeling of Recipient Governments

Any discussion of the rationale for one type or another of intergovernmental transfer program must be predicated, implicitly or explicitly, on some model or theory about how recipient governments are likely to behave in response to such a program. The discussion above has utilized the simplest and best-known such behavioral model, one which straightforwardly extends the theory of consumer behavior to the local jurisdiction. A community is viewed as having preferences, represented by an indifference map over (aggregate) consumption of private and public goods. It faces a budget constraint reflecting the limited income of the community, and the terms on which it can exchange private for public expenditures. Intergovernmental grants are analyzed in terms of their effects on this budget constraint, which changes the level of local public spending in the same fashion as changes in prices and income affect household choices, as set out in the standard theory of the consumer.

Like the theory of consumer behavior itself, this model has implications that can be tested, and some efforts have been made to carry out such tests.[19] In some respects, the theory seems to hold up reasonably well. Many studies use observations on a large group of localities at a given point in time. They postulate a relationship according to which local public expenditure in any given locality depends on its population, income, amount of lump-sum grants received, amount of matching grants received, and possibly many other variables as well. Statistical techniques are then used to quantify this relationship, producing estimates of how sensitive local public spending is to each of these variables. One result that typically emerges from such studies is that a dollar transferred to a locality in matching form tends to result in a larger increase in local public spending than a dollar transferred in lump-sum form. This result is, of course, predicted by the theory presented above; specifically, in subsection (a), we saw how a matching grant would increase local spending more than a lump-sum transfer of equal dollar amount.

Modeling a locality as if it were a household yields other testable implications as well. Let us recall Fig. 15–2, but interpret it slightly differently. Let us focus on the division of the locality's expenditures between private goods and local public goods. Let X measure total local public expenditure, and let "other expenditures" refer only to private expenditure. Then, in the absence of grants, OC represents the community's total private income, which, if no local public expenditures were carried out, would be entirely spent on private consumption. The budget line CD shows the menu of choices open to the community if it sacrifices private consumption through higher local taxes, and uses the proceeds to finance local public goods. As we saw previously, a lump-sum grant shifts the budget line up parallel to CD, for example, to FG. It is obvious that an increase in the community's private income, for example to OF, would have exactly the same impact on the community's budget line, shifting it to FG as well. Neither a lump-sum grant, nor an increase in income, changes the effective price of local public expenditures relative to private goods, and so the slope of FG should be the same as that of CD. But the fact that lump-sum grants and increases in income have identical impacts on the budget constraint immediately implies that a one-dollar increase in lump-sum grants should have exactly the same effect on local spending as a one-dollar increase in community income. Note that the theory does not specify what either of these propensities to spend must be. That depends on the indifference map, and more specifically on the shape of the income-expansion path, or income elasticity of demand for public goods. But the theory does specify that the two propensities should be identical.

Unfortunately, from the viewpoint of this simple theory, the data seem to refute this prediction in practice. Rather, cross-section statistical analyses generally show that a dollar of lump-sum grants increases local government spending more than an equal increase in aggregate community income does. This is sometimes referred to as the "flypaper effect," because the money transferred to local governments "sticks where it hits," that is, it is spent by localities, rather than being used to reduce local taxes, thus allowing an increase in private expenditures. Since the theory is incompatible with these empirical studies, efforts have been made to revise the theory in some appropriate fashion that encompasses what is actually observed. There are two revisions that we shall briefly describe here.

The first, proposed by Courant, Gramlich, and Rubinfeld (1979), Oates (1979), and others, supposes that voter-households are not perfectly informed about the amount and type of grants received by their jurisdictions, and that they may, in fact, suffer from a particular type of fiscal illusion. The argument is that households observe the level of local public expenditures and the level of their personal local tax payments, and from this they derive an *average* tax-price for local public expenditures. If individual i pays local taxes of T_i when the community spends X, the cost to i per dollar of local spending, or the average tax-price to i, would be T_i/X. The household is then assumed to use this average tax-price as a measure of the *marginal* tax-price (that is, the extra tax paid by the individual per extra dollar of local spending), and to use this perceived marginal tax price in deciding whether or not to vote for more or less local spending. If voters actually perceive marginal tax prices in this way, it is easy to see how lump-sum grants could stimulate local spending more than extra private income could. Lump-sum grants increase the amount of local expenditure per dollar of local taxes, and thus would lower the average tax prices T_i/X for all voters. This is true whether the lump-sum grants are initially used to finance more local spending with taxes constant (in which case T_i/X falls because X rises), or whether they are rebated through tax cuts, with spending held fixed (in which case T_i/X falls because T_i falls). A falling average tax price, by hypothesis, is falsely perceived as a falling marginal tax price, making local public expenditure appear to be relatively less expensive at the margin. As a result, voters will demand more local public expenditures, more than would be the case if they had received, in the aggregate, an equal increase in private income, which would not have the effect of lowering the perceived effective price of local public goods.

A second approach to the problem of the "flypaper effect" can be built on the model of the budget-maximizing bureaucrat studied in Chapter 6, as discussed by Romer and Rosenthal (1980). Suppose that the level of expenditure most preferred by the median voter is less than the "reversion level" of expenditure that will be selected if the voters oppose the budget proposal offered by the bureaucrats. An increase in the incomes of voters will increase their most preferred expenditure levels, assuming local public goods are normal. However, if the median voter's most preferred point is still less than the reversion level after the income change,[20] the equilibrium level of spending will remain unchanged at the reversion level. Thus an increase in private income would have *no effect at all* on public spending.

An equivalent increase in lump-sum grants, by contrast, can have quite a different effect. Suppose that the reversion level is increased dollar for dollar by any such grants, a possible legal constraint that Romer and Rosenthal suggest might apply in some United States localities. Then it follows immediately (provided that private goods are normal) that an increase in lump-sum grants will increase the reversion level by more than the increase in the desired expenditure level of the median voter. If we suppose, as before, that the median voter's preferred point is initially less than the reversion level, then the new equilibrium level of public spending will be at the new reversion level, having increased by the *full* amount of the grant. Thus, it is possible in this setting to find a zero effect on public spending from private income changes, while lump-sum grants increase spending dollar for dollar—a most extreme form of the flypaper effect.

Of course, these results apply under the assumption that the reversion level exceeds the preferred point of the median voter. This is only a special case, and Romer and Rosenthal show that many different possibilities can arise under different, and perhaps, in most cases, more plausible, assumptions. It can happen, for instance, that an increase in lump-sum grants results in a *reduction* in local spending, if the reversion level is pushed up closer to the median voter's preferred point. The main conclusion for us to note, perhaps, is that recipient government's response to grants can depend importantly on the precise mechanism by which public expenditure decisions are made. The simple community utility maximization model introduced earlier, though it yields many useful insights, may be seriously inadequate or incomplete. It remains for future theoretical and empirical studies to show what the preferred alternative(s) to this model should be.

CONDITIONAL AND UNCONDITIONAL GRANTS IN THE UNITED STATES

15–5 Intergovernmental grants have assumed a central role in the functioning of the United States federal system. Their importance is documented in Table 15–2. While very little revenue flows from states to the federal government, or from localities to states, the flows from higher- to lower-level governments are quite large. For example, about 20 percent of state revenues are provided by the federal government. At the local level, the percentage is much higher. Thirty-seven percent of local revenues come from higher-level governments, with the bulk (82 percent of intergovernmental revenue) coming from the states, and the remainder from the federal government. Primarily these transfers take the form of conditional grants. An exception to this is the revenue-sharing program, whereby the federal

Table 15–2 Sources of Revenue of Federal, State, and Local Governments, 1981–82 ($ Millions)

	Federal	*State*	*Local*
Total revenue*	687,647	330,949	313,131
Own revenue	685,835	261,784	197,168
Intergovernmental revenue:	1,812	69,166	115,963
from federal	—	66,026	20,919
from state	1,812	—	95,044
from local	—	3,139	—

* Total revenue includes taxes and charges, utility revenue, liquor store revenue, and insurance trust revenue. It excludes debt issue.

Source: United States Department of Commerce (1983a), Table 4, p. 19.

government transfers funds to the state and local governments, which transfers can be used for essentially any governmental function. This program, however, has stayed fairly small since its inception in 1972, with a peak total outlay of about $8.5 billion in 1980, and reductions occurring since then as transfers to states are phased out.

It would be impossible to discuss this rather complicated system of intergovernmental transfers in any detail. (For further discussion, see Break [1980].) In this section we shall, however, present some of the important issues of grant design, and describe some of the characteristics and functions of existing grant programs. First, we consider conditional grants, and later we discuss revenue sharing.

(a) Conditional Grant Programs

Conditional grants are transfers of money from one level of government to another that must be used for a specific purpose. The size of each conditional grant, or *grant-in-aid* as it is often called, depends upon a specific formula that varies considerably from grant to grant. Some of the features that appear frequently in various grants-in-aid are as follows:

(i) *Fiscal Capacity* The amount of the transfer for a particular program frequently depends upon the fiscal capacity of the recipient. By fiscal capacity is meant the ability of a jurisdiction to raise revenues to finance public expenditures. Most often, per capita income is used as the approximate measure for fiscal capacity in grant formulas. However, it is only an accurate measure of fiscal capacity for raising income tax revenues, whereas many recipient governments rely much more heavily on other sources of tax revenue, such as sales taxes and property taxes. A more accurate reflection of fiscal capacity might require taking into consideration the ability to raise revenues from a variety of sources. For example, in determining the fiscal capacities of various states one might find out how much revenue per capita could be raised in each state by applying a common set of tax rates to each state's tax bases. The common set of rates might be the national average of the various state taxes levied in all 50 states.[21]

(ii) *Need* Even if two jurisdictions have the same fiscal capacity and levy the same tax rates, they may not be able to provide the same level of public services. This may be reflected in grant formulas by the inclusion of an index of "need." This index will reflect the difference in the ability of different jurisdictions to provide particular services due to such things as cost differentials and number of users per capita. For example, the ability to provide educational services out of given revenue will depend upon the number of school children per capita, and welfare services will depend upon the number of welfare recipients per capita. Also, the provision of highway services may depend upon the geographical characteristics of the terrain. Depending on the specific program, grants may vary according to one of these indices. In many cases, the population is used as a very crude indicator of need, and the grant is based on a per capita measure.

(iii) *Matching Requirements*   Over 80 percent of grants-in-aid are based on matching formulas such that the donor government agrees to pay a predetermined proportion of the total expenditures undertaken by the recipient government. In almost all cases, the recipient government decides upon how much it will spend, and the donor government passively makes available the funds according to the matching formula (and sometimes subject to an upper bound as discussed below). Such programs are identical to subsidies as discussed in Section 15–4. Some grants, called project grants, require approval of a requested project by the donor government before the grant is given. The matching or subsidy rate available may be uniform across all recipients, or it may vary from one to another. Usually, under variable matching rates, the rate will depend upon the fiscal capacity (per capita income) of the recipient. The higher the per capita income, the lower the rate of subsidy. Sometimes, the rate of subsidy varies directly with an index of need. Matching formulas may follow a method other than that described above. For example, in many states, grants to local governments for education are given on the condition that the local government contribute to educational expenditures the equivalent of a specific tax rate applied to a particular base.

(iv) *Closed-ended Grants*   Almost all grants-in-aid specify an upper limit on the amount of funds that may be received by each recipient under the grant's formula. Since the limit is usually quite moderate, it is frequently binding. The specification of the limit for each recipient may vary according to the need (e.g. population) and/or the fiscal capacity of the recipient jurisdiction (e.g. per capita income). In some instances, the upper bound may be determined by the physical characteristics of the expenditure being undertaken. For example, the federal and state governments may negotiate the amount of expenditures allotted to a particular project under the interstate highway program.

In summary, the typical grant-in-aid program may be based upon a formula that provides for a matching rate that may vary with fiscal capacity or need, and an upper bound on total transfers that may be determined by fiscal capacity or need. Before looking at the actual allocation of grant funds to various programs, it is worth considering the extent to which grant formulas, such as those discussed, are justified on economic grounds. We argued earlier that intergovernmental grants fulfill two roles. First, they serve to internalize interjurisdictional spillovers, by providing the emitter of the spillover with an incentive for taking into consideration all the benefits of its activities. Second, they are a means to transfer purchasing power from one level of government to another, to overcome any fiscal imbalance in the system or to pursue the goal of fiscal equity among jurisdictions. Furthermore, we argued that the appropriate form of grant to use to correct for spillovers is the conditional grant with a rate of subsidy equal to the rate of spillover. The best way to transfer purchasing power would be in the form of unconditional grants, whose allocation among jurisdictions might be determined on equity grounds by such indicators as fiscal capacity or need.[22]

Grants-in-aid in the United States do not conform to those prescribed on the basis of our economic reasoning. Presumably, one main role of the grant-in-aid is to correct for interjurisdictional spillovers arising from such things as education, transportation, health, and welfare expenditures. Matching grants are obviously appropriate for this role. Yet, there is no apparent reason why the matching rates applicable should be related to fiscal capacity or need, since there is no reason why the rate of spillover should be directly related to these. Furthermore, there is no reason to think, on efficiency grounds, that the grant should be of the closed-end form. This would imply that after some level of activity no further spillovers were generated.

The problem, as discussed by Oates (1972) and Thurow (1966), is that in addition to attempting to correct for spillovers, the system of grants-in-aid has simultaneously attempted to achieve two other goals: the equalization of fiscal effort across jurisdictions, and the achievement of a minimum level of each public service throughout the nation. The former goal is presumably motivated by a desire to achieve fiscal equity as we have described it, while the latter is a goal that is based upon other (political) motives. One can explain the variable matching formulas and the upper limit to grants in terms of these goals. The basing of the matching rate, and the maximum transfer on fiscal capacity and/or need, makes the grant structure more equalizing than it otherwise would be. Also, by making the subsidy rate high for poorer jurisdictions, and by making the transfer to them larger, there is a built-in incentive for poorer jurisdictions to increase their public services more, and to equalize service levels across jurisdictions.

Unfortunately, the adjustment of these grant formulas for fiscal capacity and need conflicts with the efficiency aims of the grants. At the same time, the matching-grant approach is not the most appropriate way to pursue the other two stated objectives of fiscal equity and establishing minimum service levels. The problem is that one tool is being used in the pursuit of three conflicting ends, whereas three separate tools should, in principle, be used. Conditional open-ended grants are appropriate for the correction of spillovers, with the rates equal to the rate of spillover. Admittedly, there is a genuine informational problem involved in determining the correct rate. The achievement of an assured minimum level of service could be accomplished by the use of conditional lump-sum grants for particular expenditures (as are sometimes used now). This is a fairly expensive way for the donor to ensure that the minimum level of expenditure is achieved, and it may well be possible to achieve the minimum level with a matching-grant scheme. The goal of fiscal equity among regions is best pursued by a system of unconditional grants.

There has recently been some movement towards diversifying the tools available for making transfers. For one thing, some of the previously fragmented matching-grant programs in particular areas have been consolidated into *bloc grants*. Bloc grants are lump-sum conditional grants given for the use of recipient jurisdictions within a particular area of expenditures. For example, in 1976, $2.55 billion was committed by the federal government to the *community development grant progam*. The funds are allocated on the basis of need to local governments, to be used for a wide variety of community development activities with only a minimum of review. This program replaced seven grant-in-aid programs that included such activities as urban renewal and model cities. To the extent that local governments would not have spent that much money otherwise, the program will be successful in achieving minimum expenditures. If funds would have been spent by local governments out of their own sources, the program is ultimately the same as an unconditional grant. The other comparatively recent change was the institution of general revenue sharing in 1972, discussed later.

The funds allocated in fiscal year 1981–82 under various grant-in-aid schemes by the federal and state governments are summarized in Table 15–3. State payments are almost entirely to local governments, and about 61 percent of them were for education. These were payments to local governments for the support of public schools. About 14 percent of state grants went to local governments for welfare services. This proportion varied greatly from state to state, since different states assign the various welfare functions to different levels of government (state and local). Almost all of the transfers for transportation were to be used by local governments for highways and roads. In the health category, most of the transfers were for the provision of health services by local governments. State grants to localities for housing and urban renewal were relatively insignificant.

Federal intergovernmental transfers include both those supporting state expenditures and those going to local governments. The largest category

Table 15–3   Intergovernmental Grant-in-Aid Transfers by Federal and State Governments, Selected Functions, 1981–82 ($ Millions)

Function	Federal Payments	State Payments
Education	11,971	60,685
Public Welfare	34,414	13,744
Transportation	8,339	5,112
Health and Hospitals	3,231	2,886
Housing and urban renewal	5,716	290
Natural Resources	2,183	321
General Revenue Sharing	4,575	—
Other	15,591	15,706
Total	86,014	98,743

Source: United States Department of Commerce (1983a), Table 10, p. 32.

of transfers is public welfare which represents 40 percent of total federal transfers. These are mainly grants given to support welfare schemes made under state programs, including Aid to Families with Dependent Children and Medicare. Some of this money is transferred to local governments in states which so delegate the responsibility for welfare programs. In fact, most of local government expenditures on public welfare are financed by transfers from upper levels of government. Public welfare transfers, in addition to being the largest current type of federal transfer, have also been the most rapidly growing ones in recent years.

Education is the next largest category of federal grants, making up about 14 percent of total federal transfers. A large portion of these transfers went to support local schools, including grants to operate school lunch and school milk programs. Almost half of local government expenditures on education come from grants from federal and state governments. The remainder of the federal transfers for education were to the states for the support of scientific research and development, especially by institutions of higher education. Much of the funding of education grants is through matching grants, although there are some bloc-grant funds for certain educational purposes, such as educational innovation and instructional resources.

Transportation grants comprise 9.7 percent of all federal grants. Over three-quarters of this represents transfers to the states for interstate highways. A lesser amount goes for urban mass transit expenditures by local governments, in the form of formula grants. There is also a limited amount available for discretionary capital grants for mass transit. Finally, $339 million was paid as federal grants for air transportation.

Federal grants for housing and urban renewal are self-explanatory. Grants for natural resources include water resource development and waste treatment funds. These are directed mostly to local governments. As mentioned earlier, much of the housing and urban renewal assistance has been consolidated into a bloc grant. In the health and hospital area, grants consist mainly of payments to assist the states in the provision of medical services. Some funds are available for public health programs, and a small amount of grants are provided for hospital construction.

Finally, grants are provided for a variety of other purposes. One of the more important is manpower training and manpower services. Grants are given under the Comprehensive Employment and Training Act to states and localities to finance local training and employment plans. Some funds are provided to states and localities for public service employment programs and to states for job matching services.

(b) General Revenue Sharing

After some years of debate, Congress, in 1972, enacted the State and Local Fiscal Assistance Act, providing for transfers of funds from the federal government to the state and local governments through a program known as general revenue-sharing. These funds were authorized for a five-year period, ending in 1977; in 1977, the program was extended for another three years. In 1980, the program was again renewed, but only for three years, and only for aid to local governments; and, in 1983, another three-year extension was made. Prior to 1980, total transfers amounted to over $6 billion per year, whereas about $4.5 billion annually has been allocated to transfers to localities since then.

Revenue-sharing, as originally conceived (see, for example, Heller et al. [1967]), would have been limited neither in dollar amount nor in duration. The spirit of the original revenue-sharing proposals was that a given percentage of federal revenues, or perhaps of a specific source of federal revenues such as the individual income tax, would be allocated on an indefinite basis to lower-level governments. In this way the funds would grow automatically with the increases in the federal tax base; in particular, they would not be eroded in real value by inflation. They would also be available on a more or less permanent basis, so that recipient governments could plan their expenditures accordingly. The existing program has met neither of these desiderata: The program has been limited in duration, especially recently, and it has shrunk in real value. It has been argued that the limited authorization periods for the program have been too short to allow effective long-range planning for spending the funds. If the recipient governments do not know how much funding, if any, will be forthcoming after the allotment period, they may treat it as a one-shot source of funds and use it for once-and-for-all expenditures. It has been argued that the funds have been heavily devoted to financing capital and once-over expenditures, rather than recurring expenditures. Unfortunately, it is difficult to test this empirically, since it is not known how many of the capital expenditures would have been undertaken in the absence of these transfers.

While the revenue-sharing program provided assistance to both states and localities prior to 1980, it has, since then, supported only local governments. The allocations are determined on a state-by-state basis, and under the old formulae one-third of each state's allocation would go to the state government. The remaining two-thirds would go to the localities in each state, again according to a precise formula. Since 1980, all of the funds have gone to the local governments, but the allocation procedure remains basically intact. To understand how the system works, then, one must begin with the determination of the funds to be allocated to each state. We shall therefore present a brief description of the mechanics of this part of the program, and then turn to the allocation of state funds to individual localities.

(i) *Allocation to State Governments*   Each year, the total entitlement of funds is allocated among states using two formulas, a three-factor formula and a five-factor formula, discussed below. Using the three-factor formula, the way in which the total funds would be allocated to each state is calculated; and the way they would be allocated using the five-factor formula is also calculated. Each state is then assigned the allocation of whichever of these two gives it the most funds. Then, since the sum of the best allocation for each state would exceed the total fund, all allocations are reduced in the same proportion so as to exhaust the funds.

The three-factor formula weights the state's share by population, relative income, and tax effort.[23] Population and tax effort both contribute positively to the share, and per capita income negatively. The population factor adds some equalizing element to the formula. An allocation of funds on a per capita basis would tend to redistribute income among states, when one takes into consideration that the funds were raised by federal taxation. The states that paid the most tax would not receive as much back on a per capita basis. The population factor also affords some benefit to densely populated areas. The tax effort factor is included for incentive reasons, to reward those states that exploit their tax bases most. It presumably has no strong equalizing effect, if any. The per capita income factor strengthens considerably the equalizing potential of general revenue-sharing. It is intended to reflect the fiscal capacity of the state.

The five-factor formula includes those three factors plus two others: urbanized population and state personal income tax collections.[24] The urbanized population factor is intended to increase relief to urban areas, which are said to be in more need of funds than non-urban areas. The state personal income tax factor is intended to provide an incentive for states to rely more on the personal income tax to finance their expenditures. In fact, the same act which established general revenue-sharing also included provision for federal collection of state personal income taxes, with the aim of reducing the administrative costs of income tax collection. To avail themselves of the service (so-called "piggy-back" collection), states were required to adopt a uniform set of tax rules. To date, the combined effect of the personal income tax factor in general revenue-sharing and the piggy-back collection system do not appear to have induced much increase in state use of the personal income tax.

On the whole, general revenue-sharing funds appear to be mildly equalizing. Table 15–4 shows the allocations of funds to the five richest and poorest states, in terms of per capita income, including the District of Columbia. Clearly, there is a tendency to treat lower-income states more generously, although the correspondence is far from perfect. (For more detailed discussion of the impact of revenue sharing, consult Nathan et al. [1975, 1977].)

(ii) *Allocation to Local Governments*　　Formerly, two-thirds of each state's allocation was required to be "passed through" to local governments. Since 1980, however, all funds accrue to local governments. All general-purpose local governments (including cities, counties, townships in some states, and others) are eligible for revenue-sharing funds, provided that they are entitled to at least $200 according to the legislative formula. Funds must be allocated within each state according to the same three-factor formula based on population, per capita income, and tax effort as discussed ὲbove.[25] However, two further stipulations are added to the allotment: No municipal or township

Table 15–4   Federal General Revenue Sharing Receipts,
Total and per Capita, Selected States, 1981–82

Five States with Highest per Capita Personal Income, 1981	Per Capita Personal Incomes 1981	Revenue Sharing Receipts, 1980–81		
		Total ($1,000's)	Per Capita	Per $1,000 Personal Income
Alaska	$13,763	15,780	$39.25	2.78
District of Columbia	13,539	18,657	29.24	2.18
Connecticut	12,816	56,021	18.02	1.39
New Jersey	12,127	152,524	20.71	1.70
California	11,923	514,900	21.76	1.78
Five States with Lowest per Capita Personal Income, 1981				
Utah	8,313	32,666	22.36	2.59
Alabama	8,219	72,131	18.52	2.24
Arkansas	8,044	43,143	18.87	2.34
South Carolina	8,039	64,823	20.76	2.55
Mississippi	7,408	61,603	24.44	3.28

Source: United States Department of Commerce (1983a), Table 27, p. 96, and Table 6, p. 29.

government, or country area, may receive more than 145 percent or less than 20 percent of the average state-wide per capita entitlement. And, no local government can receive more than 50 percent of the sum of its taxes and intergovernmental transfers. These maximum and minimum rules are sometimes binding, and have been criticized. The maximum rule has tended to restrict the amounts of funds going to large cities, which presumably need it most. At the same time, the 20 percent minimum has tended to increase the allotments going to smaller levels of government and relatively affluent suburbs. The 20 percent minimum rule has also tended to perpetuate some obsolete types of local government that have relatively few services to perform.

These formulae are really at the heart of the revenue-sharing program. The funds that are allocated to the recipient governments can be used for virtually any desired governmental function, with the significant exception of education. The rationale for the program, then, must be that it is useful to allocate funds according to these formulae, and that federal government transfers of this unconditional type are worthwhile. As we have already discussed, the program does have some equalizing features; it, or a similar, but expanded, program, could have some important effects on interjurisdictional equity, or efficiency of resource allocation. Given its present small and decreasing size, however, revenue-sharing may gradually disappear from the fiscal scene.

It is interesting to note that revenue-sharing has, at times, been justified in terms of an overall fiscal imbalance between the federal and lower-level governments. Some have argued that the federal government tax system, based as it is on income, tends to produce more rapidly-rising revenue over time than the systems of the states and localities. It has also been argued that the functions traditionally assumed by the federal government do not "require" rapidly rising expenditures over time, whereas state and local public expenditure "requirements" tend to grow relatively quickly. The basis for these contentions has never been made very clear; indeed, they seem somewhat difficult to support in any straightforward way at a time of large federal government deficits. The potential for an expanded unconditional transfer program always exists, however. It is possible that the existing system of many conditional grants will gradually evolve in the direction of greater and greater consolidation, with fewer and fewer restrictions on recipient government use of funds, even if revenue-sharing itself eventually passes from the scene.

CHAPTER NOTES

1. In the economic sense, a federal system of government is simply one in which the expenditure and tax functions are divided among different levels of government. This is a considerably looser interpretation of the term federal than is used in, say, political science. For a discussion of this, as well as many other issues that arise in this chapter, see Oates (1972).

2. We are concerned here only with resource allocation functions of government including income redistribution. There is also a segment of the literature related to the assignment of the stabilization or macro-policy functions of government. There seems to be some agreement among authors that such functions ought to be given to the central government. See, for example, Oates (1972), esp. pp. 21–30, and Musgrave (1959), pp. 181–2.

3. The property tax can be viewed, at least partially, as a tax on a mobile factor, capital. This gives rise to inefficiencies in the allocation of capital as we discussed in Chapter 12.

4. For an analysis of this phenomenon, see Boskin (1973), Oates (1972), and Starrett (1980).

5. That is, $\partial U^i/\partial Y^i$, $\partial U^i/\partial W^A$, $\partial U^i/\partial W^B \geq 0$; $\partial U^i/\partial P^A$, $\partial U^i/\partial P^B \leq 0$.

6. Of course, the optimal levels of W^A and W^B from Eqs. (15-4) and (15-5) depend upon the method of financing the transfers as is always the case with public goods. This nonseparability of efficiency from equity aspects was discussed above in Chapter 4.

7. Two communities could provide the same level of public services and yet have different property tax rates, if the values of property in the two differed, if economies of scale existed, or if grants from higher levels of government differed.

8. That is, the nominal tax rate times the ratio of assessed property value to actual value. The latter differs considerably over communities.

9. These included the distance of the community from Manhattan, the median number of rooms per owner-occupied house, the percentage of houses built since 1950, the median family income, and the percentage of families with annual incomes less than $3000.

10. The regression technique used was two-stage least squares, to take account partly of the fact that both tax rates and expenditure per pupil may also depend upon property values. That is, there exists some simultaneous equation bias. An increase in the property tax rate from 2 to 3 percent was found to cause a reduction in house values of about $1500. Increases in expenditure per pupil from $350 to $450 caused house values to rise by $1200.

11. Pauly (1976) provides a proof of this for the case in which the supply of property in each community is fixed.

12. Meadows includes both educational expenditures per pupil and municipal expenditures per resident as separate estimates of local public services.

13. Flatters, Henderson, and Mieszkowski (1974) show that tax bills will be equal if workers have a compensated price elasticity of demand for public goods of unity. They also provide an analytical proof of the equal tax efficiency condition for a two-region model with identical workers and one local public good.

14. Lump-sum grants that are tied to specific expenditures are ultimately the same as unconditional grants, unless the size of the grant is larger than the amount the jurisdiction would otherwise have spent on the specific expenditure. The jurisdiction is always free to release funds it otherwise would have used here and use them for other purposes. See the discussion in Oates (1972), pp. 75-7.

15. Of course, if the number of jurisdictions involved is small, it might be possible to come to a voluntary bargaining solution to internalize the externality without recourse to the central government. This discussion ignores the fact that there may also be spillovers on the tax side. That is, part of the taxes collected in one jurisdiction may be paid for by residents of other jurisdictions. This phenomenon, known as "tax exporting," would make the marginal cost of all expenditure activities to a jurisdiction lower than the marginal cost to the nation as a whole. McLure estimated that as much as 25 percent of state and local taxes may be exported across state boundaries. See McLure (1967). On the other hand, this effect is offset to the extent that the mobility of factors of production discourages a local jurisdiction from raising tax rates.

16. The rate of subsidy, as in the externality case, should equal the marginal spillover benefit at the optimum. There are obvious informational problems in determining the appropriate size of subsidy, especially in the reciprocal spillover case where each jurisdiction's output level affects that of the other. For a full discussion of the problems involved in determining the optimal set of subsidies under reciprocal externalities, see Davis and Whinston (1962), and Oates (1972).

17. Once again, we assume that the residents of *A* behave in a collectively efficient manner. One of the objections to revenue-sharing grants of this sort is that lower levels of government will behave irresponsibly in spending those funds, since they have not had to accept the responsibility for raising the taxes to finance them. The validity of that objection can only be determined by an analysis of the positive aspects of local decision-making. Unfortunately, no such analysis is available now.

18. It might be noted that if these residence-based tax collections were fully equalized, and if all states behaved identically after the equalization, the result would be the same as if the state were a unitary one, with one nationwide income tax system financing a uniform provision of public services across the country.

19. See Gramlich (1977) for a review of some of the large empirical literature on this topic.

20. Let us assume, here and below, that the identity of the median voter does not change as incomes or grant levels change. If this assumption is relaxed, the range of possible outcomes in the bureaucratic model increases.

21. For a discussion of various formulas for fiscal capacity, see Musgrave (1961). This approach to measuring fiscal capacity is used in Canada to determine the allocation of equalization (unconditional) grants to the provinces.

22. Musgrave (1961) has suggested that another index which might be used to allocate funds is *tax effort*. By this is meant the extent to which the government is actually obtaining tax revenue relative to its capacity. For example, the tax effort of a jurisdiction might be measured by the amount of tax revenue being raised as a proportion of the amount of tax revenue that would be raised using the national average tax rate. As we shall see below, tax effort is one of the factors which determines the allocation of federal revenue sharing funds.

23. In particular, the share of the total fund going to each state is determined by the following formula:

$$S_i = \frac{P_i(E_i/Y_i)}{\sum\limits_{j=1}^{50} P_i(E_i/Y_i)}$$

where S_i is the share of state i, P_i is population, E_i is an index of tax effort, and Y_i is per capita income. Tax effort E_i is the total state and local tax collections divided by total state personal income.

24. The share going to each state is determined by a weighted average of the five factors as follows:

$$S_i = \frac{2}{9}\frac{P_i}{\Sigma P_j} + \frac{2}{9}\frac{U_i}{\Sigma U_j} + \frac{2}{9}\frac{P_i/Y_i}{\Sigma P_j/Y_j} + \frac{1}{6}\frac{E_i}{\Sigma E_i} + \frac{1}{6}\frac{T_i}{\Sigma T_j}$$

where S_i, P_i, and E_i are defined as in footnote 23, U_i is the urbanized population in state i, and T_i is total personal income tax collections in state i.

25. The tax effort formula does not include that part of local revenues used to finance education.

References

Aaron, H. J. (1974, May). A new view of property tax incidence. *American Economic Review, 64,* pp. 212–21.

Aaron, H. J. (1975). *Who pays the property tax?* Washington, DC: The Brookings Institution.

Aaron, H. J. (1976a, May). Inflation and the income tax. *American Economic Review* (Papers and Proceedings), *19,* 193–199.

Aaron, H. J. (1976b). Inflation and the income tax: An introduction. In H. J. Aaron (Ed.), *Inflation and the income tax.* Washington, DC: The Brookings Institution.

Aaron, H. J., & Boskin, M. J. (1980). *The economics of taxation.* Washington, DC: The Brookings Institution.

Aaron, H. J., & Pechman, J. A. (Eds.). (1981). *How taxes affect economic behavior.* Washington, DC: The Brookings Institution.

Advisory Committee on Intergovernmental Relations. (1967). *Fiscal balance in the American federal system.* Washington, DC: USGPO.

Ahsan, S. M. (1976, April–May). Taxation in a two-period temporal model of consumption and portfolio allocation. *Journal of Public Economics, 5,* 337–52.

Alchian, A. A. (1953, March). The meaning of utility measurement. *American Economic Review, 42,* pp. 26–50.

Allingham, M. G. (1975, November). Towards an ability tax. *Journal of Public Economics, 4,* 361–76.

Ando, A., & Modigliani, F. (1963, March). The life cycle hypothesis of saving: Aggregate implications and tests. *American Economic Review, 53,* pp. 55–84.

Archibald, C., & Donaldson, D. (1976, August). Non-paternalism and externalities. *Canadian Journal of Economics, 9,* 492–507.

Arrow, K. J. (1951a). An extension of the basic theorems of classical welfare economics. *Proceedings of the Second Berkeley Symposium* (pp. 507–532). Berkeley, CA: University of California Press.

Arrow, K. J. (1951b). *Social choice and individual values.* New York: Wiley.

Arrow, K. J. (1963a). *Social choice and individual values* 2nd ed. New York: Wiley.

Arrow, K. J. (1963b). Uncertainty and the welfare economics of medical care. *American Economic Review, 53,* pp. 942–973.

Arrow, K. J. (1970). *Essays in the theory of risk-bearing* (ch. 4). Amsterdam: North Holland Publishing Co.

Arrow, K. J. (1973, July). Higher education as a filter. *Journal of Public Economics, 2,* 193–216.

Arrow, K. J., & Lind, R. C. (1970, June). Uncertainty and the evaluation of public investment decisions. *American Economic Review, 60,* pp. 364–378.

Arrow, K. J., Minhas, B. S., Chenery, H. B., & Solow, R. M. (1961). Capital–labor substitution and economic efficiency. *Review of Economics and Statistics, 43,* pp. 225–250.

Asimakopulos, A., & Burbidge, J. B. (1974, June). The short-period incidence of taxation. *Economic Journal, 84*, 267–288.

Atkinson, A. B. (1977). Optimal taxation and the direct versus indirect tax controversy. *Canadian Journal of Economics, 10*, 590–606.

Atkinson, A. B., & Stern, N. (1974). Pigou, taxation and public goods. *Review of Economics Studies*, pp. 119–128.

Atkinson, A. B., & Stiglitz, J. E. (1972, April). The structure of indirect taxation and economic efficiency. *Journal of Public Economics, 1*, 97–119.

Atkinson, A. B., & Stiglitz, J. E. (1976, July–August). The design of tax structure: Direct versus indirect taxation. *Journal of Public Economics, 6*, 55–75.

Atkinson, A. B., & Stiglitz, J. E. (1980). *Lectures on public economics.* New York: McGraw-Hill.

Auerbach, A. J. (1979, August). Wealth maximization and the cost of capital. *Quarterly Journal of Economics, 93*, 433–46.

Auerbach, A. J. (1982a, September). Whither the corporate tax? Reform after ACRS. *National Tax Journal, 35*, 275–86.

Auerbach, A. J. (1982b). The new economics of accelerated depreciation. *Boston College Law Review, 23*, 1327–1355.

Auerbach, A. J. (1983, May). Welfare aspects of current U.S. corporate taxation. *American Economic Review* (Papers and Proceedings), *73*, pp. 76–81.

Averch, H., & Johnson, L. L. (1962, December). Behavior of the firm under regulatory constraint. *American Economic Review, 52*, pp. 1053–1069.

Azariadis, C. (1975, November–December). Implicit contracts and unemployment equilibria. *Journal of Political Economy, 83*, 1183–1202.

Bailey, M. J. (1954, June). The marshallian demand curve. *Journal of Political Economy, 62*, 255–61.

Baily, M. N. (1974, January). Wages and employment under uncertain demand. *Review of Economic Studies*, pp. 37–50.

Baily, M. N. (1977). On the theory of layoffs and unemployment. *Econometrica, 45*, pp. 1043–1063.

Baily, M. N. (1978). Some aspects of optimal unemployment insurance. *Journal of Public Economics, 10*, 379–402.

Ballentine, J. G. (1978). The incidence of a corporation income tax in a growing economy. *Journal of Political Economy, 86*, 863–75.

Ballentine, J. G., & McLure, C. E. (1980, March). Taxation and corporate financial policy. *Quarterly Journal of Economics, 94*, 351–72.

Barlow, R., Brazer, H. E., & Morgan, J. N. (1966). *Economic behavior of the affluent.* Washington, DC: The Brookings Institution.

Barlow, R., & Sparks, G. R. (1964, June). A note on progression and leisure. *American Economic Review, 54*, 372–77.

Barlow, B., & Sparks, G. R. (1966, March). A note on progression and leisure: Reply. *American Economic Review, 56*, p. 180.

Barr, J. L., & Davis, O. A. (1966, October). An elementary political and economic theory of the expenditures of local governments. *Southern Economic Journal, 33*, 149–65.

Barro, R. J. (1974). Are government bonds net wealth? *Journal of Political Economy, 82*, 1095–1117.

Barro, R. J. (1976, April). Reply to Feldstein and Buchanan. *Journal of Political Economy, 84* (2), 343–349.

Baumol, W. J. (1967). The macroeconomics of unbalanced growth: The anatomy of urban crisis. *American Economic Review, 57*, pp. 415–426.

Baumol, W. J. (1972, June). On taxation and the control of externalities. *American Economic Review, 62*, pp. 307–322.

Baumol, W. J., & Bradford, D. F. (1970, June). Optimal departures from marginal cost pricing. *American Economic Review, 60*, pp. 265–283.

Baumol, W. J., & Bradford, D. F. (1972, May). Detrimental externalities and non-convexity of the production set. *Economica*, (N.S. 39) pp. 160–176.

Baumol, W. J., & Klevorick, A. K. (1970). Input choices and rate of return regulation: An overview of the discussion. *Bell Journal of Economics, 1*, 162–190.

Baumol, W. J., & Malkiel, B. (1967, November). The firm's optimal debt-equity combination and the cost of capital. *Quarterly Journal of Economics, 18*, 547–578.

Baumol, W. J., & Oates, W. (1975). *The theory of environmental policy.* Englewood Cliffs, NJ: Prentice-Hall, Inc.

Beach, C. M., & Balfour, F. S. (1983, February). Estimated payroll tax incidence and aggregate demand for labour in the United Kingdom. *Economica, 50*, pp. 35–48.

Bentham, J. (1907). *An introduction to the principles of morals and legislation.* Oxford: Clarendon Press.

Bentick, B. L. (1979, August). The impact of taxation and valuation practices on the timing and efficiency of land use. *Journal of Political Economy, 87,* (4), 859–868.

Bergson, A. (1938, February). A reformulation of certain aspects of welfare economics. *Quarterly Journal of Economics, 52,* 314–44.

Bergstrom, T. C., & Goodman, R. P. (1973, June). Private demands for public goods. *American Economic Review, 63,* pp. 290–296.

Bhatia, K. B. (1979, February). Corporate taxation, retained earnings and capital formation. *Journal of Public Economics, 11,* 123–134.

Bishop, R. L. (1968, May). The effects of specific and ad valorem taxes. *Quarterly Journal of Economics, 82,* 198–218.

Black, D. (1948, February). On the rationale of group decision making. *Journal of Political Economy, 56,* 23–34.

Blinder, A. S. (1975). Distribution effects and the aggregate consumption function. *Journal of Political Economy, 83,* 447–476.

Blinder, A. S. (1976). Intergenerational transfers and life cycle consumption. *American Economic Review, 66,* pp. 87–93.

Blinder, A. S., Gordon, R. M., & Wise, D. E. (1980). Reconsidering the work disincentive effects of social security. *National Tax Journal, 33,* 431–442.

Boadway, R. W. (1974, December). The welfare foundations of cost-benefit analysis. *Economic Journal, 84,* 926–939.

Boadway, R. W. (1975, June). The welfare foundations of cost-benefit analysis: Reply. *Economic Journal, 86,* 359–361.

Boadway, R. W. (1979). Long-run tax incidence: A comparative dynamic approach. *Review of Economic Studies, 46,* pp. 505–511.

Boadway, R. W., & Bruce, N. (1979). Depreciation and interest deductions and the effect of the corporation income tax on investment. *Journal of Public Economics, 11,* 93–105.

Boadway, R. W., & Bruce, N. (1984). *Welfare economics.* Oxford: Basil Blackwell.

Boadway, R. W., Bruce, N., & Mintz, J. M. (1982, May). Corporate taxation and the cost of holding inventories. *Canadian Journal of Economics, 15,* 278–293.

Boadway, R. W., Bruce, N., & Mintz, J. (1983, February). On the neutrality of flow of funds corporate taxation. *Economica, 50,* pp. 49–61.

Boadway, R. W., & Flatters, F. R. (1982, November). Efficiency and equalization payments in a federal system of government: A synthesis and extension of recent results. *Canadian Journal of Economics, 15,* 613–633.

Boadway, R. W., & Kitchen, H. M. (1984). *Canadian Tax Policy* (2nd ed.). Toronto: Canadian Tax Foundation.

Boadway, R. W., & Treddenick, J. M. (1978, August). A general equilibrium computation of the effects of the Canadian tariff structure. *Canadian Journal of Economics, 11,* 424–446.

Board of Trustees of the Federal Old-Age and Survivors Insurance and Disability Insurance Trust Funds. (1983). 1983 Annual Report. In *House Documents of the 98th Congress, 1st Session.* Washington: USGPO.

Borcherding, T. E., & Deacon, R. T. (1972, December). The demand for the services of nonfederal governments. *American Economic Review, 62,* pp. 891–901.

Boskin, M. J. (1972). The effects of taxes on the supply of labor: With special reference to income maintenance programs. *Proceedings of the 64th Annual Conference on Taxation of the National Tax Association,* 684–698.

Boskin, M. J. (1973, January–February). Local tax and product competition and the optimal provision of public goods. *Journal of Political Economy, 81,* 203–210.

Boskin, M. J. (1975, February). Efficiency aspects of the differential tax treatment of market and household economic activity. *Journal of Public Economics, 4,* 1–25.

Boskin, M. J. (1976, January–February). Estate taxation and charitable bequests. *Journal of Public Economics, 5,* 27–56.

Boskin, M. J. (1977). Social security and retirement decisions. *Economic Inquiry, 15,* pp. 1–25.

Boskin, M. J. (1978, April). Taxation, saving, and the rate of interest. *Journal of Political Economy, 86,* S3–S27.

Bowen, H. R. (1943, November). The interpretation of voting in the allocation of economic resources. *Quarterly Journal of Economics, 58,* 27–48.

Bradford, D. F. (1975, December). Constraints on government investment opportunities and the choice of a discount rate. *American Economic Review, 65,* pp. 887–899.

Bradford, D. F. (1980). Tax neutrality and the investment tax credit. In H. J. Aaron & M. J. Boskin (Eds.), *The economics of taxation* (pp.

281–298). Washington, DC: The Brookings Institution.

Break, G. F. (1957, September). Income taxes and incentives to work: An empirical study. *American Economic Review, 47,* pp. 529–549.

Break, G. F. (1974). The incidence and economic effects of taxation. In *The Economics of Public Finance* (pp. 119–240). Washington, DC: The Brookings Institution.

Break, G. F. (1980). *Financing government in a federal system.* Washington, DC: The Brookings Institution.

Brechling, F. (1975). *Investment and employment decisions.* Manchester, UK: Manchester University Press.

Brennan, G., & Buchanan, J. M. (1980). *The power to tax: Analytical foundations of a fiscal constitution.* Cambridge, UK: Cambridge University Press.

Breton, A. (1965, May). A theory of government grants. *Canadian Journal of Economics and Political Science, 31,* 175–187.

Brittain, J. A. (1972). *The payroll tax for social security.* Washington, DC: The Brookings Institution.

Brittain, J. A. (1978). *Inheritance and the inequality of material wealth.* Washington, DC: The Brookings Institution.

Broome, J. (1978, February). Trying to value a life. *Journal of Public Economics, 9,* 91–100.

Browning, E. K. (1973, March). Alternative programs for income redistribution: The NIT and NWT. *American Economic Review, 63,* pp. 38–49.

Browning, E. K. (1976). The marginal cost of public funds. *Journal of Political Economy,* 283–298.

Brueckner, J. K. (1979, April). Property values, local public expenditure, and economic efficiency. *Journal of Public Economics, 11,* 223–246.

Buchanan, J. M. (1950, September). Federalism and fiscal equity. *American Economic Review, 40,* pp. 583–599.

Buchanan, J. M. (1952, June). Federal grants and resource allocation. *Journal of Political Economy,* 208–217.

Buchanan, J. M. (1965a, February). An economic theory of clubs. *Economica, 32,* pp. 1–14.

Buchanan, J. M. (1965b, November). Joint supply, externality and optimality. *Economica* (N.S. 33), pp. 404–415.

Buchanan, J. M. (1968). *The demand and supply of public goods.* Chicago: Rand McNally.

Buchanan, J. M. (1976). Barro on the Ricardian

Equivalence Theorem. *Journal of Political Economy, 84,* 337–342.

Buchanan, J. M., & Goetz, C. J. (1972, April). Efficiency limits of fiscal mobility: An assessment of the Tiebout model. *Journal of Public Economics, 1,* 25–43.

Buchanan, J. M., & Stubblebine, W. (1962, November). Externality. *Economica* (N.S. 20), 371–384.

Buchanan, J. M., & Tullock, G. (1962). *The calculus of consent.* Ann Arbor, MI: The University of Michigan Press.

Buchanan, J. M., & Wagner, R. (1970). An efficiency basis for federal fiscal equalization. In J. Margolis (Ed.), *The Analysis of Public Output.* New York: Columbia University Press.

Burns, M. E. (1973, June). A note on the concept and measure of consumer's surplus. *American Economic Review, 63,* pp. 335–344.

Burrows, P. (1979, August). Pigovian taxes, polluter subsidies, regulation, and the side of a polluting industry. *Canadian Journal of Economics, 12,* 494–501.

Calvo, G. A., Kotlikoff, L. J., & Rodriguez, C. A. (1979, August). The incidence of a tax on pure rent: A new(?) reason for an old answer. *Journal of Political Economy, 87,* 869–874.

Calvo, G. A., & Wellisz, S. (1979, October). Hierarchy, ability, and income distribution. *Journal of Political Economy, 87,* 991–1010.

Caves, R. E., & Jones, R. W. (1973). *World trade and payments.* Boston: Little, Brown and Co.

Cheung, S. N. S. (1970, April). The structure of a contract and the theory of a nonexclusive resource. *Journal of Law and Economics, 13,* 49–70.

Clarke, E. H. (1971, Fall). Multi-part pricing of public goods. *Public Choice, 11,* 17–33.

Coase, R. H. (1960, October). The problem of social cost. *Journal of Law and Economics, 3,* 1–44.

Cooper, G. (1980). *A voluntary tax? New perspectives on sophisticated estate tax avoidance.* Washington, DC: The Brookings Institution.

Corlett, W. J., & Hague, D. C. (1953–54). Complementarity and the excess burden of taxation. *Review of Economics Studies, 21,* pp. 21–30.

Courant, P. N., Gramlich, E. M., & Rubinfield, D. L. (1979). The stimulative effects of intergovernmental grants: Or why money sticks where it hits. In Mieszkowski & Oakland (Eds.), 5–22.

Cragg, J. C., Harberger, A., & Mieszkowski, P. M. (1967, December). Empirical evidence of the incidence of the corporation income tax. *Journal of Political Economy, 75,* 811–821.

Cragg, J. C., Harberger, A., & Mieszkowski, P. M. (1970, July–August). Empirical evidence of the incidence of the corporation income tax: A rejoiner. *Journal of Political Economy, 78,* 768–775.

Dales, J. (1968). *Pollution, property rights and prices.* Toronto: University of Toronto Press.

Darby, M. R. (1979). *Effects of social security on income and the capital stock.* Washington, DC: American Enterprise.

Dasgupta, P., Marglin, S. A., & Sen, A. K. (1972). *Guidelines for project evaluation.* United Nations: UNIDO.

David, M. (1968). *Alternative approaches to capital gains taxation.* Washington, DC: The Brookings Institution.

David, P. A., & Scadding, J. L. (1974). Private savings: Ultra rationality, aggregation and Denison's Law. *Journal of Political Economy, 82,* 225–249.

Davis, O. A., & Whinston, A. (1962, June). Externalities, welfare, and the theory of games. *Journal of Political Economy, 70,* 241–262.

Deaton, A., & Muellbauer, J. (1980). *Economics and consumer behaviour.* Cambridge: Cambridge University Press.

Diamond, P. A. (1975, August). Inflation and the comprehensive tax base. *Journal of Public Economics, 4,* 227–244.

Diamond, P. A. (1977). A framework for social security analysis. *Journal of Public Economics, 8,* 275–298.

Diamond, P. A., & Mirrlees, J. A. (1971, March and June). Optimal taxation and public production. *American Economics Review, 61,* pp. 8–27 (Mar.), pp. 261–78 (Jun.).

Diamond, P. A., & Mirrlees, J. A. (1978, December). A model of social insurance with variable retirement. *Journal of Public Economics, 10,* 295–336.

Diewert, E. W. (1974, August). Unions in a general equilibrium model. *Canadian Journal of Economics, 3,* 475–495.

Domar, E. D., & Musgrave, R. A. (1944, May). Proportional income taxation and risk taking. *Quarterly Journal of Economics, 58,* 387–422.

Dorfman, R. (1962). Basic economic and technological concepts: A general statement. In A. Maass et al. (Ed.), *Design of water resource systems,* pp. 129–58. Cambridge, MA: Harvard University Press.

Downs, A. (1957). *An economic theory of democracy.* New York: Harper & Row.

Dusansky, R. (1972, November). The short-run shifting of the corporation income tax in the United States. *Oxford Economic Papers, 24,* pp. 357–371.

Edel, M., & Sclar, E. (1974, September–October). Taxes, spending, and property values: Supply adjustment in the Tiebout-Oates Model. *Journal of Political Economy, 82,* 941–954.

Epple, D., Zelenitz, A., & Visscher, M. (1978, June). A search for testable implications of the Tiebout Hypothesis. *Journal of Political Economy, 86,* 405–426.

Feldstein, M. S. (1972a). The inadequacy of weighted discount rates. In R. Layard (Ed.), *Cost-benefit analysis,* (pp. 311–32). Harmondsworth, Middlesex, UK: Penguin Books Ltd.

Feldstein, M. S. (1972b, March). Distributional equity and the optimal structure of public sector prices. *American Economic Review, 62,* pp. 32–36.

Feldstein, M. S. (1973a). Tax incentives, corporate saving and capital accumulation in the United States. *Journal of Public Economics, 2,* 159–171.

Feldstein, M. S. (1973b). Unemployment compensation, adverse incentives, and distributional anomalies. *National Tax Journal.*

Feldstein, M. S. (1974a, October). Incidence of a capital income tax in a growing economy with variable savings rates. *Review of Economic Studies, 19,* pp. 505–513.

Feldstein, M. S. (1974b). Tax incidence in a growing economy with variable factor supply. *Quarterly Journal of Economics, 88,* 551–573.

Feldstein, M. S. (1974c). Social security, induced retirement and aggregate capital accumulation. *Journal of Political Economy, 82,* 905–926.

Feldstein, M. S. (1976a, July–August). On the theory of tax reform. *Journal of Public Economics, 6,* 77–104.

Feldstein, M. S. (1976b, October). Temporary layoffs in the theory of unemployment. *Journal of Political Economy, 84,* 937–958.

Feldstein, M. S. (1976c). Perceived wealth in bonds and social security: A comment. *Journal of Political Economy, 84,* 331–336.

Feldstein, M. S. (1977a). Does the United States save too little? *American Economic Review, 67,* pp. 116–121.

Feldstein, M. S. (1977b, April). The surprising incidence of a tax on pure rent: A new answer to an old question. *Journal of Political Economy, 85,* 349–360.

Feldstein, M. S. (1977c). Facing the social security crisis. *The Public Interest, 47,* pp. 88–100.

Feldstein, M. S. (1978a, April). The welfare cost of capital income taxation. *Journal of Political Economy, 86,* S29–S51.

Feldstein, M. S. (1978b, December). The effect of unemployment insurance on temporary layoff unemployment. *American Economic Review, 68,* pp. 834–853.

Feldstein, M. S. (1982, June). Social security and private saving: Reply. *Journal of Political Economy, 90,* 630–642.

Feldstein, M. S., & Clotfelter, C. (1976, January–February). Tax incentives and charitable contributions in the United States: A microeconomic analysis. *Journal of Public Economics, 5,* 1–26.

Feldstein, M. S., & Flemming, J. S. (1964). The problem of time stream evaluation: Present value versus internal rate of return rules. *Bulletin of Oxford University Institute of Economics and Statistics, 26,* pp. 79–85.

Feldstein, M. S., & Friedman, B. (1977). Tax subsidies, the rational demand for insurance and the health care crisis. *Journal of Public Economics, 7,* 155–178.

Feldstein, M. S., & Green, J. (1983, March). Why do companies pay dividends? *American Economic Review, 73,* pp. 17–30.

Feldstein, M. S., Green, J., & Sheshinski, E. (1978, April). Inflation and taxes in a growing economy with debt and equity finance. *Journal of Political Economy (Part 2), 86* (2), S53–S70.

Fields, D. B., & Stanbury, W. T. (1970). Incentives, disincentives and the income tax: Further empirical evidence. *Public Finance, 25,* pp. 381–415.

Fisher, I. (1930). *The theory of interest.* New York: Macmillan.

Flatters, F. R., Henderson, J. V., & Mieszkowski, P. M. (1974, May). Public goods, efficiency and regional fiscal equalization. *Journal of Public Economics, 3,* 99–112.

Foster, C. D., & Beesley, M. E. (1963). Estimating the social benefit of constructing an underground railway in London. *Journal of the Royal Statistical Society* (Series A126), pp. 46–92.

Foster, E. (1976, June). The welfare foundations of cost-benefit analysis: A comment. *Economic Journal, 86,* 353–358.

Friedman, M. S. (1952, February). The welfare effects of an income and an excise tax. *Journal of Political Economy, 60,* 25–33.

Friedman, M. S. (1957). *A theory of the consumption function.* Princeton, NJ: Princeton University Press.

Friedman, M. S. (1964). *Capitalism and freedom.* Chicago: University of Chicago Press.

Friedman, M. S., & Savage, L. J. (1948, August). The utility analysis of choices involving risk. *Journal of Political Economy, 56,* 279–304.

Gillespie, I. W. (1965). Effects of public expenditures on the distribution of income. In R. Musgrave (Ed.), *Essays in fiscal federalism* (pp. 122–186). Washington, DC: The Brookings Institution.

Gillespie, I. W. (1976, July–August). On the redistribution of income in Canada. *Canadian Tax Journal, 24,* 417–450.

Gordon, H. S. (1954, April). The economic theory of a common property resource: The fishery. *Journal of Political Economy, 62,* 124–142.

Gordon, H. S. (1980). *Welfare, justice, and freedom.* New York: Columbia University Press.

Gordon, R. J. (1967, September). The incidence of the corporation income tax in U.S. manufacturing, 1925–1968. *American Economic Review, 57,* pp. 731–58.

Gould, J. P. (1968). Adjustment costs in the theory of investment of the firm. *Review of Economic Studies, 35,* 111–120.

Graaff, J. de Van (1957). *Theoretical welfare economics.* Cambridge, UK: Cambridge University Press.

Gramlich, E. M. (1977). Intergovernmental grants: A review of the empirical literature. In W. E. Oates (Ed.), *The political economy of fiscal federalism.* Lexington, MA: D.C. Heath.

Green, C. (1967). *Negative income taxes and the poverty problem.* Washington, DC: The Brookings Institution.

Green, H. A. J. (1971). *Consumer theory.* Harmondsworth, Middlesex, UK: Penguin Books.

Green, J., & Laffont, J. J. (1977, March). Characterization of satisfactory mechanisms for the revelation of preferences for public goods. *Econometrica, 45,* pp. 427–438.

Green, J., & Laffont, J. J. (1979). *Individual incentives in public decision-making.* Amsterdam: North-Holland.

Green, J., & Sheshinski, E. (1978). Optimal capital-gains taxation under limited information. *Journal of Political Economy, 86,* 1153–1158.

Green, J., & Sheshinski, E. (1979). Approximating the efficiency gain of tax reforms. *Journal of Public Economics, 11,* 179–195.

Grieson, R. E. (1975, February). The incidence of profits taxes in a neoclassical growth model. *Journal of Public Economics, 4,* 75–85.

Groves, T., & Ledyard, J. (1977, May). Optimal allocation of public goods: A solution to the "free rider" problem. *Econometrica, 45,* pp. 783–809.

Groves, T., & Loeb, M. (1975, August). Incentives and public inputs. *Journal of Public Economics, 4,* 211–226.

Haig, R. M. (1921). *The federal income tax.* New York: Columbia University Press.

Hall, R. E. (1978, December). Stochastic implications of the life cycle–permanent income hypothesis: Theory and evidence. *Journal of Political Economy, 86,* 971–987.

Hall, R. E., & Jorgenson, D. W. (1967, June). Tax policy and investment behavior. *American Economic Review, 57,* pp. 391–414.

Hamilton, B. W. (1976, June). The effects of property taxes and local public spending on property values: A theoretical comment. *Journal of Political Economy, 84,* 647–654.

Harberger, A. C. (1954, May). Monopoly and resource allocation. *American Economic Review Papers and Proceedings, 4,* 77–87.

Harberger, A. C. (1962, June). The incidence of the corporation income tax. *Journal of Political Economy, 70,* 215–240.

Harberger, A. C. (1964). Taxation, resource allocation and welfare. *The role of direct and indirect taxes in the federal revenue system* (pp. 25–70). (Conference Report of NBER and the Brookings Institution.) Princeton, NJ: Princeton University Press.

Harberger, A. C. (1969). Professor Arrow on the social discount rate. In *Cost benefit analysis of manpower policies.* Proceedings of a North American Conference, G. G. Somers and W. D. Wood (Eds.), Kingston, Ontario: Industrial Relations Center, Queen's University.

Harberger, A. C. (1971a, September). Three basic postulates of applied welfare economics: An interpretive essay. *Journal of Economic Literature, 9,* 785–797.

Harberger, A. C. (1971b). On measuring the social opportunity cost of labour. *International Labour Review, 103,* pp. 559–579.

Harberger, A. C. (1978, April). On the use of distributional weights in social cost–benefit analysis. *Journal of Political Economy, 86,* S87–S120.

Harberger, A. C. (1980). Tax neutrality in investment incentives. In H. J. Aaron & M. J. Boskin (Eds.), *The economics of taxation* (pp. 299–313). Washington, DC: The Brookings Institution.

Harris, J. R., & Todaro, M. P. (1970, March). Migration, unemployment, and development: A two-sector analysis. *American Economic Review, 60,* pp. 126–142.

Harrison, A. J., & Quarmby, D. S. (1972). The value of time. In R. Layard (Ed.), *Cost-benefit analysis* (pp. 173–208).

Harsanyi, J. C. (1955, August). Cardinal welfare, individualistic ethics, and interpersonal comparisons of utility. *Journal of Political Economy, 63,* 309–321.

Hause, J. C. (1975, December). The theory of welfare cost measurement. *Journal of Political Economy, 83,* 1145–1182.

Hausman, J. A. (1981a, September). Exact consumer's surplus and deadweight loss. *American Economic Review, 71,* pp. 662–676.

Hausman, J. A. (1981b). Labor Supply. In H. J. Aaron & J. A. Pechman (Eds.), *How taxes affect economic behavior* (pp. 27–72). Washington, DC: The Brookings Institution.

Head, J. (1966, March). A note on progression and leisure: Comment. *American Economic Review, 56,* pp. 172–179.

Heller, W. et al. (1967). *Revenue sharing and its alternatives: What future for fiscal federalism?* Washington, DC: USGPO.

Helliwell, J. F. (1969, May). The taxation of capital gains. *Canadian Journal of Economics, 2,* 314–318.

Helliwell, J. F. (Ed.). (1976). *Aggregate investment.* Harmondsworth, Middlesex, UK: Penguin Education.

Henderson, J. M., & Quandt, R. E. (1980). *Microeconomic theory: A mathematical treatment* (3rd ed.). New York: McGraw-Hill.

Hicks, J. R. (1939, December). Foundations of welfare economics. *Economic Journal, 49,* 696–712.

Hicks, J. R. (1943, Winter). The four consumer's surpluses. *Review of Economic Studies, 11,* pp. 31–41.

Hicks, J. R. (1946). *Value and capital.* (2nd ed.). Oxford: Clarendon Press.

Hicks, J. R. (1956). *A revision of demand theory.* Oxford: Clarendon Press.

Hirshleifer, J. (1976). *Price theory and applications.* Englewood Cliffs, NJ: Prentice-Hall, Inc.

Hochman, H. M., & Rogers, J. D. (1969, September). Pareto optimal redistribution. *American Economic Review, 59,* pp. 542–557.

Holland, D. M. (1970). The effect of taxation on effort: Some results for business executives. *Proceedings of the 66th Annual Conference on Taxation of the National Tax Association* (pp. 428–517).

Holt, C. C., & Shelton, J P. (1962, December). The lock-in effect of the capital gains tax. *National Tax Journal, 15,* 337–352.

Hotelling, H. (1938, July). The general welfare in relation to problems of taxation and of railway and utility rates. *Econometrica, 6,* pp. 242–269.

Howrey, P. E., & Hymans, S. H. (1978). The measurement and determination of loanable-funds saving. *Brookings Papers on Economic Activity, 3,* pp. 655–705.

Inman, R. P. (1979). The fiscal performance of local governments: An interpretative review. In P. Mieszkowski & M. Straszheim (Eds.), (pp. 270–321). Baltimore, MD: Johns Hopkins University Press.

James, E. (1975, March). A note on uncertainty and the evaluation of public investment decisions. *American Economic Review, 65,* pp. 200–205.

Johnson, B. M. (1964, January–April). On the economics of road congestion. *Econometrica, 32,* pp. 137–150.

Johnson, H. G. (1971). *The two sector model of general equilibrium.* Chicago: Aldine-Atherton Press.

Johnson, H. G., & Mieszkowski, P. M. (1970). The effects of unionization on the distribution of income: A general equilibrium approach. *Quarterly Journal of Economics, 84,* 539–561.

Jones, R. W. (1965, December). The structure of general equilibrium models. *Journal of Political Economy, 75,* 557–572.

Jones–Lee, M. W. (1976). *The value of life: An economic analysis.* Chicago: University of Chicago Press.

Jorgenson, D. W. (1963). Capital theory and investment behavior. *American Economic Review, 53,* pp. 247–259.

Jorgenson, D. W. (1967). The theory of investment behavior. In R. Ferber (Ed.), *A conference of the universities—National Bureau Committee for Economic Research.* New York: Columbia University Press.

Kaizuka, K. (1965, May). Public goods and decentralization of production. *Review of Economics and Statistics, 47,* pp. 118–120.

Kalachek, E. D., & Raines, F. Q. (1970). Labor supply of low income workers. *President's Commission on Income Maintenance Programs, Technical Studies* pp. 159–181.

Kaldor, N. (1939, September). Welfare propositions of economics and interpersonal comparisons of utility. *Economic Journal, 49,* 549–552.

Kaldor, N. (1955). *An expenditure tax.* London: Unwin University Books.

Kalecki, M. (1937, September). A theory of commodity, income and capital taxation. *Economic Journal, 47,* 444–450.

Kay, J. A., & King, M. A. (1978). *The British tax system.* London: Oxford University Press.

Kesselman, J. R. (1973, February). A comprehensive approach to income maintenance: SWIFT. *Journal of Public Economics, 2,* 59–88.

Kesselman, J. R. (1976, April–May). Egalitarianism of earnings and income taxes. *Journal of Public Economics, 5,* 285–301.

Kindleberger, C. (1973). *International economics.* (5th ed.). Homewood, IL: Richard D. Irwin.

King, M. A. (1977). *Public policy and the corporation.* London: Chapman and Hall.

King, M. A., & Fullerton, D. (Eds.). (1983). *The taxation of income from capital: A comparative study of the U.S., U.K., Sweden, and West Germany.* Chicago: The University of Chicago Press.

Knight, F. H. (1924, August). Some fallacies in the interpretation of social cost. *Quarterly Journal of Economics, 38,* 582–606.

Kosters, M. (1969). Effects of an income tax on labor supply. In A. C. Harberger and M. J. Bailey (Eds.), *Taxation of income from capital* (pp. 301–324). Washington, DC: The Brookings Institution.

Kotlikoff, L. J., & Summers, L. M. (1979, November). Tax incidence in a life cycle model with variable labor supply. *Quarterly Journal of Economics, 93,* 705–718.

Kotlikoff, L. J., & Summers, L. M. (1981). The role of intergenerational transfers in aggregate capital accumulation. *Journal of Political Economy, 89,* 706–732.

Kramer, G. M. (1973, March). On a class of equilibrium conditions for majority rule. *Econometrica, 41,* pp. 285–297.

Kraus, M., Mohring, H., & Pinfold, T. (1976, September). The welfare costs of non–optimum pricing and investment policies for freeway transportation. *American Economic Review, 66,* pp. 532–547.

Krause, M. B., & Johnson, H. G. (1972, November). The theory of tax incidence: A diagrammatic analysis. *Economica* (N.S. 39), 357–382.

Krzyzaniak, M., & Musgrave, R. A. (1964). *The shifting of the corporation income tax.* Baltimore, MD: Johns Hopkins University Press.

Krzyzaniak, M., & Musgrave, R. A. (1970, July–August). Corporate tax shifting: A response. *Journal of Political Economy, 78,* 768–775.

Layard, P. R. G., & Walters, A. A. (1978). *Microeconomic theory,* pp. 351–382. New York: McGraw-Hill.

Layard, R. (Ed.). (1972). *Cost-benefit analysis.* Harmondsworth, Middlesex, UK: Penguin Books Ltd.

Leibenstein, H. (1966, June). Allocative efficiency vs. X-efficiency. *American Economic Review, 56,* pp. 392–415.

Leimer, D. R., & Lesnoy, S. D. (1982, June). Social security and private saving: New time-series evidence. *Journal of Political Economy, 90,* 606–629.

Lerner, A. P. (1944). *The economics of control.* New York: Macmillan.

Lindahl, E. (1958). Just taxation: A positive solution. In R. A. Musgrave and A. T. Peacock (Eds.), *Classics in the theory of public finance* (pp. 168–177). London: Macmillan.

Lipsey, R. G., & Lancaster, K. (1956–7). The general theory of second best. *Review of Economic Studies, 24,* pp. 11–32.

Little, I. M. D. (1951, September). Direct vs. indirect taxes. *Economic Journal, 61,* 577–584.

Little, I. M. D. (1960). *A critique of welfare economics.* Oxford: Oxford University Press.

Little, I. M. D., & Mirrlees, J. A. (1968). *Manual of industrial project analysis in developing countries, vol. 2, social cost-benefit analysis.* Paris: Development Center of OECD.

Lucas, R. E. (1967). Optimal investment policy and the flexible accelerator. *International Economic Review, 8,* 78–85.

Marglin, S. A. (1963a, February). The social rate of discount and the optimal rate of investment. *Quarterly Journal of Economics, 77,* 95–112.

Marglin, S. A. (1963b, May). The opportunity costs of public investment. *Quarterly Journal of Economics, 77,* 274–289.

Markowitz, H. M. (1959). *Portfolio selection.* New York: John Wiley & Sons.

Marshall, J. M. (1976). Moral hazard. *American Economic Review, 66,* pp. 880–890.

McKelvey, R. D. (1976). Intransitivities in multidimensional voting models and some implications for agenda control. *Journal of Economic Theory, 12,* 472–482.

McKelvey, R. D. (1979, September). General conditions for global intransitivities in formal voting models. *Econometrica, 47,* pp. 1085–1112.

McLure, C. E., Jr. (1967, March). The interstate exporting of state and local taxes: Estimates for 1962. *National Tax Journal, 20,* 49–77.

McLure, C. E., Jr. (1974). A diagrammatic exposition of the Harberger Model with one immobile factor. *Journal of Political Economy, 82,* 56–82.

McLure, C. E., Jr. (1975a, February). General equilibrium incidence analysis: The Harberger Model after ten years. *Journal of Public Economics, 4,* 125–161.

McLure, C. E., Jr. (1975b, September). The case for integrating the income taxes. *National Tax Journal, 28,* 257–264.

McLure, C. E., Jr. (1977). The new view of the property tax: A caveat. *National Tax Journal, 30,* 69–76.

McLure, C. E., Jr. (1978). *Must corporate income be taxed twice?* Washington, DC: The Brookings Institution.

Meade, J. E. (1952, March). External economies and diseconomies in a competitive situation. *Economic Journal, 62,* 54–76.

Meade, J., et al. (1978). *The structure and reform of direct taxation.* London: Allen and Unwin.

Meadows, G. R. (1976, August). Taxes, spending, and property values: A comment and further results. *Journal of Political Economy, 84,* 869–880.

Menchik, P. L. (1979, November). Inter-generational transmission of inequality: An empirical study of wealth mobility. *Economica, 46,* pp. 349–362.

Menchik, P. L. (1980, March). Primogeniture, equal sharing, and the U.S. distribution of wealth. *Quarterly Journal of Economics, 94,* 299–316.

Mieszkowski, P. M. (1967, June). On the theory of tax incidence. *Journal of Political Economy, 75,* 250–262.

Mieszkowski, P. M. (1969, December). Tax incidence theory: The effects of taxes on the distribution of income. *Journal of Economic Literature, 7,* 1103–1124.

Mieszkowski, P. M. (1972, April). The property tax: An excise tax or a profits tax. *Journal of Public Economics, 1,* 73–96.

Mieszkowksi, P. M. (1980). The advisability and feasibility of an expenditure tax system. In H. J. Aaron and M. Boskin (Eds.), *The Economics of Taxation* (pp. 179–201). Washington, DC: The Brookings Institution.

Mieszkowski, P. M., & Oakland, W. H. (Eds.). (1979). *Fiscal federalism and grants-in-aid.* Washington, DC: The Urban Institute.

Mill, J. S. (1921). In W. J. Ashley (Ed.), *Principles of political economy.* London: Longmans, Green & Co. Ltd.

Minhas, B. (1962, April). The homophypallagic production function, factor intensity reversals, and the Heckscher-Ohlin Theorem. *Journal of Political Economy, 70,* 138–157.

Mirer, T. W. (1979, June). The wealth-age relation among the aged. *American Economic Review, 69,* pp. 435–443.

Mirrlees, J. A. (1971, April). An exploration in the theory of optimal income taxation. *Review of Economic Studies, 38,* pp. 175–208.

Mishan, E. J. (1960, June). A survey of welfare economics: 1939–1959. *Economic Journal, 70,* 197–265.

Mishan, E. J. (1967, November). Pareto optimality and the law. *Oxford Economic Papers, 19,* pp. 255–287.

Mishan, E. J. (1971a). *Cost-benefit analysis.* (ch. 11). London: Allen and Unwin, Ltd.

Mishan, E. J. (1971b, March). The postwar literature on externalities: An interpretative essay. *Journal of Economic Literature, 9,* 1–28.

Mishan, E. J. (1971c, July). Evaluation of life and limb: A theoretical approach. *Journal of Political Economy, 79,* 687–705.

Modigliani, F., & Miller, M. (1958). The cost of capital, corporation finance and the theory of investment. *American Economic Review,* pp. 261–297.

Mohring, H. (1970, September). The peak-load pricing problem with increasing returns and pricing constraints. *American Economic Review, 60,* pp. 693–705.

Mossin, J. (1968, February). Taxation and risk-taking: An expected utility approach. *Economica, 35,* 74–82.

Mueller, D. C. (1979). *Public choice.* Cambridge, UK: Cambridge University Press.

Munnell, A. H. (1974). *The effect of social security on personal savings.* Cambridge, MA: Ballinger Publishing Co.

Munnell, A. H. (1977). *The future of social security.* Washington, DC: The Brookings Institution.

Musgrave, R. A. (1955). The incidence of the tax structure and its effects on consumption. *Federal tax policy for economic growth and stability of the Joint Committee on the Economic Report,* (84). Congress 1 Session.

Musgrave, R. A. (1959). *The theory of public finance.* New York: McGraw-Hill.

Musgrave, R. A. (1961). Approaches to a fiscal theory of political federalism. In *Public finances: Needs, sources, and utilization* (pp. 97–122). Princeton, NJ: Princeton University Press, National Bureau of Economic Research.

Musgrave, R. A. (1969a). Provision for social goods. In J. Margolis & M. Guitton (Eds.), *Public economics* (pp. 124–145). New York: St. Martin's Press.

Musgrave, R. A. (1969b, September). Cost-benefit analysis and the theory of public finance. *Journal of Economic Literature, 7,* 797–806.

Musgrave, R. A. (1974, May). Is a property tax on housing regressive? *American Economic Review, 64,* 222–229.

Musgrave, R. A. (1976, July–August). ET, OT and SBT. *Journal of Public Economics, 6,* 3–16.

Musgrave, R. A., Case, K. E., & Leonard, H. B. (1974, July). The distribution of fiscal burdens and benefits. *Public Finance Quarterly, 2,* 259–312.

Nathan, R. P., Adams, C. F., & Associates. (1977). *Revenue sharing: The second round.* Washington, DC: The Brookings Institution.

Nathan, R. P., Manvel, A. D., Calkins, S. E., & Associates. (1975). *Monitoring revenue sharing.* Washington, DC: The Brookings Institution.

Ng, Y. K. (1973, August). The economic theory of

clubs: Pareto optimality conditions. *Economica* (N.S. 40), pp. 291–298.

Ng, Y. K. (1980). *Welfare economics. Introduction and development of basic concepts.* New York: John Wiley & Sons.

Niskanen, W. A. (1971). *Bureaucracy and representative government.* Chicago: Aldine-Atherton.

Oakland, W. H. (1972a, August). Corporate earnings and tax shifting in U.S. manufacturing: 1930–1962. *Review of Economics and Statistics, 54,* pp. 235–244.

Oakland, W. H. (1972b, November). Congestion, public goods, and welfare. *Journal of Public Economics, 1,* 339–357.

Oates, W. E. (1969, November). The effects of property taxes and local public spending on property values: An empirical study of tax capitalization and the Tiebout Hypothesis. *Journal of Political Economy, 77,* 957–971.

Oates, W. E. (1972). *Fiscal federalism.* New York: Harcourt Brace Jovanovich.

Oates, W. E. (1979). Lump-sum intergovernmental grants have price effects. In Mieszkowski & Oakland (Eds.). 23–30.

Owens, J. D. (1971, January–February). The demand for leisure. *Journal of Political Economy, 79,* 56–76.

Patinkin, D. (1963). Demand curves and consumer's surplus. In C. E. Christ (Ed.), *Measurement in Economics* (pp. 83–112). Stanford, CA: Stanford University Press.

Pauly, M. V. (1968). The economics of moral hazard. *American Economic Review, 58,* pp. 531–537.

Pauly, M. V. (1973, February). Income redistribution as a local public good. *Journal of Public Economics, 2,* 35–58.

Pauly, M. V. (1974, February). Overinsurance and public provision of insurance: The roles of moral hazard and adverse selection. *Quarterly Journal of Economics, 88,* 44–62.

Pauly, M. V. (1976, October). A model of local government expenditure and tax capitalization. *Journal of Public Economics, 6,* 231–242.

Pechman, J. A. (1977). *Federal tax policy* (3rd ed.). Washington, DC: The Brookings Institution.

Pechman, J. A. (1980). *What should be taxed: Income or expenditure?* Washington, DC: The Brookings Institution.

Pechman, J. A. (1983). *Federal tax policy* (4th

ed.). Washington, DC: The Brookings Institution.

Pechman, J. A., Aaron, H. J., & Taussig, M. K. (1968). *Social security: Perspectives for reform.* Washington, DC: The Brookings Institution.

Pechman, J. A., & Okner, B. A. (1974). *Who bears the tax burden?* Washington, DC: The Brookings Institution.

Pigou, A. C. (1918). *The economics of welfare.* London: Macmillan.

Pigou, A. C. (1951). *Public finance* (3rd ed.). London: Macmillan.

Plott, C. R. (1967, September). A notion of equilibrium and its possibility under majority rule. *American Economic Review, 57,* pp. 787–806.

Plott, C. R. (1976, August). Axiomatic social choice theory: An overview and interpretation. *American Journal of Political Science,* 511–596.

Rae, D. N. (1969, March). Decision-rules and individual values in constitutional choice. *American Political Science Review, 63,* pp. 40–56.

Ramsey, F. P. (1927, March). A contribution to the theory of taxation. *Economic Journal, 37,* 47–61.

Rawls, J. (1971). *A theory of justice.* Cambridge, MA: Harvard University Press.

Report of Royal Commission on Taxation. (1966). Ottawa: The Queen's Printer.

Richter, M. K. (1960, June). Cardinal utility, portfolio selection, and taxation. *Review of Economic Studies, 27,* 152–166.

Romer, T. (1975, February). Individual welfare, majority voting, and the properties of a linear income tax. *Journal of Public Economics, 4,* 163–185.

Romer, T., & Rosenthal, H. (1979a). The elusive median voter. *Journal of Public Economics, 12,* 143–170.

Romer, T., & Rosenthal, H. (1979b). Bureaucrats versus voters: On the political economy of resource allocation by direct democracy. *Quarterly Journal of Economics, 93,* 563–587.

Romer, T., & Rosenthal, H. (1980). An institutional theory of the effect of intergovernmental grants. *National Tax Journal, 33* (4), 451–458.

Rothschild, M., & Stiglitz, J. E. (1976). Equilibrium in competitive insurance markets. *Quarterly Journal of Economics, 90,* 629–650.

Royal Commission on Taxation. (1954). *Report of the Royal Commission on the taxation of profits and income* (Cmnd. 9474). London: HMSO.

Sadka, Efraim (1976, December). On progressive income taxation. *American Economic Review, 66*, 931–35.

Samuelson, P. A. (1950, January). Evaluation of real national income. *Oxford Economic Papers* (N.S. 2), pp. 1–29.

Samuelson, P. A. (1954, November). Pure theory of public expenditures. *Review of Economics and Statistics, 36*, pp. 387–389.

Samuelson, P. A. (1955, November). Diagrammatic exposition of a theory of public expenditures. *Review of Economics and Statistics, 37*, pp. 350–56.

Samuelson, P. A. (1956, February). Social indifference curves. *Quarterly Journal of Economics, 70*, 1–22.

Samuelson, P. A. (1958). An exact consumption-loan model of interest with or without the social contrivance of money. *Journal of Political Economy, 66*, 467–482.

Samuelson, P. A. (1964, December). Tax deductibility of economic depreciation to insure invariant valuations. *Journal of Political Economy, 72*, 604–606.

Sandmo, A. (1972, April). Optimality rules for the provision of collective factors of production. *Journal of Public Economics, 1*, 149–157.

Sandmo, A. (1973, October). Public goods and the technology of consumption. *Review of Economic Studies, 40*, pp. 517–528.

Sandmo, A. (1974, March–April). Investment incentives and the corporate income tax. *Journal of Political Economy, 82*, 287–302.

Sandmo, A. (1976, July–August). Optimal taxation: An introduction to the literature. *Journal of Public Economics, 6*, 37–54.

Sargent, T. J. (1979). *Macroeconomic theory*. New York: Academic Press.

Sato, K. (1967). Taxation and neo-classical growth. *Public Finance, 22*, pp. 346–370.

Scarf, H. E. (1969). An example of an algorithm for calculating general equilibrium prices. *American Economic Review, 59*, pp. 669–677.

Scarf, H. E. (with the collaboration of T. Hansen). (1973). *The computation of economic equilibria*. New Haven, CT: Yale University Press.

Schall, L. D. (1972, February). Interdependent utilities and Pareto optimality. *Quarterly Journal of Economics, 86*, 19–24.

Scitovsky, T. (1941, November). A note on welfare propositions in economics. *Review of Economic Studies, 9*, 77–88.

Scitovsky, T. (1954, April). Two concepts of external economies. *Journal of Political Economy, 62*, 143–151.

Scott, A. D. (1955, April). The fishery: The objectives of sole ownership. *Journal of Political Economy, 63*, 116–124.

Sen, A. K. (1967, February). Isolation, assurance and the social rate of discount. *Quarterly Journal of Economics, 81*, 112–124.

Sen, A. K. (1970). *Collective choice and social welfare*. San Francisco: Holden-Day.

Sen, A. K. (1972, March). Control areas and accounting prices: An approach to economic evaluation. *Economic Journal, 82*, 486–501.

Sen, A. K. (1973). *On economic inequality*. Oxford: Clarendon Press.

Sen, A. K. (1977a). On weights and measures: Information constraints in social welfare analysis. *Econometrica, 45*, pp. 1539–1572.

Sen, A. K. (1977b). Social choice theory: A re-examination. *Econometrica, 45*, pp. 53–89.

Shavell, S., & Weiss, L. (1979). The optimal payment of unemployment insurance benefits over time. *Journal of Political Economy, 37*, 1347–1362.

Shoven, J. B., & Whalley, J. (1972, November). A general equilibrium calculation of the effects of differential taxation of income from capital in the U.S. *Journal of Public Economics, 1*, 281–321.

Silberberg, E. (1972). Duality and the many consumer's surpluses. *American Economic Review, 62*, 942–952.

Silberberg, E. (1974). A revision of comparative statics methodology in economics. *Journal of Economic Theory, 7*, 159–172.

Simons, H. C. (1938). *Personal income taxation*. Chicago: University of Chicago Press.

Slemrod, J., & Yitzhaki, S. (1983, March). On choosing a flat-rate income tax system. *National Tax Journal, 36*, 31–44.

Smith, B., & Stephen, F. H. (1975, December). The welfare foundations of cost–benefit analysis. Comment. *Economic Journal, 85*, 902–905.

Smith, V. L. (1963, January). Tax depreciation policy and investment theory. *International Economic Review, 4*, pp. 80–91.

Smith, V. L. (1968, June). Economics of production from natural resources. *American Economic Review, 58*, 409–431.

Solow, R. M. (1956, February). A contribution to

the theory of economic growth. *Quarterly Journal of Economics, 70,* 65–94.

Sonstelie, J. C., & Portney, P. R. (1978, April). Profit maximizing communities and the theory of local public expenditure. *Journal of Urban Economics, 5,* 263–277.

Sonstelie, J. C., & Portney, P. R. (1980, January). Gross rents and market values: Testing the implications of Tiebout's hypothesis. *Journal of Urban Economics, 7,* 102–118.

Spence, M. (1974). *Market signalling.* Cambridge, MA: Harvard University Press.

Starrett, D. (1979). Second best welfare economics in the mixed economy. *Journal of Public Economics, 12,* 329–350.

Starrett, D. (1980). On the method of taxation and the provision of local public goods. *American Economic Review, 70,* pp. 380–392.

Stein, B. (1980). Social security and pensions in transition. New York: The Free Press.

Stern, N. H. (1976, July–August). On the specification of models of optimum income taxation. *Journal of Public Economics, 6,* 123–162.

Stiglitz, J. E. (1969, May). The effects of income, wealth, and capital gains taxation on risk-taking. *Quarterly Journal of Economics, 83,* 263–83.

Stiglitz, J. E. (1974, November). The demand for education in public and private school systems. *Journal of Public Economics, 3,* 349–386.

Stiglitz, J. E. (1975, June). The theory of "screening," education, and the distribution of income. *American Economic Review, 65,* 283–300.

Stiglitz, J. E. (1977). The theory of local public goods. In M. S. Feldstein & R. P. Inman (Eds.), *The economics of public services.* New York: Macmillan.

Stolper, W. F., & Samuelson, P. A. (1941, November). Protection and real wages. *Review of Economic Studies, 9,* pp. 58–73.

Summers, L. H. (1981, September). Capital taxation and accumulation in a life cycle growth model. *American Economic Review, 71,* 533–544.

Tax Foundation, Inc. (1981). *Facts and figures on government finance.* New York: Tax Foundation, Inc.

Tideman, N., & Tullock, G. (1976, December). A new and superior process for making social choices. *Journal of Political Economy, 84,* 1145–1160.

Tiebout, C. M. (1956, October). A pure theory of local expenditures. *Journal of Political Economy, 64,* 416–424.

Thaler, R., & Rosen, S. (1975). The value of saving a life. In *Conference on income and wealth, household production, and consumption.* New York: NBER.

Thurow, L. C. (1966, December). The theory of grants-in-aid. *National Tax Journal, 19,* 373–377.

Thurow, L. C. (1971, May). The income distribution as a pure public good. *Quarterly Journal of Economics, 85,* 327–336.

Thurow, L. C. (1975, June). The economics of public finance. *National Tax Journal, 28,* 185–194.

Tobin, J. (1969). Raising the income of the poor. In K. Gordon (Ed.), *Agenda for the nation.* Washington, DC: The Brookings Institution.

Tobin, J. (1970, October). On limiting the domain of inequality. *Journal of Law and Economics, 13,* 263–277.

Tomes, N. (1981). The family, inheritance, and the intergenerational transmission of inequality. *Journal of Political Economy, 89,* 928–958.

Topel, R., & Welch, F. (1980). Unemployment insurance: Survey and extensions. *Economica, 47,* pp. 351–379.

Tulkens, H., & Schoumaker, F. (1975). Stability analysis of an effluent charge and the polluters pay principle. *Journal of Public Economics, 4,* 245–269.

Turvey, R. (1963, August). On divergences between social cost and private cost. *Economica* (N.S. 30), pp. 309–313.

U.S. Department of Commerce. (1975). *Historical statistics of the United States: Colonial times to 1970.* Washington, DC: USGPO.

U.S. Department of Commerce. (1983a). *Governmental finances in 1981–82.* Washington, DC: USGPO.

U.S. Department of Commerce. (1983b). *Statistical abstract of the United States, 1982–83.* Washington, DC: USGPO.

U.S. Department of Health, Education and Welfare. (1973, December). *Summary report: New Jersey graduated work incentive experiment.* Washington, DC: Office of Assistant Secretary for Planning and Evaluation, HEW.

U.S. Department of Labor. (1983). *Employment and earnings.* Washington, DC: USGPO.

United States Treasury. (1977). *Blueprints for basic tax reform.* Washington, DC: USGPO.

Usher, D. (1973). An imputation to the measure of economic growth for changes in life expectancy. In M. Moss (Ed.), *The measurement of economic and social performance.* New York: NBER.

Usher, D. (1977). The welfare economics of the socialization of commodities. *Journal of Public Economics, 8,* 151–168.

Usher, D. (1983). The private cost of public funds. Unpublished.

Vandendorpe, A. F., & Friedlaender, A. F. (1976, October). Differential incidence in the presence of initial distorting taxes. *Journal of Public Economics, 6,* 205–229.

Varian, H. R. (1980). Redistributive taxation as social insurance. *Journal of Public Economics, 14,* 49–68.

Vickrey, W. S. (1947). *Agenda for progressive taxation.* New York: Ronald Press.

Vickrey, W. S. (1961, May). Counterspeculation, auctions and competitive sealed tenders. *Journal of Finance, 16,* 8–37.

Viner, J. (1931). Cost curves and supply curves. *Zeitschrift fur Nationalokonomie: Vol. 3* (pp. 23–46). (Reprinted in American Economic Association, 1952. *Readings in price theory* (pp. 198–232). Homewood, IL: Richard D. Irwin, Inc.)

Von Furstenberg, G. (1981). Savings. In H. J. Aaron & J. A. Pechman (Eds.), *How taxes affect economic behavior* (pp. 327–402). Washington, DC: The Brookings Institution.

Walker, M. A. (1983). *On flat-rate tax proposals.* Vancouver: The Fraser Institute.

Walters, A. A. (1961, October). The theory and measurement of private and social costs of highway congestion. *Econometrica, 29,* pp. 676–699.

Weber, W. E. (1970). The effect of interest rates on aggregate consumption. *American Economic Review, 60,* 591–600.

Weisbrod, B. A. (1968). Income redistribution effects and benefit-cost analysis. In S. B. Chase, Jr. (Ed.), *Problems in public expenditure analysis.* Washington, DC: The Brookings Institution.

Wheaton, W. C. (1975). Consumer mobility and community tax bases: The financing of local public goods. *Journal of Public Economics, 4,* 377–384.

Wheaton, W. C. (1978, Autumn). Price-induced distortions in urban highway investment. *Bell Journal of Economics, 9,* 622–632.

Wildasin, D. E. (1979a). Public good provision with optimal and non-optimal commodity taxation. *Economics Letters, 4,* pp. 59–64.

Wildasin, D. E. (1979b). Local public goods, property values, and local public choice. *Journal of Urban Economics, 6,* 521–534.

Wildasin, D. E. (1980). Locational efficiency in a federal system. *Regional Science and Urban Economics, 10,* 453–471.

Wildasin, D. E. (1984). On public good provision with distortionary taxation. *Economic Inquiry, 22.*

Wilde, J. A. (1968, September). The expenditure effects of grants-in-aid programs. *National Tax Journal, 21,* 340–348.

Williamson, O. E. (1966, September). Peak-load pricing and optimal capacity under indivisibility constraints. *American Economic Review, 56,* 810–827.

Willig, R. D. (1976, September). Consumer's surplus without apology. *American Economic Review,* 589–597.

Wright, C. (1969). Saving and the rate of interest. In A. C. Harberger & M. J. Bailey (Eds.), *The taxation of income from capital.* Washington, DC: The Brookings Institution.

Zeckhauser, R. (1969). Uncertainty and the need for collective action. In *The analysis and evaluation of public expenditures: The PPB system.* Joint Economic Committee, U.S. Congress. (Reprinted in R. Haveman & J. Margolis (Eds.). (1970). *Public expenditures and policy analysis.* Chicago: Markham).

Zeckhauser, R. (1970, March). Medical insurance: A case study of the tradeoff between risk spreading and appropriate incentives. *Journal of Economic Theory, 2,* 10–26.

Zeckhauser, R. (1971, June). Optimal mechanisms for income transfers. *American Economic Review, 63,* 324–334.

Index